Portrait of Paul

&

An Appeal

Portrait of Paul

By

John Fletcher

Compiled and edited by
Jeffrey L. Wallace

ISBN-10: 0-9886253-7-7
ISBN-13: 978-0-9886253-7-2

A *Heritage of Truth* Book
Reclaiming the Wisdom of the Past

Heritage of Truth
Reclaiming the Wisdom of the Past

Published by:
Apprehending Truth Publishers
Brookfield, Missouri
2017

Buy the Truth and sell it not. ~Proverbs xxiii, 23

AT 10 9 8 7 6 5 4 3 2 1
170901

Other Titles published by Apprehending Truth:

Defining Biblical Holiness

The Works of John Fletcher:
Volume One: Five Checks To Antinomianism
Volume Two: Creeds and Scripture Scales
Volume Three: Doctrines of Grace and Justice
Volume Four: Portrait of Paul & An Appeal
Volume Five: A Vindication of the Faith (forthcoming)
Volume Six: Outlines & Miscellany (forthcoming)

Adam Clarke's Christian Theology

Defining Biblical Holiness

New Testament Holiness

God's Crucible: Life in a Biblical Church

Did Jesus Correct Moses?

Salvation – Strait & Narrow

Antinomianism and the Gospel

-----

www.ATPublishers.net

Jean Guillaume de la Flechere

The Works

of

John Fletcher

Volume Four

Portrait of Paul

An Appeal

Apprehending Truth Publishers
Brookfield, Missouri
2017

CONTENTS

I. PORTRAIT OF ST. PAUL.

II. THE PORTRAIT OF LUKEWARM MINISTERS AND FALSE APOSTLES.

III. THE PORTRAIT OF ST. PAUL. -- PART SECOND.

The dispensation of the Holy Spirit is now in force, and the minister who preaches

IV. THE PORTRAIT OF ST. PAUL -- PART THIRD. -- AN ESSAY ON THE CONNECTION OF DOCTRINES WITH MORALITY.

V. APPEAL TO MATTER OF FACT AND COMMON SENSE.

THE

PORTRAIT OF ST. PAUL

OR,

THE TRUE MODEL

FOR

CHRISTIANS AND PASTORS,

TRANSLATED FROM A FRENCH MANUSCRIPT OF THE LATE

REV. JOHN WILLIAM DE LA FLECHERE,

VICAR OF MADELEY.

———

BY THE REV. JOHN GILPIN,

VICAR OF ROCKWARDINE, IN THE COUNTY OF SALOP.

INTRODUCTION.

THE following work was begun and nearly completed in the course of Mr. Fletcher's last residence at Nyon, where it formed a valuable part of his private labours, during a long and painful confinement from public duty. On his return to England he suffered the manuscript to lie by him in a very loose and disordered state, intending, at his leisure, to translate and prepare it for the press. In the meantime he entered upon the arduous task of revising and enlarging a French poem, which he had lately published at Geneva under the title of "La Louange, " and which was reprinted at London in the year 1785, under the title of "La Grace et la Nature." The second appearance of this poem was speedily followed by the dissolution of the author. Soon after this melancholy event had taken place, Mrs. Fletcher, in looking over the papers of the deceased, discovered the first part of the Portrait of St. Paul, with the perusal of which she favoured the translator, who finding it a work of no common importance, was readily induced to render it into English. From time to time different parts of the work were discovered, and though the manuscript was so incorrect and confused, as frequently to stagger the resolution of the translator, yet a strong persuasion that the work was calculated to produce the most desirable effects, encouraged him to persevere till he had completed his undertaking.

It is scarcely necessary to inform the intelligent reader that the Portrait of St. Paul was originally intended for publication in the author's native country, to which its arguments and quotations apply with peculiar propriety. It may be more necessary to observe, that had the life of Mr. Fletcher been prolonged the traits of St. Paul's moral character would have been rendered abundantly more copious and complete.

THE AUTHOR'S PREFACE.

MANY celebrated writers have offered excellent treatises to the public, sonic on the character of a true Christian, and others on the duties of a good pastor. It were to be wished that these two objects might be so closely united as to fall under the same point of view: and to effect such union is the design of this work, in which may be seen, at one view, what were the primitive Christians and the apostolic pastors; and what they are required to be, who are called to follow them in the progress of piety.

As *example* is more powerful than *precept,* it was necessary that some person should be singled out, who was both an excellent Christian, and an eminent minister of Jesus Christ. The person we fix upon is St. Paul, in whom these two characters were remarkably united, and a sketch of whose wondrous portrait we endeavour to exhibit in the following pages. When this apostle is considered as a Christian, his diligence in filling up the duties of his vocation, his patience in times of trial, his courage in the midst of dangers, his perseverance in well doing, his faith, his humility, his charity, all sweetly blended together, constitute him an admirable model for every Christian. And when we regard him as a dispenser of the mysteries of God, his inviolable attachment to truth, and his unconquerable zeal, equally distant from fanaticism and indifference, deserve the imitation of every minister of the Gospel.

The Holy Scriptures furnish materials in abundance for the present work; *the Acts of the Apostles,* from chapter viii, containing little else than a narration of the labours of St. Paul, or an abridgment of his sermons and apologies. The New Testament, beside the Acts, contains twenty-two different books, fourteen of which were composed by this apostle himself, with all the frankness suited to the epistolary style, and all the personal detail into which he was obliged to enter when writing in an uncommon variety of circumstances, to his friends, his brethren, and his spiritual children. It is on such occasions that a man is most likely to discover what he really is; and it is on such occasions that the moral painter may take an author in the most interesting positions, in order to delineate, with accuracy, his sentiments, his circumstances, and his conduct.

Let it not be said that, in proposing this apostle as a model to Christians, we do but cast discouragements in the way of those who are at an immense distance behind him, with respect both to grace and diligence. The masterly skill that Raphael and Rubens have discovered in their pieces, serves not to discourage modern painters, who rather labour to form themselves by such grand models. Poets and orators are not disheartened by those *chef d' oeuvres* of poetry and eloquence which Homer and Virgil, Demosthenes and Cicero, have transmitted to posterity; why then should we be discouraged by considering the eminent virtues and unwearied labours of this great apostle? The greater the excellence of the pattern proposed, the less likely is the laboured copy to be incomplete.

It is granted that all the faithful are not called to be ministers, and that all ministers are not appointed, like St. Paul, to establish new Churches: but it is maintained, that all Christians, in their different states, are to be filled with the piety of that apostle. If the most inconsiderable trader among us is not allowed to say, "I deal only in trifling articles, and therefore should be indulged with a false balance,"–if such a trader is required to be as just in his shop, as a judge on his tribunal; and if the lowest volunteer in an army is called to show as much valour in his humble post, as a general officer in his more exalted station; the same kind of reasoning may be applied to the Christian Church: so that her youngest communicant is not permitted to say, "My youth, or the weakness of my sex, excuses me from exercising the charity, the humility, the diligence, and the zeal which the Scriptures prescribe."

It should be laid down as an incontrovertible truth, that the same zeal which was manifested by St. Paul for the glory of God, and the same charity that he displayed, *as an apostle,* in the very extensive scene of his labours, a minister is called to exercise, *as a pastor*, in his parish, and a private person, *as father of a family,* in his own house. Nay, even every woman, in proportion to her capacity, and as the other duties of her station permit, should feel the same ardour to promote the salvation of her children and domestics, as St. Paul once discovered to promote that of the ancient Jews and Gentiles. Observe, in the harvest field, how it fares with the labourers, when they are threatened with an impetuous shower. All do not bind and bear the weighty sheaves. Every one is occupied according to their rank, their strength, their age, and their sex; and all are in action, even to the little gleaners. The true Church resembles this field. The faithful of every rank, age, and sex, have but one heart and one mind. According to their state, and the degree of their faith, all are animated to labour in the cause of God, and all are endeavouring to save either communities, families, or individuals, from the wrath to come; as the reapers and gleaners endeavour to secure the rich sheaves, and even the single ears of grain, from the gathering storm.

If, in the course of this work, some truths are proposed which may appear new to the Christian reader, let him candidly appeal, for the validity of them, to the Holy Scriptures, and to the testimony of reason, supported by the most respectable authorities, such as the confessions of faith adopted by the purest Churches, together with the works of the most celebrated pastors and professors who have explained such confessions.

Among other excellent ends proposed in publishing the following sheets, it is hoped that they may bring back bigoted divines to evangelical moderation, and either reconcile, or bring near to one another the orthodox professor, the imperfect Christian, and the sincere deist.

THE FIRST TRAIT
IN THE MORAL CHARACTER OF ST. PAUL.

His early piety.

IF great apostle of the Gentiles bore no resemblance to those who reject the service of God, till they are rendered incapable of gratifying their unruly passions. He was mindful of his Creator from his early youth, and as an observer of religious rites outstripped the most exact and rigid professors of his time; so that the regularity of his conduct, the fervour of his devotion, and the vivacity of his zeal, attracted the attention of his superiors in every place. Observe the manner in which he himself speaks on this subject, before the tribunal of Festus: "My manner of life, from my youth, which was at the first among mine own nation at Jerusalem, know all the Jews, which knew me from the beginning, (if they would testify,) that after the straitest sect of our religion I lived a Pharisee," Acts xxvi:4, 5. Having occasion afterward to mention the same circumstances, in his Epistle to the Galatians, he writes thus: "Ye have heard of my conversation in time past, how I profited in the Jews' religion above many my equals in mine own nation, being more exceedingly zealous of the traditions of my fathers," Galatians i:13, 14. And to what an extraordinary pitch of excellence he had carried his morality, may be inferred from the following short, but solemn declaration, which was made in the presence of persons who were very well competent to have convicted him of falsehood, had there been found the least blemish in his outward conduct: "Men and brethren, I have lived in all good conscience before God unto this day," Acts xxiii, 1. Such was the early piety of St. Paul; and such was the righteousness in which he trusted, when, through zeal for the Church and state, of which he was a member, he persecuted Christians as disturbers of the public peace.

Having seen the beautiful side of this apostle's early character, let us now consider his defects. As a member of the Jewish Church he was inspired with zeal, but that zeal was rigid and severe; as a member of society, his manners were probably courteous, but on some occasions his behavior was tyrannical and inhuman; in a word, he possessed the whole of religion, except those essential parts of it, humility and charity. Supercilious and impatient, he would bear no contradiction. Presuming upon his own sufficiency, he gave himself no time to compare his errors with truth: and hence, covering his cruelty with the specious name of zeal, he breathed out "threatenings and slaughter against the disciples of the Lord," Acts ix:1. He himself, speaking of this part of his character, makes the following humiliating confession: "I was a blasphemer and a persecutor, and injurious," 1 Timothy i:13. "I verily thought

The Works of John Fletcher

with myself that I ought to do many things contrary to the name of Jesus of Nazareth. Which thing I also did in Jerusalem, and many of the saints did I shut up in prison, having received authority from the chief priests; and when they were put to death I gave my voice against them. And I punished them oft in every synagogue, and compelled them to blaspheme; and being exceedingly mad against them, I persecuted them even unto strange cities," Acts xxvi:9-11.

Nevertheless, this rigid Pharisee, who carried his devotion to bigotry, and his zeal to fury, had an upright heart in the sight of God. "I obtained mercy," says he, after his conversion, "because I did it ignorantly in unbelief," 1 Timothy i:13; imagining, that when I persecuted the disciples of Jesus, I was opposing a torrent of the most dangerous errors.

Piety is that knowledge of God and his various relations to man, which leads us to adore, to love, and obey him in public and in private. This great virtue is the first trait in the moral character of St. Paul; and it is absolutely necessary to the Christian character in general, since it is that parent of all virtues, to which God has given the promise of the present life, and of that which is to come. But it is more particularly necessary to those who consecrate themselves to the holy ministry; since being obliged by their office to exhibit before their flock an example of piety, if they themselves are destitute of godliness, they must necessarily act without any conformity to the sacred character they have dared to assume.

If Quintilian the heathen has laid it down as a general principle, that it is impossible to become a good orator without being a good man, surely no one will deny that piety should be considered as the first qualification essential to a Christian speaker. Mons. Roques, in his "Evangelical Pastor," observes that "the minister, by his situation, is a man retired from the world, devoted to God, and called to evangelical holiness. He is," continues he, "according to St. Paul, 'a man of God,' that is, a person entirely consecrated to God; a man of superior excellence; a man, in some sense, divine; and to answer, in any degree, the import of this appellation, it is necessary that his piety should be illustrious, solid, and universal." Without doubt this pious author had collected these beautiful ideas from the writings of St. Paul, who thus addresses Titus upon the same subject: "A minister must be blameless as the steward of God; not self-willed, not soon angry, not given to wine, no striker, not given to filthy lucre: but a lover of hospitality, a lover of good men, sober, just, holy, temperate; holding fast the faithful word, that he may be able, by sound doctrine, both to exhort and convince the gainsayers," Titus i:7-9. "He must use sound speech, that cannot be condemned: in doctrine showing uncorruptness, gravity, sincerity; that he who is of the contrary part may be ashamed, having no evil thing to say of him," Titus ii:7, 8.

A pastor without piety disgraces the holy profession which he has made choice of, most probably from the same temporal motives which influence others to embrace the study of the law, or the profession of arms. If those who are called to serve tables were to be "men of honest report, full of the Holy Ghost and wisdom," Acts vi:3, it is evident that the same dispositions and graces should be possessed, in a more eminent degree, by those who are called to minister in holy things. "When thou art converted," said Christ to Peter, "strengthen thy brethren," Luke xxii:32.

No sight can be more absurd than that of an impenitent infidel engaged in calling sinners to repentance and faith. Even the men of the world look down with contempt upon a minister of this description, whose conduct perpetually contradicts his discourses, and who, while he is pressing upon others the necessity of holiness, indulges himself in the pleasures of habitual sin. Such a preacher, far from being instrumental in effecting true conversions among his people, will generally lead his hearers into the same hypocrisy which distinguishes his own character: since that which was said in ancient times holds equally true in the present day, "Like people, like priest," Hosea iv:9. Lukewarm pastors make careless Christians; and the worldly preacher leads his worldly hearers as necessarily into carnal security, as a blind guide conducts the blind into the ditch. And to this unhappy source may be traced the degenerate manners of the present age, the reproach under which our holy religion labours, and the increasing triumphs of infidelity.

"The natural man," saith St. Paul, "receiveth not the things of the Spirit of God: for they are foolishness unto him; neither can he know them, because they are spiritually discerned," 1 Corinthians ii:14. Now, if a minister, who is destitute of Scriptural piety, is counted unable to comprehend the doctrines of the Gospel, how much less is he able to publish and explain them? And if those, who live according to the vain customs of the world, have not the righteousness of the Pharisees, with what propriety can they be called, I will not say, true ministers, but even pious Deists?

Though every candidate for the sacred ministry may not be in circumstances, to declare with St. Paul, "I have lived in all good conscience before God unto this day:" yet all who aspire to that important office should, at least, be able to say with sincerity, "Herein do I exercise myself, to have always a conscience void of offence, toward God and toward man," Acts xxiv:16. Such were the morals and the conduct of a Socrates and an Epictetus: and worshippers like these, "coming from the east and from the west," shall enter into the kingdom of heaven, "while the children of the kingdom shall be cast out into outer darkness," Matthew viii:11, 12.

TRAIT II.

His Christian piety.

IT has been made sufficiently plain, under the preceding article, that St. Paul was possessed of a good degree of piety from his very infancy. Having been brought up in the fear of God by his father, who is supposed to have been a zealous Pharisee, he was afterward instructed at the feet of Gamaliel, a pious doctor of the law, to whose wisdom and moderation St. Luke has borne an honourable testimony, Acts v:34. And so greatly had he profited in his youth by these inestimable privileges, that "touching the righteousness which is of the law," he was blameless. But this piety was not sufficient under the New Testament.

To become a Christian and a true minister of the Gospel, it is necessary to have not only the piety of a sincere Deist, or of a devout Jew, as St. Paul had before his conversion, but also those higher degrees of piety which that apostle possessed, after he had received the two-fold gift of deep repentance toward God and living faith in Jesus Christ. The basis of piety among the Jews was a knowledge of God, as Creator, Protector, and Rewarder: but, in order to have Christian piety, it is necessary, that to this knowledge of God as Creator, &c, should be added that of God the Redeemer,

God the destroyer of all evils, God our Saviour; or in other words, the knowledge of Jesus Christ. "This is life eternal, that they might know thee, the only true God, and Jesus Christ whom thou hast sent," John xvii:3.

But who can truly know, I will not say his Saviour, but merely his need of a Saviour, without first becoming acquainted with his own heart, and receiving there a lively impression both of his sin and his danger? A student in theology, who has not yet submitted himself to the maxim of Solon, "Know thyself;" and who has never mourned under that sense of our natural ignorance and depravity which forced Socrates to confess the want of a Divine instructer:—a candidate, I say, who is wholly unacquainted with himself, instead of eagerly soliciting the imposition of hands, should rather seek after a true understanding of the censure which Christ once passed upon the pastor of the Laodicean Church: "Thou art wretched, and miserable, and poor, and blind, and naked," Revelation iii:17.

If a young man steals into the ministry without this knowledge, far from being able to preach the Gospel, he will not even comprehend that first evangelical principle, "Blessed are the poor in spirit, for theirs is the kingdom of heaven," Matthew v:3. And instead of devoutly offering up to God the prayers of an assembled congregation, he will constantly begin the sacred office by an act of hypocrisy, in saying, "Almighty Father we have erred and strayed from thy ways like lost sheep. We have offended against thy holy laws. There is no health in us. But thou, O Lord, have mercy upon us, miserable sinners." After making these confessions in public, when he is interrogated in private respecting that misery and condemnation, under a sense of which he so lately appeared to groan, he will not scruple immediately to contradict what he has so plainly expressed: thus discovering to every impartial observer, that when he prays in public, he prays either as a child who understands not what he repeats, or as a deceiver, who appears to believe what he really gives no credit to, and that merely, for the sake of enjoying the pension of a minister, and his rank in society.

What is here said of ministers is equally applicable to Christians in general. If any one dares to approach the sacramental table, there to make a profession of being redeemed from eternal death by the death of Christ, before he is deeply humbled under a sense of the condemnation due to his sin: can such a one be said to perform an act of piety? Is he not rather engaged in performing an act of vain ceremony and presumptuous dissimulation in the presence of God? The feigned humiliation of such a communicant would resemble that of a rebel subject, who, without any consciousness that his actions had merited death, should cast himself, from motives of interest, at the feet of his prince, and affect to rejoice under a sense of that undeserved clemency which permitted him to live. All our professions of faith in Christ are tinctured, more or less, with hypocrisy, unless preceded by that painful conviction of past errors, whence alone can cordially flow those humiliating confessions, with which we are accustomed to begin our sacred services.

The true Christian, and, consequently, the true minister, is constrained to cry out, with St. Paul, when he discovered the purity of Jehovah's law, and the greatness of his own guilt: "The law is spiritual," and demands an obedience correspondent to its nature; "but I am carnal, sold under sin: for what I would, that I do not; but what I hate, that I do. I know that in me, that is, in my flesh, dwelleth no good firing. O wretched man that I am! who shall deliver me from the body of this death?" Romans vii:14-24.

The Portrait of St. Paul

In this manner the true penitent, weary and heavy laden, makes his approaches to the Saviour; and while he continues to implore his grace and favour, an incomprehensible change takes place in his soul. His groans are suddenly turned into songs of deliverance, and he is enabled to adopt the triumphant language of the great apostle: "I thank God, through Jesus Christ our Lord; for the law of the Spirit of life in Christ Jesus hath made me free from the law of sin and death. There is therefore now no condemnation to them which are in Christ Jesus, who walk not after the flesh, but after the Spirit," Romans vii:25; viii:1, 2.

Every true follower of Christ, therefore, and especially every true minister of the Gospel, has really experienced the evil of sin, the inability of man to free himself from such evil, and the efficacy of that remedy, which endued the first Christians with so extraordinary a degree of purity, power, and joy. And in testimony of the virtue of this sovereign remedy, every such follower has a right to declare with his happy predecessors, "We give thanks unto the Father, who hath made us meet to be partakers of the inheritance of the saints in light: who hath delivered us from the power of darkness, and hath translated us into the kingdom of his dear Son; in whom we have redemption through his blood, even the forgiveness of sins," Colossians i:12-14.

When a preacher is possessed of Christian piety; or, in other words, when he has made his peace with God, by that deep repentance which enables us to die unto sin, and by that living faith which unites us to Christ, he naturally invites the world to embrace a Saviour who has wrought for him so wonderful a deliverance: and this invitation he enforces with all the power and warmth which must ever accompany deep sensibility. After having believed with the heart to the obtaining of righteousness, he is prepared to confess with his lips, and to testify of his salvation: crying out, as sincerely as Simeon, but in a sense far more complete, "Lord, now lettest thou thy servant depart in peace; for, according to thy word, mine eyes have seen thy salvation." "Here," says Mr. Ostervald, "may be applied what was spoken by our blessed Lord, 'A good man, out of the good treasure of his heart, bringeth forth good things.' Erasmus speaks the same thing, *Nihil potentius ad excitandos bonos affectus, quam piorum affectuum fonten habere in pectore. Si vis me flere, dolendum est, &c:* that is, following the idea of the author, you will never win others over to a religious life, unless you yourself are first possessed of piety. This inspires thoughts, dispositions, and words, which nothing else can produce. It is this that animates the voice, the gesture, and every action of the Christian preacher. When he is thus grounded in piety, it is difficult to conceive with what facility, and with what success he labours, still enjoying an unspeakable sweetness in himself. Then it is that he is truly sensible of his vocation; then he speaks in the cause of God, and then only he is in a proper situation to affect others."

It appeared so necessary to the fathers, who composed the synod of Berne, that every minister should be possessed of solid piety, that they believed it impossible for a man to be a good catechist without it. After recommending it to pastors to explain among the youth, the Lord's prayer and the apostles' creed, they add: "This will be abundantly more effectual, if, first of all, we are careful that Jesus Christ may arise in our own hearts. The fire, with which we should then be animated, would soon stir up and warm the docile minds of children. Otherwise, that which reason alone draws from books, and is taught by other men, is no more than a human work, and will be ineffectual, till the great Master, the Holy Spirit itself, becomes of the party, creating, renewing, and regenerating to a celestial and eternal life." (*Acts of the Synod* chap. xxxiv.):—

REFLECTIONS

Upon the second trait of the character of St. Paul.

1. THE experimental knowledge of our misery as sinners, and of our salvation as sinners redeemed, is the portion of every believer under the Gospel. If we are destitute of this two-fold knowledge, we are yet in a state of dangerous ignorance, and are denominated Christians in vain: for Christian humility has its source in the knowledge of our corruption, as Christian charity flows from the knowledge of the great salvation which Christ has procured for us: and if these two graces are not resident in our hearts, our religion is but the shadow of Christianity.

2. As there are some persons whose physiognomy is strongly marked, and who have something peculiarly striking in the whole turn of their countenance; so there are some, the traits of whose moral character are equally striking, and whose conversion is distinguished by uncommon circumstances. Such was the Apostle Paul. But a train of wonderful occurrences is by no means necessary to conversion. For example—It is not necessary that all believers should be actually cast to the earth: or that groaning beneath the weight of their sins, and under the conviction of a two-fold blindness, they should continue in prayer for three days and nights, without either eating or drinking. But it is absolutely necessary that they should be sensible of an extreme sorrow for having offended a gracious God; that they should condemn themselves and their vices by an unfeigned repentance, and that, confessing the depravity of their whole heart, they should abandon themselves to that sincere distress which refuses all consolation, except that which is from above. Neither is it necessary that they should hear a voice from heaven, that they should see a light brighter than the sun, or behold, in a vision, the minister chosen to bring them consolation in the name of the Lord Jesus. But it is absolutely necessary that they should hear the word of God, that they should be illuminated by the Gospel, and receive directions from any messenger sent for their relief; till, placing their whole confidence in God through a gracious Redeemer, they feel a new and heavenly nature produced within them. This sincere repentance and this living faith, or, which is the same thing, this Christian piety, is strictly required of every believer under the New Testament.

3. Christian piety constitutes the great difference that is observed between true ministers and unworthy pastors. The latter preach, chiefly, either in order to obtain benefices, or to preserve them, or, perhaps, to relieve one another in the discharge of those duties which they esteem heavy and painful. But the desire of communicating to sinners that spiritual knowledge, which is more precious than rubies, is the grand motive for preaching with the true ministers of God. They publish Christ, like St. Paul, from sentiment and inclination; exposing themselves even to persecution on account of preaching the Gospel, like those faithful evangelists, who, when commanded to teach no more in the name of Jesus, answered with equal respect and resolution: "Whether it be right, in the sight of God, to hearken unto you more than unto God, judge ye; for we cannot but speak the things which we have seen and heard," Acts iv:19, 20.

4. It is worthy of observation, that St. Paul supplicates, not only for all public teachers, but for every private believer in the Church, the highest degrees of grace and Christian experience. "I cease not," saith he to the Ephesians, "to make mention of you in my prayers: that the God of our Lord Jesus Christ, the Father of glory, may give unto you the spirit of wisdom and revelation in the knowledge of him; the eyes of your understanding being enlightened, that ye may know what is the hope of his calling, and what the riches of the glory of his inheritance in the saints: and what is the exceeding greatness of his power to us-ward, who believe," Ephesians i:16-19. And the same end which this apostle proposed to himself in his private supplications, St. John also proposed to himself in writing his public Epistles: "That which we have seen and heard declare we unto you, that ye may also have fellowship with us; and truly our fellowship is with the Father, and with his Son, Jesus Christ. And these things write we unto you, that your joy may be full," 1 John i:3, 4. As though he had said, We write, if haply we may excite you to seek after higher degrees of faith, charity, and obedience; "that being rooted and grounded in love, ye may be able to comprehend with all saints, the love of Christ, which passeth knowledge; that ye may be filled with all the fulness of God," Ephesians iii:17-19. The attentive reader will easily perceive, that what was once the subject of St. Paul's most ardent prayers, is at this day considered by nominal Christians in general, as a proper subject for the most pointed raillery.

5. Those ministers who are not yet furnished with Christian experience, and who are not seeking after it as the pearl of great price, held out to us in the Gospel, are not yet truly converted to the Christian faith: and (I repeat it after Mr. Ostervald) being destitute of Christian piety, far from being in circumstances to preach the Gospel, they are not even able to comprehend it. These are they, "who, having a form of godliness, deny the power thereof," 2 Timothy iii:5. And the greatest eulogium that can be pronounced upon such characters, is that with which St. Paul honoured the unbelieving zealots of his time: "I bear them record that they have a zeal for God;" but that zeal is unaccompanied with any true knowledge, either of man's weakness, or the Redeemer's power: "for they, being ignorant of God's righteousness, and going about to establish their own righteousness, have not submitted themselves unto the righteousness of God. For Christ is the end of the law for righteousness to every one that believeth," Romans x:2-4.

6. Whoever has not experienced that conviction of sin, and that repentance, which is described by St. Paul in the Seventh chapter of his Epistle to the Romans, though, like Nicodemus, he may be "a doctor in Israel," yet he shall never see the kingdom of God. Totally carnal, and satisfied to continue so, he neither understands nor desires that regeneration which the Gospel proposes and insists upon. He endeavours not to fathom the sense of these important words: "Verily, verily, I say unto thee, except a man be born again, he cannot see the kingdom of God," John iii:8. He considers those who are born of the Spirit as rank enthusiasts, and disdains to make any serious inquiry respecting the foundation of their hope. If his acquaintance with the letter of the Scripture did not restrain him, he would tauntingly address the artless question of Nicodemus to every minister who preaches the doctrine of regeneration: "How can a man be born when he is old? Can he enter the second time into his mother's womb, and be born?" John iii:4. And unless he was withheld by a sense of politeness, he would rudely repeat to every zealous follower of St. Paul the ungracious expression of Festus: "Thou art beside thyself; much" mystic "learning doth make thee mad," Acts xxvi:24.

7. On the contrary, a minister who is distinguished by the second trait of the character of St. Paul, at the same time proportionably possesses every disposition necessary to form an evangelical pastor: since it is not possible for Christian piety to exist without the brilliant light of truth, and the burning zeal of charity. And every minister who has this light and this love, is enriched with those two powerful resources which enabled the first Christians to act as citizens of heaven, and the first ministers as ambassadors of Christ.

TRAIT III.
His intimate union with Christ by faith.

"I AM come," said the good Shepherd, "that my sheep might have life, and that they might have it more abundantly," John x:10, 11. "I am the light of the world," John viii:12. "I am the way, the truth, and the life," John xiv:6. "I am the vine; ye are the branches," John xv:5. The faithful minister understands the signification of these mysterious expressions. He walks in this way, he follows this light, he embraces this truth, and enjoys this life in all its rich abundance. Constantly united to his Lord, by an humble faith, a lively hope, and an ardent charity, he is enabled to say, with St. Paul, "The love of Christ constraineth me; because we thus judge, that if one died for all, then were all dead; and that he died for all, that they which live should not henceforth live unto themselves, but unto Him who died for them and rose again," 2 Corinthians v:14. "We are dead, and our life is hid with Christ in God. When Christ, who is our life, shall appear, then shall we also appear with him in glory," Colossians iii:3, 4. "For if we have been planted together in the likeness of his death, we shall be also in the likeness of his resurrection. Knowing that Christ, being raised from the dead, dieth no more; but liveth unto God. We likewise reckon ourselves to be dead indeed unto sin, but alive unto God, through Jesus Christ our Lord," Romans vi:5, 9, 11.

This living faith is the source from whence all the sanctity of the Christian is derived, and all the power of the true minister. It is the medium through which that sap of grace and consolation, those streams of peace and joy, are perpetually flowing, which enrich the believing soul, and make it fruitful in every good work; or, to speak without, a metaphor, from this powerful grace proceeds that love of God and man which influences us to think and act, either as members or as ministers of Jesus Christ. The character of the Christian is determined according to the strength or weakness of his faith. If the faith of St. Paul had been weak or wavering, his portrait would have been unworthy of our contemplation: he would necessarily have fallen into doubt and discouragement; he might probably have sunk into sin, as St. Peter plunged into the sea; he must, sooner or later, have lost his spiritual vigour, and have made the same appearance in the Church as those ministers and Christians who are influenced by the maxims of the world. The effects of faith are still truly mysterious, though our Lord has explained them in as intelligible a manner as their nature will permit: "He that abideth in me," by a living faith, "and in whom I abide," by the light of my word and by the power of my Spirit, "the same bringeth forth much fruit; for without me ye can do nothing. If any man abide not in me, he is cast forth as a branch, and" being "withered, is cast into the fire and burned. Herein is my Father glorified, that," united to me as the branches to the vine, "ye bear much fruit; so shall ye be my disciples," John xv:6, 7, 8.

Penetrated with these great truths, and daily cleaving more firmly to his living Head, the true minister expresses what the natural man cannot receive, and what few pastors of the present age are able to comprehend, though St. Paul not only experienced it in his own heart, but openly declares it in the following remarkable passage: "I am crucified with Christ: nevertheless, I live; yet, not I, but Christ liveth in me, and the life which I now live in the flesh, I live by the faith of the Son of God, who loved me, and gave himself for me," Galatians ii:20.

TRAIT IV.

His extraordinary vocation to the holy ministry, and in what that ministry chiefly consists.

EVERY professor of Christianity is acquainted with the honour which our Lord conferred upon the Apostle Paul, in not only calling him to a participation of the Christian faith, but by appointing him also to publish the everlasting Gospel. A just sense of this double honour penetrated the heart of that apostle with the most lively gratitude: "I give thanks," saith he, "to Christ Jesus our Lord, for that he counted me faithful, putting me into the ministry; who was before a blasphemer, and a persecutor, and injurious. But I obtained mercy, because I did it ignorantly in unbelief: and the grace of our Lord was exceeding abundant in me, with faith and love, which is in Christ Jesus. Howbeit, for this cause I obtained mercy, that in me first Jesus Christ might show forth all long-suffering, for a pattern to them which should hereafter believe on him to everlasting life," 1 Timothy i:12, 16. The evangelical ministry, to which St. Paul was immediately called, is in general the same through every age enlightened by the Gospel, and consists in publishing the truth after such a manner that the wicked may be converted, and the faithful edified. The commission which this great apostle received from Christ contains, essentially, nothing more than the acknowledged duty of every minister of the Gospel. Leave out the miraculous appearance of our Lord; pass over the circumstance of a commission given in an extraordinary manner; substitute the word sinners for that of Gentiles, and instead of Jews, read hypocritical professors; and you will perceive that, with these immaterial alterations, the commission of St. Paul is the commission of every faithful minister of the Church. Observe the tenor of it. In person, or by my ambassadors, in a manner either extraordinary or ordinary, "I appoint thee a minister, and a witness of those things which thou hast seen, [or experienced,] and of those things in the which I will appear to thee; and I will deliver thee from the hands of the people, and from the

Gentiles," that is, from the hands of hypocritical professors, and from ignorant sinners, "unto whom I now send thee, to open their eyes, and to turn them from the darkness of error to the light of truth, and from the power of Satan to God," that is, from sin, which is the image of Satan, to holiness, which is the image of God, "that they may receive forgiveness of sins, and an inheritance among them which are sanctified, by faith that is in me," Acts xxvi:16-18. Such was the office to which St. Paul was appointed, more especially among the Gentile nations; and such, without doubt, is the office of every pastor, at least within the limits of his particular parish. As for taking the ecclesiastical habit, reading over some pages of a liturgy, solemnizing marriages, baptizing infants, keeping registers, and receiving stipends, these things are merely accidental; and every minister should be able to say, with St. Paul, "Christ sent me, not [principally] to baptize, but to preach the Gospel," 1 Corinthians i:17.

It is evident, from various passages in the different offices of our Church, that our pious reformers were unanimously of opinion, that Christ himself appoints, and, in some sort, inspires all true pastors; that he commits the flock to their keeping, and that their principal care is the same with that of the first evangelists, namely, "the conversion of souls." And truly, the same Lord who appointed his disciples as apostles, or ocular witnesses of his resurrection, has also appointed others as pastors, or witnesses of a secondary order, and suffragans of the first evangelists. If the witnesses of a higher order were permitted to see Christ after his resurrection, these of a secondary order have felt the efficacy of his resurrection, "being raised together with him," or regenerated through the reception of "a lively hope, by the rising again, of Christ from the dead," 1 Peter i:3; Colossians iii:1. So that every true minister who bears his testimony to the truths of the Gospel, whether it be from the pulpit or before tribunals, is supported by his own particular experience of Christ's resurrection, as well as by a conviction founded upon the depositions of the first witnesses. Now this conviction and this experience are by no means confined to the ministering servants of God; but the hearts of the faithful, in their several generations, have been influenced by them both; if it be true, that they have constantly stood prepared to seal with their blood these two important truths, Jesus Christ "died for our sins, and rose again for our justification." Millions of the laity have been called to give this last proof of their faith, and, beyond all doubt, it is abundantly more difficult to bear testimony to the truth upon a scaffold than from a pulpit.

If St. Paul and the other apostles are considered as persons of rank far superior to ours, they themselves cry out, "O sirs! we also are men of like passions with you," Acts xiv:15. If it be said that God inspired the apostles with all the wisdom and zeal necessary to fulfil the duties of their high vocation; it may be replied, that our Churches implore for their established pastors the same wisdom and zeal, grounding such prayers upon the authority of many plain passages of Holy Scripture. "Now unto him that is able to do exceeding abundantly above all that we ask or think, according to the power that worketh in us, unto him be glory in the Church, by Christ Jesus, throughout all ages, world without end," Ephesians iii:20, 21.

Moreover, it is an error to suppose that the apostles needed no augmentation of that Divine light by which spiritual objects are discerned. St. Paul, who was favoured with an extraordinary inspiration, and that sufficient to compose sacred books, in which infallibility is to be found, writes thus to believers: "Now we see through a glass darkly; but then face to face. Now I know in part; but then shall I know even as also I am known," 1 Corinthians xiii:12. An humble, but happy confession! which, on the one hand, will not suffer us to be discouraged when we are most sensible of our inadequate light; and teaches us, on the other, how necessary it is to make incessant application to the "Father of lights;" equally guarding us against the pride of some, who imagine themselves to have apprehended all the truth; and the wilful ignorance of others, who pronounce spiritual knowledge to be altogether unattainable.

Now, if the Apostle Paul could but imperfectly discern the depths of evangelical truth, and if angels themselves "desire to look into these things," 1 Peter i:12, who can sufficiently wonder at the presumption of those men, who are so far persuaded of their own infallibility that they regard all truths which they are unable to fathom as the mere reveries of fanaticism? But, turning our eyes at present from the pernicious error of these self-exalted Christians, let us consider a subject in which we are more interested than in the extraordinary vocation of St. Paul to the holy ministry.

REFLECTIONS.
Upon the ordinary vocation to the holy ministry.

"THE harvest truly is plenteous, but the labourers are few: pray ye, therefore, the Lord of the harvest, that he will send forth labourers into his harvest," Matthew ix:37, 38. Retaining in memory these remarkable words of our Lord, the conscientious man is incapable of thrusting himself into the holy ministry, without being first duly called thereto by the Lord of the harvest, the great "Shepherd and Bishop of souls."

The minister of the present age is not ordinarily called to the holy ministry, except by carnal motives, such as his own vanity, or his peculiar taste for a tranquil and indolent life. Perhaps his vocation to the ministry is principally from his father and mother, who have determined that their son shall enter into holy orders. Very frequently if the candidate for holy orders had sincerity enough to discover the real inclination of his heart, he might make his submissions to the dignitaries of our Church, and say, "Put me, I pray you, into one of the priest's offices, that I may eat a piece of bread," 1 Samuel ii:36.

It is not thus with the real believer who consecrates himself to the holy ministry. He is not ignorant that "Christ glorified himself to be made a high priest:" and he is perfectly assured that no man has a right to take upon himself the sacerdotal dignity "but he that is called of God," either in an extraordinary manner, as Aaron and St. Paul, or at least in an ordinary manner, as Apollos and Timothy, Hebrews v:4, 5. As it is a matter of the utmost importance to understand by what tokens this ordinary vocation to the holy ministry may be discovered, the following reflections upon so interesting a subject may not be altogether superfluous:—

If a young man of virtuous manners is deeply penetrated with this humiliating truth, "All have sinned and come short of the glory of God," Romans iii:23: if, farther, he is effectually convinced of this consolatory truth, "God so loved the world that he gave his only begotten Son, that whosoever believeth in him should not perish, but have everlasting life," John iii:16: if his natural talents have been strengthened by a liberal education: if the pleasure of doing good is sweeter to him than all the pleasures of sense: if the hope of "converting sinners from the error of their way" occupies his mind more agreeably than the idea of acquiring all the advantages of fortune: if the honour of publishing the Gospel is superior in his eyes to the honour of becoming the ambassador of an earthly prince: in short, if by a desire which springs from the fear of God, the love of Christ, and the concern he takes in the salvation of his neighbour, he is led to consecrate himself to the holy ministry: if, in the order of Providence, outward circumstances concur with his own designs; and if he solicits the grace and assistance of God with greater eagerness than he seeks the outward vocation from his superiors in the Church by the imposition of hands; he may then satisfy himself, that the great High Priest of the Christian profession has set him apart for the high office to which he aspires.

When, after serious examination, any student in theology discovers in himself the necessary dispositions mentioned above; then having received imposition of hands, with faith and humility, from the pastors who preside in the Church, he may solidly conclude that he has been favoured with the ordinary vocation. Hence, looking up to the source of the important office with which he is honoured, he can adopt with propriety the language of St. Paul: "I thank Jesus Christ our Lord, for that he hath counted me faithful, putting me into the ministry," 1 Timothy i:12. "Though I preach the Gospel, I have nothing to glory of; for necessity is laid upon me, yea, wo is unto me if I preach not the Gospel;" for then I should be found unfaithful to my vocation, 1 Corinthians ix:16. "God was in Christ reconciling the world unto himself, and hath committed unto us the word of reconciliation. Now then we are ambassadors for Christ," 2 Corinthians v:19, 20. And if he becomes not like that "wicked and slothful servant," who refused to administer to the necessities of his master's household, he will be able, at all times, to say, "Therefore, seeing we have this ministry, as we have received mercy, we faint not: but have renounced the hidden things of dishonesty, not walking in craftiness, nor handling the word of God deceitfully, but by manifestation of the truth commending ourselves to every man's conscience in the sight of God," 2 Corinthians iv:1, 2.

A person of this description, searching the depths of the human heart, of which he has acquired a competent knowledge by the study of his own, meditating with attention upon the proofs, and with humility upon the mysteries of our holy religion, giving himself up to the study of Divine things, and, above all, to prayer and to good works; such a pastor may reasonably hope to grow in grace, and in the knowledge of that powerful Saviour, whom he earnestly proclaims to others. Nor is it probable that such a one will labour altogether in vain. Gradually instructed in the things which concern the kingdom of God, he will become like the father of a family, bringing forth out of his treasures things new and old: and whether he speaks of the old man, the earthly nature, which he has put off with such extreme pain, or the new man, the heavenly nature, which he has put on with equal joy, Esphesians 4:22, 24, he will speak with a conviction so powerful, and a persuasion so constraining, that the careless must necessarily be alarmed, and the faithful encouraged.

TRAIT V.

His entire devotion to Jesus Christ.

THE true Christian, called to become a disciple of the blessed Jesus, rather than refuse the offered privilege, renounces his, all. If this token of devotion to Christ is discernible in the character of every true Christian, it is still more conspicuous in the character of every true minister. Such a person inwardly called by the grace of God to a state of discipleship with Christ, and outwardly consecrated to such a state by the imposition of hands, gives himself unreservedly up to the service of his condescending Master. He withstands no longer that permanent command of our exalted Lord, to which his first disciples showed so cheerful a submission, "Follow me." Nor is he discouraged, while Christ continues, "If any man will come after me, let him deny himself, take up his cross, and follow me," Matthew xvi:24. "No man having put his hand to the plough, and looking back, is fit for the kingdom of God," Luke ix:62. "He that loveth father or mother, son or daughter, more than me, is not worthy of me." He that findeth his life shall lose it: and he that loseth his life for my sake, shall find it," Matthew x:37-39. If there be found any pastor who cannot adopt the solemn appeal of the first ministers of Christ, "Lo, we have left all, and followed thee," Luke xviii:28, that man is in no situation to copy the example of his forerunners in the Christian Church, and is altogether unworthy the character he bears; since without this detachment from the world, and this devotion to the Son of God, he flatters himself in vain, that he is either a true minister or a real member of Jesus Christ.

Observe the declaration of one whose attachment to his Divine Master deserves to be had in everlasting remembrance: "Those things which were gain to me, I counted loss for Christ. Yea, doubtless, and I count all things but loss for the excellency of the knowledge of Christ Jesus my Lord for whom I have suffered the loss of all things, and do count them but dung, that I may win Christ and be found in him, having the righteousness which is of God by faith," Philippians iii:7, 8, 9. "For none of us," true Christians or true ministers, "liveth to himself, or dieth to himself; but whether we live, we live unto the Lord; and whether we die, we die unto the Lord," Romans xiv:7, 8.

Professing to be either a minister or a believer of the Gospel without this entire devotion to Jesus Christ is to live in a state of the most dangerous hypocrisy: it is neither more nor less than saying, Lord! Lord! without having a firm resolution to do what our gracious Master has commanded.

TRAIT VI.

His strength and his arms.

THE ministers of the present age are furnished in a manner suitable to their design. As they are more desirous to please than to convert their hearers, so they are peculiarly anxious to embellish the inventions of a seducing imagination. They are continually seeking after the beauty of metaphors, the brilliancy of antitheses, the delicacy of description the just arrangement of words, the aptness of gesture, the modulations of voice, and every other studied ornament of artificial eloquence. While the true minister, effectually convinced of the excellence of the Gospel, relies alone for the effect of his public ministry upon the force of truth, and the assistance of his Divine Master.

Observe the manner in which St. Paul expresses himself upon this subject: "We, having the same spirit of faith according as it is written, I believed and therefore have I spoken; we also believe, and therefore speak, 2 Corinthians iv:13. And I, brethren, came not with excellency of speech, or of wisdom, declaring unto you the testimony of God: for I determined not to know any thing among you, save Jesus Christ, and him crucified. And my speech and my preaching was not with enticing words of man's wisdom, but in demonstration of the Spirit and of power: that your faith should not stand in the wisdom of men, but in the power of God," 1 Corinthians ii:1-5 "For the weapons of our warfare are not carnal, but mighty, through God, to the pulling down of strong holds: casting down imaginations, and every high thing that exalteth itself against the knowledge of God, and bringing into captivity every thought to the obedience of Christ," 2 Corinthians x:4, 5.

The true minister, following the example of St. Paul, after having experienced the power of these victorious arms, exhorts every soldier of Christ to provide himself with the same spiritual weapons. "Finally, my brethren, be strong in the Lord, and in the power of his might. Put on the whole armour of God, that ye may be able to stand. For we wrestle not merely against flesh and blood, but against principalities, against powers, against the rulers of the darkness of this world, against spiritual wickedness in high places. Wherefore take unto you the whole armour of God, that ye may be able to withstand in the evil day, and having done all, to stand.

Stand, therefore, having your loins girt about with truth, having on the breastplate of righteousness, and your feet shod with the preparation of the Gospel of peace: above all, taking the shield of faith, wherewith ye shall be able to quench all the fiery darts of the wicked. And take the helmet of salvation, and the sword of the Spirit, which is the word of God." And that you may perform heroical service with these arms, "pray always with all prayer and supplication in the Spirit," Ephesians vi:10-18.

So long as the faithful minister, or servant of Christ wears and wields these Scriptural arms, he will be truly invincible. But no man can gird himself with these invisible weapons, except he "be born of the Spirit;" nor can any Christian soldier employ them to good purpose, unless he be first endued with all that Divine power which flows from the love of God and man: he must feel, at least, some sparks of that fire of charity which warmed the bosom of St. Paul, when he cried out, "Whether we be beside ourselves, it is to God: or whether we be sober, it is for your cause. For the love of Christ and of souls constraineth us," 2 Corinthians v:13, 14.

"From the time that the eyes of St. Paul were opened to a perception of the Gospel," says Mons. Romilly, pastor of a church in Geneva, "we find him no longer the same person. He is another man, he is a new creature who thinks no more but on Gospel truths, who hears nothing, who breathes nothing but the Gospel; who speaks on no other subject, who attends to no other thing but the voice of the Gospel; who desires all the world to attend with him to the same voice, and wishes to communicate his transports to all mankind. From this happy period, neither the prejudices of flesh and blood, neither respect to man, nor the fear of death, nor any other consideration is able to withstand him in his course. He moves on with serenity in a path sown thick with reproaches and pain. What has he to fear? He despises the maxims of the world, nay, the world itself; its hatred as well as its favour, its joys as well as its sorrows, its meanness as well as its pomp. Time is no longer an object with him, nor is his economy regulated by it. He is superior to every thing; he is immortal. Though the universe arms itself against him, though hell opens its abysses, though affliction assaults him on every side, he stands immovable in every storm, looking with contempt upon death, conscious that he can never die. Superior to all his enemies, he resists their united attempts with the arms of the Gospel, opposing, to time and hell, eternity and heaven."

TRAIT VII.

His power to bind, to loose, and to bless, in the name of the Lord.

THE armour of God, described in the preceding article: is common to all Christians; but the true minister is girded with weapons of a peculiar temper. As a Christian, his sword is the word of God in general; but, as a minister, it is especially those parts of the Gospel by which he is invested with authority to preach the word of God, and to perform the functions of an ambassador of Jesus Christ. "Go," said our blessed Master to his first disciples, "and preach the Gospel to every creature. He that believeth my doctrine shall be saved: but he that believeth not shall be damned," Mark xvi:15, 16. "All power is given unto me in heaven and in earth. Go ye, therefore, and teach all nations, baptizing them in the name of the Father, and of the Son, and of the Holy Ghost; teaching them to observe all things whatsoever I have commanded you. And lo, I am with yea alway, even unto the end of the world," Matthew xxviii:18. "Verily, verily, I say unto you, he that receiveth whomsoever I send, receiveth me; and he that receiveth me, receiveth Him that sent me," John xiii:20. "Verily I say unto you, whatsoever ye shall bind on earth, shall be bound in heaven; and whatsoever ye shall loose on earth," according to the spirit of my Gospel, "shall be loosed in heaven," Matthew xviii:18.

Behold from whence the ministers of Christ have authority to absolve true penitents, and to excommunicate obstinate sinners. An authority which some have called the power of the clergy; a power which unrighteous pastors so much abuse, and which the faithful never presume to exercise but with the utmost solemnity: a power which, nevertheless, belongs to them of Divine right, and which can be denied them with no more reason than they can refuse the sacramental cup to the people. Such, at least, is the judgment of many excellent and learned divines, among whom may be reckoned Mons. Ostervald and Mons. Roques. It may, however, be inquired with propriety in this place, Can ecclesiastics be justified in still making use of their authority in these respects, unless they do it with prudence and impartiality? And would it not become them to exercise the ecclesiastical discipline, in an especial manner, upon unworthy pastors, following the maxim of St. Peter, "The time is come, that judgment must begin at the house of God!" 1 Peter iv:17.

The Works of John Fletcher

Invested with the authority which Christ has conferred upon him, the true minister is prepared to denounce the just judgments of God against obstinate sinners, to console the dejected, and to proclaim the promises of the Gospel to every sincere believer, with an energy unknown to the worldly pastor, and with a power which is accompanied by the seal of the living God. Thus, when such a minister clearly discerns the profound malice of another Elymas, he is permitted to say, with the authority of an ambassador of Jesus Christ, "O full of all subtlety and all mischief, thou child of the devil, thou enemy of all righteousness, wilt thou not cease to pervert the right ways of the Lord? Behold! the hand of the Lord shall be upon thee," Acts xiii:10, 11. But the true minister is careful never to abuse this lawful power. "We can do nothing," says St. Paul, "against the truth, but for the truth; I write these things being absent, lest being present I should use harshness, according to the power which the Lord hath given me to edification, and not to destruction," 2 Corinthians xiii:8, 10. The denunciation of vengeance is to the minister of Christ what the execution of judgment is to the God of love, his painful and strange work.

The good pastor, conscious that the ministration of mercy exceeds in glory the ministration of condemnation, places his chief glory and pleasure in spreading abroad the blessings of the new covenant. He knows that the promises are yea, and amen, in that beneficent Redeemer, who gave the following charge to his first missionaries: "Into whatsoever house ye enter, first say, Peace be to this house. And if the son of peace be there, your peace shall rest upon him: if not, it shall turn to you again," Luke x:5, 6. The wishes and prayers of a minister who acts and speaks in conformity to the intent of this benign charge, really communicate the peace and benediction of his gracious Master to those who are meet for their reception: and, according to the degree of his faith, he can write to the faithful of distant Churches with the confidence of St. Paul,—I am persuaded that "when I come unto you, I shall come in the fulness of the blessing of the Gospel of Christ," Romans xv:29. Whenever he salutes his brethren, his pen or his lips become the channel of those evangelical wishes which flow from his heart: "Grace be unto you, and peace, from God our Father, and from the Lord Jesus Christ," Philippians i:2. "The grace of our Lord Jesus Christ, and the love of God, and the communion of the Holy Ghost, be with you all," 2 Corinthians xiii:14. Thus the true minister approves himself a member of the royal priesthood, a priest of the Most High, "after the order of Melchisedec," who blessed the Patriarch Abraham: or rather, a ministering servant of the Son of God, who was manifested in the flesh, that "in him all the families of the earth might be blessed."

Great God! grant that the whole company of Christian pastors may be men after thine own heart. Leaving to the ignorant those compliments which a slavish dependence has invented, may thy ministers perpetually carry about them the love, the gravity, and the apostolic authority, which belongs to their sacred character. May all the benedictions which thou hast commissioned them to pronounce, cause them still to be received "as angels of God," Galatians iv:14. Far from being despised as hypocrites, shunned as troublesome guests, or feared as men of a covetous and tyrannical disposition, may that moment always be esteemed a happy one, in which they enter any man's habitation: and whenever they make their appearance upon these charitable occasions, may those who compose the family, each seeking to give the first salute, cry out, "How beautiful are the feet of them that preach the Gospel of peace!" Romans x:15.

The power of pronouncing exhortations and blessings is not the exclusive privilege of pastors, but belongs to all experienced believers. The patriarchs had a right to bless their children; and Jacob blessed not only his sons and grandsons, but also the king of Egypt himself. If the followers of Christ, then, are deprived of this consolatory power, the children of ancient Israel were more highly privileged than the members of the Christian Church, who are called, nevertheless, to receive more precious benedictions, and to be, as our Lord expresses it, "the salt of the earth," and "the light of the world." When St. Paul writes to believers, "Desire spiritual gifts; but rather that ye may prophesy: for he that prophesieth speaketh unto men to edification, to exhortation, and comfort," 1 Corinthians xiv:1, 3, he doubtless excites them to ask of God that overflowing charity, and that patriarchal authority, without which it is impossible for them fully to comply with the following apostolic injunction, "Bless and curse not, knowing that ye are thereunto called, that ye should inherit a blessing;" and without a high degree of which they cannot sincerely obey those distinguished precepts of our blessed Lord, "Love your enemies; do good. to them that hate you; and pray for them which despitefully use you, and persecute you," Romans xii:14; 1 Peter iii:9; Matthew v:44.

TRAIT VIII.
The earnestness with which he began, and continued to fill up the duties of his vocation.

THE true penitent, having renounced himself for the honour of following his exalted Lord, stands faithfully in his own vocation, whether it be secular or ecclesiastic. He is prepared, upon all occasions, to perform the will of his gracious Master: and if he is commissioned to act as a minister of Christ, after furnishing himself with "the whole armour of God," he will expose himself, without fear, to the most threatening dangers, that he may compel sinners to come in to the marriage supper of the Lamb. "I rejoice," saith St. Paul, "in my sufferings for the body of Christ, which is the Church, whereof I am made a minister, according to the dispensation of God which is given to me for you to fulfil the word of God; even the mystery, which hath been hid from ages, but which is now made manifest to his saints; to whom God would make known what is the riches of the glory of this mystery among the Gentiles, which is Christ in you, the hope of glory; whom we preach, warning every man, and teaching every man in all wisdom, that we may present every man perfect in Christ Jesus; whereunto I also labour, striving according to his working which worketh in me mightily. For I would that ye knew what great conflict I have for you," and for all those among whom the word of God is preached, "that their hearts might be comforted, being knit together in love, and unto all riches of the full assurance of understanding to the acknowledgment of the mystery of God, even of the Father and of Christ; in whom are hid all the treasures of wisdom and knowledge," Colossians i:24, 29; ii:1, 2, 3.

Such are the great ideas which the Apostle Paul entertained of the ministry he had received; and observe the assiduity with which he discharged the duties of so important an office: "Ye know," says he, speaking to the pastors, to whom he committed the care of one of his flocks, "from the first day that I came into Asia, after what manner I have been with you at all seasons, serving the Lord with all humility of mind, and with many tears and temptations: and how I kept back nothing that was profitable unto you, but have showed you, and have taught you publicly, and from house to house, testifying both to the Jews, and also to the Greeks, repentance toward God and faith toward our Lord Jesus Christ. Wherefore I take you to record this day that I am pure from the blood of all men. For I have not shunned to declare unto you all the counsel of God. Take heed, therefore, unto yourselves; for I know this, that after my departing shall grievous wolves," unfaithful pastors, "enter in among you, not sparing the flock. Therefore, watch; and remember, that by the space of three years I ceased not to warn every one night and day with tears," Acts xx:18, 31. In every place he discharged the obligations of a minister with the same application and zeal, travelling from city to city, and from church to church, bearing testimony to "the redemption that is in Jesus," and declaring the great truths of the Gospel. When the synagogues were shut against him, he preached in the schools of philosophers, upon the sea shore, on shipboard, and even in prisons; and while he dwelt a prisoner in his own house at Rome, "he received all that came in unto him, to whom he expounded and testified the kingdom of God, persuading them concerning Jesus, both out of the law of Moses, and out of the prophets, from morning till evening," Acts xxviii:23.

Thus the Son of God himself once publicly laboured for the conversion of sinners, sometimes going through all "Galilee, teaching in their synagogues, and preaching the Gospel," Matthew vi:31. And at other times instructing the multitudes, who either followed him into the fields, or resorted to the house where he lodged; "for there were many coming and going, and they had no leisure so much as to eat;" Mark vi:31. And when, through the pleasure of bringing the Samaritans acquainted with spiritual truth, he disregarded the necessities of nature, his disciples requesting him to partake of the food they had prepared, received from him this memorable answer: "I have meat to eat that ye know not of: my meat is to do the will of him that sent me, and to finish his work," viz. the glorious work of enlightening and saving of sinners, John iv:31, 34.

Thus St. Paul was diligently and daily occupied in fulfilling the duties of his apostolic vocation; and thus every minister of the Gospel is called to labour in his appointed sphere. It remains to be known, whether all who do not labour, according to their ability, are not condemned by the following general rule: "If any will not work, neither should he eat," 2 Thessalonians iii:10. For these words signify, applied to the present case, that they who will not labour as pastors, should by no means be permitted to eat the bread of pastors; an evangelical precept this, which deserves the strictest attention, as the bread of pastors is, in some sort, sacred bread, since it is that which the piety of the public has set apart for the support of those who have abandoned every worldly pursuit, that they might dedicate themselves freely and fully to the service of the Church.

TRAIT IX.

The manner in which he divided his time between prayer, preaching and thanksgiving.

THE minister of the present age is but seldom engaged in publishing to his people the truths of the Gospel; and still more rarely in supplicating for them the possession of those blessings which the Gospel proposes. It is chiefly before men that he lifts up his hands, and affects to pour out a prayer from the fulness of his heart; while the true minister divides his time between the two important and refreshing occupations of preaching and prayer; by the former, making a public offer of Divine grace to his hearers, and by the latter, soliciting for them in secret the experience of that grace. Such was the manner of the blessed Jesus himself, who, after having reproved his disciples for the low degree of their faith, retired either into gardens, or upon mountains, praying that their "faith might not fail." The good pastor, who constantly imitates the example of his Divine Master, is prepared to adopt the following language of St. Paul, in addressing the flock upon which he is immediately appointed to attend: "For this cause I bow my knees unto the Father of our Lord Jesus Christ, of whom the whole family in heaven and earth is named, that he would grant you, according to the riches of his glory, to be strengthened with might by his Spirit in the inner man; that Christ may dwell in your hearts by faith; that ye, being rooted and grounded in love, may be filled with all the fulness of God," Ephesians iii:14, 19. "And this I pray, that your love may abound more and more in knowledge, and in all judgment; that ye may approve things that are excellent; that ye may be sincere and without offence till the day of Christ; being filled with the fruits of righteousness, which are, by Jesus Christ, unto the glory and praise of God," Philippians i:9, 11. By prayers, like these the Apostle Paul was accustomed to water, without ceasing, the heavenly seed which he had so widely scattered through the vineyard of his Lord, manifesting an increasing attachment to those among whom he had at any time published the tidings of salvation, and breathing out, in all his epistles to distant Churches, the most earnest desire that God would "fulfil" in them "all the good pleasure of his goodness, and the work of faith with power; that the name of the Lord Jesus Christ might be glorified in them, and they in him," 2 Thessalonians i:11, 12.

Pastors who pray thus for their flocks, pray not in vain. Their fervent petitions are heard; sinners are converted, the faithful are edified, and thanksgiving is shortly joined to supplication. Thus the same apostle: "I thank my God always on your behalf for the grace of God which is given you by Jesus Christ: that in every thing ye are enriched by him, in all utterance, and in all knowledge. So that ye come behind in no gift, waiting for the coming of our Lord Jesus Christ," 1 Corinthians i:4, 7. "Having heard of your faith in the Lord Jesus, and your love unto all the saints, I cease not to give thanks for you," Ephesians i:15, 16.

Worldly ministers have no experience of the holy joy that accompanies these secret sacrifices of praise and thanksgiving. But this can by no means be considered as matter of astonishment. Is their attachment to Christ as sincere as that of his faithful ministers? Are they as solicitous for the salvation of their hearers? Do they teach and preach with equal zeal? Do they pray with the same ardour and perseverance?

TRAIT X.

The fidelity with which he announced the severe threatenings and consolatory promises of the Gospel.

THE worldly minister has neither the courage nor the tenderness of the true pastor. He is fearful of publishing those truths which are calculated to alarm the careless sinner; and he knows not in what manner to apply the promises of the Gospel for the relief of those who mourn. If ever he attempts to descant upon the consolatory truths of the Gospel, he only labours to explain what is nearly unintelligible to himself; and all his discourses on subjects of this nature are void of that earnest persuasion, and that unction of love which characterize the ministers of Christ. On the other hand, his dread of giving offence will not suffer him to address sinners of every rank with the holy boldness of the Prophet Samuel: "If ye will not obey the voice of the Lord, but rebel against the commandment of the Lord, then shall the hand of the Lord be against you. If ye still do wickedly, ye shall be consumed," 1 Samuel xii:15, 25. The faithful pastor, on the contrary, conscious that the harshest truths of the Gospel are as necessary as they are offensive, courageously insists upon them, in the manner of St. Paul, "Thinkest thou, O man, that doest such things, that thou shalt escape the judgment of God?" Know this, that "after thy hardness and impenitent heart thou treasurest up unto thyself wrath against the day of wrath, and revelation of the righteous judgment of God:" for "indignation and wrath, tribulation and anguish shall be upon every soul of man that doeth evil," Romans ii:3, 5, 9. "If every transgression," under the first covenant, "received a just recompense of reward, how shall we escape if we neglect so great salvation, which at the first begun to be spoken by the Lord, and was confirmed unto us by them that heard him?" Hebrews ii:2, 3. "This ye know, that no unclean person, nor covetous man, hath any inheritance in the kingdom of Christ and of God: let no man deceive you with vain words; for because of these things cometh the wrath of God upon the children of disobedience," Ephesians v:5, 6. "See that ye refuse not him that speaketh; for if they escaped not, who refused him that spake on earth," viz. the Prophet Moses; "much more shall not we escape, if we turn away from him that speaketh from heaven," viz. the Saviour Jesus Christ. "Wherefore let us serve God acceptably, with reverence and godly fear: for our God is a consuming fire," Hebrews xii:25, 29.

But though the true minister courageously announces the most severe declarations of the word to the unbelieving and the impenitent; yet he is never so truly happy, as when he invites the poor in spirit to draw forth the riches of grace from the treasury of God's everlasting love. "God hath not," saith St. Paul, "appointed us to wrath; but to obtain salvation by our Lord Jesus Christ," 1 Thessalonians v:9. "This is a faithful saying, and worthy of all acceptation, that Christ Jesus came into the world to save sinners," 1 Timothy i:15. "Ye are not come unto the mount that burned with fire, nor unto blackness, and darkness, and tempest. But ye are come unto Mount Sion, and unto the city of the living God, and to Jesus the Mediator of the new covenant, and to the blood of sprinkling, that speaketh better things than that of Abel. Having, therefore, brethren, boldness to enter into the holiest by the blood of Jesus, and having a High Priest over the house of God, let us draw near with a true heart, in full assurance of faith," Hebrews xii:18, 24; x:19, 22. "If, when we were enemies, we were reconciled to God by the death of his Son, much more, being reconciled, we shall be saved by his life. He that spared not his own Son, but delivered him up for us all, how shall he not with him also freely give us all things? Who shall lay any thing to the charge of God's elect? It is God that justifieth: who is he that condemneth? It is Christ that died, yea, rather that is risen again, who is even at the right hand of God, who also maketh intercession for us," Romans v:10; viii:32, 34.

When these exhilarating declarations are found insufficient "to revive the heart of the contrite," the evangelical preacher fails not to multiply them in the most sympathizing and affectionate manner. "I say unto you, " continues he, "all manner of sin and blasphemy shall be forgiven unto men: for the blood of Jesus Christ cleanseth from all sin," Matthew xii:31; 1 John i:7. "And by him all, who believe, are justified from all things, from which ye could not be justified by the law of Moses," Acts xiii:39. "There is, therefore, now no condemnation to them which are in Christ Jesus," Romans viii:1: "for where sin abounded, grace did much more abound," Romans v:20.

Such are the cordials which the faithful evangelist administers to those who are weary and heavy laden: precious cordials which the worldly pastor can never effectually apply; which he either employs out of season, or renders useless by such additions of his own, as are contrary to the spirit of the Gospel.

TRAIT XI.
His profound humility.

THERE is no evil disposition of the heart, with which the clergy are so frequently reproached, as pride. And it is with reason that we oppose this sinful temper, especially when it appears in pastors, since it is so entirely contrary to the spirit of the Gospel, that the Apostle Paul emphatically terms it, "The condemnation of the devil," 1 Timothy iii:6.

There is no amiable disposition which our Lord more strongly recommended to his followers, than lowliness of mind. From his birth to his death, he gave himself a striking example of the most profound humility, joined to the most ardent charity. After having washed the feet of his first disciples, that is, after he had taken the place of a slave at their feet, he addressed them as follows:—"Know ye what I have done unto you? Ye call me Master and Lord: and ye say well; for so I am. If I then, your Lord and Master, have washed your feet; ye also ought to wash one another's feet. For I have given you an example, that ye should do as I have done to you. Verily, verily, I say unto you, the servant is not greater than his Lord; neither he that is sent, greater than he that sent him," John xiii:12-16. Again he says to the same effect, Ye know that the princes of the Gentiles exercise dominion over them, and they that are great exercise authority upon them. But it shall not be so among you: but whosoever will be great among you, let him be your minister: and whosoever will be chief among you, let him be your servant: even as the Son of man came not to be ministered unto, but to minister," Mark x:42; ii:45.

Real Christianity is the school of humble charity, in which every true minister can say, with Christ, according to his growth in grace, "Learn of me, for I am meek and lowly in heart; and ye shall find rest unto your souls." And unhappy will it be for those who, reversing Christianity, say, by their example, which is more striking than all their discourses, "Learn of us to be fierce and revengeful, at the expense of peace both at home and abroad." They who receive the stipends of ministers, while they are thus endeavouring to subvert the religion they profess to support, render themselves guilty, not only of hypocrisy, but of a species of sacrilege.

It is supposed that St. Peter had the pre-eminence among the apostles, at least by his age: it is certain that he spake in the name of the other apostles, that he first confessed Christ in two public orations; that our Lord conferred particular favours upon him; that he was permitted to be one of the three witnesses of his Master's transfiguration and agony; and that on the day of pentecost he proved the power of his apostolic commission, by introducing three thousand souls at once into the kingdom of Christ. Far, however, from arrogating, upon these accounts, a spiritual supremacy over his brethren, he assumed no other title but that which was given in common to all his fellow labourers in the ministry: "The elders which are among you," says he, "I exhort, who am also an elder: feed the flock of God which is among you, taking the oversight thereof, not for filthy lucre, but of a ready mind: neither as being lords over God's heritage, but being ensamples to the flock," 1 Peter v:1, 3. A piece of advice this, which is too much neglected by those prelates who distinguish themselves from their brethren, yet more by an anti-christian pride, than by those ecclesiastical dignities to which they have made their way by the intrigues of ambition.

All pastors should seek after humility with so much the greater concern, since some among them, seduced with the desire of distinguishing themselves as persons of eminence in the Church, after making certain ecclesiastical laws contrary to the word of God, have become persecutors of those who refused submission to their tyrannical authority. Observe here the injustice of some modern philosophers, who, misrepresenting the Christian religion, a religion which breathes nothing but humility and love, set it forth as the cause of all the divisions, persecutions, and massacres, which have ever been fomented or perpetrated by its corrupt professors. Disasters, which, far from being the produce of real Christianity, have their principal source in the vices of a supercilious, uncharitable, and antichristian clergy.

The Church will always be exposed to these imputations, till every ecclesiastic shall imitate St. Paul, as he imitated Christ. That apostle, ever anxious to tread in the steps of his Divine Master, was peculiarly distinguished by his humility to God and man. Ever ready to confess his own native poverty, and to magnify the riches of his grace, he cries out, "Who is sufficient for these things?" Who is properly qualified to discharge all the functions of the holy ministry? "Such trust have we in Christ to Godward: not that we are sufficient of ourselves to think any thing as of ourselves; but our sufficiency is of God, who also hath made us able ministers of the New Testament: not of the letter, but of the Spirit; for the letter killeth, but the Spirit giveth life," 2 Corinthians ii:16; iii:4, 6. "Who is Paul, and who is Apollos, but ministers by whom ye believed, even as the Lord gave to every man? I have planted, Apollos watered; but God gave the increase. So then, neither is he that planteth any thing, neither he that watereth: but God that giveth the increase," 1 Corinthians iii:5, 7. "I am the least of the apostles, that am not meet to be called an apostle: but by the grace of God I am what I am," 1 Corinthians xv:9. "God hath shined in our hearts to give the light of the knowledge of the glory of God, in the face of Jesus Christ: but we have this treasure in earthen vessels, that the excellency of the power may be of God, and not of us," 2 Corinthians iv:6, 7.

If the humility of St. Paul is strikingly evident in these remarkable passages, it is still more strongly expressed in those that follow:—"Ye see, brethren, that not many wise men after the flesh, not many mighty, not many noble are called. But God hath chosen the foolish things of the world to confound the wise, and the weak things of the world to confound the things which are mighty; and base things of the world, and things which are despised, hath God chosen, yea, and things which are not, to bring to nought things that are: that no flesh should glory in his presence," 1 Corinthians i:26, 29. "Unto me who am less than the least of all saints, who am nothing, who am the chief of sinners, is this grace given, that I should preach the unsearchable riches of Christ," Ephesians iii:2; 2 Corinthians xii; 1 Timothy i:15.

Reader, if thou hast that opinion of thyself, which is expressed in the foregoing passages, thou art an humble Christian. Thou canst truly profess thyself the servant of all those who salute thee; thou art such already by thy charitable intentions, and art seeking occasions of demonstrating, by actual services, that thy tongue is the organ, not of an insidious politeness, but of a sincere heart. Like a true disciple of Christ, who concealed himself when the multitude would have raised him to a throne, and who presented himself, when they came to drag him to his cross, thou hast a sacred pleasure in humbling thyself before God and man, and art anxious, without hypocrisy or affectation, to take the lowest place among thy brethren.

The humble Christian, convinced of his wants and his weakness, feels it impossible to act like those proud and bashful poor, who will rather perish in their distress, than solicit the assistance of their brethren. St. Paul had nothing of this false modesty about him. Penetrated with a deep sense of his unworthiness and insufficiency, after imploring for him. self the gracious assistance of God, he thus humbly solicits the prayers of all the faithful:—"Brethren, pray for us," 1 Thessalonians v:25. "I beseech you, brethren, for the Lord Jesus Christ's sake, and for the love of the Spirit, that ye strive together in your prayers for me," Romans xv:30. "Pray always for all saints; and for me, that utterance may be given me, that I may open my mouth boldly, to make known the mystery of the Gospel, for which I am an ambassador in bonds: that therein I may speak boldly as I ought to speak," Ephesians vi:18, 19. "You also [continuing] to help by prayer for us, that for the gift bestowed upon us by the means of many persons, thanks may be given by many on our behalf," 2 Corinthians i:11.

Thus humility, or poverty of spirit, which is set forth by Christ as the first beatitude, leads us, by prayer, to all the benedictions of the Gospel, and to that lively gratitude which gives birth to thanksgiving and joy. Lovely humility! penetrate the hearts of all Christians, animate every pastor, give peace to the Church, and happiness to the universe.

TRAIT XII.

The ingenuous manner in which he acknowledged and repaired his errors.

IT is difficult for a proud man to confess himself in an error: but they who are possessed of humility and love can make such an acknowledgment with cheerfulness. When St. Paul was called upon to justify his conduct before the tribunal of the Jews, the same spirit of resentment which animated his persecutors suddenly seized upon the more passionate of his judges, when the high priest, still more exasperated than the rest, commanded them who stood near Paul "to smite him on the mouth." It was in that moment of surprise and indignation that the apostle, unacquainted with the author of so indecent a proceeding, and not imagining that the president of an august assembly could so far forget his own dignity as to act with so reprehensible an impetuosity, gave this sharp reply to so unjust an order. "God shall smite thee, thou whited wall; for sittest thou to judge me after the law, and commandest me to be smitten contrary to the law?" Immediately those who stood by, reproaching him with his apparent disrespectful carriage, inquired with the utmost indignation, "Revilest thou God's high priest?" Here the apostle, far from justifying his own conduct in resenting the severity of a judge who had degraded himself by an act of the most flagrant injustice, immediately acknowledged his error: and lest the example he had given should encourage any person to withhold the respect due to a magistrate, still more respectable by his office than blamable by his rigorous proceedings, he endeavoured to make instant reparation for his involuntary offence, by citing a penitent passage from the law, answering with all meekness: "I wist not, brethren, that he was the high priest: for it is written, Thou shalt not speak evil of the ruler of thy people," Acts xxiii:2, 5.

There is another instance of the indiscretion and candour of this apostle. Paul and Barnabas going forth to publish the Gospel, took for their companion John Mark, the nephew of Barnabas. The young evangelist, however, staggered by the dangers which those apostles were constantly obliged to encounter, forsook them at Pamphilia in the midst of their painful labours. But afterward, repenting of his former irresolution, he offered to accompany them in another journey. Barnabas, who had charity enough to hope all things of his nephew, wished to afford him a second trial: while Paul, whose prudence taught him to fear every thing from a young man who had already given an indisputable proof of his inconstancy, refused his consent. At length the two apostles, unable to decide the matter to their mutual satisfaction, took the resolution of separating one from another. Paul went to preach the Gospel in Syria with Silas; while Barnabas, accompanied by his nephew, proceeded to proclaim Christ in the isle of Cyprus. Thus the separation of true Christians, without producing any schism in the Church, frequently tends to the propagation of the Gospel.

Time alone could determine whether Barnabas was deceived by an abundance of *charity,* or St. Paul through an excess of *prudence.* The event turned the balance in favour of the judgment of Barnabas; the conduct of John Mark on this second mission was irreproachable. From that time, St. Paul, with his usual candour, forgetting the former instability of Mark, placed the utmost confidence in him, received him with joy as the companion of his labours, revoked the order he had formerly given respecting him, and recommended him to the Churches as a faithful minister. Thus much may be inferred from the following passage in his epistle to the Colossians: "Aristarchus, my fellow prisoner, saluteth you, and Marcus, sister's son to Barnabas, touching whom ye receive, I commandments; if he come unto you, receive him," Colossians iv:10.

Thus the sincere followers of Christ are ever anxious to repair their involuntary faults: faults which we, as well as the apostles, are always exposed to the commission of, and which should constrain us to say, with St. Paul, "Now we know" things and persons "in part." This imperfection in our knowledge will sometimes produce errors in our judgment, and those errors may probably influence our conduct. But, if in these failings there be no mixture of malice; if we sin through ignorance, and in the integrity of our hearts, God imputes not to us those errors; provided that we are always prepared, like St. Paul, to confess and repair them. To err is the lot of humanity: obstinacy in error is the character of a demon: but humbly to acknowledge, and anxiously to repair an error, is to exhibit a virtue more rare and valuable than innocence itself, when accompanied with any degree of conceit and pride. They who give the portraits of legendary saints generally paint them without a single failing. But they who wish faithfully to imitate the sacred authors, are obliged to employ shades as well as lights, even in their most celebrated pieces. If this part of the portrait of St. Paul should not appear brilliant, it will serve, at least, to manifest the reality of the original, the liberality of the apostle, and the fidelity of the painter.

TRAIT XIII.

His detestation of party spirit and divisions.

WHILE the spirit of the world is confessedly a spirit of particular interest, pride, and division, the spirit of true religion is manifested, among its sincere professors, as a spirit of concord, humility, and brotherly love. The true minister, animated in an especial manner by this Divine spirit, losing sight of his own reputation and honour, is unweariedly engaged in seeking the glory of God, and the edification of his neighbour. Perfectly satisfied with the lowest place, and distinguished as much by condescension to his brethren, as by respect to his superiors, he is ever on his guard against that spirit of party which is continually seeking to disturb the union of the Church, whether it be by too great a fondness for particular customs, by an obstinate zeal for any system of doctrines, or by too passionate an attachment to some eminent teacher.

Without persecuting those who are led by so dangerous a spirit, the good pastor employs every effort to reunite them under the great Head of the Church. Arguing against the folly of those who are ready to separate themselves from the company of their brethren, he takes up the language of St. Paul, and says, "O foolish *Christians*, who hath bewitched you, that ye should not obey the truth, before whose eyes Jesus Christ hath been evidently set forth, crucified among you? Are ye so foolish? Having begun in the Spirit, are ye now made perfect by the flesh?" Galatians iii:1, 3. "Ye have," indeed, "been called unto liberty: only use not liberty as an occasion to the flesh, but by love serve one another. For all the law is fulfilled in one word, even in this: thou shalt love thy neighbour as thyself. But if ye bite and devour one another, take heed that ye be not consumed one of another. Now the works of the flesh are manifest, *among which are these,* hatred, variance, emulations, wrath, strife, seditions, and heresies: of the which I tell you before, as I have also told you in time past, that they which do such things, shall not inherit the kingdom of God. But the fruit of the Spirit is love, joy, peace, long-suffering, gentleness, faith, meekness, temperance. If we live in the Spirit, let us walk in the Spirit. Let us not be desirous of vain glory, provoking one another," Galatians v:13, 26. "There is one body, and one Spirit, even as ye are called in one hope of your calling; one Lord, one faith, one baptism, one God and Father of all, who is above all, and through all, and in you all. Endeavour, *therefore,* to keep the unity of the Spirit in the bond of peace," Ephesians iv:3, 6.

When the people seek to honour a true minister by placing him at the head of any party in the Church, he refuses the proffered dignity with an humble and holy indignation. His soul is constantly penetrated with those sentiments, under the influence of which the Apostle Paul thus nobly expressed himself: "I seek not my own profit, but the profit of many, that they may be saved," 1 Corinthians x:33. "I beseech you, brethren, by the name of our Lord Jesus Christ, that ye all speak the same thing, and that there be no divisions among you; but that ye be perfectly joined together in the same mind. For it hath been declared unto me that there are contentions among you: and that every one of you saith, I am of Paul, and I am of Apollos, and I of Cephas, and I of Christ. But is Christ divided? Was Paul crucified for you? Or were you baptized in the name of Paul?" 1 Corinthians i:10, 13. "Who is Paul, but a minister by whom ye believed? Therefore, let no man glory in men, whether Paul, or Apollos, or Cephas," 1 Corinthians iii:5, 21, 22; but rather in "our Lord Jesus Christ, of whom the whole family in heaven and earth is named," Ephesians iii:14, 15.

By such exhortations it is, and by maintaining at the same time a conduct conformable to the nature of such exhortations, that every faithful minister endeavours to engage Christians of all denominations to walk together "in love, as Christ also walked," Ephesians v:2. "Proving what is acceptable unto the Lord," Ephesians v:10, "and submitting one to another in the fear of God," Ephesians v:21, till the arrival of that promised period, when the whole company of the faithful shall be of one heart and of one mind.

But after all these exertions for the extirpation of a sectarian spirit from the Church they who content themselves with the exterior of Christianity, as the Pharisees were contented with the ceremonies of the Mosaic worship, will, sooner or later, accuse every evangelical pastor of attempting to form a particular sect. When modern Pharisees observe the strict union which reigns among true believers, a union which every faithful minister labours to establish among his people, as well by example as by precept; when they behold penitent sinners deeply sensible of their guilt, and frequently assembling together for the purpose of imploring the blessings of "wisdom, righteousness, sanctification, and redemption," they immediately take the alarm, and cry out, "These men do exceedingly trouble our city, teaching customs which are not lawful for us to receive," and maintaining such a conduct as is most inconvenient for us to follow, Acts xvi:20, 21.

Happy are those cities in which the minister of Christ is able to discover a Nicodemus, a Gamaliel, or some worshippers possessed of as much candour as the

Jews of Rome, who desired to hear what the persecuted Paul had to offer in behalf of that newly-risen sect, which was "every where spoken against," Acts xxvii:22. Till this amiable candour shall universally prevail among the nominal members of the Church, true Christianity, even in the centre of Christendom, will always find perverse contradiction, and sometimes cruel persecution.

TRAIT XIV.
His rejection of praise.

THE minister of the present day labours chiefly with a view to his own advantage and honour. He endeavours to please that he may be admired of men. "He loves the chief seats in synagogues," public greetings, and honourable titles, Matthew xxiii:6, 7, thus tacitly challenging, by his unreasonable pretensions to the respect and homage of men, a part of that glory which is due to God alone.

A totally different character is maintained by the true minister. His discourses, his actions, his look, his deportment, all agree to say, "Not unto us, O Lord, not unto us, but unto thy name give glory, for thy mercy and for thy truth's sake," Psalm cxv:1. If the arm of the Omnipotent enables him to perform any extraordinary work, which the multitude do not immediately refer to the "Author of every good and perfect gift," he cries out with St. Peter, "Why look ye so earnestly on us, as though by our own power or holiness" we had performed what appears to excite your astonishment? "The God of our fathers hath," upon this occasion, "glorified his Son Jesus; and the faith, which is by him," hath effected this extraordinary work in the presence of you all, Acts iii:12, 13, 16. On all occasions he can say with the great apostle, "Do I seek to please men? If I yet pleased men," unless for their edification, "I should not be the servant of Christ," Galatians i:10. "With me it is a very small thing, that I should be judged of you, or of man's judgment," 1 Corinthians iv:3. "But as we were allowed of God to be put in trust with the Gospel, even so we speak, not as pleasing men, but God, who trieth our hearts. Neither at any time used we flattering words, as ye know; nor of men sought we glory, neither of you, nor yet of others," 1 Thessalonians ii:4, 6. By such a conduct he distinguishes himself as a faithful ambassador of the blessed Jesus, who expressed himself in the following lowly terms to those who had reproached him with a spirit of self-exaltation: "I do nothing of myself, but as my Father hath taught me, I speak these things. I seek not my own glory: there is one that seeketh and judgeth. If I honour myself, my honour is nothing. It is my Father that honoureth me; of whom ye say that he is your God," John viii:28, 50, 54.

There may be peculiar cases in which a ministering servant of God may be allowed to call upon Christians for a public testimony of their approbation; and when this is refused, he is justified in modestly calling their attention to every past proof of his integrity and zeal. Thus St. Paul, as a proper mean of maintaining his authority among the Corinthians, who had manifested an unjust partiality toward teachers of a very inferior order, entered into a long detail of those revelations and labours, which gave him a more than ordinary claim to the respect of every Church. But whenever he commended himself, he did it with the utmost reluctance, as one constrained by the peculiarity of his circumstances to act in immediate contrariety to his real disposition. Hence, whenever he recounts the particular favours with which God had honoured him, he speaks in the third person, as of another man: "Of such a one will I glory; yet of myself I will not glory, but in mine infirmities," 2 Corinthians xii:5. "For we dare not make ourselves of the number of those who commend themselves, measuring themselves by themselves," without any reference to the excellent graces and endowments of others. "But he that glorieth, let him glory in the Lord. For not he that commendeth himself is approved, but whom the Lord commendeth," 2 Corinthians x:12, 18.

Nothing affords greater satisfaction to false apostles than commendation and praise; while the true minister shrinks with horror from those very honours which they assume all the forms of Proteus to obtain. When the multitude, led by their admiration of a faithful preacher, follow him with unsuitable expressions of applause, he meets them with unfeigned indignation, arrests their impious plaudits, and rejects their idolatrous adulations, crying out with St. Paul, "Sirs! why do ye these things? we also are men of like passions with you; and preach unto you, that ye should turn from these vanities unto the living God," Acts xiv:13, 15. We are neither the way, the truth, nor the life: but we point to you that way which the truth has discovered, and through which eternal life may be obtained, entreating you to walk therein with all simplicity and meekness. And remember, that instead of affecting in our discourses that vain wisdom, which the world so passionately admires, we faithfully proclaim Christ: and, to humble us the more before God and man, "we preach Christ crucified," 1 Corinthians i:23.

By this humble carriage the ministering disciples of Christ are principally known. By this they copy the amiable example of John the Baptist, who cheerfully humbled himself that Christ might be exalted, crying out in the language of that self-renouncing teacher, "Behold the Lamb of God, which taketh away the sin of the world! There standeth one among you whom ye know not, whose shoes' latchet we are not worthy to unloose. We baptize with water; but he baptizeth with the Holy Ghost." Beware then of entertaining too high an idea of our ministry; and remember, that "He must increase" in your estimation, "but we must decrease," John i:26, 33; 3:30.

After beholding John the Baptist, who was accounted greater than any of the prophets, abasing himself in the presence of Christ; and after hearing St. Paul, who was far superior to the Baptist, exclaiming in the humility of his soul, "I live not; but Christ liveth in me," how can we sufficiently express our astonishment at the conduct of those titular apostles, who either set up a vain philosophy in the place of Christ, or employ the cross of their Lord as a kind of pedestal for the support of those splendid monuments, by which their pride is endeavouring to perpetuate the memory of their eloquence. Self-conceited orators! When shall we rank you with the faithful ministers of the humble Jesus? When shall we behold the character you have assumed, and the conduct you maintain, sweetly harmonizing with each other? When shall we hear you addressing your flocks with the unaffected simplicity and condescension of the great apostle: "We preach not ourselves, but Christ Jesus the Lord; and," far from elevating ourselves above you, on account of the commission we have received, "ourselves your servants for Jesus' sake," 2 Corinthians iv:5. Then we might with propriety salute you as humble imitators of St. Paul, as zealous ministers of the Gospel, and as faithful servants of that condescending Saviour, who "came not to be ministered unto, but to minister," Matthew xx:28.

TRAIT XV.
His universal love.

TRUE Christians are distinguished from Jews, Mohammedans, and all other *worshippers*, by that spirit of universal love, which is the chief ornament and glory of their profession. But among evangelical pastors this holy disposition appears in a more eminent degree. They feel for the inconsiderate and the sinful that tender compassion of which Christ has left us an example. Their conduct answers to that beautiful description of charity with which Paul presented the Corinthian Church, and which may be considered as an emblematical representation of his own character from the time of his conversion to the Christian faith. Universal love is that invigorating sap, which, passing from the *true vine* into its several branches, renders them fruitful in every good work. But this Divine principle circulates through chosen ministers with peculiar force, and in more than ordinary abundance, as so many principal boughs, by which a communication is opened between the root and the lesser branches.

The faithful pastor entertains an affecting remembrance of those benevolent expressions which the good Shepherd addressed to the Apostle Peter, and in the person of that apostle to all his successors in the ministry, repeating them even to the third time: "Lovest thou me? Feed my sheep." As though he had said, The greatest proof you can possibly give of your unfeigned attachment to me, is, to cherish the souls which I have redeemed, and to make them the objects of your tenderest regard. Such is the affectionate precept which every faithful minister has received together with his sacred commission, and to which he yields a more ready and cheerful obedience, from a firm dependence upon the following solemn declaration of his gracious Master: "When the Son of man shall come in his glory, he shall say" to all the children of love, "Verily, I say unto you, inasmuch as ye have done good unto one of the least of these my brethren," whether their wants were corporal or spiritual, "ye have done it unto me," Matthew xxv:31, 40.

The love of the evangelical pastor, like that of St. Paul, is unbounded. "God," saith that charitable apostle, "will have all men to be saved, and to come unto the knowledge of the truth: I exhort, therefore, that supplications, prayers, intercessions, and giving of thanks, be made for all men: for this is good and acceptable in the sight of God our Saviour," 1 Timothy ii:4. But not content with submitting to the exhortation of St. Paul, with respect to the duty of universal prayer, he endeavours to copy the example of that apostle in labouring for the salvation of all men: "I am made all things to all men, that I might by all means save some," 1 Corinthians ix:22. Being by regeneration "a partaker of the Divine nature," 2 Peter i:4, he bears a lovely, though imperfect resemblance to his heavenly Parent, whose chief perfection is love. Like the High Priest of his profession, he breathes nothing but charity; and like the Father of lights, he makes the sun of his beneficence to rise upon all men. To describe this lesser sun in its unlimited course, and to point out the admirable variety with which it distributes its light and its heat, is to delineate with precision the character of a faithful pastor.

TRAIT XVI.
His particular love to the faithful.

THE universal love of the true minister manifests itself in a particular manner, according to the different situations of those who are the objects of it. When he finds the whole conduct of professing Christians conformable to the nature of their sacred profession, "he loves them with a pure heart fervently," 1 Peter i:22, and giving way to the effusions of holy joy, he expresses his affection in words like these: "Brethren, we are comforted over you in all our affliction and distress by your faith: for now we live if ye stand fast in the Lord." And "what thanks can we render to God for you, for all the joy wherewith we joy for your sakes before God," 1 Thessalonians iii:7, 9. In these expressions of St. Paul an astonishing degree of affection is discovered. "Now we live;" as though he had said, We have a two-fold life, the *principal life* which we receive immediately from Christ, and an *accessary life*, which we derive from his members through the medium of brotherly love. And so deeply are we interested in the concerns of our brethren, that we are sensibly affected by the variations they experience in their spiritual state, through the power of that Christian sympathy which we are unable to describe. Thus when sin has detached any of our brethren from Christ, and separated them from the body of the faithful, we are penetrated with the most sincere distress: and, on the contrary, whenever they become more affectionately connected with us, and more intimately united to Christ our common head, our spirits are then sensibly refreshed and invigorated with new degrees of life and joy.

Reader, dost thou understand this language? Hast thou felt the power of this Christian sympathy? Or has thy faith never yet produced these genuine sentiments of brotherly love? Then thou hast spoken as a person equally destitute of sensibility and truth, whenever thou hast dared to say, "I believe in the communion of saints."

TRAIT XVII.
His love to those whose faith was wavering.

WHEN a minister, after having been made instrumental in the conversion of sinners, perceives their faith decreasing, and their love growing cold, he feels for them what the Redeemer felt when he wept over Jerusalem. Not less concerned for the remissness of his believing hearers, than St. Paul was distressed by the instability of his Galatian and Corinthian converts, he pleads with them in the same affectionate terms: "Ye know," ye who are the seals of my ministry, "how I preached the Gospel unto you at the first. And ye despised me not, but received me as an angel of God. Where is then the blessedness ye spake of? For I bear you record, that if it had been possible, ye would have plucked out your own eyes and have given them to me. Am I therefore become your enemy because I tell you the truth? My little children, of whom I travail in birth again, until Christ be formed in you," I tell you with sorrow, that after all my confidence in you, "I stand in doubt of you," Galatians iv:13-20. "Our mouth is open unto you, our heart is enlarged. Ye are not straitened in us, but ye are straitened in your own bowels. Now for a recompense in the same (I speak as unto my children) be ye also enlarged. Be ye not unequally yoked together with unbelievers; for what fellowship hath righteousness with unrighteousness? or what part hath he that believeth, with an infidel? Wherefore, come out from among them, and be ye separate, saith the Lord, and touch not the unclean thing; and I will receive you, and will be a Father unto you, and ye shall be my sons and daughters, saith the Lord Almighty. We beseech you, therefore, brethren, that ye receive not the grace of God in vain," 2 Corinthians vi:1, 11-18.

This language of the Christian pastor is almost unintelligible to the minister who is merely of man's appointing. Having never converted a single soul to Christ, he has neither spiritual son nor daughter, and is entirely unacquainted with that painful travail which is mentioned by St. Paul. His bowels are straitened toward Christ and his members, and having closely united himself to the men of the world, he considers the assembly of the faithful as a company of ignorant enthusiasts. But, notwithstanding the spiritual insensibility of these ill-instructed teachers, who never studied in the school of Christ, there is no other token by which either sincere Christians or true ministers can be discerned, except that fervent love which the Galatians entertained for St. Paul before their falling away, and which that apostle ever continued to entertain for them. "By this," saith our Lord, "shall all men know that ye are my disciples, if ye have love one to another," John xiii:35.

TRAIT XVIII.
His love to his countrymen and his enemies.

ST. PAUL, like his rejected Master, was persecuted even to death by the Jews, his countrymen, while he generously exposed himself to innumerable hardships in labouring for their good. These furious devotees, inspired with envy, revenge, and a persecuting zeal, hunted this apostle from place to place, as a public pest. And when the Gentiles, on a certain occasion, had rescued him out of their hands, forty of the most hardened among them engaged themselves by an oath, neither to eat nor drink till they had assassinated him. But, notwithstanding the most indubitable proofs of their bloody disposition toward him, his fervent charity threw a veil over their cruelty, and made him wish to die for his persecutors. "I declare," saith he, "the truth in Christ, my conscience also bearing me witness in the Holy Ghost, that I have great heaviness and continual sorrow in my heart: for I could wish that myself were accursed from Christ for my brethren, my kinsmen according to the flesh," Romans ix:1-3. As though he should say, "It is written, Cursed is every one that hangeth on a tree," Galatians iii:13. Thus Christ himself became accursed for us, and I also would lay down my life for my brethren, "that I may have fellowship with him in his sufferings, being made conformable unto his death," Philippians iii:10; "and filling up that which is behind of the afflictions of Christ, in my flesh, for his body's sake, which is the Church," Colossians i:24. It is by expressions so charitable, and by actions which demonstrate the sincerity of those expressions, that Christians avenge themselves of their enemies, and work upon the hearts of their countrymen.

If the sentiments of every sincere disciple of Christ are expressed in the preceding language of St. Paul, how deplorable then must be the state of those Christians, whose anxiety either for their own salvation, or for that of their nearest relations, bears no proportion to that eager concern which this apostle manifested for the salvation of his bitterest persecutors! And if good pastors feel so ardent a desire to behold all men actuated by the spirit of Christ, without excepting even their most malicious enemies, what shall we say to those ministers who never shed a single tear, nor ever breathed one ardent prayer for the conversion of their parishioners, their friends, or their families?

TRAIT XIX.
His love to those whom he knew only by report.

THOUGH the true minister takes a peculiar interest in every thing that concerns the salvation of his countrymen, yet his Christian benevolence is far from being confined within the narrow limits of a particular country. He desires to bear the name of his Saviour to the ends of the earth; and if he is not able to do this by his personal addresses, he will do it, at least, by his earnest wishes and his constant prayers. If Providence have not yet fixed him in a particular Church, he writes, in the manner of St. Paul, to the inhabitants of the most distant countries: "I would not have you ignorant, brethren, that I" consider myself as a "debtor both to the Greeks and to the barbarians; both to the wise and the unwise. And as much as in me is, I am ready to preach the Gospel to you that are at Rome," where error and impiety have fixed their throne. "For I am not ashamed of the Gospel of Christ: for it is the power of God unto salvation to every one that believeth," Romans i:13-16. If he writes to stranger converts, whose faith is publicly spoken of in the world, he declares his sincere attachment to them, and his longing desire to afford them every spiritual assistance, in terms like these. "God is my witness, whom I serve with my spirit in the Gospel of his Son, that without ceasing I make mention of you always in my prayers. Making request, if, by any means, I might have a prosperous journey by the will of God to come unto you. For I long to see you, that I may impart unto you some spiritual gift, to the end ye may be established; that is, that I may be comforted together with you, by the mutual faith both of you and me," Romans i:9-12.

If the Apostle Paul, when he knew the Romans no otherwise than by report, expressed so ardent a desire to see them for the sole purpose of inciting them to seek after higher degrees of faith and piety; what must be the disposition of those ministers who feel no desires of this nature, even for the members of their own flock? And in how great an error are those Christians, who frequently assemble together, either in their own houses, or in more public places, for the very purpose of mutually forgetting the restraints of piety, losing their time in frivolous conversation, and debasing their minds by puerile amusements! Farther: if the new nature of the regenerate excites in them that lively concern for the salvation of their neighbours, which St. Paul expressed for the Salvation of those who inhabited the remotest parts of the earth, is it becoming in the faithful to stifle the motions of that commendable zeal which Christian charity alone can inspire? And if there are to be found among us dignified teachers, who, far from seconding a zeal so necessary in our day, are rather disposed to extinguish the first sparks of it, wherever they are discernible; whom may they be said to take for their model, Paul the apostle, or Saul the Pharisee? Doubtless Saul, the agent of a bigoted sect, and the open persecutor of the faithful.

TRAIT XX.

*His charity toward the poor in giving or procuring
for them temporal relief.*

THOUGH our Lord came principally to save the souls of sinners, yet he was by no means unmindful of their bodies. "He went about doing good," in the most unlimited sense, daily relieving, with equal care, the corporal and spiritual maladies of the people. Thus, when he had distributed the word of God to those who were hungering and thirsting after righteousness, he expressed an anxious concern for the support of those among his followers who were sensible of no other wants, except such as were of a temporal nature: "I have compassion on the multitude, because they have now been with me three days, and have nothing to eat"—and not content with barely expressing his concern for their corporal necessities, he wrought an astonishing miracle for their immediate relief, Mark viii:2. The true minister cheerfully imitates the conduct of his gracious Master, by a strict and affectionate attention to the spiritual and temporal wants of his people. "James, Cephas, and John," saith St. Paul, "gave to me and Barnabas the right hand of fellowship, that we should go unto the heathen: only they would that we should remember the poor: the same which I also was forward to do," Galatians ii:9, 10.

When the liberality of St. Paul toward his necessitous brethren was restrained by his own excessive indigence, he employed the most effectual means to procure for them the generous benefactions of their wealthier companions in the faith of the Gospel. The following passages, extracted from his epistles, may serve as sufficient proofs of this: "Brethren," I cannot but inform you "of the grace of God bestowed on the Churches of Macedonia; how that, in a great trial of affliction, the abundance of their joy and their deep poverty abounded unto the riches of their liberality. For to their power, I bear record, yea, and beyond their power, they were willing of themselves; praying us, with much entreaty, that we would receive the gift, and take upon us the fellowship of the ministering to the saints. Therefore, as ye abound in faith, in utterance, in knowledge, in all diligence, and in your love to us, see that ye abound in this grace also. I speak by occasion of the forwardness of others, and to prove the sincerity of your love. For ye know the grace of our Lord Jesus Christ, that though he was rich, yet for your sakes he became poor, that ye, through his poverty, might be rich. Wherefore, show ye, before the Churches, the proof of your love, and of our boasting on your behalf," 2 Corinthians viii:1-24.

Not yet content with these earnest solicitations in behalf of the poor, the apostle thus proceeds to enforce his importunities: "I thought it necessary to exhort the brethren that they should go before unto you, and make up beforehand your bounty, that the same might be ready, as a matter of bounty, and not as of covetousness. But this I say, he that soweth sparingly, shall reap also sparingly; and he that soweth bountifully, shall reap also bountifully. God loveth a cheerful giver. And God is able to make all grace abound toward you; that ye, always having all sufficiency in all things, may abound to every good work: as it is written, He hath dispersed abroad; he hath given to the poor; his righteousness remaineth for ever. Now he that ministereth seed to the sower, both minister bread for your food, and multiply your seed sown, and increase the fruits of your righteousness; *that ye may be* enriched in every thing to all bountifulness, which causes through us thanksgiving to God. For the administration of this service not only supplieth the wants of the saints, but is abundant also by many thanksgivings unto God: while, by the experiment of this ministration, they glorify God for your professed subjection unto the Gospel of Christ, and for your liberal distribution unto them, and unto all men," 2 Corinthians ix:5-13. Who could possibly refuse any thing to a godly minister pleading the cause of the poor, with all this apostolic dignity, simplicity, and zeal?

After having obtained alms for the poor, the Apostle Paul cautiously avoided all suspicion of appropriating any part of them to the relief of his own necessities; and was equally careful that they were never misemployed through the unfaithfulness of those who were appointed to distribute them. One of our brethren, adds the apostle, "chosen of the Churches, accompanies" us in our journey "with this grace, which is administered by us to the glory of the same Lord, and declaration of your ready mind: avoiding this, that no man should blame us in this abundance, which is administered by us: providing for honest things, not only in the sight of the Lord, but also in the sight of men," 2 Corinthians viii:9-21. Mentioning again his favourite employment, he writes to a distant Church, "Now I go unto Jerusalem to minister unto the saints. For it hath pleased them of Macedonia and Achaia to make a certain contribution for the poor saints, which are at Jerusalem. When therefore I have performed this, and have sealed to them this fruit, I will come by you into Spain. Now I beseech you, brethren, that ye strive together in your prayers for me, that I may be delivered from them that do not believe in Judea; and that the service which I have for Jerusalem may be accepted of the saints," Romans xv:25-31.

Thus to wait upon the Churches, and particularly thus to attend upon the poor, is to merit the name of a faithful minister.

TRAIT XXI.

His charity toward sinners in offering them every spiritual assistance.

TO solicit alms for those who are destitute of food and raiment, and at the same time to withhold the word of God from those "who hunger and thirst after righteousness," is to manifest an unhappy inconsistency of character. Such inconsistencies, however, are frequently discoverable even among pastors, who pique themselves upon their disposition to works of benevolence and charity.

Man has an immortal soul. This soul, which is properly himself, is rendered, by disobedience, so totally ignorant and completely miserable, that she seeks to enrich herself with the vanities of the world, and to gratify her inclinations with the pollutions of sin. In pity to the soul in this state of wretchedness, the truths of the

The Portrait of St. Paul

Gospel are proposed by a compassionate God, as a sacred remedy, adapted to the nature of her innumerable wants: they illumine the blind with spiritual light and knowledge; they clothe the naked with the robe of righteousness; they feed the hungry; they heal the sick; they burst the captive's bands; they give eternal life to those who are dead in trespasses and sin: in a word, they make us partakers of the great salvation of God, To publish this Gospel, then, or to procure the preaching of it to sinners, is undoubtedly to give them an important proof of the most excellent charity; while, on the other hand, to refuse them the word of God, or to avoid any occasion of administering it, is absolutely or occasionally to deny them those spiritual alms and assistances which the Saviour of the world has appointed for their daily relief. The pastor who acts in this unbecoming manner resembles a physician, or an almoner, who, having received a charge from his prince to supply the poor with food, or the sick with medicine, not only refuses to acquit himself with his acknowledged duty with diligence and impartiality, but strenuously opposes those who endeavour to supply his lack of service. Such a minister seems to maintain a system as absurd and cruel as would be that of either of those characters just alluded to, who should pretend that no one had authority to administer alms to the poor, or medicine to the sick, except such as received pensions from the prince for that purpose; and that even these would act in a disorderly manner, if they should dare to distribute alms or remedies except on the Sabbath day, and then only during particular hours.

So long as any pastor seeks his own glory, so long he will be subject to some degree of that contemptible jealousy, which will not suffer him to behold with pleasure the more abundant and successful labours of his brethren. But the faithful minister of Christ, whose chief desire is the prosperity of the Church, is actuated by a totally different spirit. Though he has a peculiar satisfaction in beholding the success of his own spiritual labours; yet when he hears the Gospel published by others, and even by such as are apparently influenced by unworthy motives, he greatly rejoices in their success. His charity, which neither envies another's prosperity, nor seeks his own particular advantage, expresses itself, upon so delicate a subject, in the language of St. Paul: "Some indeed preach Christ even of envy and strife, supposing to add affliction to my bonds. What then? notwithstanding every way, whether in pretence or in truth, Christ is preached; and I therein do rejoice, yea, and I will rejoice," Philippians i:15-18.

Influenced by envy, or rendered insensible by their lukewarmness, worldly ministers are absolute strangers to the generous pleasure here mentioned by the apostle; nor have they the least idea of acting in a criminal manner, when they will not permit the truths of the Gospel to be freely declared by all who are disposed to announce them.

The good pastor, by whatever name he may be distinguished, lives only to publish the Gospel, and to convert the souls committed to his charge: to restrain him then from attending to these important labours, is to force him aside from the true end of his calling, and must appear to every enlightened mind a greater act of cruelty, than to withhold the rich from giving alms, or to detain an expert swimmer from saving his drowning brethren. If such a pastor, in any period of his life, has acted like a monopolist of the Gospel, and, by denying to the "poor in spirit," what was freely given for their support, has caused in any place a "famine of the word;" he believes himself abundantly more culpable than those avaricious merchants, who, by forming a monopoly of grain in the East Indies, caused a grievous famine in that country, by which an innumerable multitude of its inhabitants perished. Those covetous men denied to the bodies of their neighbours a perishable nourishment; but he has withheld from the souls of his brethren that precious manna, which might have preserved them to everlasting life. Such was the crime of those whom our Lord addressed in the following words: "Wo unto you, scribes and Pharisees, hypocrites! for ye shut up the kingdom of heaven against men; for ye neither go in yourselves, neither suffer ye them, that are entering, to go in," Matthew xxiii:13. Observe St. Paul's sentiments of such characters. With respect to those Jews, "who both killed the Lord Jesus, and their own prophets, and have persecuted us; they please not God, and are contrary to all men, forbidding us to speak to the Gentiles, that they might be saved," filling up by this means the measure of their sin: "for the wrath is come upon them to the uttermost," 1 Thessalonians ii:15, 16.

If the character which the apostle here describes was odious in a Jew, without doubt it is more so in a Christian, and still doubly detestable in a minister of the Gospel, whose heart should continually be animated with a fervent desire for the conversion of sinners, and the salvation of all mankind. Were it possible for those who are distinguished by this trait of the character of Antichrist to discover the turpitude of their own conduct, they would acknowledge themselves abundantly more guilty than the robber, who should force away from a famished pauper the morsel of bread he had begged in his distress. They would pronounce, without hesitation, that the foster-mother who neglects the infant she has undertaken to cherish, and prevents her charitable neighbours from affording it any nourishment, is still more excusable than the pastor, who, not content with refusing to feed the flock of Christ, endeavours to scatter his sheep wherever they are found feeding, seeking out accusations against those who have led them to a refreshing pasture, and studying, by every mean, to withdraw the Gospel from those penitent sinners, who, "as new-born babes, desire the sincere milk of the word. that they may grow thereby," 1 Peter ii:2.

Happy will be the age in which Christian pastors shall no longer be found, like the scribes in the days of St. Paul, labouring to fill up the measure of their iniquities! Then truth and piety shall no longer be restrained by the fetters of prejudice and bigotry! Then the faithful shall worship God, and publish the Gospel, with as much freedom as the dissipated indulge themselves in the sports of the age, or the malevolent in slandering their neighbours!

TRAIT XXII.
The engaging condescension of his humble charity.

CHARITY avoids all appearance of haughtiness, and is never seen to act in an unbecoming manner. On the contrary, full of courtesy, she fears lest she should give offence to any; and, full of benevolence, she labours for the edification of all. Here the charitable pastor cannot act otherwise than with a holy condescension toward all men, and especially toward the ignorant and poor, with whom the ministers of the present age will scarcely deign to converse: and, without ever slipping his foot into the pit of error, he sometimes approaches it with a happy mixture of compassion and prudence, for the relief of those who are unable to extricate themselves from it. "Though I am free from all men," writes St. Paul, "yet I have made myself servant unto all, that I might gain the more. Unto the Jews I became as a Jew, that I might gain the Jews: to them that are without law, as without law, that I might gain them that are without a written law. To the weak became I as weak, that I might gain the weak: I am made all things to all men, that I might by all means save some. And this I do for the Gospel's sake," 1 Corinthians ix:19-23. "All things are lawful for me," continues he, "but all things are not expedient: all things are lawful for me, but all things edify not," 1 Corinthians x:23. "When ye sin against the brethren by wounding their weak conscience, ye sin against Christ. Wherefore, if meat make my brother to offend, I will eat no flesh while the world standeth, lest I make my brother to offend," 1 Corinthians viii:12, 13. "Whether, therefore, ye eat or drink, or whatsoever ye do, do all to the glory of God. Even as I please all men in all things, not seeking mine own profit, but the profit of many, that they may be saved," 1 Corinthians x:32, 33.

Behold that sweet prudence of charity which our Lord recommended to his disciples, when he pointed out the folly of putting new wine into such bottles as were unable to resist the force of the fermenting liquor. And of this affectionate discretion he himself gave them a striking example, when he said, "I have many things to say unto you, but ye cannot bear them now." If this condescending carriage was lovely in the blessed Jesus, it will ever appear amiable in his humble imitators, who can say, with the Apostle Paul, to the weaker members of the Church, "We have fed you with milk, and not with meat; for hitherto ye were not able to bear it," 1 Corinthians iii:2.

Special care is, however, to be taken that this charitable condescension may never betray the interests of truth and virtue. "Abstain," saith St. Paul, "from all appearance of evil," 1 Thessalonians v:22. "Be ye followers of me, even as I also am of Christ," 1 Corinthians xi:1. For "herein do I exercise myself to have always a conscience void of offence toward God and toward men," Acts xxiv:16. And "our rejoicing is this, the testimony of our conscience, that in simplicity and godly sincerity, not with fleshly wisdom, but by the grace of God, we have had our conversation in the world, and more abundantly to you-ward," among whom we have laboured in the Gospel, 2 Corinthians i:12.

If there exist pastors who lack this condescension toward the poor, or who are destitute of that humble charity which can familiarize itself with the most ignorant for their edification and comfort: if there are ministers to be found who are ever meanly complaisant to the rich, and who are void of holy resolution in the presence of the great, instead of conducting themselves with that mingled humility and dignity which are suitable to the character they sustain,—may the one and the other be convinced of the grievous error into which they are fallen, while they contemplate this opposite trait in the character of St. Paul.

Upon what consideration is founded the humiliating distinction which is generally made between the rich and the poor? Was Christ manifested in a state of earthly grandeur? Did he not chiefly associate with the poor? Far from flattering the rich, did he not insinuate that they would, with the utmost difficulty, enter into the kingdom of God? Did he not affirm it were better for a man to be cast into the sea with a millstone about his neck, than to offend the poorest believer? Did he not declare that he would consider the regard shown to the meanest of his followers as though he himself had been the immediate object of it? When St. James assures us that "he who converteth a sinner from the error of his way," performs the best of all possible good works, because, by preventing a multitude of sins, he places the soul in the road to every virtue,—can this declaration be supposed to lose any of its force when applied to the soul of a poor man? Are not the lowest of men immortal as the most elevated? Did not Christ humble himself to the death of the cross for the poor as well as the rich? "Hath not God chosen the poor of this world, rich in faith, and heirs of the kingdom?" And, finally, were the angels less ready to convey the soul of perishing Lazarus to paradise than that of wealthy Abraham? Perish then for ever that unchristian prejudice which dishonours the poor, nourishes the pride of the rich, and leads us to the violation of that great command, by which we become as guilty as though we had transgressed the whole law, the spirit of which is love. And let us remember it is only out of the ruins of so despicable a partiality, that the engaging condescension, of which St. Paul has left us so lovely an example, can possibly be produced.

TRAIT XXIII.
His courage in defence of oppressed truth.

"CHARITY rejoiceth in the truth," 1 Corinthians xiii:6. These two amiable companions are closely united together, and mutually sustain each other. It is possible, however, when an error has the suffrages of many persons, respectable on account of their wisdom, their age, their rank, their labours, or their piety, that a sincere Christian may be tempted to sacrifice truth to authority, or rather to a mistaken charity. But the enlightened pastor, putting on the resolution of St. Paul, will never suffer himself to be imposed upon by the appearance of either persons or things; and though he should see himself standing alone on the side of evangelical truths, he will not fear, even singly, to act as their modest and zealous defender.

In these circumstances a lukewarm minister loses all his courage. Behold his general plea for the pusillanimity of his conduct—"I am alone, and what success can I expect in so difficult all undertaking? The partisans of this error are persons whom I both love and honour. Some of them have shown me great kindness, and others have sufficient credit to prejudice the world against me. Moreover, it would be looked upon as presumption in me, who am weaker than a reed, to oppose myself to a torrent, which bears down the strongest pillars of the Church." Such is the manner in which he apologizes for the timidity of his conduct in those situations, where his love of truth is publicly called to the test: not considering, that to reason thus is to forget at once the omnipotence of God, the force of truth, and the unspeakable worth of those souls which error may poison and destroy.

On the contrary, the faithful minister, who, on all occasions, rejoices in the truth, "conferring not with flesh and blood," courageously refuses to bear the yoke of any error that must evidently be accompanied with evil consequences. In the most trying situations of this nature he imitates the conduct of the great apostle, who, when he saw a shameful error making its way in the Church, placed himself in the gap, and gave way to the emotions of his honest zeal, as related in the following passage:

"False brethren came in privily to spy out our liberty which we have in Christ Jesus, that they might bring us into bondage. To whom we gave place by subjection, no not for an hour; that the truth of the Gospel might continue with you. And when Peter was come to Antioch, I withstood him to the face, because he was to be blamed. For before that certain came from James, he did eat with the Gentiles: but when they were come, he withdrew and separated himself, fearing them which were of the circumcision. And the other Jews dissembled likewise with him, insomuch that Barnabas also," under the specious pretence of not offending his neighbour, "was carried away with their dissimulation. But when I saw that they walked not uprightly according to the truth of the Gospel, I said unto Peter before them all, If thou, being a Jew, livest after the manner of the Gentiles, and not as do the Jews, why compellest thou the Gentiles to live as do the Jews?' Galatians ii:4, 14.

This reasonable reprimand is, perhaps, one of the greatest proofs which St. Paul ever gave of the uprightness of his intention, and the steadiness of his resolution.

Ye men of integrity! ye, who have proved how much it costs to defend the rights of truth, when they stand opposed to that deference which condescending love obliges us to show in a thousand instances to respectable authority; you alone are able to make a proper judgment of the holy violence which was exercised by St. Paul upon this occasion. But whatever they may be called to endure in so honourable a cause, happy are those Christians, and doubly happy those pastors who have so great a love for truth, and so true a love for their brethren, that they are ready at all times, with this faithful apostle, to sacrifice to the interests of the Gospel every inferior consideration, every servile fear, and every worldly hope.

TRAIT XXIV.
His prudence in frustrating the designs of his enemies.

THERE is no kind of calumny which the incredulous have not advanced, in order to render Christianity either odious or contemptible. According to the notions of these men, to adopt the maxims of evangelical patience argues a want of sensibility; and to regulate our conduct according to the dictates of Christian prudence, is to act the hypocrite. What we have to say, in this place, will chiefly respect the latter charge.

It has been asserted, by modern infidels, that the gentleness and forbearance which the Gospel requires of its professors, must necessarily make them the dupes of designing men, and lead them unreluctantly into the snares of their persecutors. But to draw this inference from some few passages of Scripture, understood in too literal a sense, is to set truth at variance with itself, merely for the purpose of charging Christians with all the evil, which, it is presumed, they might have avoided by prudence, or have overcome by resolution. The example of our Lord, and that of St. Paul, might have rectified the ideas of cavillers upon this point. When Christ exhorted his disciples to be "harmless as doves," he admonished them at the same time to be "wise as serpents:" and of this harmless wisdom he himself gave a striking example, when he was interrogated by the Jews respecting the lawfulness of paying tribute unto Cesar. Well acquainted with the different sentiments of that people with regard to the Roman yoke, without directly combatting the prejudices of any party, he returned a satisfactory answer to all parties, by an inference drawn from "the image and superscription" borne upon their current coin,—"Render therefore unto Cesar the things that are Cesar's, and unto God the things that are God's," Matthew xxii:21.

The sincere Christian, and the faithful minister, have frequently occasion for this happy prudence, as well as St. Paul, who, more than once, employed it with success. The Jews, irritated against this apostle, sought occasion to destroy him, on account of the zeal with which he published the Gospel among the Gentiles. Hoping to soften the prejudices they entertained against his conduct, he recounted to them how Jesus, being raised from the dead and appearing to him in an extraordinary manner, had expressly sent him to the Gentiles, Acts xxii:21, when the Jews, more irritated than before, would have torn him in pieces, had he not been rescued out of their hands by the Roman garrison. By this means Paul was preserved for a more peaceful hearing. And on the morrow, when he stood before the Jewish council, perceiving that the assembly was composed partly of Sadducees, who say there is "no resurrection, neither angel, nor spirit;" and partly of Pharisees, who believe equally in the existence of spirits and the resurrection of the body; he immediately availed himself of this circumstance, and cried out, "Men and brethren, I am a Pharisee, the son of a Pharisee: of the hope and resurrection of the dead I am called in question," Acts xxiii:6. As though he had said, The great cause of the violent persecution that is now raised against me is, that I preach "Jesus and the resurrection." Our fathers, indeed, were not absolutely assured of a life to come; but the important doctrine of the resurrection, and of the judgment that shall follow, is now demonstrated; since God has given an incontestable proof of it, in raising up his son Jesus from the dead. And I myself have been an eye witness of his resurrection, to whom he has appeared two several times; once as I journeyed to Damascus, and afterward as I prayed in the temple. But when I mentioned this second appearance of a risen Saviour, my incredulous accusers began vehemently to cry out, "Away with such a fellow from the earth." By this just exposition of the fact, and by his prudent selection of "the resurrection of Christ" from among the other great doctrines of Christianity, St. Paul happily caused a division to take place among his judges. And the event answered his expectation: for "the scribes that were of the Pharisees' part, arose, saying, We find no evil in this man; but if a spirit," that is, a man risen from the dead, "or an angel, hath spoken to him, let us not fight against God," Acts xxiii:9. There is still another instance of the wisdom of the serpent reconciling itself with the innocence of the dove, in the conduct of this apostle, when marking the disposition of his Athenian judges, he took advantage of their taste for novelty by announcing to them "The unknown God," to whom they had already erected an altar, Acts xvii.

This Christian prudence, equally distant from the duplicity of hypocrites and the stupidity of idiots, merits a place among the traits which characterize this great apostle, not only because it is worthy of our imitation, but also because it has been indirectly represented, by a modern Celsus, as mere cunning and artifice. The author here alluded to, who deserves rather to be called a great poet than a faithful painter, having disfigured this trait of St. Paul's character with a pencil dipped in the gall of prejudice, we gladly take this occasion of setting forth the injustice of his imputations, so illiberally cast both upon Christianity itself, and the most eminent of its defenders. This witty philosopher, who has said so many good things against the spirit of persecution, never perceived that he himself was actuated by an intolerant spirit: so true it is, that the most sagacious are liable to be blinded by passion or prejudice. The same spirit of persecution which excited the Athenians to discountenance the justice of Aristides as a dangerous singularity, and to punish the piety of Socrates as a species of atheism, led the author of the Philosophical Dictionary to represent the prudence of St. Paul as the duplicity of a hypocrite.

Had this severe judge occupied the seat of Ananias, he might, perhaps, with an affected liberality, have overlooked the peculiarities of the apostles' creed; but, in the end, his innate detestation of piety would have assisted him, according to the general custom of persecutors, to feign some just cause for treating him with the utmost rigour. And this he has done in our day as far as his circumstances would permit, since, not being able to disgrace him by the hand of a public executioner, he has studied to do it with his pen, by ravishing from him, not only his reputation for extraordinary piety, but even his claim to common honesty.

Persecutor! whoever thou art, be content that thy predecessors have taken away the lives of the righteous, and spare them, what they prefer infinitely before life itself, "the testimony of a good conscience."

TRAIT XXV.

His tenderness toward others, and his severity toward himself.

THOUGH perfectly insensible to the warm emotions of brotherly love, the worldly pastor frequently repeats, in his public discourses, those affectionate expressions which flow so cordially from the lips of faithful ministers, "My dear brethren in Christ!" These expressions from the pulpit are almost unavoidable upon some occasions; but, in general, they are to be regarded in no other light than the civil addresses of a haughty person, who concludes his epistles by assuring his correspondents that he considers it an honour to subscribe himself their obedient servant. But while the worldly minister affects a degree of benevolence which he cannot feel, the good pastor, out of the abundance of a heart overflowing with Christian charity, addresses his brethren with the utmost affection and regard, not only without any danger of feigning what he has not experienced, but even without a possibility of expressing the ardour of his brotherly love. His exhortations to the faithful, like those of St. Paul, are seasoned with an unction of grace, and accompanied with a flow of tenderness which frequently give them an astonishing effect upon his brethren, and which always evince the interest he takes in the concerns of the Church. "Rebuke not an elder," says St. Paul, "but entreat him as a father, and the younger men as brethren: the elder women as mothers, the younger as sisters, with all purity," 1 Timothy v:1. Such was the exhortation of this apostle to a young minister, nor was his example unsuitable to his counsel. "I beseech you, brethren, by the mercies of God, that ye present your bodies a living sacrifice, holy, acceptable to God. Dearly beloved, be not overcome of evil, but overcome evil with good," Romans xii:1, 19, 21. "I write not these things to shame you, but as my beloved sons I warn you," 1 Corinthians iv:14. "I, the prisoner of the Lord, beseech you, that ye walk worthy of the vocation wherewith ye are called," Ephesians iv:1. "If there be any consolation in Christ, if any comfort of love, if any fellowship of the

Spirit, if any bowels and mercies, fulfil ye my joy, that ye be likeminded, being of one accord My beloved, work out your own salvation with fear and trembling," Philippians ii:1, 2, 12. "We beseech you, brethren and exhort you by the Lord Jesus, that as you have received of us how ye ought to walk, and to please God, so ye would abound more and more," 1 Thessalonians iv:1. "Though I might be much bold in Christ, to enjoin thee that which is convenient, yet for love's sake I rather beseech thee, being such a one as Paul the aged, and now also a prisoner of Jesus Christ. I beseech thee for my son Onesimus, whom I have begotten in my bonds; who in time past was unto thee unprofitable, but now profitable unto thee and me, whom I have sent again. Thou therefore receive him, that is, mine own bowels. Yea, brother, let me have joy of thee in the Lord; refresh my bowels in the Lord," Philemon i:8, 12, 20. Such was the tenderness and affection with which St. Paul was accustomed to address his believing brethren. But the language of this apostle was very different when he spoke of himself, and of that body of sin which constrained him to cry out, "O wretched man that I am!"

It is the character of too many persons to be severe toward the failings of others, while they show the utmost lenity toward themselves, with respect both to their infirmities and their vices. Always ready to place the faults of their neighbours in an odious light, and their own in the most favourable point of view, they seem to be made up of nothing but partiality and self love; while the true minister reserves his greatest indulgence for others, and exercises the greatest severity toward himself. "All things are lawful for me," writes St. Paul, "but I will not be brought under the power of any," 1 Corinthians vi:12. "Know ye not that they which run in a race, run all, but one receiveth the prize? And every one that striveth for the mastery is temperate in all things: now they do it to obtain a corruptible crown, but we an incorruptible. I therefore so run, not as uncertainly; so fight I, not as one that beateth the air: but I keep under my body, and bring it into subjection: lest that by any means, when I have preached to others, I myself should be a cast-away," 1 Corinthians ix:24-27.

One reflection naturally finishes this trait of the character of St. Paul. If this spiritual man, if this great apostle thought himself obliged to use such strenuous efforts, that he might not be rejected before God at the last, in how great danger are those careless pastors and Christians, who, far from accustoming themselves to holy acts of self denial, satisfy their natural desires without any apprehension, and treat those as enthusiasts who begin to imitate St. Paul, by regarding their baptismal vow, and renouncing their sensual appetites.

TRAIT XXVI.

His love never degenerated into cowardice, but reproved and consoled, as occasion required.

THE charity of the true minister bears no resemblance to that phantom of a virtue, that mean complaisance, that unmanly pliancy, that unchristian cowardice, or that affected generosity, which the ministers of this day delight to honour with the name of charity. According to these insufficient judges, to be charitable is only to give

The Portrait of St. Paul

some trifling alms out of our abundant superfluities, to tolerate the most dangerous errors, without daring to lift up the standard of truth, and to behold the overflowings of vice, without attempting to oppose the threatening torrent. Such would be the mistaken charity of a surgeon, who, to spare the mortifying arm of his friend, should suffer the gangrene to spread over his whole body. Such was the charity of the high priest Eli toward Hophni and Phinehas; an impious charity, which permitted him to behold their shameful debaucheries with too favourable an eye; a fatal charity, which opened that abyss of evil which finally swallowed them up, and into which they dragged with them their father, their children, the people of Israel, and the Church, over which they had been appointed to preside.

The good pastor, conscious that he shall save a soul from death, if he can but prevail with a sinner to forsake his evil way, uses every effort to accomplish so important a work. And among other probable means, which he employs on the occasion, he tries the force of severe reprehension, rebuking the wicked with a holy authority; and, if it be necessary, returning to the charge with a spark of that glowing zeal with which his Master was influenced, when he forced from the temple those infamous buyers and sellers who had profaned it with their carnal merchandise. Thus St. Paul, on receiving information that scandalous errors had been discovered in the conduct of a member of the Corinthian Church, immediately wrote to that Church in the following severe and solemn manner: "It is reported that there is fornication among you. And ye are puffed up, and have not rather mourned, that he that hath done this deed might be taken away from among you. Know ye not that a little leaven leaveneth the whole lump," and that the plague in any single member of a society is sufficient to infect the whole company? "Purge out therefore the old leaven, and put away from among yourselves that wicked person. If any that is called a brother be a fornicator, keep not company with such a one, no not to eat. Be not deceived: fornicators shall not inherit the kingdom of God. Know ye not that your bodies are the members of Christ? Flee fornication, therefore, and avoid the company of fornicators. For ye are bought with a price: therefore glorify God in your body and in your spirit, which are God's. Farther, I verily, as absent in body, but present in spirit, have judged already concerning the lascivious person that is among you, to deliver such a one unto Satan for the destruction of the flesh, that the spirit may be saved in the day of the Lord Jesus," 1 Corinthians v:6.

When the true minister has passed the severest censures upon sinners, and beholds those censures attended with the desired effect, he turns to the persons he lately rebuked with testimonies of that unbounded charity that "beareth all things, and hopeth all things." More ready, if possible, to relieve the dejected than to humble the presumptuous, after having manifested the courage of a lion he puts on the gentleness of a lamb, consoling and encouraging the penitent offender, and never ceasing to intercede for him, till his pardon is obtained both from God and man. Thus St. Paul, who had so sharply rebuked the Corinthians in his first epistle, gave them abundant consolation in his second, and exhorted them to receive with kindness the person whom he had before enjoined them to excommunicate. It is easy to recognize the tenderness of Christ in the following language of this benevolent apostle: "I wrote unto you my first epistle out of much affliction and anguish of heart, with many tears, not that ye should be grieved, but that ye might know the love which I have more abundantly unto you," 2 Corinthians ii:4. "Great is my glorying of you: I am filled with comfort, I am exceeding joyful in all our tribulation. God, that comforteth them that are cast down, comforted us by the coming of Titus, my messenger, when he told us your earnest desire, your mourning, and your fervent mind toward me. For though I made you sorry with a letter, I do not repent, though I did repent. Now I rejoice, not that ye were made sorry, but that ye sorrowed to repentance. For ye were made sorry after a godly manner. For behold, what carefulness it wrought in you! What clearing of yourselves! What holy indignation! What fear! What vehement desire! What zeal! What revenge! In all things ye have approved yourselves to be clear in this matter. Moreover, we were comforted in your comfort. Yea, and exceedingly the more joyed we for the joy of Titus, because his spirit was refreshed by you all. And his inward affection is more abundant toward you, while he remembereth the obedience of you all, and how you received him, together with my reproof, with fear and trembling. I rejoice, therefore, that I have confidence in you in all things," 2 Corinthians vii. And with respect to the person who has caused us so much distress, "Sufficient to such a man is this punishment, which was inflicted of many. So that now ye ought rather to forgive him, and comfort him, lest perhaps such a one should be swallowed up with overmuch sorrow. Wherefore, I beseech you, that ye would confirm your love toward him. To whom ye forgive any thing, I forgive also: Nay, I have already forgiven him for your sakes, as in the presence of Christ," 2 Corinthians ii:6-10.

Great God! appoint over thy flock vigilant, charitable, and courageous pastors, who may discern the sinner through all his deceitful appearances, and separate him from thy peaceful fold, whether he be an unclean goat or a ravenous wolf. Permit not thy ministers to confound the just with the unjust, rendering contemptible the most sacred mysteries, by admitting to them persons with whom virtuous heathens would blush to converse. Touch the hearts of those pastors who harden thy rebellious people, by holding out tokens of thy favour to those who are the objects of thy wrath: and permit no longer the bread of life, which they carelessly distribute to all who choose to profane it, to become in their unhallowed hands the bread of death. Discover to them the impiety of offering their holy things to the dogs: and awaken in them a holy fear of becoming accomplices with those hypocritical monsters, who press into thy temple to crucify thy Son afresh; and who, by a constant profanation of the symbols of our holy faith, add to their other abominations the execrable act of eating and drinking their own damnation, and that with as much composure as some among them swallow down the intoxicating draught, or utter the most impious blasphemies.

AN OBJECTION ANSWERED.

BEFORE we proceed to the consideration of another trait of the character of St. Paul, it will be necessary to refute an objection to which the preceding trait may appear liable. "Dare you," it may be asked, "propose to us as a model, a man who could strike Elymas with blindness, and deliver up to Satan the body of a sinner?"

ANSWER. The excellent motive, and the happy success of the apostle's conduct in both these instances, entirely justify him. He considered affliction not only as the crucible in which God is frequently pleased to purify the just, but as the last remedy to be employed for the restoration of obstinate sinners. Behold the reason why the charity of the primitive Church demanded, in behalf of God, that the rod should not be spared, when the impiety of men was no longer able to be restrained by gentler means: determining, that it was far better to be brought to repentance, even by the sharpest sufferings, than to live and die in a sinful state. To exercise this high degree of holy and charitable severity toward a sinner, was, in some mysterious manner, "to deliver up his body to Satan," who was looked upon as the executioner of God's righteous vengeance in criminal cases. Thus Satan destroyed the first-born in Egypt, smote the subjects of David with the pestilence, and cut off the vast army of Sennacherib. St. John has thrown some light upon this profound mystery by asserting, "There is a sin unto death," 1 John v:16: and the case of Ahab is fully in point; for when that king had committed this sin, a spirit of error received immediate orders to lead him forth to execution upon the plains of Ramoth-Gilead, 1 Kings xxii:20, 22. This awful doctrine is farther confirmed by St. Luke, when he relates, that in the same instant, when the people, in honour of Herod, "gave a shout, saying, It is the voice of a god and not of a man, the angel of the Lord smote him, because he gave not God the glory: and he was eaten up of worms, and gave up the ghost," Acts xii:22, 28. The punishment thus inflicted, by the immediate order of God, was always proportioned to the nature of the offence. If the sin was "not unto death," it was followed by some temporary affliction, as in the cases of Elymas and the incestuous Corinthian. If the crime committed was of such a nature that the death of the sinner became necessary, either for the salvation of his soul, for the reparation of his crime, or to alarm those who might probably be corrupted by his pernicious example, he was then either smitten with some incurable disease, as in the case of Herod; or struck with immediate death, as in the case of Ananias and Sapphira, who sought to veil their hypocrisy with appearances of piety, and their doubledealing with a lie. Had M. Voltaire considered the Christian Church as a well-regulated species of theocracy, he would have seen the folly of his whole reasoning with respect to the authority of that Church in its primitive state. And convinced that God has a much greater right to pronounce, by his ministers, a just sentence of corporal punishment, and even death itself, than any temporal prince can claim to pronounce such sentence by his officers: that daring philosopher, instead of pointing his sarcasms against an institution so reasonable and holy, would have been constrained to tremble before the Judge of all the earth.

Finally. It is to be observed, that when this kind of jurisdiction was exercised in the Church, the followers of Christ, not having any magistrates of their own religion, lived under the government of those heathenish rulers, who tolerated those very crimes which were peculiarly offensive to the pure spirit of the Gospel. And on this account God was pleased to permit the most eminent among his people, on some extraordinary occasions, to exercise that terrible power, which humbled the offending Church of Corinth, and overthrew the sorcerer Elymas in his wicked career. If it be inquired, What would become of mankind, were the clergy of this day possessed of the extraordinary power of St. Paul? We answer, The terrible manner in which St. Paul sometimes exercised the authority he had received, with respect to impenitent sinners, is not left as an example to the ecclesiastics of the present day, unless they should come (which is almost impossible) into similar circumstances, and attain to equal degrees of discernment, faith, and charity, with this apostle himself.

TRAIT XXVII.
His perfect disinterestedness.

IF "charity seeketh not her own;" and if it is required, that the conversation of the faithful should be without covetousness, it becomes the true minister, in an especial manner, to maintain an upright and disinterested conduct in the world.

Though it be true, that "they which wait at the altar are partakers with the altar;" yet nothing is so detestable to the faithful pastor as the idea of enriching himself with the sacred spoils of that altar. Observe how St. Paul expresses himself upon this subject: "We brought nothing into this world, and it is certain we can carry nothing out. Having, therefore, food and raiment, let us be therewith content. But they that will be rich fall into temptation and a snare, and into many foolish and hurtful lusts, which drown men in perdition. For the love of money is the root of all evil: which, while some have coveted after, they have erred from the faith, and pierced themselves through with many sorrows. But thou, O man of God," who art set apart as a minister of the everlasting Gospel, "flee these things; and follow after righteousness, godliness, faith, love, patience, meekness," 1 Timothy vi:7-11. With regard to myself, "I have learned, in whatever state I am, therewith to be content. Every where, and in all things, I am instructed both to be full and to be hungry; both to abound and to suffer need," Philippians iv:11, 12. "Neither at any time used we flattering words, as ye know, nor a cloak of covetousness; God is witness. For ye remember our labour and travail, because we would not be chargeable unto any of you. Ye are our witnesses, and God also, how holily, and justly, and unblamably, we behaved ourselves among you that believe, 1 Thessalonians ii:5, 10. Behold, the third time I am ready to come to you; and I will not be burdensome to you; for I seek not yours, but you: for the children ought not to lay up for the parents, but the parents for the children. And I will very gladly spend and be spent for you," 2 Corinthians xii:14, 15. Behold the disinterestedness of the faithful shepherd, who is ever less ready to receive food and clothing from the flock than to labour for its protection and support! Behold the spirit of Christ! And let the pastor, who is influenced by a different spirit, draw that alarming inference from his state, which he is taught to do by the following expression of St. Paul: "If any man have not the Spirit of Christ, he is none of his," Romans viii:9.

Happy would be the Christian Church were it blessed with disinterested pastors! Avaricious ministers, who are more taken up with the concerns of earth than with the things of heaven, who are more disposed to enrich their families than to supply the necessities of the poor, who are more eager to multiply their benefices, or to augment their salaries, than to improve their talents, and increase the number of the faithful: such ministers, instead of benefiting the Church, harden the impenitent, aggravate their own condemnation, and force infidels to believe that the holy ministry is used, by the generality of its professors, as a comfortable means of securing to themselves the perishable bread, if not the fading honours, of the present life.

TRAIT XXVIII.

His condescension in laboring at times with his own hands, that he might preach industry by example, as well as by precept.

SUCH is the disinterestedness of the true minister, that though he might claim a subsistence from the sacred office to which he has been solemnly consecrated, yet he generously chooses to sacrifice his rights when he cannot enjoy them without giving some occasion for reproach. To supply his daily wants, he is not ashamed to labour with his own hands, when he is called to publish the Gospel, either among the poor, or in those countries where the law has not appointed him a maintenance, as among heathen nations and savage tribes: nor will he refuse to do this when his lot falls among a slothful people, animating them to diligence in their several vocations by his prudent condescension, that the Gospel may not be blamed. In such circumstances, if his own patrimony be insufficient for his support, no disciple of Jesus will blush to follow the example of St. Paul, who gives the following representation of his own conduct in cases of a like nature'" Have I committed an offence in abasing myself that you might be exalted, because I have preached to you the Gospel of God freely? When I was present with you and wanted, I was chargeable to no man: in all things I have kept myself from being burthensome unto you, and so will I keep myself. As the truth of Christ is in me, no man shall stop me of this boasting in the regions of Achaia. Wherefore? because I love you not? God knoweth. But that I may cut off occasion from them that desire occasion," and who would not fail to represent me as a self-interested person, were they able to charge me with the enjoyment of my just rights among you, 2 Corinthians xi:7-12. "I have coveted no man's silver, or gold, or apparel: ye yourselves know that these hands have ministered unto my necessities, and to them that were with me. I have showed you all things, how that so labouring ye ought to support the weak; and to remember the words of the Lord Jesus, how he said, It is more blessed to give than to receive," Acts xx:33, 35. Ye know how ye ought to follow us: for we behaved not ourselves disorderly among you, neither did we eat any man's bread for nought; but wrought with labour and travail night and day, that we might not be chargeable to any of you; not because we have not power but to make ourselves an ensample unto you. For even when we were with you, this we commanded you, that if any would not work, neither should he eat. For we hear that there are some which walk among you disorderly, working not at all, but are busybodies," 2 Thessalonians iii:7-11. Happy were those times of Christian simplicity, when the apostles of Christ thought it no disgrace to follow some useful occupation for the relief of their temporal necessities: when, instead of eating the bread of idleness, they cast their net alternately for fishes and for men: when they quitted the tabernacles, in which they were wont to labour, for the sacred recreation of setting before sinners "a building of God, a house not made with hands, eternal in the heavens." Of how much greater value were the nets of St. Peter than dogs of the chase; and the working implements of St. Paul than those tables of play, at which many of his unworthy successors are now seeking amusement!

But notwithstanding all the circumspection and prudence of the faithful pastor, even though he should think it necessary to preach industry by example as well as by precept, yet if his exhortations are more frequent than those of his lukewarm brethren, he will be reproached by the irreligious part of the world, as an indirect advocate for indolence. The enemies of piety and truth are still ready to renew the old objections of Pharaoh against the service of God: "Wherefore do ye let the people from their works? The people of the land are many, and you make them rest from their burdens. They be idle: therefore they cry, saying, Let us go and sacrifice to our God. Let there more work be laid upon the men, and let them not regard vain words," Exodus v:4, 9. Such is the erroneous judgment which is generally formed respecting the most zealous servants of God: but while they feel the bitterness of these unmerited reproaches, they draw more abundant consolation from the encouraging language of their gracious Master: "Blessed are ye when men shall say all manner of evil against you falsely for my sake. Rejoice and be exceeding glad, for great is your reward in heaven: for so persecuted they the prophets, which were before you," Matthew v:11, 12.

The declared adversaries of religion are not, however, the only persons who accuse a laborious minister of diverting the people from their business, by the too frequent returns of public exhortation and prayer. There are others, not wholly destitute of piety, who frequently add weight to these unjust accusations. Such are the half converted, who, not yet understanding the inestimable worth of that bread which nourisheth the soul to everlasting life, are chiefly engaged in labouring for the broad which perisheth. Men of this character, engaging themselves in a vast variety of earthly concerns, incessantly "disquiet themselves in vain," and consider those hour's as running to waste, in which a zealous pastor detains them from worldly cares and frivolous enjoyments. While he is engaged in teaching, that "one thing [only] is [absolutely] needful," they are grasping at every apparent good that solicits their affections: and while he is insisting upon the necessity of choosing "that good part that shall not be taken away," these formal professors are ready to reason with him, as Martha with Jesus, Dost thou not know how greatly we are cumbered with a multiplicity of vexatious concerns; and "carest thou not" that our assistants and dependents are detained from their necessary avocations by an indolent attendance upon thy ministry?

These false sentiments, with respect both to the ministers and the word of God, which too generally prevail among nominal Christians, have their source in that direct opposition, which must always subsist between the grand maxim of the children of God, and the distinguishing principle of worldly men: "Seek ye first the kingdom of God, and his righteousness," saith the blessed Jesus, "and all these things," which are farther necessary to your welfare, "shall be added unto you, "Matthew vi:33. No, replies the prince of this world; seek ye first the enjoyments of time and sense, and all other things, that are needful to your well being, shall be added over and above. From these two opposite principles results that entire contrariety, which has been observed in all ages, between those who are laying up treasures upon earth, and those who have set their affections upon things that are above. Happy are the faithful, and doubly happy the pastors, who, constantly imitating the great apostle, according to their several vocations, pray and labour at the same time, both for their daily bread, and the bread of eternal life! In thus observing the twofold command of Moses and of Christ, some reasonable hope may be entertained, that their good works will at length overcome the aversion of their enemies, as those of the first Christians overcame the deep-rooted prejudices of the heathen world.

TRAIT XXIX.

The respect he manifested for the holy estate of matrimony, while Christian prudence engaged him to live in a state of celibacy.

SOME ministers have carried their disinterestedness to so high a pitch, that they have refused to enter into the marriage state, merely with this view; that being free from all superfluous care and expense, they might consecrate their persons more entirely to the Lord, and their possessions less reservedly to the support of the poor, whom they considered as their children, and adopted as their heirs. But all pastors are not called to follow these rare examples of abstinence and disinterested piety.

When we examine into the life of a celebrated man, we generally inquire whether he passed his days in a state of marriage or celibacy, and what it was that determined his choice to the one or the other of these states. Such an inquiry is peculiarly necessary with respect to St. Paul, as many of the faithful, in the earliest ages of the Church, deluded by the amiable appearance of celibacy, embraced the monastic life,—a state to which the clergy and the religious of the Romish Church still dedicate themselves: whence those disgraceful accusations which divers philosophers have preferred against the Christian religion, as destructive of society in its very origin, which is the conjugal bond. But leaving the reveries of legend, if we seek for Christianity in the pure Gospel of Christ, we shall find this accusation to be totally groundless: since one view of the Christian Legislator, in publishing that Gospel, was to strengthen the nuptial tie, by declaring that an immodest glance is a species of adultery, by revoking the permission formerly given to the husband to put away his wife for any temporary cause of dissatisfaction, and by absolutely forbidding divorce, except in case of adultery. Matthew v:28, 32. Nay, so far did this Divine Lawgiver carry his condescension in honour of the marriage state, that he was present at one of those solemn feasts, which were usually held upon such occasions, attended by the holy virgin and his twelve disciples. And not content with giving this public testimony of his respect for so honourable an institution, he accompanied it with the first miraculous proof of his almighty power.

St. Paul, it is true, passed the whole of his life in a state of celibacy; but he never enjoined that state to any person: and if he occasionally recommended it to some, to whom it was indifferent whether they married or not, it was chiefly on account of the distress and persecution of those times, 1 Corinthians vii:26. To engage the most pious persons ordinarily to live in a state of celibacy, is not less contrary to nature and reason, than to the spirit of the Gospel. This is to oppose the propagation of the best Christians, and the most faithful subjects. It is to suppose that those persons who join example to precept in the cause of virtue, and who, for that very reason, are peculiarly qualified for the education of children, are the only persons in the world who ought to have none. The absurdity of this opinion constrained the Apostle Paul publicly to combat it, by declaring to the Hebrews, that "marriage, and the bed undefiled, are honourable among all men," Hebrews xiii:4. He farther affirmed, that "a bishop must be the husband of one wife, one that ruleth well his own house, having his children in subjection with all gravity," 1 Timothy iii:2, 4. And if he wished the Corinthians to continue in the state which he himself had chosen, on account of the peculiar advantages accruing from it, at that season, to the persecuted members of the Christian Church: "nevertheless, to avoid fornication," he counselled, that "every man should have his own wife," and "every woman her own husband," 1 Corinthians vii:2. "I will," saith he to Timothy, "that the younger women marry, bear children, and guide the house," 1 Timothy v:14. And lastly, he cautioned the same Christian bishop against the error of those who, in the last times, should "depart from the faith, giving heed to the doctrines of devils," and "forbidding to marry;" earnestly exhorting his young successor to guard the brethren against a doctrine so fatal to the Church in particular, and so destructive of society in general, 1 Timothy iv:1, 6.

But it may be urged—If St. Paul really entertained such high ideas of marriage, and represented it as the most perfect emblem of that strict union which subsists between Christ and his Church, why did he not recommend it by his example? I answer—Although St. Paul was never married, yet he expressly asserted his right to that privilege, as well as St. Peter, and some others of the apostles, 1 Corinthians ix:5, intimating, at the same time, that prudence and charity inclined him to forego his right in that respect. When a man is perpetually called to travel from place to place, prudence requires that he should not encumber himself with those domestic cares, which must occasion many unavoidable delays in the prosecution of his business. Or, if he derives his maintenance from the generosity of the poor, charity should constrain him to burden them as little as possible. This zealous apostle could not prevail upon himself to expose a woman and children to those innumerable dangers which he was constantly obliged to encounter. The first peril, from which he made his escape, was that which compelled him to descend from the wall of Damascus in a basket. Now, if a family had shared with him the same danger, what an addition would they have made to his affliction and care! Is it not evident that, in such circumstances, every man who is not obliged to marry, from reasons either physical or moral, is called to imitate the example of this disinterested apostle, from the same motives of prudence and charity? This indefatigable preacher, always on a mission, judged it advisable to continue in a single state to the end of his days. But, had he been fixed in a particular church; had he there felt how much it concerns a minister neither to tempt others nor be tempted himself; and had he known how much assistance a modest, provident, and pious woman is capable of affording a pastor, by inspecting the women of his flock—he would then probably have advised every resident pastor to enter into the marriage state, provided they should fix upon regenerate persons, capable of edifying the Church, in imitation of Phebe, a deaconess of Cenchrea and Persis, who was so dear to St. Paul on account of her labours in the Lord, Romans xvi:1, 12; or copying the example of those four virgins, the daughters of Philip, who edified, exhorted, and consoled the faithful by their pious discourses, Acts xxi:9*.

---

* The attention of ministers, in choosing such companions as may not hinder their success in the ministry, is of so great importance, that in some countries the conduct of a pastor's wife, as well as that of the pastor himself, is supposed either to edify or mislead the flock. Nay, the minister himself is frequently condemned for the faults of his wife. Thus, in the Protestant Churches of Hungary they degrade a pastor whose wife indulges herself in cards, dancing, or any other public amusement, which bespeaks the gayety of a lover of the world, rather than the gravity of a Christian matron. This severity springs from the supposition that the woman, having promised obedience to her husband, can do

The Christian doctrine on this point may be reduced to the following heads. 1. In times of great trouble, and grievous persecutions, the followers of Christ should abstain from marriage, unless obliged thereto by particular and powerful reasons, Matthew xxiv:19. 2. The faithful, who mean to embrace the nuptial state, should be careful, on no account to connect themselves with any persons except such as are remarkable for their seriousness and piety, 2 Corinthians vi:14. 3. If a man is married before he is converted; or if, being converted, he is deceived in choosing a woman, whom he supposes to be pious, but discovers to be worldly; instead of separating himself from his wife, in either of these cases, he is rather called to give all diligence in bringing her acquainted with the truth as it is in Jesus, 1 Corinthians vii:16. 4. Missionaries ought not to marry, unless there be an absolute necessity. 5. A bishop, or resident pastor, is usually called to the marriage state, 1 Timothy iii:12; Titus i:6. Lastly, a minister of the Gospel, who is able to live in a state of celibacy "for the kingdom of heaven's sake," that he may have no other care, except that of preaching the Gospel, and attending upon the members of Christ's mystical body; such a one is undoubtedly called to continue in a single state. For having obtained the gift of continence, he is dispensed from carnally giving children to the Church, because he begets her spiritual sons and daughters. And such a one, instead of being honoured as the head of a particular household, should be counted worthy of double honour, as a spiritual father in his Lord's family, Matthew xix:12.

TRAIT XXX.
The ardour of his love.

THE passions are the springs by which we are usually actuated. Reason alone is too weak to put us in motion so often as duty requires; but when love, that sacred passion of the faithful, comes in to its assistance, we are then sweetly constrained to act in conformity to the various relations we sustain in civil and religious life. Thus the God of nature has rooted in the hearts of mothers a fond affection, which keeps them anxiously attentive to the wants of their children. And thus the Spirit of God implants in the bosom of a good pastor that ardent charity which excites him to watch over his flock with the most affectionate and unwearied attention. The love of a father to his son, the attachment of a nurse to her foster child, the tender affection of a mother to her infant, are so many emblems employed in the Holy Scriptures to

---

nothing but what he either directs or approves. Hence they conclude, that example having a greater influence than precept, the wife of a minister, if she is inclined to the world, will preach worldly compliance with more success by her conduct, than her husband can preach the renunciation of the world by the most solemn discourses. And the incredulity of the stumbled flock will always be the consequence of that unhappy inconsistency, which is observable between the serious instructions of a well-disposed minister, and the trifling conduct of a woman with whom he is so intimately connected. Nor are there wanting apostolic ordinances sufficient to support the exercise of this severe discipline:— *Even so must their wives be grave, not slanderers, sober, faithful in all things.* Let the bishop or deacon be *one that ruleth well his own house, having his children,* and every part of his family, *in subjection with all gravity. For if a man know not how to rule his own house, how shall he take care of the Church of God?* 1 Timothy iii:4, 5, 11.

set forth the sweetness and ardour of that Christian love which animates the true minister to the performance of his several duties. "You know," says St. Paul, "how we exhorted, and comforted, and charged every one of you, as a father doth his children: we were gentle among you, even as a nurse cherisheth her children. So, being affectionately desirous of you, we were willing to have imparted unto you, not the Gospel of God only, but also our own souls, because ye were dear unto us," 1 Thessalonians ii:7, 8, 11. "God is my record, how greatly I long after you all in the bowels of Jesus Christ," Philippians i:8. "Receive us; for ye are in our hearts to die and live with you," 2 Corinthians vii:2, 3. Worldly pastors can form no idea of that ardent charity which dictates such benevolent language, and accompanies it with actions which demonstrate its sincerity. This is one of those mysterious things which are perfectly incomprehensible to the natural man, and which frequently appear to him as the extremest folly. This fervent love improves us into new creatures, by the sweet influence it maintains over all our tempers. This holy passion deeply interests the faithful pastor in the concerns of his fellow Christians, and teaches him to rejoice in the benefits they receive, as though his own prosperity were inseparably connected with theirs. "I thank my God," writes the great apostle to the benefactor of his brethren, "making mention of thee always in my prayers, hearing of thy love and faith, which thou hast toward the Lord Jesus, and toward all saints; that the communication of thy faith may become effectual, by the acknowledging of every good thing which is in you in Christ Jesus. For we have great joy and consolation in thy love, because the bowels of the saints are refreshed by thee, brother," Philippians v:4-7. The sorrow and the joy of this zealous imitator of Christ were generally influenced by the varying states of the faithful. When any, who had once run well, were seen loitering by the way, or starting aside from the path of life, he expressed the most sincere affliction on their account. There are some, "of whom I have told you often, and now tell you even weeping, that they are the enemies of the cross of Christ," Philippians iii:18. On the other hand, the progress of believers was as marrow to his bones, and as the balsam of life to his heart: "We are glad when we are weak, and ye are strong: and this also we wish, even your perfection," 2 Corinthians xiii:9. "My brethren, dearly beloved and longed for, my joy and crown, stand fast in the Lord, my dearly beloved. Be blameless and harmless, the sons of God without rebuke, holding forth the word of life, that I may rejoice in the day of Christ, that I have not run in vain, neither laboured in vain," Philippians iv:1; ii:15, 16.

Reader, whoever thou art, permit me to ask thee an important question. Art thou acquainted with that ardent charity that influenced the Apostle Paul? If his Christian love was like a rapid and deep river; is thine at least like a running stream whose waters fail not? Do thy joys and thy sorrows flow in the same channel, and tend to the same point, as the sanctified passions of this benevolent man? Relate the chief causes of thy satisfaction and thy displeasure, and I will tell thee whether, like Demas, thou art a child of this present world, or a fellow citizen of heaven, with St. Paul.*

---

* Have you more joy when your preaching augments your income, than when you observe a wandering sheep conducted into the right way? Then conclude that you preach more for mammon than for Christ.—M. ROQUES.

TRAIT XXXI.

His generous fears and succeeding consolations.

WHEN the Church is threatened with a storm, the worldly pastor has no fears except for himself and his relations. But the true minister, if he be at all disquieted with fear, when the Lord's vessel is driven with the winds, or appears to be in danger through the indiscreet conduct of false or unloving brethren, he feels much less for his own safety than for the security of his companions in tribulation. He fears especially for the weak of the flock, and for those of the faithful who are exposed to violent temptation. And these generous fears, which equally prove his holy zeal and brotherly love, without robbing him of all his joy, afford him frequent opportunities of exercising his faith, his resignation, and his hope. "We are troubled," saith St. Paul, "on every side; without were fightings, within were fears. I fear, lest by any means, as the serpent beguiled Eve through his subtilty, so your minds should be corrupted from the simplicity that is in Christ. I fear, lest when I come, I shall not find you such as I would," 2 Corinthians vii:5; xi:3; xii:20. "When we could no longer forbear, we sent Timothy to establish you, and to comfort you concerning your faith, that no man should be moved by these afflictions: for yourselves know that we are appointed thereto. For verily, when we were with you, we told you before, that we should suffer tribulation; even as it came to pass. For this cause, when I could no longer forbear, I sent to know your faith, lest by some means the tempter should have tempted you, and our labour be in vain," 1 Thessalonians iii:1, 5.

Though these "fightings without," and these "fears within," are always painful to the flesh, yet they are as constantly beneficial to the soul. If they subject the true minister for a season to the keenest affliction, they prepare him in the end for "strong consolation." Observe the manner in which the great apostle expresses himself upon this point: "We would not, brethren, have you ignorant of our trouble, which came to us in Asia, that we were pressed out of measure, above strength, insomuch that we despaired even of life. We had the sentence of death in ourselves, that we should not trust in ourselves, but in God which raiseth the dead: who delivereth us from so great a death, and doth deliver: in whom we trust that he will yet deliver us," 2 Corinthians i:8, 10. "I would ye should understand, brethren, that the things which happened unto me have fallen out rather unto the furtherance of the Gospel; so that my bonds in Christ are manifest in all the palace, and in all other places; and many of the brethren in the Lord, waxing confident by my bonds, are much more bold to speak the word without fear," Philippians i:12, 14. Hence, "we glory in tribulations: knowing that tribulation worketh patience; and patience, experience; and experience, hope; and hope maketh not ashamed, because the love of God is shed abroad in our hearts by the Holy Ghost which is given unto us," Romans v:3, 5. "Blessed be God, the Father of mercies, and the God of all comfort; who comforteth us in all our tribulation, that we may be able to comfort them which are in any trouble, by the comfort wherewith we ourselves are comforted of God. For as the sufferings of Christ abound in us, so our consolation also aboundeth by Christ," 2 Corinthians i:2, 5.

If those who are honoured with a commission to publish the Gospel were fully convinced how gracious and powerful a Master they serve, instead of being alarmed at the sight of those labours and dangers which await them in the exercise of their ministry, they would stand prepared to run all hazards in his service; as courageous soldiers who fight under the eye of a generous prince, are ready to expose their lives for the augmentation of his glory. Can it become good pastors to manifest less concern for the salvation of their brethren, than mercenary warriors for the destruction of their prince's foes? And if the Romans generously exposed themselves to death in preserving the life of a fellow citizen, for the trifling reward of a civic wreath, how much greater magnanimity should a Christian pastor discover in rescuing the souls of his brethren from a state of perdition, for the glorious reward of a never-fading crown?

TRAIT XXXII.

The grand subject of his glorying, and the evangelical manner in which he maintained his superiority over false apostles.

THE disposition of a faithful pastor is, in every respect, diametrically opposite to that of a worldly minister. If you observe the conversation of an ecclesiastic who is influenced by the spirit of the world, you will hear him intimating either that he has, or that he would not be sorry to have, the precedency among his brethren, to live in a state of affluence and splendour, and to secure to himself such distinguished appointments as would increase both his dignity and his income, without making any extraordinary addition to his pastoral labours. You will find him anxious to be admitted into the best companies, and occasionally forming parties for the chase or some other vain amusement. While the true pastor cries out in the self-renouncing language of the great apostle: "God forbid that I should glory, save in the cross of our Lord Jesus Christ, by whom the world is crucified unto me, and I unto the world," Galatians vi:14.

If the minister who is really formed to preside in the Church, were singled out from among his brethren, and placed in an apostolic chair, he would become the more humble for his exaltation. If such a one were slighted and vilifled by false apostles, he would not appeal, for the honour of his character, to the superiority of his talents, his rank, or his mission; but rather to the superiority of his labours, his dangers, and his sufferings. Thus, at least, St. Paul defended the dignity of his character against the unjust insinuations of his adversaries in the ministry: "Are they ministers of Christ? (I speak as a fool) I am more." But in what manner did he attempt to prove this? Was it by saying, I have a richer benefice than the generality of ministers; I am a doctor, a professor of divinity, I bear the mitre, and dwell in an episcopal palace? No: instead of this he used the following apostolic language: "In labours I am more abundant, in stripes above measure, in prisons more frequent, in deaths oft. In journeyings often, in perils in the city, in perils in the wilderness, in perils in the sea, in perils by the heathen, in perils among false brethren: in weariness and painfulness, in watchings often, in hunger and thirst, in fastings often, in cold and nakedness. Beside those things that are without, that which cometh upon me daily, the care of all the Churches. Who is weak and I am not weak? Who is offended and I burn not? If I must needs glory, I will glory in the things which concern mine infirmities," 2 Corinthians xi:23-30. "From henceforth let no man trouble me: for I bear in my body the marks of the Lord Jesus," Galatians vi:17. Such are the appeals of holy prelates. But for a man to glory at having obtained a deanery, a professor's chair, or a bishopric, is in reality to boast of his unfaithfulness to his vocation, and to prove himself unworthy of the rank to which he has been injudiciously raised.

Ye who preside over the household of God, learn of the Apostle Paul to manifest your real superiority. Surpass your inferiors in humility, in charity, in zeal, in your painful labours for the salvation of sinners, in your invincible courage to encounter those dangers which threaten your brethren, and by your unwearied patience in bearing those persecutions which the faithful disciples of Christ are perpetually called to endure from a corrupt world. Thus shall you honourably replace the first Christian prelates, and happily restore the Church to its primitive dignity.

TRAIT XXXIII.

His patience and fortitude under the severest trials.

"CHARITY is not easily provoked," but on the contrary "thinketh no evil." Full of patience and meekness, Christ distinguished himself by his abundant love to those from whom he received the most cruel treatment. Thus also the ministers of Christ are distinguished, who, as they are more or less courageous and indefatigable in the work of the ministry, are enabled to adopt the following declaration of St. Paul with more or less propriety: "Being reviled, we bless; being persecuted, we suffer it; being defamed, we entreat: we are made as the filth of the world, and are as the offscouring of all things unto this day," 1 Corinthians iv:12, 13. "Giving no offence in any thing, that the ministry be not blamed: but in all things approving ourselves as the ministers of God in much patience, in afflictions, in necessities, in distresses, in stripes, in imprisonments, in tumults, in labours, in watchings, in fastings; by pureness, by knowledge, by long suffering, by kindness, by the Holy Ghost, by love unfeigned, by the word of truth, by the power of God, by the armour of righteousness on the right hand and on the left," which enables us to attack error and vice, while it shields us from their assaults; "by honour and dishonour; by evil report and good report; as deceivers, and yet true; as unknown, and yet well known; as dying, and behold we live; as chastened, and not killed; as sorrowful, yet alway rejoicing; as poor, yet making many rich; as having nothing, and yet possessing all things," 2 Corinthians vi:3, 10.

Far from being discouraged by the trials which befall him, the true minister is disposed in such circumstances to pray with the greater fervency; and according to the ardour and constancy of his prayers, such are the degrees of fortitude and patience to which he attains. "We have not received," saith St. Paul, "the spirit of bondage again to fear; but we have received the spirit of adoption, whereby we cry, Abba, Father. The Spirit itself," amidst all our distresses, "beareth witness with our spirit, that we are the children of God. Likewise the Spirit also helpeth our infirmities. For we know not what we should pray for as we ought: but the Spirit itself maketh intercession for us with groanings which cannot be uttered," Romans viii:15, 26. "I besought the Lord thrice, that *this trial* might depart from me. And he said unto me, My grace is sufficient for thee: for my strength is made perfect in weakness. Therefore I take pleasure in infirmities, in reproaches, in necessities, in persecutions, in distresses, for Christ's sake: for when I am weak, then am I strong," 2 Corinthians xii:8-10. "I can do all things through Christ which strengtheneth me," Philippians iv:13.

What an advantage, what an honour is it, to labour in the service of so gracious and powerful a Master! By the power with which he controls the world, he overrules all things "for good to them that love him." Their most pungent sorrows are succeeded by peculiar consolations: the reproach of the cross prepares them for the honours of a crown; and the flames, in which they are sometimes seen to blaze, become like that chariot of fire which conveyed Elijah triumphantly away from the fury of Jezebel.

TRAIT XXXIV.
His modest firmness before magistrates.

SUPPORTED by a strong persuasion that God and truth are on his side, the faithful minister is carried above all those disheartening fears which agitate the hearts of worldly pastors. Depending upon the truth of that solemn prediction, "They will deliver you up to the council, and ye shall be brought before governors and kings for my sake, for a testimony against them and the Gentiles;" he expects in times of persecution to appear before magistrates, and possibly before kings, for the cause of Christ and his Gospel. Nor is he affected at such a prospect. Relying on the promise of that compassionate Redeemer, who once appeared for him before Annas and Caiaphas, Herod and Pontius Pilate, without anxiously premeditating what he shall answer, and resting assured that wisdom shall be given him in every time of need, he cries out with the holy determination of the psalmist, "I will speak of thy testimonies also before kings, and will not be ashamed," Psalm cxix:46.

When he is brought as a malefactor before the judge, while his accusers, actuated by a malicious zeal, agree to say, "We have found this man a pestilent fellow, a mover of sedition among the people," and one of the ringleaders of a new and dangerous sect; he justifies himself by answering, The witnesses who appear against me this day, neither found me trampling under foot the authority of my superiors, nor sowing the seeds of sedition among the people; "neither can they prove the things whereof they now accuse me. But this I confess, that after the way which they call heresy, so worship I the God of my fathers, believing all things which are written in the law and the prophets; and have hope toward God, which they themselves allow, that there shall be a resurrection of the dead, both of the just and unjust." And supposing his accusers are not only deists, but professors of the Christian faith, he will add, This also I confess, that in conformity to those principles, which pretended philosophers term superstitious, and which lukewarm Christians call enthusiastic, "I believe" not only "in God the Father Almighty," but also in Jesus Christ his only Son, whom I acknowledge to be "King of kings, and Lord of lords, and who, after having suffered for our sins, rose again for our justification." Farther: I joyfully subscribe to that confession of faith, which is frequently in your own mouths, "I believe in the Holy Ghost," who regenerates and sanctifies every true member of "the holy catholic Church:" and I participate with those members the common advantages of our most holy faith, which are an humble consciousness of "the forgiveness of sins," a lively hope of "the resurrection of the body," and a sweet anticipation of "everlasting life." "And herein do I exercise myself, to have always a conscience void of offence toward God and toward men," Acts xxiv:5, 16. If his judge, already prejudiced against him, should unbecomingly join issue with his accusers, and charge him with extravagance and fanaticism; he will answer after St. Paul, with all due respect, "I am not mad: but speak forth the words of truth and soberness. And I would to God, that not only thou, but also all who hear me this day were altogether such as I am, except these bonds," Acts xxvi:24, 29.

After a pastor has had experience of these difficult trials, he is then in a situation to confirm younger ministers in the manner of St. Paul: "I know whom I have believed, and I am persuaded that he is able to keep that which I have committed unto him against that day. At my first answer no man stood with me; but all men forsook me: notwithstanding, the Lord stood with me and strengthened me: that by me the preaching might be fully known, and that all the Gentiles might hear the Gospel: and I was delivered out of the mouth of the lion. And the Lord shall deliver me from every evil work, and will preserve me unto his heavenly kingdom: to whom be glory for ever and ever," 2 Timothy i:12; iv:16, 18.

Behold the inconvenience and dangers to which not only Christian pastors, but all who follow the steps of the Apostle Paul, will be exposed in every place, where the bigoted or incredulous occupy the first posts in Church or state! And whether we are called to endure torments, or only to suffer reproach in the cause of truth, let us endeavour to support the sufferings that shall fall to our lot, with that resolution and meekness, of which St. Paul and his adorable Master have left us such memorable examples.

TRAIT XXXV.
His courage in consoling his persecuted brethren.

PERSUADED that "all who will live godly in Christ Jesus," and particularly his ministers, "shall suffer persecution," 2 Timothy iii:12, the good pastor looks for opposition from every quarter; and whenever he suffers for the testimony he bears to the truths of the Gospel, he suffers not only with resolution, but with joy.

The more the god of this degenerate world exalts himself in opposition to truth, the more he disposes every sincere heart for the reception of it. The Gospel is that everlasting rock upon which the Church is founded, and against which the gates of hell can never prevail; and though this rock is assailed by innumerable hosts of visible and invisible enemies, yet their repeated assaults serve only to demonstrate, with increasing certainty, its unshaken firmness and absolute impenetrability. A clear sight of the sovereign good, as presented to us in the Gospel, is sufficient to make it universally desirable. The veil of inattention, however, conceals, in a great measure, this sovereign good, and the mists of prejudice entirely obscure it. But by the inhuman conduct of the persecutors of Christianity, their false accusations, their secret plots, and their unexampled cruelty, these mists are frequently dissipated, and these veils rent in twain from the top to the bottom. Error is by these means unwittingly exposed to the view of the world; while every impartial observer, attracted by the charms of persecuted truth, examines into its nature, acknowledges its excellence, and at length triumphs in the possession of that inestimable pearl which he once despised. Thus the tears of the faithful, and the blood of confessors, have been generally found to scatter and nourish the seed of the kingdom.

Ye zealous defenders of truth! let not the severest persecutions alarm your apprehension, or weaken your confidence, since every trial of this kind must necessarily terminate in your own advantage, as well as in the establishment and glory of the Christian faith. Error, always accompanied with contradictions, and big with absurd consequences, will shortly appear to be supported by no other prop than that of prejudice or passion, or the despotism of a usurped authority, which renders itself odious by the very means employed for its support. The more the partizans of every false doctrine sound the alarm against you, the more they resemble a violent multitude opposing the efforts of a few who are labouring to extinguish the fire that consumes their neighbours' habitations; the different conduct of the one and the other must, sooner or later, manifest the incendiaries. Error may be compared to a vessel of clay, and truth to a vase of massy gold. In vain is calumny endeavouring to render the truth contemptible by overheaping it with every thing that is abominable; in vain would prejudice give error an amiable appearance by artfully concealing its defects: for whenever the hand of persecution shall furiously hurl the latter against the former, the solid gold will sustain the shock unhurt, while the varnished clay shall be dashed in pieces. The experience, however, of seventeen ages has not been sufficient to demonstrate to persecutors a truth so evident; nor are there wanting inexperienced believers in the Church who are ready to call it in question, and who, "when persecution ariseth because of the word," are unhappily observed to lose their Christian resolution. But, "why do the heathen rage, and the people imagine a vain thing, the kings of the earth stand up, and the rulers take counsel together against the Lord, and against his anointed? He that dwelleth in heaven shall laugh them to scorn," and make their malice serve to the accomplishment of his great designs, Psalm ii:1-4.

Thus the Jews, in crucifying Christ, contributed to lay the grand foundation of the Christian Church; and afterward, by persecuting the Apostle Paul to death, gave him an opportunity of bearing the torch of truth to Rome, and even into the palaces of its emperors. And it was from Rome itself, as from the jaws of a devouring lion, that he comforted the faithful, who were ready to faint at his afflictions, and encouraged them to act in conformity to their glorious vocation. "I suffer trouble as an evil doer, even unto bonds; but the word of God is not bound. Therefore I endure all things for the elect's sake, that they may also obtain the salvation which is in Christ Jesus, with eternal glory. It is a faithful saying; for if we be dead with him, we shall also live with him; if we suffer, we shall also reign with him; if we deny him, he will also deny us. Be not thou therefore ashamed of the testimony of our Lord, nor of me his prisoner; but be thou partaker of the afflictions of the Gospel, according to the power of God, who hath called us according to his own purpose and grace, which was given us in Christ Jesus, who hath abolished death, and hath brought life and immortality to light through the Gospel. Whereunto I am appointed a preacher and an apostle, for the which cause I also suffer these things; nevertheless 1 am not ashamed. Thou, therefore, endure hardness as a good soldier of Jesus Christ," 2 Timothy ii:9-12; i:8-12; ii:3.

Happy is the faithful minister of Christ amid all the severe afflictions to which he is sometimes exposed! Though "troubled on every side," yet he is "not distressed;" though "perplexed," yet "not in despair;" though "persecuted," yet "not forsaken;" though "cast down," yet "not destroyed." All the violent attacks of his enemies must finally contribute to the honour of his triumph, while their flagrant injustice gives double lustre to the glorious cause in which he suffers.

TRAIT XXXVI.

His humble confidence in producing the seals of his ministry.

A PASTOR must, sooner or later, convert sinners, if he sincerely and earnestly calls them to repentance toward God, and faith in our Lord Jesus Christ. Nevertheless, though filled with indignation against sin, with compassion toward the impenitent, and with gratitude to Christ, he should, like St. Paul, in proportion to his strength, wrestle with God by prayer, with sinners by exhortation, and with the flesh by abstinence; yet, even then, as much unequal to that apostle as that apostle was unequal to his Master, he may reasonably despair of frequently beholding the happy effects of his evangelical labours. But if he cannot adopt the following apostolic language, "Thanks be unto God, who always causeth us to triumph in Christ, and maketh manifest the savour of his knowledge by us in every place;" he will at least be able to say in his little sphere, "We are unto God a sweet savour of Christ, in them that are saved, and in them that perish; to the one we are the savour of death unto death; and to the other the savour of life unto life," 2 Corinthians ii:14-16. If he has not, like St. Paul, planted new vines, he is engaged with Apollos in watering those which are already planted; he is rooting up some withered cumberers of the ground, he is lopping off some unfruitful branches, and propping up those tender sprigs which the tempest has beaten down.

He would be the most unhappy of all faithful ministers, had he not some in his congregation to whom he might with propriety address himself in the following terms:—"Do we need epistles of commendation to you? Ye are manifestly declared to be the epistle of Christ, ministered not by us, written not with ink, but with the Spirit of the living God; not in tables of stone, but in fleshly tables of the heart," 2 Corinthians iii:1-3. "Are not ye my work in the Lord? If I be not an apostle unto others, yet doubtless I am to you; for the seal of mine apostleship are ye in the Lord. For though ye have ten thousand instructers in Christ, yet have ye not many fathers; for in Christ Jesus have I begotten you through the Gospel," 1 Corinthians ix:2; iv:15.

When a minister of the Gospel, after labouring for several years in the same place, is unacquainted with any of his flock, to whom he might modestly hold the preceding language, it is to be feared that he has laboured too much like the generality of pastors in the present day; since "the word of God," when delivered with earnestness and without adulteration, is usually "quick and powerful, and sharper than any two-edged sword, piercing even to the dividing asunder of soul and spirit, and of the joints and marrow," Hebrews iv:12. "He that hath my word, let him speak my word faithfully. What is chaff to the wheat? saith the Lord. Is not my word like a fire; and like a hammer that breaketh the rock in pieces? Behold, I am against them that cause my people to err by their lies and by their lightness: therefore they shall not profit this people at all, saith the Lord," Jeremiah xxiii:28-32.

Those ministers who are anxious so to preach and so to conduct themselves as neither to trouble the peace of the formal, nor to alarm the fears of the impenitent, are undoubtedly the persons peculiarly alluded to in the following solemn passage of Jeremiah's prophecy:—"Mine heart within me is broken because of the prophets; all my bones shake because of the Lord, and because of the words of his holiness. For both prophet and priest are profane; yea, in my house have I found their wickedness, saith the Lord. They walk in lies, [either actually or doctrinally,] they strengthen also the hands of evil doers, that none doth return from his wickedness. From the prophets of Jerusalem is profaneness gone forth into all the land. They speak a vision of their own heart, and not out of the mouth of the Lord. They say unto them that [secretly] despise me, The Lord hath said, Ye shall have peace; and they say unto every one that walketh after the imagination of his own heart, No evil shall come upon you. I have not sent these prophets, yet they ran: I have not spoken to them, yet they prophesied. But if they had stood in my counsel, and had caused my people to hear my words, then they should have turned them from their evil way, and from the evil of their doings," Jeremiah xxiii:9-22.

Behold the reason why nothing can so much afflict a faithful minister as not to behold, from time to time, unfeigned conversions effected among the people by means of his ministry. The husbandman, after having diligently prepared and plentifully sowed his fields, is sensibly afflicted when he sees the hope of his harvest swept away at once by a furious storm; but he feels not so lively a sorrow as the charitable pastor who, after having liberally scattered around him the seeds of wisdom and piety, beholds his parish still overrun with the noxious weeds of vanity and vice. If Nabals are still intoxicated; if Cains are still implacable; if Ananiases are still deceitful, and Sapphiras still prepared to favour their deceit; if Marthas are still cumbered with earthly cares; if Dinahs are still exposing themselves to temptation, even to the detriment of their honour, and to the loss of that little relish which they once discovered for piety; and if the former still continue to approach God with their lips while their hearts are far from him—a good pastor, at the sight of these things, is pierced through with many sorrows, and feels, in a degree, what Elijah felt, when, overburdened with fatigue and chagrin, "he sat down under a juniper tree, and said, It is enough, now, O Lord, take away my life: for I am not better than my fathers," 1 Kings xix:4.

Indifference, in a matter of so great importance, is one of the surest marks by which an unworthy pastor may be discerned. Of what consequence is it to a worldly minister whether the flock about which he takes so little trouble is composed of sheep or goats? He seeks not so much to benefit his people, as to discharge the mere exterior duties of his office in such a way as may not incur the censure of his superiors in the Church, who, possibly, are not a whit less lukewarm than himself. And if a tolerable party of his unclean flock do but disguise themselves three or four times in a year, for the purpose of making their appearance at the sacramental table, he is perfectly satisfied with the good order of his parish, especially when the most detestable vices, such as extortion, theft, adultery, or murder, are not openly practised in it. This outward kind of decency, which is so satisfactory to the worldly minister, and which is ordinarily effected by the constraining force of the civil laws, rather than by the truths of the Gospel, affords the faithful pastor but little consolation. He is solicitous to see his people hungering and thirsting after righteousness, working out their salvation with fear and trembling, and engaging in all the duties of Christianity with as much eagerness as the children of the world pursue their shameful pleasures or trifling amusements; and if he has not yet enjoyed this satisfaction, he humbles himself before God, and anxiously inquires after the reason of so great an unhappiness, he is conscious that if his ministry be not productive of good fruit, the sterility of the word must flow from one or other of the following causes: either he does not publish the Gospel in its full latitude and purity, in a manner sufficiently animating, or in simplicity and faith. Perhaps he is not careful to second his zealous discourses by an exemplary conduct: perhaps he is negligent in imploring the blessing of God upon his public and private labours; or probably his hearers may have conceived inveterate prejudices against him, which make them inattentive to his most solemn exhortations; so that, instead of being received among them as an ambassador of Christ, he can apply to himself the proverb formerly cited by his rejected Master, "No prophet is accepted in his own country," where he is accustomed to be seen without ceremony, and heard without curiosity. If the fault appears to be on his own side, he endeavours to apply the most speedy and efficacious remedies, redoubling his public labours, and renewing his secret supplications with more than ordinary fervour of spirit. But if, after repeated trials, he is convinced that his want of success chiefly flows from the invincible hatred of his flock to the truths of the Gospel, or from the sovereign contempt which his parishioners manifest both to his person and labours, he is then justified in following the example of his unerring Master, who refused to exercise his ministry in those places where prejudice had locked up the hearts of the people against the reception of his evangelical precepts.

When, in such a situation, a pastor is fearful of following the example of our Lord, lest he should be left destitute of a maintenance, in how deplorable a state must he drag through the wearisome days of a useless life! If every sincere Christian is ready to take up his cross, to quit friends and possessions, yea, to renounce life itself, on account of the Gospel, can we consider that minister as a man really consecrated to the service of Christ, who has not resolution sufficient to give up a house, a garden, and a salary, when the welfare of his own soul and the interests of the Church require such a sacrifice?

When a preacher of the Gospel counts less upon the promises of his Master than upon the revenues of his benefice, may we not reasonably conclude, that he is walking in the footsteps of Balaam, rather than in those of St. Paul? And is it for such a man to declare the statutes of the Lord, or to recite the words of his covenant? Psalm l:16. Is he not attempting to publish, before he effectually believes, the truths of the Gospel? And has he not a front of brass, when, with the dispositions of a Demas, he mounts the pulpit, to celebrate the bounty of that God who supplies the wants of "sparrows, who feeds the young ravens that call upon him," opening his hand and filling all things living with plenteousness? Let such a one consider, that the character of a virtuous preceptor, or an honest tradesman, is abundantly more honourable than that of a mercenary priest.

In general, it may be reasonably supposed, that if a pastor faithfully exercise his ministry in any place, to which he has been appointed by the providence of God, he will either benefit those among whom he is called to labour, or his hardened hearers will, at length, unite to drive him from among them, as the inhabitants of Nazareth forced Jesus away from their ungrateful city. Or if he should not be forcibly removed from his post, as was the case of our Lord in the country of the Gada-renes, yet believing it incumbent upon him to retire from such a part, he will seek out some other place in his Master's vineyard, that shall better repay the pains of cultivation, whatever such a removal may cost him in the judgment of the world. And, indeed, such a mode of conduct was positively prescribed by our Lord to his first ministers, in the following solemn charge: "Into whatsoever city or town ye shall enter, inquire who in it is worthy. And whosoever shall not receive you, nor hear your words; when [slighted and reproached by its unworthy inhabitants,] ye [are constrained to] depart out of that house or city, shake off the dust of your feet," as a testimony against those who prefer the maxims of the world before the precepts of the Gospel, Matthew x:11, 14.

If any pastor refuse to adopt this method of proceeding, after patience has had its perfect work; if he still fear to give up an establishment, as the sonsin- law of Lot were afraid of forsaking their possessions in Sodom, he then acts in direct opposition to the command of Christ; he obstinately occupies the place of a minister, against whom, very probably, less prejudice might be entertained, and whose ministry, of consequence, would be more likely to produce some salutary effect; he loses his time in casting pearls before swine; and instead of converting his parishioners, he only aggravates the condemnation due to their obduracy.

The faithful pastor, however, is not soon discouraged, though he beholds no beneficial consequences of his ministry. His unbounded charity suffers, hopes, and labours long, without fainting. The more sterile the soil appears, which he is called to cultivate, the more he waters it, both with his tears and with the sweat of his brow; the more he implores for it the dew of heaven, and the influences of that Divine Sun which spreads light and life through every part of the Church. It is not, therefore, (let it be repeated,) till after patience has had its perfect work, that a conscientious minister takes the final resolution of quitting his post, in order to seek out some other situation, in which his labours may be attended with the greater profit.

TRAIT XXXVII.
His readiness to seal with his blood the truths of the Gospel.

HE who is not yet prepared to die for his Lord, has not yet received that "perfect love" which "casteth out fear:" and it is a matter of doubt, whether any preacher is worthy to appear in the pulpit, whose confidence in the truths of the Gospel is not strong enough to dispose him, in certain situations, to seal those truths with his blood. If he really shrink from the idea of dying in the cause of Christianity, is it for him to publish a Saviour, who is "the resurrection and the life?" And may he not be said to play with his conscience, his auditors, and his God, if, while he is the slave of sin and fear, he presents himself as a witness of the salvation of that omnipotent Redeemer, who, "through death, has destroyed him that had the power of death;" and who, by his resurrection, has "delivered them who, through fear of death, were all their lifetime subject to bondage?" Hebrews ii:14, 15. Love, in the language of

Solomon, "is strong as death:" but the true minister glows with that fervent love to Christ and his brethren, which is abundantly stronger than those fears of death which would prevent him, in times of persecution, from the faithful discharge of his ministerial functions. Such was the love of St. Paul, when he cried out to those who would have dissuaded him from the dangerous path of duty: "What mean ye to weep, and to break mine heart? for I am ready not to be bound only, but also to die at Jerusalem for the name of the Lord Jesus," Acts xxi:13. "And now, behold, I go bound in the spirit unto Jerusalem, not knowing the things that shall befall me there: save that the Holy Ghost witnesseth in every city, saying, that bonds and afflictions abide me. But none of these things move me, neither count I my life dear unto myself, so that I may finish my course with joy, and the ministry which I have received of the Lord Jesus," Acts xx:22-24. "For I know that this shall turn to my salvation, through your prayer, and the supply of the spirit of Jesus Christ, according to my earnest expectation, that Christ shall be magnified in my body, whether it be by life or by death. For me to live is Christ, and to die is gain. And if I be offered upon the sacrifice and service of your faith, I joy and rejoice with you all," Philippians i:19-21; ii:17.

Thus "the good shepherd giveth his life for the sheep: but he that is a hireling, and not the shepherd, seeth the wolf coming, and leaveth the sheep, and fleeth; and the wolf catcheth them, and scattereth the sheep," John x:11, 12. Happy is that Church whose pastor is prepared to tread in the steps of "the great Shepherd and Bishop of souls!" St. Paul would not have been ashamed to acknowledge such a one as his companion and fellow labourer in the work of the Lord.

TRAIT XXXVIII.

The sweet suspense of his choice between life and death.

WHATEVER desire the faithful pastor may have to be with Christ, and to rest from his labours, yet he endures with joy his separation from the person of his Saviour, through the sacred pleasure he experiences in the service of his members. The sweet equilibrium in which his desire was suspended between life and death, is thus expressed by the Apostle Paul: "We know that if our earthly house of this tabernacle were dissolved, we have a building of God, a house not made with hands, eternal in the heavens. For in this we groan, earnestly desiring to be clothed upon with our house which is from heaven: knowing that while we are at home in the body, we are absent from the Lord," 2 Corinthians v:1-6. "Yet what I shall choose I wot not. For I am in a strait betwixt two, having a desire to depart, and to be with Christ, which is far better: nevertheless, to abide in the flesh is more needful for you. And having this confidence, I know that I shall abide and continue with you all, for your furtherance and joy of faith," Philippians i:22-25.

It is chiefly when believers have the unconquerable love of St. Paul, "that all things work together for their good." Whether they live, or whether they die, every occurrence turns out a matter of favour. If they live, it is that they may support their companions in tribulation, and insure to themselves a greater reward, by maintaining, for a long season, the victorious fight of faith. If they die, it is that they may rest from their labours, and come to a more perfect enjoyment of their Master's presence. "Blessed are the dead which die in the Lord: they rest from their labours, and their works do follow them," Revelation xiv:13. And in the meantime, blessed are the living who live in the Lord: for they are honourably engaged in those important conflicts which will daily add to their spiritual strength, and augment the brilliancy of their final triumph.

TRAIT XXIX.

The constancy of his zeal and diligence to the end of his course.

LIVING or dying, the faithful servant of Christ never acts unworthy of his character. "Blameless and harmless in the midst of a crooked and perverse generation, a child of God without rebuke, he shines," to the end of his course, "as a light in the world," Philippians ii:15. He beholds death, whether it be natural or violent, always without fear, and generally with pleasure, regarding it as a messenger appointed for his safe conduct into that glorious state, where they rejoice together who have continued faithful to the end. He is anxious only that his Lord may find him occupied in the grand business he was commissioned to perform: and the nearer his hour approaches, the more earnest he is that he may finish his ministry with joy. If he be no longer able to exhort the brethren in person, he writes to them in the manner of St. Peter: "I will not be negligent to put you always in remembrance of these things," the doctrines, precepts, threatenings, and promises of the Gospel, "though ye know them, and be established in the present truth. Yea, I think it meet, as long as I am in this tabernacle, to stir you up by putting you in remembrance; knowing, that shortly I must put off this tabernacle, even as our Lord Jesus Christ hath showed me," 2 Peter i:12-14. He desires, at such a season, to address the faithful, and especially young ministers, as St. Paul addressed the Corinthians and Timothy: "My beloved brethren, be steadfast, unmovable, always abounding in the work of the Lord; forasmuch as ye know that your labour is not in vain in the Lord," 1 Corinthians xv:58. "Thou, Timothy, hast fully known my doctrine, manner of life, purpose, faith, long suffering, charity, patience, persecutions, afflictions, which came unto me at Antioch, at Iconium, at Lystra; what persecutions I endured: but out of then, all the Lord delivered me. Yea, and all that will live godly in Christ Jesus shall suffer persecution. But watch thou in all things, endure afflictions, do the work of an evangelist, make full proof of thy ministry; for I am now ready to be offered, and the time of my departure is at hand," 2 Timothy iii:10-12; iv:5, 6.

Thus triumphantly St. Paul advanced toward the end of his course. And thus the faithful minister, pouring fresh oil into his lamp as the night advances, goes forth to meet his approaching God, whom his faith already considers as a merciful Judge, and his hope as a munificent Rewarder.

TRAIT XL.

His triumph over the evils of life, and the terrors of death.

THE living faith that sustains a good pastor, or a believer in Christ, amid all the difficulties and afflictions of life, causes him more especially to triumph at the approach of death in all its terrific appearances. Ever filled with an humble confidence in Him, who is the resurrection and the life, he frequently expresses the assurance of his victorious faith, at this solemn season, in the manner of St. Paul: "Thanks be unto God, which always causeth us to triumph in Christ," 2 Corinthians ii:14. "Knowing, that He who raised up the Lord Jesus shall raise up us also by Jesus, and shall present us with you: therefore we faint not: but though our outward man perish, yet the inner man is renewed day by day. For our light affliction, which is but for a moment, worketh out for us a far more exceeding and eternal weight of glory," 2 Corinthians iv:14. Thus holding up the shield of faith to quench the fiery darts of the wicked one, and to receive the piercing arrows of the angel of death, he expects his last hour without fear or impatience; cheerfully leaving the time, the place, the manner, and the circumstances of this concluding trial, to the disposal of that God whose wisdom, goodness, and power, are all combined to insure him the victory. Whether he be called by the providence of God, in a chamber or upon a scaffold, to taste the bitter cup of which his Master drank so deeply, he prepares himself to accompany a suffering Saviour, encouraged with the hope that he shall not be tempted above his strength; and that, if he should suffer and die with the King of glory, he shall also rise and reign together with him.

At length the fatal shaft is thrown,—whether by accident, by disease, or by the hand of an executioner, is of little consequence; the true Christian, prepared for all events, sees and submits to the order of Providence. He receives the mortal blow, either with humble resignation, or with holy joy. In the first case, his soul is sweetly disengaged from its earthly tabernacle, while he breathes out the supplicatory language of happy Simeon, "Lord, now lettest thou thy servant depart in peace, for mine eyes have seen thy salvation." But in the second case, he leaves the world in a state of holy triumph, crying out in the fullest assurance of faith, My persuasion takes place of sight, and without the help of vision I endure, as seeing him that is invisible; as effectually sustained, as though, contemplating with Stephen an open heaven, I saw the Son of man standing at the right hand of God, ready to save and glorify my soul. Of these two manners of holy dying, the most enviable appears to have been the lot of St. Paul, if we may judge from the anticipated triumph he describes in several of his epistles, and particularly in the last he addressed to Timothy from Rome, where he received the crown of martyrdom. "I desire to depart and to be with Christ, for whom I have suffered the loss of all things, and do count them but dung, that I may know him, and the power of his resurrection, and the fellowship of his sufferings, being made conformable unto his death," Philippians i:13; iii:8-10. "I have fought a good fight, I have finished my course, I have kept the faith. Henceforth there is laid up for me a crown of righteousness, which the Lord, the righteous Judge, shall give me at that day: to whom be glory for ever and ever," 2 Timothy iv:7, 8, 18. "Who shall separate us from the love of Christ? Shall tribulation, or distress, or persecution, or the sword? Nay, in all these things we are more than conquerors, through him that loved us. For I am persuaded, that neither death, nor life, nor angels, nor principalities, nor powers, nor things present, nor things to come, nor height, nor depth, nor any other creature, shall be able to separate us from the love of God, which is in Christ Jesus," Romans viii:35, 39. "O death, where is thy sting? O grave, where is thy victory? Thanks be to God, who giveth us the victory through our Lord Jesus Christ," 1 Corinthians xv:55-57.

Thus the great apostle went forth to meet his last trial, counting it an honour to suffer in the cause of truth, and rejoicing in hope of the glory of God. The enemies of Christianity rendered him at last conformable to Christ in his death:* but while they severed his head from his body, they united his happy spirit more intimately to that exalted Jesus, who had once met him in the way, and who now was waiting to receive him at the end of his course. Happy are the faithful, who, like this faithful apostle, live unto the Lord! yet happier they, who, like him, are enabled to die unto the Lord! "Their works do follow them, while they rest from their labours," and wait in peace the resurrection and the sublime rewards of the righteous.

---

* Tradition informs us, that St. Paul, in the second journey he made to Rome, received the crown of martyrdom under the Emperor Nero, about thirty-five years after the crucifixion of our blessed Lord. St. Clement, the contemporary of St. Paul, speaks of that apostle in the following terms, in his first epistle to the Corinthians: "By means of jealousy, Paul has received the prize of perseverance. Having been seven times in bonds; having been evil entreated and stoned; having preached in the east and in the west, he has obtained the glorious prize of his faith. After having instructed all the world in righteousness, coming into the west, he has suffered martyrdom under those who command; and thus quitting the world, after having shown in it a great example of patience, he has gone into the holy place."

THE PORTRAIT

OF

LUKEWARM MINISTERS AND FALSE APOSTLES.

CHAPTER I.

THE essence of painting consists in a happy mixture of light and shade, from the contrast of which an admirable effect is produced, and the animated figure made to rise from the canvass. Upon this principle we shall oppose to the Portrait of St. Paul, that of lukewarm ministers and false apostles, whose gloomy traits will form a back ground peculiarly adapted to set off the character of an evangelical pastor.

If the primitive Church was disturbed and misled by unfaithful ministers, it may be reasonably presumed that, in this more degenerate period of its existence, the Church of God must be miserably overrun with teachers of the same character. There is, however, no small number of ministers who form a kind of medium between zealous pastors and false apostles. These irresolute evangelists are sincere to a certain point. They have some desire after the things of God, but are abundantly more solicitous for the things of the world: they form good resolutions in the cause of their acknowledged Master, but are timid and unfaithful when called upon actual service. They are sometimes actuated by a momentary zeal, but generally influenced by servile fear. They have no experience of that ardent affection, and that invincible courage with which St. Paul was animated. Their wisdom is still carnal, 2 Corinthians i:12; they still confer "with flesh and blood," Galatians i:16. Such was Aaron, who yielded, through an unmanly weakness, to the impious solicitations of his people. Such was Jonah, when he refused to exercise his ministry at Nineveh. That this prophet was possessed of a holy confidence in God, and a desire for the salvation of his fellow creatures, we have every reason to believe: but we find, that neither the one nor the other was sufficiently powerful to engage him in a service which appeared likely to endanger his reputation among men. Such were also the apostles before they were endued with power from on high. To every pastor of this character, that expression of Christ, which was once addressed to the most courageous man among his disciples, may be considered as peculiarly applicable: "Thou art an offence unto me, for thou savourest not the things that be of God, but those that be of men," Matthew xvi:23.

Lukewarmness, false prudence, and timidity, are the chief characteristics by which ministers of this class may be distinguished. Perceiving the excellence of the Gospel in an obscure point of view, and having little experience of its astonishing effects, they cannot possibly discover that religious zeal which is indispensably necessary to the character they affect to sustain.

The pious Bishop Massillon gives the following representation of these unqualified teachers, and the ill effects of their unfaithfulness. "Manners are every day becoming more corrupt among us, because the zeal of ministers is daily becoming colder; and because there are found among us few apostolical men, who oppose themselves, as a brazen wall, to the torrent of vice. For the most part, we behold the wicked altogether at ease in their sins, for the want of hearing more frequently those thundering voices, which, accompanied with the Spirit of God, would effectually rouse them from their awful slumber. The want of zeal, so dearly discernible among pastors, is chiefly owing to that base timidity which is not hardy enough to make a resolute stand against common prejudice, and which regards the worthless approbation of men, beyond their eternal interests. That must needs be a worldly and criminal consideration, which makes us more anxious for our own glory than for the glory of God. That must truly be fleshly wisdom, which can represent religious zeal under the false ideas of excess, indiscretion, and temerity: a pretext this, which nearly extinguishes every spark of zeal in the generality of ministers. This want of courage they honour with the specious names of moderation and prudence. Under pretence of not carrying their zeal to an excess, they are content to be entirely destitute of it. And while they are solicitous to shun the reeks of imprudence and precipitation, they run, without fear, upon the sands of indolence and cowardice. They desire to become useful to sinners, and, at the same time, to be had in estimation by them. They long to manifest such a zeal as the world is disposed to applaud. They are anxious so to oppose the passions of men, that they may yet secure their praises; so to condemn the vices they love, that they may still be approved by those they condemn. But when we probe a wound to the bottom, we must expect to awaken a degree of peevishness in the patient, if we do not extort from him some bitter exclamation."

"Let us not deceive ourselves," continues the same author; "if this apostolical zeal, which once converted the world, is become so rare among us, it is because, in the discharge of our sacred functions, we seek ourselves, rather than the glory of Christ, and the salvation of souls. Glory and infamy were regarded by the apostle with equal indifference, while he filled up the duties of his important office. He knew it impossible to please men, and to save them; to be the servant of the world, and the servant of Christ. Nevertheless, there are many among us who are seeking to unite these different services, which the apostle believed to be irreconcilable."

Mons. Roques agrees with the pious bishop in condemning those ministers who neglect to copy the example of St. Paul. "The little piety that is to be found among ministers," says this excellent writer, "is the most effectual obstacle to the progress of the Gospel. By piety, I mean that sincere and ardent love for religion, which deeply interests a man in all its concerns, as well as in every thing that respects the glory of God, and of our Lord Jesus Christ. If this Divine love were found reigning in the hearts of those who proclaim Christ; if every preacher of the Gospel were enabled to say, with the sincerity of Peter, "Lord! thou knowest all things; thou knowest that I love thee," John xxi:15; thou knowest that I have no ambition but for thy glory, and that my highest pleasure consists in beholding the increase of thy kingdom—we should then perceive the sword of God in their hands like a two-edged sword, cutting asunder the very deepest roots of sin. But as the Gospel is preached more through contention, through vain glory, and through the desire of getting a livelihood by serving at the altar, than through an ardent zeal to advance the glory of God; hence it is that ministers fall into several errors, giving evident proofs of that indolence and unconcern, which afford matter of scandal rather than of edification."—*Evangelical Pastor.*

Mons. Ostervald speaks the same language in his Third Source of the Corruption which reigns among Christians. "A great part of our ecclesiastics," says this writer, "may be justly charged with the corruption of the people, since there are among them many who oppose the reestablishment of a holy discipline; while others render the exercise of it totally useless, by an ill-timed softness, and a shameful indulgence."

"I except those," continues this venerable pastor, "who ought to be excepted. But on a general view, in what do ecclesiastics differ from other men? Do they distinguish themselves by an exemplary life? Their exterior, indeed, is somewhat different: they lead a more retired life; they, in some degree, save appearances; though all do not go thus far. But beyond this, are they not equally attached to the world, as much engaged with earthly things, as wholly taken up with secular views, as constantly actuated by interest and passion, as the generality of mankind?"

Christian prudence required that these portraits of lukewarm ministers should be exhibited as the designs of pastors who have been eminent for their piety, their rank, and experience, and who, on that account, had a peculiar right to declare those truths, which might give greater offence were they to come from less respectable persons.

CHAPTER II.

The portrait of false apostles.

BETWEEN the state of careless ministers, and that of false apostles, there is not, in reality, so vast a difference as many are apt to imagine. An unworthy labourer in the spiritual vineyard gives speedy proofs of a lukewarm temper in the service of his Lord; shortly after his heart becomes entirely cold with respect to piety; and what is still more lamentable, he frequently manifests as warm a zeal for error and vice as the true minister can possibly discover in the cause of truth and virtue. Such is the state of those who may properly be termed preachers of the third class, and who are spoken of by St. Paul under the title of "false apostles," 2 Corinthians xi:13.

These unworthy ministers are known by their works. Like many of St. Paul's unfaithful fellow labourers, 2 Timothy i:15, they prefer the repose and pleasure of the world before the service and reproach of Christ. Like Judas and Simon the sorcerer, they love the honours and revenues of ministers, while they abhor the crosses and labours of the ministry. Like Hophni and Phinehas, they are sons of Belial, and know not the Lord. Their sin is very great before the Lord. For, on their account, many "abhor the offering of the Lord," 1 Samuel ii:12, 17. Like the wicked servant, described by their reputed Master, instead of providing "meat for his household in due season, they begin to smite," or to persecute those of their fellow servants who are intent upon discharging their several duties; while they pass away their time in mirth and festivity with the riotous and the drunken, Matthew xxiv:48, 49. They may justly be compared to lamps extinguished in the temple of God. "Instead of shining there to his praise," says Bishop Massilion, "they emit black clouds of smoke which obscure every object about them, and become a savour of death to those who perish.

The Works of John Fletcher

They are pillars of the sanctuary, which, being overthrown and scattered in public places, become stones of stumbling to every heedless passenger. They are the salt of the earth, and were appointed to preserve souls from corruption But having lost all their savour, they begin to corrupt what they were intended to preserve." They are physicians who carry to their patients infection instead of health. From the spiritually diseased they withhold the healing word of God, Psalm cvii:20, while they distribute among them the dangerous poison of a lax morality, setting before them an example of bitter zeal against the truth, puffing them up with that wisdom which is "earthly, sensual, and devilish," James iii:14, 15.

"A false pastor," says Mons. Roques, or a false apostle, "is a minister whose heart is not right before God, and who lives not in such a manner as to edify his flock. He knows the holy course of life to which Christians in general, and ministers in particular, are called; but in spite of all his knowledge and his apparent zeal, he fears not to trample under foot those very maxims of the Gospel which he has publicly established and preached with the utmost energy. Every day he performs acts of the most detestable hypocrisy. Every time he preaches and censures, he bears open testimony against his own conduct. But he publicly accuses, without ever intending to correct himself. He is a constant declaimer against vice in the pulpit; but a peculiar protector of it while he is engaged in the common concerns of life. While he exhorts his hearers to repentance, he either imagines himself above those laws which he proposes to others on the part of God; or he believes himself under no other necessity of holding them forth, except his own engagements to such a work, and the salary he receives for the performance of it."

Mons. Ostervald, in a work already referred to, makes mention of these pastors in the following terms: "How many do we see who regard their holy vocation in no other light than the means of procuring for them a comfortable maintenance. Are there not many who bring a scandal upon their profession by the licentiousness of their manners? Do we not see them hasty and outrageous? Do we not observe in them an extreme attachment to their own interests? Are they careful to rule their families well? Has it not been a subject of complaint, that they are puffed up with pride, and are implacable in their hatred? I say nothing of many other vices and defects which are equally scandalous in the clergy, such as vain and loose conversation, an attachment to diversion and pleasure, a worldly disposition, slothfulness, craft, injustice, and slander."

"It is impossible to find a person," adds Mons. Ostervald, "surrounded with more powerful motives to piety, than a man whose ordinary occupation is to meditate upon religious things, to discourse of them among others, to reprove vice and hypocrisy, to perform Divine service, to administer the holy sacraments, to visit the afflicted and the dying; and who must one day render to God an account of the souls committed to his charge. I know not whether it be possible to find any stronger marks of impiety and hypocrisy than those which may be discovered in the character of a person, who, in the midst of all these favourable circumstances, is, nevertheless, an unrighteous man. Such a one may be said to divert himself with the most sacred things of religion, and to spend the whole of his life in performing the part of an impostor. And this he does to his cost; since there is no profession in the world that will more effectually secure a sentence of condemnation than that of the priesthood, when exercised in so unfaithful a manner."

The Portrait of St. Paul

But it is chiefly in the Holy Scriptures where these unworthy pastors are portrayed in so strong a point of view, that every attentive inquirer may readily discern their distinguishing features. "Son of man," saith the Lord, "prophesy against the shepherds of Israel, and say unto them: Ye eat the fat, and ye clothe you with the wool, ye kill them that are fed; but ye feed not the flock. The diseased have ye not strengthened, neither have ye bound up that which was broken, neither have ye brought again that which was driven away, neither have ye sought that which was lost: but with force and with cruelty have ye ruled them. Therefore thus saith the Lord God, Behold, I am against the shepherds; and I will require my flock at their hand," Ezekiel xxxiv:2, 10. "As Jannes and Jambres withstood Moses, so do these also resist the truth. Men of corrupt minds, reprobate concerning the faith," 2 Timothy iii:8. "Wo unto them; for they have gone in the way of Cain, and ran greedily after the error of Balaam for reward, and perished in the gain-saying of Korah. Clouds they are without water, carried about of winds; trees without fruit, twice dead, plucked up by the roots; raging waves of the sea, foaming out their own shame; wandering stars, to whom is reserved the blackness of darkness for ever," Jude i:11, 12.

St. John has not only drawn the character; but has likewise given us the name of a certain tyrannical teacher, who began to disturb the peace of the primitive church: "I wrote unto the Church," saith he to Gaius, concerning the reception of stranger evangelists; but Diotrephes, who loveth to have the pre-eminence among them, receiveth us not. If I come, I will remember his deeds which he doeth, prating against us with malicious words. And not content therewith, neither doth he himself receive the brethren, and forbiddeth them that would, and casteth them out of the Church," 3 John. Behold a striking description of proud and persecuting ecclesiastics!

But, perhaps, the most complete description of these is given by our Lord himself, where he treats of worthless pastors in general, under the particular names of scribes and Pharisees. Here a Divine and impartial hand delineates the jealousy, the pride, the feigned morality, the malice, and the persecuting spirit which characterize this class of men in every age of the world. "Do not ye," saith Christ, "after their works, for they say, and do not. All their works they do to be seen of men. They love the chief seats in the synagogues, and greetings in the markets. Wo unto you, hypocrites! For ye shut up the kingdom of heaven against men: ye neither go in yourselves, neither suffer ye them that are entering to go in. Ye neglect judgment, mercy, and faith. Ye outwardly appear righteous unto men, but within ye are full of hypocrisy and iniquity. Because ye garnish the sepulchres of the righteous," ye vainly imagine yourselves free from a persecuting spirit, while in other matters, as "the children of them which killed the prophets," ye are labouring to "fill up the measure of your fathers. Behold, I send unto you prophets" and zealous preachers of the word, "and some of them ye shall kill, and some of them ye shall persecute from city to city," Matthew xxiii:3, 34.

We need take but a cursory view of the New Testament, for sufficient proof that these worldly-minded scribes and these furious bigots above represented, were the very persons who pursued the first evangelists with such deadly rancour. Nay, had it not been for Annas and Caiaphas, Herod and Pilate would silently have permitted the preaching of Jesus himself. These, who were the chief men of the state, after refusing to embrace the word of God, on their own part, would most probably have contented themselves with denying its truths, and ridiculing its followers. But they would never have passed a sentence of death upon persons of so admirable a character as Christ and his forerunner.

The peculiar opposers of Jesus and his disciples were powerfully influenced by jealous pride; and with the same malignant disposition every false apostle in the Christian Church is deeply infected. The prelate, whose pen we have already borrowed, gives the following lively description of this unhappy temper: "This despicable jealousy not only dishonours zeal, but supposes it extinguished in the heart. It is an infamous disposition which afflicts itself even for the conversion of sinners, and for the progress of the Gospel, when it is through the ministry of others that God is pleased to work these miracles. The glory of God seldom interests us so much as when our own glory appears to be mingled with his. We endure, with some kind of regret, that God should be glorified: and I will dare to add, that some of us could behold our brethren perishing, with pleasure, rather than see them rescued from death by other labours, and other talents than our own. St. Paul rejoiced to see the Gospel spread abroad, though it were by the ministry of those who sought to disgrace him among the faithful; and Moses desired that all his brethren might receive the gift of prophecy. But we are anxious to stand alone, and to share with no person the glory and success of the holy ministry. Every thing that eclipses our own brightness, or shines too near us, becomes insupportable, and we appear to regard the gifts of God in others, merely as a shame and reproach to ourselves." Observe here the true source of those specious pretexts, which are professedly drawn from the order, the customs, and even from the prejudices of the world. Pretexts under which we dare oppose the zeal of our brethren, to withstand the word of God in its course, and to render the cross of the ministry more burthensome to those who carry it farther than we are disposed to do. One distinguishing mark of these turbulent evangelists, is that of being thorns in the sides of true ministers, whom they never fail to represent as deceivers or novices, causing the truest piety to wear the semblance of enthusiasm and folly. "They speak evil of the things they understand not," 2 Peter ii:12; and by the most malicious discourses, which have always an appearance of zeal for religion and order, they are gradually rousing anew that spirit of persecution, by which the name of Christ has been so universally disgraced in the world.

In the earliest age of the Christian Church, these false apostles, swelling with envy at the success of more faithful ministers, made use of every effort to render them contemptible, by giving false representations of their holy zeal, and their exemplary actions. Thus they accused St. Paul of walking "according to the flesh;" and asserted, that though "his letters were weighty and powerful," yet "his bodily presence was weak, and his speech contemptible," 2 Corinthians x:2, 10. Nay, so anxious were they in seeking occasions for offence in the conduct of this apostle, that he believed himself obliged in the end publicly to expose them. "These are false apostles," says he, "deceitful workers, transforming themselves into the apostles of Christ. And no marvel, for Satan himself is transformed into an angel of light. Therefore it is no great thing if his ministers also be transformed, as the ministers of righteousness; whose end shall be according to their works," 2 Corinthians xi:13-15. As our Lord foresaw that these strenuous opposers of real religion would bring his Church to the very brink of ruin, he exhorted his disciples continually to stand upon their guard against them, Matthew vii:15. And the apostles, after steadily following their Master's important advice, were diligent in transmitting it to the latest of their followers, Acts xx:28, 30; 2 Peter ii:1.

One necessary remark shall conclude this chapter. In the Portrait of St. Paul we have seen that of an evangelical pastor. In the preceding chapter we have marked the character of a careless minister; and in this we behold the faithful representation of a false apostle. Let us remember, that one of these three portraits must agree, more or less, with every preacher of the Gospel. I say more or less, because the various traits here marked out may be varied to an almost inconceivable degree. Moreover, so inconstant is man, that a minister, who to-day is possessed of zeal sufficient to rank him with preachers of the first class, may, to-morrow, by an unhappy remissness, sink into the second, as once did John, whose surname was Mark; or even into the third, as Hymeneus and Philetus, Diotrephes and Demas. On the contrary, a man, who now discovers many of those traits by which Saul the Pharisee was once distinguished, may, ere long, become an humble imitator of the zeal and charity of Paul the apostle.

CHAPTER III.
An answer to the first objection which may be made against the Portrait of St. Paul.

OBJECTIONS are the ordinary weapons with which error makes war upon truth, and these are sometimes so powerful, that, till they are effectually repelled, we see truth deprived of its rights. The first that will probably be advanced against the Portrait of St. Paul, is this: "The model placed before us is too exalted for those who are not endued with the miraculous gifts of St. Paul."

To this, and every other objection, we shall offer a variety of replies, in as concise a manner as possible. To the present objection a sufficient answer has been already returned by a truly respectable author: "This excuse," says Mons. Roques, "might have some weight, if, in proposing the example of Christ to persons who are honoured with the holy ministry, we insisted upon their keeping pace with the Saviour of mankind. But this excuse is altogether frivolous, when nothing more is required of ministers than continually to place Christ as a model before their eyes, and to imitate him with all the exactness of which they are capable." "This excuse," continues he, "is still more unreasonable, when applied to prophets and apostles, who were men of like passions with ourselves; and who, of consequence, may be placed before us as models, whose perfections are attainable by means of the very same succours which supported them, and which are never refused to those who have sincere and apostolical intentions." (*Evangelical Pastor.*)

To the answer of this pious divine we shall subjoin a few observations.

1. In the Portrait of St. Paul there is found no large description of miraculous gifts, but a faithful representation of those Christian virtues, which are found in every believer, according to his vocation, and without which it is impossible for us to fill up our several duties—such as humility, faith, charity, zeal, and assiduity.

2. The morality which was practised by St. Paul was no other than the morality of the Gospel, which is the same in every age, and for every condition: whence it follows, that the moral character of this apostle belongs not only to all true pastors, but even to every sincere believer. If St. Paul was truly humble, charitable, and pious, his humility, his charity, and his piety, are as essential to the religion of every Christian, as three angles are essential to the nature of every triangle. It is granted, that the piety of this apostle was greater than that of a thousand other ministers, just as one triangle may be greater than that of a thousand others. But as the angles of the most diminutive triangle are of the same quality with those which compose a triangle of uncommon magnitude, so the moral character of St. Paul is, with regard to essentials, the moral character of every true Christian.

3. This apostle informs us, that he was obliged to "keep his body in subjection, lest after having preached to others he himself should become a castaway," 1 Corinthians ix:27. This single acknowledgment sufficiently proves that he was exposed to all those dangers with which Christians are generally beset, and that he saw no way of escaping them, but by the use of those very precautions which the weakest believer is instructed to take. Now, if St. Paul was so fearful of falling away; if St. Peter was really seen to stumble and fall; and if Judas, an elected apostle, irremediably plunged himself into the depths of perdition; it is but reasonable to suppose that, by a faithful improvement of our privileges, we may attain to a good degree of that exalted piety, from which one apostle fell for a season, and another for ever.

4. In the whole Portrait of St. Paul there is not a stronger trait than the eighteenth, which describes the ardour of his love for the Jews, who pursued him even to death: a love that made him willing to be accursed in dying for them, as his gracious Master had been in dying for the world. Now this charity is so far from being an attainment too exalted for true ministers, that it is indiscriminately required of every professing Christian. "Hereby," saith St. John "perceive we the love of God, because he laid down his life for us: and we ought to lay down our lives for the brethren," 1 John iii:16. And our Lord himself hath said, "By this shall all men know that ye are my disciples, if ye have love one to another," John xiii:35. It is by a new commandment to this effect that the morality of the Gospel is peculiarly distinguished from that of the law. And shall we impiously attempt to enervate evangelical morality? Let us rather declare, upon all occasions, that "he who loveth not knoweth not God," 1 John iv:8. Let us cry out with the apostle, "If any man love not the Lord Jesus Christ, let him be anathema maranatha." And if a man love not his brethren, he loves not the Lord Jesus; for "he that loveth not his brother, whom he hath seen, how can he love God, whom he hath not seen?" 1 Corinthians xvi:22.

On the other hand, when we love our brethren "with a pure heart fervently," 1 Peter i:22, when, disposed to universal benevolence, we can look upon our very enemies with sentiments of pity and affection, we are then assuredly possessed of that Christian charity, which forms the most brilliant trait in the moral character of St. Paul.

5. St. Paul was for three years the resident pastor of a single Church. The city of Ephesus was his parish. And while he resided there, he gave an example, which every minister, by the most solemn engagements, is bound to follow, whether he be commissioned to labour in a city or a village. During two other years of his life this apostle was confined within narrower limits than any pastor of a parish. Shut up at Rome in a house that served him for a prison, and constantly guarded by a soldier, he was unable to extend the sphere of his labours. Yet, even in these circumstances, he continued in the diligent exercise of the holy ministry, "preaching the kingdom of God to all them that came in unto him, and teaching those things which concern the Lord Jesus Christ," Acts xxviii:30.

Surely nothing can appear more perfectly reasonable, than that every pastor should discover as much zeal in his particular parish, as St. Paul was accustomed to manifest in the Roman empire when he was at liberty, and in his own apartment when loaded with chains.

6. If the ardent charity and the incessant labours of St. Paul were happily imitated by Timothy, why may they not be copied by every pastor in the present day? That youthful minister was anxious to tread in the steps of this apostle, and they, who are otherwise minded, assuredly fall under those apostolical censures, which are thus indirectly expressed in his Epistle to the Philippians: "I trust to send Timotheus shortly unto you, for I have no man like-minded, who will naturally care for your state. For all seek their own, not the things which are Jesus Christ's. But ye know the proof of him, that as a son with the father, he hath served with me in the Gospel," Philippians ii:19-22.

7. The destruction of the eastern Churches commenced in the falling away of their pastors, who gradually abated in the fervours of that holy zeal, with which they had begun to labour in the vineyard of their Lord. Of such unfaithful teachers Christ affectingly complained in the earliest period of his Church, and accompanied his complaints with the most terrible menaces. "Write unto the angel of the Church of Ephesus," said he to St. John, "I know thy former works, and thy labour, and thy patience, and how thou canst not bear them which are evil. And thou hast tried them which say they are apostles, and are not; and hast found them liars, &c. Nevertheless, I have somewhat against thee, because thou hast left thy first love. Remember, therefore, from whence thou art fallen, and repent, and do the first works: or else I will come unto thee quickly, and will remove thy candlestick out of his place, except thou repent," Revelation ii:2-5.

The warning was unattended to, and, at length, the threatened blow was struck. Thus fell the Church of Ephesus, and thus every Church upon earth is fallen, making way for that "mystery of iniquity," and that general apostasy, which have been so long foretold. So true is it, that apostolical charity, that charity which was first lighted up on the day of pentecost, is still absolutely necessary to every pastor, to every Church, and, of consequence, to every believer.

From the combined force of these seven argumentative observations, we have a right to conclude, that the virtues of St. Paul are far from being inimitable, and that the first objection against his portrait is void of solidity.

CHAPTER IV.
A second objection argued against.

THEY who follow the example of Diotrephes rather than that of St. Paul, add to the preceding another objection, to discredit, if possible, the imitators of this great apostle. "Do you pretend," say they, "to be the successors of St. Paul, and the other apostles, whom you presumptuously cite as your models?"

To such objectors the following reflections will serve as a sufficient reply:—

1. We have heard St. Paul, in the character of a believer, proposing himself as an example to all believers; and, as a minister of the Gospel, exhorting every pastor to tread in his steps, 1 Corinthians xi:1; Philippians iii:17.

2. John the Baptist preached repentance. The apostles proclaimed remission of sins in the name of Jesus Christ, "who was delivered for our offences, and was raised again for our justification," Romans iv:25; and every true minister still continues to insist upon these important doctrines. Now, as he who takes the place of a person deceased, is accounted the successor of such person; so these faithful pastors should be regarded as teachers appointed to succeed both the forerunner and apostles of Christ. It must be allowed that the apostles, as elders in the family of our Lord, were in possession of privileges which we are not permitted to enjoy. But if the Gospel is unchangeable, and if the kingdom of God still remains under its ancient form of government, the priesthood must, for the most part, of necessity continue the same.

3. There was a time in which the Jewish priests had lost the Urim and Thummim with which Aaron and his sons were at first invested. There was a time in which God no longer manifested himself to his own appointed priests, as he had been accustomed to do. But as, notwithstanding the loss of that glory which formerly rested upon the Jewish Church, every pious priest, such as Zacharias, was a true successor of Aaron; so, during the eclipse of that glory which once illuminated the Christian Church, every pious minister may justly be accounted a true successor of St. Paul.

4. The word *apostle* signifies *one who is sent,* and answers to the term *angel* or *messenger.* "Our brethren," says St. Paul, who accompany Titus, "are the messengers," or apostles, "of the Churches," 2 Corinthians viii:23. Every minister, therefore, who carries with sincerity the messages of his Lord, may, with propriety, be ranked among his angels or messengers. Nor do such immediately lose their title when they neglect to perform the duties of their office. They may, like Judas, go under the name of apostles even to their death, though utterly unworthy of such an honourable appellation. Thus, after the pastors of Ephesus and Laodicea had outlived the transient fervours of their charity and zeal, they were still addressed as the angels of their several Churches. And thus St. Paul gave the title of apostles to the worldly ministers of his time. In quality of ministers they were apostles; but in quality of worldly ministers they were false apostles.

5. As the name of Cesar is ordinarily applied to the twelve first Roman emperors, so the name of apostle is ordinarily applied to the twelve first ministers of the Gospel who had been permitted to converse with their Lord, even after his resurrection, and to St. Paul who was favoured with a glorious manifestation of his exalted Saviour. In this confined sense it is acknowledged that the name of apostle belongs, in an especial manner, to those who were sent forth by Christ after having received their consecration and commission immediately from himself. But as the name of Cesar, in a more general sense, may be given to all the emperors of Rome, so the name of apostle may be applied to every minister of the everlasting Gospel. Thus Barnabas,

Andronicus, and Junia, who were neither of the number of the twelve, nor yet of the seventy, were denominated apostles as well as St. Paul, Acts xiv:14; Romans xvi:7.

6. It is the invariable opinion of slothful Christians that the zeal of ministers, and the piety of believers in the present day, must necessarily fall far below what they were in the apostles' time: as though the promises of Christ were unhappily limited to the primitive Church. This error has been frequently refuted in vain by a variety of Christian writers, since nothing can be more conformable to that spirit of incredulity which reigns among us, than to renounce, at once, the most important promises of the New Testament. Had the same promises been made respecting temporal honours and profits, we should see a different mode of conduct adopted; "For the children of this world are, in their generation, wiser, than the children of light," Luke xvi:8.

Mons. Roques bears the following testimony to the truth contended for in this place. "The ministers of the Gospel esteem themselves, and with reason, the successors of the apostles. Their employment is essentially the same; though the apostles were honoured with many glorious prerogatives, as being the first to lay the foundation of the Church."

"The minister of Christ," says the same writer, "cannot be said vainly to flatter himself when he counts upon the gracious assistance of his Master. He takes the promise of that Master for the solid foundation of his hope. 'I am with you alway,' said Christ to his apostles, and, in their persons, to all those who should succeed them in the ministry, 'even unto the end of the world,'"Matthew xxviii:20.

"It was this Divine promise," continues he, "a promise more steadfast than earth or heaven, that filled the apostles with such an ardent zeal, as enabled them to rejoice evermore; placing them above the fury of tyrants, and beyond the reach of fear; assisting them to endure excessive fatigue and toilsome journeys, the inclemency of the seasons, and the resistance of obdurate hearts." Impressed with a just sense of this important promise, the venerable writer concludes with this fervent prayer: "Holy Jesus! who hast promised to continue for ever with thine apostles, and to give them that wisdom which no man shall ever be able to resist, give me to experience a participation of these signal favours, that, animated by the same spirit with which thy first disciples were inspired, I may lead some soul a happy captive to the obedience of thy word." These beautiful quotations will make their own apology for appearing in this place.

7. If any are disposed to condemn Monsieur Roques as an enthusiast in this point, they consider not how many great and honourable names they disgrace by such a precipitate judgment; since all those pious fathers who are looked upon as the reformers of corrupted doctrines and degenerate manners, were unanimously of the same opinion.

From the preceding reflections it seems but reasonable to conclude, that all the true ministers of Christ in every nation are to be considered as the true successors of the apostles, and particularly of St. Paul, who, by way of eminence, is entitled the apostle of the Gentiles, and who, on that account, may, with the greater propriety, be proposed to them as a model.

CHAPTER V.
A third objection replied to.

THEY who will allow neither believers nor pastors to become imitators of St. Paul, very rarely forget to propose a third objection against such imitation. "If you pretend," say they, "to be the apostles' successors, then prove your mission by the performance of miracles equal to theirs."

To this objection we reply:—

1. That no mention is made of the miracles of Andronicus, Junia, and Barnabas, who were real apostles; nor any miracles attributed to Titus or Timothy, though they were undoubted successors of the apostles. Farther: it is expressly said that John the Baptist, though he was greater than the prophets, did no miracle, John x:41. On the other hand, some miraculous gifts were common in the Church of Corinth, even among those who were neither apostles nor evangelists; and these gifts were so far from being essential to apostolic zeal, that many unworthy brethren, and many false apostles, as well as the traitor Judas. were endued with them. This we are taught, in the most express terms, by our Lord himself, Matthew vii:22.

2. If any of those pastors who make a profession of following St. Paul, are observed to publish another Gospel, or to depart from the order established by the apostles, the world has then reason to require miracles at their hands as a demonstration that their doctrines are Divine, and that their recent customs are preferable to those which were formerly adopted in the Church of Christ. But if they simply proclaim that glorious Gospel which has been already confirmed by a thousand miracles, and are observed to adopt no other method than that of the apostles; it is absurd, in the highest degree, to insist upon miracles as the only sufficient evidences of their mission. From worldly pastors such attestations of their sacred commission might, with propriety, be required. These are the persons who turn aside from the beaten track of Christ and his disciples, both with respect to doctrine and discipline; and these should be required by the Church to give incontestable proofs that their novel customs are better than those of St. Paul and the ancient evangelists.

3. No sufficient reason can be given why the humble imitators of St. Paul should be required to evidence their spiritual mission by extraordinary actions. On the one hand, they do but simply declare those religious truths of which they have had the most convincing experience: and on the other, they earnestly solicit the wicked to become partakers of the same invaluable blessings with themselves. Now the certainty of such declaration, and the sincerity of such invitation, may be solidly established upon two kinds of proofs; the first upon those proofs which support the Gospel in general, and the second upon the holy conduct of those who bear this testimony, and repeat these invitations, by which they demonstrate the efficacy of their doctrine, and indisputably prove that true Christians are dead indeed unto sin, but alive unto God, Romans vi:11. That pastor who is unable to produce the former proofs, cannot possibly be regarded as a true successor of the great apostle; and he whose uniform conduct is insufficient to supply the latter, is no other than a false apostle.

4. External miracles, which effect no change in the heart, nor rescue the soul from a state of spiritual blindness and death; miracles which serve only to repair the organs of a body that must shortly be consigned to the grave; miracles which tend merely to modify matter, such as causing green trees to wither, withered trees to spring, and waters to gush out of the flinty rock: miracles of this nature are far less important than those which cause the thorns of vice to wither, the seeds of grace to spring, and streams of sacred consolation to flow through those very hearts which were formerly barren as a desert, and hard as the rock that Moses smote.

5. "If you wish for miracles," says a Christian writer, "if you are anxious to experience them in yourselves; if, in the secret of your heart, you would become witnesses of his almighty power by whom that heart was formed, then ask of him that sublime virtue [that charity] from which all your inclinations and habits detain you at so vast a distance that you are in no situation to form any just idea of it, nor even to conceive the possibility of its existence." (*Professor Crousaz's Sermon* upon 1 Corinthians xiii:13.)

6. That Divine charity, and those sacred consolations, which were as "a well of water springing up into everlasting life" in the hearts of Christ's first disciples, may be made to abound even in ours, since the source of these inestimable graces can never be exhausted, Hebrews xiii:8, and the faithful, who experience in themselves this gracious miracle, stand in need of no other prodigy to establish them in the faith of the Gospel.

7. The most important miracles were those which were wrought by the apostles when, as fellow workers together with God, they opened the eyes of sinners, turning them "from darkness to light, and from the power of Satan unto God," Acts xxvi:18. True miracles of mercy these, and memorable conversions, which the word of God, in the mouths of his ministers, is continually operating in every age!

8. The charity which is discovered by a faithful pastor who humbly cooperates with God in the conversion of his inveterate enemies, should be regarded by the world as the truest test of his apostleship. "Whether there be prophecies, they shall fail; whether there be tongues, they shall cease; but charity never faileth. And though I have all faith, so that I could remove mountains," and perform the most unheard of prodigies, "if I have not CHARITY, I am nothing," 1 Corinthians xiii.

The preceding replies are abundantly sufficient to demonstrate the weakness of their third objection, who are the professed enemies of apostolic zeal.

CHAPTER VI.
A fourth objection refuted.

THE objection here proposed has been abundantly more prejudicial to the cause of piety, than any of the preceding. "You suppose," say formal professors, "that every pastor is called to labour for the salvation of souls, in the present day, with all that zeal which animated St. Paul in primitive times. But their circumstances differ in a very material way. The apostles were commissioned to preach the Gospel, either to obstinate Jews or idolatrous heathens: whereas our pastors are called to exercise their ministry among such as have received the truth from their earliest infancy. Is it not then contrary to common sense, that the same laborious efforts should be thought necessary for the instruction of Christians, which St. Paul was formerly constrained to make use of for the conversion of idolaters?"

As this specious objection has been more frequently repeated than properly refuted, it becomes necessary, in this place, to expose all its weakness, and to demonstrate that the difference between sinners who are baptized, and those with whom St. Paul had to do, is by no means in favour of indolent pastors.

1. There are found swarms of infidels and idolaters in every Christian country upon earth. We need not look beyond Protestant Churches to discover multitudes of impious Christians, who not only despise the Gospel in secret, but who even dare to make it the subject of public ridicule: men, who "have set up their idols in their hearts," Ezekiel xiv:2 and who perfectly answer the apostle's description of degenerate professors, 2 Timothy iii:2-5.

2. St. Paul himself sufficiently answers this very objection, as follows:—"In Christ Jesus, neither circumcision availeth any thing, nor uncircumcision, but a new creature: and as many as walk according to this rule, peace be on them," Galatians vi:15, 16. If there are any who make a profession of receiving the Christian faith, and who follow not this evangelical rule, the apostle thus addresses them with a holy warmth: "Examine yourselves, whether ye be in the faith; prove your own selves; know ye not your own selves how that Jesus Christ is in you, except ye be reprobates?" 2 Corinthians xiii:5. "Be not deceived: neither covetous persons, nor drunkards, nor revilers, nor extortioners, shall inherit the kingdom of God," 1 Corinthians vi:9, 10.

3. Observe how the same objection is combated again in another of St. Paul's epistles. "Behold, thou art called a Christian, and makest thy boast of God, and knowest his will, being instructed out of the *twofold* law of *Moses and of Christ.* Thou, that makest thy boast of *this* law; *if* thou, through breaking the law, dishonourest God, the name of God is *then* blasphemed among the Gentiles through thee. Therefore, thou art inexcusable, O man, whosoever thou art, that judgest" *the heathen*, as sinners more hopeless than thyself: "for wherein thou judgest another, thou condemnest thyself; for thou that judgest doest the same things. And thinkest thou, O man," that thy privileges unimproved will assist thee to "escape the judgment of God? Or despisest thou the riches of his goodness; not knowing that the goodness of God leadeth thee to repentance?" Beware lest, "after the hardness of thine impenitent heart, thou treasurest up unto thyself wrath against the day of wrath," Romans ii:1-24.

If every Scriptural threatening is denounced against those who are without that holiness which the Gospel requires, it would ill become us to flatter either ourselves or others, with being the true followers of Christ, merely on account of that external profession of Christianity, which is generally apparent among us. Is it not undeniably evident, that such a profession, unless it be accompanied with strict holiness, will subject us to more and heavier stripes, than if we had never known the will of our heavenly Father, nor ever acknowledged Christ as our rightful Lord? Luke xii:47, 48. Did not our gracious Master himself once openly manifest a greater degree of abhorrence toward the lukewarm Christian, than toward the notorious sinner? Revelation iii:16. And has he not plainly declared, that myriads of righteous heathens shall be permitted to sit down in the kingdom of God, while multitudes of his professing people shall be cast into outer darkness? Luke xiii:28, 29.

5. After infants have been baptized, and after young persons have been admitted to the holy communion, the true pastor, instead of taking it for granted that they are become unfeigned Christians by partaking of these ordinances, examines them with diligence from time to time, and, from an attentive observation of their conduct, forms a judgment of their faith. If, after the strictest scrutiny, he discovers some among them who hold the form without experiencing the power of godliness, he renews his work with increasing ardour. The most painful part of his duty is still before him, when he attempts to convert those sinners, who are baptized, and those infidels who are communicants: since, before he can lead them to that faith which worketh by love, as St. Paul was accustomed to lead unprejudiced heathens, he must first unmask them with a holy severity, as the blessed Jesus was accustomed to unmask the Pharisees of his day.

6. If unregenerate Christians are heathens by their worldly dispositions; if they are Pharisees by their presumption, and confirmed in their Pharisaism by the fallacious opinions they indulge of their prerogative under the Gospel; it follows that every modern pastor is called to a performance of the twofold duty above described, and if this be the case, how unreasonable is it to imagine, that the ministers of our own time have a much less difficult task before them than those who were formerly commissioned to publish the Gospel!

7. All pastors have an important task assigned them, and, till this is performed, they are required to labour without fainting. Observe in what this task consists:—"He that descended from heaven," saith St. Paul, "gave some apostles, and some pastors and teachers, for the perfecting of the saints, for the work of the ministry, for the edifying of the body of Christ: till we all come, [both pastors and flocks,] unto the measure of the stature of the fulness of Christ," Ephesians iv:11-13. When every Christian has attained to this exalted state, the ministers of the Gospel may then assert their work to be complete, and need no longer imitate the diligence of St. Paul. But while we are surrounded with baptized swearers, Sabbath breakers, slanderers, gamesters, drunkards, gluttons, debauchees, blasphemers, and hypocrites, who are using every effort to render Christianity despicable before infidels, and execrable in the eyes of philosophers; at such a time, it cannot be reasonably imagined, that any individual labourer is permitted to stand idle in the spiritual vineyard. And yet, in this very time of universal degeneracy, there are not wanting many among us, who inconsiderately cry out: "St. Paul, without doubt, had reason to labour with unremitting assiduity for the conversion of idolatrous heathens; but we are converted already, and see no necessity for that burning zeal, and those strenuous efforts among our modern teachers, which were formerly commendable in that apostle."

8. If it be objected, that Christians are here represented in a more deplorable point of view, than candour or observation can warrant; we make our appeal to those proclamations which have been made with a view to repress the single sin of profaning the name of God, by impious oaths and horrible imprecations. These must undoubtedly be considered as public testimonies of public guilt. In such proclamations, all Christian governments, whether Catholic or Protestant, equally complain, that all the civil laws by which they have endeavoured to enforce the law of God, have proved insufficient to prevent the overflowings of a crime as insipid as it is disgraceful. In vain have new penalties and punishments been decreed; in vain are they constantly held forth from the pulpits of preachers and the thrones of kings; this despicable vice still reigns undisturbed among us, insulting over the broken laws of earth and heaven. Now, if it has hitherto been found impossible to prevent the commission of a sin, which has neither pleasure nor profit to plead in its favour, what can we expect concerning all those thousand vices which allure with promises of both? Are not dissimulation and perjury, injustice and covetousness, lasciviousness and luxury, apparent among the members of every Church? Do not rapine, revenge, and murder, defile every part of Christendom, in spite of prisons, banishment, and death? It is a truth too notorious to be controverted, that every crime, with which human nature has ever been polluted, is still continually practised in the most enlightened parts of the world.

We might here mention, if it were necessary, the contempt in which marriage is held, the instability of that holy estate, and the facility with which so sacred a bond is broken. We might go on to bewail the frequent commission of suicide in Christian communities. But to speak of these, with many other sins which are increasing around us to an alarming degree, would be only to echo back those sad complaints which are every day breathed from the lips of the righteous. The above remarks may possibly appear uncharitable to some: but, if they be without foundation, how many unmeaning expressions do we find in our liturgy! What hypocrisy in our public confessions! What false humility in our prayers!

From all these observations, it is evident that the most heathenish manners are common among Christians, so called, and that the most scandalous vices are prevalent, even in those countries where reformed Christianity has erected its standard. Let the impartial inquirer then declare, whether it be not peculiarly necessary to preach repentance among those whose rebellion against God is accompanied with perfidiousness and hypocrisy?

CHAPTER VII.
The same subject continued.

1. WERE it even certain, that professing Christians in general walk according to their holy vocation, would it be commendable in pastors to show less concern for the salvation of Christ's apparent disciples, than was anciently discovered by St. Paul for the conversion of persecuting heathens? Christians are our brethren. The Church, our common mother, has nourished us with the same spiritual milk, and calls us to a participation of the same heavenly inheritance. Christians are no more strangers; and even those who are bad citizens, and unfaithful domestics, are, nevertheless, in some sense citizens of the same city with ourselves, and "of the household of God," Ephesians ii:19. Hence, as we compose but one household, so whenever we are disposed to neglect any part of this family, we may apply to ourselves the following words of the apostle: "If any provide not for his own, and especially for those of his own house, he has denied the faith, and is worse than an infidel," 1 Timothy v:8. Let ministers, then, be placed in the happiest imaginable circumstances, and it will still become them to cry out, with the pious benevolence of St. Paul, "As we have opportunity, let us do good unto all men, especially unto them who are of the household of faith," Galatians v:10.

2. We may here pursue the idea which Christ himself has given us, by comparing his Church to a vineyard. If it be necessary to graft those stocks which are naturally wild, is it less necessary to cultivate those which have been already grafted? We see the husbandmen bestowing most culture upon those vines which produce the most excellent fruit. Let ministers attend to this general rule: and since they only can be fruitful in the sacred vineyard, who receive the word of God in faith, let them study to train up believers to the highest state of maturity. Thus the heavenly husbandman is represented as purging every fruitful branch, "that it may bring forth more fruit," John xv:2.

3. The word of God must be offered to sinners as a remedy suited to the disease of their souls: but to the faithful it must be administered as nourishing food. Hence, as the order of grace resembles that of nature, it is necessary, in a spiritual sense, to minister nutriment to the healthy in much greater quantities, than medicine to those who are diseased. Thus believers, who constantly hunger and thirst after greater degrees of grace, should more frequently receive the living word, that they "may abound yet more and more in knowledge," till they are "filled with the fruits of righteousness," Philippians i:9-11.

4. We find the following expressions in the Epistle of St. Paul to the Romans: "I am persuaded of you, my brethren, that ye are full of goodness, filled with all knowledge, able to admonish one another. Nevertheless, I have written the more boldly unto you, as putting you in mind. And I long to see you, that I may impart unto you some spiritual gift, to the end ye may be established," Romans xv:14, 15; i:11. Now, if St. Paul could express so earnest a desire to instruct those Christians, who were perfect strangers to him, and who were already so Divinely enlightened; far from being imitators of this great apostle, do we not forfeit all pretensions to charity, while we suffer those ignorant Christians to perish "for lack of knowledge," Hosea iv:6, who are not only of our neighbourhood, but probably of our very parish?

5. Though St. Paul was assisted with miraculous endowments, yet how anxiously did he endeavour to fill up the twofold duties of a believer in Christ, and a minister of his Gospel! And shall we refuse to labour with equal earnestness, whose gifts are so mean, and whose graces are so inconsiderable? Appointed, like the primitive preachers of Christianity, to be "fishers of men," is it not perfectly reasonable that we should manifest as great activity with our feeble lines, as St. Paul was accustomed to discover in the use of his capacious net? If that apostle, filled with holy zeal, was enabled to convert more sinners by a single discourse, than many pastors are known to convert in a thousand sermons, should we not, by our uncommon assiduity, supply, as much as possible, the want of that incomprehensible energy which accompanied his ministerial labours?

6. Ministers are compared to labourers, who go forth to cultivate the lands of their master. Now St. Paul, as the foremost of these labourers, wrought night and day with an extraordinary instrument, which marked out furrows of an uncommon depth, and ploughed up entire provinces on a sudden. He made the fullest proof of his ministry, and by the most astonishing efforts spread the seed of the Gospel "from Jerusalem round about unto Illyricum," Romans xv:19. How vast a difference between the former and latter pastors of the Christian Church! Many of us are content to stand altogether idle, till "the night cometh, in which no man can work," John ix:4; while others, who are disposed to some little occupation, employ themselves as workmen who have need to be utterly ashamed of their insignificant labours, 2 Timothy ii:15. At best, we hold but a tardy instrument; an instrument which, with immense toil, will but barely graze the earth we are called to cultivate. And shall we, thus unhappily circumstanced, permit our ploughshares to gather rust during six successive days, and then leisurely employ them by an hour upon the seventh? Surely such a mode of conduct is as contrary to common sense as to the example St. Paul has left us.

7. So astonishing is the inconstancy, the weakness, and the depravity of the human heart, that in spite of all the persevering industry of this apostle in the vineyard of his Lord, it still brought forth briers and thorns, to the anguish of his soul. "Behold," saith he to the Corinthians, "the third time I am ready to come unto you for your edifying. For I fear, lest, when I come, I shall not find you such as I would, and that I shall be found unto you such as ye would not: lest there be debates, envyings, wraths, strifes, backbitings, whisperings, swellings, tumults: and lest when I come my God will humble me among you, and that I shall bewail many which have sinned already, and have not repented," Romans xii:14-21.

We shall close this chapter by proposing the following queries, which may be reasonably grounded upon the preceding passage. If the natural and supernatural talents of St. Paul; if his zeal, his diligence, and his apostolic authority, were insufficient to engage his flock to conduct themselves as followers of Christ; if their want of piety drew from him tears of lamentation, and obliged him to renew his painful efforts with redoubled solicitude; can those pastors be said to possess the spirit of the Gospel, who behold with indifference the disorders of that falling Church which Christ has purchased with his own blood? And if the extraordinary labours of St. Paul were not sufficient fully to answer the design of the sacred ministry, is it not presumption indeed to imagine, that our trivial services are sufficiently complete?

CHAPTER VIII.
A farther reply to the same objection.

WHEN we attack a prejudice that is obstinately defended, it is frequently as needful to multiply arguments as it is necessary in a siege to multiply assaults. Pursuing this method, we shall endeavour, upon new grounds, to establish the doctrine contended for in the two last chapters.

1. After exhorting Timothy to labour without ceasing, St. Paul assigns the following reason for such injunction: "Know," saith he, "that in the last times" of the Christian Church, "men," who make a profession of faith, "shall be lovers of their own selves, despisers of those that are good— lovers of pleasure more than lovers of God; having a form of godliness, but denying the power thereof." Now, if Timothy was exhorted to use all diligence in opposing those evils which were then only making their approach, is it reasonable that we should be remiss, who are unhappy enough to see those last times, in which the decay of piety, predicted by the apostle, is become universal? On the contrary, is not this the moment in which we should strenuously

resist the overflowings of ungodliness, and fortify those who are not yet swept away by the impetuous torrent?

2. When the great apostle benevolently carried the word of God to sinners of every different nation, he thereby armed against himself the authority of magistrates and priests, as well Jewish as Pagan. His universal philanthropy exposed him to the most cruel persecutions. Thousands and ten thousands were set in array against him, and the inhabitants of every kingdom seemed determined to resist or destroy him in his spiritual progress. He saw these surrounding dangers; but he saw them without discovering any symptom of fear; and rather than discontinue his painful labours, he cheerfully proceeded to encounter every threatening evil. We, on the contrary, are appointed to build up the children of the kingdom in their most holy faith. And shall we labour less because we can labour with less danger? Shall we neglect the duties of our sacred function because our superiors in Church and state permit us to convert sinners, command us to preach the Gospel, erect us temples for the public celebration of Divine worship, and allow us salaries, that our ministry may never be interrupted by secular cares? The ministerial services, which St. Paul performed with such unabating zeal, when his reward was imprisonments and stripes, must we be engaged to discharge by emoluments and honours? And, after all, shall we limit our constrained obedience precisely to that point, which will merely secure us from public depositions and disgrace?

3. What was the error of Demas; a man as notorious by his fall among the evangelists as Judas among the apostles? Demas "loved this present world," 2 Timothy iv:10, and, ceasing to imitate the diligence of St. Paul, ungratefully left him to labour almost without a second. And will unfaithful evangelists presume, that they may imitate without fear the apostasy of Demas, and renounce with impunity the example of St. Paul? If such be their unhappy persuasion, we submit the following queries to their serious consideration:—Are the souls of men less valuable; is sin of any kind less detestable, or the law of God less severe in the present day, than in the earlier ages of the Christian Church? Have pastors a right to be remiss while the night of incredulity is blackening around them? Are the attacks of antichristian philosophers less frequent and audacious at present than in former times? Or, finally, is the appearance of our omnipotent Judge no longer expected in the world?

4. If the apostles and primitive pastors have removed many threatening impediments out of our way: if they have procured for us our present advantages, by the most amazing exertions, and at the prodigious price of their blood; surely it can never be imagined that they acted with so much resolution, and suffered with so much constancy, that we might become the indolent readers of their unparalleled history. Was it not rather, that, animated with a becoming sense of their great example, we might make the highest improvement of our inestimable privileges?

5. The mountains are now laid low, the valleys are filled up, the crooked ways are made straight, and we have only to carry that salvation to sinners, for which such wonderful preparations have been made. And are we negligent in running the errands of everlasting love? And are we backward in bearing the happiest tidings to the most hapless of creatures? No excuse then can possibly be made for this coldness, except that which the author of Emilius has put into the mouth of a fictitious character: "Of what importance is it to me," says the vicar Savoyard, "what becomes of the wicked?

I am but little concerned in their future destiny." An excuse for the want of zeal, which can never be pleaded without reflecting the utmost disgrace upon humanity.

6. Ye pastors of a flock ever prone to wander! choose whom you will follow, philosophers or apostles; the indefatigable zeal of St. Paul, or the cruel indifference of the skeptical vicar? But, if you take the latter for your model, we solemnly entreat you to lay aside the profession While you so shamefully renounce the duties of the holy ministry. "As I live, saith the Lord God, I have no pleasure in the death of the wicked; but that the wicked turn from his way and live," Ezekiel xxiii:11. With you, however, it is a matter of very inconsiderable importance, whether the wicked be finally saved or destroyed. And yet, careless as you are of its weal or wo, you presume to appear as ministers of the Church, and as pastors over that little flock, for which the good Shepherd was content to lay down his life. To rank with the watchful attendants of the fold is an honour of which you are altogether unworthy; but you may with propriety be counted in the number of those ungrateful hirelings, who "care not for the sheep," John x:13.

8. It is true, you are not without companions, as well ancient as modern. You have Hophni and Phinehas, Gehazi and Balaam, to keep you in countenance; you have the prophets of Jezebel to plead in your favour, and every worldly ecclesiastic of the present day to approve your choice: but apostolical men will resolutely withstand you, like Elisha and his master, in the cause of deserted truth. Ye slothful domestics of the most diligent Master! Ye cruel attendants of the tenderest Shepherd! say, have ye never heard that Master crying out, with the voice of affection, "Feed my sheep?" John xxi:17. Have ye not seen him conducting his flock to an evangelical pasture, in the temple, in synagogues, in villages, in houses, in deserts, on the sea shore, and on the tops of mountains? He anxiously sought out the miserable. Truth was the guide of his way, charity accompanied his steps, and his path was marked with blessings. His secret efforts were more painful than his public labours: he publicly instructed through the day, but he privately agonized in prayer through the night. His first disciples were anxious to tread in the steps of their adorable Master. They exercised their ministry within sight of torments and death. And will you dare to neglect it, now the cry of persecution is hushed? Will you equally despise both the promises and threatenings of the Gospel? Will you hasten the time of antichrist by an antichristian conduct? And when the Son of man shall come, shall he find you trampling under foot the Gospel of his grace? Or, shall he surprise you distributing cards round the tables of your friends, rather than earnestly inviting those friends to the table of your Lord?

O that we could prevail upon you to stand in your proper post, and act in conformity to your professional character! While you dream of security, you are surrounded with the most alarming dangers. "Stand, therefore, having your loins girt about with truth; having on the breastplate of righteousness, and your feet shod with the preparation of the Gospel of peace: above all, taking the shield of faith, wherewith ye shall be able to quench all the fiery darts of the wicked. And take the helmet of salvation, and the sword of the Spirit, which is the word of God; praying always with all prayer, and watching thereunto with all perseverance, and supplications for all saints, [and for the ministers of the Gospel in particular,] that *they* may open *their* mouths boldly, to make known the mystery of the Gospel, *and diffuse abroad* the unsearchable riches of Christ," Ephesians vi:14- 19; iii:8. Thus quitting yourselves like men in this sacred warfare, after steadily resisting, you shall finally overcome all the strength of the enemy, "by the word of truth, by the power of God, by the armour of righteousness on the right hand and on the left," 2 Corinthians vi:7: till, having weathered out the evil day, continuing "faithful unto death," ye shall be rewarded with "a crown of *everlasting* life," Revelation ii:10.

CHAPTER IX.
A farther refutation of the same objection.

(1.) WHEN we see a number of persons in perilous circumstances, charity constrains us to make our first efforts in favour of those who appear to be in the most imminent danger. Such are unholy Christians. Sinful heathens are doubtless in danger; obstinate Jews in still greater peril; but impenitent Christians are in a situation abundantly more lamentable than either; since they offend against clearer light and knowledge, equally inattentive to the most gracious promises on the one hand, and the most terrible menaces on the other. To sin with the New Testament in our hand, and with the sound of the Gospel in our ears: to sin with the seal of baptism on our forehead, and the name of Christ in our lips: to sin and receive the holy communion: to ratify and break the most solemn engagements; what is this, but earnestly labouring out our own damnation, and plunging ourselves into those abysses of wretchedness which Pagans and Jews are unable to fathom? How eagerly then should every believer attempt to rescue his falling brethren; and especially how anxious should they be to arrest those leaders of the blind who are drawing their followers to the brink of perdition! As this is one of those arguments upon which the truth here pleaded for must principally rest, we shall consider it in the several points of view under which it is presented to us in the Gospel.

(2.) The commission of St. Paul was particularly directed to the Gentiles; yet, before he visited their benighted nations, he judged it his duty to make a full and a free offer of the everlasting Gospel to the people of the Jews. For the conduct of the apostle in this respect, the following reasons are to be assigned. *First,* The promises pertained to the Jews in a peculiar manner, Romans ix:4. *Secondly,* The children of Abraham, according to the flesh, had a more threatening prospect before them, in case of final impenitence, than any other people upon earth. "Tribulation and anguish shall be upon every soul of man that doeth evil, of the Jew first, and also of the Gentile," Romans ii:9.

(3.) The same reasons, though chiefly the latter, are still to be urged, why the ministers of Christ should principally labour among Christians. For if sinners of the circumcision shall be more severely punished than the ignorant heathen, so the apostle declares that sinners, who are baptized into the name of Christ, shall be treated with still greater rigour than impenitent Jews. "He that despised Moses' law," saith he, "died without mercy under two or three witnesses. Of how much sorer punishment, then, suppose ye, shall he be thought worthy, who hath trodden under foot the Son of God, and hath done despite unto the Spirit of grace?" Hebrews x:28, 29. If this consideration were accompanied with its due effect, it would fire us with the most unconquerable zeal for the salvation of the negligent Christians.

(4.) In one of the last discourses our Lord addressed to the cities of Galilee, we find him reading over to them this dreadful sentence of condemnation: "Wo unto thee, Chorazin, wo unto thee, Bethsaida! for if the mighty works which were done in you had been done in Tyre and Sidon, they would have repented long ago in sackcloth and ashes. But I say unto you, It shall be more tolerable for Tyre and Sidon at the day of judgment, than for you. And thou, Capernaum, which [by thy religious privileges,] art exalted unto heaven, shalt, [for the non-improvement of them,] be brought down to hell." Yea, "it shall be more tolerable, in the day of judgment, for the land of Sodom, [which has been already consumed with fire from above,] than for thee," Matthew xi:21-24.

(5.) To draw the just consequences from this affecting menace, we must recollect that, when it was pronounced, the inhabitants of the above mentioned cities had been favoured, but for a very short interval, with the ministry of Christ and his messengers. And if the death and resurrection of Jesus were afterward published among them, it is more probable that these important facts were published only in a desultory and transient way. Nevertheless, the sinners of Capernaum were thought worthy of greater punishment than the sinners of Sodom. Hence, we conclude, that if the sinners of London, Paris, Rome, and Geneva, have hardened themselves against the truths of the Gospel for a much longer continuance than the citizens of Capernaum were permitted to do, there as every reason to apprehend that their sentence will not only be more dreadful than the sentence of Sodom, but abundantly less tolerable than that which was pronounced upon the inhabitants of Galilee.

(6.) While we consider the various proportions in which future punishment shall be administered to the wicked of different classes, we may turn to those remarkable expressions of St. Peter and St. Paul: "If after having escaped the pollutions of the world, through the knowledge of the Lord and Saviour Jesus Christ, they are again entangled therein and overcome; the latter end is worse with them than the beginning. For it had been better for them not to have known the way of righteousness, than, after they have known it, to turn from the holy commandment delivered unto them," 2 Peter ii:20, 21. "If we sin wilfully after we have received the knowledge of the truth, there remaineth no more sacrifice for sins, but a certain fearful looking for of judgment, and fiery indignation, which shall devour the adversaries," Hebrews x:26, 27. These declarations assist us to discover the true ground of that apostolic exhortation, with which we shall close this chapter: "Of some have compassion, making a difference: and others save with fear, pulling them out of the fire," Jude i:22, 23.

From this last view of the subject, we may perceive into how dangerous an error those persons are fallen, who presume to object against imitating the zeal of St. Paul.

CHAPTER X.
A fifth objection answered.

THE solidity of the preceding remarks may be acknowledged by many pastors, who will still excuse themselves from copying the example of St. Paul.

"It is unreasonable," they will say, "to require that we should preach the word of God, in season and out of season, as St. Paul once did, and as Timothy was afterward exhorted to do. We find it, in this day, a matter of difficulty to prepare any public address that may be either acceptable to the people, or honourable to ourselves."

To this objection we return the following replies:—

(1.) He, who spake as never man spake, rejected the arts of our modern orators, delivering his discourses in a style of easy simplicity and unaffected zeal.

(2.) We do not find that St. Paul and the other apostles imposed upon themselves the troublesome servitude of penning down their discourses. And we are well assured, that when the seventy and the twelve were commissioned to publish the Gospel, no directions of this nature were given in either case.

(3.) St. Paul gives the following pastoral instructions to Timothy: "Give attendance to reading, to exhortation, to doctrine. Neglect not the gift that is in thee. Meditate upon these things: give thyself wholly to them. Take heed unto thyself and to thy doctrine; continue in them: for in doing this, thou shalt both save thyself, and them that hear thee," 1 Timothy iv:13, 16. "Preach the word; be instant in season, out of season. Reprove, rebuke, exhort, with all long suffering and doctrine," 2 Timothy iv:2. Now, had it ever entered into the mind of the apostle that it would be proper for pastors to compose their sermons in the manner of rhetoricians, and to deliver them as public orators, he would most probably have given some intimation of this to his disciple. In such case he would have held out to his pupil in divinity some instructions of the following nature: "O Timothy, my son! I have frequently commanded thee to labour in the work of the Lord, according to my example. But as thou art not an apostle, properly so called, and hast not received the gift of languages, I advise thee to write over thy sermons as correctly as possible. And after this, do not fail to rehearse them before a mirror, till thou art able to repeat them with freedom and grace: so that when thou art called upon public duty, thou mayest effectually secure the approbation of thine auditors. Furthermore: when thou art about to visit any distant Churches, lay up in thy portmanteau the choicest of thy sermons. And wherever thou art, take care to have, at least, one discourse about thee, that thou mayest be prepared for any sudden emergency, and never appear unfurnished in the eyes of the people." The idea of such a passage in the Epistles of St. Paul, whether public or private, is too absurd to be endured.

(4.) If advocates, after hastily considering a question of difficulty, are ready to plead the cause of their client before a court of judicature; can it be possible, that, after several years of meditation and study, a minister should still be unprepared to plead the cause of piety before a plain assembly of his unlearned parishioners?

(5.) When we are deeply interested in a subject of the last importance, do we think it necessary to draw up our arguments in an orderly manner upon paper, before we attempt to deliver our sentiments upon the matter in hand? Are not the love and penetration of a parent sufficient to dictate such advice as is suited to the different tempers and conditions of his children? After perceiving the house of our neighbour on fire, we do not withdraw to our closet to prepare a variety of affecting arguments, by way of engaging him to save both himself and his family from the flames. In such case, a lively conviction of our neighbour's danger, and an ardent desire to rescue him from it, afford us greater powers of natural eloquence than any rules of art can furnish us with.

(6.) Horace observes, that neither matter nor method will be wanting upon a well-digested subject:—

Cui lecta potenter erit res,
Nec facundia deseret hunc, nec lucidus ordo.

With how much facility then may suitable expressions be expected to follow those animating sentiments which are inspired by an ardent love to God and man; especially when subjects of such universal concern are agitated, as death and redemption, judgment and eternity! Upon such occasions, out of the abundance of the heart the mouth will speak, "nor will the preacher be able to repeat a tenth part of the truths which God has communicated to him, while meditating upon his text." (*Act of Synod*, chap. 11.) If malice can furnish those persons with an inexhaustible fund of conversation, who delight in malice, how much more may we suppose the charity of a pastor to furnish him with an inexhaustible fund of exhortation, instruction, and comfort!

(7.) It has been a plea with many ministers of the Gospel, that they neglect to proclaim that Gospel during six days in the week, lest they should be unprepared to address their parishioners, with propriety, upon the seventh. With teachers, who are thus scrupulously tenacious of their own reputation, we may justly be allowed to reason in the following manner: to what purpose are all those oratorical appendages, with which you are so studious to adorn your discourses: and who hath required all this useless labour at your hand? Isaiah i:11, 12. If a servant, after being charged by his master with a message of the utmost importance, should betake himself to his chamber, and defer the execution of it day after day, would not such a delay be esteemed an unpardonable neglect? Or, if he should attempt to apologize for the omission, by alleging that he had been busily engaged in learning to repeat, with precision, the message he had received, and to move upon his errand with dignity and grace; would not such an excuse be regarded as an instance of the highest presumption and folly? And can we imagine that our heavenly Master will overlook that neglect in his public messengers, which would appear in the conduct of a private domestic so justly condemnable?

(8.) What advantage has accrued to the Church, by renouncing the apostolic method of publishing the Gospel? We have indolence and artifice, in the place of sincerity and vigilance. Those public discourses, which were anciently the effects of conviction and zeal, are now become the weekly exercises of learning and art. "We believe and therefore speak," 2 Corinthians iv:13, is an expression that has grown entirely obsolete among modern pastors. But nothing is more common among us than to say, As we have sermons prepared upon a variety of subjects, we are ready to deliver them as opportunity offers.

(9.) Many inconveniences arise from that method of preaching, which is generally adopted in the present day. While the physician of souls is labouring to compose a learned dissertation upon some plain passage of Scripture, he has but little leisure to visit those languishing patients who need his immediate assistance. He thinks it sufficient to attend upon them every Sabbath day, in the place appointed for public duty. But he recollects not, that those to whom his counsel is peculiarly necessary, are the very persons who refuse to meet him there. His unprofitable employments at home leave him no opportunity to go in pursuit of his wandering sheep. He meets with them, it is true, at stated periods, in the common fold: but it is equally true, that during every successive interval, he discovers the coldest indifference with respect to their spiritual welfare. From this unbecoming conduct of many a minister, one would naturally imagine that the flock were rather called to seek out their indolent pastor, than that he was purposely hired to pursue every straying sheep.

(10.) The most powerful nerve of the sacred ministry is ecclesiastical discipline. But this nerve is absolutely cut asunder by the method of which we now speak. When a pastor withdraws fatigued from his study, imagining that he has honourably acquitted himself with regard to his people, he is too apt to neglect that vigilant inspection into families, upon which the discipline of the Church depends. Such a spiritual instructer may justly be compared to a vain-glorious pedagogue, who, after drawing up a copy, and adorning it, for several days together, with all the embellishments of his art, should yet imagine that he admirably performed his part, in preparing it, at length, for his scholars, without any visible defects. And what could reasonably be expected from the pupils of such a teacher, but that, fearing neither scholastic discipline, nor particular inspection, they should neglect to transcribe what their master, with so much unprofitable toil, had produced?

(11.) Since the orator's art has taken place of the energy of faith, what happy effect has it produced upon the minds of men? Have we discovered more frequent conversions among us? Are formal professors more generally seized with a religious fear? Are libertines more universally constrained to cry out, "Men and brethren, what shall we do?" Acts ii:37. Do the wicked depart from the Church to bewail their transgressions in private; and believers to visit the mourners in their affliction? Is it not rather to be lamented, that we are at this day equally distant from Christian charity and primitive simplicity?

(12.) Reading over a variety of approved sermons is generally supposed to be preaching the Gospel. If this were really so, we need but look out some school boy of a tolerable capacity, and after instructing him to read over, with proper emphasis and gesture, the sermons of Tillotson, Sherlock, or Saurin, we shall have made him an excellent minister of the word of God. But if preaching the Gospel is to publish among sinners that repentance and salvation which we have experienced in ourselves; if it is to imitate a penitent slave, who, freed from misery and iron, returns to the companions of his former slavery, declaring the generosity of their prince, and persuading them to sue for mercy;—if this is to publish the Gospel of peace, then it is evident that experience and sympathy are more necessary to the due performance of this work, than all the accuracy and elocution that can possibly be acquired.

(13.) When this sacred experience and this generous sympathy began to lose their prevalence in the Church, their place was gradually supplied by the trifling substitutes of study and affectation. Carnal prudence has now for many ages solicitously endeavoured to adapt itself to the taste of the wise and the learned. But while "the offence of the cross" is avoided, Galatians v:11, neither the wise nor the ignorant are effectually converted. The Gospel is abundantly better suited to the "poor in spirit," than to those who value themselves as men of sagacity and science. "I thank thee, O Father," said the lowly Jesus, "that thou hast hid these things from the wise and the prudent, and hast revealed them unto babes," Matthew xi:25. These babes, however, in the language of Christ, are the very persons who have been usually neglected by us, for the mere gratification of reputed sages. Alas! how many thousand proofs do we require to convince us, that the wisdom of this world will continue to trample under foot the pearl of the Gospel, though, in order to secure its reception, it should be presented among the artificial pearls of a vain philosophy?

(14.) In consequence of the same error, the ornaments of theatrical eloquence have been sought after with a shameful solicitude. And what has been the fruit of so much useless toil? Preachers, after all, have played their part with much less applause than comedians; and their curious auditors are still running from the pulpit to the stage, for the pleasure of hearing fables repeated with a degree of sensibility which the messengers of truth can neither feel nor feign.

Notwithstanding the above remarks have been expressed in the most pointed manner, we mean not to insinuate that the errors already exposed are the only mistakes to be guarded against. Extremes of every kind are to be avoided with equal care. We condemn the carnal prudence of Christian orators; but we as sincerely reprobate the conduct of those enthusiasts who, under pretence that Christ has promised to continue with his disciples to the end of the world, exhibit the reveries of a heated imagination for the truths of the Gospel. Too many of these deluded fanatics are found, who, taking their slothfulness and presumption for the effects of a lively faith, and an apostolical confidence, repeatedly affront the Almighty, and justly offend those candid hearers who are least disposed to take offence. Offences will undoubtedly come; but it behooves us to make a just distinction between the real offence of the cross, and that which is given by an unlicensed presumption on our own part.

If we are honoured with the pastoral office, let us consider the Holy Scriptures as an inexhaustible mine of sacred treasures. In the law of the Lord let us meditate day and night. Before we attempt to deliver evangelical truths in public, let it be our first care to penetrate our hearts in private with an adequate sense of those truths. Let us arrange them in the most suitable order; let us adduce and compare the several passages of Sacred Writ, which appear to support or explain the particular doctrines we mean to insist upon. But, above all, joining faith and prayer to calm meditation, after becoming masters of our subject, let us humbly ask of God that warrhsia, that lively and forcible elocution, which flows from the unction of grace.

And here, instead of resting contented with barely requesting, we should labour to acquire what we seek, by frequently stirring up the gift that is in us. Let us embrace every opportunity of exhorting both believers and catechumens. Let us carry, with unwearied constancy, instruction to the ignorant, and consolation to the afflicted. Let us be faithful in reproving sinners of every class, and diligent in training up the children of our parish.

It is necessary indeed to be scrupulously cautious, lest we abuse the liberty of preaching from meditation, by becoming followers of those who are more worthy of censure than imitation. There are pastors of this kind who, having acquired a good degree of spiritual knowledge, and a wonderful facility of expression, unhappily begin to pique themselves upon appearing before a numerous assembly without any previous study. Conscious of their own ability, these self-sufficient preachers make little or no preparation for one of the most solemn duties that can possibly be discharged. They hasten to a crowded auditory without any apparent concern, and coming down from the pulpit with an air of the same easy confidence with which they ascended it, contentedly return to that habitual listlessness, which had been interrupted by the external performance of a necessary work. Alas! if these presuming pastors could be prevailed upon to write over their sermons, to how much better purpose might they thus employ their hours, than by heedlessly trifling them away in frivolous conversation and shameful inactivity!

It is not to imitate examples of this nature that we solicit the ministers of Christ to recover those hours which are usually employed in composing their weekly discourses. How many are the important occupations of which the faithful pastor has his daily choice! The wicked are to be reclaimed, and the righteous established. Hope must be administered to the fearful, and courage to the tempted. The weak are to be strengthened, and the strong to be exercised. The sick must be supported, and the dying prepared for dissolution. By frequent pastoral visits to hamlets, schools, and private houses, the indefatigable minister should continually be moving through the several parts of his parish; discovering the condition of those intrusted to his care, and regularly supplying the necessities of his flock; diffusing all around instruction and reproof, exhortation and comfort. To sum up his duties in a single sentence, he should cause the light that is in him to shine out in every possible direction, before the ignorant and the learned, the rich and the poor; making the salvation of mankind his principal pursuit, and the glory of God his ultimate aim.

Thus, after having faithfully performed the work of an evangelist, when he is about to be removed from his charge by death, or by any otherprovidential appointment, he may take an affectionate leave of his people, and say, "Remember, my children, that while I have sojourned among you, I have not ceased to warn every one of you,[*] night and day; and if my word has not always been accompanied with tears, Acts xx:31, yet it has constantly flowed from the truest sincerity and affection."

CHAPTER XI.
A reply to the fifth and last objection, which may be urged against "the Portrait of St. Paul."

THOSE persons who have already so earnestly resisted the truths for which we contend, will not fail to exclaim in the last place, by way of an unanswerable argument, "What you require of pastors is unreasonable in the highest degree. If they are indeed called to labour for the salvation of souls, with the zeal and assiduity of St. Paul, the holy ministry must be regarded as the most painful of all professions, and, of consequence, our pulpits will be shortly unoccupied."

Monsieur Ostervald, who foresaw this objection, has completely answered it in his *Third Source of the Corruption which reigns among Christians*. "It will not fail to be objected," says this venerable author, "that if none were to be admitted to holy

---

[*] It is highly reasonable that pastors should give evening instructions to those who have been engaged, through the course of the day, in their different callings. This season, whether it be in the most dreary or the more pleasing part of the year, is peculiarly suited to works of devotion. Such a custom might, at least, prevent many young persons from mixing with that kind of company, and frequenting those places, which would tend to alienate their minds from religion and virtue.

orders, except those who are possessed of every necessary qualification, there could not possibly be procured a sufficient number of pastors for the supply of our churches. To which I answer, that it would be abundantly better to expose ourselves to this inconvenience, than to violate the express laws of the written word. A small number of chosen pastors is preferable to a multitude of unqualified teachers. [One Elijah was more powerful than all the prophets of Baal.] At all hazards we must adhere to the command of God, and leave the event to Providence. But, in reality, this dearth of pastors is not so generally to be apprehended. To reject those candidates for holy orders whose labours in the Church would be altogether fruitless, is undoubtedly a work of piety; and such alone would be repulsed by the apprehension of a severe scrutiny, and an exact discipline. Others, on the contrary, who are in a condition to fulfil the duties of the sacred office, would take encouragement from this exactness and severity; and the ministry would every day be rendered more respectable in the world." Behold an answer truly worthy an apostolical man!

If it still be objected by the generality of pastors, that what we require is as unreasonable as it is unusual: permit me to ask you, my lukewarm brethren, whether it be not necessary that you should use the same diligence in your sacred profession with which your neighbours are accustomed to labour in their worldly vocations and pursuits?

The fisherman prepares a variety of lines, hooks, and baits; he knows the places, the seasons, and even the hours that are most favourable to his employment; nor will he refuse to throw his line several hundred times in a day. If he be disappointed in one place, he cheerfully betakes himself to another; and if his ill success be of any long continuance, he will associate with those who are greater masters of his art. Tell me, then, ye pastors, who make the business of a fisherman the amusement of many an idle hour, do ye really imagine that less ardour and perseverance are necessary to prepare souls for heaven, than to catch trout for your table? The huntsman rejoices in expectation of the promised chase. He denies himself some hours of usual repose, that he may hasten abroad in pursuit of his game. He seeks it with unwearied attention, and follows it from field to field with increasing ardour. He labours up the mountain: he rushes down the precipice: he penetrates the thickest woods, and overleaps the most threatening obstacles. He practises the wildest gestures, and makes use of the most extravagant language; endeavouring, by every possible means, to animate both dogs and men in the furious pursuit. He counts the fatigues of the chase among the number of its pleasures: and through the whole insignificant business of the day he acts with as much resolution and fervour as though he had undertaken one of the noblest enterprises in the world.

The fowler with equal eagerness pursues his different game. From stubble to stubble, and from cover to cover, he urges his way. He pushes through the stubborn brake, and takes his way along the pathless dingle. He traverses the gloomy mountain, or wanders devious over the barren heath: and, after carrying arms all day, if a few trifling birds reward his toil, he returns rejoicing home.

Come, ye fishers of men! who, notwithstanding your consecration to God, are frequently seen to partake of these contemptible diversions; come, and answer, by your conduct, to the following questions:—Is the flock committed to your charge less estimable than the fowl which you so laboriously pursue? Or are you less interested in the salvation of your people, than in the destruction of those unhappy quadrupeds which give you so much silly fatigue, and afford you so much brutal pleasure?

Permit me still farther to carry on my argument. Was the panting animal which usually accompanies your steps in the last mentioned exercise incautiously to plunge into a dangerous pit; though faint with the labours of the day, and now on your return, would you carelessly leave him to perish? Would you not rather use every effort to extricate him from apparent death? Could you even sleep or eat till you had afforded him every possible assistance? And yet you eat, you sleep, you visit; nay, it may be you dance, you hunt, you shoot, and that without the least inquietude, while your flocks are rushing on from sin to sin, and falling from precipice to precipice. Ah! if a thousand souls are but comparable to the vilest animal, and if these are heedlessly straying through the ways of perdition, may we not reasonably exhort you to use every effort in preserving them from the most alarming danger, and in securing them from the horrors of everlasting death?

But, passing by those amusements which so generally engage your attention, let me reason with you from one of the most laborious occupations of life. You are called to be "good soldiers of Jesus Christ," 2 Timothy ii:3. And can you possibly imagine that less resolution and patience are required in a spiritual warrior, than in an earthly soldier? Behold the mercenary, who, for little more than food and clothing, is preparing to go on his twentieth campaign! Whether he is called to freeze beneath the pole, or to melt under the line, he undertakes the appointed expedition with an air of intrepidity and zeal. Loaded with the weapons of his warfare, he is harassed out with painful marches: and after enduring the excessive fatigues of the day, he makes his bed upon the rugged earth, or, perhaps, passes the comfortless night under arms. In the day of battle he advances against the enemy amid a shower of bullets, and is anxious, in the most tremendous scenes, to give proofs of an unconquerable resolution. If through the dangers of the day he escape unhurt, it is but to run the hazard of another encounter; perhaps to force an intrenchment, or to press through a breach. Nothing, however, discourages him; but, covered with wounds, he goes on unrepining to meet the mortal blow. All this he suffers, and all this he performs in the service of his superiors, and with little hope of advancement on his own part.

Behold this dying veteran, ye timorous soldiers of an omnipotent Prince! and blush at your want of spiritual intrepidity. Are you not engaged in the cause of humanity, and in the service of God? Are you not commissioned to rescue captive souls from all the powers of darkness? Do you not fight beneath his scrutinizing eye who is King of kings, and Lord of lords? Are you not contending within sight of eternal rewards, and with the hope of an unfading inheritance? And will you complain of difficulties, or tremble at danger? Will you not only avoid the heat of the engagement, but even dare to withdraw from the standard of your sovereign Lord? Let me lead you again into the field; let me draw you back to the charge; or, rather, let me shame your cowardice by pointing you to those resolute commanders who have formerly signalized themselves under the banners of your Prince. Emulate their example, and you shall share their rewards.

But if, hitherto, you have neither contemplated the beauty, nor experienced the energy of those truths by which St. Paul was animated to such acts of heroism, it is in vain that we exhort you to shine among the foremost ranks of Christians as inextinguishable lights, holding up, against every enemy, as a "two-edged sword,"

Hebrews iv:12, "the word of *everlasting* life," Philippians ii:15, 16. Instead of this, it will be necessary to place before you the excellence and efficacy of this apostle's doctrines, together with the infinite advantages which they procure to those who cordially embrace them. And this we shall endeavour to do in the second part of this work. Meanwhile, we will conclude this first part with a short exhortation from St. Chrysostom's fifty-ninth sermon upon St. Matthew. "Since the present life is a continual warfare; since we are at all times surrounded by a host of enemies, let us vigorously oppose them, as our royal Chieftain is pleased to command. Let us fear neither labour, nor wounds, nor death. Let us all conspire mutually to assist and defend one another. And let our magnanimity be such as may add firmness to the most resolute, and give courage to the most cowardly."

THE PORTRAIT OF ST. PAUL.

PART II.

The doctrines of an evangelical pastor.

THE minister of the present age, being destitute of Christian piety, is neither able to preach, nor clearly to comprehend the truths of the Gospel. In general, he contents himself with superficially declaring certain attributes of the Supreme Being; while he is fearful of speaking too largely of grace or its operations, lest he should be suspected of enthusiasm. He declaims against some enormous vice, or displays the beauty of some social virtue. He affects to establish the doctrines of heathen philosophers: and it were to be wished that he always carried his morality to so high a pitch as some of the most celebrated of those sages. If he ever proclaims the Lord Jesus Christ, it is in but a cursory way, and chiefly when he is obliged to it by the return of particular days. He himself continues the same through all seasons; and the cross of Christ would be entirely laid aside, unless the temporal prince, more orthodox than the minister, had appointed the passion of our Lord to be the preacher's theme during certain solemnities of the Church.

With the evangelical pastor it is wholly otherwise. "Jesus Christ," he is able to say with St. Paul, "sent me to preach the Gospel, not with wisdom of words, lest the cross of Christ should be made of none effect. For the preaching of the cross is to them that perish foolishness; but unto us which are saved, it is the power of God. For it is written, I will destroy the vain wisdom of the wise, and will bring to nothing the false understanding of the prudent. Hath not God made foolish the wisdom of this world? For after that the world by this wisdom, [this boasted philosophy,] knew not God, [but rested in materialism and idolatry,] it pleased God, by the foolishness of preaching, to save them that believe," 1 Corinthians i:17-21. The preaching of the true minister, which commonly passes for folly in a degenerate world, is that through which God employs his power for the conversion of sinners, and the edification of believers. It comprehends all that is revealed in the Old and New Testament: but the subjects on which it is chiefly employed are the precepts of the decalogue, and the truths of the apostles' creed. They may be reduced to four points: (1.) True repentance toward God. (2.) A lively faith in our Lord Jesus Christ. (3.) The sweet hope which the Holy Spirit sheds abroad in the hearts of believers. (4.) That Christian charity which is the abundant source of every good work. In a word, the good pastor preaches repentance, faith, hope, and charity. These four virtues include all others. These are four pillars which support the glorious temple of which St. Paul and St. Peter make the following mention: "Ye are God's building. Ye also, as lively stones, are built up a spiritual house."

By searching into the solidity of these four supports, we may observe how vast a difference there is between the materials of which they are composed, and that untempered mortar with which the ministers of the present day are striving to erect a showy building upon a sandy foundation.

The evangelical pastor preaches true repentance toward God.

THE true minister, convinced, both by revelation and experience, that Jesus Christ alone is able to recover diseased souls, employs every effort to bring sinners into the presence of this heavenly Physician, that they may obtain of him spiritual health and salvation. He is fully persuaded that he who is not "weary and heavy laden," will never apply for relief; that he who is not "poor in spirit," will constantly despise the riches of the Gospel; and that they who are unacquainted with their danger, will turn an inattentive ear to the loudest warnings of a compassionate Saviour. His first care, then, is to press upon his hearers the necessity of an unfeigned repentance; that, by breaking the reed of their confidence, he may constrain them with the "poor," the "miserable," the "blind," and the "naked," to fall before the throne of Divine justice. Whence, after seeing themselves condemned by the law of God, without any ability to deliver their own souls, he is conscious that they will have recourse to the throne of grace, entreating, like the penitent publican, to be "justified freely by the grace of God, through the redemption that is in Christ Jesus," Romans iii:25. It is in this state of humiliation and compunction of heart, that sinners are enabled to experience the happy effects of that evangelical repentance, which is well defined in the fourteenth chapter of the Helvetic Confession. "By repentance," say our pious Reformers, "we mean that sorrow, or that displeasure of soul, which is excited in a sinner by the word and Spirit of God, &c. By this new sensibility, he is first made to discover his natural corruption, and his actual transgressions. His heart is pierced with sincere distress. He deplores them before God. He confesses them with confusion, but without reserve; he abhors them with a holy indignation; he seriously resolves, from the present moment, to reform his conduct, and religiously apply himself to the practice of every virtue during the remainder of his life. Such is true repentance: it consists, at once, in resolutely renouncing the devil, with every thing that is sinful; and in sincerely cleaving to God, with every thing that is truly good. But we expressly say, this repentance is the mere gift of God, and can never be effected by our own power," 2 Timothy ii:25.

It appears, by this definition, that our Reformers distinguished that by the name of repentance, which many theologians have called the awakening of a soul from the sleep of carnal security; and which others have frequently termed conversion. But, if sinners understand and obtain the disposition here described, no true minister will be over anxious that they should express it in any particular form of words.

How sin and the necessity of repentance entered into the world.

OBSERVE the account which the evangelical minister gives, after Moses and St. Paul, of the manner in which that dreadful infection made its way into the world, that corrupt nature, that "old man," that "body of death," which Christ, the seed of the woman, came to destroy. "When the *tempted* woman saw that [the fruit of the tree, which God had forbidden her to touch,] was pleasant to the eyes, good for food, and to be desired to make one wise, she took thereof and did eat, and gave also unto her husband with her, and he did eat," Genesis iii:6. Thus entered into the very fountain head of our nature that moral evil, that complicated malady, "that lust of the flesh, that lust of the eyes, and that pride of life," 1 John ii:16, which the second Adam came to crucify in the flesh, and which is still daily crucified in the members of his mystical body.

If Jesus Christ never publicly discoursed concerning the entry of sin into the world, it was because his sermons were addressed to a people who had been long before instructed in a matter of so great importance. On this account, he simply proposed himself to Israel, as that promised Messiah, that Son of God and Son of man, who was about to repair the error of the first Adam, by becoming the resurrection and the life of all those who should believe in his name.

St. Paul was very differently circumstanced, when labouring among those nations which were unacquainted with the fall, except by uncertain and corrupt tradition. Behold the wisdom with which he unfolds to the heathen that fundamental doctrine, which was not contested among the Jews. "The first man Adam," the head of the human species, "was made a living soul;" but Jesus Christ, "the last Adam, was made a quickening spirit;" and he also is the head of the human species; for "the head of every man is Christ," 1 Corinthians xi:3. "The first man is of the earth, earthy: the second man is the Lord from heaven. As is the earthy, such are they also that are earthy [worldly:] and as is the heavenly, such are they also that are heavenly [regenerate.] And as we have borne the image of the earthy, we, [whose souls are already regenerate,] shall also bear the complete image of the heavenly. When this mortal shall have put on immortality: *for the* flesh and blood, [which we have from the first Adam,] cannot inherit the kingdom of God," 1 Corinthians xv:45-53.

As human pride is continually exalting itself against this humiliating doctrine, so the true minister as constantly repeats it, crying out in the language of this great apostle: "All *unregenerate* men are under sin, there is none that understandeth, there is none that seeketh after God: they are all gone out of the way, they are together become unprofitable. The way of peace have they not known: there is no fear of God before their eyes. We know that whatsoever things the law saith, [the natural or the Mosaic law,] it saith to them that are under the law; that every mouth may be stopped, and all the world may become guilty before God," Romans iii:9-19. "There is no difference; for as all have sinned and come short of the glory of God, [so all equally need the merits and assistance of] Jesus Christ, whom God hath set forth to be a propitiation, through faith in his blood," Romans iii:22-25. All those, therefore, who, neglecting Christ, rely upon "the works of the law, are under the curse;" and all their endeavours to deliver themselves by their imperfect obedience, are totally vain. "For it is written, Cursed is every one that continueth not in all things, which are written in the book of the law to do them." Thus, by denouncing maledictions, as dreadful as the thunders from Mount Sinai, against every act of disobedience, "the law *becomes* our schoolmaster to bring us unto Christ, that we might be justified by faith," Galatians iii:10-24.

This doctrine is maintained by all the Christian Churches.

WHEN an evangelical minister insists upon the fall, the corruption and the danger of unregenerate man, he acts in conformity to the acknowledged opinions of the purest Churches. As I chiefly write for the French Protestants, I shall here cite the Confession of Faith now in use among the French Churches. "We believe," say they in the ninth, tenth, and eleventh articles of their creed, "that man, having been created after the image of God, fell by his own fault from the grace he had received; and thus became alienated from God, who is the fountain of holiness and felicity; so that having his mind blinded, his heart depraved, and his whole nature corrupted, he lost all his innocence. We believe that the whole race of Adam is infected with this contagion, that in his person we forfeited every blessing, and sunk into a state of universal want and malediction: we believe also that sin, &c, is a perverseness producing the fruits of malice and rebellion!"

The Reformed Churches of Switzerland make as humiliating a confession. "Man," say they, "by an abuse of his liberty, suffering himself to be seduced by the serpent, forsook his primitive integrity. Thus he rendered himself subject to sin, death, and every kind of misery; and such as the first man became by the fall, such are all his descendants, Romans v:12. When we say, man is subject to sin, we mean by sin, that corruption of nature, which from the fall of the first man, has been transmitted from father to son; vicious passions, an aversion to that which is good, an inclination to that which is evil, a disposition to malice, a bold defiance and contempt of God. Behold the unhappy effects of that corruption, by which we are so wholly debilitated, that of ourselves we are not able to do, nor even to choose, that which is good." (*Helvetic Confession*, chap. viii.) Every man may find in himself sufficient proofs of those painful truths. "God is the Creator of man," say the fathers who composed the Synod of Berne, "and he intended that man should be entirely devoted to his God. But this is no longer his nature; since he looks to creatures, to his own pleasure, and makes an idol of himself." (*Acts of Synod*, chap. viii.)

This doctrine is also set forth in the Augsburg Confession; as well as in the ninth and tenth articles of the Church of England, where it is expressed in the following terms: "Original sin standeth not in the following of Adam, but it is the fault and corruption of the nature of every man, whereby he is very far gone from original righteousness, and is, of his own nature, inclined to evil, so that the flesh lusteth always contrary to the Spirit; and therefore, in every person born into the world, it deserveth God's wrath and damnation." "The condition of man after the fall of Adam is such that he cannot turn and prepare himself, by his own natural strength and good works, to faith and calling upon God. Wherefore we have no power to do good works, pleasant and acceptable to God, without the grace of God by Christ preventing us, that we may have a good will, and working with us when we have that good will."

Nothing less than a lively conviction of the corruption, weakness, and misery described in these confessions of faith, can properly dispose a man for evangelical repentance.

The Portrait of St. Paul

Without evangelical repentance, a lively faith in Christ, or regeneration by the Holy Spirit, will appear not only unnecessary, but absurd.

As the knowledge of our depravity is the source from whence evangelical repentance and Christian humility flow, so it is the only necessary preparation for that living faith, by which we are both justified and sanctified. He who obstinately closes his eyes upon his own wretchedness, shuts himself up in circumstances which will not suffer him to receive any advantage from that glorious Redeemer, whom "God hath anointed to preach the Gospel to the poor;" to heal the "broken hearted; to preach deliverance to the captives, and recovering of sight to the blind; to set at liberty them that are bruised; to preach the acceptable year of the Lord," Luke iv:18, 19. Reason itself declares, that if sinful man is possessed of sufficient ability to secure his own salvation, he needs no other Saviour, and "Christ is dead in vain," Galatians ii:21. In short, so far as we are unacquainted with our degenerate estate, so far the important doctrine of regeneration must necessarily appear superfluous and absurd.

Here we may perceive one grand reason why the ministers of the present day, who are but superficially acquainted with the depravity of the human heart, discourse upon this mysterious subject in a slight and unsatisfactory manner.

The true minister, on the contrary, following the example of his great Master, speaks upon this momentous change with affection and power. Observe the terms in which our Lord himself declares this neglected doctrine: "Verily, verily, I say unto you, Except a man be born of water, and of the Spirit, he cannot enter into the kingdom of God," John iii:5. As though he should say, The natural man, how beautiful an appearance soever he may make, is possessed of a heart so desperately wicked, that unless it be broken by the repentance which John the Baptist preached, and regenerated by the faith which I declare, he can never become a citizen of heaven. For the doors of my kingdom must remain everlastingly barred against those "ravening wolves," who disguise themselves as sheep, Matthew vii:15; and those painted hypocrites, who salute me as their Lord, without embracing my doctrines, and observing my commands. "Verily," therefore, "I say unto you," my first disciples and friends, "Except ye be converted, and become as little children," who are strangers to envious, ambitious, or impure thoughts, "ye shall not enter into the kingdom of heaven," Matthew xviii:3.

Such is the doctrine that is still able to convert every inquiring Nicodemus. At first it may perplex and confound them; but, at length, submitting to the wisdom of their heavenly Teacher, they will cry, "Impart to us, Lord, this regenerating faith:" and when once they have obtained their request, they will adopt the prayer of the disciples, Luke xvii:5, and proceed, like them, from faith to faith, till all things in their regenerate hearts are become new.

But if this doctrine is a savour of life unto some, it is also a savour of death unto others. It gives offence to blinded bigots, while modern infidels strengthen themselves against it, as Pharaoh once strengthened himself against the authority of Jehovah. "Thus saith the Lord," said Moses to that obstinate monarch, "Let my people go, that they may serve me," Exodus viii:1; and the haughty infidel replied, "Who is the Lord, that I should obey his voice? I know not the Lord, neither will I let

Israel go," Exodus v:2. Come up out of mystic Egypt, saith the Son of God to every sinful soul: "Follow me in the regeneration," Matthew xix:28, and I will teach you to "worship God in spirit and in truth," John iv:24. "And who is the Son of God?" replies some petty Pharaoh: "I know neither him nor his Father, nor conceive myself in any wise obliged to obey his commands."

Impious as this language may appear, the conduct of every irreligious Christian must be considered as equivalent to it, according to those words of our Lord, "He that despiseth" my servants, and my doctrines, "despiseth me; and he that despiseth me, despiseth him that sent me," Luke x:16. Whatever mask such a Pharisaical professor may wear, he "loves the world:" therefore "the love of the Father is not in him," 1 John ii:15. He hates both Christ and his Father, John xv:24, his repentance is superficial, his faith is vain, and, sooner or later, his actions or his words will testify that he is an utter enemy to Christ and his members.

How the faithful pastor leads sinners to repentance.

WHAT was spoken by God to Jeremiah, may in some sort be applied to the true minister: "I have set thee to root out and to plant, to pull down and to build," Jeremiah i:10. For before the sacred vine can be planted, the thorns of sin must be rooted up, together with the thistles of counterfeit righteousness. And before the strong tower of salvation can be erected, that spiritual Babel must be overthrown, by which presumptuous men are still exalting themselves against heaven.

To lead sinners into a state of evangelical repentance, the true minister discovers to their view the corruption of the heart, with all the melancholy effects it produces in the character and conversation of unregenerate men. After he has denounced the anathemas of the law against particular vices, such as swearing, lying, evil speaking, extortion, drunkenness, &c, he points out the magnitude of two general or primitive sins. The greatest offence, according to the law, he declares to be that by which its first and great command is violated: consequently, those who love not God beyond all created beings, he charges with living in the habit of damnable sin; since they transgress that most sacred of all laws, which binds us to love the Deity with all our heart, Matthew xxii:37, 38. Hence he goes on to convict those of violating a command like unto the first, who love not their neighbour as themselves, Matthew xxii:32; and to these two sins, as to their deadly sources, he traces all the crimes which are forbidden in the law and in the prophets, Matthew xxii:40.

And now he proceeds to lay open, before the eyes of professing Christians, the two greatest sins which are committed under the Gospel dispensation. If the two great commands of God, under the new covenant, are to this effect, that we believe on his Son Jesus Christ, and love one another, 1 John iii:23, it is evident that the two greatest sins under the Gospel are, the want of that living faith which unites us to Christ, and that ardent charity, which binds us to mankind in general, as well as to believers in particular, with the bands of cordial affection. As darkness proceeds from the absence of the sun and moon, so from these two sins of omission flow all the various offences which are prohibited by the evangelical law. And if those who are immersed in these primitive sins be withheld from the actual commission of enormous offences, they are not on this account to be esteemed radically holy, since they are possessed of that very nature from which every crime is produced. Sooner or later temptation and opportunity may cause some baneful shoots to spring forth in their outward conduct, in testimony that a root of bitterness lies deep within, and that the least impious of men carry about them a degenerate nature, a body of sin and death.

To give more weight to these observations, he sets forth the greatness of the Supreme Being, enlarges on his justice, and displays the severity of his laws. He tramples under foot the Pharisaical holiness of sinners, that he may bring into estimation the real virtues of the "new man, which after God is created in righteousness and true holiness." To awaken those who are sleeping in a state of carnal security, he denounces the most alarming maledictions, calling forth against them the thunders of Mount Sinai, till they are constrained to turn their faces Zion ward; till they seek for safety in the Mediator of the new covenant, and hasten to "the sprinkling of that blood, which speaketh better things than the blood of Abel," Hebrews xii:24.

By this method, he conducts his wandering flock to the very point where ancient Israel stood, when God had prepared them to receive the law by his servant Moses. Now, after the people had heard the thunderings, and "the noise of the trumpet;" after they had seen "the lightning, and the mountain smoking," Exodus xx:18; when, unable any longer to gaze on the dreadful scene, "they said unto Moses, Speak thou with us and we will hear; but let not God speak unto us, *without a Mediator*, lest we die," Exodus xx:19. Then it was that Moses began to console them in the following words: "Fear not: for God is come to prove you, and that his fear may be before your faces, that ye sin not," Exodus xx:20. So in the present day, they only who are brought to this poverty of spirit are properly disposed to receive the riches of Divine mercy. As soon, therefore, as the evangelical minister has sufficiently alarmed a sinner with the terrors discovered upon Mount Sinai, he anxiously prepares him for the consolations of the Gospel, by a sight of the suffering scene upon Calvary.

Many pious divines have supposed that by preaching the cross of Christ alone, mankind might be brought to true repentance. What the fathers of the Synod of Berne have said upon this point deserves the attention of those who desire successfully to use that spiritual weapon which is "sharper than any two-edged sword," Hebrews iv:12.

"The knowledge of sin," say they, "must of necessity be drawn from Jesus Christ. The apostle writes thus: 'God commendeth his love toward us, in that while we were yet sinners Christ died for us,' Romans v:8. It follows, that sin must have made us abominable and extremely hateful, since the Son of God could no other way deliver us from the burden of it, than by dying in our stead. Hence we may conceive what a depth of misery and corruption there is in the heart, since it was not able to be purified, but by the sacrifice of so precious a victim, and by the sprinkling of the blood of God," that is, of a man miraculously formed, in whom dwelt "all the fulness of the Godhead bodily," Colossians ii:9. "The apostles have clearly manifested the sinfulness of our nature by the death of Christ; whereas the Jews, after all their painful researches, were not convinced of sin by the law of Moses. After a solid knowledge of sin has been drawn from the passion of our Lord, there will naturally flow from this knowledge a true repentance; that is, a lively sorrow for sin, mingled with the hope of future pardon. To this necessary work the Holy Spirit also powerfully contributes, bringing more and more to the light, by its mysterious operations, the hidden evils and unsuspected corruptions of the heart; daily purifying it from the filthiness of sin, as silver is purified by the fire." (*Acts of Synod*, chap. viii, ix, xiv.)

How the prophets, Jesus Christ, his forerunner, and his apostles, prepared sinners for repentance.

EVER faithful to the word of God, the minister of the Gospel endeavours to humble the impenitent, by appealing to the sacred writers, and particularly to the declarations of Jesus Christ.

The corruption of the heart is the most ancient and dreadful malady of the human race. Man had no sooner made trial of sin, but he was driven by it from an earthly paradise, Genesis iii:24. And so terrible were its first effects, that the second man was seen to assassinate the third, Genesis iv:8. This moral contagion increased through every age, to so astonishing a degree, that, before the deluge, "God saw that the wickedness of man was great in the earth, and that every imagination of the thoughts of his heart was only evil continually," Genesis vi:5. "After the flood God still declared the imagination of man's heart to be evil from his youth," Genesis viii:21. "The heart of man," saith he again, long after that time, "is deceitful above all things, and desperately wicked: who can know it? I the Lord search the heart, I try the reins," Jeremiah xvii:9, 10.

Our Lord himself, who perfectly "knew what was in man," John ii:25, being the Physician who alone is able to heal us, and the Judge who will render to every one according to his works,—our Lord has described mankind alienated from the chief good, filled with aversion to his people, and enemies to God himself. "I send you forth," saith he to his disciples, "as lambs among wolves," Luke x:3. "If the world hate you, ye know that it hated me before it hated you. If ye were of the world, the world would love his own; but because I have chosen you out of the world," that ye should walk in my steps, "therefore the world hateth you. If they have persecuted me, they will also persecute you," John xv:18, 19, 20. "All these things will they do unto you for my name's sake, because," notwithstanding their Deism and Polytheism, "they know not him that sent me. For he that hateth me hateth my Father also," John xv:21, 23. "These things have I told you, that, when" they shall chase you from their Churches, as demons would chase an angel of light, "ye may remember that I told you of them," John xvi:4.

The Jews were, doubtless, in one sense, the most enlightened of all people; seeing they offered the true God a public worship unmixed with idolatry, were in possession of the Law of Moses, the Psalms of David, together with the writings of the other prophets, in which the duties required of man, both with respect to God and his neighbour, are traced out in the most accurate manner. Nevertheless, Jesus Christ represents this enlightened people as universally corrupted, in spite of all these advantages. "Did not Moses," saith he to them, "give you the law? And yet none of you keepeth the law," John vii:19.

The Portrait of St. Paul

What appears most extraordinary in the sermons of our Lord, is the zeal with which he bore his testimony against the virtues of those Jews who were reputed men of uncommon devotion. Although they piqued themselves upon being eminently righteous, he declared to his disciples that, unless their righteousness should "exceed the righteousness of the scribes and Pharisees," they should "in no case enter into the kingdom of heaven," Matthew v:20. And observe the manner in which he generally addressed those religious impostors: "Wo unto you, scribes and Pharisees, hypocrites! for ye make clean the outside of the cup and of the platter, but within they are full of extortion and excess [full of covetous desires and disorderly passions.] Thou blind Pharisee, cleanse first that which is within, that the outside may be clean also," Matthew xxiii:25, 26.

Nothing is more common than that blindness which suffers a man to esteem himself better than he really is, and this blindness is, in every period, and in every place, the distinguishing characteristic of a Pharisee. This species of hypocrisy, with which St. Paul was once elated, agrees perfectly well with the ordinary sincerity of nominal Christians, who blindly regard amusements the most trifling and expensive as allowable and innocent pleasures; who look upon theatres as schools of virtue; intrigue and deceit as prudence and fashion; pomp and profusion as generosity and decorum; avarice as frugality; pride as delicacy of sentiment; adultery as gallantry; and murder as an affair of honour.

To all such modern Christians may we not, with propriety, repeat what our Lord once openly addressed to their predecessors? Without doubt, we are authorized to cry out against them, with a holy zeal, "Wo unto you, hypocrites! for ye are like unto whited sepulchres, which indeed appear beautiful outward, but are within full of dead men's bones and of all uncleanness," Matthew xxiii:27. "Ye outwardly appear righteous unto men, but within ye are full of hypocrisy and iniquity." Of *hypocrisy*, because your virtues have more of appearance than solidity; and of *injustice*, because you render not that which is due to God, to Cesar, or to your fellow creatures, whether it be adoration, fear, honour, support, or good will, Matthew xxiii:28.

But if the depravity of the Jews in general, and of the Pharisees in particular, appears abundantly evident; must we suppose there were no happy exceptions among them? It is true the royal prophet declares, "The Lord looked down from heaven upon the children of men, to see if there were any that did understand and seek God. They are all gone aside, they are all together become filthy. There is none that doeth good, no, not one," Psalm xiv:2, 3. But were not the disciples of our Lord to be considered in a different point of view? No. Even after the extraordinary assistance afforded them by the Son of God, the apostles themselves did but confirm the sad assertion of the psalmist. Our Lord, upon whom no appearances could impose, once testified to James and John that, notwithstanding their zeal for his person, they were unacquainted with his real character; and that, instead of being influenced by his Spirit, they were actuated by that of the destroyer, Luke ix:55. "Ye, then, being evil," said he to all his disciples, Matthew vii:11. "Have not I chosen you twelve, and one of you is a devil?" John vi:70. "One of you shall betray me,"—Peter, who is the most resolute to confess me, shall "deny me thrice—and all ye shall be offended because of me," Matthew xxvi:21, 34, 31. *Lastly:* our Lord constantly represented the unregenerate as persons diseased and condemned. "They that are whole," said he, "have no need of the physician, but they that are sick. I came not to call the righteous, but sinners to repentance," Mark ii:17. "Ye are of this world, therefore I said unto you that ye shall die in your sins; for if ye believe not that I am He," and refuse to observe the spiritual regimen I prescribe, "ye shall die in your sins," John viii:23, 24. "Except ye repent, ye shall perish," Luke xiii:5.

It is notorious, that John the Baptist prepared the way of his adorable Master by preaching the same doctrine. "O generation of vipers," said he to the Pharisees and Sadducees, to the profane and professing part of the nation, "who hath warned you to flee from the wrath to come? Bring forth, therefore, fruits meet for repentance," Matthew iii:7, 8.

It is equally well known that the disciples were instructed by Christ himself to tread in the steps of his forerunner. "It behooved," said he, "Christ to suffer; and that repentance should be preached in his name among all nations," Luke xxiv:46, 47. Hence an apostle was heard to cry out: "God now commandeth all men every where to repent," Acts xvii:30. And at other times, the same divine teacher was inspired to write as follows: "We, who are Jews by nature, and not sinners of the Gentiles, were by nature the children of wrath even as others," Galatians ii:15; Ephesians ii:3. "For we were sometimes foolish, disobedient, deceived, serving divers lusts and pleasures, living in malice and envy, hateful, and hating one another," Titus iii:3.

The same doctrine was constantly held forth by the other apostles, as well as by St. Paul. "In time past," saith St. Peter, "we have wrought the will of the Gentiles, walking in lasciviousness, lusts, revellings," &c. 1 Peter iv:3. "The whole world lieth in wickedness," saith the beloved John, 1 John v:19; and St. James solemnly testifies, that every "friend of the world is the enemy of God," James iv:4.

This humiliating doctrine, which the world universally abhors, is a light too valuable to be hidden under a bushel: and till it be raised, as it were, upon a candlestick of gold, we can never hope to see the visible Church enlightened and reformed.

Observations upon the repentance of worldly men.

IF it be inquired, Do not all ministers preach repentance? we answer, that, ordinarily, true ministers alone preach true repentance. The preachers of the day, as they are conformable to the world in other things, so they are perfectly contented with practising the repentance of worldly men. Now, as he who receives only base coin, cannot possibly circulate good money, so he who satisfies his own heart with a short-lived sorrow for sin, cannot possibly give free course to that evangelical repentance which the Gospel requires. And it is observable, that the hearers of such ill-instructed scribes generally fix those bounds to their repentance which are satisfactory to their impenitent pastors.

The repentance we here condemn may be known by the following marks:—

1. It is superficial, and founded only upon the most vague ideas of our corruption. Hence, it cannot, like that of David and Jeremiah, trace sin to its source, and bewail the depravity of the whole heart, Psalm li:5; Jeremiah xvii:9.

2. It is Pharisaical, regarding only outward sins. The righteousness of the Pharisees rested upon the most trifling observances, while they neglected those weighty commands of the law which respect the love of God and our neighbour, Matthew xxiii:23. They afflicted themselves when they had not scrupulously paid the tenths of their herbs: but they smote not upon their breasts when they had rejected the glorious Gospel of Jesus Christ. In the same dangerous circumstances are those penitents of the present day who are less sorrowful on account of having offended God and rejected Christ, than that they are become objects of ridicule, contempt, or punishment, by the commission of some impious or dishonourable action. We frequently hear these false penitents bewailing the condition to which they have reduced themselves, and giving vent to the most passionate expressions of sorrow. But when are they seen to afflict themselves because they have not been wholly devoted to God? Or when do they shed a single tear at the recollection that they have not cherished their neighbour as themselves? Are they ever heard to lament the want of that faith in Christ "which worketh by love?" Galatians v:6. Are they ever engaged in seeking after that communion of saints by which believers become of one heart and one soul? Alas! so far are they from this, that they continue equally tranquil under the maledictions of the Gospel as under those of the law. They hear, without terror, those dreadful words of the apostle, "If any man love not the Lord Jesus Christ, let him be anathema maranatha," 1 Corinthians xvi:22. And though they neither love nor know him, yet they vainly look upon themselves as godly mourners and unfeigned penitents.

3. This repentance is unfruitful, inasmuch as those who repent after this manner, are utter strangers to compunction of heart. None of these are constrained to cry out, "Men and brethren, what shall we do?" Acts ii:37. They come not to the Redeemer among such as "are weary and heavy laden," Matthew xi:28. They have no experience of that godly sorrow by which the true penitent dies to sin: and so far are they from being born again of the Spirit, that they neither expect nor desire any such regeneration. In short, this repentance is rarely as sincere as that of Judas, who confessed his sin, justified the innocent, subdued his ruling passion, and returned the money he had so dearly obtained.

Evangelical repentance is an incomprehensible work to the generality of ministers. Wherever it appears they are prepared to censure it; and are earnest in exhorting men to flee from it, rather than request it as a gift from God. Thus, when they behold any one truly mourning under a sense of sin, smiting upon his breast with the publican, stripping off, with St. Paul, the covering of his own righteousness, and inquiring, with the convicted jailer, "What must I do to be saved?" Acts xvi:30, they suppose these to be certain signs of a deep melancholy. They imagine the conversation of some enthusiast has driven the man to despair, and will not scruple to affirm that he has lost the proper use of his reason. So true it is, that "the natural man receiveth not the things of the Spirit of God," 1 Corinthians ii:14; nor is even able to form any just ideas of that repentance, which is the first duty imposed upon us by the Gospel, and the first step toward that holiness, without which no man shall see the Lord.

The moralists of the present time acknowledge that all men are sinners; but they neglect to draw the just consequences from so sad a truth. To be found a sinner before an infinitely holy and just God, is to forfeit, at once, both our felicity and existence. To appear as an offender in the eyes of our all-seeing Judge, is to lie in the

The Works of John Fletcher

condition of a broken vessel, which the potter throws aside as refuse: it is to stand in the circumstances of a criminal, convicted of violating the most sacred laws of his prince. The two most important laws of God, are those which require piety toward himself, and charity toward our neighbour. Now if we have violated both the one and the other of these laws, and that times without number, if becomes us not only to confess our transgression, but to consider our danger. When a traitor is convicted of treason, or an assassin of murder, he immediately expects to hear his sentence pronounced. And thus, when a sinner confesses himself to be such, he makes a tacit acknowledgment that sentence of death might justly be pronounced upon him.

Some persons are naturally so short sighted, that they can only discover the most striking objects about them. Many in the moral world are in similar circumstances, to whom nothing appears as sin, except impieties of the grossest kind. If we judge of God's commands according to the prejudices of these men, idolatry is nothing less than the act of prostrating ourselves before an idol; and murder is merely the act by which a man destroys the life of his fellow creature. But if these deluded persons could contemplate sin in a Scriptural light; if they could avail themselves of the law of God, as of an observatory erected for sacred meditation, their moral view would be sufficiently strengthened to discover the following truths:—

1. If we have not, at all times, placed a greater confidence in the Creator than in any of his creatures; if we have either feared or loved any one more than our celestial Parent, we have then really set up another God, in opposition to the Lord of heaven and earth.

2. If, neglecting to worship the Almighty in spirit and truth, we have suffered ourselves to be seduced by any splendid vanity of the age, we have sinned in the same degree, as though we had fallen down before a molten image.

3. If, in our conversation, our reading, or our prayers, we have ever irreverently pronounced the "name of God," we have then taken that "sacred name in vain:" and God himself declares that he will not hold such a one guiltless.

4. If we have refused to labour diligently, through the week, in the work of our particular calling; or if we have ever made the Sabbath a day of spiritual indolence and frivolous amusement; then we have neglected and broken that law which we are peculiarly commanded to "remember and keep."

5. If we have, at any time, been wanting in obedience, respect, or love to our parents, our pastors, our magistrates, or to any of our superiors; or if we have neglected any of those duties, which our relations in society, or our particular vocation has imposed upon us, we have merited that God should cut us off from the land of the living.

6. If we have weakened our constitution by excess of any kind; if we have struck our neighbour in a moment of passion; if we have ever spoken an injurious word; if we have ever cast a look directed by malice; if we have ever formed in our hearts a single evil wish against any person whatever, or if we have ever ceased to love our brother;—we have then, in the sight of God, committed a species of murder, 1 John iii:15.

7. If we have ever looked upon a woman with any other feelings than those of chastity, Matthew v:28; or if we have at any time cast a wishful glance upon the honours and pleasures of the world; we have sufficiently proved the impurity of our nature, and must be considered as living in enmity with God, James iv:4.

8. If we have received the profit annexed to any post or employment, without carefully discharging the duties incumbent upon us in such situation; or if we have taken advantage either of the ignorance or the necessity of others, in order to enrich ourselves at their expense; we may justly rank ourselves with those who openly violate the eighth command.

9. If we have ever offended against truth in our ordinary conversation; if we have neglected to fulfil our promises; or have ever broken our vows, whether made to God or man; we have reason, in this respect, to plead guilty before the tribunal of immutable truth.

10. If we have ever been dissatisfied with our lot in life; if we have ever indulged restless desires, or have given way to envious and irregular wishes; we have then assuredly admitted into our hearts that covetousness which is the root of every evil.

When St. Paul considered the law, in this point of view, he cried out, "It is spiritual; but I am carnal, sold under sin," Romans vii:14. And when Isaiah, passing from the letter to the spirit, discovered the vast extent of the decalogue, he exclaimed, "Wo is me! for I am a man of unclean lips, and I dwell in the midst of a people of unclean lips," Isaiah vi:5. If our selfapplauding moralists would be persuaded to weigh their piety in the same balance, they would find it as defective at least as that of Isaiah and St. Paul.

Here, perhaps, some objecting Pharisee may say, "If I have sinned in some degree, yet I have not committed such crimes as many others have done, and I trust that God will not be severe in attending to trifling sins." But, (1.) These pretended trifling sins are ordinarily of so great a number, that the multitude of them becomes equivalent to the enormity of those crimes which are rarely committed; so mountains and seas are but collections of grains of sand and drops of water.

2. Every voluntary transgression argues a real contempt of the legislator's authority; and in such contempt there is found the seed of every sin that can possibly be committed, in opposition to his express command. All the commands of God, whether they be great or small, have no other sanction than that which consists in his Divine authority, and this authority is trampled under foot by every petty delinquent, as well as by every daring transgressor.

3. Those which we usually esteem trivial sins, are the more dangerous on account of their being less attended to. They are committed without fear, without remorse, and generally without intermission. As there are more ships of war destroyed by worms than by the shot of the enemy, so the multitude of those who destroy themselves through ordinary sins, exceeds the number of those who perish by enormous offences.

4. We have a thousand proofs that small sins will lead a man, by insensible degrees, to the commission of greater. Nothing is more common among us than the custom of swearing and giving way to wrath without reason; and these are usually regarded as offences of an inconsiderable nature. But there is every reason to believe, that they who have contracted these vicious habits, would be equally disposed to perjury and murder, were they assailed by a forcible temptation, and unrestrained with the dread of forfeiting their honour or their life. If we judge of a commodity by observing a small sample; so by little sins, as well as by trivial acts of virtue, we may form a judgment of the heart. Hence the widow's two mites appeared a considerable oblation in the eyes of Christ, who judged by them how rich an offering the same

woman would have made, had she been possessed of the means. For the same reason, those frequent exclamations, in which the name of God is taken in vain, those poignant railleries, and those frivolous lies, which are produced in common conversation, discover the true disposition of those persons, who, without insult or temptation, can violate the sacred laws of piety and love. The same seeds produce fruit more or less perfect, according to the sterility or luxuriance of the soil in which they are sown. Thus the very same principle of malice which leads a child to torment an insect, acts more forcibly upon the heart of a slanderous woman, whose highest joy consists in mangling the reputation of a neighbour; nor is the cruel tyrant actuated by a different principle, who finds a barbarous pleasure in persecuting the righteous and shedding the blood of the innocent.

If prejudice will not allow these observations to be just, reason declares the contrary. The very same action that, in certain cases, would be esteemed a failing, becomes, in some circumstances, an offence; and, in others, an enormous crime. For instance: if I despise an inferior, I commit a fault; if the offended party is my equal, my fault rises in magnitude; if he is my superior, it is greater still: if he is a respectable magistrate—a beneficent prince—if that prince is my sovereign lord, whose lenity I have experienced after repeated acts of rebellion; who has heaped upon me many kindnesses; who means to bestow upon me still greater favours: and if, after all, I have been led to deny and oppose him, my crime is undoubtedly aggravated, by all these circumstances, to an extraordinary degree. But if this offended benefactor is Lord of lords, and King of kings—the Creator of man—the Monarch of angels—the Ancient of days, before whom the majesty of all the monarchs upon earth disappears, as the lustre of a thousand stars is eclipsed by the presence of the sun—if this glorious Being has given his beloved Son to suffer infamy and death, in order to procure for me eternal life and celestial glory—my crime must then be aggravated in proportion to my own meanness, the greatness of benefits received, and the dignity of my exalted Benefactor. But our imagination is bewildered, when we attempt to scan the enormity which these accumulated circumstances add to those acts of rebellion, denominated sins.

They who are not working out their "salvation with fear and trembling," Philippians ii:12, must necessarily live in the practice of some constitutional sin; and this self indulgence, however secret it may be, will not suffer them to perceive the demerit of their daily transgressions. An old debauchee, whose chief delight has been in seducing women, or an infamous murderer, who has shed human blood like water, may as easily conceive the horror that adultery and murder excite in virtuous souls.

Before we can form a rational judgment of sin, and the punishment it deserves, it becomes us to entertain just ideas of moral order, to mark the obligation laid upon the supreme Legislator to maintain that order by wholesome laws, and to discover, in some degree, the sanctity, the excellence, and the extent of those absolute commands. It is necessary to understand the dependence of the creature upon the Creator; since the image formed by the presence of an object before a mirror, is not more dependent upon that object, than all orders of created beings depend upon the Creator; if he withdraw his protecting hand, they are no more; if he stretch out the arm of his vengeance, they are plunged, at once, into an abyss of misery. We must reflect upon all the various obligations under which we lie to the Almighty, as Creator, Preserver, Redeemer, and Comforter. We must consider those examples of his vengeful justice, which he has placed before our eyes, on purpose to awaken our fears, together with the unmerited favours by which he has constantly sought to engage our grateful affections. It becomes us likewise to observe the vanity of all those appearances by which we are allured into sin: and lastly, it is necessary to remember that "God will bring every work into judgment, with every secret thing," Ecclesiastes xii:14. While we pay not a proper attention to every one of these circumstances, we must necessarily form an imperfect judgment concerning the nature of sin, the severity with which God has determined to punish it, and the greatness of that expiatory sacrifice by virtue of which his justice and his mercy unite in pardoning the penitent.

When the law of God is wilfully transgressed, it is ridiculous in any man to attempt the justification of himself, by pleading that he has committed no enormous crimes; or that, if ever he has been guilty of any such offences, his good actions have always been sufficient to counterbalance their demerit. Frivolous excuses! Is not one treasonable act sufficient to mark the traitor? Is not that soldier punished as a deserter, who flies his colours but a single time? And does not a woman forfeit her honour by one moment of weakness?

Though we grant, there are some sins of a peculiarly atrocious kind; yet as murder will always appear, before an earthly tribunal, according to its horrible nature, so sin will ever be considered as such before an infinitely holy God. If a man, accused of having wilfully poisoned a fellow creature, should address his judge in terms like these: "The charge brought against me is just; but let it be considered that the person I have destroyed was only an infant—that he was the child of a common beggar—and that this is the only murder I have committed through the whole of my life. On the other hand, I have been a constant benefactor to the poor; and surely a thousand acts of charity will abundantly outweigh one little dose of arsenic." "No:" the judge would answer, "when you prolonged the life of the indigent by your alms, you merely performed a duty which is universally required of every worthy citizen; and the law allows you nothing on this account. But if you have given the smallest dose of poison to any human creature, with an intent to destroy his life, the law pronounces you a murderer, and will punish you as such."

After our first parents had offended by eating the forbidden fruit, they had but vainly excused themselves in saying, "We have only gathered that which appeared to be of little worth: we have tasted it but once: moreover, our labour in the garden is of much greater value than the fruit we have taken. Lord! condemn us not to death for so inconsiderable an offence." Such, however, are the frivolous excuses with which every blinded moralist contents his seared conscience, and with which he hopes to satisfy his omniscient Judge. When St. Paul was one of this class, he practised upon himself the same delusions. Capable only of natural sentiments, the hidden truths of a spiritual law were not only incomprehensible, but vain and foolish things in his estimation. This we learn from the following passage in his Epistle to the Romans: "I was alive without the law once," paying little attention to the spirituality of its precepts, or the severity of its threatenings, and indulging no suspicion either of my corruption or of my condemnation. "But when the commandment came," in its spiritual energy, "sin revived," assuming an appearance suited to its infernal nature, and, receiving a sentence of death in myself, "I died. I had not then known sin, but by the law; for I had not known lust," which is the source of every evil, and the first

ancient Pharisees' hope: but Christ and his apostles overthrew their vain confidence, by the same arguments which evangelical ministers are still obliged to turn against multitudes of religious professors, who indulge an exalted opinion of their own contemptible merits.

The Gospel requires, say these faithful pastors, that to the external marks of religion, you should be careful to add humility and charity: and if these two capital graces are wanting, your religion is but a body without a soul. You have received the holy sacraments of our Church but what salutary effects have they produced in your life and conversation? The circumcision, which saved the Jews, was not the circumcision of the flesh, but that of the heart, Romans ii:29: and the baptism, which saves Christians, is not that by which the body is sprinkled with water, but that which purifies the soul, 1 Peter iii:21. So the passover, which was acceptable to God on the part of the Jews, consisted not simply in eating the paschal lamb, but in penetrating their souls with gratitude, on recollecting the many wonderful deliverances which the Almighty had wrought for his people. And the communion, which is acceptable on the part of Christians, consists not merely in receiving the consecrated elements, as various classes of sinners are accustomed to do; but in uniting themselves to the Lord by a living faith, and to all his members by an ardent charity. You pray—and did not the Pharisees so? Yea, they were remarkable for their long and zealous prayers: but, alas! while they acknowledged "God with their lips, their hearts were far from him," Isaiah xxix:13. You give alms, but, if you mean with these to purchase heaven, you do but deceive your own souls, while your pretended charity degenerates into insolence: or, if you merely seek to procure the reputation of being charitably disposed; you have your reward. You fast—but if you do this chiefly through custom, or through respect to the orders of your prince, your fast can no more be counted religious than the regimen prescribed you by a physician. And if these facts have not produced in you a sincere repentance, and a true conversion, however you may regard them as acts of devotion, they are in reality no other than acts of hypocrisy. Moreover, the Pharisees fasted twice in the week; while you, it may be, are among the number of those who imagine they have made a valuable sacrifice to God, by abstaining from a single repast in a year.

As Pharisaical moralists "have sought out so many inventions," Ecclesiastes vii:29, to evade the necessity of an unfeigned repentance; and as philosophizing Christians rise up with one consent against this doctrine of the Gospel, we shall conclude this subject by disclosing the sources of their common error.

1. There are phantoms of virtue, or virtues purely natural, which pass in the world for Divine. But who ever imagined the dove to be really virtuous because she is not seen, like the eagle, to make a swoop at birds of a weaker frame than herself? Or who supposes wasps to be generous insects, because they are observed mutually to defend themselves when their nest is attacked? Is not the conjugal and maternal tenderness of the human species apparent, in an eminent degree, among various tribes of the feathered kind? And do we not see among bees and ants that ardent patriotism which was so highly extolled among the Romans? Does not the spider exhibit as manifest proofs of ingenuity and vigilance as the most industrious artist? And do not carnivorous animals discover all that fearless intrepidity which is so universally boasted of by vain-glorious heroes? Let us not mistake in a matter of so much importance: as nothing but charity can give to our alms the value of good works, so

nothing less than the fear of God, and a sincere intention of pleasing him, can give to our most valuable propensities the stamp of solid virtues. If we could completely expose the worthless alloy, which worldly men are accustomed to pass off as sterling virtue, many of those who now esteem themselves rich in good works, would be constrained to "abhor themselves, and repent in dust and ashes," Job xlii:6.

2. Many persons indulge too favourable ideas of the human heart, through their ignorance of that unsullied purity which God requires of his intelligent creatures. They judge of themselves and others as a peasant judges of a theme replete with solecisms, who, far from expressing the discernment of a critic, admires the vast erudition of the young composer. Thus some external acts of devotion are applauded by undiscerning Christians as commendable works, which, in the sight of God, and before holy spirits, appear altogether polluted and worthy of punishment.

3. If we are sometimes deceived by our own ignorance, we more frequently impose upon others by our innate hypocrisy. Unregenerate men, after having thrown a cloak over their distinguishing vices, are anxious to make a parade of virtues which they do not possess. The proud man is sometimes observed putting on the garb of humility, and with the most lowly obeisance, professing himself the very humble servant of an approaching stranger. Immodesty is frequently masked with an affected air of chastity and bashfulness; hatred, envy, and duplicity, veil themselves under the appearances of good nature, friendship, and simplicity: and this universal hypocrisy contributes to render its practitioners less outwardly offensive than they would otherwise be; as an unhandsome woman appears less defective to a distant beholder, after having nicely varnished over the blemishes of her face.

4. It frequently happens, that one vice puts a period to the progress of another. Thus vanity, at times, obliges us to act contrary to the maxims of avarice, avarice contrary to those of indolence, and indolence contrary to those of ambition. A refined pride is generally sufficient to overcome contemptible vices, and may influence its possessor to the performance of many apparently virtuous actions: hence the impious and sordid Pharisee went regularly to the temple: he prayed, he fasted, he gave alms; and, by all these appearances of piety and benevolence, acquired the commendation of the world. Society makes a kind of gain by these acts of dissimulation, which are as the homage paid to virtue by vice, and by impiety to devotion. But, notwithstanding every plausible appearance that can possibly be put on, when the minister of the Gospel declares the fall of man, together with the absolute need of regeneration, he is supported at once by revelation, reason, and experience.

5. If the moral disorder, with which human nature is infected, appear not always at its utmost height, it is because regeneration having commenced in many persons of every rank, the wicked are overawed by the influence of their example. Add to this, that God restrains them, as with a bridle, by his providence, and by those motions of conscience which they vainly endeavour to stifle. It is notorious, that the fear of public contempt and punishment is sometimes able to arrest the most abandoned in their vicious career; since they cannot discover what they really are, without arming against themselves the secular power. Thus the terror which prisons and gibbets inspire, constrains ravening wolves to appear in the garb of inoffensive sheep. But is it possible, that innocence so constrained should be accounted of any value even

among heathens themselves? It is impossible, since we find one of their own poets declaring—

Oderunt peccare mali, formidine poenæ.

The wicked abstain from mischief through fear of punishment. And all the recompense he conceives due to such guiltless persons, consists in not becoming the food of ravens upon a gibbet:—

Non pastes in cruce corvos.

6. If servile fear is sometimes the cause of our innocence, necessity is more commonly the cause of our apparent virtues. A youth of any modesty is generally cautious among his superiors, who afford him neither money to indulge, nor liberty to discover his inclinations. Now, if this forced discretion should, at length, become habitual to him, he may in such circumstances esteem himself a virtuous man, because he has not, like the son of a dissolute courtier, plunged himself into every kind of impiety. Whereas had he enjoyed but equal liberty with the licentious rake, he might have surpassed him in every sinful excess. On the other hand, when an infamous voluptuary, enfeebled either by age or by his frequent debaucheries, finds it absolutely needful to live in a more sober and orderly style, immediately he takes himself for another Cato; not considering that necessity alone is the source of his temperance. The least excess disorders his health, and the weakness of his stomach obliges him to abstain from those luxurious feasts, of which he can still converse with so much satisfaction. If such a one be virtuous, because no longer able to rush into his former excesses, then we may prove the most incorrigible robber to be an honest man, while the irons are on his hands, or when scared by the officers of justice, he flies to some secret retreat. Has that woman any reason to boast of her virtuous conduct, who was never solicited by those men who were most likely to have triumphed over her modesty? And yet, many such, filled with self approbation, will frequently applaud their own innocence, placing that to the account of virtue, which was merely owing to providential circumstances; or, perhaps, to the want of personal attraction. Such plausible appearances no more merit the commendation due to solid virtue than the sickly wolf, who peaceably passes by a flock of sheep, can be said to deserve the caresses which a shepherd bestows upon his faithful dog.

7. Effectually to impose upon others by a beautiful outside, we practise a deeper deceit upon our own hearts; and very frequently we succeed as well, in hiding from ourselves our own evil dispositions, as in concealing from others our unworthy actions. Could we discover all that secretly passes in the world, we should not want demonstrative proofs of the depravity of the human heart. But why need we go abroad in search of a truth, which is easily evidenced at home? Had we ourselves but dared to have executed openly, what we have acted in imagination, when our irascible or concupiscible passions have been roused, where should we have hidden our guilty heads, or how should we have escaped the sword of justice? Convinced too late of our degenerate nature, we should, haply, have smitten upon our breasts, with the repentant publican, adopting long ago his humiliating confession, in the anguish of our souls. Every thinking person must allow, that had evil intentions fallen under the

cognizance of human laws, and had the secular power possessed equal ability to punish them, as it punishes those actions, of which they are the very root and soul, the whole earth must, in such case, have become as vast a scaffold, as it is now a place of graves. Can it be necessary to multiply observations upon this head, when the Almighty, whose mercy and justice are infinite, sufficiently declares the universal depravity of mankind, by the variety of scourges with which he is constrained to punish both individuals and commonwealths?

8. If the children of this world are unable to form any just conception of the human heart and its evil propensities, it is because they are in the number of those natural men, of whom the Apostle Paul makes mention, 1 Corinthians ii:14. And such, having a natural antipathy to the Gospel, while they are ever ready to cast reproach upon the faithful, are equally prepared to favour those of a like disposition with themselves. Thus Herod, Caiaphas, and Pilate, mutually overlooked the faults of each other, while they united in accusing and persecuting Christ.

It is usual with many, who are destitute of true religion, to esteem some of their sinful companions as moral and well-disposed men. But, were they themselves to be really converted, their error, in this respect, would soon become apparent. Upon daring to oppose any torrent of impiety with the zeal of their heavenly Master, instead of finding among their associates any natural disposition to real virtue, they would meet with indisputable proofs, in spite of a thousand amiable qualities, that all unregenerate men resemble one another in their "enmity against God," Romans viii:7. Yes; whether they inhabit the banks of the Thames or the Seine; the lake of Genesareth or that of Geneva; they are, in the sight of God, as filthy swine trampling under foot the pearls of the Gospel, Matthew vii:6, or like "ravening wolves," Matthew vii:15, outrageously tearing in pieces the Lamb of God.

It might, perhaps, have been objected that this portrait is overcharged, had not Christ himself, who is immutable Truth, and unsearchable Love, penciled out the gloomiest traits observable in it. Following such a guide, though we may give much offence, yet we can never err.

The second point of doctrine, insisted upon by the true minister, is a living faith.

To show the necessity of repentance, without publishing the remission of sins, through faith in Jesus Christ, would be to open a wound without binding it up. It would be leading sinners to the brink of a tremendous gulf, and cutting off all possibility of their retreat. But nothing can be more contrary to the intention of the faithful minister, than to sport with the miseries of man, or ultimately to aggravate his distress.

When he has discovered to his hearers that natural propensity to evil, which manifests its existence in every heart, by a variety of external transgressions: when he has convinced them, by the word of God, and by all appeal "to every man's conscience," 2 Corinthians iv:2, that they are unable to deliver themselves, either from that fatal propensity, or its dreadful consequences: after he has thus demonstrated the need in which they stand of a Redeemer, who hath "all power in heaven and in earth," Matthew xxviii:18; if they "harden not their hearts," Psalm xcv:8; if they stand, like the first sinner, naked and trembling before God, Genesis iii:10, having received the sentence of death in themselves, 2 Corinthians i:9: in a word, when they cry out, like the publicans and soldiers alarmed by the preaching of John, "What shall we do?" Luke iii:12; they are then properly disposed to receive "the glorious Gospel of Christ," 2 Corinthians iv:4, and will be enabled to experience its powerful effects. From this time, the evangelical pastor affectionately preaches remission of sins through faith in the name of a merciful Redeemer.

This is the very same method which Christ and his forerunner pursued. "Behold the Lamb of God, which taketh away the sin of the world," was the cry of John the Baptist, John i:29. And "blessed," said our Lord, "are the poor in spirit; for theirs is the kingdom of heaven," Matthew v:3. "God so loved the world, that he gave his only begotten Son, that whosoever believeth in him should not perish, but have everlasting life," John iii:16. "He that believeth on the Son hath everlasting life; and he that believeth not the Son, shall not see life; but the wrath of God abideth on him," John iii:36. "Whosoever shall drink of the water that I shall give him, shall never thirst; but it shall be in him a well of water, [a source of sacred consolation,] springing up into everlasting life," John iv:14. Again, when it was inquired by the multitude, "What shall we do, that we may work the works of God? Jesus said unto them, This is the work of God, that ye believe on him whom he hath sent. And this is the will of him that sent me, that every one which seeth the Son, and believeth on him, may have everlasting life: and I will raise him up at the last day," John vi:28, 29, 40. Thus it was, that our adorable Master proclaimed salvation through faith in himself. And, indeed, it was for this end alone that he appeared upon earth; as we learn from the last address he made to his disciples: "It behooved," said he, "Christ to suffer, and to rise from the dead the third day, that remission of sins should be preached in his name among all nations, beginning at Jerusalem," the abode of his murderers, Luke xxiv:46.

Observe the great commission given to those messengers of peace. "Go ye into all the world, and preach the Gospel to every creature. He that believeth and is baptized shall be saved; but he that believeth not shall be damned," Mark xvi:15, 16. To the same purpose was the commission with which the Apostle Paul was afterward honoured. I have "appeared unto thee," said the persecuted Jesus, "for this purpose, to make thee a minister and a witness to the Gentiles, unto whom I now send thee, to open their eyes, to turn them from darkness to light, and from the power of Satan unto God, that they may receive forgiveness of sins, and inheritance among them that are sanctified, by faith that is in me," Acts xxvi:16, 17, 18.

The apostles unanimously preached in obedience to the orders, and in conformity to the example of their benevolent Lord. And all true ministers, instructed by the same Divine Teacher, continue to proclaim the glad tidings of the Gospel, through faith in Jesus Christ; laying as much stress, in all their sermons, upon this efficacious grace, as the apostle of the Gentiles was accustomed to do in all his epistles. Take a few instances of St. Paul's usual custom in this respect. After having convinced the Romans of their corruption and misery, he sets before them "the redemption that is in Christ Jesus, whom God hath set forth to be a propitiation through faith in his blood, to declare his righteousness for the remission of sins that are past: that he might be just, and the justifier of him that believeth in Jesus," Romans iii:24, 25, 26. "Therefore," continues he, "being justified by faith, we have peace with God, through our Lord Jesus Christ," Romans v:1. To the Corinthians he writes: "Brethren, I declare unto you the Gospel which I preached unto you, which also ye have received, and wherein ye stand; by which also ye are saved, unless ye have believed in vain," 1 Corinthians xv:1, 2. For "ye are justified in the name of the Lord Jesus," 1 Corinthians vi:11. "God hath reconciled us to himself by Jesus Christ, and hath committed unto us the word of reconciliation; to wit, that God was in Christ reconciling the world unto himself, not imputing their trespasses unto them: for he hath made him to be sin for us, who knew no sin, that we might be made the righteousness of God in him," 2 Corinthians v:18, 21. To the Galatians: "Knowing that a man is not justified by the works of the law, but by the faith of Jesus Christ, even we have believed in Jesus Christ, that we might be justified by faith, and not by the works of the law," Galatians ii:16. Before "faith came, we were kept under the law. Wherefore the law was our schoolmaster to bring us unto Christ. But after that faith is come, we are no more under a schoolmaster. For ye are all the children of God by faith in Christ Jesus," Galatians iii:23-26. To the Ephesians: "Blessed be the God and Father of our Lord Jesus Christ, who hath made us accepted in the Beloved: in whom we have redemption through his blood, the forgiveness of sins," Ephesians i:3, 6, 7. "By grace are ye saved through faith; and that not of yourselves: it is the gift of God. Not of works, lest any man should boast," Ephesians ii:8, 9. "Finally, my brethren—put on the whole armour of God—above all, taking the shield of faith, wherewith ye shall be able to quench all the fiery darts of the wicked," Ephesians vi:10, 11, 16. To the Philippians: "Stand fast in one spirit, with one mind, striving together for the faith of the Gospel," Philippians i:27. "We rejoice in Christ Jesus, and have no confidence in the flesh. Yea, I count all things but loss, that I may win Christ, and be found in him, not having mine own righteousness, which is of the law, but that which is through the faith of Christ, the righteousness which is of God by faith," Philippians iii:3, 8, 9. To the Colossians: "It pleased the Father, that in him [the Son] should all fulness dwell; and (having made peace through the blood of his cross) by him to reconcile all things unto himself. And you that were sometimes alienated, and enemies in your mind by wicked works, hath he reconciled in the body of his flesh through death, to present you holy and unblamable in his sight; if ye continue grounded and settled in the faith," Colossians i:19, 23. "As ye have therefore received Christ Jesus the Lord, so walk ye in him. Rooted and built up in him, and established in the faith, as ye have been taught, abounding therein with thanksgiving," Colossians ii:6, 7. To the Thessalonians: "Let us, who are of the day, be sober, putting on the breastplate of faith. For God hath not appointed us unto wrath, but to obtain salvation by our Lord Jesus Christ, who died for us, that whether we wake or sleep, we should live together with him," 1 Thessalonians v:8, 10. "We are bound to thank God always for you, brethren, because that your faith groweth exceedingly. Now the Lord shall come to be glorified in his saints, and to be admired in all them that believe. Wherefore we pray that our God would fulfil in you the work of faith with power; that the name of our Lord Jesus Christ may be glorified in you, and you in him," 2 Thessalonians i:3, 12. To Timothy: "This is a faithful saying, and worthy of all acceptation, that Christ Jesus came into the world to save sinners, of whom I am chief. Howbeit, for this cause I obtained mercy, that in me first Jesus Christ might show forth all long suffering, for a pattern to them which should hereafter believe on him to life everlasting," 1 Timothy i:15, 16. "For God our Saviour will have all men to be saved, and to come to the knowledge of the truth. For there is one God, and one Mediator between God and man, the man Christ Jesus, who gave himself a ransom for all," 1 Timothy ii:3, 6.

Great is the mystery of godliness: God was manifest in the flesh, justified in the Spirit, seen of angels, preached unto the Gentiles, believed on in the world, received up into glory," 1 Timothy iii:16. "God hath saved us, [that is to say, hath put us in possession of the same present salvation, which the sinful woman experienced, who, while she prostrated herself at the feet of Jesus, in faith and prayer, received from him these consolatory sentences, "Thy sins are forgiven thee; thy faith hath saved thee; go in peace," Luke vii:48, 50.] God hath saved us, not according to our works, but according to his own grace, which was given us in Christ Jesus—who hath abolished death, and hath brought life and immortality to light through the Gospel," 2 Timothy i:8, 10. To Titus: "Paul, an apostle of Jesus Christ, to Titus, mine own son after the common faith: grace, mercy, and peace from God the Father, and the Lord Jesus Christ our Saviour," Titus i:1, 4, "who gave himself for us, that he might redeem us from all iniquity, and purify unto himself a peculiar people, zealous of good works," Titus ii:14. "We ourselves were sometimes disobedient: but after that the kindness and love of God our Saviour toward man appeared, not by works of righteousness which we have done, but according to his mercy he saved us—that being justified by his grace, we should be made heirs of eternal life," Titus iii:3, 7. To Philemon, he writes: "Grace be to you, and peace from God our Father, and the Lord Jesus Christ. I thank my God, hearing of thy faith, which thou hast toward the Lord Jesus Christ. The grace of our Lord Jesus Christ be with your spirit," Philem. Thus, a persecuted Saviour became the Alpha and the Omega of this great apostle.

In his Epistle to the Hebrews he uses the same language. It begins and concludes with Him who is "the beginning and the end" of all things, Revelation xxii:13. "God," saith he, "hath in these last days spoken unto us by his Son, by whom also he made the worlds. Who being the brightness of his Father's glory, and the express image of his person, and upholding all things by the word of his power, when he had by himself purged our sins, sat down on the right hand of the Majesty on high," Hebrews i:1, 2, 3. "It became Him, for whom are all things, in bringing many sons unto glory, to make the Captain of their salvation perfect through sufferings. Forasmuch then as the children are partakers of flesh and blood, he also himself took part of the same; that through death he might destroy him that had the power of death, that is, the devil; and deliver them who, through fear of death, were all their lifetime subject to bondage," Hebrews ii:10-15. "Though he were a son, yet learned he obedience by the things which he suffered; and being made perfect, he became the author of eternal salvation," Hebrews v:8, 9. "This man, because he continueth ever, hath an unchangeable priesthood. Wherefore he is able to save them to the uttermost that come to God by him, seeing he ever liveth to make intercession for them," Hebrews vii:24, 25. "Having, therefore, a High Priest over the house of God, let us draw near in full assurance of faith," Hebrews x:21, 22. "Now faith is the substance of things hoped for, the evidence of things not seen: for by it the elders obtained a good report, who through faith subdued kingdoms, wrought righteousness, obtained promises, stopped the mouths of lions, quenched the violence of fire, escaped the edge of the sword, out of weakness were made strong, waxed valiant in fight, turned to flight the armies of the aliens," Hebrews xi:1, 2, 33, 34. "Wherefore, seeing we are compassed about with so great a cloud of witnesses, let us run with patience the race that is set before us, looking unto Jesus, the author and finisher of our faith," Hebrews xii:1, 2. "Now the God of peace—make you perfect in every good work to do his will, working in you that which is well pleasing in his sight, through Jesus Christ; to whom be glory for ever and ever," Hebrews xiii:20, 21.

The same Saviour whom St. Paul was so anxious to declare in his epistles, he as constantly preached in his sermons. He was no sooner converted, but "straightway," says St. Luke," he preached Christ in the synagogues, that he is the Son of God," Acts ix:20. Take an abridgment of the first of his sermons which is left upon record, and which was preached at Antioch, in Pisidia. After asserting the fulfilment of that glorious promise which had been anciently given respecting the birth of our omnipotent Saviour, he cries out, "Men and brethren, children of the stock of Abraham, and whosoever among you feareth God, to you is the word of this salvation sent." For the inhabitants and rulers of Jerusalem, "because they knew him not," nor understood the sense of those prophecies which are read "every Sabbath day," have given them their sad completion, by condemning the Lord of life and glory. "Though they found no cause of death in him, yet desired they Pilate that he should be slain. And when they had fulfilled all that was written of him, they laid him in a sepulchre." But God, after three days, raised him triumphantly from the grave. "And he was seen many days" of his wondering disciples, whom he continued to visit and instruct, even after his resurrection, that they might become "his witnesses to the people." And now, "we declare unto you, that God hath fulfilled the promise which was made unto the fathers, in that he hath raised up Jesus from the dead. Be it known unto you, therefore, men and brethren, that through this man is preached unto you the forgiveness of sins; and by him all that believe are justified from all things, from which ye could not be justified by the law of Moses. Beware, therefore, lest that come upon you, which is spoken of in the prophets, Behold, ye despisers, and wonder, and perish: for I work a work in your days, a work which you will in no wise believe, though a man declare it unto you," Acts xiii. When the cross of Christ and its happy effects are thus faithfully declared, the word of God is never wholly preached in vain. Some, it is true, will always reject and count themselves unworthy of everlasting life, Acts xiii:46. But others will rejoice in the truth, glorifying the word of the Lord; and all those who, by a true poverty of spirit, are disposed for eternal life, shall effectually believe, verse 48.

Some time afterward, St. Paul delivered a sermon in the prison at Philippi, the capital of Macedonia. St. Luke, his historian, has not favoured us with this discourse, but he has transmitted to us the subject matter of it. Despairing sinner, said the apostle to the affrighted jailer, who lay trembling at his feet, "believe on the Lord Jesus Christ, and thou shalt be saved, and thy house." After hearing thus much, the astonished man collected his family together, and the apostle continued his discourse, declaring unto them all "the word of the Lord." Such are the small remains we are able to collect of this excellent sermon. But though we are unacquainted with its several parts, we know that it was attended with the happiest effects: for, before the return of day, this converted jailer, snatched from the very brink of destruction, was seen, with all his believing family, rejoicing in God, Acts xvi.

When the same apostle was afterward appointed to speak before the senate at Athens, he could not, with propriety, set before those unhumbled philosophers "the mystery of the Gospel," Ephesians vi:19. But after bearing a public testimony against their superstition and idolatry, he pressed upon them the necessity of an unfeigned repentance; announcing Christ as an omniscient Judge, that he might afterward proclaim him as the compassionate Saviour of men, Acts xvii. To the same purpose was that other sermon of his, which was delivered before the tribunal of Felix, when the Roman governor was seen to tremble under the power of an apostle's preaching, Acts xxiv:25. The little effect produced by these two last mentioned discourses may be brought as a proof, that the most momentous truths are hidden "from the wise and prudent," while they are "revealed unto babes," Matthew xi:25.

It was by proclaiming the same mighty Saviour, that St. Stephen obtained for himself the first crown of martyrdom among the Christians. Behold an abridgment of his celebrated apology: "Men, brethren, and fathers," you accuse me of having spoken blasphemously against Moses. But, on the contrary, I publicly acknowledge him as the deliverer of our fathers, and gladly embrace this opportunity of reasoning with you from the character of that favoured prophet. "He once supposed," that, by certain of his actions, "his brethren would have understood how that God, by his hand, would deliver them." But so far were they from understanding any such matter, that one of them thrust him away, crying out in an insulting manner, "Who made thee a ruler and a judge over us?" This Moses, however, whom they thus refused, was chosen of God to be their future prince and deliverer. "This is that Moses who said unto the children of Israel, A prophet shall the Lord your God raise up unto you of your brethren, like unto me." A prophet whom you will at first reject, as you rejected me; but who, nevertheless, when you shall receive him, will deliver you out of spiritual Egypt, as I once delivered you from the land of bondage, when you gave credence to my word. This promised Saviour has already made his appearance among us, whom ye have rejected to your own condemnation. As our fathers rejected Moses in the wilderness, thrusting him from them, and in their hearts turning back again into Egypt, so you have rejected your greater Deliverer. "Ye uncircumcised in heart and ears, ye do always resist the Holy Ghost as your fathers did, so do ye. Which of the prophets have not your fathers persecuted? And they have slain them which showed before of the coming of the Just One, of whom ye have been now the betrayers and murderers; ye who have received the law by the disposition of angels, and have not kept it," Acts vii.

That the powerful preaching of the Gospel is sometimes made "the savour of death unto death," 2 Corinthians ii:16, is sufficiently clear from the following account. After Stephen had finished this discourse, the hearts of his hearers were transported with rage, insomuch that "they gnashed upon him with their teeth." Meanwhile the holy martyr continued to proclaim Christ; and, far from being intimidated by their threatenings, looking steadfastly up to heaven in a kind of ecstasy, produced by the strength of his faith, the vigour of his hope, and the ardour of his love, he cried out, "I see the heavens opened, and the Son of man standing on the right hand of God." And while the multitude ran upon him with stones, after committing his own soul to the care of his exalted Saviour, he cried, with a loud voice, "Lord, lay not this sin to their charge." Behold an apology, which was looked upon by the preachers of that day as replete with ignorance and fanaticism, though delivered by an evangelist who was filled with faith and power, and with the Holy Ghost!

The same doctrine was preached by the evangelists, who were dispersed abroad by the persecution excited against Stephen, and was followed by the benediction of the Lord. For we find that some of them, entering into the city of Antioch, spake unto the Grecians there, preaching the Lord Jesus; and the hand of the Lord was with them, so that "a great number believed and turned unto the Lord," Acts xi:19, 20, 21.

We shall go on to select a few proofs, that all the apostles were of one heart in this matter, preaching Jesus Christ as the Saviour of all those who believe in him.

Though St. James professedly wrote his epistle against the error of those who had destroyed the law of charity, by an imaginary faith in Christ, yet so far is he from despising the substantial faith of believers, that, as "the servants of God, and of our Lord Jesus Christ," he exhorts false brethren to seek after and manifest it by its proper fruits. He even employs a species of irony to point out the necessity of this powerful grace: "Show me thy faith without thy works, and I will show thee my faith by my works," James ii:18. He intimates that our faith must be tried by "divers temptations," in order to our becoming "perfect and entire" before God. Whence we learn that, according to his judgment, the perfection of Christians absolutely depends upon the perfection of their faith, James i:2-4. On this account he exhorts us to ask wisdom in faith. And lastly, he declares, that the prayer of faith shall be powerful enough to procure health for the sick, and remission for the sinful, James v:15.

There needs no more than an attentive perusal of this epistle, to convince us that St. James announces a faith which saves the Christian, by producing in him hope, charity, and every good work.

The same doctrine was inculcated by St. Peter, both in his sermons and epistles. Three thousand souls were converted, while he cried out, upon the day of pentecost, "Ye men of Israel, Jesus of Nazareth, a man approved of God among you, by miracles, and wonders, and signs; him, being delivered by the determinate counsel of God, ye have taken, and by wicked hands have crucified and slain. Whom God hath raised up, having loosed the pains of death, because it was not possible that he, who is the resurrection and the life, John xi:25, should be holden of it. This Jesus, therefore, being by the right hand of God exalted, hath shed forth this which ye now see and hear. Therefore, let all the house of Israel assuredly know, that God hath made that same Jesus, whom ye have crucified, both Lord and Christ." Now, when the convicted multitude inquired, in their distress, "Men and brethren, what shall we do?" Peter answered and said, "Repent and be baptized, every one of you, [that is to say, first cordially believe, and then by baptism make a public confession of that faith,] in the name of Jesus Christ, for the remission of sins, and ye shall receive the gift of the Holy Ghost," Acts ii.

His second discourse was to the same effect. "The God of our fathers hath glorified his Son Jesus, whom ye delivered up and denied in the presence of Pilate, when he was determined to let him go. But ye desired a murderer to be granted unto you, and killed the Prince of life, whom God hath raised from the dead; whereof we are witnesses. And faith in his name hath made this man strong, whom ye see and know; yea, the faith which is by him hath given him this perfect soundness in the presence of you all. And now, brethren, repent ye, and be converted, that your sins may be blotted out, when the times of refreshing shall come from the presence of the Lord," Acts iii:13-19.

His apology before the council was founded upon the same Divine truths. Be it known unto you all, and to all the people of Israel, that by the name of Jesus of Nazareth, whom ye crucified, whom God raised from the dead, even by him doth this man stand here before you whole. This is the stone that was set at nought of you builders, which is become the head of the corner. Neither is there salvation in any other: for there is none other name under heaven given among men whereby we must be saved," Acts iv:10, 12. Thus St. Peter," filled with the Holy Ghost, spake the word of God with boldness, and with great power gave witness to the resurrection of the Lord Jesus," Acts iv:31, 33. Even after being commanded to speak no more in the name of Jesus, he departed from the council, rejoicing that he was counted worthy to suffer shame for his Master's sake, "and daily in the temple and in every house, he ceased not to teach and preach Jesus Christ," Acts v:40, 42.

The fourth sermon of this apostle perfectly corresponds with the foregoing. This discourse was delivered in the house of Cornelius, the centurion, to whom an angel had before revealed that Peter should declare unto him things whereby both himself and his house should be saved. Of all the sermons which have ever been preached, this was, perhaps, the most effectual; since it is observed, that "the Holy Ghost fell on all them which heard the word." Take an abridgment of this powerful discourse. God hath proclaimed peace "to the children of Israel by Jesus Christ, whom they slew and hanged on a tree. But he," being raised again by the power of God, "commanded us to preach unto the people, and to testify that it is he which was ordained of God to be the Judge of quick and dead. To him give all the prophets witness, that whosoever believeth in him shall receive remission of sins," 10:36, 43.

And, as in his sermons, so also in his epistles, St. Peter was ever anxious to declare salvation through faith in the name of Jesus Christ.

"Peter, an apostle of Jesus Christ, to the elect of God. Blessed be God, who hath begotten us again unto a lively hope by the resurrection of Jesus Christ from the dead, to an inheritance incorruptible, reserved in heaven for you, who are kept by the power of God through faith unto salvation," 1 Peter i:1-5. "It is contained in the Scripture, Behold, I lay in Sion a chief corner stone, elect, precious: and he that believeth on him shall not be confounded. Unto you, therefore, which be disobedient, he is made a stone of stumbling and a rock of offence," 1 Peter ii:6-8.

The second Epistle of St. Peter was written for the confirmation of the weak and the establishment of the strong. In the first verse, Christ is represented as the author and finisher of our faith: in the last, the glory of our salvation is expressly ascribed to the same Divine Person. And these two verses may be given as an abridgment of the whole epistle.

This powerful faith, and this adorable Saviour, were as constantly proclaimed by the Apostle John. Though St. Luke has not transmitted to us any extracts from his discourses, yet his doctrine is sufficiently manifested in his epistles.

"If any man sin," saith this favoured apostle, "we have an advocate with the Father, Jesus Christ the righteous: and he is the propitiation for our sins," 1 John ii:1, 2. "He was manifested to take away our sins. And this is the commandment of God, that we should believe on the name of his Son Jesus Christ," 1 John iii:5, 23. "Whosoever believeth, is born of God—whatsoever is born of God, overcometh the world: and this is the victory that overcometh the world, even our faith," 5:1, 4. "These things have I written unto you that believe on the name of the Son of God, that ye may know that ye have eternal life, and that ye may" yet more steadfastly believe, ver. 13.

"Many deceivers," continues the same apostle in his second epistle, "have entered into the world, who confess not that Jesus Christ is come in the flesh. This is a deceiver and an antichrist. Whosoever abideth not in the doctrine of Christ, hath not God: he that abideth in the doctrine of Christ, hath both the Father and the Son," 2 John i:7, 9. Here St. John, foreseeing the melancholy revolution that would one day be effected in the Church by these antichristian teachers, notwithstanding his natural gentleness, cries against them with a holy indignation: "If there come any unto you, and bring not this doctrine, receive them not into your house, neither bid them God speed. For he that biddeth him God speed, is partaker of his evil deeds," 10, 11.

In his third epistle he expresses the utmost joy over Gaius, on account of his steady adherence to the truth; assuring him, that he had no greater joy than to hear that his children continued to walk in the truths of the Gospel. He commends his charity toward the people of God, and exhorts him to continue a fellow helper to the truth, by affording a hospitable reception to those who, with a view of spreading that truth, were journeying from place to place.

St. Jude, in his short epistle, writes thus: "Beloved, when I gave all diligence to write unto you of the common salvation, it was needful for me to exhort you, that ye should earnestly contend for the faith which was once delivered unto the saints. For there are certain men crept in unawares, denying the only Lord God, and our Lord Jesus Christ," Jude i:3, 4. "But ye, beloved, building up yourselves on your most holy faith, praying in the Holy Ghost, keep yourselves in the love of God, looking for the mercy of our Lord Jesus Christ unto eternal life," verses 20, 21.

The concluding book of the New Testament abounds with striking testimonies to the foregoing truths, and was added for the consolation of the Church in every age. It opens with a sublime eulogy pronounced upon that incomprehensible Saviour, who is "the Alpha and the Omega, the faithful Witness, the first begotten of the dead, and the Prince of the kings of the earth, who hath loved and washed us from our sins in his own blood, and hath made us kings and priests unto God and his Father, for ever and ever," Revelation i:5, 6.

The faithful, who groan in secret to behold their Master rejected by Deists, and neglected by the greater part of Christians, attend with holy transport to the representations here given by St. John. Here they perceive that condescending Saviour, who was dishonoured upon earth, acknowledged and adored by the hosts of heaven. They see the prostrate elders, and behold the innumerable multitude of the redeemed assembled before the throne. They hear that new song of adoration, in which angels and the spirits of just men made perfect unanimously cry out, "Worthy is the Lamb that was slain, to receive power, and riches, and wisdom, and strength, and honour, and glory, and blessing," Revelation v:12. These are scenes which the believer is assisted to realize by means of a lively faith, and in which he already bears an humble part, ascribing, with his more exalted brethren, "Blessing, and honour, and glory, and power, unto him that sitteth upon the throne, and unto the Lamb, for ever and ever," ver. 13.

This mysterious book concludes with that short prayer of St. John, which shall one day be offered up with the energy of the Holy Spirit, by ten thousand times ten thousand of the faithful, "Come, Lord Jesus," fully to accomplish thy gracious promises, Revelation xxii:20.

The Portrait of St. Paul

If it be here inquired, "Do not all ministers maintain this Scriptural faith?" I answer, It is a rare thing with the generality of ministers to treat on a point of so vast importance: and even when they are heard to speak of this mighty grace, they represent it as something manifestly different from that living faith by which we are regenerated. If ever they discourse with their catechumens on this subject, they speak as men who attempt to teach what they have yet to learn. They frequently repeat the word faith, but are unable to open its spiritual signification. They take it for granted that all their neighbours are possessed of this grace, except those who openly rejected the word of God; and thus they become perfectly satisfied with that species of faith against which St. Paul and St. James were authorized to denounce the anathemas of the Gospel. On this account, one of the last texts a worldly pastor would make choice of, is that solemn exhortation of the apostle, "Examine yourselves, whether ye be in the faith: prove your own selves: know ye not your own selves, how that Jesus Christ is in you, except ye be reprobates?" 2 Corinthians xiii:5. The faith with which he contents himself, and which he publishes to others, may be equally possessed by those who are conformable to this present evil world, and those who "have crucified the flesh with the affections and lusts," Galatians v:24. It belongs to self-exalting Pharisees, who boast of their own righteousness, as well as to those humble believers who count themselves unworthy of the benefits they have received.

Farther: so far is the ill-instructed minister from preaching the true faith, that he is always prepared to plead against it. In confirmation of this melancholy truth, take the following relation:—

A believer, whose circumstances frequently engaged him in conversation with a worldly man of his neighbourhood, once took occasion to offer him such advice as brotherly charity suggested. After the customary civilities, Sir, said he, we have lived as neighbours long enough to know one another; and, I presume, the intimacy of our acquaintance authorizes us to speak to each other without any reserve. It has given me real satisfaction to observe your constant attendance at our church, and your strict attention to her most solemn services. Nevertheless, permit me to express my fears that you are not seeking the kingdom of God with that earnestness and solicitude without which it can never be obtained. Though you are constant at church, yet you are as constant at tables of festivity; and an approaching entertainment appears to afford you greater pleasure than an approaching sacrament. I regularly observe the gazette upon your table, with a variety of new and ingenious publications; but I have never found you perusing the sacred pages of a more important volume. I have heard you speak in an agreeable manner upon twenty different things; but cannot recollect that your conversation ever turned upon what our Lord has described as "the one thing needful," Luke x:42. In short, sir, I apprehend, from your conduct, that you are altogether unacquainted with evangelical faith; and if so, your hope is as fallacious as your devotion is Pharisaical.

Neighbour. I am obliged, sir, by the interest you appear to take in my salvation; but allow me to say, with Solomon, "There is a time for all things."

Believer. Yes, sir; for all that is good. But, if you really believe there is a time for all things, is it not amazing, that after you have found four seasons in every day convenient for eating and drinking in your family, you should find no proper opportunity, through the whole course of a week, to pour out your prayers with that family before God?

N. It is true, I do not pique myself upon my piety: and I will confess to you, that I frequent the church and the holy communion, rather out of decency than choice. But, notwithstanding this, my faith is as orthodox as that of my neighbours. We all believe in God as our Creator, and in Christ as our Redeemer, except some few persons, who glory in trampling all revelation under foot. For my own part, I have never erred, from the faith since I first became acquainted with the apostles' creed: and that was so early in life, that I cannot now recollect who first instructed me in it.

B. It seems, then, neighbour, that you imbibed your faith as you drew in your nurse's milk: and you have learned to believe in Christ, rather than in Mohammed, because you happened to be taught the English rather than the Turkish language.

N. That may be. However, if I had been a Mohammed, I trust I might also have been an honest man. I give to every one his due. This is the grand principle upon which I have always acted, and from this I leave every rational man to form a judgment of my faith.

B. Ah, sir! if such are the principles by which your conduct is regulated, then make a full surrender of your heart to God, and consecrate to his service those powers of body and soul which you have received from his bounty, and to which he has so just a title. But, alas! without piety, your strict justice is like the fidelity of a subject, who fulfils his engagements with a few particular persons, while he withholds the homage due to his rightful sovereign. If such a subject can be termed faithful, then may you, with propriety, be accounted just, while you offer not to God that tribute of love, gratitude, adoration, and obedience, which is your reasonable service. You made a confession but now, that you piqued not yourself upon your piety: it would not have astonished me more had you said, that you piqued not yourself upon paying your debts, and acting with common honesty in the world. Alas, sir, your boasted principles do but confirm the fears to which your conduct had given rise. I entreat you, in the most solemn manner, "to examine yourself, whether you be in the faith."

N. What do you call *faith?*

B. The Scriptures teach us, that we must believe with the heart, and that "faith is the substance of things hoped for, and the evidence of things not seen," Hebrews xi:1. He, therefore, who truly believes in the Father, the Son, and the Holy Ghost, carries within him a lively demonstration of the Almighty's presence, which penetrates him with sentiments of fear, respect, and love, for a Being so powerful, just, and good: he possesses an internal evidence of the affection of that Redeemer upon whom alone he grounds his hope of salvation, saluting him, with Nathanael, as "the Son of God, the King of Israel," John i:49: and he discovers in his own heart the most indisputable testimonies of the sanctifying and consoling operations of the Holy Spirit. Now, from this threefold demonstration he is enabled to say, with suitable sentiments of gratitude and devotion, "Behold what manner of love the Father hath bestowed upon us, that we should be called the sons of God," 1 John iii:1. "He hath made us accepted in the Beloved, in whom we have redemption through his blood, the forgiveness of sins," Ephesians i:6, 7; and "the Spirit itself beareth witness with our spirit, that we are the children of God," Romans viii:16. Tell me, then, since you boast of having received the Christian faith, have you ever experienced those salutary effects of faith, which I have now described!

N. If that demonstration, and that lively representation of which you speak, are essential to Christian faith, I must confess that to such a faith I am a perfect stranger.

But the writings of St. Paul, whose definition of faith you have just cited, are generally looked upon as remarkably dark and mysterious; I wish you had rather quoted St. John.

B. I doubt, sir, whether you will gain any thing by such an appeal. "Whosoever believeth that Jesus is the Christ," saith St. John, "is born of God. This is the victory that overcometh the world, even our faith. Who is he that overcometh the world, but he that believeth that Jesus is the Son of God?" 1 John v:1-5. You perceive, sir, that, according to this apostle, faith is a principle of grace and power sufficiently forcible and victorious to regenerate and make us partakers of the Divine nature, enabling us to triumph equally over the most seducing, as well as the most afflicting occurrences in the world. Have you obtained, or have you even sought the faith of which such excellent things are spoken.

N. You embarrass me. I never heard the least intimation of such a faith in this country.

B. Indeed, sir, you are in an error, since this very faith is plainly set forth in the sixteenth chapter of the Helvetic Confession. "The Christian faith," say the pious ministers who composed that work, "is not a mere human opinion or persuasion, but a state of full assurance: it not only gives a constant and clear assent to, but also comprehends and embraces the truths of God, as proposed to us in the apostles' creed. The soul, by this act, unites itself to God, as to its only, eternal, and sovereign good, and to Jesus Christ as the centre of all the promises." Have you, then, this Divine persuasion, this full assurance of the truths of our holy religion? And have you experienced this act, by which the soul is united to God, through Christ, as to its sovereign good?

N. I have, undoubtedly, a persuasion that the word of God is true. But how may I absolutely determine, whether or no I am a possessor of the faith of which you speak?

B. If you are possessed of faith, you have some experimental knowledge of those happy effects of that grace, which are thus enumerated in the same confession: "True faith restores peace to the conscience. It procures a free access to God, enabling us both to approach him with confidence, and to obtain from him the things which we need. It retains us in the path of obedience, enduing us with power to fulfil our several duties both to God and our neighbour. It maintains our patience in adversity, and disposes us, at all times, to a sincere confession of our confidence. To sum up all in a single word, it produces every good work." "Let it be observed," says the same confession, "that we do not here speak of a pretended faith, which is vain, ineffectual, and dead, but of a living, effectual, and vivifying faith. This is a doctrine which St. James cannot be understood to combat, seeing he speaks of a vain and presumptuous confidence, of which some were known to boast, while they had not Christ living in them by means of faith."

N. "Christ living in them by means of faith!" I pray, sir, what is to be understood by this expression? I do not comprehend the thing. But, if I recollect, I shall have an opportunity, in a few hours, of mentioning the matter to our pastor, whom I expect here this evening to make up a party at cards. The true believer, after thanking his worldly neighbour for the patience with which he had listened to his conversation, took his leave and withdrew, apprehending every evil consequence from the decision of a pastor who was known to indulge a taste for play and vain amusement. His fears were too well founded. The minister, true to his engagement, arrived at the appointed hour, and the gentleman thus eagerly addressed him: "I have been receiving some singular advice from a person of a very unaccountable turn, who appears to agree either with the Mystics or the Pietists. He spoke much of faith, asserting that all true Christians are really regenerate, and that they have Christ living in them by faith. What think you, sir, of such assertions as these?" "I will tell you freely," replied the minister, "that these abstruse points of doctrine are among those profound mysteries, which neither you nor I are appointed to fathom. It is usual with enthusiasts to speak in this manner: but such mystic jargon is now out of season. There have been ages in which divines were accustomed to speculate concerning this faith, and publicly to insist upon it in their sermons. But, in an age like this, enlightened by sound philosophy and learned discoveries, we no longer admit what we cannot comprehend. I advise you, as a friend, to leave these idle subtilties close shut up in the unintelligible volumes of our ancient theologists. The only material thing is to conduct ourselves as honest men. If we receive revelation in a general sense, and have good works to produce, there can be no doubt but that our faith is of a proper kind, and highly acceptable before God." To this short discourse the card table succeeded, which served to strengthen the bands of intimacy between our careless clergyman and his deluded neighbour: so perfectly alike were their faith and their manners.

The circumstances alluded to in the above relation are not imaginary; and there is every reason to fear, that circumstances of the same nature are no less common in other Christian countries, than in that which gave birth to the writer of these pages.

Thus the worldly minister, instead of preaching this important doctrine in its purity, seeks to destroy even the curiosity which would engage an irreligious man to inquire into the necessity, the nature, the origin, and the effects of evangelical faith. And while the generality of those who are required to publish this victorious grace are seen to reject it with contempt, no wonder that the true minister esteems himself obliged to contend for it, with increasing earnestness, both in public and private, Jude i:3.

To close this section. When the Christian minister proclaims salvation by faith, he adheres, not only to the Holy Scriptures, but also to those public confessions of faith, which are in common use among the Churches of Christ. "We believe," say the Churches of France, "that every thing necessary to our salvation was revealed and offered to us in Christ, who is made unto us wisdom, righteousness, sanctification, and redemption," Art. 13. "We believe that we are made partakers of righteousness by faith alone; since it is said, that he [Christ] suffered in order to procure salvation for us, and that whosoever believeth in him shall not perish," Art. 20. "We believe that, by this faith, we are regenerated to newness of life, being by nature in bondage to sin. So that faith, instead of cooling in us the desire of living righteously and godly, naturally tends to excite such desire, and necessarily produces every good work," Art. 22.

Such also is the doctrine of the Helvetic Confession: "We believe, with St. Paul, that sinful man is justified by faith alone in Jesus Christ, and not by the law. Faith receives Jesus, who is our righteousness; and on this account justification is attributed to faith. That by means of faith we receive Jesus Christ, he himself has taught us in the Gospel, where he significantly uses the terms applied to eating for believing: for, as by eating we receive bodily nourishment, so by believing we are made partakers of

Christ," chap. 15. "Man is not regenerated by faith, that he should continue in a state of indolence, but rather that he should apply himself, without ceasing, to the performance of those things which are useful and good: since the Lord hath said, 'Every good tree bringeth forth good fruit,' Matthew vii:19: 'he that abideth in me, and I in him, the same bringeth forth much fruit,' John xv:6."

The Church of England expresses herself in the following terms upon salvation by faith, and the good works produced by that faith:—"We are accounted righteous before God only for the merit of our Lord and Saviour Jesus Christ, by faith, and not for our own works and deservings. Wherefore, that we are justified by faith only is a most wholesome doctrine, and very full of comfort," Art. 11. "Good works do spring out necessarily of a true and lively faith, insomuch that by them a lively faith may be as evidently known, as a tree discerned by the fruit," Art xii.

The true minster goes on to announce a lively hope.

"GODLINESS with contentment is great gain," 1 Timothy vi:6. And the pastor, who is possessed of so invaluable a blessing, cannot be backward in soliciting all, within the circle of his acquaintance, to share it with him. Happy in the enjoyment of that precious secret, which enables him to rejoice without ceasing, he readily communicates it to the afflicted, by leading them to that lively hope which consoles and sustains the heart of every believer.

In a word, where the bitterness of evil is continually increasing; where we discover the scourges of a God, who will not fail to chastise his rebellious creatures; where disappointment and death successively deprive us of our dearest comforts, and where the forerunners of death are continually weakening all our imperfect enjoyments; in such a world, it is evident, that the most exalted pleasure we are capable of, must spring from a wellgrounded hope of those immortal joys which are reserved for the righteous. The language of mortality is too feeble to describe either the power or the sweetness of such a hope. Here we can only cry out with the psalmist, "O taste, and see how gracious the Lord is," Psalm xxxiv:8, in providing so potent a cordial for those who are travelling through a vale of tears.

The lively hope which gives birth to a believer's felicity, is one of the most exhilarating fruits of his faith, and is inseparably connected with it, since "true faith is the substance of things hoped for." In proportion as the truths and promises, upon which faith is founded, are evidenced and apprehended, such will be the hope with which that faith is accompanied. If Moses then, by the faith which he professed, was enabled to renounce the prospect of an earthly crown, with the hope of obtaining a more glorious inheritance; if he esteemed "the reproach of Christ greater riches than the treasures of Egypt, having respect unto the recompense of reward," Hebrews xi:26; what may not be expected from a hope founded upon those precious promises, which have been sealed with the blood of that condescending Saviour, who "brought life and immortality to light through the Gospel?" 2 Timothy i:10. "The law," saith the apostle, "made nothing perfect, but the bringing in of a better hope did; by the which we draw nigh unto God," Hebrews vii:19. "Seeing then that we have such hope," continues the same apostle, "we all, with open face, beholding as in a glass the glory of the Lord, are changed into the same image, from glory to glory," 2 Corinthians iii:12, 18.

We every day observe the men of the world exulting in the hope of some temporal advantage. The prospect of an honourable title, an augmentation of fortune, an advantageous marriage, or even a poor party of pleasure, is sufficient to allure, to animate, to enrapture them. They will even acknowledge, that the flattering hope of future pleasure is sweeter than enjoyment itself. Who then shall attempt to declare those transports, which flow from the lively hope of a triumphing Christian? A hope which is founded upon the Rock of ages, and which has, for its multifarious object, riches, honours, and pleasures, as much superior to those of worldly men, as the soul is superior to the body, heaven to earth, and eternity to the present fleeting moment.

The true minister publicly announces this hope to the world, persuaded that, if mankind were once happy enough to possess it, they would exchange a load of misery for a prospect of blessedness. But since he knows that this hope can never be admitted into hearts replete with sin, his first concern is to overthrow the vain confidence of the impenitent, to undermine the presumption of the Pharisaical, and to point out the true distinction between a sinner's groundless expectation, and the wellfounded hope of a believer in Christ.

In every place there are many to be found, who, without "evangelical faith or hope," are filled with a presumption as blind as that of the Pharisees, and as fatal as that of heathens hardened in their sin. To every such person, the true minister uniformly declares that he is "without Christ, without hope, and without God in the world," Ephesians ii:12. These very men, it is probable, may offer to the Deity a formal worship, and indulge high expectations from the mercy of a Divine Mediator, though they are totally destitute of an unfeigned "repentance toward God, and a true faith toward our Lord Jesus Christ," Acts xx:21. Thus far the unconverted may proceed in a seemingly religious course. But the regenerate alone can truly say, "The grace of God that bringeth salvation hath appeared unto all men, teaching us, that denying ungodliness and worldly lusts, we should live soberly, righteously, and godly, in this present world: looking for that blessed hope, and the glorious appearing of the great God, and our Saviour Jesus Christ," Titus ii:11-13.

The hope of unrighteous men is founded upon pride, false notions of the Deity, ignorance of his law, and upon those prejudices, which the irreligious communicate one to another. On the contrary, the hope of believers has, for its basis, the word of Him "who cannot lie," Titus i:2. "Whatsoever things were written aforetime," saith the apostle, "were written for our learning, that we [the children of God] through patience and comfort of the Scriptures might have hope," Romans xv:4. It is founded not only upon the word, but equally upon the oath of God.

Men verily swear by the greater; and an oath for confirmation is to them an end of all strife. Wherein God, willing more abundantly to show unto the heirs of the promise the immutability of his counsel, confirmed it by an oath: that by two immutable things, in which it was impossible for God to lie, [namely, his word and his oath,] we might have strong consolation, who have fled for refuge to lay hold upon the hope set before us: which hope we have as an anchor of the soul, both sure and steadfast," Hebrews vi:16-19.

The Portrait of St. Paul

When the faithful minister has rooted up every false hope, he then announces Jesus Christ, who hath brought in a better hope than that of heathens or Jews. Observe here the reason why those pastors who preach not Christ are incapable of doing any thing toward the furtherance of that living faith, of which Christ is the grand object, and that lively hope, of which he is the inexhaustible source. "Jesus Christ," saith St. Paul, "is our hope," 1 Timothy i:1: and we declare unto you "the mystery, which hath been hid from ages," and is still hidden from worldly men, "which is Christ in you, the hope of glory." Thus the everlasting Son of the Father is made to his true followers the beginning and the consummation of hope, as well as "the author and finisher of faith," Hebrews xii:2.

By the mercy of God, and through the redemption that is in Jesus Christ, the believer has already received the promise of a free pardon for past offences; otherwise he deserves not to be termed a believer: at least, he is destitute of evangelical faith. Now, when the believer sincerely receives the glad tidings of redeeming grace, he then assuredly receives Jesus Christ, in whom "all the promises are yea and Amen," 2 Corinthians i:20; and he would conduct himself in a manner contrary to that which both reason and Scripture prescribe, if he should refuse to rejoice in God his Saviour. By such a mode of acting, he would prove his want of gratitude for that which Christ hath already done, and of hope for that which he hath promised still to perform. But when he gives himself up to a joy, as reasonable as it is refreshing, he then answers the gracious designs of his benevolent Lord. Continually taken up with more satisfactory enjoyments, he despises the seducing pleasures of sin. He carries in his own bosom a source of celestial pleasure, while the man of the world disquiets his heart in the vain pursuit of earthly joys. The difference between the enjoyments of these two characters is as great as between the rational pleasures of those who gather their wheat into the barn, and the puerile mirth of children, who are busied in collecting the scattered straws and thorns; the former are securing an inestimable treasure, while the latter have nothing more in view, than to dance round a short-lived blaze, the truest emblem of a sinner's satisfaction.

In the Holy Scriptures very excellent things are spoken of the hope which produces this sacred joy. (1.) It is a Divine hope, since it has for its object the enjoyment of God, and because it draws supplies of strength from that Holy Spirit which discovers to believers the greatness and stability of Gospel promises. Thus St. Paul teacheth us that "the Father of glory *giveth us* the Spirit of wisdom and revelation: enlightening the eyes of our understanding, that we may know what is the HOPE of our calling, and what the riches of the glory of his inheritance among the saints," Ephesians i:17, 18.

2. It gives honour to the faithfulness and power of God. Abraham, saith St. Paul, against all human probability, believing "in HOPE, staggered not at the promise; but was strong in faith, giving glory to God; being fully persuaded, that what he had promised he was able also to perform," Romans iv:18-21. "Therefore, being justified," like Abraham, "by faith, we rejoice," continues the apostle, with a confidence like his, "in hope of the glory of God. And this hope maketh not ashamed," Romans v:1-5. How unlike the fallacious hope of worldly men, who are frequently put to shame by their blasted expectations!

3. This hope is said to fill us with a holy joy. "Blessed be the God and Father of our Lord Jesus Christ," saith St. Peter, "who hath begotten us again to a lively hope,

by the resurrection of Jesus Christ from the dead. Wherein ye greatly rejoice," 1 Peter i:3, 6. And on this account it was, that the Apostle Paul prayed with so much ardour for an increase of hope among believers. "Now the God of hope fill you with all joy and peace in believing, that ye may abound in hope through the power of the Holy Ghost," Romans xv:13.

4. It actually saves us, as St. Paul himself declares in the following words: "I reckon that the sufferings of the present time are not worthy to be compared with the glory which shall be revealed in us. And," supported by this sweet persuasion, "we wait for the adoption, to wit, the redemption of our body. For," in this respect, "we are saved by hope," Romans viii:18, 24.

5. It is equally sweet and solid; since it rests upon the right which the children of God may claim to the inheritance of their heavenly Father; a sacred right, which is confirmed to them with the utmost solemnity in the New Testament. Now every man who receives, with sincerity, the Lord of life and glory, receives with him a title to everlasting possessions, and ranks, from that moment, among "the sons of God," John i:12. So that to such the following passages may, with propriety, be applied: "He hath made us accepted in the Beloved—in whom ye also trusted, after that ye heard the word of truth, the Gospel of your salvation: in whom also, after that ye believed, ye were sealed with that Holy Spirit of promise, which is the earnest of our inheritance, until the redemption of the purchased possession," Ephesians i:6, 12, 14.

6. It purifies us. "Now are we," saith St. John, "the sons of God, and it doth not yet appear what we shall be; but we know, that when he shall appear, we shall be like him; for we shall see him as he is. And every man that hath this hope in him purifieth himself, even as he is pure. Whosoever is born of God [or regenerated by a true faith and a lively hope] doth not commit sin; for his seed remaineth in him; and he cannot sin, because he is born of God," 1 John iii:2, 3, 9. The truth of this assertion is clear to the eye of reason. We fall into sin, because we suffer ourselves to be seduced by the allurements of some transitory good, which presents itself either to our senses or imagination. But when we are once persuaded that infinite enjoyments await us, we can then look with contempt upon those deceitful appearances; and after our hearts are animated with a confident hope of possessing those invisible realities, the charm of sin is broken. In such a state, we break through temptations with as much resolution as a prince who is going to take possession of a kingdom, renounces the little amusements that occupied his thoughts before they were engrossed by a concern of so vast importance. "Who is he that overcometh the world," but the man who believes with that faith which affords him a lively representation of things hoped for? Compare 1 John v:5, with Hebrews xi:1.

7. This lively hope produces charity in the soul. "We give thanks to God," saith the apostle, "praying always for you, since we heard of the love which ye have to all the saints; for the HOPE which is laid up for you in heaven, whereof ye heard before in the word of the truth of the Gospel," Colossians i:3-5. Nay, of so prevailing an influence is this solid hope, that the apostle intimates, in the same chapter, that believers shall be presented before God, holy and unblamable, provided they be not "moved away from the HOPE of the Gospel," Verses 22, 23. "For," continues he, "we are made partakers of Christ, if we hold the beginning of our confidence steadfast unto the end," Hebrews iii:14. "And we desire that every one of you do show the same diligence to the full assurance of hope unto the end: that ye be not

slothful, but followers of them who through faith and patience inherit the promises," Hebrews vi:11, 12.

8. This hope is full of consolation. "We who remain," saith the apostle, "shall be caught up to meet the Lord in the air, and so shall we ever be with the Lord. Wherefore comfort one another with these words," 1 Thessalonians v:17, 18. "Now our Lord Jesus Christ himself, and God, even our Father, which hath loved us, and hath given us everlasting consolation and good hope through grace, comfort your hearts," 2 Thessalonians ii:16, 17. When we observe among us some who are disquieted and cast down, who want courage to support affliction without impatience, and to fill up their duties with cheerfulness, we then behold persons who never enjoyed, or who have unhappily lost, the lively hope of true Christians. If all ministers of the Gospel had experienced the sweetness and power of this hope, with what pleasure would they publish it to the afflicted! And with what perseverance would they join to their discourses the most ardent prayers, that all their hearers might come to the enjoyment of so invaluable a blessing!

When the true minister leads his flock to this lively and joyful hope, he treads in the footsteps of his Divine Master. Christ, it is true, began his ministry by preaching repentance, Matthew iv:17. But immediately after we find him placing before the believer's eye beatitudes and promises of the most consolatory nature, verse 1, &c. In a vast variety of affecting passages, he exhorts his followers to the exercise of a joyful hope in the severest trials, making that an indispensable duty, which is indeed a glorious privilege. "Fear not them," saith he, "which are not able to kill the soul. Whosoever shall confess me before men, him will I confess also before my Father which is in heaven," Matthew x:28, 32. "Fear not, little flock; for it is your Father's good pleasure to give you the kingdom," Luke xii:31. "I give unto my sheep eternal life, and they shall never perish, neither shall any pluck them out of my hands," John x:27, 28.

He appears anxious that his people should be partakers of his peace, his joy, and his hope, till they come to the possession of consummate blessedness. "These things have I spoken," saith he, "that in me ye might have peace. In the world ye shall have tribulation; but be of good cheer: I have overcome the world," John xvi:33. "Let not your heart be troubled. I go to prepare a place for you. And if I go to prepare a place for you, I will come again and receive you unto myself, that where I am there may ye be also," 14:1-8. "Ye now have sorrow: but I will see you again, and your heart shall rejoice, and your joy no man taketh from you," John xvi:22. He exhorts them continually to expect his return, Luke xii:40, and even condescends to mention the very terms in which he will, at that time, salute every waiting believer.

The prayers of Christ, as well as his exhortations and promises, tend to produce and support the most exalted hope in the souls of believers. He has graciously interceded for them; he still continues to make intercession, and his prayer is always prevalent. Mark a few sentences of that memorable prayer, which he once offered up for all his followers, and which forms the seventeenth chapter of St. John's Gospel. "O Father! I pray not for the world, but for them which thou hast given me. Holy Father! keep, through thine own name, those whom thou hast given me, and sanctify them through thy truth. Neither pray I for these alone, but for them also which shall believe on me through their word; that they may all be one, even as we are one.

Father! I will that they whom thou hast given me be with me where I am, that they may behold my glory."

A lively hope, founded upon these prayers and declarations of the blessed Jesus, enabled the primitive Christians to triumph over every affliction. In the midst of the most terrible persecutions they could congratulate one another on their common blessedness, and say, "Our life is hid with Christ in God. And when Christ, who is our life, shall appear, then shall we also appear with him in glory," Colossians iii:4. For "he shall yet come to be glorified in his saints, and to be admired in all them that believe," 2 Thessalonians i:10.

The apostles, agreeable to the example of their Master, were unanimous in publishing this glorious hope; and St. Paul very frequently insists upon it, as a most important duty. "Let us," saith he, "who are of the day, be sober, putting on the breastplate of faith and love, and for a helmet the hope of salvation," 1 Thessalonians v:8. "I beseech you, brethren, present your bodies a living sacrifice unto God— rejoicing in hope," Romans xii:1, 12. "Rejoice in the Lord alway, and again I say, rejoice," Philippians iv:4. This evangelical hope will ever be experienced, as a never failing source of consolation and thankfulness; and hence, wherever the hope of the Gospel is preached, there believers continue to be filled with unspeakable joy, Acts xiii:52. How truly happy would Christians be were such a hope to flourish among them! Far from disputing any longer for the trifles of time and sense, they would joyfully renounce them all, in expectation of an eternal inheritance; and instead of running to the frivolous amusements of the world for a momentary recreation, every passing day would appear too short for the exhilarating duties of praise and thanksgiving.

It is asserted by many, that this Divine hope is usually insisted upon by every minister. That preachers in general are accustomed to exhort their hearers, in a cold and languid manner, to hope in the Divine mercy, will readily be granted. But that such do not publish the real, evangelical hope of Christians, may be easily proved beyond the possibility of a doubt. We have seen, in the preceding sections, that the minister of the present day is unacquainted with this hope; that he is even without any just ideas of that true repentance, and that living faith, from which alone this hope can flow. And hence it is impossible for him, in the nature of things, to publish it in the Church of God. In vain has Christ himself declared that the broad way will conduct multitudes to destruction, and that "except a man be born again, he cannot enter into the kingdom of God," John iii:5. In spite of these solemn declarations, the worldly pastor still imagines that this very way will conduct him to life, and that he shall be counted among the inhabitants of that kingdom without Scriptural regeneration. He supposes, at least, that he is sufficiently sanctified, though his righteousness exceeds not that of the Pharisees, nor his devotion that of the Laodicean Church. Thus, entertaining a vain hope in his own heart, and indulging a confidence which is repugnant to the concurrent testimonies of every sacred writer, he necessarily leads his hearers into the same dangerous delusions.

As in order solidly to found our hopes upon a benefactor, or a surety, it is necessary to have an acquaintance with the person who presents himself in either of these characters, so the lively hope of which we speak must flow from an experimental knowledge of God, by Jesus Christ. "This is eternal life, that they may know thee, the only true God, and Jesus Christ, whom thou hast sent," John xvii:3.

But the children of this world, whether they be laymen or ecclesiastics, are destitute of this knowledge. They know neither the Father nor the Son; and were it otherwise, the love of the world would not have dominion over them.

This lively hope can never dwell in an unregenerate heart. The child that is not born cannot possibly rejoice in hope of possessing the heritage of his father; since he is equally unacquainted with his parent, and the patrimony that is likely to be reserved for him. It is, therefore, absolutely necessary to be born of God, before we can exercise this exhilarating hope. Now a man is thus born when he is regenerated by that spirit of adoption, which God hath promised to those who sincerely believe in Jesus Christ. But they who are conformable to the maxims of the world are not able to receive this vivifying spirit. "I will pray the Father," said Christ to his disciples, "and he shall give you another Comforter, that he may abide with you for ever, even the Spirit of truth, whom the world cannot receive, because it seeth him not, neither knoweth him; but [being already regenerated in part] ye know him; for he dwelleth with you, and shall be in you," when you are fully born of the Spirit, John xiv:16, 17. It is not till after the accomplishment of this promise has been experienced, that the following expressions can be fully understood: "Know ye not that your body is the temple of the Holy Ghost?" 1 Corinthians vi:19. "Now the God of hope fill you with all joy and peace in believing, that ye may abound in hope, through the power of the Holy Ghost," Romans xv:13.

Far from preaching this primitive hope, the worldly minister is alarmed at the bare mention of it. Let it here be observed again, that this celestial plant can flourish only in those hearts where the word of God, sharper than any two-edged sword, has cut down every unfruitful appearance of Pharisaical hope. Now when a true minister is engaged in performing this preparatory work, cutting away the mortified members of the old man, and plucking from pride its unprofitable supports, the inexperienced minister preposterously takes offence at his holy zeal, and censures this necessary severity, as leading souls into the horrors of despair. Slow of understanding in spiritual concerns, he comprehends not that they who recline upon a broken reed must give up all the confidence they foolishly place in so slender a prop, before they can effectually choose the Rock of ages for their support.

The true character of these false apostles is not generally known. Covering their impiety with the cloak of religion, they are supposed by many to act on the part of Christ, and are frequently esteemed as pillars in the Church. But there are occasions on which they unwittingly throw off the mask, and make an open discovery of their secret thoughts. Some few persons are found in the world, who, refusing to attend card assemblies, rejoice to be present in those less polite assemblies which are formed for the purpose of prayer. Here it is usual for consenting neighbours to take sweet counsel together, and wrestle with ardour for the hope of the Gospel, in words like these: "Gracious Father! forgive the sins of thy returning children, and grant us an increase of spiritual strength. Sensible of our own unworthiness, assist us to place all our confidence in thy unbounded mercy, manifested through Jesus Christ. Increase our faith in the Son of thy love, and confirm our hope in thine unchangeable promises. O thou Divine Saviour! descend this day into our hearts, as thou didst once descend upon thy first disciples. Consecrate us thy living temples, fill us with thy graces, and, during the time of our earthly pilgrimage, vouchsafe to lead us with the right hand of thy power. Let not thy Spirit of illumination and holiness, thy Spirit of consolation and joy, abandon us for a moment, as we pass through this valley of tears. May its potent operations subdue in us the power of sin, and produce in our outward conversation the happy fruits of righteousness, peace, and joy. Permit us, at this time, to return to our houses with a consciousness of thy love, and an assurance of thy favour; and grant that, after having been the temples of thy Spirit upon earth, we may one day be received into the temple of thine eternal glory in the heavens."

A worldly minister, on a certain time, entering into an assembly of this kind, heard the prayer of these humble believers; and, as much surprised to see the ardour with which they offered their petitions, as to observe the time and place in which they were presented, withdrew from their society, with as much indignation as a good pastor would retire from a company of jugglers. But having understood that one of his own parishioners was of the religious party, he took the earliest opportunity of testifying the utmost disapprobation of his conduct. "What was it," said he, "that you was doing with those people the other day, in such a place? Conventicles of that kind are contrary to order, and unworthy of toleration. The church is the only proper place for the performance of Divine worship. Moreover, I heard you foolishly praying for I know not what consolation, light, and power, of the Holy Spirit. Receive in good part the advice I offer you. Look upon inspirations and illuminations of this sort as no other than the idle fancies of visionaries and enthusiasts. Renounce the imaginary assurance, with which you do but deceive yourself, and repose upon the hope which I have constantly preached to you; a hope with which you, and your neighbours, may very well rest contented." Confounded with a discourse of this kind, a weak and inexperienced Christian might have been drawn aside from the narrow path of truth. But the person here alluded to, by citing Ephesians i:17, 18, was enabled to prove that the very same illumination and power which were treated so contemptuously by his opponent, were nevertheless absolutely necessary, as the groundwork of a solid hope. Nay, he pushed the matter still farther; and asserted, that the prayer against which the zealous pastor had so angrily exclaimed, was used in exact conformity to those very petitions which he himself was incessantly heard to offer at the feast of pentecost, and at other solemn seasons.

If this little relation faithfully describes the manner of thinking which is too common among the clergy of the day, is it not evident that they are more disposed to ridicule than to preach the Christian hope: and abundantly more earnest to obstruct, than to farther their parishioners in the pursuit of everlasting blessedness?

When the dawn of this glorious hope first began to glimmer; when, at the descent of the Mount of Olives, the whole company of disciples began to praise God with a loud voice, strewing the way by which their Lord was to pass with garments and branches of trees, and crying out before him, "Hosanna to the Son of David: blessed is he that cometh in the name of the Lord: hosanna in the highest!" Some of the Pharisees, who had mixed among the multitude, rudely exclaimed, "Master, rebuke thy disciples." And when he had entered into the temple, "the chief priests and scribes [those models by which the generality of ministers seem anxious to form themselves] seeing the wonderful things that he did, and the children crying Hosanna, were sore displeased, and said unto him, Hearest thou what these say?" And Jesus answered them, "Yea; have ye never read, Out of the mouths of babes and sucklings thou hast perfected praise? I tell you, that if these should hold their peace, the stones would immediately cry out," Matthew xxi; Luke xix. There still exists the same opposition between those who cordially embrace the Gospel, and those who ungratefully reject it. As often as the former are perceived to give a loose to the transports of their gratitude, rejoicing in hope of the glory of God, the worldly minister, displeased to observe any thing that appears to reproach his own lukewarmness, is prepared to stifle the motions of that joyful hope, which he deems no better than the confidence of presumptuous fanatics. While the faithful minister, who imitates St. Paul, on observing such a scene, will cry out with that great apostle, "Now the God of hope fill you with all joy and peace in believing, that ye may abound in hope through the power of the Holy Ghost," Romans xv:13.

If penitents are not pointed to the blessedness of this hope, they will strive, like Cain, to stifle their remorse by passionately abandoning themselves to the business and enjoyments of the present world: or, like the Israelites, who found not sufficient pleasure in religion to banish the recollection of Egypt's vanities, they will indulge that spirit of trifling which the apostle thus describes: "The people sat down to eat and drink, and rose up to play," 1 Corinthians x:7. On the contrary, when the Christian is directed to the hope of his high calling, he finds it a source of unutterable consolation, and having discovered the treasure hidden in the Gospel field, "for joy thereof he selleth his all," in order to purchase that field. He now renounces, without pain, what before had hindered him in running the heavenly race, counting nothing dear to himself, that he may finish his course with joy, and insure the crown of everlasting life. So powerfully were the first Christians supported by this Gospel hope, that they remained immovable amidst the sorest calamities of life, and suffered death itself with a courage that astonished the persecutors. But when they lost their confidence, like Demas, they began to indulge the fond hopes and foolish fears of the present world, becoming altogether weak, as other men. And such are the generality of Christians at this day. The love of many is waxing cold, while the Church of God is evidently falling into ruins. And how shall we assist to rekindle that love, or to repair that Church, but by zealously proclaiming abroad the "hope of the Gospel?"

The true minister preaches Christian charity.

IF the evangelical pastor proclaims repentance, faith, and hope, it is with a view of leading sinners to that Christian charity which is justly esteemed the crown of every grace. In preaching repentance, he lays the axe to the root of every corrupt tree. In publishing evangelical faith, he plants the tree of life. When he proclaims the hope of the Gospel, he causes that tree to put forth a beautiful blossom. But when he preaches Christian charity, he calls forth the rich fruit from every vigorous branch. And while he is engaged in performing the various parts of this important work, he denounces the anathemas of the Gospel against that repentance, faith, and hope, which are superficial, unfruitful, and delusive.

The minister of the day piques himself upon preaching morality, which he is ordinarily accustomed to do in the manner of a heathen philosopher. Unacquainted with the importance and power of the doctrines of Christianity, he is ashamed to walk in the traces of St. Paul. If he is enabled to paint, with any degree of ability, the serpents of envy, the inquietudes of avarice, and the delights of charity, he imagines that he shall readily dispose his neighbours to love as brethren. He knows not that "the law of the Spirit of life in Christ Jesus" is that alone which can make any man "free from the law of sin and death," by delivering him from that envy, that avarice, that ambition, that indifference, trod those worldly fears which are incompatible with evangelical charity. "What the law could not do in that it was weak through the flesh," i.e. our degenerate nature, which has need of stronger motives and more powerful supports than those which the law proposes, "God sending his own Son in the likeness of sinful flesh, and for sin, condemned sin in the flesh:" that by the new motives, and the Divine assistance offered in the Gospel, "the righteousness of the law might be fulfilled in us," who, being regenerate, "walk not after the flesh, but after the Spirit," Romans viii:4.

The judicious pastor, observing the same connection between the morals and doctrines of Christianity, as between the root and fruit of a vigorous tree, is constrained incessantly to preach those important truths, which naturally give rise to the three first-mentioned graces: and he is perfectly assured, that wherever these truths are permitted to take root, he shall shortly rejoice over the inestimable fruits of Christian charity. This mode of acting is equally conformable to reason and revelation. By publishing those doctrines upon which the necessity of repentance is founded, he exterminates pride and inordinate self love, which are the greatest obstacles to charity. By preaching the doctrines of faith, he gives rise to that universal love which extends to God and man. Thus when a sinner sincerely believes that "God is love," 1 John iv:16; when, penetrated with admiration and gratitude, he can say with the apostle, "I live by the faith of the Son of God, who loved me and gave himself for me," Galatians ii:20: at that moment he necessarily feels a degree of affection toward the creating Father, and the redeeming Son, whom he longs to imitate, and whom he rejoices to obey. This love is as boundless as it is ardent, and reaches to the most unworthy of his fellow creatures, enabling him, after the example of Christ, to sacrifice for his very enemies, not only outward comforts, but even life itself. Hence the Christian faith is said to work by love. Now if this lively persuasion of the unspeakable blessings which God hath already given us in Christ Jesus, is sufficient to produce in the soul a high degree of Scriptural charity, it is evident that a wellgrounded hope of greater blessings still to come, must necessarily serve to quicken and increase this charity. And if we are fully persuaded that our labours of love shall never be forgotten; that even a cup of cold water, imparted for the love of Christ, shall not go unrewarded; how vast an influence may such a hope be expected to exert in opening the heart to universal benevolence, and in producing all the fruits of evangelical love!

Convinced that to plead for charity, without insisting upon the doctrines by which it must be supported, would be building a house without laying a solid foundation, the true minister industriously labours to explain the nature, to exhibit the motives, and represent the effects of this wondrous grace, in the clearest manner. To some, indeed, such discourses are vain; but others among his hearers are found, who, ravished with the loveliness of this virtue, and constrained by those motives which the Gospel proposes, betake themselves to the exercise of it, with as much ardour as the voluptuous run to their sensual entertainments.

Darkness differs not more from light, than the charity of the faithful minister differs from that of a scribe ill instructed in the mysteries of the kingdom. The love of the good pastor "rejoiceth not in iniquity, but rejoiceth in the truth," 1 Corinthians xiii:6, which frequently comes to humble human pride. On the contrary, the charity which every false apostle preaches is no more than the phantom of a virtue, consoling the heart in the midst of sin, rejoicing in a lie, and resting upon assurance altogether contrary to the word of God. To be charitable is, according to the notions of these men, to indulge a persuasion that there is much to be abated of the threatenings contained in the Gospel, and that St. Paul is far beside the truth when he declares, that "no unclean or covetous person hath any inheritance in the kingdom of Christ," Ephesians v:5. It is to believe that the Holy Spirit was too severe, when it dictated to St. James, that "he who is a friend of the world is the enemy of God," and violates his baptismal vow in as full a sense as adulterers violate the sacred vow of conjugal fidelity, James iv:4. It is to insinuate that Christ himself overpassed the bounds of reason when he publicly cried out, "Whosoever shall say to his brother, Thou fool, shall be in danger of hell fire," Matthew v:22. "Judge not," saith the Redeemer, "that ye be not judged," Matthew vii:1. But, according to the sentiments of those erring guides, to be Divinely charitable, is to conclude from this precept that a man may even revoke the judgments of Christ himself; thus, under pretext of not judging those who are evidently walking in the road to perdition, they indirectly give judgment against the Redeemer, as bearing a false testimony. In errors like these it is that the world will needs have the greatest part of charity to consist.

The true minister attacks this false grace as an enemy to the truth of the Gospel, while he pleads for that Christlike charity which may properly be called the sister of truth. He asserts the dignity and power of truth; holding it up to the veneration and love of those who would not wilfully offend the God of truth. Let us, continues he, "speaking the truth in love, grow up into him in all things, which is the head, even Christ," Ephesians iv:15; and having first "purified our souls in obeying the truth," let us "love one another with a pure heart fervently," 1 Peter i:22. Between these Scriptural companions he will suffer no separation to take place; and when they are treated by the injudicious as enthusiastic and heretical, he will dare to stand forth in defence of these two confederate virtues.

Another opinion that generally prevails among the professors of Christianity, is, that charity consists in giving alms to the poor. And this opinion is earnestly contended for by many, although the Pharisees, who were regarded by our Lord as "serpents and vipers," Matthew xxii:33, through their want of unfeigned charity, were yet remarkable for their generosity in almsgiving. St. Paul manifestly opposes this erroneous notion, where he declares that it is possible for a man to "give all his goods to feed the poor," and yet be destitute of charity, 1 Corinthians xiii:3. The faithful pastor, it is true, maintains that every charitable person is constrained to assist the poor, according to his ability: but he adds, that almsgiving is as uncertain a mark of charity, as a constant attendance upon the sacramental table is an equivocal evidence of faith, since it is as possible to relieve the poor from weakness or vanity, as to receive the holy communion through timidity or custom.

If the charity of worldly men is ever found to exceed this description, yet it will always be limited to the necessities of the body. As they know not how far the immortal spirit is superior to the perishing body, which must soon be blended in the dust of a thousand carcasses, it is no wonder that their chief concern is engrossed by the latter. The welfare of their own souls is attended to with a very small degree of solicitude: and while this is the case, it cannot be imagined that they should manifest any extraordinary degree of affection toward the souls of their neighbours. They behold without sorrow those deluded partisans, who make war upon each other for the sake of their particular errors. They can even gaze, without pity, upon those obdurate souls who are desperately plunging from one abyss of sin to another. How different were the feelings of David, when, like a true penitent, he not only wept for his own offences, but shed torrents of tears for those who transgressed the law of God," Psalm cxix:136. And how contrary was the character of St. Paul, who went through a kind of spiritual travail till the degenerate were born again," Galatians iv:19. In like manner the primitive Christians exposed themselves to imminent dangers, that they might give proofs of the most exalted charity, by snatching souls from sin and death. And when they were not able to effect this by their external labours, they then wrestled in their closets, with secret prayers and tears, for the conversion of the ungodly. Where there is no desire after the salvation of others, there Christian charity is unknown. For while a man disregards the soul of his neighbour, all the interest he takes in his temporal affairs can manifest no more than the charity of a disciple of Epicurus, which is as far below the charity of Christ's disciples, as materialism is inferior to Christianity.

In opposition to all the erroneous notions, which too generally prevail upon this important subject, the ministry of the New Testament teaches, that evangelical charity is the image of God. And that eternal and infinite charity is nothing less than God himself. One apostle declares that "God is love;" and another assures us, that we are called to be made "partakers of the Divine nature," 2 Peter i:4; whence the sacred preacher infers, that "the new creature," of which St. Paul makes mention, 2 Corinthians v:17, must necessarily consist in charity. When a Christian is filled with charity, he is then regenerate and born of God. Christ is then formed in his heart, the Holy Spirit rests upon him, and he is "filled with all the fulness of God," Ephesians iii:16, 19. He keeps the first commandment of the law, by making a full surrender of his heart to God, from a consciousness that he is in himself the sovereign Good; but he chiefly loves him in the person of Christ, through whom the Father is pleased peculiarly to shine forth as a God of love. In a secondary sense, he loves the works of God in all their wonderful variety, as they shadow forth his matchless perfections, and place them within the reach of man's understanding. And his esteem for these admirable productions is in proportion to the nearer or more distant relation in which they stand to that eternal Wisdom which formed them all. Guided by this principle, he loves all mankind with an extraordinary degree of affection. The soul of man is peculiarly dear to him, because created in the image of God, and redeemed with the blood of his beloved Son: while, as the organized vehicle of the soul, he admires and loves the perishable body. As the souls of the poor and the rich are equally immortal, he is never meanly prejudiced in favour of the latter; but, on the contrary, is ever ready to prefer a poor and pious beggar, before a sensual and supercilious noble. Thus the true Christian cherishes the faithful, not only for love of the Creator and Redeemer, but also for love of the sanctifying Spirit, unto whom their souls are consecrated as living altars, and their bodies as hallowed temples, 1 Corinthians vi:19, 20. From this Divine charity good works of every kind proceed, as from an inexhaustible fountain; a fountain which is making, as it were, continual efforts to enrich the barren soil around it. But, where this is wanting, all external appearances are without any real value. The lavish giver loses his worth before pious men, and the zealous martyr his reward before a righteous God.

Uniting in his own heart the love of God with the love of his neighbour, the true minister anxiously endeavours to demonstrate the folly of those who seek to separate these kindred virtues. He maintains, that charity without piety is but a mere natural virtue, which discovers itself as frequently in the brute creation, as among unregenerate men. Thus, the swallow and the bat are careful of their young—the beaver and the ant are observed to labour for the respective societies of which they are individuals, and the she bear is ready to meet death in defence of her cubs. On this account, the good pastor furnishes his flock with those exalted motives to Christian love, which, by imparting an evangelical principle to mutual charity, ennobles it in man, and renders it Divine.

As charity, without piety, is no more than a natural virtue, and may be the effect of Pharisaical or diabolical pride, so devotion, without brotherly love, is to be considered as a species of hypocrisy. This our Lord himself teaches in the following passage: "If thou bring thy gift to the altar, and there rememberest that thy brother hath aught against thee; leave there thy gift before the altar, and go thy way; first be reconciled to thy brother, and then come and offer thy gift," which would otherwise be rejected, as an abomination, by the God of love, Matthew v:23, 24. True charity embraces all men, because, being made of one blood, they compose but one vast family, of which God himself is the great Parent. And here our Lord permits us not to except even our most cruel enemy. "Ye have heard," saith he, "that it hath been said, Thou shalt love thy neighbour and hate thine enemy. But I say unto you, Love your enemies, bless them that curse you, do good to them that hate you, and," manifesting a concern for their souls, as well as all attention to their persons, "pray for them that despitefully use and persecute you; that ye may be the children of your Father which is in heaven. For he maketh his sun to rise on the evil and on the good," Matthew v:43-45.

Charity consists of two parts, patience and benevolence. By the one, we suffer every kind of indignity, without entertaining a thought of revenge; and by the other, we heap upon our enemies unsolicited favours. Our adorable Master, whose conduct has furnished us with examples of the most perfect charity, discovers to us the extent of this virtue, in the following passages: The world hath "hated both me and my Father," John xv:24; nevertheless, "God so loved the world, that he gave his only begotten Son, that whosoever believeth in him should not perish, but have everlasting life," John iii:16. "It hath been said, An eye for an eye, and a tooth for a tooth;" and the time is coming, when it shall be said, A thrust with a sword for an abusive word; a pistol shot for a satirical expression. "But I say unto you, Resist not," according to the maxims of those by whom you are evil entreated; but whosoever shall smite thee on thy right cheek, turn to him the other also:" that is, suffer two insults rather than revenge one. Follow the same rule likewise with respect to your worldly substance, "and if any man will sue thee at the law, and take away thy coat, let him have thy cloak also:" that is, far from exacting with rigour, be ready to remit much of thy right, for the maintenance of peace; since it is better to suffer a double injustice, than to lack condescension and charity. "And whosoever shall compel thee to go a mile, go with him twain:" that is, merely yielding to others in things that are good, or indifferent, is not enough: thy charity should rather prevent and surprise them with unexpected acts of civility and kindness. From these expressions it appears that our Lord would have his disciples to possess a charity not only extraordinary in some degree, but altogether Divine. In point of quality, he requires that it should be equal to the inexpressible love of the Father; as a drop taken from the ocean is of the same nature with those mighty waves that roll over the unfathomable deep. "If ye love them," saith he, "that love you, what reward have you? Do not even the publicans so? Be ye therefore perfect, [in charity,] even as your Father which is in heaven is perfect," Matthew v.

Faith, unspeakably excellent as it is, would be void of any real worth, unless it produced this happy disposition. "In Christ," saith the apostle, "the whole body, [of the faithful,] fitly joined together, and compacted by that which every joint supplieth, according to the effectual working in the measure of every part, maketh increase of the body, unto the edifying of itself in love," Ephesians iv:15, 16. "In Jesus Christ neither circumcision availeth any thing, nor uncircumcision; but faith, which worketh by love," Galatians v:6. "And though I have all faith, so that I could remove mountains, and have not charity, I am nothing," 1 Corinthians xiii:4. This celestial grace runs through the whole circle of Christian virtues. Thus, when St. Paul enumerates the fruits or effects of the Spirit, he points to charity, as the foremost of the train. And when St. Peter recounts the virtues which a Christian should add to his faith, he concludes with the finishing graces of "brotherly kindness and charity," Galatians v:22; 2 Peter i:7. Both these ideas are afterward united by the great apostle, where he exhorts the Colossians "to put on charity, as that bond of perfectness," Colossians iii:14, without which the Christian character would be incomplete, and which may be said to include all the graces of the Spirit, as a thousand ears of corn are united in the same sheaf, by one common band.

It was with these sublime views of charity, that St. Paul thus addressed his converts. "By love serve one another; for all the law is fulfilled in one word, even in this, Thou shalt love thy neighbour as thyself," Galatians v:13, 14. "Owe no man any thing, but to love one another, for he that loveth another, [in obedience to Christ's command,] hath fulfilled the law," Romans xiii:8. "Charity never faileth;" inasmuch as it is the source of heavenly joy. "Now, [in the Church militant,] abide faith, hope, and charity; but the greatest of these is charity," which shall certainly animate the Church triumphant, 1 Corinthians xiii:8, 13.

Even here on earth it is counted as the beginning of eternal life to know, by faith, that "God is love," and that he seeks to gain our affections by blessings without number, John xvii:3. A discovery of this kind cannot but give rise to some grateful return in the soul; since it is impossible firmly to believe these ravishing truths, without crying out like the first Christians, "We love him, because he first loved us," 1 John iv:19. If God has mercifully made the first advances toward his rebellious creatures, if notwithstanding the distance between him and us be infinite, and the obstacles to our union innumerable, he yet graciously presents himself, in spite of all, within our reach; if he yet inclines to pardon the guilty, and endeavours to reconcile the world unto himself by Jesus Christ, 2 Corinthians v:18; what conscious heart can be unaffected with these tokens of his love, or what tongue can be silent in his praise?

This God of charity thus affectionately addressed an ancient class of his servants:" I have loved thee with an everlasting love, therefore with loving kindness have I drawn thee," Jeremiah xxxi:3. The favour here expressed toward the Jewish Church is great; but that which is testified by the same adorable Jehovah to the Christian Church, is still more astonishing. His Son, the living and eternal image of his Father, humbles himself to the dust, and invests himself with our nature, that raising us from our low estate, he may at length place us at the right hand of the majesty on high. "He loved the Church," saith St. Paul, "and gave himself for it, that he might sanctify and cleanse it, and that he might present it to himself a glorious Church, not having spot or wrinkle, or any such thing," Ephesians v:25, 27. Thus he has given to believers an example of the love which they ought to entertain for all their Christian brethren, and to husbands a pattern of the attachment they should feel to their wives; since he left the bosom of his Father for the very purpose of suffering with and for his Church, which, in the language of Scripture, is called his spouse, Revelation xix:7. But, adds the apostle, "this is a great mystery," Ephesians v:32. Now the true minister is happily initiated into this grand mystery of charity. He can say, With Peter, "Lord! thou knowest all things; thou knowest that I love thee." He can testify, with Paul, "The love of Christ constraineth me." And, at other times, when the emotions of his heart are too tender for utterance, tears of gratitude and joy silently cry out, like those of dissolving Mary, "Lord, thou art worthy of all my love, since thou hast graciously pardoned all my sin." Animated with this love, he publicly resists upon universal charity, with all the ardour of St. John, testifying that it flows from the knowledge of God, and must be considered as the root of Christian obedience. "Hereby," saith he, "perceive we the love of God, because he laid down his life for us; and we ought to lay down our lives for the brethren. My little children, let us not love in word, neither in tongue; but [according to the example of Christ] in deed and in truth," 1 John iii:16- 18. For, if "God so loved us, we ought also to love one another," and remember, "he that loveth not, knoweth not God, for God is love," 1 John iv:11, 8.

Although Christ evidently came to break down the wall of separation between the Jews and Gentiles, by preaching the doctrine of universal charity; yet he willed that believers should love one another with a peculiar degree of affection. We are required to meet the unregenerate with a love of benevolence; but believers should be bound to each other by ties so tender and powerful, that the world may acknowledge them to be men of one heart and one soul. "By this," saith our Lord, "shall all men know that ye are my disciples, if ye have love one to another, John xiii:35. And who can describe the generosity, the sweetness, the strength, and the constancy, of this enlivening grace? It is more active than the penetrating flame; it is stronger than death. The communion of saints is received among Christians as a sentence in their established creed. Happy would it be did it constitute a part of their religious experience! As to the difference between Christian charity and that which was required under the law, it seems to be satisfactorily pointed out by St. John in the following passage: "Brethren, I write no new commandment unto you, but an old commandment, which ye had from the beginning:" for Moses himself earnestly exhorted his people to maintain among themselves the holy fire of fraternal love. "Again, a new commandment I write unto you," 1 John ii:7, 8; new, in relation to Christ, who hath loved us not only as himself, but even more than himself; since he offered up his life a ransom for the rebellious. Moses tasted not of death for Pharaoh, as Jesus did for Pilate, Herod, and Caiaphas. The Christian Legislator alone requires a charity of this perfectly disinterested nature; and for the support of so exalted a precept, he has seconded it with his own great example. "Herein is love," continues the apostle, "not that we loved God, but that he loved us, and sent his Son to be the propitiation for our sins." Love, then, is undoubtedly of God; flowing from him, as from an inexhaustible spring; "and he that loveth [after the same pure and fervent manner] is born of God, and knoweth God," 1 John iv:7, 11.

This charity is set forth by St. Paul as a source of consolation. "If," saith he to the Philippians, "there be any comfort in love, be ye like-minded, having the same love [one to another;] and let this mind be in you, which was also in Christ Jesus," Philippians ii:1, 6. And, in another epistle he cries out, "I have a great conflict for them at Laodicea, that their hearts might be comforted, being knit together in love," Colossians ii:1, 2.

1. Charity may be considered as a spring of comfort, because it frees us from the fear of death, and delivers us from a thousand other terrors, which trouble the peace of worldly men. "There is no fear in love; but perfect love, hoping all things, tasteth out fear; because fear hath torment. He therefore that feareth is not made perfect in love," 1 John iv:18.

2. Charity is consoling, because it assists and encourages us in the discharge of our several duties. When we glow with affection to God and our neighbour, works of piety and charity are performed not only without pain, but with heartfelt sensations of secret delight. "This is the love of God, that we keep his commandments;" and to those who sincerely love him, "his commandments are not grievous," 1 John v:3. Thus a tender mother loses her repose without repining, that she may tend to the wants of her restless infant; thus an affectionate father labours with pleasure for the support and education of his children; and thus, with every testimony of joy, the primitive Christians relieved and supported one another. The admirable effects produced by this unfeigned love are described by St. Luke in the following terms: "The multitude of them that believed were of one heart and one soul; neither said any of them that aught of the things which he possessed was his own; but [losing sight of every self-interesting view] they had all things common," Acts iv:32.

Here we behold *that* eminently accomplished by Christ which was anciently prefigured unto Moses in the desert, when the manna was so equally distributed among the people, that "he who gathered much had nothing over, and he who gathered little had no lack," Exodus xvi:18.

Happy were these fleeting days of Christian fellowship! Days that had long been promised by God, and of which a foretaste had been given in the land of Canaan, when it was ordained that, during the year of Jubilee, the poor should be permitted to share the comforts of their richer neighbours. It must be allowed, that a multitude of insincere professors overspreading the Church in these melancholy times, will not permit this method to be generally adopted among us, which would nevertheless be entirely practicable in a country inhabited by the affectionate followers of Jesus. But at the same time it is no less true, that every individual who is possessed of real charity, is still treading in the steps of his elder brethren, and waiting only the return of favourable times to prove that "Jesus Christ is the same yesterday, to-day, and for ever," Hebrews xiii:8, and that unfeigned charity, in the same circumstances, will ever produce the same effect.

It is impossible too highly to exalt this charity, which springs from a grateful sense of the redemption that is in Jesus. He who is unacquainted with this grace is a stranger to every real virtue, and utterly destitute of that "holiness without which no man shall see the Lord," Hebrews xii:14. Hence we find the Apostle Paul so frequently connecting holiness with love; or rather, pressing the latter as the ground of the former. "God," saith he, "hath chosen us in Christ, that we should be holy and without blame before him in love," Ephesians i:3, 4. "Let Christ dwell in your hearts by faith; that ye, being rooted and grounded in love, may be able to comprehend, with all saints, what is the breadth, and length, and depth, and height; and to know the love of Christ, which passeth knowledge, that ye might be filled with all the fulness of God," Ephesians iii:17, 18. "The Lord make you to increase and abound in love one toward another, and toward all men; to the end that he may establish your hearts unblamable in holiness before God," 1 Thessalonians iii:12, 13.

"Knowledge [alone] puffeth up, but charity [added to knowledge] edifieth," 1 Corinthians vii:1, and conducts the soul from grace to grace, "unto the measure of the stature of the fulness of Christ," Ephesians iv:13. Happy they who have attained to this high degree of spirituality, from which, with a look of pure beneficence, they can smile on all around them! Such may join the first professors of Christianity, and say, "We have known and believed the love that God hath to us," and, penetrated with a deep sense of his affection, we declare, from happy experience, that "God is love; and he that dwelleth in love, dwelleth in God and God in him," 1 John iv:16. The love of these persevering disciples may, in a Scriptural sense, be termed "perfect;" since it enables them to bear a just, though faint resemblance to the God of love, 1 John iv:17. Their hearts are as replete with charity as sparks are filled with fire; and doubtless the smallest spark may be said to shine with a degree of perfection, in its little sphere, as well as the brighter sun in his more boundless course.

St. Paul, who preached this charity with so much fervency, declares, that it was kindled in his heart by the love of Christ; and upon this account he labours to found it upon those doctrines which are universally despised by every class of Deists. In his Epistle to the Romans, which contains sixteen chapters, he employs eleven in laying this solid foundation, while the duties of charity are declared only in the five remaining chapters. Like a wise master-builder, before he attempts to raise this sacred edifice, he endeavours to remove out of the way the ruins of corrupted nature, and the rubbish of self love. But had he endeavoured to do this without calling in to his aid the doctrines of the Gospel, he would have acted as ridiculously as Archimedes, had that philosopher attempted the removal of the earth without having first secured a solid footing suited to his purpose.

The most powerful motives employed by this apostle in urging us to the practice of Christian charity, are the love of God and the compassion of Christ. "God," saith he, "commendeth his love toward us, in that while we were yet sinners Christ died for us," Romans v:8; and, "ye know the grace of our Lord Jesus Christ, that though he was rich, yet for your sakes he became poor, that ye, through his poverty, might become rich," 2 Corinthians viii:9. Now, whoever is sensible of the power, and tastes the sweetness, of these two grand truths, feels himself at the same time carried to every good work, in the same manner as the miser is led to those actions which serve to increase his hoard. For, "being saved by grace, through faith," in these very truths, "we are created by Christ Jesus unto good works," Ephesians ii:8, 10. "Who gave himself for us," on this sole account, "that he might redeem us from all iniquity, and purify unto himself a peculiar people zealous of good works," Titus ii:14. The consolatory doctrine of a gratuitous pardon offered to sinners as a token of God's unfathomable love, is another motive frequently made use of to the like purpose. "Put on," continues the same apostle," as the elect of God, bowels of mercies, kindness, humbleness of mind, meekness, long suffering; forbearing one another, and forgiving one another, if any man have a quarrel against any: even as Christ forgave you, so also do ye," Colossians iii:12, 13. "Above all things have fervent charity among yourselves; for charity shall cover the multitude of sins," 1 Peter iv:8. Yes, it not only covers the sins of others, by considering their doubtful actions in the most favourable point of view, and by overlooking the most unpardonable of their failings; but may, in some measure, be said to cover our own offences, since God, for Christ's sake, has promised to overlook our transgressions, as we give proof of a forgiving temper toward our brethren. Discord entered into the world by sin. Hence we see unregenerate men not only separated from God, but divided among themselves: and hence, by the rebellion of his growing passions against his enfeebled reason, every unrighteous man is at war with himself. Dreadful as these evils are, we are here presented with a perfect remedy for them all. He who created man upright, has sent his Son to re-establish harmony in the world, to reduce our passions under the dominion of universal benevolence, to subject our reason to the authority of truth, and to subdue the whole man under the sweet yoke of charity manifested in the flesh; that charity which is destined to reign for ever, and whose happy empire is called the "kingdom of heaven." "The Father of glory," says St. Paul, "hath put all things under the feet of Christ, and hath given him to be the head over all things to the Church, which is his body, the fulness of him that filleth all in all," Ephesians i:17, 23. "Ye, who sometimes were far off, are now made nigh by the blood of Christ. For he is our peace" between Jews and Gentiles, between man and man, "who hath made both one, and hath broken down the middle wall of partition between us, that he might reconcile both unto God in one body, by the cross, having slain the enmity" by that perfect charity of which he gave so many wonderful proofs. "Now therefore," we, who are actuated by the same spirit of love, "are no more strangers and foreigners, but fellow citizens with the saints and of the household of God; and are built upon the foundation of the apostles and prophets, Jesus Christ himself being the chief corner stone. In whom the whole building, fitly framed together, groweth unto a holy temple in the Lord: in whom also ye are builded together for a habitation of God, through the Spirit" of charity, Ephesians ii:13, 22.

The minister who feels the force of these constraining motives, cannot fail to place them continually before his hearers. The various parts of his public discourses as naturally incline to this grand point, as the several parts of a solid edifice mutually rest upon the common foundation. "There is one body," saith he with the apostle, "and one Spirit even as ye are called in one hope of your calling; one Lord, one God and Father of all, who is above all, and through all, and in you all," Ephesians iv:4, 6. "As we have many members in one body; so we, being many, are one body in Christ, and every one members one of another. Let love be, therefore, without dissimulation: be kindly affectioned one to another, with brotherly love; in honour preferring one another. Rejoice with them that do rejoice; and weep with them that weep. Be of the same mind one toward another. Avenge not yourselves, but rather give place unto wrath. If thine enemy hunger, feed him; if he thirst, give him drink. Be not overcome of evil; but overcome evil with good," Romans xii:4, 21. In a word, "let all things be done with charity," 1 Corinthians xvi:14.

To conclude. The evangelical pastor points out the excellence of charity, and urges every motive that can lead to the practice of it, till worldly men are constrained to cry out, with all the admiration of the ancient heathens, "See how these Christians love one another!" Lucian, indeed, could look with ridicule upon the zeal with which the primitive Christians succoured one another: "For," says he, "their legislator has made them believe that they are all brethren; and hence they have all things common among them, despising even death itself, through the hope of immortality." The good pastor, however, is anxious to do that which this heathen writer was impious enough to censure in Christ. He admonishes believers to address the Almighty as their common parent, Luke xi:2; conscious that so soon as they receive power to cry, "Abba," that is, *Father*, by the Holy Spirit, they will necessarily forget every scrupulous distinction between mine and thine, and put up, with unfeigned sincerity, that universal prayer, "Give us this day our daily bread." This petition is commonly used by every member of our degenerate Church, while their hearts are comparatively insensible to the wants of their necessitous brethren. But were the love of ancient days to revive among us, we should not only solicit common blessings from above, but rejoice to share them with each other, as brethren partake of a repast provided for them at the table of their common parent.

Happy days! when the Gospel of Christ was seen to flourish in the earth. Surely that sacred season might, with propriety, be termed the golden age of the Church. O that we could recall the felicity we have forfeited, and see the joys of unanimity restored to a distracted world. But while we give vent to our lamentations, let us not sink into despair, since, however deplorable our present circumstances may be, they are not totally remediless. Though for so many ages, self love has usurped the throne of charity: though mankind are prone to injure one another, in their reputation by slander; in their property by injustice; and in their persons by murder, whether perpetrated in the character of an assassin, or that of a duellist; though wars are fomented on the slightest pretences, and Christian princes appear eager to wash their hands in the blood of thousands: though "all the earth is full of darkness and cruel habitations," Psalm lxxiv:21, yet will we not give up our hope. These unhappy times were foretold by our gracious Master, Matthew xxiv:12. And as he had prescience enough to predict the decays of Christian love, and the calamities consequent thereupon; so he is possessed of sufficient power to re-establish the empire of charity in the world. Believers, then, amidst all their afflictions, may patiently and confidently expect those "times of refreshing" which shall assuredly "come from the presence of the Lord;" looking forward to that promised "restitution of all things," concerning "which God hath spoken by the mouth of all his holy prophets since the world began," Acts iii:19, 21. In the meanwhile, let those who are hastening, by their prayers, this desirable revolution, be careful to preserve in their own hearts those sparks of charity which shall one day kindle the universe into a sacred flame. And let the ministers of the Gospel make a constant display of those evangelical truths which were formerly sufficient to light up this glorious fire; that, by stirring up the dying embers of grace, the little light, which still remains in the Church, may be preserved from total extinction.

Should it be here objected—Are not all the ministers of our Church to be considered as preachers of Christian charity? We answer, By no means. The charity, concerning which we speak, must flow from a union with Christ; a union which

The Works of John Fletcher

ministers of the present day are accustomed to treat as enthusiastic and vain. This excellent grace "is shed abroad in our hearts by the Holy Ghost which is given unto us," Romans v:5. But he who dares openly to plead for this Scriptural truth, is esteemed by such preachers no better than a deluded fanatic. These insincere preachers are frequently heard, indeed, to speak of Christian charity, but far from endeavouring to spread it through the world, they use every effort to destroy the very seeds of this grace in the Church of God. If, in a parish that is unhappy enough to have a pastor of this kind, a few persons are happily converted to God, and united together in Jesus Christ; if, having one heart, and one soul, they frequently join together in prayer and in praise, mutually exhorting and provoking one another to love and good works; the worldly minister, instantly alarmed, imagines that these persons, for the sake of forming a new sect, are destroying the unity of the Church; when, on the contrary, they are but just about to experience the communion of saints. And, if he be possessed of zeal, or party spirit, he will labour to make it appear that these Christians, who are beginning to love as brethren, are forming conventicles to disturb the order both of Church and state. Such a minister will give encouragement to companies of jugglers, dancers, and drunkards, rather than tolerate a society which has Christian charity for its object and basis.

The true minister believes and preaches the three grand promises of God, together with the three great dispensations of grace.

WE have seen, in the preceding chapters, that believers are saved by a lively faith and a joyful hope, which mutually serve to excite and increase in their souls the superior grace of charity. Now this faith and this hope must necessarily have for their foundation some promise of God. A promise already accomplished is embraced by faith alone; but a promise, whose accomplishment is protracted, is equally the object of faith and of hope. He, therefore, who is appointed by Christ a preacher of the everlasting Gospel, is solicitous to obtain clear ideas of the great promises of God. He is constantly engaged in meditating upon their past or future accomplishment, in order to maintain in his own heart those inestimable graces with which he is desirous to animate the souls of others. Observe the order in which he considers, embraces, and preaches them.

Under the dispensation of the Father, the grand promise was that which respected the external manifestation of the Son. The original promise, as made to Adam, was expressed in the following terms:—"The seed of the woman shall bruise the head of the serpent," Genesis iii:15. As the Messiah was to descend from Abraham, according to the flesh, the same promise was thus renewed to that patriarch: "In thee shall all families of the earth be blessed," Genesis xii:3. In the days of Moses, it was repeated to all Israel, as follows: "The Lord thy God will raise up unto thee a prophet, from the midst of thee, of thy brethren, unto him shall ye hearken," Deuteronomy xviii:15. David and the other prophets powerfully confirmed this prophecy, and Malachi thus recapitulates the promises which had been given before his time: "The Lord whom ye seek, shall suddenly come to his temple, even the Messenger of the covenant whom ye delight in; behold, he shall come, saith the Lord of Hosts," Malachi iii:1. "Unto you, that fear my name, shall the Sun of righteousness arise with healing in his wings; and ye shall go forth," out of your present obscure dispensation, "and grow up," in spiritual strength, "as calves of the stall," Malachi vi:2. Thus speaks the last of the prophets, under the dispensation of the Father.

Immediately upon the accomplishment of these promises, while the dispensation of the Son was but darkly opened by his precursor, another promise was given for the exercise of faith and hope, under this new economy, respecting the full manifestation of the Holy Ghost, as a Spirit of truth and love. Behold this grand promise as announced by John the Baptist: "I am not the Christ; I am the voice of one crying in the wilderness, Make straight the way of the Lord," John i:20, 23. "I baptize you with water unto repentance," as a preparation for the spiritual king dom and baptism of the Messiah: "but he that cometh after me is mightier than I, whose shoes I am not worthy to bear." He shall introduce a more spiritual dispensation, and administer a more efficacious baptism: for "he shall baptize you with the Holy Ghost and with fire," shedding abroad those gifts and graces of his Spirit, which shall penetrate and purify your hearts, as metals are penetrated and purified by material fire," Matthew iii:11. This promise is of so great importance that it was thought necessary to be repeated by the four evangelists.

Our Lord, continuing the dispensation which his forerunner had opened, "made and baptized more disciples than John, though Jesus himself baptized not, with water, but his disciples," John iv:1, 2. The baptism which he was about to administer, was as far superior to the baptism of John, and that of his own disciples, as the water of which he spake to the woman of Samaria was superior to the water of Jordan, or that of Jacob's well. "Whosoever shall drink of the water that I shall give him," said he to that inquiring woman; whosoever shall come to my baptism, and let down his vessel into the inexhaustible fountain of my grace, "shall never thirst: but the water that I shall give him, shall be in him a well of water," a source of righteousness, peace, and joy, "springing up into everlasting life," John iv:14.

In order to strengthen the hope of those who had been baptized with water, our Lord publicly ratified the promise which had been so frequently repeated to them by John the Baptist. "In the last day, that great day of the feast, Jesus stood and cried, If any man thirst, let him come unto me and drink. He that believeth on me, as the Scripture hath said, out of his belly shall flow rivers of living water. But this he spake of the Spirit, which they that believe on him, in every age, should receive. For the Holy Ghost was not yet fully given, because that Jesus was not yet glorified," John vii:37-39. An inestimable promise this, which deserves to be deeply engraven in the minds of those who are merely acquainted with Christ, according to his exterior appearance in the world. Observe here the method by which the blessed Jesus endeavours to prepare all such, in every country and in every period, for his manifestation in the Spirit: "If you love me, keep my commandments;" be faithful to the present dispensation of my Gospel, "and I will pray the Father, and he will give you another Comforter, that he may abide with you for ever. At that day," when ye shall experience the fulness of his presence, "ye shall know that I am in my Father, and ye in me, and I in you." For "he that loveth me, shall be loved of my Father, and I will love him, and we will come unto him, and make our abode with him," John xiv:15-23. By comparing these words with the seventeenth and twenty-sixth verses of the same chapter, it is evident, that by this spiritual manifestation of the Father and

The Works of John Fletcher

the Son, nothing less can be intended than the full measure of that Holy Spirit "which proceedeth from the Father," John xv:26, and which is expressly called "the Spirit of the Son," Galatians iv:6.

Our Lord, who knew the stupidity of those who were under the inferior dispensation of his Gospel, and how "slow of heart" they were "to believe" what either the prophets or himself had spoken, judged it expedient to repeat the grand promise of the Spirit again and again. "When the Comforter is come," said he, "whom I will send unto you from the Father, he shall testify of me," John xv:26. "It is expedient for you that I go away: for if I go not away, the Comforter will not come unto you; but if I depart, I will send him unto you," John xvi:7. "Behold I send the promise of my Father upon you," Luke xxiv:49.

The abundant effusion of the Holy Spirit was termed by our Lord the promise of the Father, for two reasons: first, because, coming to instruct mankind how to worship the Father "in spirit and in truth," it became him to refer all things to that Father. And this he was strictly and constantly accustomed to do. Secondly, because "the Father of lights" is to be considered as the author of "every good and perfect gift." It was he who so loved the world, that he gave his only begotten Son to die for the world, and from him proceeds that Holy Spirit, which Jesus Christ still continues to shed abroad among his faithful followers. The Father had already promised, under the law, that he would grant unto his people a general outpouring of his Spirit, under the reign of the Messiah. The memorable prophecy of Joel, as quoted by St. Peter, is generally known; and the following promises equally merit the attention of believers. "In that day I will pour upon the house of David, and upon the inhabitants of Jerusalem, the spirit of grace and of supplications. And they shall look upon me, whom they have pierced, and they shall mourn for him, as one mourneth for his only son," Zechariah xii:10. "I will pour water upon him that is thirsty, and floods upon the dry ground. I will pour my Spirit upon thy seed, and my blessing upon thine offspring," Isaiah xliv:3. "I will sprinkle clean water upon you, and ye shall be clean. I will put my Spirit within you, and cause you to walk in my statutes," Ezekiel xxxvi:25-27. "I will give them one heart: I will take the stony heart out of their flesh, and will give them a heart of flesh," Ezekiel xi:19. That man must be prejudiced to an extreme degree, who perceives not that these gracious prophecies began to receive their accomplishment upon the day of pentecost, when the multitude of them that believed were "of one heart and one soul."

The last day our risen Saviour passed upon earth was employed in strengthening the faith of his disciples, with respect to this promise. After having assembled them together, "he commanded them to wait for the promise of the Father, which," continued he, "ye have heard of me. For John truly baptized with water," and ye have done the same by my direction, "but ye shall be baptized with the Holy Ghost not many days hence," Acts i:4, 5.

After the grand promise under the dispensation of the Son was in part accomplished; when the disciples were filled with faith, and with the Holy Ghost, another promise was given to exercise their faith, to fix their attention, and to perfect their patience; the promise of Christ's second coming to "gather his wheat into the garner, and to burn up the chaff with unquenchable fire," Matthew iii:12. "This same Jesus," said the angels who appeared to the disciples on the day of their Master's ascension, "this same Jesus, which is taken up from you into heaven, shall so come, in like manner as ye have seen him go into heaven," Acts i:11. This important promise was afterward repeated by St. Paul and the other apostles. "The Lord Jesus shall be revealed from heaven, with his mighty angels, in flaming fire, taking vengeance on them that obey not the Gospel; who shall be punished with everlasting destruction from the presence of the Lord, when he shall come to be glorified in his saints, and to be admired in all them that believe," 2 Thessalonians i:7-10. "Behold, he cometh with clouds, and every eye shall see him, and they also which pierced him; and all kindreds of the earth shall wail because of him," Revelation i:7. "The day of the Lord will come as a thief in the night," 2 Peter iii:10.

This coming of Christ, which is disregarded by many, for the reason assigned by St. Peter, 2 Peter iii:9, 10, is so fully expected by those who live under the dispensation of the Spirit, that they are constantly "looking for, and hastening to, the coming of the day of God," 2 Peter iii:12. According to St. Paul, sinners are converted from the error of their ways, that they may "serve the living and true God, and wait for his Son from heaven, whom he raised from the dead," 1 Thessalonians i:9, 10. "Looking for that blessed hope, and the glorious appearing of the great God and our Saviour Jesus Christ," Titus ii:13. This second coming of Christ was the object of this apostle's highest hopes, after which he represents himself as groaning with the most fervent desire, Romans viii:23. "Yea, I count all things but loss," continues he, "that I may know him, and the power of his resurrection. Our conversation is in heaven, from whence also we look for the Saviour, who shall change our vile body, that it may be fashioned like unto his glorious body, according to the working whereby he is even able to subdue all things unto himself," Philippians iii:20, 21.

As God had afforded believers, under the Old Testament, a perspective view both of the manifestation of the Redeemer in a mortal body, and of that dispensation of the Spirit, which he was to open among his followers under the New Testament; so he had likewise foretold, by his prophets, the glorious return of that Saviour to the earth. "The Lord cometh with ten thousand of his saints to execute judgment," Jude i:14. "Behold, he shall come, saith the Lord of hosts. But who may abide the day of his coming? And who shall stand when he appeareth? For he is like a refiner's fire, and like fullers' soap," Malachi iii:1, 2.

Mark the terms in which our Lord himself declared this sublime dispensation. "The love of many shall wax cold. False prophets shall arise, and ye shall see the abomination of desolation, spoken of by the Prophet Daniel, standing in the holy place. Immediately after the tribulation of those days, the powers of the heaven shall be shaken. And then shall appear the sign of the Son of man in heaven. Then shall all the tribes of the earth mourn, and they shall see the Son of man coming in the clouds of heaven, with power and great glory. But of that day and hour knoweth no man. Watch, therefore; for ye know not what hour your Lord doth come," Matthew xxiv. Thus Jesus himself testified of his second coming; and his first disciples, in conformity to their Master's declaration, addressed a large assembly in the following terms, almost immediately after his ascension: "Repent ye, and be converted, that your sins may be blotted out, when the times of refreshing shall come from the presence of the Lord; and he shall send Jesus, which before was preached unto you; whom the heavens must receive, until the time of restitution of all things, which God hath spoken by the mouth of all his holy prophets, since the world began," Acts iii:19-21.

So long as a minister embraces these different promises; so long as, with a lively faith, which is "the evidence of things not seen," he believes that the Father sent his Son for the redemption of sinners, and his Holy Spirit for the sanctification of believers,—so long as, with a faith which is "the substance of things hoped for," he believes that Christ shall one day return for the glorification of his saints; so long he is saved by that faith and hope which enable him to preach the Gospel in all its wondrous extent: so long he not only comprehends but experiences the power of that Gospel in his own soul, while he labours to make it manifest before the world, by his public discourses, and by the whole tenor of his conduct.

The true minister studies the different dispensations, in order to qualify himself for the discharge of every part of his duty.

THE pastor who is ill instructed in the mysteries of our holy religion, loses himself, and leads his sheep astray. The good pastor, on the contrary, having found out the way to everlasting life, presses forward therein at the head of his flock, and exhorts every heedless wanderer to follow his steps. He is conscious, not only that he has a mixture of sheep and goats in his fold, but he knows that, among the former, there are some to whose spiritual condition the sincere milk of the word is much better adapted than stronger food. To all of these he studies to address himself in a suitable manner. To those who are dead in trespasses and sin, equally destitute both of love and fear, he proclaims the first principles of the Gospel, such as "repentance from dead works, faith toward God, and an eternal judgment," Hebrews vi:1, 2. Those who had already awakened from the delusions of sin, he anxiously leads into the paths of grace; and endeavours to conduct those to evangelical perfection, who have felt the powers of the world to come, verse 6. He easily distinguishes the mixed multitude of his hearers into a variety of classes. The unbelieving and the impenitent, who are to be considered as without God and without hope in the world, are such as go on, without any symptom of fear, toward the gulf of perdition; whether it be by the high road of vice, with the notoriously abandoned, or through the by-path of hypocrisy, with Pharisaical professors. Converted sinners, or believers, are either under the dispensation of the Father, under that of the Son, or under that of the Holy Ghost, according to the different progress they have made in spiritual things. And the faithful pastor is as perfectly acquainted with their various attainments, as a diligent tutor is acquainted with the different abilities of his several pupils.

Believers, under the dispensation of the Father, are ordinarily surrounded with a night of uncertainty and doubt, though visited, at times, with a few scattered rays of hope. Under the dispensation of his Son, the doubts of believers are dissipated, like those of the two disciples who journeyed to Emmaus, while they discover more clearly, and experience more powerfully, the truths of the Gospel. But under the dispensation of the Spirit, they "walk in the light," 1 John i:7, and are led into all truth by "the Spirit of truth," John xvi:13; "the anointing which they have received abideth in them, and teacheth them of all things" necessary to salvation, 1 John ii:27.

The Portrait of St. Paul

A father of the Church, paraphrasing upon those words of the apostle, "Lord, save us; we perish," apostrophizes thus with the doubting disciples: "You have your Saviour with you, what danger can you fear? We are yet, they reply, but children, and have attained but to a small degree of strength: hence we are afraid. The descent of the Holy Spirit, that Divine protector which has been graciously promised, has not yet filled us with full assurance. This has been the cause of our unsteadiness hitherto: and hence the Saviour so frequently reproaches us with the weakness of our faith." (*Origen Hom.* Matthew viii:23-28.) Now all those Christians, who have not yet received the spiritual baptism so frequently mentioned in the New Testament, are shut up in this state of weakness and doubt. But so soon as they are born of the Spirit, they cry out no longer with trembling fear, "Save us; we perish!" But they cry out, in transports of gratitude, "God, according to his mercy, hath saved us, by the washing of regeneration and renewing of the Holy Ghost, which he hath shed on us abundantly, through Jesus Christ our Saviour," Titus iii:5, 6.

Under the dispensation of the Father, believers constantly experience the fear of God, and, in general, a much greater degree of fear than love. Under the economy of the Son, love begins to gain ascendancy over fear. But under the dispensation of the Holy Spirit, "perfect love casteth out fear," 1 John vi:18; because it is the peculiar office of the Comforter to deliver the soul from every thing that is liable to distress and torment it.

Under the economy of the Father, the believer is frequently heard to exclaim, "O wretched man that I am! who shall deliver me from the body of this death?" Romans vii:24. Under that of the Son, he gratefully cries out, "I thank God," who hath effectually wrought this deliverance, "through Jesus Christ our Lord," Romans vii:25. But under the perfect Gospel, which is the dispensation of the Spirit, all believers are enabled to say with one voice, "We have not received the spirit of bondage again to fear; but we have received the Spirit of adoption, whereby we cry, Abba, Father! The Spirit itself beareth witness with our spirit, that we are the children of God, and joint heirs with Christ," Romans viii:15-17.

St. Paul thus distinguishes the different states of advancement in the Christian faith. "The heir, as long as he is a child, [and such is the case with believers, under the dispensation of the Father,] differeth nothing from a servant, though he be lord of all; but is under tutors and governors till the time appointed of his father. Even so we were once in a state of bondage; but when the fulness of time was come, God sent forth his Son to redeem them that were under the law, that we might receive the adoption of sons. And because ye are sons, God hath sent forth the Spirit of his Son into your hearts, crying, Abba, Father. Wherefore, thou art no more a servant, but a son; and if a son, then an heir of God, through Christ," Galatians iv:1-7, "by whom we have access into this grace, and rejoice in hope of the glory of God," Romans v:2.

Our Lord himself evidently pointed out the progressive state of the Church, when, turning to his disciples, he said, "Blessed are the eyes which see the things that ye see: for I tell you, that many prophets and kings have desired to see those things which ye see, and have not seen them; and to hear those things which ye hear, and have not heard them," Luke x:23, 24. Nevertheless, when their gracious Master held this language, he was at that time neither glorified nor crucified: and it is well known that the glory of the Gospel was to follow his sufferings and his triumph.

The Works of John Fletcher

The same subject is treated by St. Peter in his first epistle, where he speaks of that full salvation which is to be considered as the end or recompense of faith, 1 Peter i:9. "Of which salvation," saith he, "the prophets have inquired and searched diligently, who prophesied of the grace that should come unto you: searching what, or what manner of time, the Spirit of Christ, which was in them, did signify, when it testified beforehand the sufferings of Christ, and the glory that should follow. Unto whom it was revealed, that not unto themselves, but unto us, they did minister the things which are now reported unto you, by them that have preached the Gospel unto you, with the Holy Ghost sent down from heaven, which things the angels desire to look into," 1 Peter i:10-12. "Happy are ye! for the Spirit of glory and of God resteth upon you," 1 Peter iv:14. "Ye are a chosen generation, a peculiar people, that ye should show forth the praises of him who hath called you out of darkness into his marvellous light," 1 Peter ii:9.

Without an experimental knowledge of these several states, a minister can no more lead sinners to evangelical perfection, than an illiterate peasant can communicate sufficient intelligence to his rustic companions, to pass an examination for the highest degree in a university.

It may here be necessary to mark out the grand truths by which these dispensations are severally characterized.

The common language under the dispensation of the Father is as follows: "God hath made of one blood all nations of men, and hath appointed the bounds of their habitation; that they should seek the Lord, if haply they might feel after him and find him, though he be not far from every one of us," Acts xvii:26, 27. "The grace of God that bringeth salvation, hath appeared [in different degrees] to all men," Titus ii:11. "For the living God is the Saviour of all men, especially of those that believe," 1 Timothy iv:10. "God is no respecter of persons; but in every nation he that feareth him and worketh righteousness, is accepted with him," Acts x:34, 35. "Without faith it is impossible to please him: for he that cometh unto God must believe that he is, and that he is a rewarder of them that diligently seek him," Hebrews xi:6. "He hath showed thee, O man, what is good; and what doth the Lord require of thee but to do justly, and to love mercy, and to walk humbly with thy God?" Micah vi:8.

Observe the language of the Son's dispensation, "Glory to God in the highest, and on earth peace, good will toward men. I bring you good tidings of great joy, which shall be to all people: for unto you is born this day, in the city of David, a Saviour, which is Christ the Lord," Luke ii:10-14. "Grace and truth came by Jesus Christ," John i:17, "who hath abolished death, and hath brought life and immortality to light through the Gospel," 2 Timothy i:10. "The hour cometh and now is, when the true worshippers shall worship the Father in Spirit and in truth," John iv:23. "Ye believe in God, believe also in me," John xiv:1. "If the Son shall make you free, ye shall be free indeed," John viii:36. "This is the work of God, that ye believe on him whom he hath sent. No man can come unto me, except the Father, which hath sent me, draw him: and every man that hath heard, and hath learned of the Father, cometh unto me," John vi:29, 44, 45. "He that believeth on the Son, hath everlasting life: and he that believeth not the Son, shall not see life; but the wrath of God abideth on him," John iii:36.

The dispensation of the Spirit is again distinguished by the following peculiar language: "This is that which was spoken by the Prophet Joel: In the last days, [or under the last dispensations of my grace,] saith God, I will pour out of my Spirit upon all flesh, upon my servants, and upon my handmaidens: and they shall prophesy. Jesus, being by the right hand of God exalted, and having received of the Father the promise of the Holy Ghost, hath shed forth this [plenitude of grace, the effects of] which you now see and hear. Repent, therefore, and be baptized every one of you, in the name of Jesus Christ, for the remission of sins, and ye shall receive the Holy Ghost. For the promise is unto you and to your children, and to all that are afar off, even as many as the Lord our God shall call," Acts ii:16, 39.

If at any time it is to be apprehended that believers are still carnal, and unrenewed by the Spirit of God, the pastor who is conversant with these different economies of grace, inquires with St. Paul, "Have ye received the Holy Ghost since ye believed?" Acts xix:2. When others among his flock demonstrate, both by their conversation and conduct, that they are influenced by the Spirit of Christ, he exhorts them in a manner suitable to the glorious dispensation under which they live. "Ye are washed, ye are sanctified, ye are justified, in the name of the Lord Jesus, and by the Spirit of God. Your body is the temple of the Holy Ghost; therefore glorify God in your body and your spirit, which are God's," 1 Corinthians vi:11, 20. "Grieve not the Holy Spirit of God, whereby ye are sealed unto the day of redemption," Ephesians iv:30. "Be filled with the Spirit; speaking to yourselves in psalms and hymns, and spiritual songs, making melody in your hearts unto the Lord," v:18, 19. "Rejoice evermore. Pray without ceasing. In every thing give thanks," 1 Thessalonians v:16-18.

This language is too elevated for natural men, who understand it no more than illiterate persons comprehend the most abstruse parts of science. Hence it is necessary that the faithful minister should acquaint himself with the different conditions and capacities of all his hearers, if he would happily accommodate spiritual things to spiritual men. Without this knowledge, he will, under every dispensation, run the hazard of refusing to advanced Christians the solid nourishment they need, and of presenting to the natural man that celestial manna which his very soul abhors.

The different dispensations are produced by that lovely variety with which the Almighty is pleased to distribute his favours.

IF the light of the Gospel had been due from God to every individual sinner; if he had not been left entirely free, in every sense of the word, to impart it to whom, at what time, and in what degree soever was most pleasing to himself; his impartial justice would then have engaged him equally to illuminate all mankind, and he must have caused the Sun of righteousness, immediately after the fall, to have shone out in its meridian brightness. In such case, there would have been but one dispensation of grace; and the light of the Gospel would not have proceeded to its highest glory by such just gradations as are observable in all the productions of nature.

But the Almighty has proceeded in the work of our redemption, according to the dictates of his own unerring wisdom, and not upon the plans of our pretended sages. The day of the Gospel, whether it be considered as enlightening the world in general, or the heart in particular, rises, like the natural day, from one degree of brightness to another, till all its glories are fully manifested.

The confusion which many divines have spread over this part of theology, makes it necessary to go into particulars, that we may place in a just point of view, both the gradations and the harmony of these three dispensations, which collectively form the glorious Gospel of God.

If some naturalists were determined to confine their observations upon the rainbow, to those lines in it that are manifestly red: if naturalists of another class were as obstinate in contemplating those of an orange hue; and if others were as resolutely bent in singling out those of a blue colour, they would contradict and dispute with each other in as ridiculous a manner as many ignorant worshippers of the triune God are observed to do at this day. Thus Deists dispute for the honour of God the Creator; and while some Christians pay all their homage to God the Redeemer, others are as wholly taken up with God the Sanctifier. Amid all the confusion of these jarring sentiments, the prudent pastor admits, in their proper place, the various dispensations of evangelical light, conducting his followers from faith to faith, till he beholds them illuminated with all the truths, and experiencing all the power of the Christian religion.

We acknowledge that God is just, though the light of the natural sun approaches us only in a gradual manner, producing a constant variety both in our days and seasons. We do not accuse the Supreme Being of injustice, because he is not pleased to bring the fruits of the earth, in an instant, to their highest maturity; or because the same species of fruit, which is esteemed for its delicious flavour in one climate, is found worthless and insipid in another. And if the Sovereign of the world is not expected to ripen, on a sudden, either the reason of individuals or the knowledge of nations, it should not be matter of surprise to observe him acting in his usual manner, with respect to things of a spiritual nature. His plans are all equally wise: but it is impossible for man to form a perfect judgment of them, unless the creature could stand for a moment in the place of the Creator, and take one comprehensive view of earth and heaven, time and eternity. If "one day is with the Lord as a thousand years," when he is pleased, in an unexpected manner, to fulfil his grand designs; "and a thousand years as one day," 2 Peter iii:8, when he sees good to accomplish his purposes in a more gradual way; why should it so strangely afflict and amaze us, that he has left the human race in a state of suspense, with regard to his unsearchable counsels, for near six thousand years? The time is coming when he will discover to us that stupendous plan, which, in our present circumstances, we contemplate with every disadvantage; and just as an animalcule, whose life is limited to six hours, would contemplate the plan of an immense palace, which a skilful architect had promised to complete in as many years. Supposing such an insect, endued with reason, and coming into existence during the night, should blindly crawl among the loose materials of which the intended edifice was to be constructed; what opinion could it form either of the architect or his plan? Would not this insignificant creature be led to judge of these matters as the pretended philosopher inconsiderately judges of that mysterious plan upon which the Almighty is erecting the temple of truth, and creating an incorruptible world? If the Creator thought it necessary to employ six days in completing the beauties of the material world; and if the Redeemer judges it expedient progressively to perfect the more lasting beauties of a spiritual world, during six of his more ample days; how little reason have we to despise the comprehensive design; especially when we consider six thousand years are far more inconsiderable in comparison with eternity, than six atoms in comparison with this terrestrial globe!

Now, if such a plan is not only reasonable, but has been evidently adopted by Him who "giveth not account of any of his matters," Job xxxiii:13; it is undoubtedly true, that those who have lived in different periods of time, have not been permitted to enjoy all the various truths which God has successively revealed to man. Nevertheless, it is equally certain that every man, in what period of time, and in what peculiar circumstances soever he found himself placed, has received sufficient light to discover, as well as sufficient power to perform, what God has been pleased to require at his hands.

The day of evangelical truth is graciously allowed to all mankind, that they may thereby be assisted to discover, to love, and to obey their celestial Parent: and, finally, that they may reach the mark of their high destination, which is the enjoyment of those different degrees of blessedness which are reserved for the different classes of the faithful. Let us consider the morning of this sacred day. When the first man had extinguished in his heart the light of truth and the fire of charity—when he became sufficiently stupid to think of concealing himself from his God among the trees of the garden, and sufficiently impious to throw the blame of his offence upon his companion in transgression, instead of confessing his disobedience with all its aggravations—it is evident, that man was then without Christ, that is, without a Saviour, without "hope, and without God in the world," Ephesians ii:12. In that night of error and confusion, and probably of despair, the promise of a powerful Redeemer was given to our first parents, whence certain beams of hope were produced, which formed the earliest twilight of the Gospel day.

The tradition of this gracious promise, which was made to Adam and confirmed to Noah; the natural law, which is nothing less than the remains of the Creator's image in the human heart; and the secret grace of the Redeemer, which is more or less operative in every man; these collectively formed that evangelical dawn, which was for a long time universally experienced in the world, and which may with propriety be termed, either Gentilism, the religion of the first patriarch, the Gospel of the heathen, or the dispensation of the Father. In this low dispensation, and under these faint glimmerings of truth, the generality of mankind are still unhappily observed to live. And though clouds of prejudice, together with vain tradition, deprive Pagan nations, in part, of this inestimable light, yet sufficient remains among them for the direction of those who are seeking after the light of a less obscure dispensation.

When mankind had become almost universally unfaithful to the grace of Gentilism, and unmindful of the past vengeance of God in destroying the world: when they had plunged themselves into the most impious excesses, and were wholly given up to the greatest idolatry; at that time the Almighty resolved to separate from the corrupted nations a single people, who should preserve among them the Divine worship in its purity; a people, among whom the Messiah should be born, and who should spread around them both the expectation and the promise of so wonderful a Deliverer.

The Works of John Fletcher

Moses, Aaron, and Joshua, were the representatives of this extraordinary Person. Moses, as a prophet and legislator; Aaron, as a high priest appointed of God; and Joshua, as an illustrious conqueror, dividing the kingdoms of Canaan among those who had followed him through the dangers of a tedious warfare. Thus the Jews became a preaching people to the rest of the world, preserving in it the light of the Father's dispensation, and preparing it for the farther dispensation of the Son: insomuch, that the expectation of a Divine Restorer was spread over many parts of the earth, as we learn from two Pagan historians,* whose testimony deserves credit. Nay, the Sibyls, and even Virgil himself, took occasion, from this general expectation, of applying to Augustus the predictions of a sublime conqueror, who was to issue from the east, renewing the face of things.

Judaism, then, seems to have been nothing more than the dispensation of the Father, though undoubtedly more luminous than it had formerly appeared before the calling of Abraham. The moral law, given by Moses, was but a new edition of the natural law, which had been given long before, and the ceremonial law was added thereto, as a farther confirmation of the original promise. This was, however, a remarkable advance toward the dispensation of the Son and that of the Holy Ghost, since the mysteries of both were shadowed forth by the interior parts of the temple, by sacrifices, by ablutions, by anointings, by perfumes, by burning lamps, and sacred fires.

The universal creed, under this ancient dispensation, still forms a part of that which is received among Christians. And there is no true worshipper under this economy but who can say, with sincerity, "I believe in God, the Father Almighty, the Creator and Preserver of heaven and earth, the Avenger of sin, and the Rewarder of those who faithfully serve him. And I trust the time is coming when some Divine instructer will enable me more fully to know and obey this incomprehensible Father of the universe." May such an instructer soon appear! was the united prayers of Socrates and Plato. "Let him hasten his coming," says the true Jew, and the pious Theist, "under whatever appellation he may choose to appear. Let him be called the Seed of the woman, the Seed of Abraham, or the Son of David; let his name be the Messiah, the Son of God, the Logos, Emmanuel, Joshua, Jesus, Saviour; or only the Prophet, the Angel of the Covenant, or the Messenger of God; it is of little consequence. If he bring but life and immortality to light, I will receive him with gratitude and joy." Such is the faith by which those Jews, Mohammedans, and Pagans, whose hearts are principled with humility, candour, and the fear of God, have been, and still continue to be, saved in every part of the world. For the Father of mercies, who knoweth whereof we are made, will no more absolutely condemn such worshippers, on account of the extraordinary respect they have discovered for Moses, Mohammed, and Confucius, than he will finally reject some pious Christians, for the sake of that excessive veneration which they manifest for particular saints and reformers. Nor will he punish either because their guides have mingled prejudice with truth, and legendary fables with the doctrines of theology.

---

* Percrebuerat Oriente toto vetus et constans opinio, esse in fatis ut Judea profecti rerum potirentur.—SUETONIUS.
Pluribus persuasio inerat, antiquis sacerdotum libris contineri eo ipso tempore fore, ut valesceret Oriens, profectique Judea rerum potirentur.—TACITUS.

The Portrait of St. Paul

As a prudent physician proportions his medicines to the different ages and habits of his patients, so the enlightened pastor, who feels himself concerned for the spiritual health of his flock, sees it necessary to act with equal care and discretion. He preaches the dispensation of the Son to those who, like Socrates and Plato, are longing for a Divine instructer, as well as to those who, like Simeon, Nicodemus, and Cornelius, are waiting for the consolation of Israel. He leads them either from the law of Moses, or from the law of nature, to the Gospel of Christ; explaining, with precision, those parts of the New Testament, which exhibit the commencement of the Son's dispensation, together with all he taught and suffered, while he continued upon earth.

Lastly, to such as have devoutly embraced this part of the Gospel, he publishes the glorious economy of the Holy Spirit, which was not fully opened till after the bodily appearance of the Redeemer was withdrawn from the world. Then it was that he descended in the fulness of the Spirit, directing and supporting his disciples, animating and sanctifying his members, and manifesting that kingdom of God, that dispensation of righteousness, peace, and joy, which is so largely treated of in the Acts and Epistles of the Apostles.

These three dispensations have one common end. They mutually tend to manifest the different perfections of the Supreme Being, to raise man from his present low estate, and to perfect his nature. This three-fold design is apparent under the dispensation of the Father; it unfolds itself more clearly under that of the Son; and shines out with increasing lustre under that of the Holy Spirit. As it is one and the same sun that animates every thing in the natural world, so it is one and the same God who operates every thing in the kingdom of grace. He, whom we address as our heavenly Father, in that sacred form of prayer which is common among Christians, is the very God in whose name the ancient patriarchs were accustomed to bless their children. The Word, through which we address him, is no other than that "Light of the world," by which the antediluvian fathers were illuminated in their several generations: and the Holy Ghost, by which the souls of the faithful are divinely regenerated, is the same Spirit that primarily "moved upon the face of the waters," Genesis i:2; of which also it was said in the days of Noah," My Spirit shall not always strive with man," Genesis vi:3.

There never was a time in which the Son and the Spirit were not occupied in completing the salvation of believers. But there was a time when the Son became manifest upon the earth, making a visible display of his astonishing labours; and then it was that his particular dispensation had its commencement. So likewise there was a time when the Holy Ghost, more abundantly shed forth by the Father and the Son, began to work his mysterious operations in a more sensible manner, and at that time commenced the particular dispensation of the Spirit, which serves to perfect the dispensation of the Son, as that of the Son was given to perfect the dispensation of the Father.

These distinctions are founded upon reason, upon revelation, and upon the apostles' creed.

1. Reason suggests, that mankind must for ever remain under the sovereignty of their omnipotent Creator, and accountable to him for the use they make of his innumerable favours. Reason farther discovers, that if man should admit the darkness of error into his understanding, and the fatal influence of sin into his will, he cannot

possibly recover his pristine state, except through the manifestation of a new light, and the exertions of a stronger influence. But who shall produce the former, except that Saviour who is "the Light of the world," John viii:12, or who shall supply the latter, except that energetic Spirit which "helpeth our infirmities?" Romans viii:26.

2. These distinctions are founded upon revelation. The volume of truth informs us, that the Creator foretold the coming of a Redeemer, and that the Redeemer, during his outward manifestation, proclaimed the near approach of "another Comforter," John xiv16, 17. It is undoubtedly true, that some earnests of redeeming grace, together with the first fruits of the Spirit, were experienced even by the most ancient inhabitants of the earth. It is true, also, that by means of those earnests and first fruits, many myriads of mankind have been saved in every age of the world. But it is no less true, that the plenitude of these sacred girls was reserved to a very distant period of time; since, after the first promise of a Redeemer was given, near four thousand years elapsed before he made his public appearance; and while he continued upon earth it is expressly said, that "the Holy Ghost was not yet given, [in its full measure,] because that Jesus was not yet glorified," John vii:39.

3. Christians are taught to distinguish these different degrees of evangelical grace, and to rejoice in all the advantages of these three dispensations, when they are solemnly baptized in the name of the Father, the Son, and the Holy Ghost. And this they publicly profess to do, so often as they repeat the three principal articles of the apostles' creed. Happy would it be, if, through the demonstration of that Holy Spirit, in which they affect to believe, they were enabled experimentally to confess their almighty Father and his redeeming Son. Every one of them might then thankfully add, "I experience the communion of saints and the forgiveness of sins: I joyfully and confidently expect the resurrection of the body, and life everlasting."

It is presumed, that no doctrines can come more strongly recommended to the consideration of professing Christians, than those which are undeniably founded upon reason and revelation, upon that outward form of baptism and that primitive creed, which are universally received in the Christian world.

The attentive reader will easily perceive, that the difference between these several dispensations is formed by those different degrees in which the Redeemer is manifested. Under Gentilism and Judaism, or under the general and particular dispensations of the Father, the Redeemer is both announced and expected; he is announced by the Father's original promise, by tradition, by types, by prophecies; and he is expected as a Saviour who shall sooner or later make his appearance. Under the baptism of John, and under that imperfect Christianity which is received by a baptism of water, the Redeemer is apprehended, in some measure, by sense; or by a faith which merely respects the history of the Gospel: but he is apprehended only as a Saviour manifested in the flesh, to accomplish the external act of redemption. It is otherwise under that perfect Christianity to which we are introduced by the mysterious baptism of the Spirit, in which the Redeemer is manifested after a manner abundantly more glorious. He is now received as coming in the Spirit, after having died for our sins and risen again for our justification. Now he performs the spiritual work of redemption in the soul, delivering his people from the power of sin, by communicating to them the special efficacy of his death, his resurrection, and his triumph. Henceforth he is a Comforter, not only with, but in us; where he spiritually exercises his acknowledged offices, instructing, purifying, and finally subduing all things to himself.

The different preachers under these different dispensations.

PERSUADED that confusion is the source of a thousand errors, the prudent minister endeavours to place the truths of the Gospel in their proper order; and reflecting upon those preachers who have formerly proclaimed them, he is enabled to produce something upon their separate testimonies which may serve to edify the different classes of his hearers. Thus St. Paul, when preaching to the Athenians, judged it convenient to cite one of their own poets rather than Moses; and thus, in addressing those teachers who leave the Gospel in order to set up a vain philosophy, the true minister may find it necessary to produce the description which Epictetus has given of a real philosopher.

Every dispensation has had its peculiar preachers, and the pastor who is led into all truth is anxious to second these preachers, by publishing, in their proper place, those sacred truths which they have respectively delivered according to their different proportions of grace.

The preachers, under the dispensation of the Father, are,

1. *The works of creation.* "The heavens," saith David, "declare the glory of God, and the firmament showeth his handy Work," Psalm xix:1. "That which may be known of God," adds St. Paul, "is manifest," even among the heathen. "For the invisible things of him, from the creation of the world, are clearly seen, being understood by the things that are made, even his eternal power and Godhead: so that they are without excuse, because that when they knew God, they glorified him not as God," Romans i:19-21.

2. *Providence.* "The living God," saith the apostle, "who, in times past, suffered all nations to walk in their own ways, left himself not without witness, in that he did good, and gave us rain from heaven, and fruitful seasons, filling our hearts with food and gladness," Acts xiv:15, 17.

3. Those dreadful scourges with which an avenging God is constrained to correct a rebellious world; such as *famine, pestilence, war, &c.*

4. *Reason;* which is a ray from that Divine Word, that Eternal Logos, that "true Light which lighteneth every man that cometh into the world."

5. *Conscience.* "For the Gentiles," saith St. Paul, "which have not the law, [written by prophets and apostles,] are a law unto themselves; their conscience beating witness, and their thoughts accusing, or else excusing one another," Romans ii:14, 15.

6. Enoch, Noah, and all the holy patriarchs who lived before the flood.

7. All those pious persons who have inculcated the fear of God, and published the traditionary promise which was given to our first parents.

8. The prophets and priests among the Jews, together with the sacred poets and true philosophers among the ancient heathens.

9. Those priests who, among Jews, Mohammedans, and modern Pagans, recommend, with sincerity, holiness and the fear of God.

And, lastly, all those preachers of Christendom, who, blind to the dispensations of the Son and the Spirit, fall back into Gentilism, delivering only such moral essays as have been abundantly exceeded by philosophers of old.

As this dispensation has ever had, and still continues to have, its celebrated preachers; so it has frequently had, and may yet continue to have, its confessors and martyrs. If it were possible to come at the history of all those who have been eminently distinguished by their piety under this economy, and who have nobly suffered in the cause of godliness, we might probably discover many an Abel, and many a Zacharias, many an Aristides, and many a Socrates, in every nation under heaven. In company with these amiable and honourable characters, the evangelical pastor is constantly observed, so far as they proceed in the high way of truth; but he advances far beyond them when he would associate with the preachers of the Son's dispensation.

The heralds of truth, under this dispensation, are,

1. The priest, Zacharias, who announced the accomplishment of the promise which was made to the patriarchs, Luke i.

2. The angel who first brought down the tidings of the Messiah's birth, in company with the multitude of the heavenly host, who attended him upon that extraordinary occasion.

3. Those Jewish priests, who directed the Magi from Jerusalem to the city in which Christ was born.

4. Those celestial voices which declared, upon Mount Tabor and on the banks of Jordan, that Jesus was the beloved Son of the Father.

5. John the Baptist, who proclaimed Christ come in the flesh, and endeavoured to prepare the penitent for the dispensation of the Spirit.

6. Those seventy disciples who were commissioned by our Lord to preach the Gospel.

And, lastly, all those teachers of the present day who, like Apollos in the beginning of his ministry, perceive nothing beyond that inferior dispensation, of which an outward baptism is considered as the seal.

Under the dispensation of the Spirit, the preachers are,

1. The apostles, who entered upon their excellent ministry after being first miraculously endued with power from on high.

2. All those ministers of the Gospel who, after receiving into their own hearts "the Spirit of adoption," Romans viii:15, proclaim the coming of that Spirit to those who have already experienced "repentance toward God, and faith toward our Lord Jesus Christ," Acts xx:21. Such ministers alone may be said to proclaim the spiritual kingdom of God; and these alone can experimentally direct believers to the absolute fulfilment of every Gospel promise. The teachers of this day, instead of proclaiming the grand promise of Christianity, unhappily renounce that promise; imagining that it merely respected the first followers of Jesus, or, at most, that it was confined to the earliest ages of the Christian Church. Far from publishing the Gospel in its abundant plenitude, these unskilful evangelists are not able to preach all that imperfect Gospel which in Scripture language is called "the baptism of John," Acts xviii:25. John publicly announced the baptism of the Holy Ghost, and far from despising such baptism himself, he openly declared that he had "need to be baptized of Christ," Matthew iii:14. Nevertheless, John was put to death before the promise of the Father

was fully accomplished; and on this account our Lord declared that the "least in the kingdom of heaven, [that is, the lowest under the dispensation of the Spirit, should be accounted] greater than he," Matthew x:11. Yea, even the soldiers of Cornelius, after the Spirit had descended upon them, were assisted to publish the mysteries of that kingdom with greater clearness, and with a more lively conviction, than the forerunner of Jesus had ever done.

That prophet doubted before his death, as well as all the apostles before the day of pentecost. But under the dispensation of the Holy Spirit, the great truths of the Gospel are demonstrated by the power of an internal evidence, which leaves in the heart no more room for doubt than a mathematical demonstration leaves room for hesitation in the mind. Farther: John the Baptist barely intimated the necessity of a spiritual baptism: but the most illiterate among the centurion's servants could say, "Christ has baptized me with the Holy Ghost and with fire; and the promise, which he hath already fulfilled to me, who am a poor Gentile, he will as gloriously accomplish in favour of others, since the promise is given 'to all that are afar off, even as many as the Lord our God shall call,'" Acts ii:39. Thus, under this sublime dispensation, every faithful servant of the Lord is enabled to prophesy out of the fulness of his heart, and to speak the wonderful works of God. Thus also, every zealous minister, persevering in his pursuit after evangelical truth, becomes, at length, of the same society with those who were the first and most effectual preachers of the everlasting Gospel.

The dispensation of the Holy Spirit is now in force, and the minister who preaches this dispensation cannot justly be esteemed an enthusiast.

TO reject the Son of God manifested in the Spirit, as worldly Christians are universally observed to do, is a crime of equal magnitude with that of the Jews, who rejected Christ manifested in the flesh. Nevertheless, in vain has the Apostle Paul informed us, that "Jesus Christ is a priest for ever, after the order of Melchisedec," Hebrews vii:17; "the same yesterday, to-day, and for ever," Hebrews xiii:8. In vain has John the Baptist declared, that "he shall baptize us with the Holy Ghost and with fire," Matthew iii:11. In vain has Christ himself made a gracious offer of this baptism to all nations, Matthew xxviii:19. In spite of all these declarations, our incredulity still seeks out some plausible reason for rejecting the dispensation of the Spirit.

So long as those perilous times shall continue which were foretold by St. Paul, 2 Timothy iii:1, so long we may expect to behold multitudes of erring professors, who, like the ancient Pharisees, not only refuse to enter into the kingdom of God themselves, but resolutely withstand all those who are striving to enter in. These faithless Christians, resembling the timorous spies of old, are constantly prepared to discourage every persevering Israelite, by raising evil reports of their promised rest. Attached to this present degenerate world, as the wife of Lot was attached to her polluted city, they are ever insinuating, that there is little danger to be apprehended in their present situation. And as for that full dispensation of the Spirit, concerning which so many excellent things are spoken, they confidently assert, that it cannot be expected in the present time, without giving way to the highest presumption and folly. On these accounts it becomes absolutely necessary that the true minister should stand prepared to give every man a solid answer, "that asketh a reason of the hope that is in him," 1 Peter iii:15.

That the extraordinary gifts of the Holy Spirit were peculiarly necessary to the apostles, and that they were actually put in possession of such gifts, we readily allow. But, at the same time, we consider those gifts as entirely distinct from the Spirit itself. When the Spirit of grace takes the full possession of a particular person, he may, if the edification of the Church requires it, bestow upon that person some extraordinary gift in an instantaneous manner: as the prince, who honours any subject with an important commission, invests him with sufficient power for the execution of such commission. But the presents of a prince do not always demonstrate his actual presence; since it is very possible for a prince to lodge with one of his subjects, upon whom he has conferred no inestimable favour, while he makes a magnificent present to another, whom he has never condescended to visit in person. Thus the Holy Spirit descended upon Mary the mother of Jesus, together with several other holy women, as well as upon the apostles, with whom they continued in earnest supplication and prayer: nevertheless, it does not appear that any one of them received even the gift of tongues. On the other hand, we are well assured, that many persons, who never received the Spirit of holiness, were yet outwardly distinguished by several extraordinary gifts of the Holy Ghost. The first king of Israel gave rise to that memorable proverb, "Is Saul also among the prophets?" 1 Samuel x:12. Jonah, though he possessed neither the faith nor the charity which are common to many Christians of this age, was yet commissioned to visit Nineveh with an extraordinary message from heaven. And we are informed that Judas was endued with the power of performing miracles, as Balaam had before been honoured with the gift of prophecy. But, notwithstanding these external appearances, we may rest assured, that neither Saul, nor Balaam, nor Judas, had fully experienced that happy estate which the meanest among the primitive Christians was permitted to enjoy. When, therefore, we assert, that every sincere believer becomes a "temple of the Holy Ghost," 1 Corinthians vi:19; it is not to be understood by such expression, that they have received the power of working miracles: since in this sense St. Paul himself was not always replenished with the Spirit. But it should rather be understood, that the same Spirit of humility, of zeal, of faith, and of charity, which so eminently dwelt in Christ, continually flows from him to the meanest of his spiritual members, as the sap is known to pass from the trunk of a vine into the least of its branches, John xv:5.

The Old and New Testament sufficiently prove, that the special influences of the Spirit are to be universally experienced by the faithful in every age. Isaiah promises this invaluable blessing to those who are athirst for God, Isaiah xliv:3. Ezekiel announces the same blessing, in a variety of passages, to all those who enjoy the privileges of the new covenant. The Prophet Joel more directly promises the extraordinary effusion of the Holy Spirit, to "the young and the old [among the people of God; to] their sons and their daughters, their servants and their handmaids," Joel ii:28, 29. John the Baptist expressly repeats the same promise to all those who partake of his inferior baptism, Luke iii:16 Our Lord invites every believer freely to come and receive the long-expected blessing, John vii:37, 39. St. Peter unreservedly offers it to the truly penitent, Acts ii:38; and St. Paul every where declares that it is the common privilege of Christians to "be filled with the Spirit,"

Ephesians v:18; 1 Corinthians vi:19. Nay, he even intimates, that the name of Christian should be refused to those who have not received the promise of the Father, Romans viii:9. These few passages abundantly testify, how strangely those professors deceive themselves, who confidently affirm that the Holy Spirit was promised to the apostles alone.

Revelation is no sooner admitted, but reason itself confirms the very truth for which we contend. Why was the Holy Spirit to be poured out in its full measure upon the first followers of Christ? If in order to their sanctification; have we less need of holiness than the apostles had? If it was to shed abroad in their hearts the love of God; is that love less necessary for us than for them? If to make intercession for them with groanings which cannot be uttered; were the apostles supposed to stand in greater need of such intercession than all other men? Lastly, if the Holy Ghost was given, that believers might be enabled to cry out, "Who shall separate us from the love of Christ? Shall tribulation, persecution, or death? O death, where is thy sting? O grave, where is thy victory? Thanks be to God, who giveth us the victory, through our Lord Jesus Christ,"—if so, then it should seem, that the apostles alone were called to suffer and die in a manner so perfectly worthy of Christians.

The more we meditate upon the Scriptures of truth, the more we shall be convinced that the experience of real Christians, and the reason of natural men, coincide with that sacred volume, in demonstrating that the grand promise of a Comforter must respect every sincere believer, as well as the first disciples of Jesus. To reject, then, this precious gift, is to trample under foot the pearl of great price, and to despise the Redeemer himself in that spiritual appearance, which is of far greater importance to us than his outward manifestation in Judea. Farther: to insinuate among Christians, that the promise of Christ's spiritual coming is no longer in force, is to enervate the glorious Gospel of God, and to maintain in his Church that detestable lukewarmness, which will ultimately prove the ground of its condemnation. It is to surpass the Jews in their obstinate rejection of our only Lord and Saviour. There was no need, says the incredulous Jew, that the Messiah should suffer and die for our sins: nor is there any need, says the carnal Christian, that the Saviour should come in a spiritual manner to reign in my heart. The one destroys the body, the other the soul, of Christianity; and both are equally strangers to the renovating power of the Gospel.

The true minister, struck with the magnitude of this sin, so general in the present day, incessantly labours for the restoration of those who are deeply plunged in so destructive an error.

The evangelical pastor defends the dispensation of the Spirit against all opposers.

WHATEVER dispensation of grace the true minister announces, he is constrained, with St. Paul, to brandish his spiritual weapons on the right hand and on the left. If he publishes the dispensation of the Father, he finds it necessary to defend its important truths against the daringly profane on the one hand, and on the other against the vainly superstitious. When he preaches the dispensation of the Son, he has still greater occasion to arm himself, in every part, in defence of the doctrine he maintains. On the left hand he is attacked either by Deists, who wholly disclaim all ideas of a Saviour; or by Socinians, who despoil that Saviour of his greatest glory; and on the right he is assailed by ill-instructed Christians, who, under pretence of exalting the Son, look down with contempt upon the dispensation of the Father; not considering that by this error they oppose one principal design of Christ's appearing, which was, that we might worship the Father in spirit and in truth. But it is chiefly with respect to the third dispensation that the Christian preacher is constrained to wield, without ceasing, that "sword of the Spirit," and that "shield of faith," Ephesians vi:16, 17, with which St. Paul was so anxious to see every Christian armed. As this doctrine is abundantly more elevated than the preceding dispensations, so it stands more exposed to the shafts of innumerable enemies. On the left it is incessantly attacked by carnal professors, and on the right by fanatical zealots. These two classes of adversaries, though continually at war with each other, unhappily agree in opposing, either directly or indirectly, the progress of this glorious dispensation, obliging the faithful minister with equal intrepidity to combat both.

Observe the grand argument with which carnal Christians carry on this opposition. "The Comforter," say they, "which was graciously promised to our Lord's first disciples, was undoubtedly received by those highlyfavoured missionaries, and conducted them into all the truths Of the Gospel. From this Divine Spirit they received continual assistance in spreading that Gospel, and by him they were endued with those miraculous gifts which served as so many incontestable marks of their sacred mission. But as Christianity is at this time firmly established in the world, the letter of the Holy Scriptures is now abundantly sufficient for every, purpose: and there is no longer any necessity for that baptism and illumination of the Spirit, which were evidently requisite among the primitive Christians."

As the mistaken Jews, perfectly satisfied with the law of Moses, inscribed upon tables of stone, rejected, with obstinacy, the promised Messiah: so these carnal Christians, contented with the letter of the New Testament, perversely reject the "Holy Spirit of promise," Ephesians i:13. "Search the Scriptures; for they testify of me," John v:39, was our Lord's exhortation to these deluded formalists. And the true minister continues to press the same exhortation upon those who blindly oppose the coming of Christ's spiritual kingdom. He is anxious, with his heavenly Master, to put the matter upon this issue; fully conscious, that they who peruse those sacred pages with an unprejudiced mind, must readily observe, that, instead of superseding the necessity of a spiritual baptism, they give ample testimony that such baptism is to be considered as a privilege freely offered to the whole multitude of believers.

When Christians affirm that the manifestation of the Spirit is no longer to be sought after, except in that mysterious volume which promises this manifestation to the Church; modern Jews might as well declare that they look for no other manifestation of their Messiah, than that which is to be found in those books of Moses and the prophets, where the coming of that Messiah is repeatedly promised. But if it be said, "The Spirit of Christ was fully given to his first disciples, and that is sufficient for us;" this argument has in it as great absurdity as the following method of reasoning: "Moses instructs us, that God created the sun, and that the patriarchs were happily enlightened by it: but the supreme illumination of that sun is no longer to be discovered, except in the writings of Moses; and those labourers are downright enthusiasts, who imagine they need any other rays from that luminary, except such as are reflected upon them from the book of Genesis. The Scripture informs us, that God commanded the earth to produce a variety of fruits and plants for the nourishment of its inhabitants; covenanting, on his part, to send refreshing rains and convenient seasons. "But we do not live," exclaims a rational farmer, "in the season of miracles, nor am I enthusiastic enough to expect that rain shall be sent upon the earth. Mention indeed is made, in ancient history, of the former and the latter rain; and the books which speak of these fructifying showers, and promise a continuance of them to the latest posterity, are undoubtedly authentic: nevertheless, all the rain we can now reasonably expect, must flow from these books alone, and from those speculations which our reason can make upon the truths they contain." Who will not smile at such a method of reasoning as this?

In those things which respect our temporal interests, we are not stupid enough to be deluded by such wretched sophisms, though we frequently deceive both ourselves and others, with regard to spiritual things, by arguments no less palpably absurd. "God, says the orthodox professor, "undoubtedly caused the Sun of righteousness so effectually to shine upon believers, on the day of pentecost, that they were instantaneously baptized "with the Holy Ghost and with fire." A celestial shower, at that time, refreshed the Church; and the mystic vine, matured on a sudden, by the direct rays of so glorious a luminary, was assisted to produce, internally, all the graces, and, externally, all the fruits of the Spirit. But such extraordinary phenomena, which accompanied that dazzling sun, and those gracious showers, have long ago disappeared. Nay, that sun itself is totally eclipsed, with respect to us; and the book, which bears testimony to the constant influence of that sun, and the endless duration of those showers, now absolutely stands in the place of both." Ridiculous divinity! And shall they be called enthusiasts who oppose such absurdities as these? Then fanaticism may be said to consist in making a rational distinction between the pearl of great price and the testament that bequeaths it; between that sacred volume, in which the Comforter is merely promised, and the actual presence of that Comforter in the heart. To pretend that we have no longer any need of the Spirit of Christ, because we are in possession of an incomparable book, which declares, that "if any man have not the Spirit of Christ, he is none of his," Romans viii:9, is not this to destroy, at once, both the letter and spirit of the Gospel? And when we see those Christians who profess the utmost respect for revelation, deriding, without fear, the manifestation of that Spirit, by which alone "the love of God [can be] shed abroad in our hearts," Romans v:5, what judgment can we form of such persons, but that they are disposed to treat the Gospel of our glorified Master as Judas once treated its persecuted Author? Whatever air of devotion they may assume, while they salute the exterior of it, their secret intention is to betray the very life of the Gospel to derision and infamy. By arguments of this nature it is that Christian ministers are frequently obliged to defend the dispensation of the Spirit from the outrageous attacks of carnally-minded Christians.

But there are times in which the faithful pastor finds it equally necessary to defend this part of his doctrine against high and fanatical professors. In every Christian country there are not wanting such as have rendered the dispensation of that Spirit contemptible, by their ridiculous and impious pretensions. Protestants have blushed for the prophets of Cevennes, and Catholics for the Convulsionaries of Paris. In order successfully to oppose the progress of enthusiasm, he publicly contrasts the

The Works of John Fletcher

two different characters of a presumptuous fanatic and an enlightened Christian, in some such terms as follow. The one extinguishes the torch of reason, that he may have opportunity to display, in its room, the vain flashes of his own pretended inspirations; the other entertains a just respect for reason, following it as the surest guide, so far as it is able to direct him in the search of truth; and whenever he implores a superior light, it is merely to supply the defects of reason. The one destroys the clear sense of Scripture language, that a way may be made for his own particular manifestations: the other refers every thing "to the law, and to the testimony," fully satisfied, that if high pretenders to sanctity "speak not according to this word, it is because there is no light in them," Isaiah viii:20. The former flatters himself, that while the means are neglected, the end may be obtained, presuming that God will illuminate him in a miraculous manner, without the help of prayer, study, meditations, sermons, or sacraments. The latter unpresumingly expects the succours of grace, in a constant use of the appointed means; and, conscious that "the Holy Scriptures are able to make him wise unto salvation," 2 Timothy iii:15, he takes them for the subject of his frequent meditation, the ground of his prayers, and the grand rule of his conduct. The fanatic imagines himself independent of superior powers both in Church and state. The real Christian, a constant friend to truth and order, looking upon himself as the servant of all, not only acknowledges the respect due to his superiors, but is ready to give them an account either of his faith or his conduct, with meekness and submission; and anxious to have his principles supported by appeals to the reason and conscience of his adversaries, as well as by the testimony of revelation. The fanatic pays but little regard to the inestimable grace of charity. Like Simon, the sorcerer, he aspires after the extraordinary gifts of the Spirit, and, seduced by a vain imagination, forsakes the substance that he may pursue the shadow. The true Christian, without despising the most inconsiderable spiritual girls, implores only those which may assist him in the discharge of his several duties, and peculiarly that of charity, which is to be ranked as high above the performance of miracles, as miracles are to be esteemed above the tricks of jugglers. The fanatic conceives himself to be animated by the Spirit of God, when his body is agitated by a rapid motion of the animal spirits, excited by the sallies of an overheated imagination and augmented by hysterical or hypochondriacal vapours. The judicious Christian detests this enthusiasm, which, covering religion with a veil of delusion and frenzy, renders it contemptible in the eyes of those who are ever ready to treat devotion as fanaticism.

When the true minister unhappily falls among persons who evidence a disposition to enthusiasm, carrying mortification to an unwarrantable excess, publicly uttering long and passionate prayers, produced with the most violent efforts, he calls their attention to that beautiful passage in the history of Elijah, where God is represented as manifesting himself, neither in the wind, the earthquake, nor the fire; but in a still small voice. To inspire them with a just horror for this kind of fanaticism, he points them to those contemptible characters whose conduct they are unwittingly copying, and exhorts them to leave the horrible custom of "crying with a loud voice," together with every other species of religious extravagance, to the superstitious priests of Baal. If it be necessary, he even applies those sarcastic expressions of Elijah, "Cry aloud," &c. In performing this part of his duty, he is anxious, however, to act with the utmost discretion; not ridiculing the fanatical with an irreverent lightness, but exhorting them with all possible affection and solemnity. It appears, from the writings of St. Paul, that enthusiasm had once risen to so great a height in the Corinthian Church, that the communion was polluted by the members of that Church, and its public ordinances thrown into the utmost disorder. Now, if the apostle had himself been an enthusiast, he would have seen these disorders without regret; or had he been like the ministers of the present day, he would have rejoiced at the pretext afforded him by the fanatical Corinthians, for turning into ridicule devotion and zeal, the power of prayer, and the gift of exhortation. But, equally attached both to order and zeal, he wrote to them in the following terms: "I would that ye all spake with tongues, but rather that ye prophesied: for he that prophesieth edifieth the Church. Forasmuch, then, as ye are zealous of spiritual gifts, seek that ye may excel to the edifying of the Church. Brethren, be not children in understanding, but men. Ye may all prophesy, that all may learn, and all may be comforted." And observe this, that "the spirits of the prophets are subject to the prophets: for God is not the author of confusion, but of peace, as in all Churches of the saints. If any man think himself to be a prophet, or spiritual, let him acknowledge that the things I write unto you are the commandments of the Lord. Let all things be done decently, and in order," 1 Corinthians xiv. It is by adopting the admirable method of this apostle, that the good pastor endeavours to root up the tares of enthusiasm, without injuring the invaluable grain of devotion.

Here it may, perhaps, be inquired, "If particular manifestations of the Spirit are admitted, how is it possible to shut the door against dangerous illusions? Would it not be wiser entirely to reject the dispensation of the Spirit, while it is confessedly attended with so many difficulties? And would it not make for the happiness of the Church, were every member of it to rest contented with having all the Holy Scriptures explained according to the best rules of reason and criticism?" We answer, By no means. Bad money, indeed, is frequently put into our hands; but is it necessary, on this account, to obstruct the free course of that which is intrinsically good? And would it be reasonable to refuse a sovereign prince the right of coining for the state, lest that coin should be counterfeited or defaced? As, in society, after warning the public of their danger, we content ourselves with apprehending the man who attempts to impose upon us in this way; so we may rest fully satisfied with adopting the same mode of conduct in regard to the Church of God.

Let it be here observed, that the operations of the Holy Spirit upon the hearts of believers are to be distinguished from the effects of enthusiasm in the imagination of visionaries, just as readily as we distinguish health from sickness, wisdom from folly, and truth from falsehood. The believers of Rome could say, "The Spirit itself beareth witness with our spirit, that we are the children of God," Romans viii:16. "By one Spirit are we all baptized," say the Corinthians, "and have been all made to drink into one Spirit," 1 Corinthians xii:13. And St. Paul could testify, that many of the Ephesians were "sealed by the Holy Spirit of God, unto the day of redemption," Ephesians iv:30. "These were all enthusiasts," says a modern doctor, "unless they could restore sight to the blind, raise the dead from their graves, and fluently converse in a variety of languages, which they had never taken the trouble to study." No, insinuates the apostle, you forget the essential for the accessory, and found your system upon false suppositions. "Are all workers of miracles? Have all the gifts of healing? Do all speak with tongues?" There must, then, be some more indubitable method of distinguishing those whose bodies are become temples of the Holy Ghost; and "I show unto you this more excellent way," 1 Corinthians xii:29-31. What was

The Works of John Fletcher

meant by this excellent way, may be satisfactorily discovered by an attentive perusal of the following chapter, in which the apostle would have the examination to turn, not upon the gift of prophecy, and much less that of languages, but essentially upon all the characters of charity. This was the reasoning of Augustine, as well as of St. Paul, when he made use of the following expression: "You then speak from the Spirit of God, when you speak from a heart glowing with love."f6 This also was the method in which Christ himself was accustomed to argue on this point. "Beware," said he, "of false prophets. Every good tree bringeth forth good fruit. Wherefore by their fruits ye shall know them," Matthew vii:15, 20. And "the fruit of the Spirit," continues St. Paul, "is love, joy, peace, long suffering, gentleness, goodness, faith, meekness, temperance," Galatians v:22, 23. Now fanaticism was never known to bear such fruits as these. On the contrary, it produces divisions, foolish joy, or stupid melancholy, trouble, impatience, and excess of different kinds. Nay, it is frequently observed to produce assertions diametrically opposite both to Scripture and reason, together with absurd pretensions to new revelations.

It may be asked, in this place, with a show of reason, "If Christ still continues to reveal himself by his Spirit to every true believer, are not such manifestations to be considered as so many new revelations?" To this we reply, That when the apostle of the Gentiles petitioned for his Ephesian converts, "the Spirit of wisdom and revelation," Ephesians i:17, he was not to be understood as requesting that God would communicate to them a new Gospel, but rather that he would assist them to discover all the glory, and to experience all the power of that inestimable Gospel which had been already published among them. "'Open mine eyes," said David, "that I may behold wondrous things out of thy law," Psalm cxi:10, 18. And when God was graciously pleased to answer this prayer of the royal prophet, he undoubtedly visited him with the illumination of his Holy Spirit. But that Spirit was imparted, not for the purpose of revealing to him a new law, but merely that he might be enabled to fathom the depths of that holy law, which had been given long before. Thus also Christian believers are constantly offering up their joint supplications, that God would strengthen them "by his Spirit in the inner man," not for the experience of new revelations, but "that they may be enabled to comprehend, with all saints, the unsearchable love of Christ; and be filled with all the fulness of God," Ephesians iii:16, 19.

After having defended internal Christianity against carnal Christians and deluded fanatics, the faithful pastor is obliged, on another part. to resist the attacks of gainsaying philosophers. And this he endeavours to do, by reasoning with them upon this important subject in the following manner:—

We consider the Supreme Being as a Divine Sun, whose centre is every where, and whose circumference is no where. A Sun, whose light is truth, and whose heat is charity. The truths of Christianity we consider as so many beams issuing from this glorious Sun, for the illumination of the soul: and as the rays of the natural sun may be collected and rendered more powerful by the interposition of a properly constructed medium, so the rays of this Divine Sun are concentred and rendered more operative by the humanity of Christ. When any of these rays, passing through the understanding, begin to strike forcibly upon the heart, they melt down its stubbornness, refine its nature, and kindle in it a fire of love to God and man. Farther: we believe these changes to be effected in the soul by that secret energy which is called by many "the inspiration of the Holy Spirit," by some the "influence" of that Spirit, and by others "the grace of God."

Is there any absurdity in this doctrine? Can the intellectual world be supposed to merit the Creator's attention in a less degree than the material world? If the rays of light that incessantly issue from the sun are supposed to pass through many millions of miles in a single moment, for the illumination and support of the material world, should it appear incredible, that the most speedy and effectual succours may be imparted to holy souls, by that more glorious Sun, which enlightens and vivifies the intellectual world? From the cedar of Lebanon to the moss that covers its bark, no plant can vegetate; from the astronomer, who measures the heavens, to the animalcule that loses itself in the cup of a violet as in a vast abyss, not a creature can exist, but through the all-pervading influence of the natural sun. Beneath this wonderful star, not a single animal is found, which carries in itself its grand principle of light, heat, and motion. And if all organized bodies depend upon this indescribable luminary for their existence, their increase, and their perfection; may we not reasonably argue from the rules of analogy, that as certainly as there is a spiritual world, so there must be a spiritual Sun, which carries life and light to the inhabitants of that world?

Do you act in a rational manner, continues the true minister, if, because you cannot comprehend how this Sun may be said to act upon spirits, you shut your eyes against his light, and obstinately deny his very existence? Can you comprehend how the material sun, without suffering any decay in himself, is continually darting around him rays sufficient to illumine and cheer revolving worlds? Can you explain how these rays are impelled by such amazing velocity, through the immense space by which that sun is separated from those worlds? Or can you describe the means by which they awaken in us the sensation of sight? Moreover, is it not absurd to suppose that the Almighty is more solicitous that we should perceive the difference between white and black, than that we should discover the more important distinctions between virtue and vice, truth and error?

If you object, that the material sun is plainly perceived, and the power of his beams universally felt by mankind, it may be replied, that he is not always discoverable. Sometimes he is eclipsed; frequently he is enveloped with thick clouds; and at other times his rays glance upon us in so oblique a manner, that their influence is scarcely perceptible. It is possible also to exclude his light by means of curtains or walls, and the cataract effectually opposes his most direct beams. In the moral world there are obstacles of a similar nature, which frequently obstruct the course of celestial light. Clouds of error and vice are constantly rising around us, which, by obscuring the Sun of righteousness, leave room for the incredulous to doubt of his existence. The eye is, in general, so much dazzled with the glare of material objects, that it cannot discover the lustre of a different light. Sometimes, invincible prejudice, like a confirmed cataract, intercepts the strongest rays of truth: and at other times, we are so closely shut up within the narrow limits of self love, that the most piercing beams of uncreated love cannot penetrate into our gloomy retirement, where that spark of reason, which might have directed us to a higher light, is, at length, totally extinguished.

The light of the Gospel is never absolutely rejected, but through the influence of sin, according to those words of Christ, "Every one that doeth evil hateth the light, neither cometh to the light, lest his deeds should be reproved," John iii:20. And here we see the cause, why so many persons cast themselves headlong into materialism, denying the inspiration of the Holy Spirit, and treating every impression of his power as the workings of a disordered brain. But as the testimony of blind men can never persuade a reasonable person that he is under a delusion, while he sees, feels, and admires the material sun; so the joint testimony of all the incredulous men in the world may justly be counted of as little force, when they would prove Scriptural illumination to be downright fanaticism. Notwithstanding all the impotent arguments that can be brought against him, the Christian believer deserves not to be esteemed an enthusiast, when he declares that "faith is the evidence of things not seen;" since he has reason and revelation to plead in his favour, his own experience, and that of his brethren, together with the universal testimony of the primitive Church.

As you do not rank with professed Atheists, it is probable that you sometimes pray to the Supreme Being. Among other blessings, you implore of him, in a peculiar manner, patience to sustain those afflictions which are necessary to the perfection of virtue. Now if you are persuaded that God is able not only to hear, but to strengthen you with his might: and, farther, if you believe that when he thus strengthens you for the day of affliction, you shall have any perception of his influencing power; we are then perfectly agreed. But if you pray without a confidence that God attends to your prayer, and without ever expecting to receive the assistance you implore of him, you act like persons deprived of their reasoning powers. Through the fear of praying like enthusiasts, you pray after the manner of idiots, and afford as manifest a token of extravagant folly, as though you should entreat tempests to grow calm, or beseech rivers to return to their sources. It is by such a method of reasoning that the true minister resists the attacks of prejudiced philosophers, solicitous to make it appear that the sanctifying and consoling operations of the Holy Spirit are as conformable to reason, as they are correspondent to our urgent necessities.

But, if it still be urged by the enemies of inspiration, that we have no distinct idea of the manner in which any knowledge is conveyed to the soul, except by means of our reason, or our senses; and that to speak of things, which will admit of no clear explanation, is running into the wildest enthusiasm: no, returns the faithful pastor, it is not usual to esteem that man an enthusiast who is employed in bestowing alms upon the poor, though he can neither explain to us how his gold was produced in the mine, how his will actuates his hand, or how the feelings of charity are excited in his bosom. If nature operates every thing in a mysterious manner, it is unreasonable to expect that the operations of grace should be conducted in a less mysterious way. This is one of the arguments proposed by our Lord to Nicodemus: "Except a man be born of the Spirit, he cannot enter into the kingdom of God." But, it may be, you have no comprehension of spiritual things: marvel not, however, at this; since there are many things above your comprehension in the natural world. "The wind bloweth where it listeth, and thou hearest the sound thereof, but canst not tell whence it cometh, and whither it goeth; so is every one that is born of the Spirit:" they prove the operations of that Spirit by incontestable effects, though they are unacquainted with many things, respecting the manner in which those effects are produced, John iii:5, 8.

We may here very properly apply what Professor Vernet has said concerning the manner in which God has frequently manifested the truth to his prophets. "It is easy to conceive," says this judicious divine, "that He who created the soul as well as the body, and who for that reason is called the Father of spirits, can never be at a loss for adequate means of communicating to us, when he judges it necessary, ideas and discoveries wholly different from those which we are able to acquire either by our own powers, or through the assistance of other persons. If the most ignorant classes of men are acquainted with the art of reciprocally communicating their thoughts to each other; how much more may we imagine that God is able to act upon the soul, both externally and internally; he who has already placed within us some confused notions of primitive truth; he who holds second causes in his hands, and animates all nature." (*Verite de la Religion Chretienne*, tom. I.)

But it it be asked, "Are not prophets, properly so called, the only persons whom God is pleased to privilege with such impressions as are formed by the seal of his Spirit?" It might, with equal propriety, be inquired, whether the apostles alone were privileged with that evangelical faith, which respects invisible and incomprehensible things, Hebrews xi:1, "A soul," says the illustrious Crousaz, "upon which the Spirit of God has moved, muses upon her Creator with ineffable delight, and contemplates her Redeemer with a mixture of gratitude, admiration, and transport. O my God! such a soul is incessantly crying out, When shall I see thy face? When shall thy light illuminate me, without one darkening cloud? To approach thee is my only happiness. Happy they who praise thee without ceasing."

"I acknowledge," continues this Christian philosopher, "that these may be the natural effects of that attention, with which the Spirit of God has graciously fixed our minds upon those objects, which revelation presents to our view, and upon which it directs us to occupy our thoughts. But I am not afraid of going beyond the truth when I add, that the Spirit of God, by his own immediate agency, may inspire the soul with this sacred taste and these exalted sentiments. Corporeal objects act upon the organs of sense by a power which they undoubtedly receive from God. This may, in some measure, be understood: but in what manner their action passes from thence upon the soul, is a mystery too obscure to admit of an explanation. Christian philosophers have conceived, that the will of God, and some established order of his appointment, are the only cause of those internal sentiments, of which these impressions upon the outward organs are but the occasion. This being the case, under what pretext can we refuse to believe that the Spirit of God may give rise to such sentiments in the soul, as are abundantly more conformable to the nature of their holy cause, than those ordinary sentiments, which are, nevertheless, referred to the will of God, as their first and true cause? Such are those sentiments which St. Paul so earnestly solicited for his followers at Ephesus, and for the increase of which he implored upon them the influence of the Holy Spirit," Ephesians iii:14, 21. (*See Professor Crousaz's sermon upon* 2 Corinthians xiii:14.)

Such also are those impressions, motions, and aids of the Holy Spirit, both mediate and immediate, for which we offer up so many ardent supplications in different parts of our public service. Every Christian liturgy is filled with petitions of this nature; petitions which are equally conformable to the principles of Christianity, the voice of reason, and the necessities of sinful men; though they usually appear to the children of this world as the mere unintelligible jargon of enthusiasm. The minister who strictly follows the example of St. Paul in this respect, will most probably be regarded as a visionary by the ignorant and the profane: but while he breathes out these ardent prayers, in humble faith, accompanying them with those discourses and that conduct which are correspondent to such requests, he has, at least, a satisfactory consciousness that he has never practised the arts of an impostor with the liturgy in his hand; nor played the part of a comedian in a Christian pulpit.

As to the real advantages which may be expected to flow from our doctrine of the dispensations, though they have been adverted to in various passages of this work, yet it appears not unnecessary to take a transient review of them in this place.

1. By an accurate acquaintance with these dispensations, every evangelical preacher may become an approved workman, "rightly dividing the word of truth," 2 Timothy ii:15; and a faithful servant, distributing to every domestic of his Master's household, that peculiar portion of spiritual food which is suited to their several circumstances, Matthew xxiv:45.

2. By exactly dividing the dispensations of grace, we are enabled to mark out the boundaries of those particular states which believers of different classes are observed to enjoy. We ascertain that degree of spiritual life to which we ourselves have attained. We distinguish the various graces bestowed upon us: we discover whatever great promise is still before *us,* and solicit, without ceasing, the accomplishment of that promise. He who preaches the Gospel, without tracing out the lines which separate the three dispensations of grace, may be said to exhibit a sun dial upon which the hours are unmarked, and from which little else than confusion, if not dangerous mistakes, can be expected to flow.

3. By the light of this doctrine, true worshippers of every different class may be taught to acknowledge and esteem one another, according to their different degrees of faith. Nothing is more common in a Christian country, than to see the rigidly orthodox uncharitably treating, as hopeless outcasts, not only those virtuous Deists who are yet unacquainted with the Son, but even those pious Socinians, who are resting satisfied with that inglorious state in which the first disciples of our Lord were so long detained, and who are unable to acknowledge any more than his humanity. Let these orthodox professors become acquainted with the various dispensations of grace, and ceasing to offend either virtuous Deists or pious Socinians with their furious anathemas; they will treat the former with all the benevolence which St. Peter once expressed toward Cornelius, and the latter with that brotherly kindness which Aquila manifested in his carriage toward Apollos. On the other hand, if those Christians, who are yet carnal, had any proper idea of these different dispensations; if they could believe that the same Jesus who was once outwardly manifested among the Jews, still continues to manifest himself in the Spirit through every part of the world, to those who are anxiously pressing into the kingdom of God; if they could admit, but in theory, this eminent dispensation of grace, they would no longer argue against those, as enthusiasts, who speak of the influence of the Spirit in Scriptural terms.

So long as this glorious light shall continue in obscurity, so long we may expect to observe among Christians the most unfriendly disputes: and though they never again may kindle blazing piles for their mutual destruction, yet bitter words, interchanged among them, like so many envenomed shafts, will continue sternly to declare that war is in their hearts. Those who imagine themselves in possession of the purest Christian faith, will treat others, who indulge different sentiments, as infidels and heretics; while these, in return, will stigmatize their uncharitable brethren with the opprobrious epithets of enthusiastic and fanatic.

But when every minister of the Gospel, enlightened with truth, and glowing with charity, shall faithfully conduct the flock of Christ from grace to grace, and from strength to strength, then the foremost of that flock will manifest their religious superiority, by giving proofs of the most unfeigned affection toward the meanest and most infirm of their spiritual companions. Copying the humble courtesy of St. Paul, these unpresuming elders will cry out among their younger brethren, "Let us, as many as be like minded, forgetting those things which are behind, and reaching forth unto the things which are before, press earnestly toward the mark, for the prize of the high calling of God in Christ Jesus; and if in any thing ye be otherwise minded," that perfect charity, which hopeth all things, engages us to believe that "God shall reveal even this unto you. Nevertheless, whereto we have already attained, let us walk by the same rule, let us mind the same things," Philippians iii:13, 16.

It may not be amiss to conclude these remarks upon the three grand dispensations of grace, by observing how imperfect worshippers deceive themselves, while they refuse to proceed from faith to faith. It is the opinion of many sincere Deists, who are zealous for the dispensation of the Father, that were they to embrace the dispensation of the Son, they must necessarily detract from the honour due to the incomprehensible God. This prejudice, however, evidently flows from the want of spiritual discernment; since the Holy Scripture instructs us, that when "at the name of Jesus every knee shall bow, and every tongue confess that he is Lord of heaven and earth," such religious adoration shall be considered as ultimately heightening "the glory of God the Father," Philippians ii:10, 11. For if the Father leads us to the Son, by the drawings of his grace, as we are taught by the following passages: "No man can come unto me, except the Father draw him," John vi:44. "Simon Peter said, Thou art Christ, the Son of the living God: Jesus answered him, Blessed art thou, Simon Barjona: for flesh and blood hath not revealed it unto thee, but my Father which is in heaven," Matthew xvi:16, 17. It is equally certain, that, when we come to Christ, he teaches us both to know and worship the Father. Observe the language of our Lord, with respect to this point. "I am the way, the truth, and the life: no man cometh unto the Father but by me," John xiv:6. "Father, glorify thy Son, that thy Son also may glorify thee. This is life eternal, that they might know thee the only true God, and Jesus Christ whom thou hast sent. Righteous Father, the world hath not known thee: but I have known thee, and these have known that thou hast sent me," to make an open display of thy glory upon earth. "I have declared unto them thy name, and I will declare it, yet more perfectly, John xvii. From these passages it evidently appears, that the faith of the Son can never possibly take away from that profound veneration which is due to the Father. And what is here observed, relative to the faith of the Son, is no less true with regard to the faith of the Holy Spirit. For, if under the dispensation of Jesus, we learn to address our "Father, who is in heaven," with a degree of humble confidence, it is only under the dispensation of the Spirit that we are enabled to make those addresses with all that filial reverence and that lively fervour which the Gospel requires. This "Spirit of adoption," by witnessing "with our spirit that we are the children of God," Romans viii:15, 16, assists us to bow before our celestial Parent with that ineffable veneration and love which are due to the Supreme Being. If philosophers would duly reflect upon these important truths, they would no longer tremble under the vain apprehension of becoming idolaters and tritheists, by admitting the doctrines of the Gospel. On the contrary, we might indulge a hope that these proud reasoners would one day be seen, in company with humble believers, approaching the God of their fathers, through the intercession of the Son, and with the energy of the Holy Spirit; crying out with St. Paul, "There is one God, and one Mediator between God and man, the man Christ Jesus," 1 Timothy ii:5: "and through him we have access, by one Spirit, unto the Father," Ephesians ii:18.

There is another class of worshippers who are zealous for the dispensation of the Son, and who, wholly taken up with the "Word manifested in the flesh," imagine that his dispensation is rendered contemptible, if it be represented merely as the commencement of Christianity, while the perfection of the Gospel is declared to consist in the dispensation of the Holy Spirit. To the consideration of such, we would propose the following expression of St. Paul: "Henceforth know we no man after the flesh: yea, though we have known Christ after the flesh, yet henceforth know we him no more," after this manner, 2 Corinthians v:16. And though our Lord is acknowledged to have spoken on this wise, "Whoso eateth my flesh, and drinketh my blood, hath eternal life; and I will raise him up at the last day: for my flesh is meat indeed, and my blood is drink indeed:" yet it must likewise be confessed that he immediately added, "It is the Spirit that quickeneth; the flesh profiteth nothing," John vi:54, 63.

The following observations, it is hoped, will entirely dissipate the fears of these pious persons:—"When the Spirit of truth is come," saith our Lord, "he will guide you into all truth;" and especially into those truths which respect faith toward me, and repentance toward my Father. "He shall glorify me; for he shall receive of mine, and shall show unto you" the merits of my righteousness, the efficacy of my death, and the power of my Gospel, John xvi:13, 14. "The Father shall give you another Comforter, which ye" already know in part; "for he dwelleth with you," even now in my bodily presence, "but hereafter he shall be in you," when I shall have baptized you with the Holy Ghost sent down from heaven. "I will not leave you comfortless. I will come unto you. The world seeth me no more; but ye shall see me," in the effects of my indwelling power; and "because I live, ye shall live also. At that day ye shall know that I am in my Father, and ye in me, and I [by my Spirit] in you," John xiv:16, 23. This spiritual abode of Christ in the souls of his people, is the most glorious mystery of the Gospel: and "if any man have not the Spirit of Christ," Romans viii:9, he is, at best, either a disciple of Moses or of John the Baptist: he is not in a spiritual, but in a carnal state.

"I live, yet not I, but Christ liveth in me," Galatians ii:20. "Christ is our life," Colossians iii:4. "The mystery which hath been hid from ages, is Christ in you the hope of glory," Colossians i:26, 27. "My little children, of whom I travail in birth, until Christ be formed in you," Galatians iv:19. These, with a thousand other Scriptural expressions, must be utterly incomprehensible to those who, resting contented with a literal knowledge of the incarnate Word, admit not the internal manifestation of Christ, by his Spirit of revelation, wisdom, and power. "The deep things of God are revealed unto us by his Spirit," 1 Corinthians ii:10; and, without this Spirit, we must continue strangers to the most exalted truths of the Gospel, and be cut off from the purest springs of religious consolation. "This is he," saith St.

The Portrait of St. Paul

John, "that came by water and blood, even Jesus Christ; not by water only, but by water and blood. And it is the Spirit that beareth witness, because the Spirit is truth," 1 John v:6. As though the apostle should say, "Christ, indeed, in the first part of his ministry, proclaimed that repentance toward God, which his own disciples, as well as John the Baptist, were accustomed to seal with a baptism of water. And to this sacred ceremony he himself condescendingly submitted. But after this he proceeded farther, when, as a visible Saviour, he sealed his own dispensation of grace with a baptism of blood upon the cross. Moreover, it is the Spirit that gives testimony to the unsearchable truths of the Gospel, by his still more excellent baptism; deepening our repentance toward God, and adding a full assurance, Hebrews x:22, to our faith in Jesus Christ. Let no one then suspect that the manifestation of the Spirit must necessarily obscure the glory of the Son; especially since it is expressly declared, "that no man can say that Jesus is the Lord, but by the Holy Ghost," 1 Corinthians xii:3.

Before we close this section, we have to lament that this important part of the Gospel is so rarely published among professing Christians. The greater part of the clergy are to be ranked with the most violent opposers of spiritual religion. They insult its followers, they condemn its advocates unheard, and presumptuously "speak evil of these things which they know not," Jude i:10. As there was a time in which the Jewish Church overlooked the most important promise under the dispensation of the Father; so it was intimated that a time would come, in which the Christian Church, sunk into a state of listlessness and incredulity, should neglect the grand promise under the dispensation of the Son. "When the Son of man cometh," saith our Lord, "shall he find faith on the earth?" Luke xviii:8. He will find little indeed, if we may either rely upon our own observations, or give credit to the most solemn assertions of a predicting apostle, 2 Timothy iii:1, 5.

All our ecclesiastics, however, are not of this description. Among the thousands of this sacred order, we find many who are possessed of godly fear, Scriptural faith, and Christian charity. These pious evangelists are anxious for the salvation of those committed to their charge. They labour to spread the kingdom of God among men, though they have never experienced that kingdom according to the fulness of the promise. And though they are unacquainted with the abundant plenitude of the Gospel, yet they cease not to publish that Gospel abroad with affection and zeal. They preach the cross of Christ; but they proclaim not the spiritual coming of a risen Saviour. As their careless brethren refuse to publish the coming of the Spirit, through infidelity and prejudice, so these upright ministers neglect to preach it, through uncertainty and irresolution. If they even entertain a just opinion of the doctrine for which we plead, yet they are restrained from speaking frequently and freely upon the subject, because as many false Christians have rendered the dispensation of the Son contemptible in the eyes of Deists; so many vainly-inspired zealots have caused the dispensation of the Spirit to appear ridiculous before soberminded Christians. But, notwithstanding the reproach which many fanatics of various sects have brought upon this sublime part of the Gospel, by mingling with it the reveries of a heated imagination, yet it will constantly be regarded, by every well-instructed Christian, as the quintessence of our holy religion.

There appears little probability that this neglected doctrine will be either universally received or preached in our degenerate day. But as truth has never been left entirely destitute of witnesses, and as the generality of ministers have still courage enough to maintain, before an unbelieving world, the dispensation of the Son; we may reasonably hope that they will continue to mention the dispensation of the Spirit, at least, on every commemoration of the pentecostal glory. By this mean we may preserve among us a precious spark of sacred fire, till our returning Lord, bursting through the clouds of incredulity, shall kindle the spark into an everlasting flame. In that day the idle pretensions of enthusiasts shall no more influence believers to reject the Holy Spirit, than the vain pretensions of those false Christs, who formerly appeared among the Jews, could influence the faithful to reject their only Lord and Saviour. The dispensation of the Spirit shall then appear as glorious to the eyes of admiring Christians, as the dispensation of the Son once appeared to ravished Simeon: and every apostolic pastor shall conduct his flock from the dispensation of the Father, through that of the Son, to that of the Holy Spirit, in as rapid a manner as St. Peter is reported to have done in his first discourse.

THE PORTRAIT OF ST. PAUL.

PART III.

AN ESSAY

ON THE

CONNECTION OF DOCTRINES WITH MORALITY

Preliminary observations.

SOME divines, almost wholly occupied with the doctrines of the Gospel, are not sufficiently careful to insist upon morality; while philosophers, for the most part, as wholly taken up with morality, treat the doctrines of the Gospel with neglect and disdain. It is to reconcile, if possible, these two mistaken classes of men, that a few observations are here presented upon the importance of such doctrines and their immediate connection with morality.

Morality is the science which regulates our manners, by teaching us to know and to follow justice, rendering to every one their due, love, honour, obedience, tribute, &c. The whole of this morality is included in those maxims of natural and revealed religion: "Whatever ye would that men should do unto you, do ye even so unto them," Matthew vii:12. "Render unto Cesar the things which are Cesar's; and unto God, the things which are God's," Matthew xxii:21. Hence it follows, that pure morality must maintain some form of Divine worship.

Some moralists, it is true, imagine it possible to be strictly just, without making any profession of piety. But if justice consists in doing that to others which we desire may be done to ourselves, it is clear, that every man who honours not the Supreme Being must be unjust, as well as impious: since, if we are parents or benefactors, we manifest so deep a sensibility of the injustice of our children or dependents, when they repay our kindness with insolence and ingratitude.

Doctrines are, in general, precepts; but by doctrines are here particularly understood, those instructions which Christ and his apostles have given respecting the different relations in which we stand to God and to each other, together with the various duties consequent upon such relations.

Such instructions, as are transmitted from generation to generation, under the name of maxims or doctrines, whether they be true or false, have a prodigious effect upon the conduct of those who admit them. In the ancient world, how many hapless infants have been sacrificed among the Greeks and Romans to that barbarous maxim, that fathers have the right of life and death over their new-born children. In the modern world, how vast a number of unborn infants, and how many fanciful heroes are falling every year unfortunate victims to those maxims of false honour. It is better to destroy the fruit of an illicit love, or to plunge a sword into the bosom of a friend, than to live without that which constitutes the honour of the sexes! Overturn these maxims of a false point of honour, and you destroy the principles upon which a thousand impious actions are committed.

Mankind can no more divest themselves of all prepossession in favour of general maxims, than they can lose sight of determining motives. The Atheist and the infidel have their particular doctrines, as well as the just man and the Christian. The inconsistency of some philosophers, in this respect, is here worthy to be noted, who begin their discourses by decrying maxims in general, and conclude them by setting forth and maintaining the most dangerous doctrines. "The road to permanent happiness," say they, "is both convenient and spacious. The Almighty pays but little regard to our actions, and has endued us with passions for the very purpose of gratifying them." They insinuate, that if a man is sufficiently rich to entertain a number of women, he may innocently enjoy whatever pleasure their society can afford him; and that, when he has no longer any relish for life, he may as innocently blow out his brains. Such are the doctrines, and such is the morality, which many ill-instructed professors are preaching among us at this day; giving ample testimony that no men are more ready to set up for dog-matists than those who reject the doctrines of the Gospel.

CHAPTER I.

Philosophers, so called, exalt themselves without reason against the doctrines of the Gospel.

AS those who affect exterior acts of devotion are not always possessed of the most solid piety, so they who are foremost to magnify philosophy are not always to be regarded as the wisest of mankind. It must, however, be confessed, that many Christians have afforded philosophers too just a subject of scandal, by continually opposing faith to reason: as though, in order to be possessed of the richest Christian grace, it were necessary to renounce that noble faculty which chiefly distinguishes us from the brute creation. Like the great apostle, we may rationally oppose faith to sense; but we can never, without the highest indiscretion, oppose it to reason. We should even be cautious of saying, with M. de Voltaire and St. Louis, "Take heed how you follow the guidance of your weak reason."* The reason of man is acknowledged to be weak, when compared with the intelligence of superior beings. But whatever its weakness may be, it becomes us with gratitude to follow it as our guide; since, in a gloomy night, it is better to profit from the smallest taper that can be procured, than obstinately to shut our eyes and walk at random. If believers prefer the revelation of Christ before the philosophy of infidels, it is because the most enlightened reason influences their choice.

The true believer is not afraid of pleading against modern philosophers before the tribunal of reason. "You accuse me," he may say, "of superstition; because in

---

* A ta foible raison, garde toi de rendre.

pursuing those honours, riches, and pleasures which are eternal, I have chosen the rough and uncomfortable path of piety. But, while I act thus, I act in no less conformity to the principles of reason, than the man who, to expel a sweet poison, receives a bitter antidote, and cheerfully submits to a disagreeable regimen, till he be restored to perfect health. If the sacrifice of a few trifling enjoyments for the present will secure to me the possession of everlasting felicity, I do but imitate the prudent husbandman, who deprives himself to-day of a few bushels of grain, that, after a few months of patient expectation, he may reap from his trivial loss an abundant harvest. And is it unreasonable in me to adopt such a mode of conduct; especially when the sweet hope of promised blessings affords me, even now, a joy as solid and constant as yours is transitory and vain?"

Ye men of boasted wisdom! we dare assert, that the secret springs of your morality are weak and gross in comparison with ours. You maintain that, in order to bind a rational creature to the practice of morality, nothing farther is requisite than the consideration of his own interests. You affirm, moreover, with equal confidence, that all attempts to urge mankind to the exercise of virtue, by the consideration of evangelical motives, is but depending upon the force of ties which are too feeble to be binding. But you perceive not that the method upon which you proceed with so much self-approbation, is entirely unworthy of true moralists, since it merely opposes one evil by means of another full as detestable, in giving that to pride which it wrests from other vicious propensities. And you, undiscerning instructer of Emilius and Sophia! you, who say in your confession of faith, "Unknowing how to determine, I neither admit revelation nor reject it; rejecting only the obligation to receive it:"—if you have removed those powerful motives to true virtue, which are drawn from the Gospel, what have you given us in exchange? "Love, that you may be loved again. Become amiable that you may be happy. Make yourself esteemed, that you may be obeyed. What greater felicity can a noble soul possess, than that which flows from the pride of virtue, joined with beauty." How puerile and insufficient are these motives, when compared with those which the Gospel presents! Leading mankind to virtue by such a route as this, is it not to inspire them, at once, with all a Pharisee's pride, and a Jezebel's vanity?

When we draw a veil over the sublime objects of faith, and place before men the mere consideration of some present advantage, in order to influence their conduct; then we actually treat the rational part of the creation as we are accustomed to deal with the most brutish animals. Behold that swine making up to a heap of corn. Throw but a single handful of that heap in his way, and he will pass on no farther; since fifty grains of corn, scattered immediately before his face, will attract him more forcibly than as many bushels piled up at a distance. Were it possible to make him an offer of all the harvests in the universe, after a single hour; yet he would not sacrifice, for them all, the poor enjoyment of the present moment. He who thus fixes his attention upon temporal and sensible objects, forgets that his soul is immaterial and immortal. He who cannot be engaged to the practice of virtue but by means of such unworthy motives, may be said to infuse morality in the cup of Circe lest he should be constrained to receive it at the hand of Christ.

Why are infidel and unstable Christians observed to fall before temptation? The only reason that can be given is, that being affected in too lively a manner with the things that are immediately before them, they are in no condition to contemplate those objects which are more remote, of how great importance soever they may be. Hence the inestimable objects of faith appear to them as the fixed stars discover themselves to the vulgar, despoiled of their real magnitude and glory, and apparently of too little consequence to merit much attention. With the sincere Christian the case is wholly different. His faith, which is a gift from God, may be compared to a Divine telescope, by which the most distant objects are brought within his ken. And of this sacred help he happily avails himself, till wholly certified of the nature and importance of celestial things, he necessarily acquires ideas suitable to so grand a discovery.

Observe here the ground of St. Paul's definition of faith, Ephesians ii:8; Hebrews xi:1. Destitute of the same assistance, what wonder is it that the infidel should remain a perfect stranger to the Christian's sacred views and exalted sentiments? He foolishly rests contented with the naked eye of his reason, regardless of that ignorance and those prejudices with which it is too frequently obscured. Thus, self deluded, he despises the Divine instrument above described, and scoffs at those who are known to use it; just as the illiterate were formerly accustomed to set at nought the most profound astronomers, and to look with derision upon their mysterious apparatus.

As to the power of this faith, by which alone any spiritual discovery can be made, it is too wonderful to be credited, either by the ignorant or the impious. It "removes mountains;" and, to the possessor of it, "nothing is impossible," Matthew xvii:20. It affords the believer a perfect "victory" over the present world, 1 John v:4, by putting into his hand a "shield," which is impenetrable to "all the fiery darts of the wicked," Ephesians vi:16. Here is the Christian's security! Behind this buckler of celestial temper he remains in undisturbed tranquillity, while the incredulous philosopher, together with the abandoned sensualist, are hurling against it the feeble darts of ridicule and malice.

It must be acknowledged, that many excellent precepts of morality are found in the Koran, and in the works of modern philosophers: but it must be asserted, at the same time, that the enemies of Christ are chiefly indebted to revelation for every just conception of religious truth. The authors of the Koran, of Emilius, and the Philosophical Dictionary, before ever they began to dogmatize, were apprized that there is a God, whom it is our duty to love above all things, and who has commanded us to love our neighbour as ourselves. It is, therefore, matter of little surprise, that a lovely sentiment of this kind should here and there brighten a page of their gloomy volumes. Their false coin could never have become current in the world, unless they had artfully mingled with it some little quantity of the pure gold of Scriptural truth.

We shall conclude this chapter with a beautiful passage from Tertullian, in which he points out the difference between a true Christian and a philosopher, so called. After having spoken of the vices with which the Greek philosophers were infected, he makes the following reply to a very common objection. "It is objected, that some also among us are guilty of violating the laws of virtue. But it must be remembered, that such offenders pass no longer with us for Christians: while, among you, after the commission of many vicious actions, philosophers still preserve their reputation, and continue to be had in honour. What resemblance then is there between the Christian and the philosopher? The one is a disciple of Greece; the other of Heaven. The one seeks to establish a fair reputation; the other aspires to work out his salvation. The one speaks admirable words; the other performs good actions. The one destroys, and the other builds up. The one deals in error, and the other in truth." (*Apolog.* chap. 46.)

CHAPTER II.

The doctrines of natural religion and philosophy are insufficient to produce true charity in the heart.

THE doctrines of natural religion, such as the being of a God, an overruling providence, and a judgment to come, are the first doctrines of the Gospel: but, hitherto, they have never been found sufficient to lead men into the love and practice of solid virtue.

As the earth, deprived of its primitive fecundity, requires not only the genial influence of the sun, but must be enriched and assisted by many other means, in order to recover its lost fertility; so the truths of natural religion can never restore the degenerate soul to its lost perfection, without the powerful assistance of a revealed Gospel. On this account, the Father of mankind has condescended to instruct us in doctrines more efficacious than those which unassisted nature can discover, and abundantly better suited to our weakness; that the tree of morality, having more numerous and vigorous roots, might be assisted to throw out fruit of a more exquisite kind, and in greater abundance, than it was formerly known to produce. "What the law," says St. Paul, "could not do, [the natural or Mosaic law,] in that it was weak through the flesh, [that is, our corrupted nature, which stands in need of greater helps than those which the law can afford,] God, sending his own Son, condemned sin in the flesh, that the righteousness of the law might be fulfilled in us," by a power derived from him, Romans viii:3, 4. Hence this promised Saviour was spoken of as "the desire of all nations," Haggai ii:7. And hence that public declaration of Christ concerning the nature of his mission to the children of men: "I am come, that they might have life, and that they might have it more abundantly," John x:20.

Without revelation, we are left a prey to the most cruel uncertainty. The Almighty created man that he might partake of his own felicity: and, after having placed in his heart an ardent desire after the sovereign good, he made a benign discovery of himself, as the one only and inexhaustible source of true blessedness. But since the darkness of sin has overspread our understanding, we have lost sight of this sovereign good, and are seeking it where it cannot possibly be found. Like Ixion in the fable, while we embrace a cloud, we imagine ourselves in possession of a sublime reality. And even after repeated convictions of our folly, uninstructed by disappointment, we set out again in pursuit of objects full as frivolous as those by which we have been already beguiled. Philosophers, unable to guide mankind to true happiness, are vainly searching after it themselves in darkness and uncertainty. Divided into a variety of sects, they maintain a hundred different opinions upon a subject of so great importance. So that after all the researches of its professors, philosophy has left the world in a state of equal perplexity with a man who, having but one arrow to level at the mark, has a hundred different marks proposed to him at the same time.

In all this uncertainty, how happy is it to discover a volume which decides the momentous question in so clear a manner, that reason itself can object nothing to the decision! This book, the most ancient that can be produced, informs us that Jehovah once appeared to the father of the faithful, "and said unto him, I am the mighty,* all-sufficient God: walk before me, and be thou perfect." So "will I make my covenant between me and thee:" and thou shalt become a joyful possessor of the sovereign good, Genesis xvii:1, 2. When these truths are once cordially assented to, the perplexity of the believer is then sweetly terminated, and his high vocation completely pointed out. From this time he feels the importance of those doctrines which, like steady lights, eclipse a thousand glimmering meteors, and discover, amid surrounding dangers, a sure though narrow road to happiness. And here it is to be observed, that upon these important truths, as well as upon every other essential point, Christians of all denominations are perfectly agreed.

What is meant by "walking before God in perfection," is fully explained in the following terms: "Thou shalt love the Lord thy God with all thy heart, and thy neighbour as thyself," Matthew xxii:37, 39. Now unregenerate man, far from filling up these duties, neglects the Supreme Being, and prefers his own particular interest to that of society in general; affording the strongest proof that he possesses neither genuine piety nor undissembled charity. Hence, before such a man can become truly virtuous, it is evident that his principles must be improved and his inclinations rectified. And till these salutary changes take place in his soul, always vicious, restless, and selfish, he will continually be making some addition to his external errors and his internal misery.

Deists, while they acknowledge that we are bound to love both God and man, presume upon the sufficiency of their own ability for the due performance of these extensive duties. Were they, however, truly anxious to practise these virtues in as unreserved a manner as even natural religion requires, they would quickly perceive the weakness of humanity, and acknowledge the deepest need of Divine assistance. But so long as the piety of these persons consists in "honouring God with their lips, while their hearts are far from him," Isaiah xxix:13; and while they boast of manifesting toward mankind a love so universal, that none but their enemies are excluded from it, Matthew v:43; so long they will need no other assistance for the performance of these wretched services, than that which corrupted nature can amply afford.

It is frequently asserted, that the mysteries of redemption are utterly useless with respect to morality, and that the benignity of God, as exemplified in our creation and preservation, is a sufficient motive to affection and obedience on the part of man. But since man has become a sinful and disobedient creature, every motive to rectitude that can possibly be drawn from his creation and preservation, has lost much of its former constraining influence. How many persons may we find in the world, who, instead of being penetrated with gratitude on account of these blessings, lament, with despairing Job and Jeremiah, that ever they were born! And when the miseries of life have rendered it almost insupportable, can we reasonably imagine its repining possessor to be glowing with love to the Deity, merely as the author and preserver of his unhappy existence? Surely nothing can be more absurd than such a supposition. Yet how many boasted reasoners confidently maintain, that the very same gift, which wretched sufferers, in every age, have thrown back to the giver with

* See the original.

anguish and contempt, is nevertheless a motive sufficiently powerful to engage every transgressor of the Almighty's law to love him with all their heart, and serve him with all their power!

But let us suppose that man, unassisted by the doctrines of the Gospel, has some knowledge of the sovereign good, and the means by which it may be obtained. Yet how superficial is this knowledge! We might here produce a gloomy catalogue of those capital errors into which the ancient philosophers have fallen, with regard to these important points. It must, indeed, be allowed that modern professors have corrected many of those errors: but it must be lamented, at the same time, that they have unhappily adopted others, not a whit less glaring or fatal. Passing over, in silence, the horrible systems of atheistical writers, let us listen to philosophers of greater estimation, among whom Rousseau and Voltaire may rank as the most conspicuous characters. The former of these acquired considerable reputation by his observations upon the education of youth, and the latter, by the courage with which he contended for toleration.

"Let it be laid down," says Rousseau, "as an incontestable maxim, that the first movements of nature are always right; and that there is no such thing as original sin in the human heart." How large a stride is here toward the sentiments of La Mettie; all whose morality was wrapped up in this single sentence, "Satisfy thy desires; they are the voice of God and of nature." To enlarge this little quotation from J. J. Rousseau would be a superfluous task. It must appear evident to every unprejudiced reader, from the above assertion, that the maxims of this admired philosopher have a greater tendency to advance self gratification than to promote universal benevolence in the world.

Turn we now to the toleration of M. de Voltaire. In his epistle to Boileau, we find him writing thus: "I have consecrated my voice to sing the praises of virtue; overcoming those prejudices which are idolized by the ignorant, I dare to preach toleration to persecutors."* Now when any man comes forth, in this public manner, to plead the cause of candour and liberality, we are naturally led to admire the generosity of his conduct. And it would be well, if M. de Voltaire was really deserving of all that credit, which a stranger feels disposed to give him, when he assumes so questionable an appearance. But notwithstanding the praises which this celebrated writer has bestowed upon his own humanity, and in spite of all the beautiful things he has said upon toleration, many ungenerous sentiments may be discovered in his works, which tend to renew the most bloody persecutions. Take an instance or two.

1. "It is never necessary to rise up against the religion of the prince." Upon this principle, Jesus Christ and St. Paul were highly worthy of blame for withstanding the hypocrisy and idolatry which composed the religion of Caiaphas and Tiberius.

2. "What is called a Jansenist, is really a madman, a bad citizen, and a rebel. He is a bad citizen, because he troubles the order of the state: he is a rebel, because he disobeys. The Molinists are madmen of a more harmless kind." These two lovely

---

* *A chanter la virtu j'ai consecre ma voix;*
Vainquer des prejuges que l'imbecile essence,
J'ose aux persecuteurs precher la tolerance.

maxims of toleration are to be found in a little piece of M. de Voltaire's, entitled, *The Voice of a Philosopher and the People.*

Had the king of France attended to this voice, he would have regarded every Jansenist, and for the same reason, every Protestant, as a bad citizen, or a rebel; every spark of religious moderation would have been extinguished in his royal bosom, and an effectual door thrown open to the terrible exertions of tyrannical power. These pretended rebels might then have perished, unpitied and unheard; while the bigoted prince, convinced that *a man must cease to be a fanatic before he merits toleration,* might have gloried in the rectitude of his public conduct. Such a prince might have commanded his blood-thirsty troops to advance under the banners of modern philosophy, leaving M. de Voltaire to animate them against the innocent with, what he calls, *The Voice of a Philosopher.*

It appears, then, according to M. de Voltaire, that every subject should profess the religion of his prince. Nor is this opinion less earnestly contended for by J. J. Rousseau, who tells us in his Emilius, that "every daughter should be of her mother's religion, and that every woman should profess the religion of her husband." So that, if a man should turn from the true, and embrace a false religion, his wife and children are bound to apostatize with him: and in case of a refusal on their part, J. J. Rousseau, while he affects to plead the cause of liberty, pronounces upon them a sentence of condemnation. Upon these principles of toleration, the father of a family is authorized to persecute his non-conforming wife and children, and a prince may lawfully take up arms against such of his subjects as are esteemed fanatics. If the benevolence and morality of these candid philosophers were to be substituted in the place of that liberality and love which the Gospel requires, Mark ix:38, &c, to what a deluge of misery would it give rise, both in families and in commonwealths! Kings would tyrannize over the conscience of their subjects, husbands over that of their wives, and parents over that of their children: nor would the least religious liberty be experienced by any class of men, except the princes of the earth. Such is the imperfect charity, and such the limited freedom, for which modern philosophers have contended, with equal earnestness and approbation.

The dangerous principles of these two oracles, upon the subject of toleration, will suffice to show with how just reason the former of them could say, "I hate false maxims, but I detest evil actions yet more." Alas! the horrible actions of a murdering inquisitor terminate with his life; but the intolerant doctrines of these reputed sages may continue to scatter misery and death through the world, long after their neglected tombs are mouldered into dust.

CHAPTER III.

The great influence of doctrines upon morality.

TO ascertain the importance of doctrines in general, let us consider the influence that they have upon our conduct. Our duties in life depend upon the different relations we sustain in it; and these relations affect us only as they are understood. Thus, it is necessary that a child should know his father before he can truly love him in that character. This knowledge is the effect of certain instructions or maxims which influence our manners in proportion as they are assented to. I love the man from whom I have received my birth and education with a particular affection: but such love is founded, first, upon this general doctrine, "Every child, honourably born, should reverence and love his father," and, secondly, upon this particular truth, "That man is my father." If I am made to doubt of this general doctrine, or of this particular truth, the moral springs of that respect, love, gratitude, and obedience, which are due to my father, will necessarily be weakened; and if either the one or the other should lose all its influence over my heart, my father would then become to me as an indifferent person.

The knowledge, therefore, of the affinities which subsist between one being and another, is essential to morality. Why is it that no traces of morality can be discovered among the beasts of the field? It is because they are incapable of understanding either the relation in which creatures stand to the Creator, or the affinities which subsist among the creatures themselves. As it becomes the soldier to have a strict knowledge of his officers, that he may render to every one according to his rank the honour and obedience to which they are severally entitled; so, preparatory to the practice of morality, it behooves us to have a clear perception of our various duties, together with the proper subject of those duties. If some desperate malady has deprived us of this knowledge, we then rank with idiots, and are in no condition to violate the rules of morality. Hence the lunatic, who butchers his father, is not punishable among us as a parricide, because he has no acquaintance with these general maxims, "No man should murder another,—every son should honour his father;" nor has he any conception of this particular truth, "The man whom thou art about to destroy, is thy father."

Take away all doctrines, and you annihilate all the relations which subsist among rational creatures; you destroy all morality, and reduce man to the condition of a brute beast, allowing him to be influenced by passion and caprice, as the lowest animals are actuated by appetite and instruct. Admit only some few doctrines, and you admit only a part of your duties as well as your privileges. An example may serve to set this truth in a clear light:— suppose you have a rich father, who is entirely unknown to you, and whom the world has never looked upon as your parent; if you never receive any certain intelligence concerning him, it is plain that you can neither render him filial obedience, nor yet succeed to his estates.

Many philosophers, who cannot reasonably be suspected of fanaticism, or even partiality to evangelical principles, have yet strenuously insisted upon the importance of doctrines, as calculated to influence the conduct of mankind. A polished writer of this class seems to have entertained an idea, that if all men were possessed of an enlightened understanding, crimes of every kind would be unknown in the world. Observe, at least, in what terms he speaks of war, which is an evil of that complex nature, that it may justly be looked upon as an assemblage of every possible vice. "What is the cause of that destructive rage, which, in every period, like a contagious malady, has infected the human race? Ignorance is, undoubtedly, the source of our calamities: ignorance with respect to the relations, rights, and duties of our species. Thus, the most ignorant and unpolished people have ever been the most warlike; and those ages of the world, which have been peculiarly distinguished by darkness and barbarism, have been invariably the most fruitful in murderous wars. Ignorance prepares the way for devastation; and devastation, in its turn, reproduces ignorance.

With a clear knowledge of their rights and their reciprocal duties, which form the true and only interest of nations, it is a contradiction to suppose that those nations would voluntarily precipitate themselves into an abyss of inevitable evils."* This author, if he be supposed to speak of our relations and duties with respect to God, as well as those which regard our neighbour, had reason on his side; and especially if his views were directed to the knowledge of every powerful motive which should constrain us to fill up those duties.

Upon these principles, of what fatal neglect are those persons guilty, who, being charged with the religious instructions of princes and people, leave both immersed in a deplorable ignorance, which draws after it the horrors of war, with all the various calamities that overspread the face of Christendom!

CHAPTER IV.

How the doctrines of the Gospel come in to the succour of morality.

IF to preach the Gospel is to teach sinners the relations they sustain with respect to God, as Creator, Redeemer, and Sanctifier; if it is to announce the advantages which flow from this three-fold relation, till, penetrated with gratitude and love, mankind apply themselves to fulfil the several duties to which they stand engaged; we may challenge the world to point out any knowledge of equal importance with that which is discovered in the Gospel. To deprive us, then, of the doctrines contained in this Gospel, is it not to suppress the most important instructions we can possibly receive, and to conceal from us a testament made wholly in our favour? To decide this question, we shall here consider what influence these doctrines have upon morality.

The virtues of worldly men, as well as their vices, are little else than a kind of traffic carried on by an inordinate self love. From this impure source the most amiable of their actions flow; and hence, instead of referring all things primarily to God, they constantly act with an eye to their own immediate advantage. Christ has offered a remedy to this grand evil, by teaching us, that to love the Deity "with all our heart" is the "first commandment" of the law; and that to love ourselves, and "our neighbour as ourselves," is but a secondary commandment in the sight of God: thus leading us up to Divine love, as the only source of pure virtue. When self love is once reduced to this wholesome order, and moves in exact obedience to the Creator's law, it then becomes truly commendable in man, and serves as the surest rule of fraternal affection.

Evangelical morality ennobles our most ordinary actions, such as those of eating and drinking, requiring that" all things be done to the glory of God," 1 Corinthians x:31, *i.e.* in celebration of his unspeakable bounty. A just precept this, and founded upon the following doctrine: "All things are of God," 2 Corinthians v:18, to whom, of consequence, they ought finally to refer. If you lose sight of this doctrine, your apparent gratitude is nothing more than a feigned virtue, which has no other motives

---

* Principes de la Legislation Universelle.

or ends, except such as originate and lose themselves in self love. In such circumstances you cannot possibly assent to the justice of the grand precept above cited. But holding it up, like the author of the Philosophical Dictionary, as a subject of ridicule, you may perhaps burlesque the feelings of a conscientious man with regard to this command, as the comedian is accustomed to sport with the character of a modest woman. Thus many philosophers are emulating the morality and benevolence of those censorious religionists, concerning whom our Lord significantly declared, "Verily they have their reward."

How shall we reduce a sinner to moral order? Will it be sufficient to press upon him the following exhortations:—Love God with all thy heart: be filled with benevolence toward all men: do good to your very enemies? All this would be only commanding a rebel to seek happiness in the presence of a prince whose indignation he has justly merited. It would be urging a covetous man to sacrifice his interests, not only to indifferent persons, but to his implacable adversaries. To effect so desirous a change in the human heart, motives and assistance are as absolutely necessary as counsels and precepts.

Here the doctrines of the Gospel come in to the succour of morality. But how shall we sufficiently adore that incomprehensible Being, who has demonstrated to us, by the mission of his beloved Son, that the Divine nature is love? Or, how shall we refuse any thing to this gracious Redeemer, who clothed himself with mortality that he might suffer in our stead? All the doctrines of the Gospel have an immediate tendency to promote the practice of morality. That of the incarnation, which serves as the basis of the New Testament, expresses the benevolence of the Supreme Being in so striking a manner, that every sinner, who cordially receives this doctrine, is constrained to surrender his heart unreservedly to God. His servile fear is changed into filial reverence, and his inveterate aversion into fervent love. He is overwhelmed with the greatness of benefits received, and, as the only suitable return for mercies of so stupendous a nature, he sacrifices, at once, all his darling vices. "If the Son of God has united himself to my fallen nature," such an humble believer will naturally say, "I will not rest till I feel myself united to this Divine Mediator. If he comes to put a period to my misery, nothing shall ever put a period to my gratitude. If he has visited me with the beams of his glory, it shall henceforth become my chief concern to reflect those beams upon all around me, to his everlasting praise."

The memorable sacrifice which was once offered up in the person of Christ, as a propitiation for our sins, is wonderfully calculated to produce the same extraordinary effects. This mysterious offering sets forth the malignity of our offences, and represents the compassion of the Deity in so overpowering a manner, that, while it fills us with horror for sin, it completely triumphs over the obduracy of our hearts. From the moment we come to a real perception of this meritorious sacrifice, from that moment we die to sin, till, "rising again with Christ" into a new life, Colossians iii:1, we become, at length, wholly "renewed in the spirit of our mind," Ephesians iv:23. Point out a man who unfeignedly believes in a crucified Saviour, and you have discovered a man who abhors all manner of vice, and in whom every virtue has taken root. Such a one can thankfully join the whole multitude of the faithful, and say, "Being justified by faith, we have peace with God, through our Lord Jesus Christ," Romans v:1, "and rejoicing in hope of the glory of God," 5:2, "we have obeyed from the heart that form of doctrine which was delivered unto us." Once, indeed, when we were without the knowledge of Christ, "we were the servants of sin: but now, being made free from sin, and become servants of God, we have our fruit unto holiness, and the end everlasting life," Romans vi:17, 22.

If you ravish from such a man these consoling and sanctifying doctrines, you will leave him either in the stupid insensibility of those who give themselves up to carnal security, or in the perplexity of others, who are crying, "What shall we do to be saved?" The one or the other of these states must be experienced, in different degrees, by every man who is unacquainted with the efficacy of evangelical doctrines. And if the first moralist (Socrates) of the Pagan world was yet observed to triumph over this stupidity and confusion, it was merely through the regenerating hope he indulged, that a restoring God, of whose internal operations he had already been favoured with some faint perception would one day afford him a more clear and perfect light.

CHAPTER V.
Containing reflections upon the apostles' creed.

FOR the fullest proof that a strict connection subsists between the doctrines of the Gospel and the most perfect morality, let us cast our eyes on an assemblage of those doctrines, known by the name of the apostles' creed; a creed to which every true Christian conscientiously subscribes, and which baptized hypocrites make a solemn show of assenting to. Our prejudice against these holy doctrines must necessarily vanish, after we have duly considered the influence they naturally have upon the conduct of true believers.

This confession of faith has three parts. The first contains the principal doctrines of Deism, or natural religion, setting forth the relation in which we stand to God, as Creator. The second part of this creed includes the principal doctrines contained in the four Gospels, and places before us the relation we bear to God, considered in the character of Redeemer, or as coming to save the world by that extraordinary person, who is called the only begotten Son of God. The doctrines here enumerated are those with which the disciples of our Lord were wholly taken up till the day of their spiritual baptism. The third part presents us with a recapitulation of the principal doctrines set forth in the Acts and Epistles of the apostles. This latter part of the Christian creed instructs us in our relation to God, as Sanctifier, or as coming to regenerate man by that Spirit of truth, consolation, and power, which was promised by Christ to his followers: a Spirit, whose office is to instruct and sanctify the Church of Christ, to maintain a constant communion among its members, to seal upon their consciences the pardon of sin, to assure them of a future resurrection, and prepare them for a life of everlasting blessedness. Let us review these three parts of this apostolic creed, and observe the necessary reference they have to morality.

The first article of this creed informs us that there is an all-powerful God, who is the Creator of all things in heaven and in earth. It is evident that no man can renounce this doctrine, without renouncing natural religion, and plunging headlong into Atheism. If there is no God, there can be no Divine law, and morality becomes a mere insignificant term. Human laws may, indeed, restrain the wretch who indulges a persuasion of this nature; but were it not for the authority of such laws, he would throw off the mask of decency, and laugh at the distinction between virtue and vice.

If you admit, with Epicurus, the being of a God, without admitting an overruling providence: if you believe not that the Creator is an all-powerful Parent, and, as such, peculiarly attentive to the concerns of his immense family: you then destroy all confidence in the Supreme Being: you take from the righteous their chief consolation in adversity, and from the wicked their chief restraining curb in prosperity.

Mutilate this important doctrine by admitting only a general providence, and you destroy the particular confidence which holy men indulge, that God dispenses to his children, according to his unsearchable wisdom, both prosperity and adversity; that he listens to their supplications, and will finally deliver them out of all their afflictions. You trample under foot the most powerful motives to resignation and patience; you nourish discontent in the heart, and scatter the seeds of despair among the unfortunate. Yet all this is done by many inconsistent advocates for morality.

Heathens themselves were perfectly convinced, that the practice of morality was closely connected with the above-mentioned doctrines Cicero, in his book concerning the nature of the gods, seems to apprehend, that the whole edifice of morality would fall to the ground, were the doctrine of a particular providence to be taken away: "For," says he, "if the gods observed not what is transacted here below, what would become of religion and holiness, without which human life would be replete with trouble and confusion? I am persuaded that, in banishing the fear of the gods, we should, at the same time, banish from among as good faith, justice, and all those other virtues which are considered as forming the basis of society."

CHAPTER VI.
The connection of morality with the second part of the apostles' creed.

THE doctrines adverted to in the latter part of the preceding chapter, compose the religion of Theists, who believe in God as Creator and Preserver, but who know him not as the Restorer of fallen man. They, however, who give their unfeigned assent to the first part of this creed, will never contentedly rest at the threshold of truth. After duly attending to the blessings of creation and preservation, they will readily perceive how destitute they are of that love, that gratitude, and that obedience, which are so justly due to the Author of all their mercies. Hence gradually discovering that, even with respect to their neighbour, they are void of that justice and charity which should be mutually exercised between man and man, they will humbly acknowledge their transgressions, and begin to apprehend those mysterious truths by which the Christian religion is distinguished from Deism.

In our ancient confessions of faith, no mention is made of the misery and depravity of man. For what need was there to make so melancholy a truth an article of faith, since it has been publicly demonstrated, in every age and country, by the conduct of all classes of men? To deny that indisputable evidences of this truth are every day to be met with, is to deny that there are in the world prisons, gibbets, soldiers, fields of blood, and beds of death.

If we give up the doctrine of the fall, and, of consequence, that of the restoration, we give the lie to the general experience of mankind, as well as to that of our own hearts; we shut our eyes against the light of conviction; we cast away, in the midst of a labyrinth, the only clue that can guide us through its winding mazes. And after such an act of folly, we shall either, with infidel philosophers, disdain to implore the assistance of the Supreme Being, or, like the haughty Pharisee, we shall approach him with insolence.

If, in direct opposition to the doctrine of our depravity, we affirm, that "all things are good, and the human species as free from imperfection as the Almighty at first intended," we then neglect the only probable means of overcoming sin, and obstinately endeavour to preclude all possibility of our restoration. Thus, by persuading a loathsome leper that his malady is both convenient and becoming, we teach him to despise the most efficacious remedies, and leave him a deluded prey to deformity and corruption. But if it be once admitted that we are immersed in sin, without the least possibility of restoring ourselves to a state of innocence, we have, then, some degree of that humility which disposed St. Paul to embrace a persecuted Saviour, and by which alone we can be prevailed upon to embrace the second part of this sacred creed.

To reject that which respects either the conception, the birth, the sufferings, the death,* the resurrection, or the ascension of Jesus Christ, is to reject every thing that concerns this condescending Saviour; since it is one and the same Gospel that instructs us in all these different doctrines. To remove one of these doctrines is to break the chain of evangelical truth, by destroying one of the links of which it is composed; it is ultimately to deny the authority of revelation, if not absolutely to overthrow that grand edifice, of which Jesus Christ "is the chief corner stone." In a word, as the doctrine of our redemption by a crucified Saviour is rejected, either wholly or in part, so we reject, either in part or altogether, the most constraining motives to repentance and gratitude, obedience and purity.

An unholy course of conduct proceeds from two principal causes, pride and the rebellion of the senses: from the former arises the disorder of our irascible passions; and from the latter proceed all our irregular desires. Now, before these evils can be perfectly remedied, or the unholy become truly virtuous, it is necessary to eradicate pride from the heart, and to subdue the irregular appetites of our degenerate nature. This is undoubtedly the most difficult task to be accomplished in life; but what is impracticable to the incredulous Deist, becomes actually possible to the sincere believer. By the example of his persecuted Master, he is animated to trample upon all the pride of life; and upon the cross of his dying Lord, he is crucified to the sensual

---

* Here is no mention made of our Lord's descent into hell, because the expression itself is an equivocal one: the Greek word *hades* by no means answering to the English word *hell*. St. Paul was ever ready to make mention of every thing that respected his Divine Master; but where he speaks of his death and resurrection, he is not observed even to hint at this singular doctrine; and if, by omitting it in this place, we are judged guilty of a capital error, the great apostle himself was guilty in this respect, Romans iv:25; viii:34; 1 Corinthians xv:4. But if St. Paul and the four evangelists have made no mention of this extraordinary circumstance, it cannot certainly be considered as a fundamental article of the Christian faith.

delights of this present world. "Take my yoke upon you," says the blessed Jesus, "and learn of me; for I am meek and lowly in heart," Matthew xi:29. "Christ hath suffered for us," continues St. Peter, "leaving us an example, that ye should follow his steps," 1 Peter ii:21. "Let the same mind be in you," adds St. Paul, "which was also in Christ Jesus, who, being in the form of God," voluntarily "took upon him the form of a servant, and became obedient unto the death of the cross," Philippians ii:5, 8.

It is necessary to be well acquainted with the human heart, and to have accurately observed the influence that example has upon mankind, in order to understand the great advantage which Christians have over Deists, even allowing the morality of both parties to be equally pure. What is there of which those persons are not capable, who follow the King of kings, encouraged by his example, and supported by his power? Thus supported, no command will appear too strict to be obeyed: no burden too heavy to be sustained; but we may joyfully triumph, like the first imitators of Jesus, over that innate pride and those sensual desires upon which the incredulous continually striking, as upon dangerous rocks, make shipwreck of all their boasted morality.

The last article, recounted in this part of our creed, must be supposed to have a prodigious influence upon the minds of men. Take away the doctrine of a judgment day, in which an infinitely holy and powerful God will render unto every man according to his works; you then take from the wicked those salutary fears which restrain them in the career of vice, and from the righteous those glorious hopes which are the strongest incentives to a life of godliness.

CHAPTER VII.

The connection of morality with the third part of the apostles' creed.

THE first article, in the third part of this ancient confession of faith, respects the confidence which every believer indulges in the Divine grace, or rather, in that Holy Spirit which sanctifies the sinful and consoles the afflicted. If, by an obstinate incredulity, we reject this sacred Comforter, we refuse the wisdom and power which result from an intimate union with the Father of lights, and disclaim all fellowship with that Divine Mediator, whose humanity is far removed from the sight of men. As we could derive no possible advantage from a sun, whose rays, concentrated in himself, should neither visit our eyes with their cheering light, nor our bodies with their kindly heat, so, if the Almighty neither illuminates our minds by the Spirit of truth, nor animates our souls by the Spirit of charity, we may reasonably suppose him to have as little interest in the concerns of men as the statue of Olympian Jupiter.

The remainder of this creed respects the nature of the Church and the privileges of its members.

To destroy the doctrines which relate to the holiness of those who truly appertain to the Church of God, the universality of that Church, and "the communion of those saints" of whom it is composed;—this is to overthrow the barriers which form the pale of the Church, confounding the holy with the profane, and the sincere with the hypocritical.

Take away the doctrine that "respects the remission of sins," and you leave us in a state of the most cruel uncertainty. You take away from penitents that expectation which sustains them; and from believers the gratitude that engages them to love much, because much has been forgiven them, Luke vii:47. You destroy the most powerful motive we have to pardon the offences of our neighbour, Ephesians iv:32, and leave us in a state of solicitude incompatible with that internal peace which is the peculiar privilege of Christians, John xiv:27.

Rob us of the doctrine of a future resurrection, and you leave us weak in times of danger, alarmed in times of sickness, and wholly in bondage to the fear of death. But, while we remain in possession of this exhilarating truth, we can follow, without fear, the standard of the cross; the most cruel torments are rendered tolerable; and we can submit, without repining, to a temporary death, looking forward to a glorious resurrection and a happy immortality.

CHAPTER VIII.
Consequences of the foregoing observations.

ALL crimes are founded upon those errors which are first embraced in theory, before they are adopted in practice. Overthrow these errors by opposing to them pure and incontrovertible doctrines, and you destroy sin in the bud. On the other hand, true virtue is produced by truth. Oppose a lie to this truth, and, if it be admitted, you destroy the seeds of virtue. So long as the first man had his heart penetrated with the certainty of this doctrine, "If I am ungrateful enough to disobey my Creator, I shall die," so long he remained in a state of innocence. But to this doctrine the tempter opposed his false promises. "You shall not surely die," said he; on the contrary, "you shall become [wise and happy] as gods." No sooner were these delusive doctrines assented to on the part of Adam, but his understanding becoming necessarily clouded, his will was immediately beguiled: and thus, blindly following the temptation, he fell into an abyss of misery.

Doctrines, whether they be good or bad, still continue to have the same influence upon the conduct of men; and to suppose the contrary, is to suppose that light and darkness can never cease to produce their ordinary effects. The following doctrine, "Out of the pale of the Romish Church there is no salvation," has filled Europe with fires, scaffolds, and massacres. Eradicate this doctrine from every prejudiced heart, and plant in its room the following Scriptural truth, "God is no respecter of persons; but in every nation, he that feareth him and worketh righteousness is accepted with him," and, in the place of streaming blood, we shall see streams of charity uninterruptedly flowing through every Christian kingdom.

The miser imagines that riches are the sovereign good, and that the highest pleasure consists in counting over and over his splendid hoards. The debauched youth is confident that the sovereign good consists in sensual gratification, and the highest gratification in the enjoyment of a frail beauty, destined to be the prey of worms. Destroy these groundless persuasions by solid doctrines: demonstrate to these infatuated creatures that God himself is the sovereign good, and that this good is offered to us in Jesus Christ; and that the highest enjoyment consists in having the heart penetrated with Divine love, and in looking forward with a lively hope of being one day eternally united to God. Convince them of these momentous truths, and the charms by which they have been captivated so long, will be immediately broken. Ah! how delightful is it to behold such sensual reasoners awaking from their deathful slumber, and crying out, with St. Augustine, "O eternal sweetness! Ineffable greatness! Beauty for ever new! Truth, whose charms have been so long unnoticed, alas, how much time have I lost in not loving thee!"

Sound reason must unavoidably submit to the force of these observations, the truth of which is demonstrated by the general conduct of mankind. But, perhaps, the best method of reasoning with the incredulous, is to point out the consequences of their own system. Imagine a man, who, instead of receiving the doctrines of the Gospel, publicly presumes to make the following declaration: "I believe not in God the Creator: I trust not in any Mediator, nor acknowledge any sanctifying Spirit. And, as I believe not in God, so I believe not in what is called his Church; nor do I look upon the communion of those who worship him in any other light than that of a mere chimera. I believe not in the remission of sins. I look for no resurrection, nor indulge any hope of everlasting life. Let us eat and drink, for to-morrow we die." Were any man seriously to repeat in your hearing such a confession of his faith, would you fix upon such a one for the management of your estate? Would you intrust him with the charge of your wife, or choose him for the guardian of your children? Would it be possible for you to depend upon his word, or confide in his honesty? Now, imagine this very infidel, in some future season, convinced of his former errors, and firmly persuaded that he acts under the eye of an omniscient God, who will bring "every work into judgment, with every secret thing," Ecclesiastes xii:14: suppose him smiting upon his breast with the penitent publican, and determining, with St. Paul, to know nothing "among men save Jesus Christ and him crucified," 1 Corinthians ii:2: would you not indulge a better opinion of this man, in his believing state, than when he rejected, with modern philosophers, the doctrines of Christianity? It could not possibly be otherwise: so true it is, that, in certain cases, your conduct will give the lie to your arguments against the utility of evangelical doctrines.

J. J. Rousseau professes to have hated bad maxims less than evil actions: when, as a wise man, he should have detested the former as the cause of the latter. It is not sufficient that we profess to make the principles of virtue the ground of our conduct, unless that basis be established upon an immovable foundation. Without attending to this rule, we resemble those Indians, who suppose the world to be founded upon the back of an elephant, while that elephant is supported by the shell of a tortoise; and who, perfectly satisfied with such a discovery, attempt not to understand any more of the matter.

A system of morality, how beautiful soever it may appear, unless it be supported by doctrines of the utmost consistency and firmness, may be compared to a splendid palace erected upon the sands: in some unexpected storm it will assuredly be swept away, proving, at once, the disgrace of its builder, and the ruin of its inhabitant.

CHAPTER IX.
An appeal to experience.

EXPERIENCE goes far in the decision of many difficult questions, and before it the most subtle sophism cannot long maintain its ground. To this, therefore, we cheerfully appeal for the happy effects of the Gospel. Ye incredulous sages of the day, show us a single enemy to the doctrines of revelation, who may truly be called an humble man, conducting himself soberly, justly, and religiously, in all the trying circumstances of life. Through the whole circle of your infidel acquaintance, you will seek such a one in vain.

If it be said that J. J. Rousseau, though a professed skeptic, presented us with the portrait of a perfectly honest man: we answer, in the first place, that J. J. Rousseau rejected not the Gospel as an obstinate enemy; but rather counted it an affliction that he was unable to embrace its doctrines. And, secondly, that this philosopher was equally destitute of humility and religion.

It must be confessed that there are multitudes of inconsistent persons in the world, who constantly deceive themselves, and who frequently delude others, by their fallacious notions of faith and incredulity. We meet with many, who, while they rank themselves in the number of believers, are usually employed in the works of infidels. And, on the other hand, we observe divers penitent worshippers, who, through an excess of humility, account themselves no better than infidels, while they manifest in their conduct the fidelity of Christians. But these particular exceptions are insufficient to destroy the general rule here contended for: since the former must be looked upon as believers, and the latter as infidels, only in appearance. The first have not sincerity enough to acknowledge their secret incredulity; and the last have not light sufficient to determine their exact advancement in the Christian faith. The latter deserve our pity, while the former merit our indignation.

But turn your eyes upon an enlightened believer. Behold St. Paul, after his memorable submission to the persecuted Jesus! The love of God possesses his soul, and he consecrates all his powers to the service of his exalted Master. Appointed to instruct the ignorant, he discharges his important commission with indefatigable zeal. Carrying to the afflicted both spiritual and temporal succours, he appears to be borne from east to west, as upon the wings of an eagle. He is ready to spend and be spent for the common interests of mankind. He proves his fidelity and gratitude to Christ at the hazard of his life. His magnanimity and fortitude, his resignation and patience, his generosity and candour, his benevolence and constancy, are at once, the amazement of his enemies and the glory of his followers. Behold this converted Pharisee, and acknowledge the wondrous efficacy of evangelical doctrines.

Ye slaves of philosophical prejudice! how long will you mistake the nature of doctrines so happily adapted to humble supercilious man, so perfectly calculated to destroy both presumption and despair; to bend the most hardened under the tender pressure of mercy, and carry up grateful believers to the sublimest summit of virtue? Behold three thousand Jews submitting, at the same instant, to the constraining power of these doctrines. Through their transcendent efficacy, innumerable miracles are still daily operated among us. They dispel the mists of ignorance, they destroy the seeds of injustice, they extinguish irregular desires, and open in the heart a source of universal charity! Thus, "the multitude of them that [formerly] believed were of one heart and one soul," &c. Enjoying together the sovereign Good, it was not possible for them to contend with each other for the trifling enjoyments of time and sense. God had given them his only begotten Son; how then could they refuse any thing to their indigent brethren!

Long after St. Luke had borne testimony to the unexampled charity of Christians, we find Tertullian citing the following testimony, which his heathen cotemporaries were constrained to bear in favour of the same Christian virtue. "Behold," say they, "how these Christians love, and are prepared to die for each other!" "Yes," adds this celebrated Christian father, "we who have but one heart and one soul are not afraid to have one purse. Among us all things are common, except our wives."*

If the testimony here produced should be disregarded, because drawn from the writings of a professed advocate for Christianity, we will readily come to another test. Pliny bears witness to the pure conversation of the persecuted Christians of his time. And the Emperor Julian himself, one of the most enlightened, as well as implacable enemies of Christianity, exhorted his heathen subjects to practise among themselves the duties of charity, after the example of Christians, "who abound," said he, "in acts of benevolence." And as to the joy, with which they sacrificed their lives, when occasion so required, "they go," continues he, "to death as bees swarm to the hive." Such influence have the doctrines of our holy religion upon the conduct of its sincere professors, even by the confession of their inveterate enemies.

It appears, then, that St. Paul was employed like an experienced moralist, while he was engaged in erecting the sacred edifice of morality upon the solid foundation of evangelical truths. And the doctrines he made choice of, as peculiarly suited to this purpose, were those which respect the mercy of God in Christ Jesus. Upon these he laid the greatest stress, and from these he drew his most persuasive arguments to virtue and piety. Witness that memorable exhortation delivered to his Roman converts: "I beseech you, brethren, by the mercies of God, that ye present your bodies a living sacrifice, holy, acceptable unto God, which is your reasonable service," Romans xii:1.

To withhold from the degenerate this cheering truth that "they are bought with a price," 1 Corinthians vi:20, is to deny them one of the most powerful motives to love and glorify" God in their bodies and in their souls," which appertain to him by the endearing right of redemption, as well as by that original right of creation, to which they are generally rendered insensible by the afflictions and disappointments of life. Instruct them concerning the sanctity of the Divine law; set before them the guilt of their innumerable offences, and the just fears to which such discoveries must naturally give rise, will make existence itself an intolerable burden. But when the Gospel of our redemption begins to dissipate their doubts, and allay the anguish of their remorse, they will be enabled to go on their way rejoicing through the strictest paths of obedience and morality.

---

* *Vide, inquiunt [gentes] ut [isti Christiani] invicem se diligunt, et ut pro alterutro mori sunt parati. Qui animo animaque miscemur, nihil de rei communicatione dubitamus. Omnia indiscreta sunt apud nos, præter uxores.* Apologeticus, chap. 39.

CHAPTER X.

An objection answered, which may be drawn from the ill conduct of unholy Christians, to prove the inutility of the doctrines of the Gospel.

THEY who exalt philosophy against revelation, imagine that, to invalidate the preceding reflections, they need only make the following reply: "All Christians receive the apostles' creed; but their faith is unattended with the happy effects you have been recounting. Crimes of every kind are committed by the disciples of Jesus; and their doctrines, instead of producing charity, engender little else than dispute and persecution!" The serious nature of this objection demands a suitable reply.

A true Christian was never known to be a persecutor. The cruel disputes which have arisen among faithless Christians have not necessarily sprung from the nature of Scriptural doctrines, but rather from the pride of those tyrannical doctors, who have contended for their particular explications of such doctrines. To insinuate, then, that the doctrines of the Gospel should be utterly rejected, because some Church-men have taken occasion from them to stir up vehement contests, would scarcely be less absurd, than to contend that anarchy is to be preferred before an excellent code of laws, because unprincipled lawyers are accustomed to foment strife, and have it always in their power to protract a cause. As to the extravagant explications, which the subtilty or power of men has substituted in the place of evangelical doctrines, they can no more be said to prove the falsity or unprofitableness of such doctrines, than the detested policy of tyrants can weaken the force of that apostolic precept, "Let every soul be subject unto the higher powers," Romans xiii. But let us come to the main knot of the difficulty.

They who have unfeignedly embraced the doctrines of Christ, far from indulging in any species of vice, have carried every virtue to a degree of perfection, surpassing almost the conception of other men. Rousseau and Montesquieu acknowledge, that even in those countries where the Gospel has but imperfectly taken root, rebellions have been less frequent than in other places. The same acknowledgment must be made by every unprejudiced observer, with regard to crimes of every kind. Many offences, it must be owned, are every where common among the professors of Christianity; but they would have been abundantly more frequent if antichristian philosophers had been able to take from them the little respect they still retain for a revealed Gospel. Moreover, there are many rare virtues which chiefly flourish in secret: and they who deserve the name of Christians, might astonish incredulity itself, had not Christ commanded them to perform their best services in so private a manner, that the left hand might not know how the right was engaged.

Nothing can be more unjust than to impute those evils to the Christian religion, which evidently flow from incredulity and superstition, fanaticism, and hypocrisy. Jesus Christ requires of his followers an ardent love both to God and man; such a love as was exemplified in the whole of his own conduct through life. The incredulous deny, either wholly or in part, the debt of grateful love, which the innumerable mercies of God impose upon them; since while the Atheist refuses to acknowledge him as the Creator and Preserver of man, the Deist rejects him as the Author of our redemption and sanctification. The superstitious, indeed, acknowledge these immense debts; but they pretend to pay them with idle ceremonies and vain repetitions of tedious forms. The fanatic attempts to discharge them with unfruitful fervours, and the hypocrite with studied grimace. But these errors cannot reasonably be considered in common with our holy religion, which exposes and condemns them all.

The life of a Christian, so called, must necessarily become pure, when he is actually possessed of Christian faith, i.e. when he is strongly persuaded that he walks in the presence of the Almighty, who, being his Father by creation, becomes so in a still more affectionate and effectual manner, by the mysterious exertions of his redeeming and sanctifying grace. These three astonishing operations of the Supreme Being are undoubtedly three grand evidences of his love to man, and must be considered as so many abundant sources of Christian charity, among the members of his Church. Hence the man, who acknowledges but one of these proofs, cannot possibly be united either to his brethren, or to his God, with so ardent an affection as he who admits and experiences all the three. The Divine charity here spoken of is produced in the heart by means of faith, and from it proceeds every social virtue, with every praiseworthy action.

All this is conformable both to reason and experience. A weak subject will fear to disobey a powerful king, whose eye is actually fixed upon him: at least, so long as he is penetrated with this thought, "The king observes me." A son will never exalt himself against a good father, while he believes that his father, in every possible sense, is good with respect to him. Brethren, who cordially acknowledge each other as such, will not dare to abuse one another in the presence of a father who is infinitely powerful. And while he leads them to take possession of a kingdom, which his generosity has divided among them, they will not threaten to murder each other, under the eyes of their parent, for the possession of any little enjoyment that presents itself upon the road. The sons of Jacob had never sold their brother Joseph, if they had been firmly persuaded that Israel would one day discover their crime: and they would have conceived the greatest horror, had they really believed that their heavenly Father was present at the impious action, resolving to call them, at some future season, to a severe account, in the face of the world. A faith, which has no influence upon the conduct, is no other than the faith of hypocrites, upon whom our Lord denounces the most terrible judgments, threatening them with everlasting banishment from his presence, into that outer darkness, where shall be "weeping, and wailing, and gnashing of teeth. I will show thee my faith," saith St. James, "by my works," James ii:18. "If any man say," continues St. John, "I believe in God, I love God, and hateth his brother, he is a liar," 1 John iv:20. The same principles, which in the present moment gain the ascendency in man, give rise to the words and actions of the moment. And hence that saying of the apostle, "Whosoever abideth in him [Christ] sinneth not: whosoever sinneth hath not seen him," through the medium of a true and lively faith. 1 John iii:6.

If there are found professors of Christianity, in whom the truths of the Gospel have failed to produce a holy conversation, we may take it for granted that such persons are infidels in disguise, and totally unacquainted with the Gospel, except it be in theory. The faith which is common to these nominal Christians is purely speculative, not differing less from the solid faith of a true believer than a sun upon canvass differs from that which spreads light and heat among surrounding worlds. As a plant cannot be nourished by the superficial application of strange sap to its rind, but by a sap peculiar to its own nature, which flowing beneath its bark, penetrates, enlivens, and nourishes every part of the plant: so the conduct of a man cannot possibly be reformed by notions of doctrines collected from books, but by those which, penetrating beyond his judgment, insinuate themselves into his heart, and become incorporated with his very being.

This answer cannot justly be regarded as a vain subterfuge. To be convinced of its solidity, it will be sufficient to consider how the soul is affected according to the different degrees of any impression that is made upon it. While Jacob was still lamenting the supposed death of Joseph, Reuben informed him that his beloved son was yet alive, and enjoying the second place of dignity in Egypt. These tidings at first appeared delusive to the good old man, who was no otherwise affected by them than by some extravagant relation. But when the affirmations of Reuben were seconded by the joint testimony of his other sons, his earnest attention was immediately excited, his incredulity was gradually overcome, and his fainting heart began to revive. The wagons and presents of Joseph now appearing in confirmation of his children's report, his doubts were entirely dissipated. "My son," cried he, "is yet alive! I will go and see him before I die." This animating persuasion, *Joseph is yet alive*, seemed to restore the languishing patriarch to all the vigour of former years. He renounced a terrestrial Canaan; he turned his back upon the tombs of Isaac and Rachel; and with all the courage of youth set forward to embrace his newlydiscovered son in Egypt. So certain it is, that a truth in which we are deeply interested, will change in some degree our very nature, and modify the soul itself.

Thus the Gospel of God our Saviour affects every true believer. And why should Egypt have greater charms than heaven? Or why should an invitation from the virtuous son of Rachel have greater weight than that which comes from the Divine Son of Mary? Were the fruits which Joseph sent his father to be preferred before those of the Spirit, with which Christ replenishes his favoured Israel? Galatians v:22, 23: or did the dissembling sons of Jacob merit greater credit than the apostles of our exalted Lord, though seconded by that noble army of martyrs, who have sealed with their blood the truths of the Gospel? Alas! if the fundamental doctrines of this Gospel (for we speak not here of those human additions by which it is too frequently disfigured and weakened) had but deeply penetrated our hearts, we should bear testimony, by our conduct, to the truth of the following assertion: "If any man be [indeed a Christian,] he is a new creature; old things are passed away; all things are become new," 2 Corinthians v:17.

But why should we go back to the times of Jacob to prove that doctrines have an influence upon the conduct of men in proportion to the degree of faith with which they are received? Let us return and cast a retrospective view upon the various circumstances of our past life. If we have at any time felt a lively persuasion of the truth of the Gospel; if at our first approaching the sacramental table, or after hearing some pathetic sermon, we have really believed "that God was in Christ reconciling the world unto himself," 2 Corinthians v:19, and promising his people, in return for their temporary labours, everlasting rewards; have we not, at such a moment, perceived the love of God and man springing up in our hearts? Now, if this partial persuasion had spread itself through the whole soul, would not our devotion, our humility, and our charity have been carried to a much higher degree of perfection than we have hitherto experienced? Would not our good works, of every kind, have been abundantly more excellent and numerous than we can now possibly pretend to?

On the other hand let us look back to the days of youth, and we shall recollect a time in which the doctrines of the Gospel began to lose the little influence they had once maintained over our conduct: we shall remember, at least, when the licentious principles of worldly men and the false maxims of infidel philosophers insinuated themselves into our corrupted hearts. And have we not, since that time, experienced that the strictest connection subsists between those maxims and immorality? Have we not, from that unhappy period, become more debauched in sentiment, less circumspect in our outward behaviour, and more disposed to trample upon the principles of natural religion, as well as upon evangelical precepts? From these observations we shall proceed to draw the following inferences:—

1. If morality may be compared to a tree, whose fruit is for the nourishment of mankind, true doctrines may be considered as the roots of this tree. Take away these doctrines, under pretence that they embarrass morality, and you ridiculously cut away the roots of this sacred plant, lest they should prove an impediment to its rising perfection. Now he who thus seeks the morality of the Gospel by reprobating evangelical doctrines, would act entirely consistent with his character, were he to plant his orchards with trees deprived of their roots in order that they might produce the more excellent fruit.

2. As in the vegetable kingdom fruits are nourished and matured by that vegetative energy which draws the sap from the root, refining, and distributing it among the several branches; so in the moral world, charity and good works can only be produced by that living faith which first receives the doctrines of truth, and then becomes a kind of vehicle to their invigorating virtue. This faith was rightly characterized by Christ and his apostles, when they represented it as the grace by which we are principally saved; since this grace alone is capable of producing in us that lively hope, that ardent charity, and that universal obedience, which will ever distinguish the believer from the infidel. He, therefore, who declaims against this Scriptural faith, whether he be a novice or a philosopher, indirectly pleads the cause of vice and gives sufficient proof of his spiritual ignorance.

3. From what has been advanced, we may infer the necessity there is of avoiding the mistakes of the Gnostics on the one hand, and the error of incredulous sages on the other: the former of whom, contending for a speculative faith, salute Christ as their Lord, though they refuse to obey his commands; while the latter, holding faith in the utmost derision, and depending upon their own power for the performance of every good work, pollute, by unworthy motives, the most excellent of their actions.

CHAPTER XI.
The same subject continued.

AS many have taken great offence in observing how little effect the doctrines of the Gospel have upon the lives of Christians, so called, it becomes us here to inquire into the causes of this grand evil.

The doctrines which distinguish Christianity from Theism have this peculiarity, that no man can possibly receive them unless he has first sincerely embraced the doctrines of Theism. He must believe in God before he can believe in Christ; he must have the sincerity of an honest heathen before he comes to the possession of Christian charity. It is usual with the whole multitude of outward professors to cry out in their public services, "We believe in Jesus Christ; we believe in the Holy Ghost," &c, though their faith, it may be, is not equal to that of devils, who believe in the existence of a rewarding and avenging God, with sincerity sufficient to make them tremble before him. These hypocrites can no more be said to believe, from the heart, the latter articles of the apostles' creed, than those children who are yet unacquainted with the alphabet may be said to have perused and digested the most profound authors. The higher doctrines of the Gospel must necessarily appear both useless and absurd to those whose faith in God is not sufficient to penetrate them with a holy fear; for as we cannot arrive at manhood without first passing through the state of infancy, so we cannot cordially receive the latter part of the apostles' creed, till we have first embraced the former part by a lively and steadfast faith. Why did Caiaphas refuse to believe in Christ? Because he was but a hypocrite with respect to the Jewish faith. On the contrary, why did Cornelius, the centurion, so readily believe? It was, undoubtedly, because the sincerity of his faith in God had prepared his heart for the reception of faith in Christ. "Every man," saith this Divine Saviour, "that hath heard, and hath learned of the Father, cometh unto me," John vi:45. "Ye who believe in God, believe also in me: and I will pray the Father, and he shall give you another Comforter, even the Spirit of truth," John xiv:1, 16, 17.

These fundamental doctrines compose the ladder of evangelical truth, in which he who takes offence at any single step, runs a double hazard; that of ascending no higher, and even that of falling from the step where he has obstinately determined to take up his rest. "He that doeth truth, cometh to the light," John iii:21; but he that refuses the first truths, places himself beyond the possibility of receiving those which are of a more sublime nature. If he has not first observed the dawn of the Gospel day, he can never contemplate our Divine Sun, when shining in his meridian brightness.

The articles of the Christian faith may be compared to a course of geometrical propositions, the last of which always suppose a perfect knowledge of the first. To require of spiritual infants any high and important acts of faith in Jesus Christ, or in the Holy Spirit, before they are taught to entertain just notions of the Supreme Being, would be equally unreasonable as for a man to pretend that it is possible to make a good geometrician of an ignorant peasant, by instructing him to repeat the terms of Euclid's last propositions, without ever bringing him to a true understanding of the first. If, then, the generality of Christians are contented with learning merely to repeat our doctrinal terms, we must expect to see them as far from manifesting the virtues of St. Paul as the superficial peasant from possessing the solidity of Euclid.

CHAPTER XII.

Other reasons given for the little influence which the foregoing doctrines are observed to have upon Christians in general.

PROFITABLY to teach the doctrines of the Gospel, there are certain rules necessary to be observed; and where these rules are either unknown or neglected, the Gospel becomes of little importance.

1. A true doctrine, in order to have its due effect, must be announced with purity. It should neither be mutilated by hasty contractions, nor corrupted by vain additions. The prince of error equally serves his own interest by perplexing the truth, as by spreading a falsehood: and when errors are added to evangelical truths, those truths may be compared to excellent medicines unhappily mingled with dangerous poisons. Thus the doctrine of future punishments is not only deprived of its utility, but becomes really pernicious, by the addition of another doctrine, which teaches that a sum of money, left as the price of prayer for a departed soul, will effectually soften, and even terminate its pains.

2. A doctrine should not only be delivered in the purest manner, but they who announce it should study to demonstrate its excellency and power by the whole course of their conduct. Were leprous physicians to cry up a specific against the leprosy, it cannot be imagined that lepers in general would anxiously adopt a remedy which had been attended with so little effect upon the recommenders of it. We here intimate, not without the utmost regret, that too many of the clergy destroy the effect of their doctrines by the immorality of their conduct.

3. To give Scriptural doctrines their full effect, it is necessary to make them pass from the understanding to the will, or from the judgment to the heart of those who admit them. It would be in vain to procure for a patient the most efficacious remedy, if, instead of applying it according to the method prescribed, he should think it sufficient to touch it with his lips, or should content himself with drawing in the grateful odour exhaling from it. To such a patient, however, the greater part of Christians bear a strict resemblance, who speculate upon the Gospel without ever embracing it with that lively "faith which worketh by love," Galatians v:6.

4. It is not sufficient that these doctrines should be preached in their native purity; but it is equally necessary that they should be preserved in the same purity by those who receive them. Our Lord makes this solemn declaration to sinners: "Except ye repent, ye shall all likewise perish." Yet how is it that many thousand Christians who admit this important truth, remain in the present day in a state of impenitence? It is because they mingle with it the following pernicious error: though I spend the present moment in sin, God will assuredly give me grace to repent in the latter part of my life. Hence that lamentable inattention to the duties of religion which is so universal among us at this day.

5. Very frequently the doctrines of the Gospel are attended with no considerable effect upon those who admit them, because the salutary operation of these truths is

counteracted by the powerful influence of earthly desires indulged in the heart. Thus, in a disordered stomach, the most wholesome food is deprived of its virtue. To remedy this evil, it is necessary to enter upon a regimen too severe to be regarded by an obstinate patient, and upon the absolute necessity of which an inattentive physician will not peremptorily insist.

6. Where the doctrines of the most humiliating tendency have not first made a deep impression, there the consolatory doctrines of the Gospel tend only to uphold the sinner in a course of impiety. Those preachers who favour the false judgment of worldly men, wanting either courage or experience wisely to administer the doctrines of the Gospel so that they may alarm the impenitent and console the dejected; these preachers, instead of eradicating, do but increase the evil we lament. It cannot, indeed, be denied, that they offer many sacred truths to the world; but, while they do not nicely distinguish and apply them to the different states of their hearers, as they only draw their bow at a venture, it is no wonder that their arrows so frequently fall beside the mark. These perplexers of truth contribute as little to the conversion of sinners, as a physician would contribute to the recovery of the sick, who, without any prudent selection, compounding together all the drugs of an excellent pharmacopoeia, should indiscriminately offer the same confused recipe to every patient.

7. The doctrines of Christianity are frequently delivered as the opinions of men, rather than as the declarations of God, founded upon events much better attested than the most certain historical facts: and to this single error the inefficacy of those doctrines may, in a good degree, be imputed. Were reason and conscience made to walk in the front of the Gospel, the want of a Redeemer would be more universally experienced in the world than it has hitherto been. But while the preachers of that Gospel neglect to assert the depravity of human nature; or while they omit, in confirmation of so melancholy a truth, to make the most solemn appeals to the consciences of men, so long we may expect to see their ill-directed labours universally unsuccessful. Had these teachers in Israel an experimental acquaintance with those truths upon which they presume openly to descant, their word would speedily be attended with unusual efficacy; their example would give it weight; and in answer to their fervent prayers, the God of all grace would set his seal to the truth of the Gospel.

Whenever the messengers of religious truth shall become remarkable for the purity of their lives, and the fervency of their zeal, their doctrines will soon be attended with sufficient influence in the Christian world to overthrow the objection we have here been considering, and effectually to stop the mouth of every gainsayer.

CHAPTER XIII.

The doctrines of Christianity have an obscure side.
The reasons of this obscurity. The error of some philosophers in this respect.

"THE Gospel," says J. J. Rousseau, "is accompanied with marks of truth so great, so striking, so perfectly inimitable, that the inventor of it appears abundantly more admirable than its hero. But, after all, this Gospel is filled with incredible things, with things that are repugnant to reason, and which no sensible man can possibly conceive or admit." "Remove all the difficulties," continue the admirers of this philosopher, "dissipate all the obscurity with which its doctrines are surrounded, and we will cheerfully embrace the Gospel."

Extraordinary things appear always incredible, in proportion to our ignorance. Thus, an ignorant negro of Guinea would look upon that man as a deceiver who should assert that there are places in the world where the surfaces of rivers become so solid, at particular seasons, that, without bridge or boat, whole armies may pass them dryshod. And it is well known, that the doctrine of antipodes gave no less offence to the celebrated geographers of a former age, than is unhappily given to the Deistical sages of modern times by the doctrine of a Divine Trinity.

As we become better acquainted with spiritual things, instead of despising the truths of the Gospel as altogether incredible, we shall be truly convinced that J. J. Rousseau passed the same kind of judgment upon the doctrines of Christianity, as a savage might be expected to pass upon some late discoveries in natural philosophy. The sciences present a hundred difficulties to the minds of young students. By entering upon an obscure course, they at length attain to superior degrees of illumination: but, after all the indefatigable labours of the most learned professor, the highest knowledge he can possibly acquire will be mingled with darkness and error. If men of wisdom, however, do not look with contempt upon those sciences which are usually taught among us, because all of them are attended with difficulties, and most of them too abstruse to permit a thorough investigation: how absurd would it be in us, for these insufficient reasons, to reject that revelation which may be considered as the science of celestial things?

To despise the doctrines of the Gospel, because they are attended with some degree of obscurity, is to act in as full contrariety to the dictates of philosophy, as to those of revelation. No follower of J. J. Rousseau could blame us, without reproaching himself, if, arguing from the erroneous principles of his master, we should make the following declarations:— "Natural philosophy *abounds with incredible things which no sensible man can either conceive or admit.* I have arteries, it is said, which carry my blood, with a sensible pulsation, from the heart to the extremities of my body; and veins, which, without any pulsation, reconduct that blood to the heart: but since the union of the arteries and veins is, to me, an inconceivable mystery, I cannot admit the generally received opinion respecting the circulation of the blood. I see that the needle of the compass perpetually turns itself toward the pole, and I have observed that the loadstone communicates to it this disposition: but, as it cannot be ascertained how all this is effected, I look upon all the voyages of Anson and Cook, which are said to have been performed by means of the compass, just as infidels are accustomed to look upon the Gospel. I will no longer increase the number of those idiots who unthinkingly pass over a bridge while they are perfectly unacquainted with the plan upon which it was built; and who vulgarly depend upon their watches with regard to the regulation of time, without being thoroughly versed in the mechanism of timepieces. I will never again be persuaded to take a medical preparation till I have penetrated into the deepest mysteries of physic and chemistry. In short, I resolve neither to eat nor to drink; neither to sow my grounds, nor to gaze upon the sun, till I am enabled perfectly to comprehend whatever is mysterious in vegetation, light, and digestion." If the preceding declarations might reasonably be considered as evident tokens of a weak and puerile judgment, the following affirmation undoubtedly deserves to be considered in the same point of view:—"I grant that the science of physics has its unfathomable mysteries: but, as a philosopher of the first rank, I insist upon it, that nothing of a mysterious nature should be suffered to pass in religion, that deep metaphysical science, which has for its objects the Father of spirits, the relation in which those spirits stand to their incomprehensible Parent, their properties, their light, their nourishment, their growth, their distempers, and their remedies, their degeneracy, and their perfection." Ye who are anxious to be saluted as lovers of wisdom, if such be the absurdity of your common objections against the Gospel of God our Saviour, what poor pretensions have you to the boasted name of philosophers!

This answer may be supported by the following observations:—

In the present world we serve a kind of spiritual apprenticeship to "the truth, which is after godliness," Titus i:1; and it is not usual hastily to reveal the secrets of an art to such as have but lately bound themselves to any particular profession. This privilege is justly reserved for those whose industry and obedience have merited so valuable a testimony of their master's approbation, See John xiv:21.

A physical impossibility of discovering, at present, certain obscure truths, forms the veil by which they are effectually concealed from our view. In order to form a perfect judgment of the material sun, it is necessary, in the first place, to take a near survey of it: but this cannot possibly be done with bodies of a like constitution with ours. The same may be said of the Father of lights. God, as a spiritual Sun, enlightens, even now, the souls of the just: but while they continue imprisoned in tenements of clay, their views of his matchless glory must necessarily be indistinct, since they can only "behold him through a glass darkly," 1 Corinthians xiii:12. Hence we argue with St. Paul, that as spiritual things are spiritually discerned, the natural man can never truly comprehend and embrace them, but in proportion as he becomes spiritually minded by regeneration.

The wise Author of our existence initiates us not immediately into the mysteries which lie concealed under many of our doctrines, for the very same reason that a mathematician conceals the most abstruse parts of his science from the notice of his less intelligent pupils. If a preceptor should affect to bring children acquainted with all the difficulties of algebra, before they had passed through the first rules of arithmetic, such an attempt would deservedly be looked upon as ridiculous and vain. And is it not equally absurd to expect that the profoundest mysteries of the Gospel should be opened to us, before we have properly digested its introductory truths, or duly attended to its lowest precepts?

The Almighty will never perform a useless work, nor ever afford an unseasonable discovery. For the practice of solid piety, it is by no means necessary that we should be permitted to fathom the depth of every spiritual mystery. It is enough that fundamental truths are revealed, with sufficient perspicuity, to produce in us that faith which is the mother of charity. When the Gospel has proposed to us the truths which give rise to this humble faith, and presented us with such motives as evidently lead to the most disinterested charity, it has then furnished us with every thing we stand in need of to work out for ourselves a glorious salvation. The followers of Christ are required to tread in the steps of their Master, and not deeply to speculate upon the secret things of his invisible kingdom.

The Portrait of St. Paul

If a clear knowledge of the mysterious side of our doctrines is no more necessary to man in his present state, than an acquaintance with every thing that respects the art of printing is necessary to a child who is studying the alphabet; why then do we peevishly complain of the sacred writers, for not having thrown light sufficient upon some particular points to satisfy an inordinate curiosity? Our scruples on this head should be silenced by the constant declarations of those very writers, that the time of perfection is not yet arrived; that they themselves were acquainted but in part with the mysteries of the kingdom; and that the language of mortality is unsuitable to the sublimity of Divine things. the sea has its unfathomable abysses, and an extent unknown to the most experienced navigators: but notwithstanding all this uncertainty, the merchant is perfectly contented, if he can but glide securely over its surface to the port for which he is bound.

If we are placed here in a state of probation, it is reasonable that our understanding, as well as our will, should be brought to the trial. But how shall the Almighty proceed to make proof either of the self sufficiency, or the diffidence of our understanding? No happier method could certainly be adopted than that of pointing us to such truths as are partly manifest and partly concealed, that we may search them out with diligence, if there be a possibility of comprehending them; or, if placed above the highest stretch of our faculties, expect with patience a future revelation of them.

To acquire and manifest dispositions of a truly Divine nature, is possible only under a religious economy, whose doctrines are in some degree mysterious, and whose morality has something in it painful to human nature. Why then do those persons who affect to be wiser than their neighbours, universally take offence at such a religion? If a mysterious veil is thrown over the operations of nature and the workings of Providence, why should we expect the more wonderful operations of grace to be laid unreservedly open to every eye? Philosophy, it is presumed, will not dare thus foolishly to destroy the rules of analogy. Humility is necessary to the perfection of our understanding no less than sagacity and penetration, on which account God is pleased to bring our humility to the test. And this he does by discovering to us so much of truth as may enable us to recognize it on its first appearance; at the same time, permitting the objects of faith to be surrounded with difficulties sufficient to leave room for the exercise of that humble confidence in his veracity, and that true poverty of spirit which philosophers are pleased to hold up as just objects of ridicule. Sound knowledge, however, and unaffected humility, will always keep pace with each other. Hence that memorable confession of Socrates, "All that I know is, that I know nothing." And hence that remarkable declaration of St. Paul, "If any man think that he knoweth any thing, he knoweth nothing yet as he ought to know."

It is impossible that any thing should have a greater tendency to keep man at a distance from God, than that arrogant self sufficiency with which modern free thinkers are usually puffed up. This unhappy disposition must be totally subdued before we can come to the fountain head of pure intelligence, James i:5. And to effect this, the Almighty permits our understanding to be embarrassed and confounded, till it is constrained to bow before his supreme wisdom, in acknowledgment of its own imbecility. But it is always with the utmost difficulty, and not till after a thousand vain devices have been practised, that human nature can be forced into this state of self abasement. Here Socrates and St. Paul may be regarded as happy companions, experiencing, in common, that submissive meekness, and that profound humility, which are so terrible to many professors of wisdom. And it is but reasonable that the piety of the one, and the philosophy of the other, should have been established upon the basis of those rare virtues which formed the ground of the following address from Christ to his Father: "I thank thee, O Father! Lord of heaven and earth, because thou hast hidden these things from the wise and the prudent, and hast revealed them unto babes," Matthew xi:25.

It becomes us so much the more to moderate the sallies of an impatient curiosity, with respect to truths of a mysterious nature, since Christ himself has given us an example of the obedience due to the following apostolic precept:—"Let no man think of himself more highly than he ought to think; but let him think soberly, according as God hath dealt to every man the measure of faith," Romans xii:3. This condescending Saviour was content, as Son of man, to remain in the humble ignorance of which we speak. If, in order to have satisfied his curiosity with respect to the day of judgment, he had attempted to explore the secret counsels of the Almighty, there can be no doubt but his gracious Father would have admitted him into that impenetrable sanctuary. But he rather chose to leave among his followers an example of the most perfect respect and resignation to the will of that Father.

What was said by St. Paul concerning heresies, may, with propriety, be applied to that obscurity which accompanies the doctrines of the Gospel. "There must be heresies among you, that they which are approved may be made manifest," 1 Corinthians xi:19. Mons. de Voltaire, who saw not any utility in the proof here mentioned by the apostle, was accustomed to censure revelation, because the doctrines it proposes are incapable of such incontestable evidence as mathematical problems. He considered not that lines, circles, and triangles, falling immediately under the senses, are subjects of investigation peculiarly suited to the natural man. He recollected not that many of Euclid's demonstrations are as incomprehensible to the greater part of mankind, as the mysteries of our holy religion are incomprehensible to the generality of philosophers. And lastly, he perceived not that, if all men were to pique themselves upon their skill in mathematics, and were equally interested in the proportions of circles, squares, and triangles, as in those relations which subsist between fallen man and an incomprehensible God, there would be excited, among ignorant mathematicians, as many warm disputes as are continually arising among ill-instructed Christians.

The justness of these observations will become more apparent, if we consider the importance of that virtue, which is called, in Scripture language, "the obedience of faith," Romans xvi:26. Man originally suffered himself to be seduced with the hope of wonderful effects to be produced by the fruit of a mysterious tree; founding his frail hope upon the simple declaration of the tempter. God, in order to humble the soul, is pleased to restore us through the hope of powerful effects to be produced by the truths of a mysterious revelation; a sweet hope, whose only basis is the simple declaration of the God of truth. And it is undoubtedly reasonable, in every respect, that the cause of our restoration should be thus directly opposed to the cause of our fall. The obedience that is unattended with difficulties, can never be regarded as a reasonable proof of our fidelity to God. Had he merely commanded us to believe that "the whole is greater than a part," or that "two and two make four;" in such case no room would have been left for a reasonable distribution of rewards and punishments. The Deity could not possibly have been disobeyed, since we can no more refuse our assent to these manifest truths, than we can deny the existence of the sun, while we are rejoicing in his meridian brightness. It appears, therefore, perfectly necessary that every truth, proposed to the faith of man in his probationary state, should have an obscure as well as a luminous side, that it may leave place for the mature deliberation, and, of consequence, for the merit or demerit of those who are called to "the obedience of faith."

To desire a revelation without any obscurity, is to desire a day without night, a summer without winter, a sky without a cloud. And what should we gain by such an exchange? Or rather, what should we not lose, if those intentional obscurities, which conceal some parts of celestial truth, should be as needful to man in his present situation, as those clouds which frequently deform the face of the heavens are beneficial to the earth? The faith which is unaccompanied with any thing mysterious, no more merits the name of faith than the tranquillity of a man, who has never been in the way of danger, deserves the name of bravery. An expression of our Lord's to one of his doubting disciples is sufficient to throw the most convincing light upon this matter: "Thomas," said he, "because thou hast seen me, thou hast believed;" but what recompense or praise can be due to such a faith? "Blessed are they that have not seen, and yet have believed," John xx:29.

To conclude: What occasion would there be for the exercise of either wisdom or virtue, were the one only good path presented so clearly to our view that it would be difficult to make choice of any other? Or to what good purpose could true philosophy serve, which has no other use except that of teaching us to regulate our principles, and govern our actions, in a manner more suited to the perfection of our nature, than is customary with those who are led by prejudice and passion?

From all these observations it may justly be argued, that to insist upon having religious doctrines without obscurity, and a revelation without mystery, is to destroy the design of the Supreme Being, who hath placed us here in a state of trial. It is to confound the goal with the course, the conflict with the triumph, and earth with heaven. Nay more: it is to confound the creature with the Creator. That which is finite must never hope to comprehend the heights and depths of infinity. Archangels themselves, though endued with inconceivable degrees of wisdom and purity, will continually find unfathomable abysses in the Divine nature. And if so, is it not to abjure good sense, as well as revelation, to turn our backs upon the temple of truth, because there is found in it "a most holy place," where the profane are never suffered to enter, and the furniture of which even true worshippers can neither clearly explain nor fully comprehend?

CHAPTER XIV.

In answer to the grand objection of philosophers against the doctrines of the Gospel, it is argued, that the advantages of the redemption are extended, in different degrees, to all mankind, through every period of the world.

AS sophistical reasoners had a hundred objections to propose against the doctrine of Socrates, who was a true philosopher, so the philosophers of this age are industriously framing objections to the doctrines of that Gospel which unerring Wisdom has announced to the world. To determine, whether or not those objections are just and unanswerable, we shall here consider that which appears to be the most weighty in the balance of those two companions in error, Mons. de Voltaire and J. J. Rousseau. "If your doctrine of the redemption," say they, "is really as important as you represent it, why has it been preached only for these last eighteen centuries? If it was of so much consequence to mankind, God, without doubt, would have published it sooner, and more universally."*

ANSWER. The doctrine of the redemption was not primarily necessary to mankind: since there was a time when unoffending man stood in no greater need of a Redeemer, than a healthy person stands in need of a physician. At that time natural religion was suitable to the state of man, and the doctrines of Deism were the spiritual food of his soul. But, as medicine is not less necessary than nutriment to a sick person, so fallen man stands in need of the Gospel, as well as of natural religion. And as strong nourishment would be a species of poison to a man enervated by a raging fever, so the tenets of Theism, administered alone to a sinner, who burns with the disorderly fervours of pride, must inevitably prove fatal to the health of his soul. Thus the presumption of some philosophers is increased by the doctrines of Deism, as the fever of a debilitated patient is redoubled by those very cordials which would increase the strength of a vigorous person. And this may serve as a proof, that the natural religion of sinless man is as little adapted to man in his corrupt estate, as the sweet familiarity of an affectionate infant is suitable to the character of a daring and disobedient son.

It is necessary here to observe, that there are two kinds of Deism; that of the humble sinner, who is not yet acquainted with the Gospel, and that of the presumptuous reasoner, who rejects it with contempt. The Centurion Cornelius, who lived in the practice of piety before he was perfectly acquainted with Christ, and the penitent publican alluded to by our Lord, were Deists of the first class, and such as might well be esteemed the younger brothers of Christians. The second class is made up of those Theists who trample revelation under their feet, and who may properly be

---

* Mons. de Voltaire, in his Philosophical Dictionary, attacks Christianity, under the name of Mohammedanism, in the following words:—"If it had been necessary to the world, it would have existed from the beginning of the world; it would have existed in every place. The Mohammedan religion therefore cannot be essentially necessary to man." J. J. Rousseau was perfectly of the same opinion. "I deny," says this writer, in his Emilius, "the necessity of receiving revelation, because this pretended obligation is incompatible with the justice of God. Should there be found in the universe a single person to whom Christ had never been preached, the objection would be as forcible on the part of that neglected individual, as for the fourth part of the human race."

called the presumptuous Pharisees of the present day. It is the haughty Deism of these men that a false philosophy would substitute in the place of the Gospel. The judicious author of *The New Theological Dictionary* has characterized these two kinds of Deism with an accuracy peculiar to himself. "Deism," says he, "was once on the high way from Atheism to Christianity; but to-day it is usually found upon the road from Christianity to Atheism."

To assert that the doctrine of the redemption has been announced for no more than eighteen centuries, is to suppose there can be no appearance of light till the sun has risen above the horizon. So soon as the work of redemption became necessary, in that very day it was announced to man. When our first parents had received from their merciful Judge the sentence that condemned them to misery and death, he immediately gave them a promise, that in some future day a repairer of their evils should be born of woman, who should "bruise the head of the serpent," that is, who should crush, at once, all the power of the tempter, and the pride of the sinner. In consequence of this gracious covenant, which was, indeed, the first promulgation of the Gospel, God implanted in man an interior principle of redemption, a seed of regenerating grace, which should, in the end, spring up to everlasting life. Now this principle was nothing less than a ray from that living Word, which was afterward to be visibly united with our nature, in order to raise man from his dishonourable fall, and, finally, to procure for him a state superior to that which he originally enjoyed. Nothing can be more explicit upon this point than the following declaration of St. John: "In Him [the living Word] was life; and the life was the light of men. And the light shined in darkness; and the darkness [in general] comprehended it not. This was [however] the true light, which lighteth [more or less] every man that cometh into the world," John i:4, 9. When, therefore, a conceited free thinker superciliously exclaims, "If the doctrine of the redemption had been necessary it would have been published in the earliest ages of the world," such objection should serve as a manifest token of his ignorance in this matter, since that important doctrine was mercifully announced to the very first offender. If that doctrine was afterward corrupted by tradition; if rebellious man began to exalt himself as his own saviour; or if, through impatience, he set up false mediators, instead of patiently expecting the fulfilment of Jehovah's promise: all this evidently proves his extreme need of a Redeemer. In short, if the greater part of the Jewish nation rejected this Divine Saviour in the days of his outward manifestation, and if prejudiced Deists still continue to reject his offered assistance, all that can be proved by their unrelenting obstinacy is the greatness of their guilt, and the depth of their depravity: just as the conduct of a patient, who abuses his physician, suffices only to demonstrate the excess of his delirium.

Several reasons may be here produced, which might have engaged the Father of mercies to defer the external manifestation of our promised Redeemer for a period of four thousand years.

1. It is probable, that as every thing is discovered to operate gradually in the natural world, the same order might be established in the moral world. Even since the time of Christ's outward manifestation, the influence of his redeeming power has but gradually discovered itself in our yet benighted world. He himself compared the Gospel to a little leaven, which spreads itself by slow degrees over a bulky mass of meal; and to a small seed, from which a noble plant is produced. To this we may add, that a portion of time, which appears long and tedious to us, appears wholly different

in the eyes of the everlasting I AM, before whom a thousand years are no more than a fleeting day.

2. If, immediately after the commission of sin, God had sent forth his Son into the world to raise us from our fall, before we had experienced the melancholy effects of that fall; such a hasty act, instead of manifesting the perfections of the Deity, would have drawn a veil of obscurity between us and them. The Divine mercy, discovered in Jesus Christ, might then have appeared as insignificant to us as to the arrogant Deist, who, notwithstanding the crimes with which the world has been polluted for near six thousand years, and in spite of those which he himself has added to the prodigious sum, has yet the audacity to assert, that there is no necessity for a Redeemer, that man is good in his present state, and that he may conduct himself honourably through it, without the assistance of regenerating grace. Hence it appears, that the outward manifestation of the Messiah was wisely deferred to a period of time far removed from the commencement of the fall.

3. While the visible manifestation of Jesus was delayed, all things were put in a state of due preparation for so great an event. And in the meantime the seed of regeneration, which was received by man, after God had pronounced the first evangelical promise, was as sufficient to save every penitent sinner, as the dawn of day is sufficient to direct every erring traveller.

This merits an explanation. The first man, to whom the promise of redemption was made, contained in himself the whole of his posterity: and this promise, wonderfully powerful, as being the "word of God," Hebrews iv:12, had an indescribable effect upon the whole human race, implanting in man a seed of regeneration, a Logos, a reason, a conscience, a light, in short, a good principle, which, in every sincere inquirer after truth, has been nourished by the grace of God, and seconded by the pious traditions of patriarchs, prophets, apostles, evangelists, or true philosophers. Unhappy is it for those, who, stifling in themselves every gracious sentiment, have treated this internal principle as the Jews once treated their condescending Lord, and as obstinate sinners still continue to treat a preached Gospel. If such are not saved it is not through the want of an offered Saviour, but because they have wilfully shut their eyes against the twilight, the opening dawn, or the meridian brightness of the Gospel day.

Nothing can be more unreasonable than the objection to which we now return an answer. To argue that God would be unjust, if having given a Saviour to the world, he should not reveal that Saviour in an equal degree to all mankind, is to argue that God is unjust, because, having given a sun to the earth, he has not ordained that sun equally to enlighten and cheer every part of the globe. Again: to insinuate that Christ cannot properly be regarded as the Saviour of mankind, because innumerable multitudes of men are not even acquainted with his name, is to insinuate that the sun is utterly useless to the deaf, because they have never heard the properties of that sun described, and to the blind, because they have never seen his cheering beams. Lastly: to conclude that the Gospel is false, because it has not rapidly spread itself over the whole world, or because it is not observed to operate in a more hasty manner the happy changes it is said to produce—thus to argue, is to reason as inconclusively as a man who should say, The tree that produces Jesuits' bark is an insignificant and useless tree: for, (1.) It grows not in every country. (2.) It has not always been known. (3.) There are persons in the country where it grows, who look upon it as no extraordinary thing: and, (4.) Many, who have apparently given this medicine a proper trial, have found it unattended with those salutary effects so generally boasted of.

Turning the arguments of our philosophers against their own system, we affirm, that the Messiah was manifested in a time and place peculiarly suited to so great an event. With respect to the time, he lived and died when the human species had arrived at the utmost pitch of refinement and learning. Had he appeared two or three thousand years sooner, he must have visited the world in its infant state, while ignorance and barbarity reigned among the nations: but in the days of Augustus and Tiberius, mankind may be said to have reached the highest degree of maturity, with respect to knowledge and civilization. Now, as it is necessary that he who bears testimony to any memorable transaction should be a man and not a child, so it is equally necessary that Christ should have appeared in the most polished period of the world, as the one Mediator between God and man.

Deists sometimes tell us that the force of historic evidence is greatly diminished by lapse of time, as a taper placed at too great a distance loses much of its brightness. If Christ, then, had offered himself a ransom for all many ages sooner than unerring Wisdom had ordained, the incredulous might have urged that the history of a miraculous event, reported to have happened in so remote a period of time, was most probably corrupted by uncertain tradition, and rendered unworthy of credit.

On the other hand, if the accomplishment of the promise had been delayed some thousands of years longer, the faith and patience of believers would have been called to a proof incompatible with the weakness of humanity. And the pious might have said, concerning the first coming of Christ, what they have long ago tauntingly spoken of his second: "Where is the promise of his coming? For since the fathers fell asleep, all things continue as they were from the beginning of the creation," 2 Peter iii:4.

What is here observed with respect to the age in which the Messiah was cut off is no less true of the season, the day, and the hour. He offered himself a sacrifice for the sins of the people in the noonday, at the solemn feast of the passover, and at that season of the year which naturally invited the dispersed Jews to visit the holy city. The place was, like the time, peculiarly adapted to such an event; a country in which the promise of Christ's coming had been frequently repeated. Moreover, he became obedient unto death in the time predicted by the prophets; before a people who possessed the oracles of God; under the eyes of the high priest; before Herod the king, together with the grand council of the nation; before Pilate, who was lieutenant of the greatest prince on earth; at the gates of Jerusalem, in the centre of Judea, and nearly in the centre of the then known world. Thus the external manifestation of our glorious Redeemer may be compared to a sun, whose rising was preceded by a dawn, which benignly opened upon the first inhabitants of the earth; and whose setting is followed by a lovely twilight, which must necessarily continue till he shall again ascend above our horizon, to go down no more. In this point of view the Scriptures uniformly represent the sacrifice of Christ. St. Paul expressly declares that, "by one offering, he hath perfected for ever them that are sanctified:" that is, all those in every nation who fear God and work righteousness, Hebrews x:14; Acts x:35. We argue, therefore, with this apostle, that "as by the offence of one judgment came upon all men to condemnation, even so by the righteousness of one the free gift came upon all men unto justification of life," Romans v:18.

From these observations we conclude, *First,* That the Gospel has been more or less clearly announced ever since the time in which a Redeemer became necessary to man. *Secondly,* That Jesus Christ openly manifested himself in a time most proper for such a discovery. *Thirdly,* That the work of redemption is as necessary to mankind as the assistance of medicine is necessary to those who are struggling under some dangerous disease. *Fourthly,* That an explicit knowledge of the Redeemer and his salvation is as desirable to those who feel themselves ruined by sin, as the certain knowledge of a physician, possessed of sovereign remedies, is consoling to the patient who apprehends his life in imminent danger. *Fifthly,* As languishing infants may be restored by the medicines of a physician with whom they are totally unacquainted, so Jews, Mohammedans, and heathens, provided they walk according to the light they enjoy, are undoubtedly saved by Jesus Christ, though they have no clear conception of the astonishing means employed to secure them from perdition. And *lastly,* That the grand argument advanced against the Gospel by Mons. de Voltaire and J. J. Rousseau, is abundantly more specious than solid.

CHAPTER XV.

Reflections upon the danger to which modern Deists expose themselves.

IN refuting the objection of superficial moralists, proposed in the preceding chapter, we may, perhaps, have afforded them ground for another, full as specious and solid.

OBJECTION. "If it be allowed that in every age salvation has been extended to all the true worshippers of God, whether they have been pious Jews, such as Joseph, Hezekiah, and Josiah: just men among the Gentiles, such as Melchisedec and Aristides; or heathen philosophers who have walked in the fear of God, such as Pythagoras, Socrates, and Plato: and if these virtuous men have been saved without subscribing to the doctrines of the Gospel, why may not Deists and modern philosophers be permitted to enjoy the same salvation while they reject those doctrines?"

ANSWER. There are three grand dispensations of grace. Under the first every heathenish and unenlightened nation must be ranked; the Jews under the second; and Christians under the third, which is a dispensation abundantly more perfect than either of the former. The followers of Mohammed may be classed with modern Jews, since they are Deists of the same rank, and have equally deceived themselves with respect to that great Prophet who came for the restoration of Israel.

Those Jews, Mohammedans, and heathens, who "fear God and work righteousness," are actually saved by Jesus Christ. Christ is the Truth and the Light; and these sincere worshippers, receiving all the rays of truth with which they are visited, afford sufficient proof that they would affectionately admire and adore the Sun of righteousness himself, were the intervening mists removed by which he is concealed from their view. But it is wholly different with those who, beholding this Divine Sun, as he is revealed in the Gospel, determinately close their eyes against him, and contemptuously raise a cloud of objections to veil him, if possible, from the view of others. Every virtuous heathen has manifested a love for truth, while many of our philosophers, in the pride of their hearts, reject and despise it. The former wrought out their salvation, though favoured only with the glimmering dawn of an evangelical day: the latter, surrounded with the meridian brightness of that day, are anxiously seeking the shadowy coverts of uncertainty and error. The former were saved according to that apostolic declaration: "Glory, honour, and peace, to every man that worketh good, to the [Christian and the] Jew first, and also to the Gentile: for there is no respect of persons with God," Romans ii:10, 11. And of this number was the Apostle Paul, who "obtained mercy" because he was ignorantly a persecutor of the truth, living, at the same time, "in all good conscience before God," 1 Timothy i:13. Nor can it be doubted, but the same grace with which St. Paul was visited in these circumstances, will, in various degrees, illumine and purify every soul that resembles him in uprightness and sincerity. The latter will be condemned by virtue of the following declarations: "This is the condemnation, that light is come into the world, and men loved darkness rather than light, because their deeds were evil," John iii:19. "God will render unto them that are contentious, and do not obey the truth, indignation and wrath, tribulation and anguish, upon every soul of man that doeth evil, of the [Christian and the] Jew first, and also of the Gentile," Romans ii:5, 9.

From these citations we may infer, that, in several proportions, the salvation of virtuous heathens will differ as greatly from the salvation of faithful Christians, as the brilliancy of an agate is different from that of a diamond. "Many mansions," and different degrees of glory, are prepared "in the house of our Father," John xiv:1. "There is one glory of the sun, and another glory of the moon, and another glory of the stars; for one star differeth from another star in glory. So also will it be in the resurrection of the dead, when God will render unto every man according to his works," 1 Corinthians xv:41.

The highest degrees of glory are reserved by the righteous Judge of all the earth for the most faithful of his servants. The honourable privilege of being seated at the right hand of Christ will be conferred upon those who have trodden in their Master's footsteps, through the narrowest and most difficult paths of resignation and obedience. On the other hand, God will display the most terrible effects of his righteous anger upon those who have trampled under foot the greatest and most frequent offers of Divine grace, according to that exclamation of the apostle, "How shall we escape if we neglect so great salvation?" Hebrews ii:3; since thus obstinately to despise the highest degrees of glory which may be attained under the Gospel, and daringly to brave the threatenings denounced against those who reject that Gospel, discovers an the heart a cold indifference to real virtue, together with a sovereign contempt for the Divine Author of it.

As true virtue, like a beautiful plant, is continually rising to a state of maturity; so true philosophy is constantly aspiring after the highest attainable degrees of wisdom and purity. If any man neglects those means which conduce to the perfection of virtue, when they are once proposed to him, he gives evident proof that he has neither that instinct of virtue, nor that true philosophy, which cannot but choose the most excellent end, together with the surest means of obtaining it. What would our philosophers say to a man, who, affecting to aspire after riches, and being called to receive a large quantity of gold, should inconsistently refuse it in the following terms: "Many persons have been rich enough with a little money to prevent them from starving, and I have no inclination to exceed them in point of fortune!" The objection

The Works of John Fletcher

proposed in this chapter is founded upon a like sophism, and amounts but to an equal argument: "Jews and virtuous heathens have received assistance sufficient effectually to secure their salvation, and we have not presumption enough to desire any extraordinary advantage above them."

It is difficult to form a just idea of the conceitedness of those boasted moralists, who despise every help afforded by the Gospel, because some heathens, without such assistance, have been acceptable to God. We may compare it to the supposed self sufficiency of a contemptible subaltern officer, who, being presented with a more honourable commission from his prince, should reject it, and cry out, "The commission is false, and they who present it are no better than deceivers. I have no anxiety to quit my present post. I aspire after no greater honours than those I possess. Many thousands have faithfully served his majesty in the capacity of subalterns: nay, common soldiers themselves have received testimonies of his royal approbation: and why should my services afford him less satisfaction than theirs?" Were a corporal, in my hearing, thus to excuse his rejection of a monarch's offered kindness, I should suppose either that he had no just conceptions of the honour intended him, or that he was withheld from accepting that honour, by motives too unworthy to be avowed. But this excuse would be insolent as well as pitiful, had the terms of the commission run thus: "Either serve your prince with fidelity in the post to which he exalts you, or expect to be treated with the utmost severity."

Now such is the case with all those who obstinately reject the Gospel, and perseveringly trample under foot the richest offers of unmerited grace. They either reject the truths of revelation through haughtiness of spirit, or they are held back from embracing them through the secret gratification of some inordinate appetite. Observe here the ground of those memorable declarations of our blessed Lord: "Preach the Gospel to every creature. He that believeth and is baptized, shall be saved; but he that believeth not, shall be damned," Mark xvi:15, 16. He that believeth not the Son, [after hearing him evangelically announced,] shall not see life; but the wrath of God abideth on him. He is condemned already: for every one that doeth evil hateth the light [of the Gospel,] neither cometh to the light, lest his deeds should be reproved," John iii:18, 36.

Upon this principle, as conformable to experience as to sound reason, the Gospel is not absolutely rejected, except by those who are either visibly corrupted, as Pilate and Felix, or secretly depraved, as Judas and Caiaphas. And it was to persons of this character that Christ addressed himself in the following terms: "How can ye believe, who receive honour one of another, and seek not the honour that cometh from God only?" John v:44. "If any man will do the will of him that sent me, [and follow the light that is imparted to him,] he shall know of the doctrine, whether it be of God, or whether I speak of myself," John vii:17. Hence, when any who have been consecrated to Christ by baptism, are seen withdrawing from the footstool of their Master to the schools of philosophy, or, at least, making no advances in true holiness; we may rest assured that their decline is caused, or their spiritual growth prevented, by the secret indulgence of some vicious inclination. These philosophizing moralists, and these lukewarm disciples, may be compared to the fruit that falls before it has attained to the perfection of its species: examine such fruit, and you will find, under a beautiful appearance, either a destructive worm, or loathsome rottenness. Such is the apostatizing Deist under the most specious forms he can possibly assume.

When J. J. Rousseau expressed himself in the following terms: "It God judges of faith by works, then to be a good man is to be a real believer;" he was not far beside the truth, provided that by a good man, he intended one who lives in temperance, justice, and the fear of God; since every man, in whom these virtues are discoverable, is assuredly principled in the true faith. Such a one is a real believer, according to that economy of grace, under which Job, Josiah, and Socrates, shone out to the glory of God; men, who either possessed principles of faith, or whose best actions are no more to be admired than those of our domestic animals.

This writer had less distinct views of truth, when he added, "The true Christian is the just man; unbelievers are the wicked:" since there are just men who are not yet Christians; as there are studious persons who cannot yet be accounted profound scholars. Moreover, there are many, who, like the Centurion Cornelius, do not yet believe the Gospel, because they have never heard that Gospel explained with precision and fidelity; and surely such deserve not to be termed absolutely unjust men. The latter proposition approaches indeed nearer the truth, "unbelievers are the wicked:" yet this is false; except the term *unbeliever* be taken for one who obstinately disbelieves the Gospel, since a good man, who receives the first part of the apostles' creed, may yet, like Nathanael and Nicodemus, be so forcibly held back by involuntary prejudice, with respect to the other parts of the same creed, that he may fluctuate long between truth and error. It is by propositions so vague and insidious that our philosophers delude themselves and beguile their disciples.

"But," replies J. J. Rousseau, "have we power to believe, or not to believe? Is the not being able to argue well imputed to us as a crime? Conscience informs us not what we are to think, but what we are to do: it teaches us not to reason well, but to act well." And are all the faculties of man, except his conscience, to be considered as utterly useless with regard to this important matter? Let it, however, be granted that a wicked and haughty person has it not in his power to believe; yet it is highly necessary that he should fear the truth, so long as he gives himself up either to actions or inclinations that are manifestly evil. Thus, the conscious robber can never overcome his fear of justice so long as he is disposed to continue his iniquitous practices. But if, after making full restitution, he should become sincerely upright, maintaining a conscience void of offence toward God and toward man, he will tremble no more at the idea of judges, tribunals, or executions.

If it be asked, what secret vice it was that would not suffer so honest a man as J. J. Rousseau to embrace the Gospel? Without searching into the anecdotes of his life, we may rest satisfied with the discovery he has made of his own heart in a single sentence: "What can be more transporting to a noble soul than the pride of virtue!" Such was the pride which made him vainly presume that he had power sufficient to conquer himself, without invoking the assistance of God; and by which he was encouraged to assert that the doctrines of the Gospel were such as "no sensible man could either conceive or admit." Such was the "virtuous pride" which would not suffer the Pharisees to receive the humiliating truths of the Gospel, and which filled the heart of Caiaphas with jealousy and hatred against Christ.

There is no species of pride more insolent than that which gives rise to the following language: "It is asserted that 'God so loved the world, as to give his only begotten Son, that whosoever believeth in him should not perish, but have everlasting life.' These tidings, whether they be true or false, are highly acceptable to many; but, for my own part, I openly declare, that I reject with contempt the idea of such a favour I read with attention those writings which tend to unfold the mysteries of nature, but resolve never to turn over those authors who vainly attempt to establish the truth of the Gospel. This subject, though it has occupied the thoughts, and engaged the pens of inquiring students for these seventeen hundred years, I shall ever regard as unworthy my attention. I leave it to the vulgar, who are easily persuaded of its importance. My virtues are sufficient to expiate my crimes, and on these I will resolutely depend, as my sole mediators before God." If this be implicitly the language of every man who obstinately rejects the doctrines of the Gospel, what heights of presumption, and what depths of depravity, must lie open, in the souls of such, to the eye of Omniscience! Reason and revelation agree to condemn them. Behold the ground of their sentence: "Whosoever exalteth himself shall be abased; and he that humbleth himself shall he exalted: for God resisteth the proud, and giveth grace to the humble," Luke xiv:11; 1 Peter v:5.

Reason itself is sufficient to discover that, before the Supreme Being, nothing can appear more detestable than the pride of a degenerate and ungrateful creature. And if so, the Deists of Socrates' time must have been far less culpable than those of the present day. The former, conscious of the uncertainty with which they were encompassed, made use of every help they could procure, in the pursuit of truth, with unwearied assiduity. The latter, presuming upon their own sufficiency, decide against doctrines of the utmost importance, without impartially considering the evidences produced in their favour. The former, by carefully examining every system of morality proposed to their deliberation, discovered a candour and liberality becoming those who were anxiously "feeling after God, if haply they might find him," Acts xvii:27. The latter, by condemning revelation, without calmly attending to the arguments of its advocates, manifest a degree of prejudice that would be unpardonable in a judge, but which becomes execrable in a criminal who is pressed by the strongest reasons to search out the truth.

Plato, in the sixth book of his Republic, introduces his master marking out the dispositions necessary to a virtuous man. "Let us begin," says Socrates, "by recounting what qualities are necessary to him who would one day become an honest man and a true philosopher. The first quality is the love of truth, which he ought to seek after in every tiring and by every mean; true philosophy being absolutely incompatible with the spirit of delusion. He who has a sincere desire to obtain wisdom, cannot confine himself to things that are here below, of which he can acquire but an uncertain knowledge. He is born for truth, and he tends to it with an ardour which nothing is able to restrain." Ye who oppose philosophy to revelation, and reject, without thoroughly investigating, the doctrines of the Gospel, can you be said to discover an attachment to truth as sincere as that of Socrates? Do ye not rather esteem that an excessive fondness for truth, or even a dangerous species of enthusiasm, which the wisest heathens have looked upon as the first disposition requisite to an honest man?

Plato and his master, who scrupulously acknowledged the truth wherever they discovered it, were assuredly in a state of acceptance before God, without an explicit acquaintance with Jesus Christ: for where the Almighty hath not strewed, there will he never expect to gather; and where he hath scattered only the first fruits of the Gospel, there he never will require that precious fruit which he expects to be produced by the highest truths of revelation. Thus the husbandman is content to reap nothing but barley in a field where nothing but barley has been sown: but if, after sowing the same field with the purest wheat, it should produce only tares, with a few scattered ears of barley, he would, undoubtedly, express a degree of surprise and displeasure, at having his reasonable expectation so strangely disappointed.

In the New Testament we find a remarkable parable to this purpose, where mankind are considered as the domestics of God's immense household. In this parable, the Almighty is represented as collecting his servants together, and confiding to the care of each a separate loan, to be employed for the mutual interest of the covenanting parties. To one of his domestics he imparts five talents; to another two; while the third has no more than a single talent committed to his charge: but all are required so to occupy, that their gains may be proportionate to the several sums intrusted to their fidelity. Now, if the Christian, with five talents of spiritual knowledge, acquires no advantage over the Jew, who had received but two, is it not evident that he has acted the part of an unfaithful servant? Nay, he is to be esteemed even more unprofitable than the heathen, who suffers his single talent to lie unimproved; since amidst all his trifling gains he has slothfully concealed three valuable talents, while the other has buried but one. But were the first and the last to derive equal advantages from the disproportionate privileges permitted them to enjoy, while the latter would be received as a good and faithful servant, the former might deservedly be treated with an unusual degree of severity by his insulted Lord. This parable may assist us to conceive that a philosopher, who is called by baptism to evangelical perfection, and yet contents himself with practising the morality of a heathen, has not, in reality, so much solid virtue as a sincere Deist bred up in the bosom of Paganism.

Our progress in morality, like our advancement in science, is to be estimated by considering the circumstances in which we are placed, and the privileges we enjoy. A dramatic piece, composed by a child or a negro, might be received with plaudits, which would justly be hissed off the stage had it been produced by a Shakspeare or a Corneille. A traveller who expresses his admiration at the address with which savages manage a hatchet of stone, would express equal astonishment at the weakness of his countrymen, should he see them casting aside their axes of iron, and felling their trees with ill-formed implements of flint. Thus, after admiring the successful efforts of Socrates, who drew many sacred truths from the chaos of Paganism, how astonishing is it to behold modern philosophers patching up a confused system of Deistical morality, to be substituted in place of the sublimer doctrines and the purer morality of the Gospel! Wherever such retrograde reasoners are discovered, their insignificant labours must be universally deplored by the lovers of truth. But when these champions of false wisdom endeavour to bury, under the ruins of Christianity, those important truths which heathens themselves have formerly discovered, it is impossible to behold their impious efforts without feeling all the warmth of an honest indignation.

We shall conclude this Essay by transcribing a part of that ancient testimony which was borne by Lactantius to the power of those doctrines for which we contend.

"That which many have discovered, by the assistance of natural religion, to be their indispensable duty, but which they have never been able either to practise themselves, or to see exemplified in the conduct of philosophers; all this the sacred doctrines of the Gospel assist us to perform, because that Gospel is wisdom in its highest excellence. How shall philosophers persuade others, while they themselves continue in a state of perplexity? Or how shall they repress the passions of others, while, by giving way to their own, they tacitly confess that nature, in spite of all their efforts, is still triumphant? But daily experience testifies how great an influence the ordinances of God have upon the heart. Give me a passionate, slanderous, implacable man; and, through the power of our Gospel, I will return him to you gentle as a lamb. Give me an avaricious man, whose greediness of gain will suffer him to part with nothing; and I will return him to you so liberal, that he will give away his money by handfuls. Bring me a man who trembles at the approach of pain and death; ere long he shall look with contempt upon crosses, fires, and even the bull of Phalaris itself. Present me with a debauchee, an adulterer, a man wholly lost to good manners; you shall shortly behold him an example of sobriety, uprightness, and continence. Give me a cruel and blood-thirsty man; his ferocious disposition shall suddenly be succeeded by real clemency. Give me an unjust man, a stupid person, an extravagant sinner; you shall shortly behold him scrupulously just, truly wise, and leading a life of innocence. Such is the power of heavenly wisdom, that it is no sooner shed abroad in the heart, but, by a single effort, it chases away folly, the mother of sin. To compass these invaluable ends, a man is under no necessity of paying salaries to masters of philosophy, and passing whole nights in meditating upon their works. Every necessary assistance is imparted without delay, with ease, and free from cost; if there be not wanting an attentive ear, and a heart desirous of wisdom. The sacred source to which we point, is plenteous, overflowing, and open to all men; the celestial light we announce, indiscriminately rises upon all who open their eyes to behold it.

"What philosopher has ever done so much? Who among them is able to perform such wonders? After having passed their lives in the study of philosophy, it appears that they have neither bettered themselves nor others, when nature causes them any great resistance. Their wisdom serves rather to cover, than to eradicate their vices. Whereas our Divine instructions [i.e. the doctrines of the Gospel] so totally change a man, that you would no longer know him for the same person." (*Lact. Lib. 3.* cap. 26.)

AN APPEAL

TO

MATTER OF FACT AND COMMON SENSE:

OR

A RATIONAL DEMONSTRATION

OF

MAN'S CORRUPT AND LOST ESTATE.

———

BY THE REV. JOHN FLETCHER,

VICAR OF MADELEY, SALOP.

———

Ye pompous sons of Reason idolized,
And vilified at once; of Reason dead,
Then deified, as monarchs were of old;
Wrong not the Christian; think not Reason yours
'Tis Reason our great Master holds so dear;
'Tis Reason's injured rights his wrath resents;
'Tis Reason's voice obey'd his glorious crown;
To give lost Reason life he pour'd his own;
Believe, and show the reason of a man;
Believe, and taste the pleasure of a God;
Through Reason's wounds alone thy faith can die.—YOUNG.

The Son of man is come to seek and to save that which was lost.—LUKE.

TO THE PRINCIPAL INHABITANTS

OF THE

PARISH OF MADELEY, IN THE COUNTY OF SALOP.

GENTLEMEN,—You are no less entitled to my private labours than the inferior class of my parishioners. As you do not choose to partake with them of my evening instructions, I take the liberty to present you with some of my morning meditations. May these well-meant endeavours of my pen be more acceptable to you than those of my tongue! And may you carefully read in your closets what you have, perhaps, inattentively heard in the church! I appeal to the Searcher of hearts that I had rather impart truth than receive tithes. You kindly bestow the latter upon me; grant me, I pray, the satisfaction of seeing you favourably receive the former, from, gentlemen, your affectionate minister and obedient servant,

J. FLETCHER.

MADELEY 1772.

CONTENTS OF APPEAL.

————

INTRODUCTION.

PART I.

The doctrine of man's corrupt and lost estate is stated at large in the words of the prophets, apostles, and Jesus Christ; and recapitulated in those of the articles, homilies, and liturgy of the Church of England.

PART II.

Man is considered as an inhabitant of the natural world, and his fall is proved by arguments deduced from the misery in which he is now undeniably involved; compared with the happiness of which we cannot help conceiving him possessed, when he came out of the hands of his gracious Creator.

A view of this misery in the following particulars. I. The disorders of the globe we inhabit, and the dreadful scourges with which it is visited. II. The deplorable and shocking circumstances of our birth. III. The painful and dangerous travail of women. IV. The untimely dissolution of still-born, or new-born children. V. Our natural uncleanliness, helplessness, ignorance, and nakedness. VI. The gross darkness in which we naturally are, both with respect to God and a future state. VII. The general rebellion of the brute creation against us. VIII. The various poisons that lurk in the animal, vegetable, and mineral world, ready to destroy us. IX. The heavy curse of toil and sweat to which we are liable; instances of which are given in the hard and dangerous labours of the author's parishioners. X. The other innumerable calamities of life And, XI, the pangs of death.

PART III.

Man is considered as a citizen of the moral world, a free agent, accountable to his Creator for his tempers and conduct; and his fall is farther demonstrated by arguments drawn from XII. His commission of sin. XIII. His omission of duty. XIV. The triumphs of sensual appetites over his intellectual faculties. XV. The corruption of the powers that constitute a good head; the understanding, imagination, memory, and reason. XVI. The depravity of the powers which form a good heart; the will, conscience, and affections. XVII. His manifest alienation from God. XVIII. His amazing disregard even of his nearest relatives. XIX. His unaccountable unconcern about himself. XX. His detestable tempers. XXI. The general outbreaking of human corruption in all individuals. XXII. The universal overflowing of it in all nations. Five objections answered. XXIII. Some striking proofs of this depravity in the general propensity of mankind to vain, irrational, or cruel diversions; and XXIV. In the universality of the most ridiculous, impious, inhuman, and diabolical sins. XXV. The aggravating circumstances attending the display of this corruption. XXVI. The many ineffectual endeavours to stem its torrent. XXVII. The obstinate resistance it makes to Divine grace in the unconverted. XXVIII. The amazing struggles of good men with it. XXIX. The testimony of heathens and Deists concerning it: and, after all, XXX. The preposterous conceit which the unconverted have of their own goodness.

PART IV.

Man is considered as an inhabitant of the Christian world; and his fallen state is farther proved by six Scriptural arguments, introduced by a short demonstration of the authenticity of the Scriptures, and by a little attack upon the amazing credulity of Deists. The heads of these arguments are, XXXI. The impossibility that fallen, corrupt Adam should have had an upright, innocent posterity; with answers to some capital objections. XXXII. The spirituality and severity of God's law, which the unrenewed man continually breaks: and XXXIII. Our strong propensity to unbelief, the most destructive of all sins, according to the Gospel. XXXIV. The absurdity of the Christian religion with respect to infants and strict moralists. XXXV. The harshness and cruelty of Christ's fundamental doctrines; and XXXVI. The extravagance of the grand article of the Christian faith, IF mankind are not in a corrupt and lost estate..

PART V.

The doctrine of man's fall being established by such a variety of arguments: First, A few natural inferences are added. Secondly, Various fatal consequences attending the ignorance of our lost estate. Thirdly, The unspeakable advantages arising from the right knowledge of it.

The whole is concluded with an address to the serious reader, who inquires what he must do to be saved. And with an appendix concerning the evangelical harmony that subsists between living faith and loving obedience.

INTRODUCTION.

———

IN religious matters we easily run into extremes. Nothing is more common than to see people embracing one error under the plausible pretence of avoiding another.

Many, through fear of infidelity, during the night of ignorance and storm of passion, run against the wild rocks of superstition and enthusiasm; and frequently do it with such force that they "make shipwreck of the faith," and have little of godliness left except a few broken pieces of its *form*.

Numbers, to shun that fatal error, steer quite a contrary course: supposing themselves guided by the compass of reason, when they only follow that of prejudice, with equal violence they dash their speculative brains against the rocks of Deism and profaneness; and fondly congratulate themselves on escaping the shelves of fanaticism, while the leaky bark of their hopes is ready to sink, and that of their morals is perhaps sunk already. Thus, both equally overlook sober, rational, heart-felt piety that lies between those wide and dangerous extremes.

To point out the happy medium which they have missed, and call them back to the narrow path where reason and revelation walk hand in hand, is the design of these sheets. May "the Father of lights" so shine upon the reader's mind that he may clearly discover truth, and notwithstanding the severity of her aspect, prefer her to the most soothing error!

If the reader is one of those who affect to be the warm votaries of reason, he is entreated to be a *close* thinker as well as a *free* thinker; and with careful attention to consider reason's dictates before he concludes that they agree with his favourite sentiments. He has, no doubt, too much candour not to grant so equitable a request; too much justice to set aside *matter of fact;* and too much good sense to disregard *an appeal to common sense.*

Should he incline to the opposite extreme, and cry down our rational powers, he is desired to remember, *right reason,* which is that which I appeal to, is a ray of "the Light that enlightens every man who comes into the world;" and a beam of the eternal *Logos,* the "Sun of righteousness."

God, far from blaming a proper use of the noble faculty by which we are chiefly distinguished from brutes, graciously invites us to the exercise of it. "Come now," says he, "and let us reason together." Jesus commends the unjust steward for reasoning better upon his wrong than the children of light upon their right principles. Samuel desires the Israelites to "stand still, that he may reason with them before the Lord." St. Peter charges believers to "give an answer to every one that asketh them a *reason* of their hope:" and St. Paul, who reasoned so conclusively himself, intimates that wicked men are *unreasonable,* and declares that a total dedication of ourselves to God is our *reasonable* service. And while he challenges the vain disputers of this world, who would make jests pass for proofs, invectives for arguments, and sophistry for reason, he charges Titus to use not merely sound speech, but (as the original also means) *sound reason,* "that he who is of the contrary part may be ashamed."

Let us, then, following his advice and example, pay a due regard both to reason and revelation. So shall we, according to his candid direction, break the shackles of prejudice; "prove all things, and," by Divine grace, "hold fast that which is good."

AN APPEAL TO MATTER OF FACT, &c.

PART I.

IN every religion there is a principle of truth or error, which, like the first link of a chain, necessarily draws after it all the parts with which it is essentially connected. This leading principle in Christianity, distinguished from Deism, is the doctrine of our corrupt and lost estate. For if man is not at variance with his Creator, what need of a Mediator between God and him? If he is not a depraved, undone creature, what necessity of so wonderful a Restorer and Saviour as the Son of God? If he is not enslaved to sin, why is he redeemed by Jesus Christ? If he is not polluted, why must he be washed in the blood of the immaculate Lamb? If his soul is not disordered, what occasion is there for such a Divine Physician? If he is not helpless and miserable, why is he perpetually invited to secure the assistance and consolations of the Holy Spirit? And, in a word, if he is not "born in sin," why is a "new birth" so absolutely necessary, that Christ declares, with the most solemn asseverations, "without it no man can see the kingdom of God?"

This doctrine then being of such importance that genuine Christianity stands or falls with it, it may be proper to state it at large. And as this cannot be done in stronger and plainer words than those of the sacred writers and our pious reformers, I beg leave to collect them, and present the reader with a picture of our natural estate, drawn at full length by those ancient and masterly hands.

I. Moses, who informs us, that "God created man in his own image, and after his likeness," soon casts a shade upon his original dignity by giving us a sad account of his Fall. He represents him, after his disobedience, as a criminal under sentence of death; a wretch filled with guilt, shame, dread, and horror; and a vagabond turned out of a lost paradise into a *cursed* wilderness, where all bears the stamp of desolation for his sake, Genesis iii:17. In consequence of this apostasy he died, and "all die in him: for by one man sin entered into the world, and death by sin; and so death passed upon all men, for that all have sinned," 1 Corinthians xv:12; Romans v:12, in him who was all mankind seminally and federally collected in one individual.

The sacred historian, having informed us how the first man was corrupted, observes, that "he begat a son in his own image," sinful and mortal like himself: that his first born was a murderer: that Abel himself offered sacrifices to avert Divine wrath, and that the violent temper of Cain soon broke out in all the human species. "The earth," says he, "was filled with violence,—all flesh had corrupted its way,—and God saw the wickedness of man was great in the earth;" so great, that every imagination of the thoughts of his heart was only evil continually," Genesis vi:5. *Only* evil, without any mixture of good; and *continually*, without any intermission of the evil.

An Appeal to Matter of Fact and Common Sense

When the deluge was over, the Lord himself gave the same account of his obstinately rebellious creature. "The imagination of man's heart," said he to Noah, "is evil from his youth," Genesis viii:21. Job's friends paint us with the same colours. One of them observes, that "man is born like the wild ass's colt:" and another, that "he is abominable and filthy, and drinketh iniquity like water," Job xi:12; xv:16.

David doth not alter the hideous portrait. "The Lord," says he, "looked down from heaven upon the children of men, to see if there was any that did understand and seek God." And the result of the Divine inspection is, "They are all gone aside; they are all together become filthy; there is none that doeth good, no, not one," Psalm xiv:3. Solomon gives a finishing stroke to his father's draught, by informing us, that "Foolishness is bound in the heart of a child:" and not of a child only; for he adds, "The heart of the sons of men is full of evil; and while they live, madness is in their heart," Proverbs xxii:15; Ecclesiastes ix:3.

Isaiah corroborates the assertions of the royal prophets in the following mournful confessions: "All we, like sheep, have gone astray. We are all as an unclean thing, and all our righteousnesses are as filthy rags," Isaiah liii:6; 64:6.

Jeremiah confirms the deplorable truth where he says, "The sin of Judah is written with a pen of iron, and with the point of a diamond; it is graven upon the tables of their hearts. O Jerusalem, wash thy heart from wickedness, that thou mayest be saved." For "the heart is deceitful above all things, and desperately wicked: who can know it?" Jeremiah iv:14; xvii:1, 9.

Thus the prophets delineate mankind in a natural, impenitent state. And do the apostles dip their pencil in brighter colours? Let them speak for themselves. The chief of them informs us, that "the natural," unrenewed" man receives not the things of the Spirit of God," and that "they are foolishness to him," 1 Corinthians ii:14. And he lays it down as a matter of fact, that "the carnal mind," the taste and disposition of every unregenerate person, is not only averse to goodness, but "enmity itself against God," the adorable fountain of all excellence. A blacker line can hardly be drawn, to describe a fallen, diabolical nature, Romans viii:7.

Various are the names which the apostle of the Gentiles gives to our original corruption; which are all expressive of its pernicious nature and dreadful effects. He calls it emphatically *sin;* a sin so full of activity and energy, that it is the life and spring of all others. "Indwelling sin;" a sin which is not like the leaves and fruits of a bad tree that appear for a time and then drop off; but like the sap that dwells and works within, always ready to break out at every bud. "The body of sin," because it is an assemblage of all possible sins in embryo, as our body is an assemblage of all the members which constitute the human frame. "The law of sin," and "the law in our members," because it hath a constraining force, and rules in our mortal bodies, as a mighty tyrant in the kingdom which he hath usurped. "The old man," because we have it from the first man, Adam; and because it is as old as the first stamina of our frame, with which it is most closely interwoven. "The flesh," as being propagated by carnal generation, and always opposing the Spirit, the gracious principle which we have from Adam the second. And "concupiscence," that mystic Jezebel, who brings forth the infinite variety of "fleshly, worldly," and "mental lusts which war against the soul."

Nor are St. James and St. John less severe than St. Paul upon the unconverted man. The one observes that his wisdom, the best property naturally belonging to him, "descendeth not from above, but is earthly, sensual, and devilish;" and the other positively declares, that "the whole world lieth in wickedness," James iii:15; 1 John v:19.

Our Lord, whose Spirit inspired the prophets and apostles, confirms their lamentable testimony. To make us seriously consider sin, our mortal disease, he reminds us that "the whole have no need of a physician, but they that are sick," Luke v:31. He declares, that "men love darkness rather than light:" that "the world hates them," and that "its works are evil," John iii:19; xv:18; vii:7. He directs all to pray for the "pardon of sin," as "being evil," and "owing ten thousand talents" to their heavenly creditor, Matthew vi:12; vii:11; xviii:24. And he assures us, that "the things which defile the man, come from within;" and that "out of the heart proceed evil thoughts, adulteries, fornications, murders, thefts, covetousness, wickedness, deceit, lasciviousness, an evil eye, blasphemy, pride, foolishness," Mark vii:21; Matthew xv:19; and, in a word, *all moral evil.*

Some, indeed, confine what the Scriptures say of the depravity of human hearts to the abandoned heathens and persecuting Jews; as if the professors of morality and Christianity were not concerned in the dreadful charge. But if the apostolic writings affirm that Christ "came not to call the righteous, but sinners;" that "he died for the ungodly," and that "he suffered, the just for the unjust;" it is plain that, unless he did not suffer and die for moral men and Christians, they are by nature *sinners, ungodly,* and *unjust,* as the rest of mankind, Romans v:5; 1 Peter iii:18.

If this assertion seems severe, let some of the best men that ever lived decide the point; not by the experience of immoral persons, but by their own. "I abhor myself," says Job, "and repent in dust and ashes," Job xliii:6. "Behold, I was shapen in iniquity," says David, "and in sin did my mother conceive me," Psalm li:5. "Wo is me, for I am undone," says Isaiah, "because I am a man of unclean lips," Isaiah vi:5. "I know," says St. Paul, "that in me, that is, in my flesh, dwelleth no good thing," Romans vii:18. "We ourselves," says he to Titus, "were sometimes foolish, disobedient, deceived, serving divers lusts and pleasures, living in malice and envy, hateful, and hating one another," Titus iii:3. And speaking of himself and the Christians at Ephesus, he leaves upon record this memorable sentence, "We were, *by nature,* the children of wrath even as others," Ephesians ii:3. Such humbling thoughts have the best men entertained both of their natural estate, and of themselves!

But as no one is a more proper person to appeal to in this matter than this learned apostle, who, by continually conversing with Jews, heathens, and Christians in his travels, had such an opportunity of knowing mankind, let us hear him sum up the suffrages of his inspired brethren. "What then," says he, "are we better than they?" Better than the immoral Pagans and hypocritical Jews described in the two preceding chapters? "No, in no wise." And he proves it by observing, (1.) The *universality* of human corruption: "*All* are under sin, as it is written: There is none righteous, no, not one." (2.) The *extent* of it in individuals, as it affects the whole man, especially his mind: "There is none that understandeth" the things of God. His affections: "There is none that seeketh after God:" and his actions: "They are all gone out of the way" of duty: "There is none that doeth good, no, not one;" for "all have their conversation in the lusts of the flesh and of the mind." (3.) The *outbreakings* of this corruption through all the parts of the body: "Their throat, their lips, their mouth, their feet, their eyes, and all their members, are together become unprofitable, and instruments of unrighteousness." As for their tongue, says St. James, it "is a world of iniquity, it defileth the whole body, and sets on fire the course of nature, and is set on fire of hell." And lastly, its *malignity* and *virulence:* It is loathsome as "an open sepulchre," terrible as one who "runs to shed blood," and mortal as "the poison of asps."

From the whole, speaking of all mankind in their unregenerate state, he justly infers, that "destruction and misery are in their ways." And, lest the self righteous should flatter themselves that this alarming declaration doth not regard them, he adds, that "the Scripture concludes all under sin;" that "there is no difference, for *all* have sinned, and come short of the glory of God;" and that "the moral law" denounces a general curse against its violators, "that *every mouth* may be stopped, and *all the world* may become guilty before God," Romans iii:9-23; vi:19; Ephesians ii:2.

If man is thus corrupt and guilty, he must be liable to condign punishment. Therefore, as the prophets and apostles agree with our Lord in their dismal descriptions of this depravity, so they harmonize with him in the alarming accounts of his danger. Till he flees to the Redeemer as a condemned malefactor, and secures an interest in the salvation provided for the lost, they represent him as on the brink of ruin.

They inform us "that the wrath of God is revealed from heaven," not only against some atrocious crimes, but "against *all* unrighteousness of men," Romans i:18. "That *every* transgression and disobedience shall receive a just recompense of reward," Hebrews ii:2. That "the soul that sinneth shall die," because "the wages of sin is death," Ezekiel xviii:4; Romans vi:23. They declare, that "they are cursed who do err from God's commandments:" that "cursed is the man whose heart departeth from the Lord:" that "cursed is every one who continues not in all things which are written in the book of the law to do them:" that "whosoever shall keep the whole law, and yet offend in one point, is guilty of all:" and that "as many as have sinned without law, shall also perish without law," Psalm cxix:21; Jeremiah xvii:5; Galatians iii:10; James ii:10; Romans ii:12.

They entreat us to turn, lest we should be found with "the many," in the "broad way, to destruction," Ezekiel xviii:23; Matthew vii:13. They affectionately inform us, "that it is a fearful thing to fall into the hands of the living God:" that "our God is a consuming fire" to the unregenerate: that "indignation and wrath, tribulation and anguish, hang over every soul of man who doeth evil:" that "the Lord shall be revealed from heaven in flaming fire, to take vengeance on them who know him not, and obey not the Gospel:" that "the wicked shall be turned into hell, and all the people that forget God:" that "they shall be punished with eternal destruction, from the presence of the Lord, and from the glory of his power:" and that "they all shall be damned who believe not the truth, but have pleasure in unrighteousness," Hebrews x:31; xii:29; Romans ii:9; 2 Thessalonians i:8; ii:12; Psalm ix:17.

Nor does our Lord, who is both the fountain and pattern of true charity, speak a different language. He bids us "fear him, who is able to destroy both soul and body in hell," Luke xii:5. He solemnly charges us to oppose corrupt nature with the utmost resolution, lest we be "cast into hell, where the worm dieth not, and the fire is not quenched," Mark ix:43. With tenderness he informs us, that "whosoever shall say to his brother, Thou fool! shall be in danger of hell fire;" that not only the wicked, but "the unprofitable servant shall be cast into outer darkness, where will be weeping, wailing, and gnashing of teeth;" and that he himself, far from conniving at sin, will fix the doom of all impenitent sinners, by this dreadful sentence, "Depart from me, ye cursed, into everlasting fire, prepared for the devil and his angels," Matthew v:22; xxv:30, 41.

II. I flatter myself that the doctrine which we are to try by the touchstone of reason, has been already sufficiently established from Scripture. Nevertheless, that the reader may have the fullest view of so momentous a subject, I shall yet present him with a recapitulation of the whole, in the words of our pious reformers, taken out of the articles, homilies, and liturgy of the Church of England.

The ninth article thus describes our depravity and danger: "Original or birth sin is the fault and corruption of the nature of every man, that naturally is engendered of the offspring of Adam; whereby man is very far gone from original righteousness, and is of his own nature inclined to evil, so that the flesh lusteth always contrary to the Spirit; and therefore, in every person born into this world, it deserveth God's wrath and damnation."

The thirty-fifth article gives sanction to the homilies in the following words:— "The book of homilies contains a good and wholesome doctrine, and therefore we judge them to be read in churches, by ministers, diligently and distinctly, that they may be understood by the people." Let us then see how they set forth the good and wholesome, though lamentable and humbling doctrine of our lost estate.

The title of the second homily is, "A Sermon of the Misery of Mankind, and of his Condemnation to Death Everlasting by his Sin." In the close of it, the contents are summed up in these words:—"We have heard how evil we are of ourselves; how of ourselves, and by ourselves, we have no goodness, help, or salvation; but, on the contrary, sin, damnation, and death everlasting."

Our Church is uniform in her woful accounts of man's misery. Hear her in the first homily for Whit-Sunday: "Man *of his own nature* (since the fall) is fleshly and carnal, corrupt and naught, sinful and disobedient to God, without any spark of goodness in him, without any virtuous or godly motion, only given to evil thoughts and wicked deeds."

In the homily on the nativity, she speaks thus: "He (disobedient man) was now cursed and abhorred. Instead of the image of God, he was now become the image of the devil, the bond slave of hell: altogether spotted and defiled, he seemed to be nothing else but a lump of sin; and therefore, by the just judgment of God, he was condemned to everlasting death. Thus, in Adam, all men became universally mortal, having in themselves nothing but everlasting damnation* of body and soul."

The same doctrine is delivered with the same plainness in the second part of the homily on the passion. "Adam died the death, that is, became mortal, lost the favour of God, and was cast out of paradise, being no longer a citizen of heaven, but a firebrand of hell, and a bond slave of the devil. And St. Paul bears witness, that by

---

* Prejudiced persons, who, instead of considering the entire system of truth, run away with a part detached from the whole, will be offended here, as if our Church "damned every body." But the candid reader will easily observe, that, instead of dooming any one to destruction, she only declares, that the Saviour finds all men in a state of condemnation and misery, where they would eternally remain, were it not for the compassionate equity of our gracious God, which does not permit him to sentence to a consciousness of eternal torments, any one of his creatures, for a sin of which they never were personally guilty; and of which, consequently, they can never have any consciousness.

Adam's offence 'death came upon all men to condemnation,' who became plain reprobates and castaways, being perpetually damned to the everlasting pains of hell fire."

Agreeably to this we are taught, in the second part of the homily on repentance, that "part of that virtue consists in an unfeigned acknowledgment of our sins to God, whom by them we have so grievously offended, that if he should deal with us according to his justice, we deserve a thousand hells, if there were so many."

The same vein of wholesome though unpleasant doctrine runs through the liturgy of our Church. She opens her service by exhorting us "not to dissemble nor cloak our manifold sins and wickedness." She acknowledges, in her confessions, that "we have erred and strayed from God's ways like lost sheep,"—that "there is no health in us,"—that we are "miserable sinners, miserable offenders, to whom our sins are grievous," and "the burden of them is intolerable."

She begins her baptismal office by reminding us that "all men are conceived and born in sin." She teaches in her catechism that "we are by nature born in sin, and the children of wrath." She confesses in the collect before the general thanksgiving, that "we are tied and bound with the chain of our sins," and entreats God to "let the pitifulness of his great mercy loose us:" and in her suffrages she beseeches him to "have mercy upon us," to "spare us," and "make speed to save us;" a language that can suit none but condemned sinners.

Duly sensible of our extreme danger till we have secured an interest in Christ, at the grave she supplicates the "most holy God not to deliver us into the bitter pains of eternal death:" and in the litany she beseeches our Lord Jesus Christ, "by his agony and bloody sweat, by his cross and passion," to "deliver us from his wrath and everlasting damnation." Thus is our Church every where consistent with herself, and with the oracles of God, in representing us as corrupt, condemned creatures in Adam, till we are penitent, absolved believers in Jesus Christ.

The doctrine to be demonstrated, in this treatise being thus fully stated, in the consentaneous words of the sacred writers, and our pious reformers, I shall close this part by an appeal to the reader's candour and common sense. If such are the sentiments of our Church, are those Churchmen reasonable, who intimate that all the maintainers of them are either her open or secret enemies? And may they rank with modest, humble Christians, who, instead of the self-abasing Scripture doctrine here laid down, boldly substitute pompous, Pharisaic descriptions of the present dignity and rectitude of human nature? Without waiting for the obvious answer, I pass to the first class of arguments on which the truth of this mortifying doctrine is established.

PART II.

As no man is bound to believe what is contrary to common sense, if the above stated doctrine appears irrational, Scriptures, articles, homilies, and liturgy, are quoted in vain. When men of parts are pressed with their authority, they start from it as an imposition on their reason, and make as honourable a retreat as they possibly can.

Some, to extricate themselves at once, set the Bible aside, as full of incredible assertions. Others, with more modesty, plead that the Scriptures have been frequently misunderstood, and are so in the present case. They put grammar, criticism, and common sense to the rack, to show that when the inspired writers say the human "heart is desperately wicked," they mean that it is extremely good; or at least like blank paper, ready to receive either the characters of virtue or vice. With respect to the testimony of our reformers, they would have you to understand that in this enlightened age we must leave their harsh, uncharitable sentiments to the old Puritans, and the present Methodists.

That such objectors may subscribe as a solemn truth what they have hitherto rejected as a dangerous error; and that humbled sinners may see the propriety of a heartfelt repentance, and the absolute need of an almighty Redeemer, they are here presented with some proofs of our depravity, taken from the astonishing severity of God's dispensations toward mankind.

AXIOM.

If we consider the SUPREME BEING as creating a world for the manifestation of his glory, the display of his perfections, and the communication of his happiness to an intelligent creature, whom he would attach to himself by the strongest ties of gratitude and love; we at once perceive, that he never could form this earth, and man, in their present disordered, deplorable condition. It is not so absurd to suppose the meridian sun productive of darkness, as to imagine that *Infinite Goodness* ever produced any kind or degree of evil.

Infinite Holiness and *Wisdom* having assisted Infinite Goodness to draw the original plan of the world, it could not but be entirely worthy of its glorious Author, absolutely free from every moral defilement and natural disorder: nor could *Infinite Power* possibly be at a loss to execute what the other Divine attributes had contrived. Therefore, unless we embrace the senseless opinion of the Materialists, who deny the being of a God; or admit the ridiculous creed of the Manichees, who adore two gods; the one the gracious Author of all the good, and the other the mischievous principle of all the evil in the world, we must conclude with Moses, that every thing which God made was at first "very good;" or, in other words, that order and beauty, harmony and happiness, were stamped upon every part of the creation, and especially on man, the masterpiece of Creating Power in this sublunary world, On this axiom I raise my

FIRST ARGUMENT.

Does not the natural state of the earth cast a light upon the spiritual condition of its inhabitants? Amidst a thousand beauties that indicate what it was when God pronounced it "very good," and as the original imports, *extremely beautiful;* amidst the elegant and grand ruins which form the variety of our smiling landscapes and romantic prospects, can an impartial inquirer help taking notice of a thousand striking proofs, that a multiplied curse rests upon this globe; and that man, who inhabits it, is now disgraced by the God of nature and providence?

An Appeal to Matter of Fact and Common Sense

Here, deceitful morasses, or faithless quicksands, obstruct our way, there, miry, impassable roads, or inhospitable, sandy deserts, endanger our life. In one place we are stopped by stupendous chains of rocky mountains, broken into frightful precipices, or hideous caverns; and in another we meet with ruinous valleys, cut deep by torrents and waterfalls, whose tremendous roar stuns the astonished traveller. Many of the hills are stony, rude, and waste; and most of the plains are covered over. with strata of barren sand, stiff clay, or infertile gravel.

Thorns, thistles, and noxious weeds,* grow spontaneously every where, and yield a troublesome, never-failing crop; while the best soil, carefully ploughed by the laborious husbandman, and sown with precious seed, frequently repays his expensive toil with light sheaves or a blasted harvest.

Consider that immense part of the globe which lies between the tropics: it is parched up by the scorching beams of the vertical sun. There the tawny inhabitants fan themselves in vain; they pant, they melt, they faint on the sultry couch; and, like the birds of night, dare not appear abroad till evening shades temper the insufferable blaze of day. View the frozen countries around the poles: in summer the sun just glances upon them by his feeble, horizontal rays: in winter he totally deserts them, and they lie bound with rigorous frosts, and buried in continual night. There the torpid inhabitants know neither harvest nor vintage; the ocean seems a boundless plain of ice, and the continent immense hills of snow.

The temperate zones are indeed blessed with climates: but even here how irregular are the seasons! To go no farther than this favoured island, what means the strange foresight by which the ice of January is laid in to temper the ardours of July; and the burning mineral is stored up in June to mitigate the frost in December? But notwithstanding these precautions, what continual complaints are heard about the intenseness of the heat, the severity of the cold, or the sudden pernicious change from the one to the other.

Let us descend to particulars. In winter, how often do drifts of snow bury the starved sheep, and entomb the frozen traveller! In summer, how frequently do dreadful storms of hail cut down, or incessant showers of rain wash away the fruits of the earth! Perhaps, to complete the desolation, *water* pours down from all the neighbouring hills; and the swelling streams, joining with overflowing rivers, cause sudden inundations, lay waste their richest pastures, and carry off the swimming flocks; while the frighted inhabitants of the vale† either retire to the top of their deluged houses, or by the timely assistance of boats, fly from the imminent and increasing danger.

If heaven seems to dissolve into water in one place, in another it is like brass; it yields neither fruitful rains nor cooling dews; the earth is like iron under it, and the perishing cattle loll out their parched tongues, where they once drank the refreshing stream. Suppose a few happy districts escape these dreadful scourges for a number of

---

* Those who oppose the doctrine of the fall, say that "weeds have their use." I grant they are serviceable to thousands of people, who earn their bread by pulling the general nuisance out of our fields and gardens: but till our objectors have proved that thistles are more useful, and therefore grow more spontaneously, and multiply more abundantly, than corn, we shall discover the badness of their cause through the slightness of their objection.

† This was the case of several families in the author's parish, November, 1770.

years, are they not at last visited with redoubled severity? And, while abused affluence vanishes as a dream before the intolerable dearth, do not a starving, riotous populace,* leave their wretched cottages to plunder the houses of their wealthy neighbours, desperately venturing the gallows for a morsel of bread?

When some, secure from the attacks of water, quietly enjoy the comforts of plenty, *fire* perhaps surprises them in an instant: they awake involved in smoke and surrounded by crackling flames, through which (if it is not too late) they fly naked, at the hazard of their necks, and think themselves happy if, while they leave behind them young children or aged parents burning in the blaze of all their goods, they escape themselves with dislocated joints or broken bones. Their piercing shrieks, and the fall of their house, seem to portend a general conflagration; loud confusion increases; disastrous ruin spreads; and perhaps, before they can be stopped, a street, a suburb, a whole city, is reduced to ashes.

Turn your imagination from the smoking ruins, to fix it upon the terrifying effects of the *air,* agitated into roaring tempests and boisterous hurricanes. Before their impetuous blast, masts of ships, and cedars of Lebanon, are like broken reeds; men of war, and solid buildings, like the driven chaff. Here, they strip the groaning forests, tear the bosom of the earth, and obscure the sky with clouds of whirling sand: and there, they plough up the liquid, foaming plains, and with sportive fury turn up mountains for ridges, or cut valleys instead of furrows. As they pass along, the confounded elements dreadfully roar under the mighty scourge, the rolling sea tosses herself up to heaven, and solid land is "swept with the besom of destruction."

To heighten the horrors of the scene, *thunder,* the majestic voice of an angry God, and the awful artillery of heaven, bursts in loud claps from the lowering sky. Distant hills reverberate and increase the alarming sound, and with rocking edifices declare to man that." vengeance belongeth unto God:" and, to enforce the solemn warning, repeated flashes of *lightning,* with horrible glare, dazzle his eyes, and with forked fires strike consternation into his breast; if they do not actually strike him dead in the midst of his shattered habitation.

Nor doth heaven alone dart destructive fires; earth, our mother earth, as if it were not. enough frequently to corrupt the atmosphere by pestilential vapours, borrows the assistance of the devouring element to terrify and scourge her guilty children. By sudden, frightful chasms, and the mouth of her burning mountains, she vomits clouds of smoke, sulphureous flames, and calcined rocks; she emits streams of melted minerals; covers the adjacent plains with boiling, fiery lavas; and, as if she wanted to ease herself of the burden of her inhabitants, suddenly rises against them, and in *battles of shaking,* at once crushes, destroys, and buries them in heaps of ruin.

These astonishing scenes, like a bloody battle that is seen at a distance, may indeed entertain us: they amuse our imagination, when, in a peaceful apartment, we behold them beautifully represented by the pen of a Virgil, or the pencil of a Raphael. But to be in the midst of them, as thousands are, sooner or later, is inexpressibly dreadful: it is actually to see the forerunners of Divine vengeance, and hear the shaking of God's destructive rod. it is to behold at once a lively emblem, and an awful pledge of that "fire and brimstone, storm and tempest," which the righteous

---

* This happened some years ago in this neighbourhood.

Governor of the world will "rain upon the ungodly," when "the heavens shall pass away with a great noise, the elements shall melt with fervent heat, and the earth with all the works that are therein shall be burned up."

Now, as reason loudly declares that the God of order, justice, and goodness, could never establish and continue this fearful course of things, but to punish the disorders of the moral world by those of the natural; we must conclude that man is guilty from the alarming tokens of Divine displeasure, which, sooner or later, are so conspicuous in every part of the habitable globe.

SECOND ARGUMENT.

We have taken a view of the residence of mankind: let us now behold them entering upon the disordered scene. And here reason informs us that some mystery of iniquity lies hid under the loathsome, painful, and frequently mortal circumstances, which accompany their birth: for it can never be imagined that a righteous and good God would suffer innocent and pure creatures to come into the world skilled in no language but that of misery, venting itself in bitter cries or doleful accents.

It is a matter of fact, that infants generally return their first breath with a groan, and salute the light with the voice of sorrow: *generally*, I say, for sometimes they are born half dead, and cannot, without the utmost difficulty, be brought to breathe and groan. But all are born at the hazard of their lives: for while some cannot press into the land of the living without being dangerously bruised, others have their tender bones dislocated. Some are almost strangled; and it is the horrible fate of others to be forced into the world by instruments of torture; having their skull bored through or broken to pieces, or their quivering limbs cut or torn off from the unfortunate trunk. Again:

While some appear on the stage of life embarrassed with superfluous parts, others, unaccountably mutilated, want those which are necessary: and, what is more terrible still, a few, whose hideous, misshapen bodies seem calculated to represent the deformity of a fallen soul, rank among frightful monsters; and, to terminate the horror of the parents, are actually smothered and destroyed.

The spectators, it is true, concerned for the honour of mankind, frequently draw a veil over these shocking and bloody scenes; but a philosopher will find them out, and will rationally infer, that the deplorable and dangerous manner in which mankind are born, proves them to be degenerate, fallen creatures.[*]

---

[*] Logicians will excuse the author, if he prefers the common unaffected manner of proposing his arguments, to the formal method of the schools. But they may easily try his enthymemes by giving them the form of syllogisms, thus:-

First Argument. If the rod of God is fearfully shaken over this globe, the disordered habitation of mankind, it is a sign they are under his displeasure.

But God's rod is fearfully shaken over this globe, &c. Therefore mankind are under his displeasure.

Second Argument. A pure and innocent creature cannot be born under such and such deplorable circumstances.

But man is born under such and such deplorable circumstances. Therefore man is not a pure and innocent creature.

THIRD ARGUMENT.

If we let our thoughts ascend from the little sufferers to the mothers that bear them, we shall find another dreadful proof of the Divine displeasure, and of our natural depravity. Does not a good master, much more a gracious God, delight in the prosperity and happiness of his faithful servants? If mankind were naturally in their Creator's favour, would he not order the fruit of the womb to drop from it without any more inconveniency than ripe vegetables fall from the opening husk, or fullgrown fruits from the disburdened tree? But how widely different is the case!

Fix your attention on pregnant mothers: see their disquietude and fears. Some go beforehand through an imaginary travail, almost as painful to the mind as the real labour is to the body. The dreaded hour comes at last. Good God! What lingering, what tearing pains; what redoubled throes, what killing agonies attend it! See the curse,—or rather, see it not. Let the daughter of her who tasted the forbidden fruit without the man, drink that bitter cup without him. Flee from the mournful scene, flee to distant apartments. But in vain—the din of sorrow pursues and overtakes you there.

A child of man is at the point of being born; his tortured mother proclaims the news in the bitterest accents. They increase with her increasing agony. Sympathize and pray, while she suffers and groans, —perhaps while she suffers and dies: for it is possibly her dying groan that reaches your ear. Perhaps nature is spent in the hard travail; her son is born, and, with Jacob's wife, she closes her languid eyes and expires. Perhaps the instruments of death are upon her; the keen steel mangles her delicate frame; as Cesar's mother, she generously suffers her body to be opened, that her unborn child may not be torn from her in pieces; and the fertile tree is unnaturally cut down that its fruit may be safely gathered.

Perhaps neither mother nor child can be saved, and one grave is going to deprive a distracted mortal of a beloved Rachel, and a long-expected Benjamin. If this is the case, O earth, earth, earth! conceal these slain; cover their blood, and detain, in thy dark bosom, the fearful curse that brought them there! Vain wish! Too active to be confined in thy deepest vaults, it ranges through the world: with unrelenting fierceness it pursues trembling mothers, and forces them to lift up their voice for speedy relief: though varied according to the accents of a hundred languages, it is the same voice, that of the bitterest anguish; and while it is reverberated from hamlet to hamlet, from city to city, it strikes the unprejudiced inquirer, and makes him confess that these clouds of unbribed witnesses, by their loud consentaneous evidence, impeach sin, the tormentor of the woman and murderer of her offspring.

But suppose the case is not so fatal, and she is at last delivered: her labour may be over, yet not her pain and danger; a lingering weakness may carry her slowly to her grave. If she recovers, she maybe a mother, and yet unable to act a mother's part. Her pining child sucks her disordered breast in vain: either the springs of his balmy food are dried up, or they overflow with a putrid, loathsome fluid, and excruciating ulcers cause the soft lips of the infant to appear terrible as the edge of the sword.

If she happily escape this common kind of distress, yet she may date the beginning of some chronical disease from her dangerous lying-in; and, in consequence of her hard wrestling for the blessing of a child, may with the patriarch go halting all her days. How sensible are the marks of Divine indignation in all these scenes of sorrow! And consequently, how visible our sinfulness and guilt!

Nor can the justness of the inference be denied, under pretence that the females of other animals, which neither *do* nor *can* sin, bring forth their young with pain as well as women. For, if we take a view of the whole earth, we shall not see any females, except the daughters of Eve, who groan under a periodical disorder, that entails languor and pain, weakness and mortal diseases, on their most blooming days. Nor do we in general find any that are delivered of their offspring with half the sorrow and danger of women. These two remarkable circumstances loudly call upon us to look for the cause of sorrow which attends the delivery of female animals, where that sorrow is most sensibly felt; and to admire the perfect agreement that subsists between the observations of natural philosophers, and the assertion of the most ancient historian Genesis iii:16.

FOURTH ARGUMENT.

If we advert to mankind, even before they burst the womb of their tortured mothers, they afford us a new proof of their total degeneracy. For reason dictates that if they were not conceived in sin, the Father of mercies could not, consistently with his goodness and justice, command the cold hand of death to nip them in the unopened, or just-opened bud. This nevertheless happens every hour. Who can number the early miscarriages of the womb? How many millions of miserable embryos feel the pangs of death before those of birth, and preposterously turn the fruitful womb into a living grave! And how many millions more of wretched infants escape the dangers of their birthday, and salute the troublesome light only to take their untimely leave of it, after languishing a few days on the rack of a convulsive or torturing disorder? I ask again, Would a good and righteous God seal the death warrant of such multitudes of his unborn, or newly born creatures, if their natural depravity did not render them proper subjects of dissolution?

It is true, the young of beasts suffer and die, as well as infants; but it is only because they are involved in our misery. They partake of it as the attendants of a noble traitor share in his deserved ruin. Sin, that inconceivable, virulent, and powerful evil, drew down God's righteous curse upon all that was created for man's use, as well as upon man himself. Hence only spring the degeneracy and death that turn beasts to one promiscuous dust with mankind. Compare Genesis iii:17; Romans v:12; and 8:22. We may then justly infer, from the sufferings and death of still-born or new-born children, that man is totally degenerate, and liable to destruction, even from his mother's womb.

FIFTH ARGUMENT.

But take your leave of the infant corpse, already buried in the womb, or deposited in a coffin of a span long; fix your attention on the healthy sucking child. See him stupidly staring in his nurse's lap, or awkwardly passing through childhood to manhood. How visible is his degeneracy in every stage!

Part of the Divine image, in which he was made in Adam, consisted in purity, power, and knowledge; but now he is naturally the least cleanly, as well as the most helpless and ignorant of all animals. Yes, if the reader could forgive the indelicacy of the assertion for the sake of its truth, I would venture to show that there is no comparison between the cleanliness of the little active animals which suck the filthy swine; and of helpless infants, who suck the purer breasts of their tender mothers. But, casting a veil over the dribbling, loathsome little creatures, without fear of being contradicted, I aver, that the young of those brutes, which are stupid to a proverb, know their dams, and follow them as soon as they are dropped; while infants are months without taking any particular notice of their parents, and without being able, I shall not say to follow them, but even to bear the weight of their swaddled body, or stand upon their tottering legs.

With reference to the knowledge necessary for the support of animal life, it is undeniable that brutes have greatly the advantage of mankind. Fowls and fishes immediately, and with amazing sagacity, single out their proper nourishment among a thousand useless and noxious things: but infants put indifferently to their mouth all that comes to their hand, whether it be food or poison, a coral or a knife; and what is more astonishing still, grown-up persons scarce ever attain to the knowledge of the quantity, or quality of the meat and drink which are most suitable to their constitutions.

All disordered dogs fix at once upon the salutary vegetable that can (in some cases) relieve their distress: but many physicians, even after several years' study and practice, hurt, and sometimes kill their patients by improper medicines. Birds of passage, by mere instinct, find the north and the south more readily than mariners by the compass. Untaught spiders weave their webs, and uninstructed bees make their combs to the greatest perfection: but fallen man must serve a tedious apprenticeship to learn his own business; and with all the help of masters, tools, and patterns, seldom proves an ingenious artist.

Again: other animals are provided with a natural covering that answers the double end of usefulness and ornament; but indigent man is obliged to borrow from plants, beasts, and worms, the materials with which he hides his nakedness, or defends his feebleness; and a great part of his short life is spent in providing, or putting on and off garments, the gaudy tokens of his shame, or ragged badges of his fall.

Are not these plain proofs that man, who, according to his superior rank and primitive excellency, should in all things have the pre-eminence, is now a degraded being, cursed for his apostasy with native uncleanliness, helplessness, ignorance, and nakedness, above all other animals?

SIXTH ARGUMENT.

Man's natural ignorance, great as it is, might nevertheless be overlooked, if he had but the right knowledge of his Creator. But, alas! the holy and righteous God judicially withdraws himself from his unholy, apostate creatures. Man is not properly acquainted with Him "in whom he lives, and moves, and hath his being." This humbling truth may be demonstrated by the following observations:—

God is infinitely perfect; all the perfection which is found in the most exalted Creatures, is but the reflection of the transcendent effulgence belonging to that glorious Sun of spiritual beauty; it is but the surface of the unfathomable depths of goodness and loveliness, which regenerate souls discover in that boundless ocean of all excellence. If therefore men saw God, they could far less help being struck with holy awe, overwhelmed with pleasing wonder, and ravished with delightful admiration; than a man born blind, and restored to sight in the blaze of a summer's day, could help being transported at the glory of the new and unexpected scene: "Could we but see virtue in all her beauty," said a heathen, "she would ravish our hearts."* How much greater would our ravishment be if we were indulged with a clear, immediate discovery of the Divine beauty, the eternal original of all virtue, the exuberant fountain of all perfection and delight! But, alas! how few thus behold, know, and admire God, may easily be seen by the impious or vain conduct of mankind.

If a multitude of men ingenuously confess they know not the king; if they take his statue, or one of his attendants for him; or, if they doubt whether there be a king, or sport with his name and laws in his presence; we reasonably conclude that they neither *see* nor *know* the royal person. And is not this the case of the superstitious, who, like the Athenians, worship an "unknown God?" Of idolaters, who bow to favourite mortals, or lifeless images, as to the true God? Of infidels who doubt the very being of a God? And of open sinners, the bulk of mankind, who live every where as if there was none?

Our natural ignorance of God manifests itself still more evidently, by the confessions both of real and nominal Christians. The former, before they knew God, and were admitted to "behold his glory shining in the face of Jesus Christ," bitterly complained as Isaiah, "Verily thou art a God that hidest thyself;" or mournfully asked with David, "How long wilt thou hide thy face from me?" It is plain, then, that by nature they were as others, "without God (practical Atheists) in the world," and have as much reason as St. Paul to declare, that "the world by wisdom knew not God."

As for *nominal* Christians, though they daily pray that "the fellowship of the Holy Ghost may be with us all," it is evident they are utter strangers to communion with God by his Holy Spirit. For if we affirm that he blesses his children with a spiritual discovery of his presence, and "manifests himself to them as he doth not to the world" they say we are mad, or call us enthusiasts. This behaviour shows, beyond all confessions, that they are totally unacquainted with "the light of God's countenance:" for, what greater proof can a blind man give, that he has no knowledge of the sun, than to suspect his neighbour of lunacy, for affirming that sunshine is a delightful reality?

From this moral demonstration of our natural ignorance of God, I draw the following conclusion:—If the Lord, who is a mild and condescending King to all his loyal subjects, a Father, full of endearing and tender love to all his dutiful children, hides his face from mankind in a natural state; and if what little they know of him is only by conjecture, hearsay, or inference;† it is a proof that they are under his displeasure, and consequently that they are rebellious, fallen creatures.

---

* Si virtus conspiceretur oculis, mirabiles amotis excitaret sui.—CICERO.

† This is the *knowledge of God* mentioned Romans i:21. It is sufficient to leave *without excuse* those who do not improve it till they attain to the saving knowledge mentioned John xvii:3; 1 John v:20.

For what but rebellion could thus separate between beings so nearly related as an infinitely gracious Creator, and favourite creature, whose soul is, according to a heathen, "*divinæ particula auræ;*" and according to Moses, "the very breath of God?" We may then rationally conclude, with the evangelical prophet, that "our iniquities have separated between us and our God," and that "our sins have hid his face from us," eclipsed the Sun of righteousness, and brought such darkness on our souls, that, by nature, we know neither what we are, nor what we should be; neither whence we come, nor whither we are going; neither the grand business we have to do, nor the danger that attends our leaving it undone.

SEVENTH ARGUMENT.

If by nature mankind know not the Lord to be their God, is it surprising that beasts should not know mankind to be their lords? Nevertheless, reason agrees with Scripture in maintaining, that man, by far the noblest work of God here below, should, according to the reason and fitness of things, bear rule over all the sublunary creation. But, alas! even in this respect, "how is the crown fallen from his head!" Inferior animals have as little regard for him as he has for his God.

Notwithstanding his artful contrivances, greedy birds and mischievous beasts eat up, trample down, or destroy, part of the fruit of his rural labour. In warmer climes, armies of locusts, more terrible than hosts of men, frequently darken the air, or cover the ground, and equally mock at human power and craft. Wherever they light, all verdure disappears, and the summer's fruitfulness is turned into wintry desolation.

If locusts do not reach this happy island, caterpillars, and a variety of other seemingly insignificant, but really formidable insects, make a more constant, though less general attack upon our trees and gardens. In vain are they destroyed by millions; they cannot be fully conquered; and the yearly returning plague forces the considerate spectator to acknowledge the finger of a sin-avenging Providence.

Happy would it be for man, if rebellious animals were satisfied with the produce of his fields and orchards: but, alas! they thirst after his blood, and attack his person. Lions, tigers, rattlesnakes, crocodiles, and sharks, whenever they have an opportunity, impetuously attack, furiously tear, and greedily devour him. And what is most astonishing, the basest reptiles are not afraid to breed in his stomach, to live in his very bowels, and to consume his inward parts: while swarms of flying, leaping, or creeping insects, too vile to be named, but not to humble a proud apostate, have the insolence to fix upon his skin; and by piercing or furrowing his flesh, suck his blood, and feast upon him from his cradle to the grave.

Domestic animals, it is true, do man excellent service. But, is it not because he either forces, or bribes them to it, by continual labour and expense, with which he breaks and maintains them? What business have multitudes of men but to serve the drudges of mankind? What are smiths, farriers, farmers' servants, grooms, hostlers, &c, but the slaves of brutes, washing, currying, shoeing, feeding, and waiting upon them both by day and by night?

And yet, notwithstanding the prerogative granted to Noah's piety, Genesis ix:2, and the care taken of domestic animals, do they not rebel as often as they dare? Here, sheep, deemed the quietest of all, run astray, or break into the field of a litigious neighbour. There, the furious bull pursues and gores, or the raging dog sets upon and tears the inoffensive traveller. To-day you read that an impetuous, foaming steed hath hurried away, thrown off, and dragged along his unfortunate master, whose blood sprinkling the dust, and brains dashed upon the stones, direct the search of his disconsolate friend: and to-morrow you may hear that a vicious horse has darted his iron-fenced hoof into his attendant's breast or forehead, and has lamed or killed him on the spot.

And would the wise Governor of the world, the kind Protector of his obedient creatures, permit this rebellion, even of the tamest animals, and basest vermin, against man, if man himself was not a daring rebel against him?

EIGHTH ARGUMENT.

That a contemptible insect should dare to set upon, and be able to devour a proud monarch, a Herod in the midst of his guards, is terrible: but the mischief stops not here. Numerous tribes of other base animals are armed with poisonous tongues or stings, and use them against mankind with peculiar rage. To say nothing of mad dogs, have not asps, vipers,* tarantulas, scorpions, and other venomous serpents and insects, the destructive skill of extracting the quintessence of the curse which sin, our moral poison, hath brought upon the earth? When we come within their reach, do they not bite or sting us with the utmost fury? And by infusing their subtle venom into our blood, spread they not anguish and destruction through our agonizing frame? Answer, ye thousands who died in the wilderness of the bite of fiery serpents; and ye multitudes, who, in almost all countries, have shared their deplorable fate.

Let us descend to the *vegetable* world. How many deceitful roots, plants, and fruits, deposit their pernicious juices in the stomach of those who unwarily feed upon them! Did not Elisha, and the sons of the prophets, narrowly escape being poisoned all together, by one of them fatally mistaking a pot-herb? And do not many go quickly or slowly to their grave by such melancholy accidents?

Minerals and *metals* are not the last to enter into the general conspiracy against mankind. Under inoffensive appearances do not they contain what is destructive to the animal frame? And have not many fallen a sacrifice to their ignorance of the mischief lurking in arsenic, and other mineral productions?† Nor are metallic effluvia less hurtful to hundreds; and the health of mankind is perhaps more injured by copper alone, than it is preserved by all the mineral waters in the world. It is acknowledged that numbers are poisoned by food prepared in utensils made of that dangerous metal; and how many are insensibly hurt by the same means, is only known to a wise and righteous Providence.

Thus God leaves us in a world where mischief lurks under a variety of things apparently useful, without giving us the least intimation of destruction near. To say that *infinite Goodness* can deal thus with *innocent* creatures, is offering violence to our

---

* Some will say that vipers' flesh is useful in physic. I grant it: but is the *poison* of that creature useful? This must be proved before the argument can be invalidated.

† It is objected, that excellent remedies are prepared with antimony and mercury. But it is well known that the persons who use them only expel one poison with another; as the decayed constitutions of those who have frequent recourse to such violent medicines abundantly prove.

reason, and an affront to Divine justice. Conclude then with me, reader, that we have lost our original innocence, and forfeited our Creator's favour.

NINTH ARGUMENT.

But if the generality of mankind escape all the various sorts of poison, do they escape the curse of toil and sweat? Is not a great majority of them reduced to such sordid want, and pressing necessity, as to be obliged to do the greatest drudgery for a wretched maintenance?

When "God made men to have dominion over the works of his hands;" when he "put all things in subjection under their feet, and crowned them with glory and honour;" they filled up each happy hour in evidencing their love to him and to each other; they spent their golden moments in admiring the variety and beauty of his works, finding out the Divine signatures impressed upon them, swaying, their mild sceptre over the obedient creation, and enjoying the rich, incorruptible fruits, which the earth spontaneously produced in the greatest perfection and abundance. Thus their pleasure was without idleness or pain, and their employment without toil or weariness.

But no sooner did disobedience open the floodgates of natural evil, than arduous labour came in full tide upon mankind; and a thousand painful arts were invented to mitigate the manifold curse which sin had brought upon them.

Since the fall, our bodies are become vulnerable and shamefully naked; and it is the business of thousands to make, or sell, all sorts of garments for our defence and ornament. The earth has lost her original fertility; and thousands more with iron instruments open her bosom, to force her to yield us a maintenance; or with immense labour secure her precarious, decaying fruits. Immoderate rains deprive her of her solidity, and earthquakes or deluges destroy her evenness; numbers, therefore, are painfully employed in making or mending roads. Each country affords some only of the necessaries or conveniences of life; this obliges the mercantile inhabitants to transport, with immense trouble and danger, the produce of one place, to supply the wants of another. We are exposed to a variety of dangers: our persons and property must be secured against the inclemency of the weather, the attacks of evil beasts, and the assaults of wicked men; hence the fatigue of millions of workmen in wood and stone, metals and minerals; and the toils and hazards of millions more, who live by making, wearing, or using, the various instruments of war and slaughter.

Disorder and injustice give rise to government, politics, and a labyrinth of laws; and these employ myriads of officers, lawyers, magistrates, and rulers. We are subject to a thousand pains and maladies; hence, myriads more prescribe and prepare remedies, or attend and nurse the sick. Our universal ignorance occasions the tedious labour of giving and receiving instruction, in all the branches of human and Divine knowledge. And, to complete the whole, the original tongue of mankind is confounded, and even neighbouring nations are barbarians to each other: from hence arise the painful lucubrations of critics and linguists, with the infinite trouble of teaching and learning various languages.

The curse introduced by sin is the occasion of all these toils. They are soon mentioned, but, alas! how long, how grievous do they appear to those that feel their severity! How many sighs have they forced from the breasts, how much sweat from the bodies of mankind! Unite the former, a tempest might ensue; collect the latter, it would swell into rivers.

To go no farther than this populous parish, with what hardships and dangers do our indigent neighbours earn their bread! See those who ransack the bowels of the earth to get the black mineral we burn: how little is their lot preferable to that of the Spanish felons, who work the golden mines!

They take their leave of the light of the sun, and, suspended by a rope, are let down many fathoms perpendicularly toward the centre of the globe. They traverse the rocks through which they have dug their horizontal ways; the murderer's cell is a palace in comparison of the black spot to which they repair; the vagrant's posture in the stocks is preferable to that in which they labour.

Form, if you can, an idea of the misery of men kneeling, stooping, or lying on one side, to toil all day in a confined place, where a child could hardly stand; while a younger company, with their hands and feet on the black, dusty ground, and a chain about their body, creep and drag along, like four-footed beasts, heavy loads of the dirty mineral, through ways almost impassable to the curious observer.

In these low and dreary vaults all the elements seem combined against them. Destructive damps, and clouds of noxious dust, infect the air they breathe. Sometimes water incessantly distils on their naked bodies; or, bursting upon them in streams, drowns them, and deluges their work. At other times, pieces of detached rocks crush them to death, or the earth, breaking in upon them, buries them alive. And frequently sulphureous vapours, kindled in an instant by the light of their candles, form subterraneous thunder and lightning. What a dreadful phenomenon! How impetuous is the blast! How fierce the rolling flames! How intolerable the noisome smell! How dreadful the continued roar! How violent and fatal the explosion!

Wonderful providence! Some of the unhappy men have time to prostrate themselves; the fiery scourge grazes their back, the ground shields their breasts; they escape. See them wound up out of the blazing dungeon, and say if these are not "brands plucked out of the fire." A pestiferous steam, and clouds of suffocating smoke, pursue them. Half dead themselves, they hold their dead or dying companions in their trembling arms. Merciful God of Shadrach! Kind protector of Meshech! Mighty deliverer of Abednego! Patient preserver of rebellious Jonah! Will not *these* utter a song,—a song of praise to *thee*,—praise ardent as the flames they escape,— lasting as the life thou prolongest? Alas! they refuse! And some,—O tell it not among the heathens, lest they for ever abhor the name of Christian,—some return to the very pits where they have been branded with sulphureous fire by the warning hand of Providence; and there, sporting themselves again with the most infernal wishes, call aloud for a fire that cannot be quenched, and challenge the Almighty to cast them into hell, that bottomless pit whence there is no return.

Leave these black men at their perilous work, and see yonder barge-men hauling that loaded vessel against wind and stream. Since the dawn of day they have wrestled with the impetuous current; and now that it almost overpowers them, how do they exert all the remaining strength, and strain their every nerve! How are they bathed in sweat and rain! Fastened to their lines, as horses to their traces, wherein do they differ from the laborious brutes? Not in an erect posture of body; for through the intenseness of their toil they bend forward, their head is foremost, and their hands upon the ground. If there is any difference, it consists in this: horses are indulged with a collar to save their breast; and these, as if theirs was not worth saving, draw without one. The beasts tug in patient silence, and mutual harmony; but the men with loud contention, and horrible imprecations. O sin, what hast thou done! Is it not enough that these drudges should toil like brutes? Must they also curse one another like devils?

If you have gone beyond the hearing of their impious oaths, stop to consider the sons of Vulcan confined to these forges and furnaces. Is *their* lot much preferable? A sultry air, and clouds of smoke and dust, are the element in which they labour. The confused noise of water falling, steam hissing, fire engines working, wheels turning, files creaking, hammers beating, ore bursting, and bellows roaring, form the dismal concert that strikes the ears; while a continual eruption of flames ascending from the mouth of their artificial volcanoes, dazzle their eyes with a horrible glare. Massy bars of hot iron are the heavy tools they handle; cylinders of the first magnitude the enormous weights they heave; vessels full of melted metal the dangerous loads they carry; streams of the same burning fluid the fiery rivers which they conduct into the deep cavities of the subterraneous moulds; and millions of flying sparks, with a thousand drops of liquid, hissing iron, the horrible showers to which they are exposed. See them cast; you would think them in a bath, and not in a furnace; they bedew the burning sand with their streaming sweat. Nor are their wet garments dried up, either by the fierce fires that they attend, or the fiery streams which they manage. Certainly, of all men, these have reason to remember the just sentence of an offended God: "In the sweat of thy face shalt thou eat thy bread all the days of thy life."

All indeed do not go through the same toil; but all have their share of it, either in body or in mind. Behold the studious son of learning; his intense application hath wasted his flesh, exhausted his spirits, and almost dried up his radical moisture. Consider the man of fortune; can his thousands a year exempt him from the curse of Adam? No: he toils perhaps harder, in his sports and debaucheries, than the poor ploughman that cultivates his estate.

View that corpulent epicure who idles away the whole day between the festal board and the dozing couch. You may think that he, at least, is free from the curse which I describe: but you are mistaken. While he is living, as he thinks, a life of luxurious ease and gentle inactivity, he fills himself with crude humours, and makes way for the gnawing gout and racking gravel. See, even now, how strongly he perspires, and with what uneasiness he draws his short breath and wipes his dewy shining face: surely he toils under the load of an undigested meal. A porter carries a burden upon his brawny shoulders, but this wretch has conveyed one into his sick stomach. He will not work; let him alone, and ere long acute pains will bathe him in as profuse a sweat as that of the furnace man; and strong medicines will exercise him to such a degree that he will envy even the collier's lot.

It is evident, therefore, that mankind are under a curse of toil and sweat,[*] according to the Divine sentence recorded by Moses; and that they are frequently

---

[*] It has been asserted that the short pleasure of eating and drinking makes amends for the severest toil. The best way to bring such idle sensual objectors to reason would be to make them earn every meal by two or three hours' thrashing. Beside, what great pleasure can those have in eating, who actually starve,

condemned by Providence to as hard labour for life as wretched felons rowing in the galleys or digging in the mines.* But as it is absolutely incredible that a good God, who by a word can supply the wants of all his creatures, should have sentenced *innocent* mankind to these inconceivable hardships to procure or enjoy the necessaries of life, it is evident they are guilty, miserable offenders.

TENTH ARGUMENT.

Hard labour and sweat make up but one of the innumerable calamities incident to the wretched inhabitants of this world. Turn your eyes which way you please, and you will see some flying from others groaning under the rod of God; and the greatest number busily making a scourge for the backs of their fellow creatures or their own.

To pass over the misery of the brute creation: to say nothing of the subtlety and rapaciousness with which (after the example of men)† they lie in wait for and prey upon one another; to cast a veil over the agonies of millions that are daily stabbed, strangled, shot, and even flayed, boiled, or swallowed up alive for the support of man's life, or the indulgence of his luxury: and not to mention again the almost uninterrupted cries of feeble infancy, only take notice of the tedious confinement of childhood, the blasted schemes of youth, the anxious cares of riper years, and the deep groans of wrinkled, decrepit, tottering old age. Fix your attention on family trials; here a prodigal father ruins his children, or undutiful children break the hearts of their fond parents! There an unkind husband imbitters the life of his wife, or an imprudent wife stains the honour of her husband: a servant disobeys, a relation misbehaves, a son lies ill, a tenant breaks, a neighbour provokes, a rival supplants, a friend betrays, or an enemy triumphs. Peace seldom continues one day.

Listen to the sighs of the afflicted, the moans of the disconsolate, the complaints of the oppressed, and shrieks of the tortured. Consider the deformity of the faces of some, and distortion or mutilation of the limbs of others. To awaken your compassion,‡ here a beggar holds out the stump of a thigh or an arm: there a ragged wretch hops after you upon one leg and two crutches; and a little farther you meet

---

or, to just stay gnawing hunger, buy food coarser than that which their rich neighbours give to their dogs?

* God's image disinherited of day,
Here, plunged in mines, forgets a sun was made;
There, beings deathless as their haughty lord,
Are hammer'd to the galling oar for life,
And plough the winter's wave, and reap despair.　　　　　Young.

† Eager ambition's fiery chase I see;
I see the circling hunt of noisy men
Burst law's enclosure, leap the mounds of right,
Pursuing and pursued, each other's prey;
As wolves for rapine; as the fox for wiles;
Till death, that mighty hunter, earths them all.　　　　　Young.

‡ Some for hard masters broken under arms,
In battle lopp'd away, with half their limbs,
Beg bitter bread through realms their valour sav'd.　　　　　Young.

The Works of John Fletcher

with a poor creature using his hands instead of feet, and dragging through the mire the cumbrous weight of a body without lower parts.

Imagine, if possible, the hardships of those who are destitute of one of their senses: here the blind is guided by a dog, or gropes for his way in the blaze of noon; there the deaf lies on the brink of danger, inattentive to the loudest calls: here sits the dumb, sentenced to eternal silence; there dribbles the idiot, doomed to perpetual childhood; and yonder the paralytic shakes without intermission, or lies senseless, the frightful image of a living corpse.

Leaving these wretched creatures, consider the tears of the disappointed, the sorrows of the captives, the anxieties of the accused, the fears of the guilty, and terrors of the condemned. Take a turn through jails, inquisitions, houses of correction, and places of execution. Proceed to the mournful rooms of the languishing and wearisome beds of the sick: and let not the fear of seeing human wo, in some of its most deplorable appearances, prevent you from visiting hospitals, infirmaries, and bedlams:—

                    A place
        Before our eyes appears, sad, noisome, dark,
        A lazar house it seems, wherein are laid
        Numbers of all diseased; all maladies
        Of ghastly spasm or racking torture, qualms
        Of heart-sick agony, all fev'rous kinds,
        Convulsions, epilepsies, fierce catarrhs,
        Intestine stone, and ulcer, colic pangs,
        Demoniac frenzy, moping melancholy,
        And moon-struck madness, pining atrophy,
        Marasmus, and wide-wasting pestilence,
        Dropsies and asthmas, and joint, racking rheums.
        Dire is the tossing! Deep the groans! Despair
        Attends the sick, busiest from couch to couch:
        And over them triumphant death his dart
        Shakes; but delays to strike, though oft invok'd
        With vows, as their chief good, and final hope.   MILTON.

To close the horrible prospect, view the ruins of cities and kingdoms, the calamities of wrecks and sieges, the horrors of sea fights and fields of battle; with all the crimes, devastations, and cruelties that accompany revenge, contention, and war; and you will be obliged to conclude with Job, that corrupt "man is born to trouble as the sparks fly upward;" with David, that "the earth is full of darkness and cruel habitations;" and with every impartial inquirer, that our depravity and God's justice concur to make this world a "vale of tears" as well as a field of toil and sweat. A vast prison for rebels already "tied with the chains of their sins," a boundless scaffold for their execution, a Golgotha, an *Aceldama*, an immense field of torture and *blood.*

Some will probably say, "This picture of the world is drawn with black lines, but kinder Providence blends light and shade together, and tempers our calamities with numberless blessings." I answer: it cannot be too thankfully acknowledged, that while patience suspends the stroke of justice, God, for Christ's sake, restores us a thousand forfeited blessings, that *his goodness may lead us to repentance.* But, alas! what is the consequence where Divine grace does not prove victorious over corrupt nature? To all our sins do we not add the crime of either enjoying the favours of Providence with the greatest ingratitude, or of abusing them with the most provoking insolence?

An Appeal to Matter of Fact and Common Sense

Our actions are far more expressive of our real sentiments than our words. "Why this variety of exquisite food?" says the voluptuary, whose life loudly speaks what his lips dare not utter: "why this abundance of delicious wines, but to tempt my unbridled appetite and please my luxurious palate?" "Would God have given softness to says the self-silks, brightness to colours, and lustre to diamonds:" applauding smile of a foolish virgin who worships herself in a glass: "would he have commanded the white of the lily thus to meet the blush of the rose, and heighten so elegant a proportion of features, if he had not designed that the united powers of art, dress, and beauty, should make me share his Divine honours?" "Why are we blessed with dear children and amiable friends," says the ridiculous behaviour of fond parents and raptured lovers, "but that we should suspend our happiness on their ravishing smiles, and place them as favourite idols in the shrine of our hearts?" "And why has Heaven favoured me both with a strong constitution and an affluent fortune," says the rich slave of brutish lusts, "but that I may drink deeper of earthly joys and sensual delights?"

Thus blessings, abused or unimproved, become curses in our hands. God's indulgence encourages us to offend him: we have the fatal skill of extracting poison from the sweetest flowers, and madly turn the gifts of Providence into weapons to attack our benefactor and destroy ourselves. That there are then such perverted gifts does not prove that mankind are innocent; but that God's *patience* "endureth *yet* daily," and that a Saviour "ever liveth to make intercession for us."

Should it be farther objected, that "our pleasures counterbalance our calamities;" I answer, The greatest part of mankind are so oppressed with want and cares, toil and sickness, that their intervals of ease may rather be termed "an alleviation of misery" than "an enjoyment of happiness." Our pains are real and lasting, our joys imaginary and momentary. Could we exercise all our senses upon the most pleasing objects, the tooth ache would render all insipid and burthensome: a fit of the gout alone damps every worldly joy, while all earthly delights together cannot give us ease under it: so vastly superior is the bitterness of one bodily pain to the sweetness of all the pleasures of sense!

If objectors still urge that "sufferings are needful for our trial;" I reply, They are necessary for our *punishment* and *correction,* but not for our *trial.* A good king can *try* the loyalty of his subjects without putting them to the rack. Let Nero and Bonner *try* the innocent by all sorts of tortures, but let not their barbarity be charged upon a God strictly just and infinitely good.

However, "calamities prove a blessing to some;" and so does transportation: but whoever inferred from thence that reformed felons were transported for the *trial of their* virtue, and not for the *punishment* of their crimes? I conclude, therefore, that our calamities and miseries demonstrate our corruption as strongly as the punishments of the bastinado and pillory, appointed by an equitable judge, prove the guilt of those on whom they are frequently and severely inflicted.

ELEVENTH ARGUMENT.

Would to God the multiplied calamities of life were a sufficient punishment for our desperate wickedness! But, alas! they only make way for the pangs of death. Like traitors, or rather like *wolves* and *vipers,* to which the Son of God compares natural men, we are all devoted to destruction. Yes, as we kill those mischievous creatures, so God destroys the sinful sons of men.

If the reader is offended, and denies the mortifying assertion, let him visit with me the mournful spot where thousands are daily executed, and where hundreds make this moment their dying speech. I do not mean what some call "the bed of honour," a field of battle, but a common death bed.

Observing, as we go along, those black trophies of the king of terrors, those escutcheons which preposterous vanity fixes up in honour of the deceased, when kind charity should hang them out as a warning to the living: let us repair to those mournful apartments where weeping attendants support the dying, where swooning friends embrace the dead, or whence distracted relatives carry out the pale remains of all their joy.

Guided by their groans and funeral lights let us proceed to the dreary charnel houses and calvaries, which we decently call *vaults* and *church yards;* and without stopping to look at the monuments of some, whom my objector remembers as vigorous as himself; and of others who were perhaps his partners in nightly revel; let us hasten to see the dust of his mouldered ancestors, and to read upon yonder coffins the dear name of a parent, a child, perhaps a wife, turned off from his bosom into the gulf of eternity.

If this sight does not convince him, I shall open one of the noisome repositories, and show him the deep hollow of those eyes that darted tender sensation into his soul; and odious reptiles fastening upon the once charming, now ghastly face, he doted upon. But methinks he turns pale at the very proposal, and rather than be confronted with such witnesses, acknowledges that he is condemned to die, with all his dear relatives, and the whole human race.

And is this the case? Are we then under sentence of death? How awful is the consideration! Of all the things that nature dreads, is not death the most terrible? And is it not (as being the greatest of temporal evils) appointed by human and Divine laws for the punishment of capital offenders; whether they are named *felons* and *traitors,* or more genteelly called *men* and *sinners?* Let matter of fact decide.

While earthly judges condemn murderers and traitors to be hanged or beheaded, does not "the Judge of all" sentence sinful mankind either to pine away, with old age, or be wasted with consumptions, burned with fevers, scalded with hot humours, eaten up with cancers, putrefied by mortifications, suffocated by asthmas, strangled by quinsies, poisoned by the cup of excess, stabbed with the knife of luxury, or racked to death by disorders as loathsome and accidents as various as their sins?

If you consider the circumstances of their execution, where is the material difference between the malefactor and the sinner? The jailer and the turnkey confine the one to his cell: the disorder and the physician confine the other to his bed. The one lives upon bread and water: the other upon draughts and boluses. The one can walk with his fetters: the other loaded with blisters can scarcely turn himself. The one enjoys freedom from pain, and has the perfect use of his senses: the other complains he is racked all over, and is frequently delirious. The executioner does his office upon the one in a few minutes: but the physician and his medicines make the other linger for days before he can die out of his misery. An honest sheriff and constables, armed with staves, wait upon one; while a greedy undertaker and his party, with like emblems of authority, accompany the other: and if it is any advantage to have a numerous attendance, without comparison the felon has the greater train.

When the pangs of death are over, does not the difference made between the corpses consist more in appearance than reality? The murderer is dissected in the surgeon's hall *gratis*, and the rich sinner is embowelled in his own apartment at great expense. The robber, exposed to open air, wastes away in hoops of iron; and the gentleman, confined to a damp vault, moulders away in sheets of lead: and while the fowls of the air greedily prey upon the one, the vermin of the earth eagerly devour the other.

And if you consider them as launching into the world of spirits, is not the advantage, in one respect, on the malefactor's side? He is solemnly assured he must die; and when the death warrant comes down, all about him bid him prepare and make the best of his short time: but the physician and chaplain, friends and attendants, generally flatter the honourable sinner to the last: and what is the consequence? He either sleeps on in carnal security, till death puts an end to all his delusive dreams; or if he has some notion that he must repent, for fear of discomposing his spirits, he still puts it off till *to-morrow:* and in the midst of his delays God says, "Thou fool, *this night* thy soul shall be required of thee." What wonder is it, then, if, when the converted thief goes from the ignominious tree to paradise, the impenitent rich man passes from his "purple bed" into an awful eternity, and there "lifts up his eyes" in unexpected "torments?"

If these are truths too obvious to be denied, wilt thou, sinner, as the thoughtless vulgar, blunt their edge by saying, with amazing unconcern, "Death is a debt we must all pay to nature?" Alas! this is granting the point; for if all have contracted so dreadful a debt, all are in a corrupt and lost estate. Nor is this debt to be paid to *nature,* but to *justice;* otherwise dying would be as easy as sleeping, or any other natural action: but it is beyond expression terrible to thee from whose soul the Redeemer has not extracted *sin,* the monster's *sting:* and if thou dost not see it now in the most alarming light, it is because either thou imaginest it at a great distance, or the double veil of rash presumption and brutish stupidity is yet upon thy hardened heart.

Or wilt thou, as the poor heathen, comfort thyself with the cruel thought, that "thou shalt not die alone?" Alas! dying companions may increase, but cannot take off the horror of dissolution. Beside, though we live in a crowd, we generally die alone: each must drink the bitter cup, as if he were the only mortal in the universe.

What must we do then in such deplorable circumstances? What but humble ourselves in the dust, and bow low to the sceptre of Divine justice; confessing that since the righteous God has condemned us to certain death, and in general to a far more lingering and painful death than murderers and traitors are made to undergo, we are certainly degenerate creatures, and capital offenders, who stand in absolute need of an almighty Redeemer.

Permit me now, candid reader, to make a solemn appeal to thy reason, assisted by the fear of God. From all that has been advanced, does it not appear that man is no more the favoured, happy, and innocent creature he was, when he came out of the hands of his infinitely gracious Creator? And is it not evident that, whether we consider him as born into this disordered world, or dying out of it, or passing from the womb to the grave, under a variety of calamitous circumstances, God's providential dealings with him prove that he is by nature in a corrupt and lost estate?

A part, how small! of this terraqueous globe
Is tenanted by man, the rest a waste,
Rocks, deserts, frozen seas, and burning sands,
Wild haunts of monsters, poisons, stings, and death.
Such is earth's melancholy map! But far
More sad, this earth is a true map of man;
So bounded are its haughty lord's delights
To wo's wide empire, where deep troubles toss,
Loud sorrows howl, envenom'd passions bite,
Ravenous calamities our vitals seize,
And threatening fate wide opens to devour!   YOUNG.

———

PART III.

WE have hitherto considered man as a miserable inhabitant of a wretched world. We have seen him surrounded by multitudes of wants; pursued by legions of distresses, maladies, and woes; arrested by the king of terrors; cast into the grave; and shut up there, the loathsome prey of corruption and worms. Let us now consider him as a moral agent; and by examining his disposition, character, and conduct, let us see whether he is wisely punished, according to the sentence of impartial justice; or wantonly tormented, at the caprice of arbitrary power.

We cannot help acknowledging it is highly reasonable, *First,* that all intelligent creatures should love, reverence, and obey their Creator; because he is most eminently their Father, their Master, and their King: *Secondly,* they should assist, support, and love each other as fellow subjects, fellow servants, and children of the same universal Parent: and, *Thirdly,* that they should preserve their souls and bodies in peace and purity; by which means alone they can be happy in themselves, profitable to man, and acceptable to God. This is what we generally call *natural religion,* which is evidently founded upon eternal reason, the fitness of things, and the essential relation of persons.

The propriety of these sanctions is so self evident, that "the Gentiles, who have not the *written* law, are a law unto themselves, and do (but alas! how seldom, and from what motives!) the things contained in the law:" thus "showing that the work," the sum and substance "of the law," though much blotted by the fall, is still "written in their heart." Nor will it be erased thence in hell itself; for nothing but a sight of the equity of God's law can clear his vindictive justice in the guilty breast, give a scorpion's sting to the worm that gnaws the stubborn offender, and arm his upbraiding conscience with a whip of biting serpents.

Since the moral law so strongly recommends itself to reason, let us see how universally it is observed or broken: so shall matter of fact decide whether we are pure and upright, or polluted and depraved.

TWELFTH ARGUMENT.

Those who reject the Scriptures, universally agree that "all have sinned;" and that "in many things we offend all." Hence it appears that persons of various constitutions, ranks, and education, in all nations, religions, times, and places, are born in such a state, and with such a nature, that they infallibly commit *many* sins in thought, word, or deed.

But one transgression would be sufficient to render them obnoxious to God's displeasure, and to bring them under the fearful curse of his broken law: for, even according to the statutes of this realm, a man who *once* robs a traveller of a small sum of money, forfeits his life, as well as the bloody highwayman, who for years barbarously murders all those whom he stops, and accumulates immense wealth by his repeated barbarities.

The reason is obvious: both incur the penalty of the law which forbids robbery; for both effectually break it, though one does it oftener and with more aggravating circumstances than the other. So sure then as one robbery deserves the gallows, one sin deserves death. "The soul that sinneth," says God's law, and not the soul that committeth so many sins, of such and such a heinousness, "it shall die." Hence it is, that the first sin of the first man was punished both with spiritual and bodily death, and with ten thousand other evils. The justice of this sanction will appear in a satisfactory light, if we consider the following remarks:—

1. In our present natural state we are such strangers to God's glory and the spirituality of his law; and we are so used "to drink" the deadly poison of "iniquity like water," that we have no idea of the horror which should seize upon us after a breach of the Divine law. We are, therefore, as unfit judges of the atrociousness of sin, as lawless, hardened assassins, who shed human blood like water, are of the heinousness of murder.

2. As every wilful sin arises from a disregard of that sovereign authority which is equally stamped upon all the commandments, it hath in it the principle and nature of all possible iniquity; that is, the disregard and contempt of the Almighty.

3. There is no *proper merit* before God, in the longest and most exact course of obedience, but infinite demerit in one, even the least act of wilful disobedience. "When we have done all that is commanded us, we are *still* unprofitable servants;" for the self-sufficient God has no more need of us than a mighty monarch of the vilest insects that creep in the dust beneath his feet: and our best actions, strictly speaking, deserve absolutely nothing from our Creator and Preserver, because we owe him all we have and are, and can possibly do. But if we transgress in one point, we ruin all our obedience, and expose ourselves to the just penalty of his broken law. The following example may illustrate this observation:—

If a rich man gives a *thousand* meals to an indigent neighbour, he acts only as a *man,* he does nothing but his duty; and the judge allows him no reward. But if he gives him only *one* dose of poison, he acts as a *murderer,* and must die a shameful death. So greatly does one act of sin outweigh a thousand acts of obedience! How exceedingly absurd, then, is the common notion, that our good works counterbalance our bad ones! Add to this, that—

4. Guilt necessarily arises in proportion to the baseness of the offender, the greatness of the favours conferred upon him, and the dignity of the person offended: an insulting behaviour to a servant is a fault, to a magistrate it is a crime, to a king it is treason. And what is wilful sin, but an injury offered by an impotent rebel to the infinitely powerful Lawgiver of the universe, to the kindest of Benefactors, to the gracious Creator and Preserver of men: an insult given to the supreme Majesty of heaven and earth, in whose glorious presence the dignity of the greatest potentates and archangels as truly disappears, as the splendour of the stars in the blaze of the meridian sun? Sin, therefore, flying into the face of such a Lawgiver, Benefactor, and Monarch, has in it a kind of infinite demerit from its infinite Object; and rebellious, ungrateful, wretched man, who commits it a thousand times with a thousand aggravations, may, in the nervous language of our Church, be said, in some sense, to *deserve a thousand hells, if there were so many.*

THIRTEENTH ARGUMENT.

Our natural depravity manifests itself by constant omissions of duty, as much as by flagrant commissions of sin, and perhaps much more. Take one instance out of many that might be produced. Constant displays of preserving goodness, and presents undeservedly and uninterruptedly bestowed upon us, deserve a perpetual tribute of heartfelt gratitude: God demands it in his law; and conscience, his agent in our souls, declares it ought in justice to be paid. But where shall we find a Deist properly conscious of what he owes the Supreme Being for his "creation, preservation, and all the blessings of this life?" and where a Christian duly sensible of "God's inestimable love in the redemption of the world by our Lord Jesus Christ?" A due sense of his ever-multiplied mercies would fill our souls with never-ceasing wonder, and make our lips overflow with rapturous praise. The poet's language would suit our grateful sensations, and without exaggeration paint the just ardour of our transports:—

> Bound every heart, and every bosom burn:
> Praise, flow for ever; (if astonishment
> Will give thee leave;) our praise, for ever flow;
> Praise, ardent, cordial, constant, &c,

Is not any thing short of this thankful frame of mind a sin of omission, a degree of ingratitude, of which all are naturally guilty; and for which, it is to be feared, the best owe ten thousand talents both to Divine goodness and justice?

Throw only a few bones to a dog and you win him: he follows you; your word becomes his law: upon the first motion of your hand he flies through land and water to execute your commands: obedience is his delight, and your presence his paradise;

he convinces you of it by all the demonstrations of joy which he is capable, of giving: and if he unhappily loses sight of you, he exerts all his sagacity to trace your footsteps; nor will he rest till he finds his benefactor again.

Shall a brute be so thankful to a man for some offals, while man himself is so full of ingratitude to God who created him, preserves his life from destruction, and hourly crowns him with mercies and loving kindness! How should shame cover our guilty faces! Surely, if the royal prophet could say, "He was a beast before God," may we not well confess that in point of gratitude we are worse than the dullest and most stupid part of the brute creation? For even "the ox," says the Lord, "knoweth his owner," and "the ass his master's crib; but Israel doth not know" me, "my people do not consider" my daily favours. And if the very heathens affirmed that "to call a man ungrateful" to a human benefactor, "was to say of him all possible evil in one word;"* how can we express the baseness and depravity of mankind, who are universally so ungrateful to so bounteous a benefactor as *God himself!*

FOURTEENTH ARGUMENT.

But though we seem made of cold inattention, when the sight of Divine mercies should kindle our hearts into gratitude and praise, we soon get out of this languid frame of mind: for, in the pursuit of sensual gratifications, we are all activity and warmth; we seem an ardent compound of life and fire.

What can be the reason of this amazing difference? What but rebellious sense and wanton appetite, raised at the sight and idea of some forbidden object! The bait of pleasure appears, corrupt nature summons all her powers, every nerve of expectation is stretched, every pulse of desire beats high, the blood is in a general ferment, the spirits are in a universal hurry, and though the hook of a fatal consequence is often apparent, the alluring bait must be swallowed. The fear of God, the most inestimable of all treasures is already gone; and if the sinful gratification cannot be enjoyed upon any other term, a good reputation shall go also. Reason indeed makes remonstrances; but the loud clamours of flesh and blood soon drown her soft whispers. The carnal mind steps imperiously upon the throne; sense, that conquers the greatest conquerors, bears down all opposition; the yielding man is led captive by a brutish lust; and while angels blush, there is joy in hell over the actual and complete degradation of a heaven-born spirit.

Some indeed affirm that these conflicts suit a state of probation and trial. But it is evident that either our temptations are too violent for our strength, or our strength too weak for our temptations; since, notwithstanding the additional help of Divine grace, there never was a mere mortal over whom they never triumphed.

Nor can we exculpate ourselves by pleading that these triumphs of sense over reason are neither long nor frequent. Alas! how many perpetrate an act of wickedness in a moment, and suffer death itself for a crime which they never repeated!

See that crystal vessel. Its brightness and brittleness represent the shining and delicate nature of true virtue. If I let it fall and break it, what avails it to say, "I never broke it before: I dropped it but once: I am excessively sorry for my carelessness: I

---

* Ingratum si dixeris, omnia dicis.—*Juv.*

will set the pieces together, and never break it again?" Will these excuses and resolutions prevent the vessel from being broken—broken for ever? The reader may easily make the application.

Even heathen moralists, by their fabulous account of the companions of Ulysses turned into swine, upon drinking once of Circe's enchanted cup, teach us that one fall into sensuality turns a man into a brute, just as one slip into unchastity or dishonesty changes a modest woman into a strumpet, or an honest man into a thief. Again:

Ought not reason to have as absolute a command over appetite as a skilful rider has over a well-broken horse? But suppose we saw all horsemen universally mastered, one time or other, by their beasts; and forced, though but for a few minutes, to receive the bit, and go or stop at the pleasure of the wanton brutes: should we not wonder, and justly infer, that man had lost the kind of superiority which he still maintains over domestic animals? And what then, but the commonness of the case, can prevent our being shocked, when we see rational creatures overcome and led captive by carnal appetites? Is not this the wanton, rebellious beast mounting upon his vanquished, dastardly rider?

We may then conclude that the universal rebellion of our lower faculties against our superior powers, and the triumphs of sense over reason, demonstrate that human nature has suffered as fatal a revolution as these kingdoms did when a degraded king was seen bleeding on the scaffold, and a base usurper lording it in the seat of majesty.

FIFTEENTH ARGUMENT.

Happy would it be for us if our fall manifested itself only by some transient advantages of sense over reason. But, alas! the experience of the best demonstrates the truth of Isaiah's words: "The whole head is sick."

To say nothing of the gross stupidity, and unconquerable ignorance, that keep the generality of mankind just above the level of brutes, how strong, how clear is the UNDERSTANDING of men of sense in worldly affairs! How weak, how dark in spiritual things! How few idiots are there but can distinguish between the shadow and the substance, the cup and the liquor, the dress and the person! But how many learned men, to this day, see no difference between water baptism and spiritual regeneration, between the means of grace and grace itself, between "the form" and "the power of godliness!" At our devotions is not our mind generally like the roving butterfly: and at our favourite diversions and lucrative business, like the fastening leech? Can it not fix itself on any thing sooner than on "the one thing needful;" and find out any way before that of peace and salvation?

What can be more extravagant than our IMAGINATION? How often have we caught this wild power forming and pursuing phantoms, building and pulling down castles in the air! How frequently hath it raised us into proud conceits, and then sunk us into gloomy apprehensions! And where is the man that it never led into such mental scenes of vanity and lewdness, as would have made him the object of universal contempt, if the veil of a grave and modest countenance had not happily concealed him from public notice?

And has our MEMORY escaped unimpaired by the fall? Alas! let us only consider how easily we forget the favours of our Creator, and recollect the injuries of our fellow creatures; how little we retain of a good book or pious discourse, and how

An Appeal to Matter of Fact and Common Sense

much of a play or frivolous conversation; and how exactly we remember an invitation to a party of pleasure, while the loudest calls to turn to God and prepare for death are no sooner heard than forgotten. Let us, I say, consider these things, and we shall be forced to confess, that this useful power loses like a sieve the living water of truth, drinks in like a sponge the muddy streams of vanity, and is never so retentive as when it is excited by revenge, or some other detestable temper.

"A wretch that is condemned to die to-morrow cannot forget it," says Baxter; "yet poor sinners, who are uncertain to live an hour, and certain speedily to see the majesty of the Lord, to their inconceivable joy or terror, can forget these things, for which they have their memory; and which, one would think, should drown the matters of this world, as the report of a cannon does a whisper, or as the sun obscures the poorest glowworm. O wonderful stupidity of an unregenerate soul! O astonishing distraction of the ungodly! That ever men can forget eternal joy, eternal wo, the eternal God, and the place of their unchangeable abode; when they stand even at the door, and there is but the thin veil of flesh between them and that amazing sight, that eternal gulf, into which thousands are daily plunging!"

Nor does our REASON* make us amends for the defects of our other faculties. Its beams, it is true, wonderfully guide some persons through the circle of sciences, and the mazes of commercial or political affairs. But when it should lead us in search of "the truth which is after godliness," unless it is assisted from above, how are its faint rays obstructed by the gross medium of flesh and blood, broken by that of passion, and sometimes lost in that of prejudice! Wise sons of reason, learned philosophers, your two hundred and eighty-eight opinions concerning the *chief good*, are a multiplied proof of my sad assertion: all miss the mark. Not one of them makes the supreme felicity to consist in the knowledge and enjoyment of God, the amiable and adorable Parent of all good.

True reason, alas! is as rare as true piety. The poor thing which, in spiritual matters, the world calls *reason*, is only the ape of that noble faculty. How partial, how *unreasonable†* is this false pretender! If it does not altogether overlook the awful realities of the Invisible, which is too frequently the case, how busy is it to reason away faith, and raise objections against the most evident truth,‡ even that which I

---

* By *reason*, I mean that power by which we pass judgment upon, and draw inferences from, what the *understanding* has simply apprehended.

> † Our earth's the Bedlam of the universe,
> Where reason (undiseas'd in heaven) runs mad,
> And nurses folly's children as her own,
> Fond of the foulest.   YOUNG.

‡ late publication in vindication of Pelagianism appears to me no small instance of this. The Rev. author takes his estimate of human nature, not from universal experience, but his indulged imagination; not from *St. Paul,* the chief of the apostles, but from *Dr. Taylor,* "to whom he acknowledges his obligations for several of the best passages in his sermon." Passing over the exposition of his text, where he boldly supposes that our Lord meant, by *the drawings of God,* the natural powers of man; which is as reasonable as to suppose that when he said, "Without me you can do nothing," he meant that *me* should signify *ourselves:*—passing this over, I shall just point out his capital mistake. He tells us that "all our faculties and powers *are* good and beautiful in their order," (that they were so before the fall is fully granted,) "and tend naturally to the happiness both of the individual and the system;" and he adds, that "how weak soever and imperfect our intellectual faculties may be, yet to speak reproachfully of them in general is a species of blasphemy against our Creator." If to expose the present weakness of our

now contend for! and when right reason has been worsted by sense, how ready is the impostor to plead against the faculty which it personates! How skilful in cloaking bad habits under the genteel name of "human foibles!" And how ingenious in defending the most irrational and dangerous methods of losing time, as "innocent sports and harmless diversions!"

These observations, which must appear self evident to all who know the world or themselves, incontestably prove the degeneracy of all our rational powers, and consequently the universality of our natural corruption.

SIXTEENTH ARGUMENT.

When "the whole head is sick," is not "the whole heart faint?" Can our will, conscience, and affections, run parallel to the line of duty, when our understanding, imagination, memory, and reason, are so much warped from original rectitude? Impossible! Experience, thou best of judges, I appeal to thee. Erect thy fair tribunal in the reader's breast, and bear an honest testimony to the truth of the following assertions:—

Our WILL, in general, is full of obstinacy. We must have our own way, right or wrong. It is pregnant with inconstancy. We are passionately fond of a thing one day, and are tired of it the next. We form good resolutions in the morning, and break them before night. It is impotent. When we see what is right, instead of doing it with all our might, we frequently remain as inactive as if we were bound by invisible chains; and we wonder by what charm the wheels of duty thus stop against our apparent inclinations, till we discover that the spring of our will is broken, or naturally works the wrong way. Yes, it is not only unable to follow the good that the

---

rational faculties, and show how greatly they are disordered and impaired by the fall, is what this divine calls "speaking reproachfully of them," have not the best men been found guilty of this pretended *blasphemy?* How far the apostles and reformers carried it may be seen in the first part of this treatise. How he can clear himself of it, as a subscriber to the 9th, 10th, and 35th articles of our Church, I cannot see: and by what means he will justify his conduct to the world, in receiving hundreds a year to maintain the doctrine of the Church of England, while he publicly expresses its *species of blasphemy,* is still a greater mystery. Far from seeing that *all the faculties and powers,* by which this is done, *are good and beautiful,* I cannot help thinking some of them are materially defective; and though such a conduct may very much *tend to the* emolument *of the individual,* it has little tendency *to the happiness of the system.* For my part, were I to commence advocate for the *uprightness* of human nature, I would save appearances, lest Dr. Taylor himself should say, *Non defensoribus istis, &c.* But, dropping this point, I appeal to common sense, who is most guilty of *blasphemy against our Creator;* he who says God made man both holy and happy, affirming that the present weakness of our rational powers is entirely owing to the original apostasy of mankind; or he who intimates that the gracious Author of our being formed our intellectual faculties weak and imperfect as they now are? If it is not the latter, my understanding is strangely defective.—In vain does this learned divine tell us, that "the candle of the Lord, which was lighted up in man at first, when the inspiration of the Almighty gave him understanding, was not extinguished by the original apostasy, but has kept burning ever since," and "that the Divine flame has catched from father to son, and has been propagated quite down to the present generation:" if it is reasonable to charge with *a species of blasphemy* those who reverence their Creator too much, to father our present state of imperfection upon him, I must confess *my* reason fails: I have outlived *the Divine flame* for one, or it never *catched from* my *father* to me. A fear lest some well-meaning person should mistake the taper of Pelagius, or the lamp of Dr. Taylor, for "the candle of the Lord," and follow it in the destructive paths of error, extorts this note from my pen. See the objections that follow the twenty-second argument.

understanding approves, but full of perverseness to pursue the evil that reason disapproves. We are prone to do, contrary to our design, those things which breed remorse and wound conscience; and, sooner or later, we may all say, with the heathen princess, who was going to murder her child,—

> *Video meliora, proboque,*
> *Deteriora sequor.*[*]

Nor is CONSCIENCE itself untainted. Alas! how slow is it to reprove in some cases! In others, how apt not to do it at all! In one person it is easy under mountains of guilt; and in another it is unreasonably scrupulous about mere trifles: it either "strains at a gnat," or "swallows a camel." When it is alarmed, in some it shows itself ready to be made easy by every wrong method; in others, it obstinately refuses to be pacified by the right. To-day you may with propriety compare it to a dumb dog, that does not bark at a thief; and to-morrow to a snarling cur, that flies indifferently at a friend, a foe, or a shadow; and then madly turns upon himself, and tears his own flesh.

If conscience, the best power of the unconverted man, is so corrupt, good God! what are his AFFECTIONS? Almost perpetually deficient in some, and excessive in others, when do they attain to, or stop at, the line of moderation? Who can tell how oft he has been the sport of their irregularity and violence? One hour we are hurried into rashness by their impetuosity; the next, we are bound in sloth by their inactivity. Sometimes every blast of foolish hope, or ill-grounded fear; every gale of base desire, or unreasonable aversion; every wave of idolatrous love, or sinful hatred; every surge of misplaced admiration, or groundless horror; every billow of noisy joy, or undue sorrow, tosses, raises, or sinks our soul, as a ship in a storm, which has neither rudder nor ballast. At other times we are totally becalmed; all our sails are furled; not one breath of devout or human affection stirs in our stoical, frozen breast; and we remain stupidly insensible, till the spark of temptation, dropping upon the combustible matter in our hearts, blows up again into loud passion; and then, how dreadful and ridiculous together is the new explosion!

If experience pronounces that these reflections are just, the point is gained. Our "whole heart is faint," through the unaccountable disorders of our *will,* the lethargy or boisterous fits of our *conscience,* and the swooning or high fever of our *affections;* and we may, without hypocrisy, join in our daily confession, and say, "There is no health in us."

SEVENTEENTH ARGUMENT.

The danger of these complicated maladies of our souls evidences itself by the most fatal of all symptoms, *our manifest alienation from God.* Yes, shocking as the confession is, we must make it, if truth has any dominion in our breast:—Unrenewed man loves not his God. That eternal Beauty, for whose contemplation, that supreme Good, for whose enjoyment he was created, is generally forgotten, despised, or hated. If the thought of his holy Majesty presents itself, he looks upon it as an intruder. It

---

[*] If the reader wants to know the English of these words, he may find it, Romans vii:15.

The Works of John Fletcher

lays him under as disagreeable a restraint as that which the presence of a grave, pious master, puts upon a wanton, idle servant. Nor can he quietly pursue his sinful courses till he has driven away the troublesome idea; or imagined, with the epicure, a careless God, who wants resolution to call him to an account, and justice to punish him for his iniquity.

Does any one offer an indignity to his favourite friend, or only speak contemptibly of the object of his esteem, he feels as if he was the person insulted, and, reddening with indignation, directly espouses his cause. But every body, the meanest of his attendants not excepted, may with impunity insult the King of kings in his presence, and take the most profane liberties with his name and word, his laws and ministers; he hears the wild blasphemy, and regards it not; he sees the horrid outrage, and resents it not; and yet, with amazing infatuation, he pretends to love God!

If he goes to the play, he can fix his roving eyes and wandering mind three hours together upon the same trifling objects, not only without weariness, but with uncommon delight. If he has an appointment with a person whom he adores as a deity, his spirits are elevated, expectation and joy flutter in his dilated breast; he sweetly anticipates the pleasing interview, or impatiently chides the slowly flowing minutes: his feelings are inexpressible. But if he attends the great congregation, which he too often omits upon the most frivolous pretences, it is rather out of form and decency, than out of devotion and love; rather with indifference or reluctance, than with delight and transport. And when he is present there, how absent are his thoughts! How wandering his eyes! How trifling, supine, irrelevant his whole behaviour! He would be ashamed to speak to the meanest of his servants with as little attention as he sometimes prays to the Majesty of heaven.* Were he to stare about when he gives them orders, as he does when he presents his supplications to the Lord of lords, he would be afraid that they would think he was half drunk, or had a touch of lunacy.

Suppose he still retains a sense of outward decency, while the Church goes through her solemn offices; yet how heavy are his spirits! how heartless his confessions] how cold his prayers! The blessing comes at last, and he is blessed indeed, not with "the grace of our Lord Jesus Christ, and the fellowship of the Holy Ghost," for that he gladly leaves to "poor enthusiasts," but with a release from his confinement and tedious work. And now that he has "done his duty, and served God," he hastes away to the company that suits his taste.

See him there. Do not his very looks declare he is in his own element? With what eagerness of spirit, energy of gesture, and volubility of tongue, does he talk over his last entertainment, chase, or bargain? Does not the oil of cheerfulness make all his motions as free and easy, as if weight and friction had no place at all in his light and airy frame?

---

* Men homage pay to men,
Thoughtless beneath whose dreadful eye they bow!
In mutual awe profound, of clay to clay,
Of guilt to guilt, and turn their backs on Thee,
Great Sire! whom thrones celestial ceaseless sing;
To prostrate angels an amazing scene!   YOUNG.

Love of God, thou sweetest, strongest of all powers! didst thou ever thus metamorphose his soul, and impart such a sprightly activity to his body? And you that converse most familiarly with him, did you ever hear him say, "Come, and I will tell you what the Lord has done for my soul. Taste and see how good the Lord is?" No, never; for "out of the abundance of the heart the mouth speaketh." Nor can it be expected that God, who hath no place in his joyous reflections, should have one in his cheerful conversation. On the contrary, it will be matter of surprise to those who introduce the delightful subject of the love of God, if he does not waive it off as dull, melancholy, or enthusiastical.

But, as he will give you to understand, "he is no hypocrite, and therefore confines devotion to his closet;" follow him there. Alas! he scarce ever bends the knee to "Him that sees in secret:" or, if he says his prayers as regularly as he winds his watch, it is much in the same spirit. For suppose he does not hurry them over, or cut them as short as possible; yet the careless, formal manner in which he offers them up, indicates, as plainly as his public conduct, the aversion lurking in his heart against God. And yet he fancies he loves him. With a sneer that indicates self applause, and a Pharisaic contempt of others, "away with your feelings and raptures," says he: "this is the love of God, that we keep his commandments." But, alas! which of them does he keep? Certainly not the first,—for the Lord is not the supreme object of his hopes and fears, his confidence and joy; nor yet the last,—for discontent and wrong desires are still indulged in his selfish and worldly heart. How unfortunate, therefore, is his appeal to the commandments, by which his secret enmity to the law, government, and nature of God, is brought to the clearest light!

EIGHTEENTH ARGUMENT.

But as the heartfelt love of God is supposed to be downright enthusiasm by some moralists, who, dashing in pieces the first table of the law against the second, pretend that our duty to God consists in the love of our neighbour, let us examine the unconverted man's charity, and see whether he bears more love to his fellow creatures than to his Creator.

Nothing can be more erroneous than his notions of *charity*. He confounds it with the bare "giving of alms;" not considering that it is possible to do this kind of good from the most selfish and *uncharitable* motives. Therefore when the fear of being accounted covetous, the desire of passing for generous, the vanity of seeing his name in a list of noble subscribers, the shame of being outdone by his equals, the teazing importunity of an obstinate beggar, the moving address of a solicitor whom he would blush to deny, or the Pharisaic notion of making amends for his sins, and purchasing heaven by his alms;—when any, I say, of these sinister motives sets him upon assisting industrious poverty, relieving friendless old age, or supporting infirm and mutilated indigence, he fancies that he gives an indubitable proof of his *charity*.

Sometimes, too, he affixes to that word the idea of a fond hope that every body is going to heaven. For if you intimate that the rich voluptuary is not with Lazarus in Abraham's bosom, and that the foolish virgins are not promiscuously admitted to glory with the wise, he wonders at "your uncharitableness, and thanks God he never entertained such unchristian thoughts of his neighbours."

He considers not that *charity is* the fair offspring of the "love of God," to which he is yet an utter stranger; and that it consists in a universal, disinterested benevolence to all mankind, our worst enemies not excepted; a benevolence that sweetly evidences itself by bearing with patience the evil which they do to us, and kindly doing them all the good we possibly can, both with respect to their soul and body, their property and reputation.

If this is a just definition of charity, the unrenewed man has not even the outside of it. To prove it, I might appeal to his impatience and ill humour: his unkind words and cutting railleries, (for I suppose him too moral ever to slander or curse any one.) I might mention his supercilious behaviour to some, who are entitled to his affability as men, countrymen, and neighbours: I might expatiate on his readiness to exculpate, enrich, or aggrandize himself at the expense of *others,* whenever he can do it without exposing *himself.*

But, waiving all these particulars, I ask, Whom does he truly love? You answer, "Doubtless the person to whom he makes daily protestations of the warmest regard." But how does he prove this regard? Why, perhaps by the most artful insinuations and dangerous attempts to rob her of her virtue. Perhaps he has already gained his end. Unhappy Magdalene! How much better would it have been for thee to have fallen into the hands of a highwayman! Thou wouldst only have lost thy money, but now thou art despoiled of the honour of thy sex, and the peace of thy mind; thou art robbed at once of virgin innocence, a fair reputation, and possibly a healthy constitution. If this is a specimen of the unconverted man's love, what must be his hatred?

But I happily mistake: "he is no libertine, he has a virtuous wife and amiable children, and he loves them," say you, "with the tenderest affection." I reply, that these relations, being *immortal spirits,* confined for a few years in a tenement of clay, and continually on the remove for eternity; his laudable regard for their *frail bodies,* and proper care of their *temporal prosperity,* are not a sufficient proof that he loves them in a right manner; for even according to wise heathens,[*] our *soul* is our *better part,* our *true self.* And what tender concern does the unrenewed man feel for the soul of his bosom friend? Does he regard it more than the body of his groom, or the life of his horse? Does he, with any degree of importunity, carry it daily in the arms of love and prayer, to the throne of grace for life and salvation? Does he, by good instructions and a virtuous example, excite his children to secure an eternal inheritance? And is he at least as desirous to see them wise and pious, as well bred, rich, handsome, and great? Alas! I fear it is just the reverse. He is probably the first to poison their tender minds with some of the dangerous maxims that vanity and ambition have invented; and, supposing he has a favourite dog, it is well if he is not more anxious for the preservation of that one domestic animal, than for the salvation of all their souls.

If these observations are founded upon matter of fact, as daily experience demonstrates, I appeal to common sense, and ask, Can the natural man, with all his fondness, be said to have a true love even for his nearest relatives? And is not the regard that he manifests for their *bodies* more like the common instinct by which doves cleave to their mates, and swallows provide for their young, than like the

[*] Nos non corpora sumus: Corpus quidem vas est aut aliquod animi receptaculum.—*Cic. Tusc. Quæst. lib.* 1.

generous affection which a rational creature ought to bear to immortal SPIRITS, awfully hovering in a state of probation, which is just going to turn for hell or heaven!

NINETEENTH ARGUMENT.

Nor is it surprising that the unrenewed man should be devoid of all true love for his nearest relations; for he is so completely fallen that he bears no true love even for *himself*. Let us overlook those who cut their throats; shoot, drown, or hang themselves. Let us take no notice of those who sacrifice a year's health for a night's revel; who inflame their blood into fevers, or derive putrefaction in their bones, for the momentary gratification of a shameful appetite; and are so hot in the pursuit of a base pleasure, that they leap after it even into the jaws of an untimely grave. Let us, I say, pass by those innumerable, unhappy victims of intemperance and debauchery, who squander their money upon panders and harlots, and have as little regard for their health as for their fortune and reputation; and let us consider the case of those good-natured, decent persons, who profess to have a real value for both.

Upon the principle laid down in the last argument, may I not ask, What love have these for their immortal part, their *true self*? What do they do for their souls? Or rather, what do they not leave undone? And who can show less concern for their greatest interest than they?

Alas! in spiritual matters the wisest of them seem on a level with the most foolish. They anxiously secure their title to a few possessions in this transitory world, out of which the stream of time carries them with unabated impetuosity; while they remain stupidly thoughtless of their portion in the unchangeable world into which they are just going to launch;* they take particular notice of every trivial incident in life, every idle report raised in their neighbourhood, and supinely overlook the great realities of death and judgment, hell and heaven.

You see them perpetually contriving how to preserve, indulge, and adorn their dying bodies; and daily neglecting the safety, welfare, and ornament of their immortal souls. So great is their folly that earthly toys make them slight heavenly thrones! So wilful their self deception that a point of time† hides from them a boundless eternity!

---

* Time flies, death urges, knells call, heaven invites,
Hell threatens! all exert; in effort, all;
More than creation labours! labours more!
And is there in creation, what, amidst
This tumult universal, wing'd despatch,
And ardent energy, supinely yawns?
Man sleeps; and *man* alone; and *man*, whose fate,
Fate irreversible, entire, extreme,
Endless, hair hung, breeze shaken, o'er the gulf
A moment trembles; drops! and *man*, for whom
All else is in alarm: *man*, the sole cause
Of this surrounding storm! and yet he sleeps,
As the storm rock'd to rest.   YOUNG

† And is it in the flight of three-score years
To push eternity from human thought,
And bury souls immortal in the dust?

So perverted is their moral taste, that they nauseate the word of truth, the precious food of souls, and greedily run upon the tempter's hook, if it is but made of solid gold; or gilt over with the specious appearance of honour, or only baited with the prospect of a favourite diversion. And while, by uneasy, fretful tempers, they too often impair their bodily health; by exorbitant affections and pungent cares they frequently break their hearts, or pierce themselves through with many sorrows.

Does such a conduct deserve the name of a well-ordered *self love,* or preposterous *self hatred?* O man, sinful man, how totally art thou depraved, if thou art not only thy own most dangerous enemy, but often thy most cruel tormentor!

TWENTIETH ARGUMENT.

This depravity is productive of the most detestable brood. When it has suppressed the love of God, perverted the love of our neighbour, and vitiated self love, it soon gives birth to a variety of execrable tempers, and dire affections, which should have no place but in the breasts of fiends, no outbreaking but in the chambers of hell.

If you ask their names, I answer, *pride,* that odious vice, which feeds on the praises it slily procures, lives by the applause it has meanly courted, and is equally stabbed by the reproof of a friend, and the sneer of a foe. *The spirit of independence,* which cannot bear control, is galled by the easiest yoke, gnaws the slender cords of just authority, as if they were the heavy chains of tyrannical power; nor ever ceases struggling till they break, and he can say, "Now I am my own master." *Ambition* and *vanity,* which, like Proteus, take a thousand shapes, and wind a thousand ways, to climb up to the high seat of power, shine on the tottering stage of honour, wear the golden badge of fortune, glitter in the gaudy pomp of dress, and draw by distinguishing appearances the admiration of a gaping multitude. *Sloth,* which unnerves the soul, enfeebles the body, and makes the whole man deaf to the calls of duty, loath to set about his business, (even when want, fear, or shame drives him to it,) ready to postpone or omit it upon any pretence, and willing to give up even the interests of society, virtue, and religion, so he may saunter undisturbed, dose the time away in stupid inactivity, or enjoy himself in that dastardly indolence which passes in the world for quietness and good nature. *Envy,* that looks with an evil eye at the good things our competitors enjoy, takes a secret pleasure in their misfortunes, under various pretexts exposes their faults, slily tries to add to our reputation what it detracts from theirs, and stings our heart when they eclipse us by their greater success or superior excellences. *Covetousness,* which is always dissatisfied with its portion, watches it with tormenting fears, increases it by every sordid means, and, turning its own executioner justly pines for want over the treasure it madly saves for a prodigal heir. *Impatience,* which frets at every thing, finds fault with every person, and madly tears herself under the distressing sense of a present evil, or the anxious expectation of an absent good.

A soul immortal spending all her fires,
Wasting her strength in strenuous idleness;
Thrown into tumult, raptur'd, or alarm'd.
At aught this scene can threaten or indulge,
Resembles ocean into tempest wrought,
To waft a feather, or to drown a fly.   YOUNG.

An Appeal to Matter of Fact and Common Sense

Wrath, which distorts our faces, racks our breasts, alarms our households, threatens, curses, stamps, and storms even upon imaginary or trifling provocations. *Jealousy,* that, through a fatal skill in diabolical optics, sees contempt in all the words of a favourite friend, discovers infidelity in all his actions, lives upon the wicked suspicions it begets, and turns the sweets of the mildest passion into wormwood and gall. *Idolatrous love,* which preys upon the spirits, consumes the flesh, tears the throbbing heart, and when it is disappointed frequently forces its wretched slaves to lay violent hands upon themselves. *Hatred* of our fellow creatures, which keeps us void of tender benevolence, a chief ingredient in the bliss of angels; and fills us with some of the most unhappy sensations belonging to accursed spirits. *Malice,* which takes an unnatural, hellish pleasure in teasing beasts, and hurting men in their persons, properties, or reputation. And the offspring of malice, *revenge,*[*] who always thirsts after mischief or blood: and shares the only delight of devils, when he can repay a real or fancied injury seven-fold. *Hypocrisy,* who borrows the cloak of religion; bids her flexible muscles imitate vital piety; attends at the sacred altars to make a show of her fictitious devotion; there raises her affected zeal, in proportion to the number of the spectators; calls upon God to get the praise of man; and lifts up adulterous eyes and thievish hands to heaven, to procure herself the good things of earth. And hypocrisy's sister, narrow-hearted *bigotry,* who pushes from her civility and good nature; stops he rears against argument and entreaties; calls *huguenots, infidels, papists,* or *heretics,* all who do not directly subscribe to her absurd or impious creeds; dogs them with a malignant eye; throws stones or dirt at them about an empty ceremony, or an indifferent opinion, And, at last, if she can, sets churches or kingdoms on fire, about a turban, a surplice, or a cowl, *Perfidiousness,* who puts on the looks of true benevolence, speaks the language of the warmest affection; with solemn protestations invites men to depend on her sincerity, while she lays a deep plot for their sudden destruction; and with repeated oaths beseeches Heaven to be witness of her artless innocence, while she moves the centre of hell to accomplish her dire designs. The fatal hour is come: her stratagem has succeeded; and she now kisses and betrays, drinks health and poisons; offers a friendly embrace, and gives a deadly stab. *Despair,* who scorns to be beholden to mercy, gives a lie to all the declarations issued from the throne of grace, obstinately turns his wild eyes from the great expiatory sacrifice; and at last, impatient to drink the cup of trembling, wildly looks for some weapon to destroy himself. *Distraction,* begotten by the shocking mixture of two or more of these infernal passions, raised to the highest degrees of extravagance: *distraction,* that wrings her hands, tears her dishevelled hair, fixes her ghastly eyes, turns her swimming

---

[*] Man hard of heart to man! Of horrid things
Most horrid! Mid stupendous, highly strange!
Yet oft his courtesies are smoother wrongs;
Pride brandishes the favours he confers,
And contumelious his humanity:
What then his vengeance? Hear it not, ye stars!
And thou, pale moon! turn paler at the sound:
Man is to man the sorest, surest ill.—
Heaven's Sovereign saves all beings but Himself,
That hideous sight, a naked human heart!   YOUNG.

brains, quenches the last spark of reason; and, like a fierce tiger, must at last be chained by the hand of caution, and confined with iron bars in her dreary dwelling.

And, to close the dismal train, *self murder,* who always points wretched mortals to ponds and rivers, or presents them with cords, razors, pistols, daggers, and poison, and perpetually urges them to the choice of one of them. "You are guilty, miserable creatures," whispers he: "the sun of prosperity is for ever set: the deepest night of distress is come upon you: you are in a hell of wo: the hell prepared for Satan cannot be worse than that which you feel; but it may be more tolerable: take this, and boldly force your passage out of the cursed state in which you groan." He persuades, and his desperate victims, tired of the company of their fellow mortals, fly for refuge to that of devils: they shut their eyes; and, horrible to say, but how much more horrible to do! deliberately venture from one hell into another to seek ease; or, to speak with more truth, leap with all the miseries of a known hell, into all the horrors of one which is unknown.

And are your hearts, O ye sons of men, the favourite seats of this infernal crew? Then shame on the wretch that made the first panegyric on the dignity of human nature! He proved my point: he began in *pride* and ended in *distraction.*

Detestable as these vices and tempers are, where is the natural man that is always free from them? Where is even the child ten years old who never felt most of these vipers, upon some occasion or other, shooting their venom through his lips, darting their baleful influence through his eyes, or, at least, stirring and hissing in his disturbed breast? If any one never felt them he may be pronounced more than mortal: but if he has, his own experience furnishes him with a sensible demonstration that he is a fallen spirit, infected with the poison that rages in the devil himself.

TWENTY-FIRST ARGUMENT.

Bad roots, which vigorously shoot in the spring, will naturally produce their dangerous fruit in the summer. We may therefore go one step farther and ask, Where is the man thirty years old, whose depravity has not broke out in the greatest variety of sinful acts? Among persons of that age, who never were esteemed worse than their neighbours, shall we find a forehead that never betrayed daring insolence? A *cheek* that never indicated concealed guilt by an involuntary blush, or unnatural paleness? A *neck* that never was stretched out in pride and vain confidence? An *eye* that never cast a disdainful, malignant, or wanton look? An *ear* that an evil curiosity never opened to frothy, loose, or defaming discourse! A *tongue* that never was tainted with unedifying, false, indecent, or uncharitable language? A *palate* that never became the seat of luxurious indulgence? A *throat* that never was the channel of excess? A *stomach* that never felt the oppressive load of abused mercies? *Hands* that never plucked or touched the forbidden fruit of pleasing sin? *Feet* that never once moved in the broad downward road of iniquity? And a *bosom* that never heaved under the dreadful workings of some exorbitant passion? Where, in short, is there a *face,* ever so disagreeable, that never was the object of self-worship in a glass? And where a *body,* however deformed, that never was set up as a favourite idol by the fallen spirit that inhabits it?

If iniquity thus works by all the powers and breaks out in all the parts of the human body, we may conclude by woful experience not only that the plague of sin is begun, but that it rages with universal fury; and to use again the evangelical prophet's words, that "from the sole of the foot even to the head" of the natural man, "there is no" spiritual "soundness in him; but wounds, and bruises, and putrefying sores."

TWENTY-SECOND ARGUMENT.

What can be said of each individual may, with the same propriety, be affirmed of all the different nations of the earth. Let an impartial judge take four unconverted men or children from the four parts of the world: let him examine their actions and trace them back to their spring; and if he makes some allowance for the accidental difference of their climate, constitution, taste, and education, he will soon find their dispositions as equally "earthly, sensual," and "devilish" as if they had all been cast in the same mould. Yes, as oak trees are oaks all the world over, though by particular circumstances some grow taller and harder, and some more knotted and crooked than others; so all unregenerate men resemble one another; for all are proud, self willed, impenitent, and "lovers of pleasure more than lovers of God."

Do not sloth, gluttony, drunkenness, and uncleanness; cheating, defrauding, stealing, and oppression; lying, perjury, treachery, and cruelty; stalk openly or lurk secretly every where? Are not all these vices predominant among black and white people, among savage and civilized nations, among Turks and Jews, heathens and Christians? Whether they live on the banks of the Ganges or the Thames, the Mississippi or the Seine? Whether they starve in the snows of Lapland, or burn in the sands of Guinea?

O sin, thou fatal pest, thou soul-destroying plague, would to God thy fixed abode were *only* in the Levant! and that, like the external pestilence, thou wert chiefly confined to the Turkish dominions! But, alas! the gross immorality and profaneness, the various crimes and villanies, the desperate impiety and wild blasphemy under which every kingdom and city have groaned, and still continue to do night and day, over the face of the whole earth, are black spots so similar and symptoms so equally terrible, that we are obliged to confess they must have a common internal principle; which can be no other than a bad habit of soul; a fallen corrupted nature. Yes, the universality and equality of the effects show to an unprejudiced mind that the cause is universal, and equally interwoven with that nature which is common to all nations, and remains the same in all countries and ages.

FIVE OBJECTIONS.

I. IF the self-righteous moralist answers, that "sin and wickedness are not so universal as this argument supposes:" I reply, that the more we are acquainted with ourselves, with the history of the dead and secret transactions of the living; the more we are convinced that, if all are not guilty of *outward* enormities, all are deeply tainted with *spiritual* wickedness.

Even those excellent persons, who, like Jeremiah, have been in part "sanctified before they came forth out of the womb," can from sad experience confess with him, that "the heart is deceitful above all things;" and say with David, "My heart showeth me the wickedness of the ungodly."

Thousands indeed boast of the goodness of their hearts; they flatter themselves that to be righteous, it is enough to avoid the gross acts of intemperance and injustice: with the Pharisees they shut their eyes against the destructive nature of the love of the world, the thirst of praise, the fear of men, the love of ease, sloth, sensuality, indevotion, self righteousness, discontent, impatience, selfishness, carnal security, unbelief, hardness of heart, and a thousand other spiritual evils. Full of self ignorance, like Peter, they imagine there is no combustible matter of wickedness in their breasts, because they are not actually fired by the spark of a suitable temptation. And when they hear what their corrupt nature may one day prompt them to, they cry out with Hazael, "Am I a dog, that I should do this thing?" Nevertheless, by and by they do it, if not outwardly as he did, at least in their vain thoughts by day, or wicked, lewd imaginations by night. So true is the wise man's saying, "He that trusteth his own heart is a fool."

II. "If historians give us frequent accounts of the notorious wickedness of mankind," say the advocates for human excellence, "it is because private virtue is not the subject of history; and to judge of the moral rectitude of the world by the corruption of courts, is as absurd as to estimate the health of a people from an infirmary."

And is private vice any more the subject of history than private virtue? If it were, what folios would contain the fulsome and black accounts of all the lies and scandal, the secret grudges and open quarrels, the filthy talking and malicious jesting, the unkind, or unjust behaviour, the gross or refined intemperance which deluge both town and country?

Suppose the annals of any one numerous family were published, how many volumes might be filled with the details of the undue fondness or forbidden coldness; the variance, animosity, and strife which break out between husbands and wives, parents and children, brothers and sisters, masters and domestics, upper and lower servants, &c! What ridiculous, impertinent scenes would be open to public view! What fretfulness, dissimulation, envy, jealousy, tale bearing, deceit! What concealed suspicions, aggravated charges, false accusations, underhand dealings, imaginary provocations, glaring partiality, insolent behaviour, loud passions!

Was even the best moralist to write the memoirs of his own heart, and give the public a minute account of all his impertinent thoughts and wild imaginations, how many paragraphs would make him blush! How many pages, by presenting the astonished reader with a blank or a blot, would demonstrate the truth of St. Paul's assertion, "They are all gone out of the way, there is none that doeth good," but spoils his best works by a mixture of essential evil! Far then from finding* those vastly superior numbers, who in safe obscurity are virtuously and innocently employed, we may *every where* see the truth of the confession which our objectors make in the church, "There is no health in us."

I say *every where;* for is cabal confined to the court any more than lewdness to the army and profaneness to the navy? Does not the same spirit of self interest and

* See the note [marked †] page 261.

An Appeal to Matter of Fact and Common Sense

intrigue, which influences the choice of ministers of state, preside also at the election of members of parliament, mayors of corporate towns, burgesses of boroughs, and petty officers in a country parish? We may, then, (notwithstanding the unfortunate comparison on which this objection is founded,) conclude, without absurdity, that as all men, sooner or later, by pain, sickness, and death, evidence their natural weakness and mortality, whether they live in *infirmaries,* palaces, or cottages; so all men, sooner or later, by their thoughts, words, and actions, demonstrate their natural corruptions, whether they crowd the jail yard, the drawing room, or the obscure green of a country village.

III. The same objectors will probably reply: "If corruption is universal, it cannot be said to be equal: for numbers lead a very harmless, and not a few a very useful life."

To this I answer, that all have naturally "a heart of unbelief," forgetful of, and "departing from the living God." In this respect "there is no difference; all the world is guilty before God." But thanks be to the Father of mercies, all do not remain so. Many cherish the seed of supernatural grace, which we have from the Redeemer; they bow to his sceptre, become "new creatures, depart from iniquity, and are zealous of good works." And the gracious power that renewed them is at work upon thousands more; hourly restraining them from much evil, and daily exciting them to many useful actions.

With respect to the *harmlessness,* for which some unrenewed persons are remarkable, it cannot spring from a better nature than that of their fellow mortals; for the nature of all *men,* like that of all *wolves,* is the same throughout the whole species. It must then be owing to the restraining grace of God, or to a happier constitution, a stricter education, a deeper sense of decency, or a greater regard for their character; perhaps only to the fear of consequences and to the want of natural boldness, or of a suitable temptation and fair opportunity to sin. Nor are there few who pass for temperate, merely because the diabolical pride lurking in the heart scorns to stoop so low as to indulge their beastly appetites: while others have the undeserved reputation of good-natured, because they find more delight in quietly gratifying their sheepish indolence or brutal desires, than in yielding to the uneasy, boisterous tempers, which they have in common with devils.

As to the *virtues* by which some of the unconverted distinguish themselves from others, they either spring from God's preventing grace, or are only vices in disguise. The love of praise, the desire of honour, and the thirst of gold, excite thousands to laudable designs and useful actions. Wicked men, set on work by these powerful springs, do lying wonders in the moral world, as the magicians did in the land of Egypt.

They counterfeit Divine grace, and for a time seem even to outdo believers themselves. Hence it is that we frequently see the indolent industrious; the coward brave; the covetous charitable; the Pharisee religious; the Magdalene modest; and the dastardly slave of his lusts a bold assertor of public liberty. But the Searcher of hearts is not deceived by fair appearances: he judges of their actions according to the motives whence they spring and the ends for which they are performed. "You are," says he to all these seemingly virtuous sinners, "like whited sepulchres, which indeed appear beautiful outwardly; but within are full of dead men's bones and of all uncleanness."

Were I to describe the saints of the world by a comparison, I would say that some of them resemble persons who artfully conceal their ulcers under the most agreeable appearance of cleanliness and health. Many that admire their faces and looks, little suspect what a putrid, virulent fluid runs out of their *secret* sores. Others of them whose hypocrisy is not of so gross a kind, are like persons infected with a mortal disease, who, though the mass of their blood is tainted, and some noble part attacked, still walk about, do business, and look as fresh coloured as if they were the picture of health. Ye sons of Esculapius, who, without feeling their pulse and carefully weighing every symptom, pronounce them very well upon their look alone, do ye not blunder in physic, just as my objectors do in divinity?

IV. But still they urge, "that it is wrong to father our sinfulness upon a pretended natural depravity, when it may be entirely owing to the force of ill example, the influence of a bad education, or the strong ferments of youthful blood."

All these, I reply, like rich soil and rank manure, cause original corruption to shoot the higher, but do not form its pernicious seeds. That these seeds lurk within the heart, before they are forced up by the heat of temptation, appears indubitable, if we consider, (1.) That all children, on particular occasions, manifest some early inclination to those sins which the feebleness of their bodily organs, and the want of proper ferments in their blood, do not permit them to commit. (2.) That infants betray envy, ill humour, impatience, selfishness, and obstinacy, even before they can take particular notice of ill examples, and understand bad counsels: and, (3.) That though uncleanliness, fornication, and adultery, on account of the shame and danger attending them, are committed with so much secrecy, that the *examples* of them are seldom, if ever, given in public; they are, nevertheless, some of the crimes which are most universally or eagerly committed.

Beside, if we were not more inclined to vice than virtue, good examples would be as common, and have as much force as bad ones. Therefore, the generality of bad examples cannot arise but from the general sinfulness of man; and to account for this general sinfulness by the generality of bad examples, is *begging* the question, and not *proving* the point.

Add to this, that as weeds, since the curse, grow even in fields sown with the best wheat; so vice, since the fall, grows in the midst of the best examples, and the most excellent education: witness the barbarous crimes committed by pious Jacob's children, and penitent Adam's eldest son.

V. "But if Cain sinned," say our objectors, "and all mankind sin also, it is no more than Adam himself once did by his own free choice, though he was created as exempt from original depravity as an angel. What need is there then to suppose that he communicated to his posterity an inbred proneness to sin?"

To this I reply: It is not one accident or single event, but a continual repetition of the same event, that proves a proneness. If a man, who is perfectly in his senses, by some unforeseen accident falls into a fit of madness, we may account for his misfortune from that accident; and no certain judgment can be formed of the bodily habit of his family. But if all his children, through a hundred generations, are not only subject to the same mad fits, but also die in consequence of them, in all sorts of climates, and under all sorts of physicians; common sense will not allow us to doubt, that it is *now* a family disorder, incurable by human art. The man is Adam, the family mankind, and the madness sin. Reader, you are desired to make the application.

TWENTY-THIRD ARGUMENT.

"But all are not employed in sin and wickedness, for many go through a constant round of *innocent diversions;* and these, at least, must be *innocent* and *happy."* Let us then consider the amusements of mankind; or, rather, without stopping to look at the wise dance of the Israelites round the golden calf, and the modest, sober, and humane diversions of the heathens, in the festivals of their lewd, drunken, and bloody gods; let us only see how far *our own* pleasures demonstrate the *innocence* and *happiness* of mankind.

How excessively foolish are the plays of children! How full of mischief and cruelty the sports of boys! How vain, foppish, and frothy the joys of young people! And how much below the dignity of upright, pure creatures, the snares that persons of different sexes perpetually lay for each other? When they are together, is not this their favourite amusement, till they are deservedly caught in the net which they imprudently spread? But see them asunder.

Here a circle of idle women, supping a decoction of Indian herbs, talk or laugh all together like so many chirping birds or chattering monkeys, and, scandal excepted, every way to as good purpose. And there a club of graver men blow, by the hour, clouds of stinking smoke out of their mouth, or wash it down their throat with repeated draughts of intoxicating liquors. The strong fumes have already reached their heads; and while some stagger home, others triumphantly keep the field of excess; though one is already stamped with the heaviness of the ox, another worked up to the fierceness and roar of the lion, and the third brought down to the filthiness of the vomiting dog.

Leave them at their *manly* sport to follow those musical sounds, mixed with a noise of stamping; and you will find others profusely perspiring and violently fatiguing themselves, in skipping up and down a room for a whole night, and ridiculously turning their backs and faces to each other a hundred different ways. Would not a man of sense prefer running ten miles upon a *useful* errand, to this useless manner of losing his rest, heating his blood, exhausting his spirits, unfitting himself for the duties of the following day, and laying the foundation of a putrid fever, or a consumption, by breathing the midnight air corrupted by clouds of dust, by the unwholesome fumes of candles, and by the more pernicious steam, that issues from the bodies of many persons, who use a strong exercise in a confined place.

In the next room, indeed, they are more quiet; but are they more rationally employed? Why do they so earnestly rattle those ivory cubes, and so anxiously study those packs of loose and spotted leaves? Is happiness graven upon the one, or stamped upon the other? Answer, ye gamesters, who curse your stars as ye go home with an empty purse and a heart full of rage!

"We hope there is no harm in taking an innocent game at cards," reply a ridiculous party of superannuated old ladies; "gain is not our aim, we only play to kill time." You are not then so well employed as the foolish heathen emperor who amused himself in killing troublesome flies and wearisome time together. The delight of rational creatures, much more of Christians on the brink of the grave, is to redeem, improve, and solidly enjoy time; but yours, alas! consists in the bare, irreparable *loss* of that invaluable treasure. O, What account will you give of the souls you neglect, and the talents you bury?

> And shall we kill each day? If trifling kill,
> Sure vice must butcher: O! what heaps of slain
> Call out for vengeance on us! Time destroy'd
> In suicide, where more than blood is spilt.   YOUNG.

And are *public* diversions better evidences of our innocence and happiness? Let reason decide. In cities, some are lavish of the gold which should be laid by for the payment of their debts, or the relief of the poor, to buy an opportunity of acting under a mask an impertinent or immodest part without a blush; and others are guilty of the same injustice or prodigality, that they may be entitled to the honour of waiting upon a company of idle buffoons, and seeing them act what would make a modest woman blush, or hearing them speak what persons of true piety, or pure morals, would gladly pay them never to utter.

Are *country* amusements more rational and innocent? What shall we say of those Christian, or rather heathenish, festivals, called *wakes,* annually kept in honour of the saints to whom the parish church was formerly dedicated? Are they not celebrated with the idleness, vanity, and debauchery of the Floralia; with the noise, riots, and frantic mirth of the bacchanals; rather than with the decent solemnity, pious cheerfulness, and strict temperance, which characterize the religion of the holy Jesus?

The *Assizes* are held, the judge passes an awful sentence of transportation or death upon guilty wretches who stand pale and trembling before his tribunal; and twenty couple of gay gentlemen and ladies, as if they rejoiced in the infamy and destruction of their fellow mortals, hire, on the occasion, a band of musicians, and dance all night, perhaps in the very apartment where the distracted victims of justice, a few hours before, wrung their hands, and rattled their irons.

The *races* are advertised; all the country is in motion; neither business, rain, nor storm can prevent thousands from running for miles, and sometimes through the worst of roads, to feast their eyes upon the danger of their fellow creatures, and divert themselves with the misery of the most useful animals. Daring mortals hazard their necks upon swift coursers which are tortured by the severest lashes of the whip, and incessant pricks or tearing gashes of the spur, that they may exert their utmost force, strain every nerve, and make continued efforts even beyond the power of nature: whence (to say nothing of fatal accidents, which yet, alas! too frequently happen) they sometimes pant away their wretched lives in a bath of sweat and blood; and all this, that they may afford a barbarous pleasure to their idle, wanton, and barbarous beholders.

In one place the inhuman sport is afforded by an unhappy bird, fixed at some distance, that the sons of cruelty may long exercise their merciless skill in its lingering and painful destruction; or by two of them trained up and high fed for the battle. The hour fixed for the obstinate engagement is come; and as if it was not enough that they should pick each other's eyes out with the strong bills that nature has given them; human malice, or rather diabolical cruelty, comes to the assistance of their native fierceness. Silver spurs or steel talons, sharper than those of the eagle, are barbarously fastened to their feet; thus armed, they are excited to leap at each other, and, in a hundred repeated onsets, to tear their feathers and flesh, as if they were contending vultures; and if at last one blinded, covered with blood and wounds, and unable to stand any longer the metallic claws of his antagonist, enters into the agonies of death; the numerous ring of stamping, clapping, shouting, eagerly betting, or horridly cursing spectators, is as highly delighted, as if the tortured, dying creature was the common enemy of mankind.

In another place a multitude of spectators is delightfully entertained by two brawny men, who unmercifully knock one another down, as if they were oxen appointed for the slaughter, and continue the savage play, till one, with his flesh bruised and his bones shattered, bleeding, and gasping as in the pangs of death, yields to his antagonist, and thus puts an end to the shocking sport.

But it is, perhaps, a different spectacle that recommends itself to the bloody taste of our baptized heathens. Fierce dogs are excited by fiercer men, with fury to fasten upon the nose, or tear out the eyes of a poor confined animal, which pierces the sky with his painful and lamentable bellowings, enough to force compassion from the heart of barbarians, not totally lost to all sense of humanity: while, in the meantime, the surrounding savage mob rends the very heavens with the most horrid imprecations, and repeated shouts of applauding joy; sporting themselves with that very misery which human nature (were it not deplorably corrupted) would teach them to alleviate.*

These are thy favourite amusements, O England, thou centre of the civilized world, where reformed Christianity, deep-thinking wisdom, and polite learning, with all its refinements, have fixed their abode! But, in the name of common sense, how can we clear them from the imputation of absurdity, folly, and madness? And by what means can they be reconciled, I will not say to the religion of the meek Jesus, but to the philosophy of a Plato, or calm reason of any thinking man? How perverted must be the taste, how irrational and cruel the diversions of barbarians, in other parts of the globe! And how applicable to all the wise man's observation, "Foolishness is bound up in the heart of a child, and madness in the breasts of the sons of men!"

TWENTY-FOURTH ARGUMENT.

The total corruption of our nature appears, not only in the inclination of mankind to pursue irrational and cruel amusements, but in their general propensity to commit the most *unprofitable, ridiculous, inhuman, impious,* and *diabolical* sins.

---

* "I ever thought," says Judge Hale, in his Contemplations, "that there is a certain degree of justice due from man to the creatures, as from man to man; and that an excessive use of the creature's labour is an injustice for which he must account. I have, therefore, always esteemed it as a part of my duty, and it has been always my practice, to be merciful to my beasts; and upon the same account I have declined any cruelty to any of thy creatures, and, as much as I might, prevented it in others as a tyranny. I have abhorred those sports that consist in the torturing of thy creatures: and if any noxious creature must be destroyed, or creatures for food must be taken, it has been my practice to do it in a manner that may be with the least torture or cruelty to the creature; ever remembering, that though God has given us a dominion over his creatures, yet it is under a law of justice, prudence, and moderation; otherwise we should become *tyrants* and not *lords* over God's creatures; and, therefore, those things of this nature which others have *practised as recreations,* I have *avoided as sins.*"

1st. The most *unprofitable:* for instance, that of sporting, in profane oaths and curses, with the tremendous name of the Supreme Being. "Because of swearing the land mourneth," said a prophet, thousands of years ago; and what land even in Christendom, yea, what parish in this reformed island mourns not, or ought not to mourn, for the same provoking crime?—a crime which is the hellish offspring of practical Atheism and heathenish insolence—a crime that brings neither profit, honour, nor pleasure, to the profane wretch who commits it—a crime for which he may be put to open shame, forced to appear before a magistrate, and sent for ten days to the house of correction, unless he pays an ignominious fine; and, what is more awful still, a crime which, if persisted in, will one day cause him to gnaw his impious tongue in the severest torments. Surely man, who drinks this insipid and yet destructive iniquity like water, must have his moral taste strangely vitiated, not to say diabolically perverted.

2dly. The most *ridiculous* sins. In what country, town, or village, do not women betray their silly vanity? Is it not the same foolish disposition of heart which makes them bore their ears in Europe, and slit their noses in America, that they may unnaturally graft in their flesh pieces of glass, shining pebbles, glittering gold, or trinkets of meaner metal? And when female Hottentots fancy they add to the importance of their filthy person, by some yards of the bloody intestines of a beast twisted round their arms or necks, do they not evidence the very spirit of the ladies in our hemisphere, who too often measure their dignity by the yards of coloured silk bands with which they crown themselves, and turn the grave matron into a pitiful May queen?

3dly. The most *inhuman* sins. "A hundred thousand mad animals, whose heads are covered with hats," says Voltaire, "advance to kill or be killed by the like number of their fellow mortals, covered with turbans. By this strange procedure they want, at best, to decide whether a tract of land, to which none of them all lays any claim, shall belong to a certain man whom they call Sultan, or to another whom they name Cesar, neither of whom ever saw, or will see, the spot so furiously contended for. And very few of those creatures, who thus mutually butcher one another, ever beheld the animal for whom they cut each other's throats! From time immemorial this has been the way of mankind almost all over the earth. What an excess of madness is this! And how deservedly might a superior being crush to atoms this earthly ball, the bloody nest of such ridiculous murderers!"

The same author makes elsewhere the following reflections on the same melancholy subject: —"Famine, pestilence, and war, are the three most famous ingredients of this lower world. The two first come from God; but the last, in which all three concur, comes from the imagination of princes or ministers. A king fancies that he has a right to a distant province. He raises a multitude of men, who have nothing to do, and nothing to lose; gives them a red coat and a laced hat, and makes them wheel to the right, wheel to the left, and march to glory. Five or six of these belligerent powers sometimes engage together, three against three, or two against four. But whatever part they take, they all agree in one point, which is, to do their neighbour all possible mischief. The most astonishing thing belonging to their infernal undertaking is, that every ringleader of those murderers gets his colours consecrated, and solemnly blessed in the name of God, before he marches up to the destruction of his fellow creatures. If a chief warrior has had the good fortune of getting only two or three thousand men slaughtered, he does not think it worth his while to thank God for it. But if ten thousand have been destroyed by fire and sword, and if, to complete this good fortune, some capital city has been totally overthrown; a day of public thanksgiving is appointed on the joyful occasion. Is not that a fine art which carries such desolation through the earth; and, one year with another, destroys forty thousand men out of a hundred thousand?"

4thly. The most *impious* sins: for instance, that of *idolatry*. "Before the coming of Christ," says a late divine, "all the polite and barbarous nations among the heathens plunged into it with equal blindness. And the Jews were so strongly wedded to it, that God's miraculous interposition, both by dreadful judgments and astonishing mercies, could not, for eight hundred years, restrain them from committing it in the grossest manner."

Nor need we look at either heathens or Jews to see the proneness of mankind to that detestable crime: Christians alone can prove the charge. To this day the greatest part of them pray to dead men and dead women; bow to images of stone, and crosses of wood; and make, adore, and swallow down, the wafer god. And those who pity them for this ridiculous idolatry, till converting grace interposes, daily "set up their idols in their hearts," and, without going to the plain of Dura, sacrifice all to the king's "golden image."

And 5thly. The most *diabolical* sin; *persecution*, that favourite offspring of Satan, transformed into an angel of light. *Persecution*, that bloody, hypocritical monster, which carries a Bible, a liturgy, and a bundle of canons in one hand; with fire fagots, and all the weapons invented by cruelty in the other; and with sanctified looks, distresses, racks, or murders men, either because they love God, or because they cannot all think alike.

Time would fail to tell of those who, on religious accounts, have been stoned and sawn asunder by the Jews, cast to the lions, and burned by the heathens, strangled and impaled by the Mohammedans, and butchered all manner of ways by the Christians.

Yes, we must confess it, Christian Rome has glutted herself with the blood of martyrs, which heathenish Rome had but comparatively tasted. And when Protestants fled from her bloody pale, they brought along with them too much of her bloody spirit. Prove the sad assertion, poor Servetus! When a Romish inquisition had forced thee to fly to Geneva, what reception didst thou meet with in that reformed city? Alas! the Papists had burned thee in effigy; the Protestants burned thee in reality, and Moloch triumphed to see the two opposite parties agree in offering him the human sacrifice.

So universally restless is the spirit of persecution which inspires the unrenewed part of mankind, that when people of the same religion have no outward opposer to tear, they bark at, bite, and devour one another. Is it not the same bitter zeal that made the Pharisees and Sadducees among the Jews, and now makes the sects of Ali and Omar among the Mohammedans, those of the Jansenists and Molinists among the Papists, and those of the Calvinists and Arminians among the Protestants, oppose each other with such acrimony and virulence?

But let us look around us at home. When persecuting Popery had almost expired in the fires in which it burned our first Churchmen, how soon did those who survived them commence persecutors of the Presbyterians? When these, forced to fly to New-England for rest, got there the staff of power in their hand, did they not, in their turn, fall upon and even hang the Quakers? And now that an act of toleration binds the monster, and the lash of pens, consecrated to the defence of our civil and religious liberties, makes him either afraid or ashamed of roaring aloud for his prey; does he not show, by his supercilious looks, malicious sneers, and settled contempt of vital piety, what he would do should an opportunity offer? And does he not still, under artful pretences, go to the utmost length of his chain, to wound the reputation of those whom he cannot devour, and inflict at least *academic death** upon those whose persons are happily secured from his rage?

O ye unconverted among mankind, if all these abominations every where break out upon you, what cages of unclean birds, what nests swarming with cruel, vipers, are your "deceitful and desperately wicked hearts!"

TWENTY-FIFTH ARGUMENT.

How dreadfully fallen is man, if he has not only a propensity to commit the above-mentioned sins, but to transgress the Divine commands with a variety of shocking aggravations! Yes, mankind are prone to sin:—

I. *Immediately*, by a kind of evil instinct: as children, who peevishly strike the very breast they suck, and betray the rage of their little hearts by sobbing and swelling, sometimes till, by forcing their bowels out of their place, they bring a rupture upon themselves; and frequently till they are black in the faces, and almost suffocated. II. *Deliberately*, as those who, having life and death clearly set before them, wilfully and obstinately choose the way that leads to certain destruction. III. *Repeatedly:* witness liars, who, because their crime costs them but a breath, frequently commit it at every breath. IV. *Continually*, as rakes, who would make their whole life one uninterrupted scene of debauchery, if their exhausted strength, or purse, did not force them to intermit their lewd practices; though not without a promise to renew them again at the first convenient opportunity. V. *Treacherously*, as those Christians who forget Divine mercies and their own repeated resolutions, break through the solemn vows and promises made in their sacraments, and, sinning with a high hand *against their profession*, perfidiously fly in the face of their conscience, the Church, and their Saviour. VI. *Daringly*, as those who steal under the gallows, openly insult their parents or their king, laugh at all laws, human and Divine, and put to defiance all that are invested with power to see them executed. VII. *Triumphantly*, *as* the vast number of those who glory in their shame, sound aloud the trumpet of their own wickedness, and boast of their horrid, repeated debaucheries, as admirable and praiseworthy deeds. VIII. *Progressively*, till they have filled up the measure of their iniquities, as *individuals:* witness Judas, who, from covetousness proceeded to hypocrisy, theft, treason, despair, and self murder: or, as a *nation*, witness the Jews, who, after despising and killing their prophets, rejected the Son of God; affirmed he was mad; stigmatized him with the name of *deceiver;* said he was *Beelzebub* himself; offered him all manner of indignities; bought his blood; prayed it might be on them and their children; rested not till they had put the *Prince of Life* to the most ignominious death; and, horrible to

---

* See Pietas Oxoniensis.

say! made sport with the groans which rent the rocks around them, and threw the earth into convulsions under their feet. IX. *Unnaturally*: (1.) By *astonishing barbarities: as* the women who murder their own children; the Greeks and Romans, who exposed them to be the living prey of wild beasts: the savages, who knock their aged parents on the head; the cannibals, who roast and eat their prisoners of war; and some revengeful people, who, to taste all the sweetness of their devilish passion, have murdered their enemy, and eaten up his liver and heart. (2.) By the most *diabolical superstitions:* as the Israelites, who, when they had "learned the works of the heathens, sacrificed their sons and their daughters to devils; and, by the horrible practices of witchcraft, endeavoured to raise and deal with infernal spirits. And (3,) by the most *preposterous gratifications of sense:* witness the incests* and rapes committed in this land; the infamous fires, which drew fire and brimstone down from heaven upon accursed cities; and the horrid lusts of the Canaanites, though, alas! not confined to Canaan, which gave birth to the laws recorded Leviticus xviii:7, 23, and xx:16;† laws that are at once the disgrace of mankind, and the proof of my assertion. X. What is most astonishing of all, by *apostasy*: as those who, having "begun in the Spirit," and "tasted" the bitterness of repentance, "the good word of God, and the powers of the world to come, make shipwreck of the faith, deny the Lord that bought them, account the blood of the covenant wherewith they were sanctified an unholy thing;" and so scandalously "end in the flesh," that they are justly compared to "trees withered, plucked up by the roots, twice dead," and to "raging waves of the sea, foaming out their own shame, to whom is reserved the blackness of darkness for ever."

Good God! what line can fathom an abyss of corruption, the overflowings of which are more or less attended with these multiplied and shocking aggravations?

TWENTY-SIXTH ARGUMENT.

If the force of a torrent may be known by the height and number of the banks which it overflows, the strength of this corruption will be rightly estimated from the high and numerous dikes raised to stem it, which nevertheless it continually breaks through.

Ignorance and debauchery, injustice and impiety, in all their shapes, still overspread the whole earth; notwithstanding innumerable means used, in all ages, to suppress and prevent them.

The almost total extirpation of mankind by the deluge, the fiery showers that consumed Sodom, the ten Egyptian plagues, the entire excision of whole nations who were once famous for their wickedness, the captivities of the Jews, the destruction of

---

*The reason which engaged the publisher of these sheets to preach to some of the colliers in his neighbourhood, was the horrid length they went in immorality. One of them, whose father was hanged, upon returning himself from transportation, in cool blood attempted to ravish his own daughter, in the presence of his own wife, and was just prevented from completing his crime, by the utmost exertion of the united strength of the mother and the child. When brutish ignorance and heathenish wickedness break out into such unnatural enormities, who would not break through the hedge of canonical regularity?

† In the last century an Irish bishop was dearly convicted of the crime forbidden in those laws, and suffered death for it.

thousands of cities and kingdoms, and millions of more private judgments, never fully stopped immorality in any one country.

The striking miracles wrought by prophets, the alarming sermons preached by divines, the infinite number of good books published in almost all languages, and the founding of myriads of churches, religious houses, schools, colleges, and universities, have not yet caused impiety to hide its brazen face any where. The making of all sorts of excellent laws, the appointing of magistrates and judges to put them in force, the forming of associations for the reformation of manners, the filling of thousands of prisons, and erecting of millions of racks and gallows, have not yet suppressed one vice.

And what is most amazing of all, the life, miracles, sufferings, death, and heavenly doctrine of the Son of God; the labours, writings, and martyrdom of his disciples; the example and entreaties of millions that have lived and died in the faith; the inexpressible horrors and frightful warnings of thousands of wicked men, who have testified in their last moments that they had worked out their damnation, and were just going to their own place; the blood of myriads of martyrs, the strivings of the Holy Spirit, the dreadful curses of the law, and the glorious promises of the Gospel. All these means together have not extirpated immorality and profaneness out of one single town or village in all the world; no, nor out of one single family for any length of time. And this will probably continue to be the desperate case of mankind, till the Lord lays to his powerful hand; seconds these means by the *continued* strokes of the sword of his Spirit; "pleads by fire and sword with all flesh;" and, according to his promise, causes "righteousness to cover the earth as the water covers the sea."

Is not this a demonstration founded on matter of fact, that human corruption is not only deep as the ocean, but impetuous as an overflowing river, which breaks down all its banks, and leaves marks of devastation in every place? This will still appear in a clearer light, if we consider the strong opposition which our natural depravity makes to Divine grace in the unconverted.

TWENTY-SEVENTH ARGUMENT.

When the Lord, by the rod of affliction, "the sword of the Spirit," and the power of his grace, attacks the hard heart of a sinner, how obstinately does he resist the sharp, though gracious operation! To make an honourable and vigorous defence, he puts on the shining robes of his formality; he stands firm in the boasted armour of his moral powers; he "daubs with untempered mortar" the ruinous "wall" of his conduct; with self-righteous resolutions and Pharisaic professions of virtue, he builds, as he thinks, an impregnable tower; he musters and draws up in battle array his poor works, artfully putting in the front those that make the finest appearance, and carefully concealing the vices which he can neither disguise, nor dress up in the regimentals of virtue.

In the meantime he prepares "the carnal weapons of" his "warfare," and raises the battery of a multitude of objections to silence the truth that begins to gall him. He affirms, "The preachers of it are *deceivers* and *madmen*," till he sees the Jews and heathens fixed, even upon Christ and St. Paul, the very same opprobrious names: he calls it "a new doctrine," till he is obliged to acknowledge that it is as old as the reformers, the apostles, and the prophets. He says, "It is fancy, delusion, enthusiasm," till the blessed effects of it, on true believers, constrain him to drop the trite and slanderous assertion. He declares that it "drives people out of their senses, or makes them melancholy," till he is compelled to confess that "the fear of the Lord is the beginning of wisdom," and that none are so happy and joyful as those who truly love, and zealously serve God: he urges, that "it destroys good works," till a sight of the readiness of believers, and of his own backwardness to perform them, makes him ashamed of the groundless accusation. He will tell you twenty times over, "Where is no need of so much ado," till he discovers the folly of being careless on the brink of *eternal ruin,* and observes, that the nearness of *temporal danger* puts him upon the utmost exertion of his powers: perhaps to get himself a name among his profane companions, he lampoons the Scriptures, or "casts out firebrands and arrows" against the despised disciples of Jesus: "They are all poor and illiterate," says he, "fools or knaves, cheats and hypocrites," &c, &c, till the word of God stops his mouth, and he sees himself the greatest hypocrite with whom he is acquainted.

When by such heavy charges he has long kept off the truth from his heart, and the servants of God from his company, this kind of ammunition begins to fail; and he barricades himself with the fear of being undone in his circumstances, till experience convinces him that "no good thing shall God withhold from them that live a godly life," and that "all things shall be added to them who seek first the kingdom of God." He then hides himself in the crowd of the ungodly, and says, "If he perishes, many will share the same fate," till he sees the glaring absurdity of going to hell for the sake of company. He shelters at last under the protection of the rich, the great, the learned despisers of Christ and the cross, till the mines of their wickedness, springing on all sides around him, make him fly "to the sanctuary of the Lord;" and there he sees the ways, and "understands the ends of these men."

When all his batteries are silenced, and a breach is made in his conscience, he looks out for some secret way to leave Sodom, without being taken notice of and derided by those who fight under Satan's banner; and the fear of being taken for one of them that "fly from the wrath to come," and openly take the part of a holy God against a sinful world, "pierces him through with many sorrows."

Are the outworks taken? has he been forced to part with his gross immoralities? he has generally recourse to a variety of stratagems: sometimes he publicly dismisses Satan's garrison, "fleshly lusts which war against the" godly, and keep under the ungodly "soul;" but it is only to let them in again secretly, either one by one, or with forces *seven* times greater, "so that his last state is worse than the first." At other times he hoists up the white flag of truth, apparently yields to conviction, favours the ministers of the Gospel, admits the language of Canaan, and warmly contends for evangelical doctrines; but, alas! the place has not surrendered, his heart is not given up to God; spiritual wickedness, under fair shows of zeal, still keeps possession for "the god of this world;" and the shrewd hypocrite artfuly imitates the behaviour of a true Israelite, just as "Satan transforms himself into an angel of light."

Is he at last deeply convinced that the only means of escaping destruction, and capitulating to advantage, is to deliver up the traitor, *sin?* Yet what a long parley does he hold about it! What a multitude of plausible reasons does he advance to put it off from day to day! "He is yet young: the Lord is merciful: all have their foibles: we are here in an imperfect state: it is a little sin: it may be consistent with loyalty to God: it hurts nobody but himself: many pious men were once guilty of it: by and by he will repent as they did," &c, &c. When louder summons and increasing fears compel him to renounce "the lusts of the flesh," how strongly does he plead for *those of the mind!* And after he has given up his bosom sin with his lips, how treacherously does he hide it in the inmost recesses of his heart!

Never did a besieged town dispute the ground with such obstinacy, and hold it out by such a variety of stratagems, as corrupt man stands it out against the repeated attacks of truth and grace. If he yields at all, it is seldom before he is brought to the greatest extremity. He "feeds on the dust of the earth;" he tries to "fill his" soul "with the husks" of vanity; and fares hard on sounds, names, forms, opinions, withered experience, dry notions of faith, and empty professions of hope, and fawning shows of love, till "the famine arises," and the intolerable want of substantial bread forces him to surrender at discretion, and without reserve.

Some stand it out thus, against the God of their salvation, ten or twenty years; and others never yield, till the terrors of death storm their affrighted souls, their last sickness batters down their tortured bodies, and "the poison of the arrows of the Almighty drinks up their" wasted "spirits." What a strong proof is this of the inveteracy and obstinacy of our corruption!

TWENTY-EIGHTH ARGUMENT.

But a still stronger may be drawn from the amazing struggles of God's children with their depravity, even after they have, through grace, powerfully subdued and gloriously triumphed over it. Their Redeemer himself "is the Captain of their salvation:" they are embarked with him, and bound for heaven; they look at the compass of God's word; they hold the rudder of sincerity; they crowd all the sails of their good resolutions, and pious affections, to catch the gales of Divine assistance; they "exhort one another daily" to ply the oars of faith and prayer with watchful industry; tears of deep repentance and fervent desire often bedew their faces in the pious toil: they would rather die than draw back to perdition; but, alas! the stream of corruption is so impetuous that it often prevents their making any sensible progress in their spiritual voyage; and if in an unguarded hour they drop the oar, and faint in "the work of faith, the patience of hope," or "the labour of love," they are presently carried down into the dead sea of religious formality, or the whirlpools of scandalous wickedness. Witness the lukewarmness of the Laodiceans, the adultery of David, the perjury of Peter, the final apostasy of Judas, and the shameful flight of all the disciples.

TWENTY-NINTH ARGUMENT.

When evidences of the most opposite interest agree in their deposition to a matter of fact, its truth is greatly corroborated. To the last argument, taken from some sad experiences of God's people, I shall therefore add one, drawn from the religious rites of Paganism, the confession of ancient heathens, and the testimony of modern Deists.

When the heathens made their temples stream with the blood of slaughtered hecatombs, did they not explicitly deprecate the wrath of Heaven and impending destruction? And was it not a sense of their guilt and danger; and a hope that the punishment they deserved might be transferred to their bleeding victims, which gave birth to their numerous expiatory and propitiatory sacrifices? If this must be granted, it is plain those sacrifices were so many proofs that the considerate heathens were not utter strangers to their corruption and danger.

But let them speak their own sentiments. Not to mention their allegorical fables of Prometheus, who brought a curse upon earth by stealing fire out of heaven; and of Pandora, whose fatal curiosity let all sorts of woes and diseases loose upon mankind; does not Ovid in his Metamorphoses give a striking account of the fall, and its dreadful consequences? Read his description of the golden age, and you see Adam in paradise; proceed to the iron age, and you behold the horrid picture of our consummate wickedness.

If the ancients had no idea of that native propensity to evil, which we call *original depravity*, what did Plato mean by our "natural wickedness."* And Pythagoras, by "the fatal companion, the noxious strife that lurks within us, and was born along with us?"† Did not Solon take for his motto the well-known saying, which, though so much neglected now, was formerly written in golden capitals over the door of Apollo's temple at Delphos. "Know thyself?"‡ Are we not informed by heathen historians, that Socrates, the prince of the Greek sages, acknowledged he was naturally prone to the grossest vices? Does not Seneca, the best of the Roman philosophers, observe, "We are born in such a condition that we are not subject to fewer disorders of the mind than of the body?"§ Yea, that "all vices are in all men, though they do not break out in every one;"** and that "to confess them is the beginning of our cure?"†† And had not Cicero lamented before Seneca, that "men are brought into life by nature as a stepmother, with a naked, frail, and infirm body; and a soul prone to divers lusts?"

Even some of the sprightliest poets bear their testimony to the mournful truth I contend for. Propertius could say, "Every body has a vice to which he is inclined by nature."‡‡ Horace declared that" no man is born free from vices," and that "he is the best man who is oppressed with the least:"§§ that "mankind rush into wickedness, and always desire what is forbidden:"*** that "youth hath the softness of wax to receive vicious impressions, and the hardness of a rock to resist virtuous admonitions:"††† in a word, that "we are mad enough to attack heaven itself, and" that "our repeated crimes do not suffer the God of heaven to lay by his wrathful thunderbolts."‡‡‡

---

* Κακια εν φυσει. Hence that excellent definition of true religion. Θεραπεια ψυχης, *The cure of a diseased soul.*

　　† Αυγρη γαρ συνοπαδος ερις Βλαπτουσα λεληθεν,
　　Συμφυτος.　　　　　　　AUR. CARM.

‡ Γνωθι σεαυτον.

§ Hac conditione nati sumus; animalia obnoxia non paucioribus animi quam corporis morbis.

** Omnia in omnibus vitia sunt, sed non omnia in singulis extant.

　　†† Vitia sua confiteri sanitatis principium est.

　　‡‡ Unicuique dedit vitium natura creato.

　　§§ Nam vitiis nemo sine nascitur, optimus ille est
　　　Qui minimis urgetur.

　　*** Gens humana ruit per vetitum nefas;
　　　Nitimur in vetitum semper cupimusque negata.

　　††† Cereus in vitium fiecti, monitoribus asper.

　　‡‡‡ Cælum ipsum petimus stultitia; neque

And Juvenal, as if he had understood what St. Paul says of the "carnal mind," affirms that "nature unchangeably fixed" tends, yea, "runs back to wickedness,"* as bodies to their centre.

Thus the very depositions of the heathens, in their lucid intervals, as well as their sacrifices, prove the depravity and danger of mankind. And so does likewise the testimony of some of our modern Deistical philosophers.

The ingenious author of a book called "Philosophical Inquiries concerning the Americans," informs us it is a custom among some Indians, that as soon as the wife is delivered of a child the husband must take to his bed, where he is waited on by the poor woman who should have been brought there; and that to this day the same ridiculous custom prevails in some parts of *France*. "From this and other instances," says our inquirer, "we may collect that, however men may differ in other points, there is a most striking conformity among them in ABSURDITY."

The same philosopher, who is by no means tainted with what some persons are pleased to call *enthusiasm*, confirms the doctrine of our natural depravity by the following anecdote, and the ironical observation with which it is dosed:—The Esquimaux, (the wildest and most sottish people in all America,) call themselves *men*, and all other nations *barbarians*. "Human vanity, we see, thrives equally well in all climates; in Labrador as in Asia. Beneficent nature has dealt out as much of this comfortable quality to a Greenlander as to the most consummate French *petit-maitre.*"

The following testimony is so much the more striking, as it comes from one of the greatest poets, philosophers, and Deists, of this present free-thinking age:—"Who can, without horror, consider the whole earth as the empire of destruction? It abounds in wonders, it abounds also in victims; it is a vast field of carnage and contagion. Every species is, without pity, pursued and torn to pieces, through the earth, and air, and water. In man there is more wretchedness than in all other animals put together: he smarts continually under two scourges which other animals never feel; anxiety and listlessness in appetence, which makes him weary of himself. He loves life, and yet he knows that he must die. If he enjoys some transient good, for which he is thankful to Heaven, he suffers various evils, and is at last devoured by worms. This knowledge is his fatal prerogative: other animals have it not. He feels it every moment rankling and corroding in his breast. Yet he spends the transient moment of his existence in diffusing the misery that he suffers; in cutting the throats of his fellow creatures for pay; in cheating and being cheated, in robbing and being robbed, in serving that he may command, and in repenting of all that he does. The bulk of mankind are nothing more than a crowd of wretches, equally criminal and unfortunate, and the globe contains rather carcasses than men. I tremble upon a review of this dreadful picture, to find that it implies a complaint against Providence, and I wish that I had never been born." (*Voltaire's Gospel of the Day*.")†

Per nostrum patimur scelus
Iracunda Jovem ponere fulmina.
* Ad mores natura recurrit
Damnatos, fixa et mutari nescia.
† Wild error is often the guide, and glaring contradiction the badge, both of those who reject revelation, like Voltaire, and of those who indirectly set aside one half of it, like the Pharisees and Antinomians around us. See a striking proof of it. This very author in another book, (O, see what *antichristian morality comes to!*) represents the horrible sin of *Sodom,* as an *"excusable mistake of nature,"* and

THIRTIETH ARGUMENT.

And yet, O strange infatuation! *Vain man will be wise,* and wicked man pretends to be righteous! Far from repenting in the dust, he pleads his innocence, and claims the rewards of imaginary merit! Incredible as the assertion is, a thousand witnesses are ready to confirm it.

Come forth, ye natural sons of virtue, who with scornful boasts attack the doctrine of man's depravity. To drown the whispers of reason and experience, sound each your own trumpet: thank God "you are not as other men:" inform us you "have a good heart" and "a clear conscience:" assure us you "do your duty, your endeavours, your best endeavours," to please the Author of your lives: vow you never "were guilty of any crime, never did any harm:" and tell us you hope to mount to heaven on the strong pinions of your "good works and pious resolutions."

When you have thus acted the Pharisee's part before your fellow creatures, go to your Creator and assume the character of the publican. Confess with your lips you are "miserable sinners," who "have done what" you "ought not to have done, and left undone what" you "ought to have done:" protest "there is no health in" you: complain "that the remembrance of your sins is grievous unto you, and the burden of them intolerable:" but remember, O ye self righteous formalists, that, by this glaring inconsistency, you give the strongest proof of your unrighteousness. You are, nevertheless, modest, when compared with your brethren of the Romish Church.

These, far from thinking themselves "unprofitable servants," fancy they are, literally, "righteous overmuch." Becoming meritmongers, they make a stock of their works of supererogation, set up shop with the righteousness they can spare to others, and expose to sale indulgences and pardons out of their pretended treasury. Nor are there wanting sons of Simon, who with ready money purchase, as they think, not

---

assures us that, "at the worst of times, there is at most upon earth only one man in a thousand that can be called wicked." Now for the proof: "Hardly do we see one of those enormous crimes, that shock human nature, committed in ten years at Rome, Paris, or London, those cities where the thirst of gain, which is the parent of all crimes, is carried to the highest pitch. If men were essentially wicked, we should find, every morning, husbands murdered by their wives, &c, as we do hens killed by foxes." According to this apostle of the Deistical world, it seems that the most intense thirst of gold is no degree of wickedness: that a woman, to be very good, needs only not cut her husband's throat while he is asleep; and that it even little matters whether she omit the dire murder out of regard to *his* life or *her own.* What moral philosophy is here! Why, if the sin of *Sodom* is a peccadillo, a frolicsome mistake; and nothing is wickedness but a treacherous cutting of a husband's or a parent's throat; I extend my charity four times beyond thee, O Voltaire! and do maintain that there is not one wicked man in *five* thousand.

I insert this note to obviate the charges of severe critics, who accuse me of dealing in "gross misrepresentations, false quotations, and forgeries," because I quote some authors when they speak as the oracles of God; and do not swell my book with their inconsistencies, when they contradict the Scriptures, reason, and the truths which they themselves have advanced in some happy moments; and because I cannot force my reason to maintain with them both sides of a glaring contradiction.

O ye Deistical moralists! let me meet with more candour, justice, and mercy from you, than I have done from the *warm* opposers of the second Gospel axiom. It is enough that you discard Scripture; do not, like them, make it a part of your orthodoxy, to murder reason, and kick common sense out of doors.

livings in the Church below, but, which is far preferable, *seats* in the Church above, and *good places* at the heavenly court.

Was ever a robe of righteousness (I had almost said a fool's coat) so coarsely woven by the slaves of imposture and avarice; and so dearly bought by the sons of superstition and credulity?

O ye spiritual Ethiopians, who paint yourselves all over with the corroding *white* of hypocrisy, and after all, are artful enough to lay on *red* paint, and imitate the blush of humble modesty; ye that borrow virtue's robes to procure admiration, and put on religion's cloak to hide your shameful deformity: ye that deal in external righteousness, to carry on with better success the most sordid of all trades, that of *sin;* of the worst of sins, *pride;* of the worst pride, that which is *spiritual:* ye numerous followers of those whom the Prophet of Christians called crafty "serpents," and soft "brood of vipers;" ye to whom he declared that "publicans and harlots shall enter the kingdom of heaven before you;" if I call you *in last*, to prove the desperate wickedness of the human heart, it is not because I esteem you the weakest advocates of the truth I contend for, but because you really are the strongest of my witnesses.

And now, candid reader, forget not plain matter of fact; recollect the evidence given by reason; pass sentence upon these last arguments, which I have offered to thy consideration; and say whether man's disposition and conduct toward his Creator, his fellow creatures, and himself, do not abundantly prove that he is by nature in a *fallen* and *lost* estate.

———

PART IV.

THE preceding arguments recommend themselves to the common sense of thinking heathens, and the conscience of reasonable Deists; as being all taken from those two amazing volumes which are open to, and legible by, all, the *world* and *man.* The following are taken from a third volume, the *Bible,* despised by the wits of the age, merely because they study and understand it even less than the other two. "The Bible!" says one of them with a smile, "save yourself the trouble of producing arguments drawn from that old legend, unless you first demonstrate its authenticity by the noble faculty to which you appeal in these pages." For the sake of such objectors, I here premise, by way of digression, a few rational arguments to evince, as far as my contracted plan will allow, the Divine authority of the Scriptures.

1. The sacred penmen, the prophets, and apostles, were holy, excellent men, and *would* not,—artless, illiterate men, and therefore *could* not,—lay the horrible scheme of deluding mankind. The hope of gain did not influence them, for they were self-denying men, that left all to follow a Master who "had not where to lay his head;" and whose grand initiating maxim was, "Except a man forsake all that he hath, he cannot be my disciple," They were so disinterested that they secured nothing on earth but hunger and nakedness, stocks and prisons, racks and tortures; which, indeed, were all that they could or did expect, in consequence of Christ's express declarations. Neither was a desire of honour the motive of their actions; for their Lord himself was treated with the utmost contempt, and had more than once assured them that they should certainly share the same fate: beside, they were humble men, not above working as

mechanics for a coarse maintenance; and so little desirous of human regard, that they exposed to the world the meanness of their birth and occupations, their great ignorance and scandalous falls.

Add to this, that they were so many, and lived at such distance of time and place from each other, that had they been impostors, it would have been impracticable for them to contrive and carry on a forgery without being detected. And as they neither would nor could *deceive* the world, so they neither could nor would *be deceived* themselves: for they were days, months, and years, *eye* and *ear* witnesses of the things which they relate; and when they had not the fullest evidence of important facts, they insisted upon new proofs, and even upon sensible demonstrations; as, for instance, Thomas, in the matter of our Lord's resurrection, John xx:25. And, to leave us no room to question their sincerity, most of them joyfully sealed the truth of their doctrines with their own blood. Did *so many* and *such* marks of veracity ever meet in any other authors?

2. But even while they lived, they confirmed their testimony by a variety of miracles, wrought in divers places, and for a number of years; sometimes before thousands of their enemies, as the miracles of Christ and his disciples; sometimes before hundreds of thousands, as those of Moses. These miracles were so well known and attested, that when both Christ and Moses appealed to their authenticity, before their bitterest opposers, mentioning the persons upon whom, as well as the particular times when, and the places where, they had been performed; the facts were never denied, but passed over in silence, or maliciously attributed to the prince of the devils. By such a *pitiful slander* as this, Porphyry, Hierocles, Celsus, and Julian the apostate, those learned and inveterate enemies of Christianity, endeavoured (as the Pharisees had done before them) to sap the argument founded upon the miracles of Christ and his disciples. So sure then as God would never have displayed his arm, in the most astonishing manner, for the support of imposture,* the sacred penmen had their commission from the Almighty, and their writings are his *lively oracles.*

3. Reason itself dictates, that nothing but the plainest *matter of fact* could induce so many thousands of prejudiced and persecuting Jews to embrace the humbling, self-denying doctrine of the cross, which they so much despised and abhorred. Nothing but the clearest evidence, arising from undoubted truth, could make multitudes of lawless, luxurious heathens receive, follow, and transmit to posterity the doctrines and writings of the apostles; especially at a time when the vanity of their pretensions to miracles and the gift of tongues could be so easily discovered, had they been impostors,—at a time when the profession of Christianity exposed persons of all ranks to the greatest contempt, and most imminent danger. In this respect the case of the primitive Christians widely differed from that of Mohammed's followers: for those who adhered to the warlike, violent impostor, saved their lives and properties, or attained to honour, by their new, easy, and flesh-pleasing religion: but those who devoted themselves to the meek, self-denying, crucified Jesus, were frequently spoiled

---

* Once indeed the Lord permitted the magicians of Egypt so to use their art, as to counterfeit for a time some of Moses' miracles; but it was only to make the authenticity of others more conspicuous. This being the happy effect of the contest, when these ministers of Satan withdrew confounded, and were forced to acknowledge that the finger of God was evidently displayed through the rod of their antagonist.

of their goods, and cruelly put to death; or if they escaped with their lives, were looked upon as the very dregs of mankind.

Add to this, that some of the most profound parts of the Scriptures were addressed to the inhabitants of polite Greece and triumphant Rome;* among whom philosophy and literature, with the fine arts and sciences, were in the highest perfection; and who, consequently, were less liable to be the dupes of forgery and imposture. On the contrary, gross ignorance overspread those countries, where Mohammed first broached his absurd opinions, and propagated them with the sword: a sure sign this, that the sacred writers did not, like that impostor, avail themselves of the ignorance, weakness, and helplessness of their followers, to impose falsehood upon them.

4. When the authenticity of the miracles was attested by thousands of living witnesses, religious rites were instituted and performed by hundreds of thousands, agreeable to Scripture injunctions, in order to perpetuate that authenticity. And these solemn ceremonies have ever since been kept up in all parts of the world; the *passover* by the Jews, in remembrance of Moses' miracles in Egypt; and the *eucharist* by Christians, as a memorial of Christ's death and the miracles that accompanied it, some of which are recorded by Phlegon the Trallian, a heathen historian.

5. The Scriptures have not only the external sanction of miracles, but the internal stamp of the omniscient God, by a variety of prophecies, some of which have already been most exactly confirmed by the event predicted; witness the rise and fall of the four grand monarchies, according to Daniel's prophecy, chap. ii and vii; and the destruction of the city and temple of Jerusalem, foretold by Christ, Matthew xxiv:2, while others are every day fulfilled in the face of infidels, particularly the persecution of the real disciples of Christ in our own times, as well as in all ages; see Matthew x:22, 35; John xv:30; and Galatians iv:29; and the present miserable state of the Jews, so exactly described by Moses above three thousand years ago; see Deuteronomy xxviii:65.

6. Sometimes the plainest *prophecies*, the most public *miracles*, and the *annals* of kingdoms, well known when these books were first received, wonderfully concur to demonstrate their authenticity, Take one instance out of many. A prophet out of Judah, above three hundred years before the event, thus foretold the pollution of Jeroboam's altar at Bethel, before Jeroboam himself, who was attended by his priests, his courtiers, and, no doubt, a vast number of idolatrous worshippers: "O altar, altar, thus saith the Lord, Behold, a child shall be born unto the house of David, Josiah by name, who shall burn men's bones upon thee:" and "this is the sign: behold," this

---

* "Not many noble, not many wise, are called," says the apostle: nevertheless, some of both, even at the rise of Christianity, openly stood up for its truth. Among the *noble* we find Joseph, a member of the great Jewish council, Dionysius, one of the judges at Athens, and Flavius Clemens, a Roman senator; and among the *wise*, Quadratus, Aristides, and Athenagoras, Athenian philosophers; Clemens, Arnobius, Ammonius, Annatolius, &c, men of great learning at Alexandria; and at Rome, Justin Martyr and Tertullian, both famous apologists for the religion of Jesus; the latter of whom, in the second century, told the Roman governors, that their corporations, councils, and armies, and the emperor's palace, were full of Christians; nor is this improbable, since so early as St. Paul's days, "the saints of Cesar's household saluted" those of the Roman provinces, Philippians iv:2. How credulous are they who can believe that persons of such rank and learning could be deluded by Jewish fishermen into the worship of a crucified impostor!

very day, "the altar shall be rent, and the ashes that are upon it scattered." King Jeroboam, inflamed with anger, "stretched forth his hand against the man of God, saying," to his guards, "Lay hold on him:" but his extended hand "was dried up so that he could not pull it in again to him;" the rending of the altar and scattering of the fire instantly took place; and the capital prophecy was exactly fulfilled by pious King Josiah, as you may see by comparing 1 Kings xiii:1, &c, with 2 Kings xxiii:15, &c. Can we reasonably suppose that books, containing accounts of such public events, would have been received as *Divine* by a *divided* people, if their authenticity had not been confirmed by indubitable matter of fact? Nay, is it not as absurd to assert it, as it would be to affirm, that the offices for the fifth of November and the thirtieth of January, were forged by crafty priests; and that the Papists, Puritans, and Royalists of the last century, agreed to impose upon the world the history of the gunpowder plot and of King Charles' decollation, with which those parts of our liturgy are so inseparably connected?

7. This scattered, despised people, the irreconcilable enemies of the Christians, keep with amazing care the Old Testament,* full of the prophetic history of Jesus Christ, and by that means afford the world a striking proof that the New Testament is true; and Christians in their turn show, that the Old Testament is abundantly confirmed and explained by the New. The earl of Rochester, the great wit of the last century, was so struck with this proof, that upon reading the fifty-third chapter of Isaiah, with floods of penitential tears he lamented his former infidelity, and warmly embraced the faith which he had so publicly ridiculed.

8. To say nothing of the venerable antiquity and wonderful preservation of those books, some of which are by far the most ancient in the world; to pass over the inimitable simplicity and true sublimity of their style, they carry with them such characters of truth, as command the respect of every unprejudiced reader.

They open to us the mystery of the creation, the nature of God, angels, and man, the immortality of the soul,† the end for which we were made, the origin and connection of moral and natural evil, the vanity of this world and the glory of the next. There we see inspired shepherds, tradesmen, and fishermen, surpassing as much the greatest philosophers, as these did the herd of mankind, both in meekness of wisdom and sublimity of doctrine. There we admire the purest morality in the world,

---

* If the histories contained in the Old Testament were in general for the credit of the Jews, the *love of praise* might indeed have engaged some of them to join in a public forgery. But that book, of which they have always been so tenacious, presents the world chiefly with an account of their monstrous ingratitude, unparalleled obstinacy, perpetual rebellions, abominable idolatries; and of the fearful judgments which their wickedness brought upon them. Moses, who leads the van of their sacred authors, sums up his history of the Israelites, and draws up their character in these disgraceful words, which he spake to their face: "Ye have been rebellious against the Lord from the day that I knew you," Deuteronomy ix:24. And even David and Solomon, their greatest kings, are represented in those books as guilty of the greatest enormities. O ye Deists, I appeal to your reason, and ask, Would you *die for,* would you even *connive* at a notorious forgery, supposing the design of it were merely to impose, upon the world as *Divine,* a book that should perpetually stigmatize your ancestors, and fix horrid blots upon the names, for which you have the greatest veneration?

† It is remarkable that the wisest heathens, with all their philosophy, seldom attained to a full assurance of the immortality of the soul. Cicero himself says, *"Nescio quomodo, dum lego assentior; cum posui librum, et mecum ipse de immortalitate animorum cœpi cogitare, assentio omnis illa elabitur."* (Tusc. Quæst. lib. 1)

agreeable to the dictates of sound reason, confirmed by the witness which God has placed for himself in our breast, and exemplified in the lives of men of like passions with ourselves. There we discover a vein of ecclesiastical history and theological truth, consistently running through a collection of sixty-six different books, written by various authors, in different languages, during the space of above fifteen hundred years. There we find, as in a deep and pure spring, all the genuine drops and streams of spiritual knowledge which can possibly be met with in the largest libraries. There the workings of the human heart are described, in a manner that demonstrates the inspiration of the Searcher of hearts. There we have a particular account of all our spiritual maladies, with their various symptoms, and the method of a certain cure; a cure that has been witnessed by millions of martyrs and departed saints, and is now enjoyed by thousands of good men, who would account it an honour to seal the truth of the Scriptures with their own blood. There you meet with the noblest strains of penitential and joyous devotion, adapted to the dispositions and states of all travellers to Sion: and there you read those awful threatenings and cheering promises which are daily fulfilled in the consciences of men, to the admiration of believers, and the astonishment of attentive infidels.

9. The wonderful efficacy of the Scriptures is another proof that they are of God. When they are faithfully opened by his ministers, and powerfully applied by his Spirit, they "wound and heal," they "kill and make alive," they alarm the careless, turn or enrage the wicked, direct the lost, support the tempted, strengthen the weak, comfort mourners, and nourish pious souls. As the woman of Samaria said of Jesus, "Come, see a man that told me all that ever I did: is not this the Christ?" a good man can say of the Bible, "Come, see a book that told me all that was in my heart, and acquainted me with the various trials and dangers I have met with in my spiritual travels: a book where I have found those truths, which, like a Divinely tempered sword, have cut my way through all the snares and forces of my spiritual adversaries; and by whose directions my soul has happily entered the paradise of Divine and brotherly love: is not this the book of God?"

10. To conclude: It is exceedingly remarkable that the more humble and holy people are, the more they read, admire, and value the Scriptures; and, on the contrary, the more self conceited, worldly minded, and wicked, the more they neglect, despise, and asperse them.

As for the objections which are raised against their perspicuity and consistency, those who are both pious and learned know that they are generally founded on prepossession, and the want of understanding in spiritual things; or on our ignorance of several customs, idioms, and circumstances which were perfectly known when those books were written. Frequently also the *immaterial* error arises merely from a wrong punctuation, or a mistake of copiers, printers, or translators; as the daily discoveries of pious critics, and ingenuous confessions of unprejudiced inquirers, abundantly prove.

To the preceding arguments, I beg leave to add the following queries: Do not disbelievers, by supposing that the Scriptures are a forged book, and, consequently, that Christianity is a false religion, run upon the very rocks which they seem so afraid of? And may they not be charged with indirectly setting their seal to opinions far more incredible than those which they reject?

An Appeal to Matter of Fact and Common Sense

(1.) O ye *disputers of this world,* if ye believe that Moses and Jesus Christ, St. Peter and St. Paul, publicly worked *sham* miracles for years, in various cities and countries, before thousands of their sharp-sighted opposers, without being ever detected in any of their tricks; might you not as reasonably believe that thousands of shrewd men were once turned into stupid asses?

(2.) If you believe that the Gospel is the production of human deceit, and yet, that in the prodigious number of apostates once concerned in carrying on the amazing villainy, such as Judas, Demas, Simon Magus, Alexander the coppersmith, who did St. Paul so much evil, &c, not one was ever found that would prove the forgery: might you not as reasonably believe, that if Mr. Wilkes, and all his friends, knew of a gross villainy carried on by the ministry, in order to turn the kingdom upside down; neither he, nor any one of them, could ever be prevailed upon to disclose and prove it to the world?*

(3.) You believe that the miracles and resurrection of Christ, together with the gifts of the Holy Ghost, were nothing but enthusiastical or knavish pretensions; and yet you are forced to grant, that thousands of Jews, strongly attached to their religion, amazingly averse to that of Jesus, and guilty of persecuting him unto death, took him openly for their Saviour a few weeks after they had seen him publicly scourged; and in the very city in sight of which he had just been crucified between two thieves. Now is not this as absurd as to believe, that if a few fishermen cried up the last person hanged in London for a notorious forgery; and if they affirmed that he was the Son of God, appealing to a great number of miracles supposed to have been wrought by him in the squares and hospitals of the metropolis, and especially in St. Paul's church yard; and maintaining that some of them had been acknowledged genuine by the great council of the nation;† they could, by such notorious lies, engage thousands of citizens, and some aldermen, to put all their trust in the villain hanged *at their special request?*

(4.) You believe that Christianity is a gross imposture; and yet you cannot deny that thousands of learned Romans and wise Greeks, who agreed to despise the Jews above all other men, took for their Saviour that very Jesus, of whom his own countrymen had been ashamed, and whom they had crucified as an impostor. Is not this as absurd as to believe, that thousands of wise Englishmen, and sensible Frenchmen, could be induced by the absurd tale of two or three Hottentots, to

---

* Pliny, a learned and prudent Roman governor, who was employed by the Emperor Trajan in stopping the progress of Christianity, wrote to him, that the apostates affirmed, the whole of their crime had been to meet before day, and sing a hymn to Christ as to their God. His own words are: "*Affirmabant hanc fuisse summam vel culpæ suæ, vel erroris, quod essent soliti stato die ante lucem convenire, carmenque Christo quasi Deo dicere.*"

† Some remarkable instances of this we have in the sacred books, published when the facts mentioned therein were notorious, and when some of the persons named were probably yet alive. After the resurrection of Lazarus, "the chief priests and the Pharisees gathered a council, and said, What do we? for this man doeth many miracles. If we let him alone, all men will believe on him," John xi:47. And after Peter and John had publicly cured the cripple who used to beg at the gate of the temple, "the rulers, and elders, and scribes, and Annas the high priest, and Caiaphas, and John, and Alexander, and as many as were of the kindred of the high priest, were gathered together at Jerusalem, saying, What shall we do to these men? For that indeed a *notable miracle* hath been done by them, is manifest to *all* them that dwell in Jerusalem, and we cannot deny it," Acts iv:5-16.

The Works of John Fletcher

worship a certain Hottentot whom the whole nation of Hottentots had condemned to be hanged, as being more worthy of an ignominious death than the bloody ringleader of a seditious mob?

(5.) If you believe, with one of the popes, that the history of Christ is "a mere fable," and that there never was such an extraordinary person, you believe that the heathens, the Jews, and the Mohammedans have agreed with the Christians, their sworn enemies, to carry on the most amazing imposture. For Pliny, Tacitus, Lucian, and Suetonius, heathen authors, who lived soon after Christ, make express mention of him; as do also Mohammed, many of the rabbis, and Julian the emperor, that powerful and crafty apostate, who not only never denied Christ's existence, but openly acknowledged that Paul, Mark, Matthew, and Peter were the authors of the Gospels and Epistles which bear their name. Now is not this as ridiculous as to believe, that the pope, the mufti, and the inquisitors, have laid their heads together with Messrs. Voltaire Hume, and Rousseau, to favour a forgery subversive of popery, Mohammedanism, and infidelity?

(6.) If you deny the authenticity of the four Gospels, which are the only ancient histories that we have of our saviour, and yet believe that there was such a personage as Jesus Christ, whose fame so spread through the Roman empire, that in less than three hundred and thirty years he was not only reckoned superior to the Roman emperor, but to Jupiter himself; and that, nevertheless, not one historian, during all that time, gave the world a *particular* account of him, [which must be the case, if the four Gospels are a forgery,] might you not as reasonably suppose, that if a blazing meteor appeared in our day, and eclipsed the stars, the moon, and the sun itself, no astronomer for several centuries would take *particular* notice of so wonderful a phenomenon?

(7.) If the Gospel is a delusion, you believe that St. Paul, who was a man of sense, learning, and intrepidity, was seduced by—nobody, to preach for near thirty years with astonishing zeal and matchless hardships, an imposture, against the abettors of which he just before "breathed" nothing but "threatenings and slaughter." Would it be half so absurd to believe that Mr. Wilkes has suddenly commenced the minister's advocate, goes through the kingdom to recommend the present administration, and accounts it an honour to be mobbed, whipped, or stoned in every borough for his excessive attachment to the king?

(8.) The instantaneous conversion of thousands was wrought by means of public appeals to notorious matter of fact. Hear the language of the apostles to the Jews: "This ye yourselves *know*," Acts ii:12. "Ye *know* the thing done through *all* Judea," Acts x:37, 38. "The king *knoweth* these things." "This thing was not done in a corner," Acts xxvi:26. Now if Christianity is not founded upon indubitable facts, might you not as well believe, that twelve men broke loose from bedlam, brought last year thousands of Deists over to Christianity, by saying to them," *Ye know*"— what you are perfect strangers to; that is, "*Ye know*" that we are a pack of bedlamites!

(9.) If the Gospel is forged, you believe that the Corinthians, &c, handed down to posterity, as a sacred treasure, epistles where St. Paul mentions their amazing conversion from gross immoralities; congratulates them about the *spiritual* or miraculous *gifts,* in which they abounded, 1 Corinthians xii:1, and gives them particular directions how to use the "gift of tongues" to edification; when yet they were totally unacquainted with any such things. Might you not with equal wisdom believe that, If Mr. Wilkes wrote to the house of commons a congratulatory epistle about their having received, *by the laying on* of his *hands*, the power of speaking Turkish, Arabic, and Chinese, they would carefully transmit his letter to the next generation as a Divine performance; and that none of Mr. Wilkes' enemies would ever expose the impudence of so absurd a pretension?

(10.) If you say that the apostles were *fools*, you must believe that *foolish* fishermen laid a scheme with so much *wisdom*, and carried it on with so much *art*, *as* to deceive multitudes of Greeks noted for their acuteness, and numbers of Romans famous for their prudence. Might you not as well believe that twelve poor, unarmed *idiots* once combined to take the strongest towns in Europe, and accomplished their strange design by means that strike the profoundest politicians with astonishment?

(11.) If you affirm, that the apostles were *cheats* and *liars*, you run into as great a difficulty; for you must believe that the greatest *knaves* that ever existed, contrary to their own principles and advantage, went through the world, exposing themselves to the greatest hardships and severest tortures unto death, to recommend, both by their *example* and *precepts*, the strictest piety toward God, and the most scrupulous *honesty* toward man; perpetually denouncing eternal destruction to cheats and hypocrites, and the torments of a "lake that burneth with fire and brimstone to every one who loveth or maketh a lie." Would it be more absurd to believe that the twelve greatest epicures in England have, for a course of years, fulfilled a mutual agreement of preaching, night and day, abstinence and fasting through the three kingdoms, merely to have the pleasure of starving to death for their pains?

(12.) To conclude: if the Gospel (and consequently the Scripture) is an imposture, you suppose that some poor Galilean fishermen, only by means of an *absurd lie*, which they told without wit, and wrote without elegance, foiled the multitude of the Jewish and Pagan priests, who had prejudice, custom, profession, learning, oratory, wealth, laws, governors, and emperors on their side; yea, and *truth* also, upon your principles, at least when they decried the Gospel as a *cheat*. Would it be more ridiculous to believe that David killed Goliah with a grain of sand, and cut off his head with a spire of grass; or that our sailors sink men of war with a puff of breath, while our soldiers batter down ramparts with snow balls?

O ye sons of worldly wisdom, drop your unjust prejudices; candidly weigh both sides of the question, and you will soon see, that, in rejecting the Gospel as an imposture, you display a far greater degree of *credulity* than we do in cordially receiving it.

After this short defence of the oracles of God, and this little attack upon the persons who suspect their authenticity, I hope I may (consistently with the plan of *an appeal to reason*) produce from THE SCRIPTURES a few more arguments to prove the original depravity and lost estate of mankind.

THIRTY-FIRST ARGUMENT.

The spiritual life of the soul consists in its union with God, as the natural life of the body does in its union with the soul; and as poison and the sword kill the latter, so unbelief and sin destroy the former.

The first man was endued with this two-fold life: "God," says the Divine historian, "breathed into him the breath of lives, and he became a living" body and a

The Works of John Fletcher

living "soul:" he had both an animal life in common with beasts, and a spiritual life in common with angels. St. Paul, who calls this angelical life "the life of God," intimates that it consisted both in that experimental *knowledge* of our Creator, wherein, says our Church, "standeth our eternal life;" and "in righteousness and true holiness," the moral and most glorious image of the Supreme Being.

To suppose man was created void of this essential *knowledge* and *holy love*, is to suppose he came very wicked out of the hands of the Parent of all good; for what is a rational creature, that neither *knows* nor *loves* his Creator, but a monster of stupidity and ingratitude, a wretch actually dead to God, and deserving present destruction?

When the Lord, therefore, said to man, "In the day thou eatest thereof," that is, in the day that thou sinnest, "thou shalt surely die," it was as if he had said, "In that very day sin shall assuredly separate between thee and the God of thy life; thou shalt certainly lose the glorious view which thou hast of my boundless goodness and infinite perfections: thou shalt infallibly quench the spirit of ardent love, and stop the breath of delightful praise by which thou livest both to my glory and thy comfort: and thy soul, 'dead in trespasses and sins,' shall remain in the filthy prison of a mortal body, till death breaks it open to remove thee to thy own place."

And was not this Adam's case after his fall? Did he not "know that he was naked," stripped of the glorious image of his Creator? Did not guilty *shame* immediately prompt him to *hide* and protect, as well as he could, his degenerate and enfeebled body? Devoid of the ardent love he felt for God before, and of the pure delight he enjoyed in him, was not he left the wretched prey of tormenting *fears?* Did he not evidence his hatred of his heavenly Benefactor, by *dreading* his voice, and flying from him as hastily as he should have fled from the infernal serpent?

Was he not deprived of the knowledge by which at first sight he discovered the nature of Eve, and gave to all living creatures names expressive of their respective properties? Was he not, I say, deprived of that intuitive knowledge and excellent wisdom, when he foolishly "hid himself among the trees" from his *all-seeing, omnipresent* Creator? And is it not evident that he was lost to all sense of filial fear toward God, and conjugal love toward Eve, when, instead of self accusations, penitential confessions, and earnest pleas for mercy, he showed nothing at his trial but stubbornness, malice, and insolence?

Such was the state of corruption into which Adam had deplorably fallen, before he multiplied the human species. Now, according to the invariable laws of Providence, an upright, holy nature can no more proceed from a fallen, sinful one, than gentle lambs can be begotten by fierce tigers, or harmless doves by venomous serpents. Common sense, therefore, and natural philosophy, dictate that our first parents could not communicate the angelical life which they had lost, nor impart to their children a better nature than their own; and that their depravity is as much ours by nature, as the fierceness of the first lion is the natural property of all the lions in the world.

FOUR OBJECTIONS.

I. Should it be said, "This doctrine reflects on the attributes of God, who, as the wise and gracious Governor of the world, should have foreseen and prevented the fall of Adam:"

An Appeal to Matter of Fact and Common Sense

I answer, (1.) "God made man in his image," part of which consists in free agency, or a power to determine his own actions. And if creating a free agent is not repugnant to Divine wisdom and goodness; the wrong choice, or sin of a free agent, can be no impeachment of those perfections in the Deity.*

(2.) Suppose man had not been endued with freedom of choice he would only have ranked among admirable machines, and nothing could have been more absurd than to place him in a state of probation. And suppose, when he was in that state, Divine power had irresistibly turned the scale of his will to obedience, the *trial* would have been *prevented*, and the counsel of Divine wisdom foolishly defeated.

(3.) God did all that a wise and good ruler of rational and free creatures could do to prevent sin. He placed in Adam's heart a vigorous principle of holiness; he granted

---

* God answers thus for himself in Milton:—

> Man will fall,
> He and his faithless progeny. Whose fault?
> Whose but his own? Ingrate! he had of me
> All he could have; I made him just and right,
> Sufficient to have stood, though free to fall.
> Such I created all the ethereal powers;
> Freely they stood who stood, and fell who fell.
> Not free, what proof could they have given sincere
> Of true allegiance, constant faith or love,
> Where only what they *needs must do* appear'd;
> Not what they *would?* What praise could they receive?
> What pleasure I from such obedience paid,
> When will and reason, (reason also is choice,)
> Useless and vain, of freedom both despoil'd,
> Made passive both, had serv'd *necessity,*
> Not me? They, therefore, as to right belong'd,
> So were created, nor can justly accuse
> Their Maker, or their making, or their fate,
> As if predestination overruled
> Their will, disposed by absolute decree,
> Or high foreknowledge. They themselves decreed
> Their own revolt, not I; if I foreknew,
> Foreknowledge had no influence on their fault,
> Which had no less proved certain unforeknown.

Young expresses the same sentiment with his peculiar boldness and energy.—

> Blame not the bowels of the Deity:
> Man shall be bless'd as far as man *permits.*
> Not man alone, all *rationals,* Heaven arms
> With an illustrious, but tremendous power
> To counteract its own most gracious ends:
> And this of strict necessity, not choice;
> That power denied, *men, angels,* were no more,
> But passive engines, void of praise or blame.
> Heaven *wills* our happiness, *allows* our doom;
> Invites us ardently, but not compels:
> Heaven but persuades, almighty man decrees;
> Man is the maker of immortal fates;
> Man falls by man, if finally he falls.

him sufficient strength to continue in obedience; he indulged him with his blessed presence and converse, to encourage him in the way of duty; he strictly forbade him to sin; he enforced the prohibition by the fearful threatening of death; he promised to crown his continuance in holiness with a glorious immortality; and gave him "the tree of life" as a pledge of this inestimable blessing. To have gone farther would have been entirely inconsistent with his wisdom; an absolute restraint being as contrary to the liberty of a moral agent, and the nature of the Divine law, as chaining down a harmless man that he may not commit murder, is contrary to the freedom of Englishmen, and the laws of this realm. Nor can we, either with reason or decency, complain that God did not make us *absolutely immutable* and *perfect* like himself: this is charging him with folly for not enduing us with infinite wisdom, and knowledge every way boundless; that is, for not making us *gods* instead of *men*.

(4.) In case man fell, Divine mercy had decreed his recovery by Jesus Christ: and when the almighty Redeemer shall have brought life out of death, and light out of darkness, the mysterious drama of creation and redemption, of which we see but one or two acts, will appear, even to our objectors, every way worthy of its infinitely wise and gracious Author.

II. In the meantime they will still urge, that "Adam's posterity (then unborn) could not *justly* partake of the consequences of his transgressions." But shall cavils overthrow *matter of fact?* Do not we see in every unrenewed person, the unbelief, pride, sinful curiosity, sensuality, and alienation from God, to which our first parents were subjected at their fall? Do not women bear children with sorrow as well as Eve? Is the ground less cursed for us than for Adam? And do not we toil, suffer, and die as he did? If this order of things were *unjust,* would the *righteous* God have permitted its continuance to the present time? Beside,

Adam contained in himself, as in miniature, all his posterity. The various nations of men are nothing but different branches growing from that original root. They are *Adam,* or *man,* existing at large; as the branches of a spreading oak, with all the acorns that have grown upon, and dropped from them, during a long succession of summers, are nothing but the original acorn, unfolding and multiplying itself with all its essential properties. It is then as ridiculous to wonder that the sons of depraved Adam should naturally be depraved, as that an acorn should naturally produce an oak; and a poisonous root a malignant plant. Again:

Adam was the general head, representative, and father of mankind; and we suffer for his rebellion *legally;* as the children of those who have sold themselves for slaves are born in a state of wretched slavery; and as the descendants of a noble traitor lose the title by their ancestor's crime: *naturally,* as the sons of a bankrupt suffer poverty for their father's extravagance, or as "Gehazi's leprosy clave to him and his seed for ever:" and *unavoidably,* as an unborn child shares the fate of his unhappy mother, when she inadvertently poisons, or desperately stabs herself.

III. "But," say the same objectors, "supposing it be granted that we are naturally depraved; yet if our depravity is *natural,* it is *necessary;* and we are no more blamable for it, than lions for their fierceness, or Ethiopians for their black complexion."

(1.) Our objectors would not, I presume, be understood to insinuate by "blamable," that our depravity does not render us detestable in the eyes of a holy God, or that it is not in itself blameworthy. Do they less dislike the complexion of the Ethiopians, or less detest the destructive rage of lions, because it is *natural* to them? If moral dispositions ceased to be worthy of praise or dispraise, as soon as they are rooted, *morally necessary,* and in *that* sense *natural;* what absurd consequences would follow! Sinners would become guiltless by arriving at complete impenitency; and God could not be praised for his holiness, nor Satan dispraised for his sinfulness, holiness being as essential to God, by the absolute perfection of his nature, as sin is morally necessary to the devil, by the unconquerable habit which he has wilfully contracted, and in which he obstinately remains.

(2.) Should they mean that "we are not *answerable* or *accountable* for our depravity," I reply, Though I should grant (which I am very far from doing)* that we are *no way* accountable for our moral infection, yet it cannot be denied that we are answerable for our *obstinate refusal* of relief, and for the *wilful neglect* of the means found out by Divine mercy for our cure. Can we justly charge God with either our misfortune or our guilt? Do not parents, by the law of nature, represent their unborn posterity? If Adam ruined us by a *common transgression,* has not Christ, the second Adam, provided for us a *common salvation?* Jude i:3; Hebrews ii:3. If by "the offence of one, [Adam,] judgment came upon all men to condemnation; by the righteousness of one, [Christ,] is" not "the free gift come upon all men to justification of life?" Romans v:18. And since God has declared that "the son shall not bear the iniquity of the father" beyond the short period of this transitory life; if any suffer after death, is it not entirely for their own unbelief, and peculiar sins?† Compare John iii:18, 19, and Mark xvi:16. But what follows completely vindicates our Creator's goodness.

(3.) Do sin and misery abound by our fall in Adam? Grace and glory "abound much more" by our "redemption" in Jesus Christ, Romans v:20. And "it must be owing to our own perverseness, or our own negligence," says the ingenious Hervey,

---

* Milton introduces Adam speaking thus:—

> *Ah, why should all mankind,*
> *For one man's fault, thus guiltless be condemn'd,*
> *If guiltless? But from me what* can *proceed,*
> *But all corrupt, both mind and will depraved,*
> *Not to* do *only, but to* will *the same*
> *With* me*? How can they then acquitted stand*
> *In sight of God? Him after all disputes*
> *Forced I absolve.*

† Milton introduces God speaking thus to the Messiah:—

> Man shall not quite be lost, but saved who will,
> Yet not of will in him, but grace in me
> Freely vouchsafed: once more I will renew
> His lapsed powers;—yet once more he shall stand
> On even ground against his mortal foe,
> By me upheld. Be thou in Adam's room
> The head of all mankind, though Adam's son.
> As in him perish all men, so in thee,
> As from a second root, shall be restored
> As many as are restored; without thee, none.
> His crimes make guilty all his sons; thy merit
> Imputed shall absolve them, who renounce
> Their own both righteous and unrighteous deeds;
> And live in thee transplanted, and from thee
> Receive new life.

with great truth, "if we do not levy a tax upon our loss, and rise even by our fall."* This leaves us not the least shadow of reason to complain of the Divine proceedings respecting us.

We may then conclude that a moral depravity, which comes upon us by the *wilful* choice of a parent, in whom we *seminally* and *federally* existed,—a depravity which cleaves to us by an *obstinate neglect* of the infinitely precious means provided to remove it,—a depravity which works now by *our own personal choice*, and to which we daily give our assent by the *free* commission of sins that are avoidable, leaves us not only accountable, but *inexcusable* before God.

IV. However, the advocates for the natural purity of the human race (endeavouring to clog with difficulties what they cannot disprove to be matter of fact) still assert, "As we have souls *immediately* from God, *if* we are born sinful, he must either create *sinful* souls, which cannot be supposed without impiety, or send *sinless* souls into *sinful* bodies, to be defiled by the unhappy union, which is as inconsistent with his goodness as his justice. Add to this," say the objectors, "that nothing can be more unphilosophical than to suppose that a body, a mere lump of organized matter, is able to communicate to a pure spirit that moral pollution, of which itself is as incapable as the murderer's sword is incapable of cruelty."

This specious objection, which Dr. Watts acknowledges to be "the very chief point of difficulty in all the controversies about original sin," is wholly founded upon the vulgar notion that we have our souls immediately from God by infusion. It will therefore entirely fall to the ground, if we can prove, that we receive them, as well as our bodies, by traduction from Adam. And that this is fact, appears, if I am not mistaken, by the following arguments:—

(1.) We have no ground, from Scripture or reason, to think that adulterers can, when they please, put God upon *creating* new souls to animate the spurious fruit of their crime. On the contrary, it is said that God "rested on the seventh day from all his work" of creation.

(2.) Eve herself was not *created* but *in* Adam. God breathed no breath of life into her, as he did into her husband, to make him "a living soul." Therefore, when Adam saw her, he said, "She shall be called woman, because she [her whole self, not her body only] was taken out of man." If then the soul of the first woman sprang from Adam's soul, as her body from his body, what reason have we to believe that the souls of her posterity are immediately infused, as Adam's was when God created him?

(3.) All agree that, under God, we receive *life* from our parents; and if *life*, then certainly our *soul*, which is the *principle of life*.

(4.) Other animals have power to propagate their own species "after its kind;" they can generate *animated* bodies. Why should man be but *half* a father? When did God stint him to propagate the mere *shell* of his person, the body without the soul?

---

* Creation's great superior, man, is thine;
Thine is *redemption*. How should this great truth
Raise man o'er man, and kindle seraphs here!
Redemption! 'Twas creation more sublime;
Redemption! 'Twas the *labour* of the skies;
Far *more* than labour,—it was *death* in heaven.
A truth so strange! 'twere bold to think it true;
If not far bolder still to disbelieve.   YOUNG.

An Appeal to Matter of Fact and Common Sense

Was it when "he blessed him, and said, Be fruitful, and multiply?" When he spoke thus did he not address himself to the *soul*, as well as to the body? Can the body alone either understand or execute a command? Is it not, on the contrary, highly reasonable to conclude that, by virtue of the Divine appointment and blessing, the *whole* man can "be fruitful and multiply;" and the soul, under proper circumstances, can generate a soul, as a thought begets a thought; and can kindle the flame of life, as one taper lights another; without weakening its immortal substance, any more than God the Father (if I may be allowed the comparison) impairs the Divine essence by the *eternal* generation of his "only begotten Son?"

(5.) Does not *matter of fact* corroborate the preceding argument? A sprightly race horse generally begets a mettlesome colt; while a heavy cart horse begets a colt that bears the stamp of its sire's dulness. And is it not so with mankind in general? The children of the Hottentots and Esquimaux are commonly as *stupid*, while those of the English and French are usually as *sharp* as their parents. You seldom see a wit springing from two half witted people, or a fool descended from very sensible parents. The children of men of genius are frequently as remarkable for some branch of hereditary genius, as those of blockheads for their native stupidity. Nothing is more common than to see very passionate and flighty parents have very passionate and flighty children. And I have a hundred times discovered, not only the features, look, and complexion of a father or a mother in a child's face, but have seen a congenial soul, looking out (if I may so speak) at those windows of the body which we call *the eyes*. Hence I conclude, that the advice frequently given to those who are about to choose a companion for life, "*Take care of the breed*," is not absolutely without foundation; although some lay too much stress upon it, forgetting that a thousand unknown accidents may form exceptions to the general role; and not considering that the peculiarity of the father's breed may be happily corrected by that of the mother, (and *vice versa*,) and that as the grace of God, yielded to, may *sweeten* the *worst* temper; so sin, persisted in, may *sour* the *best*.

(6.) Again: Moses informs us, that fallen "Adam begat a son in his own likeness, and after his image." But had he generated a body without a soul, he would not have "begotten a son in his own likeness," since he was not a mere mortal body, but a *fallen, disembodied spirit*. Compare Genesis v:3, with Genesis xlvi:26.

"But upon this scheme," will objectors say, "if Adam was converted when he begat a son, he begat a converted soul." This does by no means follow; for if he was born of God after his fall, it was "by grace through faith," and not by nature through generation. He could not, therefore, communicate his *spiritual regeneration* by *natural generation*, any more than a great scholar can propagate his learning together with his species.

Should it be again objected, that "the soul is not generated, because the Scriptures declare, 'the Lord is the Father of the spirits of all flesh,' and 'the spirit returns to God who gave it:'" I answer, It is also written, that Job and David were "fearfully made and fashioned by the hands of God in the womb;" that he "formed Jeremiah in the belly;" and that "we are the offspring of Him who made of one blood all nations of men." Now, if the *latter* scriptures do not exclude the interposition of parents in the formation of their children's *bodies*, by what rule of criticism or divinity can we prove, that the *former* exclude that interposition in the production of their *souls*?

Nor can materialists, who have no ideas of generation but such as are gross and carnal like their own system, with any shadow of reason infer that "if the soul is generated with the body, it will also perish with it." For dissolution is so far from being a necessary consequence, of the spiritual generation of souls, that it would not so much as have followed the generation of our bodies, if Adam had not brought "sin into the world, and *death* by sin." Again: if wheat, a material seed, which grows out of the same earthly clod with the chaff that encloses it, can subsist unimpaired when that mean cover is destroyed; how much more can the soul. (that spiritual, vital, heavenly power, which is of a nature so vastly superior to the body in which it is confined,) continue to exist, when flesh and blood are returned to their native dust!

Should some persons reject what I say of the traduction of souls, in order to illustrate the derivation of original sin; and should they say that they have no more idea of the *generation* than honest Nicodemus had of the *regeneration of a spirit,* I beg leave to observe two things:—

First. If such objectors are converted, they will not deny the *regeneration* of souls by the Spirit of God, since they experience it, and our Lord speaks of it as a blessed reality, even while he represents it as a mystery *unknown* as to the manner of it, John iii:8-13. Now, if pious souls have been *regenerated* from the beginning of the world, without exactly knowing *how;* is it reasonable to deny that souls are *generated,* merely because we cannot exactly account for the manner in which that wonder takes place?

Secondly. Should my objectors be versed in natural philosophy, they need not be told that even the kind of generation which they allow is as much a *mystery* to man as the movement of a watch is to a child that just sees the case and the glass. If they will not believe me, let them believe him who "gave his heart to search out by wisdom concerning all things that are done under heaven," and who, touching upon our question, says, "As thou knowest not what is the way of the spirit, nor how the bones do grow in the womb of her that is with child; even so thou knowest not the works of God who maketh all," Ecclesiastes xi:5.

For my part, I do not see why the same almighty Preserver of men, who (as St. Paul tells us) *made of* ONE BLOOD the bodies of *all nations of men,* might not, of *one* ACTIVE THOUGHT, and ARDENT DESIRE, *have made* the souls of *all nations of men* also. Have not *thought* and *desire* as great affinity to the nature of the *soul,* as *blood* has to that of the *body?* And, consequently, are not our ideas of the *traduction* of the *soul* as clear as those which we can form of the *generation* of the *body?*

Having dwelt so long upon the manner in which mankind naturally propagate original corruption, together with their *whole* species, I hope I may reasonably resume the conclusion of my argument, and affirm, that if Adam corrupted the fountain of human nature in himself, we, the streams, cannot but be naturally corrupted.

THIRTY-SECOND ARGUMENT.

God being a *Spirit,* reason and revelation jointly inform us, that his law is *spiritual,* and extends to our thoughts and tempers, as well as to our words and actions. At all times, and in all places, it forbids every thing that is sinful, or has the least tendency to sin; it commands all that is excellent, and enjoins it to be done with the utmost perfection of our dispensation.

An Appeal to Matter of Fact and Common Sense

Therefore, if we have not always trusted and delighted in God, more than in all things and persons; if for one instant we have *loved* or feared "the creature more than the Creator," we "have" had "another god beside the Lord," Colossians iii:5; Philippians iii:19. Have we once omitted to adore him "in spirit and in truth" inwardly, or at any time worshipped him without becoming veneration outwardly? we have transgressed as if we had "bowed to a graven image," John iv:24. Though perjury and imprecations should never have defiled our lips; yet, if ever we mentioned God's tremendous name thoughtlessly, or irreverently, in prayer, reading, or conversation, we have "taken it in vain," and the Searcher of hearts "will not hold" us "guiltless," Philippians ii:10. And if it has not been our constant practice and delight to "enter his courts with praise," and spend the whole Sabbath in his blessed service, we have polluted that sacred day, and the guilt of profaneness may justly be charged upon us, Isaiah lviii:18.

Did we ever show any disrespect to our superiors, or unkindness to our equals and inferiors? we have violated the precept that commands us to "honour all men," and be punctual in the discharge of all social and relative duties, 1 Peter ii:17. Did we ever weaken our constitution by excess, strike our neighbour in anger, wound his character with an injurious word, or only suffer hatred to rise in our breast against him? we have committed a species of *murder*: for "whosoever shall say to his brother, Thou fool, shall be in danger of hell fire;" and "whosoever hateth his brother is a murderer," Matthew v:22; 1 John iii:15. Are we "the friends of the world?" an apostle brands us with the name of "adulterers," because we are false to our heavenly Bridegroom, James iv:4. And if we have only "looked on a woman to lust after her," Christ declares we "have committed adultery with her already in our heart," Matthew v:28. Have we overcharged our customers, exacted upon any one in our bargains, insisted on a full salary for work done by halves, defrauded the king of any part of his taxes, or taken advantage of the necessity and ignorance of others to get by their loss? we swell the numerous tribe of reputable thieves, and genteel robbers, Matthew xxii:21. Neglecting to keep our word and baptismal vow, or speaking an untruth, is "bearing false witness against our neighbour," ourselves, or Christ, who styles himself "the Truth," Revelation xxii:15. And giving place to a fretful, discontented thought, or an irregular, envious desire, is a breach of that spiritual precept, which made St. Paul say, "I had not known lust," or a wrong desire, "to be sin, except the law had said, Thou shalt not covet," Romans vii:7.

Such being the extreme spirituality of the law, who can plead that he never was guilty of breaking one, or even all of the ten commandments? And if we have broken them all, either in their literal or spiritual meaning, and are threatened for every transgression with a curse suitable to the Lawgiver's infinite Majesty, who can conceive the greatness of our guilt and danger? Till we find a sanctuary under the shadow of a Saviour's wings, are we not as liable to the strokes of Divine vengeance, as a felon, guilty of breaking all the statutes of his country, is liable to the penalty of human laws?

If this is not the case, there is no justice in the court of heaven, and the laws given with so much terror from the Almighty's throne, like the statutes of children, or the pope's bulls, are only *bruta fulmina,* words without effect, and thunders without lightnings.

Some indeed flatter themselves that "the law, since the Gospel dispensation, abates much of its demands of perfect love." But their hope is equally unsupported by reason and Scripture. The law is the eternal rule of right, the moral picture of the God of holiness and love. It can no more vary, than its eternal, unchangeable original. The Lord "will not alter the thing that is gone out of his mouth." He must cease to be what he is, before his law can lose its power to bind either men or angels; and all creatures shall break, sooner than it shall bend; for if it commands us only to "love God with all our heart, and our neighbour as ourselves," what JUST abatement can be made in so equitable a precept? Therefore man, who breaks the righteous law of God as naturally as he breathes, is, and must continue, under its fearful curse, till he has secured the pardon and help offered him in the Gospel.

THIRTY-THIRD ARGUMENT.

Nor is the Gospel itself without its threatenings; for if the Lord, on the one hand, "opens the kingdom of heaven to all believers;" he declares, on the other, that "they shall all be damned who believe not the truth," when it is proposed to them with sufficient evidence; and that "he who believeth not is condemned already, *because* he hath not believed on the name of the only begotten Son of God," 2 Thessalonians ii:12; John iii:18. From these awful declarations, I draw the following argument:—

If faith is so essential a virtue, how depraved and wretched is man, who is so excessively "slow of heart to believe" the things that concern his salvation! Matter of fact daily proves that we readily admit the evidence of men, while we peremptorily reject the testimony of God. Commodore Byron's extraordinary account of the giants in Patagonia is, or was, every where received: but that of Jesus Christ, concerning those who "walk in the broad way to destruction" is, and has always been, too generally disregarded, Matthew vii:13.

On reading in a newspaper an anonymous letter from Naples, we believe that rivers of liquid fire flow from the convulsed bowels of a mountain, and form burning lakes in the adjacent plains: but if we read in the Scripture that Tophet, the burning lake, "is prepared of old" for the impenitent, we beg leave to withhold our assent; and unless Divine grace prevents, we must fall in, and feel, before we assent and believe, Isaiah xxx:33.

Who that has seen a map of Africa, ever doubted whether there is such a kingdom as that of Morocco, though he never saw it, or any of its natives? But who that has perused the Gospel, never doubted, whether the "kingdom of heaven within us," or that state of "righteousness, peace, and joy in the Holy Ghost," which God opens to believers upon earth, is not a mere imagination? though Christ himself invites us to it, and many pious persons not only testify they enjoy it, but actually show its blessed fruits, in heavenly tempers, a blameless life, a triumphant death, Mark i:14; Luke xvii:21; Romans xiv:17; Revelation i:6.

With what readiness do we depend upon an honest man's promise, especially if it is reduced into a bond! But with what reluctance do we rely on the "many great and precious promises" of God, *confirmed by an oath*, delivered before the most unexceptionable witnesses, and sealed with the blood of Jesus Christ! 2 Peter i:4; 2 Corinthians i:20; Hebrews vi:17.

An Appeal to Matter of Fact and Common Sense

And ye numerous tribe of patients, how do ye shame those who call themselves Christians! So entire is the trust which you repose upon a physician's advice, whom perhaps you have seen but once, that you immediately abstain from your pleasant food, and regularly take medicines, which, for what you know, may be as injurious to your stomach as they are offensive to your palate. But we who profess Christianity generally quarrel with Christ's prescriptions; and if we do not understand the nature of a remedy which he recommends, we think this is a sufficient reason for refusing it. From Christ only, if we can help it, we will take nothing upon trust.

One false witness is often sufficient to make us believe that a neighbour vows to do us an injury; but twenty ministers of Jesus cannot persuade us, God "hath sworn in his wrath," that if we die in our sins, "we shall not enter into his rest," Psalm xcv:11, or that if we "come to him" for pardon and life, "he will in no wise cast us out," John vi:37. The most defamatory and improbable reports spread with uncommon swiftness, and pass for matter of fact; but when St. Paul testifies, that "if any man hath not the Spirit of Christ, he is none of his," Romans viii:9, who believes his testimony? Does not the same mind that was open to scandalous lies, prove shut against such a revealed truth?

Isaiah asks, "Who hath believed our report?" And Jesus says, "When the Son of man cometh, shall he find faith upon the earth?" Alas! there would have been no room for these plaintive questions, *if the word of God* had not been proposed to our faith; for the most groundless and absurd assertions of men find multitudes of believers. We see daily that an idle rumour about a peace or a war meets with such credit as to raise or sink the stocks in a few hours.

It is evident that man hath a foolish and "evil heart of unbelief," ready to "strain at a gnat" in Divine revelation, while he greedily "swallows up the camel" of human imposture. Now if it is part of the Gospel which Christ commands his ministers to "preach to every creature," that "he who believeth not shall be damned," Mark xvi:16, how great is the depravity, and how imminent the danger of fallen man, who has such a strong propensity to so destructive, so damnable a sin as unbelief!

THIRTY-FOURTH ARGUMENT.

But let us come still nearer to the point. If we are not "by nature conceived in sin," and "children of wrath," millions of infants who die without actual sin, have no need of the blood of Christ to wash their robes, nor his Spirit to purify their hearts. The incarnation of the eternal Word, and the influences of the Holy Spirit, are as unnecessary to them as the visits of a physician, and his remedies, to persons in perfect health. Their spotless innocency is a sufficient passport for heaven: baptism is ridiculous, and the Christian religion absurd in their case.

Nor does it appear, why it might not be as absurd with regard to the rest of mankind, did they but act their part a little better: for if we are naturally innocent, we have a natural power to remain so; and by a proper use of it, we may avoid standing in need of the salvation procured by Christ for the lost.

Nay, if innocent nature, carefully improved, may be the way to eternal life, it is certainly the readiest way; and the Son of God speaks like the grand deceiver of mankind, when he says, "I am the way; *no man* cometh unto the Father, but *by me.*"

Christians, let self-conceited Deists entertain the thought, but harbour it not a moment: in you it would be highly blasphemous.

THIRTY-FIFTH ARGUMENT.

And that you may detest it the more, consider farther, that all the capital doctrines of Christianity are built upon that fundamental article of our depravity and danger. If all flesh hath *not* corrupted its way, how severe are those words of Christ, "Except ye repent, ye shall all perish:" and "except ye be converted, ye shall not enter into the kingdom of heaven!" If all are not carnal and earthly by their first birth, how absurd is what he said to Nicodemus, "Except a man be born again, he cannot see the kingdom of heaven!" If there is any spiritual health in us by nature, how notoriously false are these assertions! "All our sufficiency is of God:" "Without me ye can do nothing." If every natural man is not the reverse of that holiness in which Adam was created, how irrational these and the like scriptures, "If any man is in Christ, he is *a new creature.*" *"In* Christ Jesus neither circumcision availeth any thing, nor uncircumcision, but *a new creature!"* To conclude: if mankind are not universally corrupt, guilty, and condemned, how unnecessarily alarming is this declaration, "He that believeth not on the Son of God, is condemned already: the wrath of God abideth on him!" and if we are not foolish, unrighteous, unholy, and enslaved to sin, why is "Christ made to us of God wisdom, righteousness, sanctification, and redemption?"

Take away then the doctrine of the fall, and the tower of evangelical truth, built by Jesus Christ, is no more founded on a rock, but upon the sand; or rather, the stately fabric is instantly thrown down, and leaves no ruins behind it, but the dry morality of Epictetus, covered with the rubbish of the wildest metaphors, and buried in the most impertinent ceremonies.

THIRTY-SIXTH ARGUMENT.

One more absurdity still remains. If man is not in the most imminent danger of destruction, nothing can be more extravagant than the great article of the Christian faith, thus expressed in the Nicene creed: "Jesus Christ, very God of very God, by whom all things were made; who for us men, and for our salvation, came down from heaven, was made man, and was crucified *for us."*

Is it not astonishing that there should be people so infatuated as to join every Lord's day in this solemn confession, and to deny the other six, the horrible danger to which they are exposed, till they have an interest in Christ? Is not the least grain of common sense sufficient to make an attentive person see, that if He, "by whom all things were made, came from heaven for *our* salvation," if he "was made man" that he might suffer and be "crucified for us;" he saw US guilty, condemned, lost, and obnoxious to the *damnation,* which we continually deprecate in the litany? Shall we charge the Son of God, in "whom are hid all the treasures of Divine wisdom," with the unparalleled folly of coming from heaven to atone for *innocent* creatures, to reprieve persons *uncondemned,* to redeem a race of free men, to deliver from the curse a people *not accursed;* to hang by exquisitely dolorous wounds, made in his sacred hands and feet, on a tree more ignominious than the gallows, for *honest men and very good sort of people*; and to expire under the sense of the wrath of Heaven, that he might save from hell, people in no danger of going there?

Reader, is it possible to entertain for a moment these wild notions without offering the utmost indignity to the Son of God, and the greatest violence to common sense? And does not reason cry, as with the sound of a thousand trumpets, "If our Creator could not save us consistently with his glorious attributes, but by becoming incarnate, passing through the deepest scenes of humiliation and temptation, distress and want, for thirty-three years; and undergoing at last the most shameful, painful, and accursed death in our place; our wickedness must be desperate, our sins execrable, our guilt black as the shadow of death, and our danger dreadful as the gloom and torments of hell?"

"*Shocking doctrine!*" says the self-conceited moralist, as he rises from his chair full of indignation, and ready to throw aside the arguments he cannot answer. Reader, if you are the man, remember that this is an appeal to *reason*, and not to *passion; to matter of fact*, and not to your vitiated taste for *pleasing error*. You may cry out at the sight of a shroud, a coffin, a grave, "*Shocking objects!*" but your loudest exclamations will not lessen the awful reality, by which many have happily been *shocked* into a timely consideration of, and preparation for, approaching death.

"But this doctrine," you still urge, "drives people to despair." Yes, to a despair of being saved by their own merits and righteousness; and this is as reasonable in a sinner who comes to the Saviour, as despairing to swim across the sea is rational in a passenger that takes ship. Our Church, far from speaking against it, says that "sinners should be dismayed at God's rightful justice, and should *despair* indeed as touching any hope that may be *in themselves.*" (*Homily on Falling from God*: part 2.)

A just despair of ourselves is widely different from a despair of God's mercy, and Christ's willingness to save the chief of sinners, who fly to him for refuge. This horrible sin, this black crime of Judas, springs rather from a sullen, obstinate rejection of the remedy, than, as some vainly suppose, from a clear knowledge of the disease: and that none may commit it, Christ's ministers take particular care not to preach the law without the Gospel, and the fall without the recovery. No sooner have they opened the wound of sin, festering in the sinner's conscience, than they pour in the balm of Divine promises, and make gracious offers of a free pardon, and full salvation, by the compassionate Redeemer, who came to "justify the ungodly," and to "save the lost."

And indeed those only who see their sin and misery will cordially embrace the Gospel; for common sense dictates that none care for the king's mercy but those who know they are guilty, condemned criminals. How excessively unreasonable is it then to object, that the preaching of man's corrupt and lost estate drives people to despair of Divine mercy, when it is absolutely the only means of showing them their need of it, and making them gladly accept it upon God's own terms!

Leaving therefore that trite objection to the unthinking vulgar, once more, judicious reader, summon all your rational powers: and, after imploring help from on high to use them aright, say, whether these last arguments do not prove that no *Christian* can deny the complete fall of mankind, without renouncing the capital doctrines of his own religion; overturning the very foundation of the Gospel, which he professes to receive; staining the glory of the Redeemer, whom he pretends to honour; and impiously, taking from his crown, *wisdom, truth,* and *charity,* the three jewels that are its brightest ornaments. Sum up then all that has been advanced concerning the afflictive dealings of God's providence with mankind, and the base conduct, or wicked temper of mankind toward God, one another, and themselves. Declare, if all the arguments laid before you, and cleared from the thickest clouds of objections that might obscure them, do not cast more light upon the black subject of our depravity than is sufficient to show that it is a melancholy truth. And finally pronounce, whether the doctrine of our corrupt and lost estate, stated in the words of the sacred writers, and of our pious reformers, is not *rationally demonstrated*, and established upon the firmest basis in the world, *matter of fact, and* the dictates of *common sense.*

PART V.

WHEN a doctrine has been clearly demonstrated, the truths that *necessarily* spring from it cannot reasonably be rejected. Let then common sense decide whether the following consequences do not necessarily result from the doctrine of the fall, established in the preceding parts of this treatise.

I. INFERENCE. If we are by nature in a corrupt and lost estate, the grand business of ministers is to rouse our drowsy consciences, and warn us of our imminent danger: it behooves them to "cry aloud and spare not, to lift up their voice like a trumpet," and "show us our transgressions and our sins:" nor are they to desist from this unpleasing part of their office till we "awake to righteousness," and "lay hold on the hope set before us."

If preachers, under pretence of peace and good nature, let the wound fester in the conscience of their hearers, to avoid the thankless office of probing it to the bottom: if, for fear of giving them pain by a timely amputation, they let them die of a mortification: or if "they heal the hurt of the daughter of God's people slightly, saying, Peace! Peace! when there is no peace;" they imitate those sycophants of old, who, for fear of displeasing the rich and offending the great, "preached smooth things and prophesied deceit."

This cruel gentleness, this soft barbarity, is attended with the most pernicious consequences, and will deservedly meet with the most dreadful punishment. "Give sinners warning from me," says the Lord to every minister: "When I say to the wicked," the unconverted, "Thou shalt surely die; and thou givest him not warning, he shall die in his iniquity," in his unconverted state; "but his blood will I require at *thy* hand." See Matthew xviii:3; Ezekiel iii:18, and xiii:10.

II. INFERENCE. If we are naturally depraved and condemned creatures, *self righteousness* and *pride* are the most absurd and monstrous of all our sins. The deepest repentance and profoundest humility become us: to *neglect* them is to stumble at the very threshold of true religion; and to *ridicule* them is to pour contempt upon reason, revelation, and the first operations of Divine grace upon a sinner's heart.

III. INFERENCE. If the corruption of mankind is universal, inveterate, and amazingly powerful, no mere creature can deliver them from it. They must remain unrestored; or they must have an almighty, omniscient, omnipresent, unwearied, infinitely patient Saviour; willing, day and night, to attend to the wants and public or secret applications of millions of wretched souls; and able to give them immediate assistance throughout the world, in all their various trials, temptations, and conflicts, both in life and in death. Is the most exalted *creature* sufficient for these things?

When such a vast body as mankind, spread over all the earth for thousands of years, made up of numerous nations, all of which consist of multitudes of individuals, each of whom has the springs of all his faculties and powers enfeebled, disordered, or broken:—when such an immense body as this is to be restored to the image of the infinitely holy, glorious, and blessed God; common sense dictates that the amazing task can be performed by no other than the original Artist, the great Searcher of hearts, the omnipotent Creator of mankind.

Hence it appears that, notwithstanding the cavils of Arius, the Saviour is "GOD OVER ALL, blessed for ever; all things were made by him, he upholds all things by the word of his power;" and every believer may adore him and say, with the wondering apostle, when the light of faith shone into his benighted soul, "My Lord and my God!"

IV. INFERENCE. If our guilt is immense, it cannot be expiated without a sacrifice of an infinite dignity: hence we discover the mistake of heathens and carnal Jews, who trusted in the sacrifices of beasts; the error of Deists, Mohammedans, and Socinians, who see no need of any expiatory sacrifice; and the amazing presumption of too many Christians, who repose a considerable part of their confidence in the proper merit of their works; instead of placing it entirely in the infinitely meritorious sacrifice of the immaculate Lamb of God, humbly acknowledging that all the gracious rewardableness of the best works of faith is derived from his precious blood and *original* merit.

V. INFERENCE. If our spiritual maladies are both numerous and mortal, it is evident we cannot *recover* the spiritual health that we enjoyed in our first parents, but by the powerful help of our heavenly Physician, the second Adam. How absurd is it then to say that we are *saw* or *recovered* by doing good works, without the quickening grace of a Saviour!

A wretched beggar is lame both in his hands and feet; an officious man, instead of taking him to a person famous for his skill in relieving such objects of distress, assures him that the only way of getting well is to run on errands for his prince, and work for his fellow beggars. You justly wonder at the cruelty and folly of such a director; but you have much more reason to be astonished at the conduct of those miserable empirics, who direct poor, blind, lame sinners, labouring under a complication of spiritual disorders, and sick even unto eternal death, to save themselves merely by serving God and doing good to their neighbours; as if they needed neither repentance toward God, nor faith in our Lord Jesus Christ, nor yet free grace, to enable them to repent, believe, and serve God acceptably.

How much more rational is the evangelical method of salvation! "We are saved," says the apostle, we are restored to saving health, and a spiritual activity to serve God and our neighbour, "not by works, not of ourselves;" but "by grace," by mere favour; "through faith," through such an entire confidence in our Physician as makes us gladly take his powerful remedies, abstain from the pleasing poison of sin, and feed on those Divine truths which communicate angelical vigour and happiness to our souls, Ephesians ii:8.

VI. INFERENCE. If our nature is so completely fallen and totally helpless, that in spiritual things "we are not sufficient of ourselves to think any thing" truly good "as of ourselves, but our sufficiency is of God;" it is plain we stand in absolute need of his Spirit's assistance to enable us to pray, repent, believe, love, and obey aright. Consequently, those who ridicule the Holy Spirit, and his sacred influence, despise the great "Helper of our infirmities," and act a most irrational, wicked, and desperate part, Romans viii:26.

VII. INFERENCE. If by nature we are *really* and *truly* born in sin, our regeneration cannot be a mere metaphor or a vain ceremony; our spiritual birth must be *real* and *positive*. How fatal therefore is the mistake of those who suppose that the *new birth* is only a figurative expression for a *decent behaviour!* How dreadful the error of those who imagine that all whose faces have been typically washed with the material water in baptism are now effectually "born again of" living "water and the" Holy "Spirit!" And how inexcusable the case of the multitudes, who, in the Church of England, are under this dangerous mistake, so prudently guarded against by our pious reformers!

In our catechism they clearly distinguish between "the outward visible sign" or form in baptism, and "the inward spiritual grace:" and by defining the latter, "a death unto sin and a new birth unto righteousness," they declare that whosoever is not "dead" or dying "to sin," and "alive to righteousness," is not truly regenerate, and has nothing of baptism but the "outward and visible sign." In the twenty-seventh of our articles they mention, that "baptism is *not the new birth, but a* SIGN of regeneration or new birth, whereby, as by an instrument, they who receive baptism rightly, are grafted into the Church." And if our Church returns thanks for the regeneration of the infants whom she has admitted to baptism, it is chiefly* upon a charitable supposition, that "they have received it rightly," and will, "for their part, faithfully perform their promises, made for them by their sureties." If they refuse to do it *when they come of age,* far from treating them as her regenerate children, she denounces a general excommunication against them, and charges them "not to come to" her "holy table, lest Satan brings them, as" he did "Judas, to destruction both of body and soul."

VIII. INFERENCE. If the fall of mankind in Adam does not consist in a capricious imputation of his personal guilt, but in a real, present participation of his depravity, impotence, and misery; the salvation that believers have in Christ is not a capricious imputation of his personal righteousness, but a real, present participation of his purity, power, and blessedness, together with pardon and acceptance.

Unspeakably dangerous then is the delusion of those whose brains and mouths are filled with the notions and expressions of "imputed righteousness;" while their poor, carnal, unregenerate hearts remain perfect strangers to "the Lord our righteousness."

IX. INFERENCE. If the corrupt nature which sinners derive from Adam spontaneously produces all the wickedness that overspreads the earth; the holy nature

---

* I say *chiefly,* because our Church gives thanks also for Christ's general grace and mercy to children, declaring herself "persuaded of the good will of our heavenly Father toward this (unbaptized) infant," through Christ, who said, that "of little children is the kingdom of heaven." The truth lies between the error of the *Pelagians,* who suppose that unbaptized infants are *sinless* like angels; and that of the *Papists,* who affirm that they are *graceless as* devils

which believers receive from Christ, is also spontaneously productive of all the fruits of righteousness described in the oracles of God; "Good works springing out, *necessarily*,* of a true and lively faith," Art. 12.

Such ministers, therefore, as clearly preach our fall in Adam, and that faith in Christ which is productive of genuine holiness and active love, will infallibly promote good works and pure morality: when those who insist only upon works and moral duties will neither be zealous of good works themselves, nor instrumental, in turning sinners from their gross immoralities. The reason is obvious: evangelical preachers follow their Lord's wise direction: "Make the tree good, and the fruit shall be good also:" but moralists will have "corrupt trees bring forth good fruit," which, in the nature of things, is impossible, Matthew xii:33; Luke vi:43. Therefore, as nothing but faith "makes the tree good," and as "without faith it is impossible to please God;" the Christian, that will "come to him" with good works, "must" not only "believe [as heathens] that he is, and that he is a rewarder of those who diligently seek him;" but also that "he was in Christ reconciling the world unto himself," &c.

X. INFERENCE. If corruption and sin work so powerfully and sensibly in the hearts of the unregenerate, we may, without deserving the name of enthusiasts, affirm, that the regenerate are sensible of the powerful effects of Divine grace in their souls; or, to use the words of our seventeenth article, we may say, "They feel in themselves the workings of the Spirit of Christ:" for "where" the poison of "sin hath abounded," and has been of course abundantly felt; "grace," the powerful antidote that expels it, does "much more abound," and consequently may be much more perceived.

Therefore "the knowledge of salvation by the forgiveness of sins," the assurance of faith, and "the peace of God passing all understanding," are the EXPERIENCED *blessings* of the converted, as certainly as a guilty conscience, the gnawing of worldly cares, the working of evil tempers, the tumults of unbridled appetites, and the uproars of rebellious passions, are the EXPERIENCED *curses* of the unconverted.

Reader, if these inferences are justly drawn, is it not evident that the principles† are generally exploded among us as enthusiastical or Methodistical, which flow from the doctrine demonstrated in this treatise, as naturally as light from the sun? These consequences lead you perhaps farther than you could wish; but let them not make you either afraid or ashamed of the Gospel. Prejudices, like clouds, will vanish away; but truth, which they obscure for a time, like the sun, will shine for ever. A great man in the law said, *Fiat justitia, ruat mundus.* Improve the noble sentiment, and say with equal fortitude, "*Stet veritas, ruat mundus:* let truth stand, though the universe should sink into ruins."

But, happily for us, the danger is all on the side of the opposite doctrine; and that you may be convinced of it, I present you next with a view of the

---

* This is to be understood of a moral, and not of an absolute irresistible necessity; for faith never unmans the believer.

† Those doctrines pointed out in the ten above mentioned inferences, are 1. The alarming severity of the law; 2. The need of a deep, heartfelt repentance: 3. The divinity of Christ; 4. The infinite merit of his sacrifice; 5. Salvation by faith in him; 6. The influences of his Holy Spirit; 7. The reality of the new birth; 8. The necessity of a present salvation; 9. The zeal of believers for good works; and 10. The comfortable assurance which they have of their regeneration

The Works of John Fletcher

DREADFUL CONSEQUENCES
Necessarily resulting from the ignorance of our depravity and danger.

1. As the tempter caused the fall of our first parents, by inducing them to believe that they "should not surely die," if they broke the Divine law: so, now we are fallen, he prevents our recovering, by suggesting "the bitterness of death is past," and "we are in a state of safety." Hence it is that you sleep on in carnal security, O ye deluded sons of men, and even dream ye are safe and righteous. Nor can ye escape for your lives till the veil of unbelief is taken away, and ye awake to a sight of your corrupt and lost estate; for there is no guarding against, nor flying from, an unseen, unsuspected evil: here, as in a conspiracy, the danger continually increases till it is happily discovered.

2. If we are not sensible of our natural corruption and the justice of the curse entailed upon us on that account, can we help thinking God a tyrant, when he threatens unconverted moralists with the severest of his judgments, or causes the black storms of his providence to overtake us and our dearest relatives? Answer, ye self-righteous Pharisees, that so bitterly exclaim against the ministers, who declare, by the authority of Scripture, that "except ye repent, ye shall all perish." Answer, fond mother, whose tears of distraction mix with the cold sweat of the convulsed, dying infant on thy lap. Dost thou not secretly impeach Divine justice, and accuse Heaven of barbarity? Ah! if thou didst but know the evil nature which thou and thy Isaac have brought into the world; if thou sawest the root of bitterness which the hand of a gracious Providence even now extracts from his heart; far from being ready to "curse God, and die" with thy child, thou wouldest patiently acquiesce in the kindly severe dispensation; thou wouldest "clear him when he is judged" by such as thyself, and even "glorify him in the evil day of this painful visitation."

3. Though man's heart is hardened as steel, it does not frequently emit the hellish sparks of such murmurings against God, because it can seldom be struck by the flint of such severe afflictions; yet the mischief is there, and will break out, if not by *blasphemous despair*, at least by its contrary, *presumptuous madness*. Yes, reader, unless thou art happily made acquainted with the strength of thy inbred depravity, thou wilt rashly venture among the sparks of temptation: with carnal confidence thou wilt ask, "What harm can they do me?" And thou wilt continue the hazardous sport till sin and wrath consume thee together. Nor will this be more surprising than that one, who carries a bag of gunpowder, and knows not the dangerous nature of his load, should fearlessly rush through the midst of flames or sparks, till he is blown up and destroyed.

4. This fatal rashness is generally accompanied with a glaring inconsistency. Do not you make the assertion good, ye saints of the present age, who pretend to have found the secret of loving both God and the world? Do not we hear you deny to men that you are *condemned*, and yet cry to God to *have mercy upon you*? But if you are not condemned, what need have you of *mercy*? And if you are, why do you deny your lost estate? Thou too, reader, wilt fall into this absurdity, unless thou knowest thy just condemnation. But the mischief will not stop here; for,

5. Ignorance of the mystery of iniquity within you must, in the nature of things, cause you to neglect prayer, or to pray out of character. As unhumbled moralists, instead of approaching the throne of grace with the self abasement of the penitent

publican, saying, "God be merciful unto me a sinner!" you will provoke the Most High, by the open profaneness of the Sadducee; or insult him by the self-conceited services of the Pharisee, boasting ye "do no harm," and thanking God, ye "are not as other men." On these rocks your formal devotion will split, till you know, that as the impenitent and prayerless shall perish, so the Lord accepts no penitential prayer, but that of "the man who knows the plague of his own heart; because he alone prays in his own character, and without hypocrisy," 1 Peter v:5; 1 Kings viii:31.

6. And as you cannot approach the throne of grace aright, while you remain insensible of your corruption; so the reading or preaching of God's word, till it answers the end of conviction, is of no service to you, but rather proves, to use St. Paul's nervous expression, the "savour of death unto death." For when the terrors of the law only suit your case, you vainly catch at the comforts of the Gospel; or rather you remain as unaffected under the threatenings of the one as under the promises of the other: you look on Mount Sinai and Mount Sion with equal indifference, and the warmth of the preacher, who invites you to "fly from the wrath to come," appears to you an instance of religious madness. Nor is it a wonder it should, while you continue unacquainted with your danger: when a mortal disease is neither felt nor suspected, a pathetic address upon its consequences and cure must be received by any reasonable man with the greatest unconcern; and the person that makes it in earnest, must appear exceedingly ridiculous. Again:

7. "My people are destroyed for lack of knowledge," says the Lord. This is true, particularly with regard to the knowledge of our depravity. Reader, if thou remainest a stranger to it, thou wilt look upon slight confessions of outward sins as true repentance; and the "godly sorrow that worketh repentance to salvation" will appear to thee a symptom of melancholy. Taking an external reformation of manners, or a change of ceremonies and opinions, for true conversion, thou wilt think thyself in a safe state, while thy heart continues habitually wandering from God, and under the dominion of a worldly spirit. In a word, some of the branches of the tree of corruption thou mayest possibly lop off, but the root will still remain and gather strength. For it is plain, that a bad root, supposed not to exist, can neither be heartily lamented, nor earnestly struck at with the axe of self denial.

Even a heathen could say,* "The knowledge of sin is the first step toward salvation from it; for he who knows not that he sins, will not submit to be set right: thou must find out what thou art before thou canst mend thyself:—therefore, when thou discoverest thy vices, to which thou wast before a stranger, it is a sign that thy soul is in a better state."

8. It is owing to the want of this discovery, O ye pretended sons of reason, that thinking yourselves born pure, or supposing the disease of your nature to be inconsiderable, you imagine it possible to be your own physicians, when you are only your own destroyers. Hence it is, that while you give to Jesus the titular honour of *Saviour,* you speak perpetually of being "saved merely by your duties and best endeavours." Hear him warning you against this common delusion: "O Israel," says

---

* Initium est salutis notitia peccati; nam qui peccare se nescit, corrigi non vult; deprehendas te oportet antequam emendes, *Sen. Ep. 28.* Et hoc ipsum argumentum est in melius translati animi, quod vitia sua, quæ adhuc ignorabat, videt, *Ep. 4.*

he, "thou hast destroyed thyself, but in *me* is thy help found. The whole need not a physician, but they that are sick," beyond all hope of recovering themselves.

9. The prescriptions of this wise Physician are excessively severe to flesh and blood, and some of his remedies as violent as our disease. Therefore, except we see the greatness of our danger, we shall beg to be excused from taking the bitter potion. Who can have resolution enough to "cut off a right hand, to pluck out a right eye," to "take up his cross daily, to deny himself, and lose even his own life," or what is often dearer, his fair reputation? Who, I say, can do this, till a sight of imminent ruin on the one hand, and of redeeming love on the other, makes him submit to the painful injunctions? Thou lovely youth, noted in the Gospel for thy harmlessness, I appeal to thy wretched experience. When the Physician of souls, at whose feet thou wast prostrate, commanded thee to "sell all and follow him," what made thee "go away sorrowful" and undone? Not barely thy "great possessions," but the ignorance of thy condition: for "all that a man hath will he give for his life," when he sees it in immediate danger, Matthew xix:22.

10. If it is a desperate step to turn away from the Prince of Life, it is a daring one to approach him with a mere compliment. Of this, nevertheless, you are guilty, ye unawakened sinners, who daily appear before the throne of grace with *thanks* and *praises* to God, "for his inestimable love in the redemption of the world by our Lord Jesus Christ." Alas! When you deny the state of sin and misery in which you are by nature, and yet presume to thank God for *redemption* from it, do you not mock him as solemnly as you would the king, were you to present him every day an address of thanks for redeeming you from Turkish slavery, when you never knew yourselves slaves in Turkey? O how provoking to God must these unmeaning thanksgivings be! Surely one day they will be ranked among the indignities offered by earthly worms to *the Majesty on high*.

11. Some, indeed, more consistent than you, openly throw off the mask. Seeing neither the unfathomable depth of their misery by the fall, nor the immense height of their aggravated iniquities, they do not trifle with, but at once "deny, the Lord that bought them." Yes, far from admiring the established method of a salvation, procured at so immense a price as the incarnation and the crucifixion of the Son of God, they are not afraid to intimate it is irrational: and upon their principles they may well do it; for if our ruin is not immense, what need is there for an immensely glorious Redeemer? And if our guilt reaches not up to heaven, why should the Son of God have come down from thence to "put away sin by the sacrifice of himself?"

12. As we slight or reject the Saviour, till we are truly convinced of the evil and danger of sin; so we worship a false god, a mere idol. For, instead of adoring Jehovah, infinite in his holiness and hatred of sin; inviolable in the truth of his threatenings against it, and impartial in his strict justice; a God in whose presence unhumbled sinners "are not able to stand," and "with whom evil cannot dwell;" we bow to a "strange god," whom pious men never knew, a god formed by our own fancy—so *unholy* as to connive at sin, so *unjust* as to set aside his most righteous law, and so *false* as to break his most solemn word, that we must "turn or die," Ezekiel xxxiii:11.

Is not this worshipping a god of our own making; or, as David describes him, a "god altogether such as ourselves?" To adore an idol of paste, made by the baker and the priest, may be indeed more foolish, but cannot be more wicked than to adore one made by our wild imagination, and impious unbelief.

13. We may go one step farther still, and affirm that till we are deeply convinced of sin, far from worshipping the true God, (which implies knowing, loving, and admiring him in all his perfections,) we hate and oppose him in his infinite *holiness* and *justice*. The proof is obvious:—Two things diametrically opposite in their nature, can never be approved of at once. If we do not side with Divine holiness and justice, abhor our corruption, and condemn ourselves as hell-deserving sinners; far from approving, we shall arise against the holy and righteous God, who sentences us to eternal death for our sin: we shall at least wish he were less pure and just than he is, which amounts to wishing him to be no God. While proud fiends betray this horrid disposition by loud blasphemies in hell, ye do it, O ye unconvinced sons of men, by your aversion to godliness upon earth. "Haters of God," is then the proper name, and "enmity against him," the settled temper of all unhumbled unconverted sinners, Romans i:30, and viii:7.

14. When the nature of God is mistaken, what wonder if his law is misapprehended? "The law is good, says St. Paul, "if a man use it lawfully;" but if we make an improper use of it, the consequence is fatal. Since the fall, the law of God, as contra-distinguished from the Gospel of Christ, points out to us the spotless holiness, and inflexible justice, of its Divine Author. It teaches us with what ardour and constancy we should love both our Creator and our fellow creatures. As a bank cast against the stream of our iniquity, it accidentally serves to make it rise the higher, and to discover its impetuosity; for "by the law is the knowledge of sin." It demonstrates man's weakness, who "consents indeed to the law that it is good, but finds not how to fulfil it," Romans vii:16, 19. As a battery erected against pride, when it has its due effect, it silences all our selfrighteous pleas, and convinces us that a returning sinner "is not justified by the works of the law, but by the faith of Christ." A broken law, a law which "worketh wrath," being absolutely unable to absolve its violater. In a word, "it is our school master to bring us to Christ," and drives us with the rod of threatened punishments, to make us touch the sceptre of mercy, held out to us from the throne of grace.

But while we remain strangers to our helpless and hopeless state by nature, far from making this proper use of the law, we trust in it, and fancy that the merit of our unsprinkled obedience to it is the way of salvation. Thus we "go about to establish our own righteousness, making light of" the atoning blood, which marks "the new and living" way to heaven. This very mistake ruined the Pharisees of old, and destroys their numerous followers in all ages, Romans ix:31.

15. And when we form such wrong apprehensions of the law, is it possible that we should have right views of the *Gospel,* and receive it with cordial affection? Reason and experience answer in the negative. What says the Gospel to sinners? "You are saved *by grace,* " through mere favour and mercy, "not" by the covenant "of works, lest any man should boast" like the Pharisee, Ephesians ii:8. Now ye decent formalists, ye fond admirers of your own virtue, are you not utterly disqualified to seek and accept a pardon in a Gospel way? For your seeking it upon the footing of mere *mercy,* implies an acknowledgment that you deserve the ruin threatened against sinners. And suppose a pardon was granted you, before you had a consciousness of your sad deserts, you could not receive it as an act of *mere grace,* but only as a reward justly bestowed upon you for the merit of your works. It is plain, then, that according to the

The Works of John Fletcher

Gospel plan, none can be fit subjects of salvation, but those who are truly sensible of their condemnation.

16. But as the grace of God in Christ is the original and properly meritorious cause of our salvation, so the grand instrumental cause of it is *faith* on our part. "Through faith are ye saved," says St. Paul. Now, if to have faith in Christ, is habitually to lift up our hearts to him, with an humble and yet cheerful confidence, seeking in him all our "wisdom, righteousness," and "strength," as being our instructing "Prophet," atoning "Priest," and protecting "King;" it is evident, that till we awake to a sight of our fallen state, we cannot believe, nor consequently be saved. O ye that never were sensible of your spiritual blindness, can you with sincerity take Jesus for your guide, and desire his "Spirit to lead you into all truth?" Does not David's prayer, "Open thou mine eyes, that I may see the wonderful things of thy law," appear to you needless, if not fanatical? And is not the Redeemer's *prophetic office* thrown away upon such sons of wisdom as you are?

Have you a greater value for Jesus than they, O ye *just men,* who have *no* sensible *need of* heart-felt *repentance,* and whose breasts were never dilated by one sigh, under a due sense of your guilt and condemnation? Can you, without hypocrisy, apply to him as the *High Priest* of the *guilty,* claim him as the *Advocate* of the *condemned,* or fly to him as the *Saviour* of the *lost?* Impossible! Ye fondly hope ye never were lost, ye were always "good livers, good believers, good Churchmen;" ye "need not make so much ado" about an interest in the blood of the new covenant.

And ye who, flushed with the conceit of your native strength, wonder at the weakness of those that continually bow at the sceptre of Jesus' grace for protection and power; can you without a smile of pity hear him say, "Without me ye can do nothing?" Is it possible that you should sincerely implore the exertion of his royal power for victory over sins which you suppose yourselves able to conquer; and for the restoration of a nature, with the goodness of which you are already so well satisfied? Your reason loudly answers, No: therefore, till you see yourselves corrupt, impotent creatures, you will openly neglect the Redeemer, give to your aggravated sins the name of "human frailties," and trust to your baffled, and yet boasted endeavours. Self deception! Art thou not of all impostors the most common and dangerous, because the least suspected?

To sum up and close these important remarks: look at those who in mystic Babylon are not truly sensible of their total fall from God, and you will see them setting their own reason above the Holy Scriptures, and their works in competition with the infinitely meritorious sacrifice of Christ. Inquire into their principles, and you will discover that they either openly explode as enthusiastical, or slightly receive as unnecessary, the doctrines of salvation by faith in Christ, and regeneration by the Spirit of God. Examine their conduct, and you will find they all "commit sin," and "receive the mark of the beast" secretly "in their right hand, or" openly "in their foreheads," Revelation xiii:16. Sort them, and you will have two bands, the one of skeptics, and the other of formalists, who, though at as great "enmity between themselves" as Pilate and Herod, are like them "made friends together," by jointly "deriding" and "condemning Jesus" in his living members.

And if with the candle of the Lord you search the Jerusalem of professing Christians, you will perceive that the want of a heart-felt, humbling knowledge of their natural depravity, gives birth to the double mindedness of hypocrites, and the miscarriages or apostasy of those who once distinguished themselves in the evangelical race; you will easily trace back to the same corrupt source the seemingly opposite errors of the *loose Antinomian,* and the *Pharisaic Legalist,* those spiritual thieves by whom the sincere Christian is perpetually reviled; and, in short, you will be convinced, that if you set your eyes upon a man who is not yet deeply conscious of his corrupt and lost estate, or whose consciousness of it has worn away, you behold either a trifler in religion, a dead-hearted Pharisee, a sly hypocrite, a loose Antinomian, a self-conceited formalist, a scoffing infidel, or a wretched apostate.

You see, reader, what a train of fatal consequences results from rejecting, or not properly receiving, the doctrine demonstrated in these sheets. And now, that you may cordially embrace it, permit me to enumerate the

UNSPEAKABLE ADVANTAGES
Springing from an affecting knowledge of our fallen and lost estate.

No sooner is the disease rightly known, than the neglected Jesus, who is both our gracious physician and powerful remedy, is properly valued, and ardently sought. "All that" thus "seek, find;" and all that find *him,* find saving health, eternal life, and heaven.

Bear your testimony with me, ye children of Abraham and of God, who see the brightness of a Gospel "day and rejoice." Say, what made you first wishfully "look to the hills, whence your salvation is come," and fervently desire to behold the sin-dispelling beams of the "Sun of righteousness?" Was it not the deep dismal night of our fallen nature, which you happily discovered, when, awaking from the sleep of sin, you first saw the delusive dreams of life as they appear to the dying? What was "the Desire of nations" to you, till you felt yourselves lost sinners? Alas! nothing; perhaps less than nothing; an object of disgust or scorn. When "the pearl of great price" was presented to you, did you regard it more than the vilest of brutes an oriental pearl? And as if it had not been enough to look at it with disdain, were not some of you ready to "turn again and rend," after the example of snarling animals, those who affectionately made you the invaluable offer? Matthew vii:6.

But when the storm that shook Mount Sinai overtook your careless souls, and ye saw yourselves sinking into an abyss of misery, did ye not cry out and say, as the alarmed disciples, with an unknown energy of desire, "Save, Lord, or we perish?" And when, conscious of your lost estate, ye began to believe that he "came to seek and to save that which was lost," how dear, how *precious* was he to you in all his offices! How glad were you to take guilty, weeping Magdalene's place, and wait for a pardon at your *High Priest's* feet! How importunate in saying to your *King,* as the helpless widow, "Lord, avenge me of mine adversary," my "evil heart of unbelief!" How earnest, how unwearied in your applications to your *Prophet,* for heavenly light and wisdom! The incessant prayer of blind Bartimeus was then yours, and so was the gracious answer which the Lord returned to him; you "received" your spiritual "sight." And O! what saw you then? The sacred "book unsealed! Your sins blotted out as a cloud! The glory of God shining in the face of Jesus Christ;" and "the kingdom of heaven opened to all believers!"

Then, and not till then, you could say from the heart, "This is a faithful saying, and worthy of all acceptation, that Christ Jesus came into the world to save sinners, of whom I am chief," 1 Timothy i:15. Then you could cry out with his first disciples, "Behold what manner of love the Father hath bestowed upon us, that we should be called the sons of God," 1 John iii:1. "We are all the children of God by faith in Christ Jesus, whom having not seen we love; in whom, though now we see him not, yet believing, we rejoice with joy unspeakable and full of glory, receiving the end of our faith, the salvation of our souls," Galatians iii:26; 1 Peter i:8. "We trusted in him, and are helped; therefore our heart danceth for joy, and in our song will we praise him," Psalm xxviii:8. "To him that hath loved us, and washed us from our sins in his own blood, and hath made us kings and priests unto God and his Father; to him be glory and dominion for ever and ever," Revelation i:5.

And this will be also your triumphant song, attentive reader, if, deeply conscious of your lost estate, you spread your guilt and misery before Him who "came to bind up the broken hearted, to proclaim liberty to the captives, and the opening of the prison to them that are bound; and to comfort all that mourn, by giving them beauty for ashes, the oil of joy for mourning, and the garment of praise for the spirit of heaviness," Isaiah lxi:1. "Your sorrow," it is true, "may endure for a night, but joy will come in the morning, the joy of God's salvation," and the pardon of your sins. "Having much forgiven," you "will" then "love much," and admire in proportion the riches of Divine wisdom, goodness, justice, and power, that so graciously contrived, and so wonderfully executed, the plan of your redemption. You will be ravished in experiencing that a condemned sinner can not only escape impending ruin, but enter into present possession of a spiritual paradise, where peace and joy blossom together, and whence welcome death will, ere long, translate your triumphant soul to those unseen, unheard of, inconceivable glories "which God hath prepared for them that love him," 1 Corinthians ii:9.

Nor will the blossoms of heavenly "peace" and "joy" only diffuse their Divine fragrancy in your soul; all "the fruits of holiness" will grow together with them, "to the glory of God," and the profit of mankind. And thou wilt not be the last, thou fair, thou blushing *humility*, to bend all the spreading branches of the "tree of righteousness." No, we cannot be vain, or despisers of others, when we see that we are all corrupted, dying shoots of the same corrupted, dead stock: we cannot be self righteous, when we are persuaded that the best fruit which we can *naturally* produce is only splendid sin, or vice coloured over with the specious appearance of virtue. We must lie prostrate in the dust, when we consider the ignominious cross where our Divine Surety hung, bled, and died, to ransom our guilty souls.

A genuine conviction of our corruption and demerit, thus striking at the very root of our pride, necessarily fills our hearts with inexpressible gratitude for every favour we receive, gives an exquisite relish to the least blessing we enjoy, and teaches us to say with the thankful patriarch, "I am not worthy of the least of all thy mercies;" and as it renders us grateful to God, and all our benefactors, so it makes us patient under the greatest injuries, resigned in the heaviest trials, glad to be reproved, willing to forgive the faults of others, open to acknowledge our own, disposed to sympathize with the guilty, tender hearted toward the miserable, incapable of being offended at any one, and ready to do every office of kindness, even to the meanest of mankind.

Again: no sooner are we properly acquainted with our helplessness, than we give over leaning on an arm of flesh, and the broken reed of our own resolutions. Reposing our entire confidence in the living God, we fervently implore his continual assistance, carefully avoid temptations, gladly acknowledge that "the help which is done upon the earth, the Lord doth it himself," and humbly give him the glory of all the good that appears in ourselves and others.

Once more: as soon as we can discover our spiritual blindness, we mistrust our own judgment, feel the need of instruction, modestly repair to the experienced for advice, carefully search the Scriptures, readily follow their blessed directions, and fervently pray that no false light may mislead us out of the way of salvation.

To conclude: a right knowledge that "the crown has fallen from our head," will make us abominate sin, the cause of our ruin, and raise in us a noble ambition of regaining our original state of blissful and glorious righteousness. It will set us upon an earnest inquiry into, and a proper use of, all the means conducive to our recovery. Even the *sense* of our guilt will prove useful, by helping to break our obdurate hearts, by embittering the baits of worldly vanities, and filling our souls with penitential sorrow. "Before honour is humility." This happy humiliation makes way for the greatest exaltation: for "thus saith the high and lofty One that inhabiteth eternity, I dwell in the high and holy place, with him also that is of a contrite and humble spirit, to revive the spirit of the humble, and the heart of the contrite," to "fill the hungry with good things," and "beautify the meek with salvation," Isaiah lvii:15.

If these advantages, which exceed the worth of earthly crowns, necessarily result from the proper knowledge of our corrupt and lost estate, who, but an infatuated enemy of his own soul, would be afraid of that self science? Who, but an obstinate Pharisee, would not esteem it, next to the knowledge of Christ, the greatest blessing which Heaven can bestow upon the self-destroyed, and yet self-conceited children of men?

Careless reader, if thou art the person; if remaining unshaken in thy carnal confidence, and supposing thyself "wiser than seven men that can render a reason," thou not only despisest the testimony of the sacred writers, and our pious reformers, laid before thee in the first part of this treatise, but disregardest the numerous arguments it contains, tramplest under foot both *matter of fact* and *common sense,* and remainest unaffected by the most dreadful consequences of self ignorance on the one hand, and by the greatest advantages of self knowledge on the other, I have done, and must take my leave of thee.

May the merciful and holy God, whose laws thou dost daily violate, whose word thou hourly opposest or forgettest, whose salvation thou dost every moment neglect, whose vengeance thou continually provokest, and whose cause I have attempted to plead, bear with thee and thy insults a little longer! May his infinite patience yet afford thee some means of conviction, more effectual than that which is at present in thy hands! Or shouldest thou look into this labour of love once more, may it then answer a better purpose than to aggravate thy guilt, and enhance thy condemnation, by rendering the folly of thy unbelief more glaring, and consequently more inexcusable!

A CONCLUDING ADDRESS

TO

THE SERIOUS READER

WHO INQUIRES,

"WHAT MUST I DO TO BE SAVED?"

Is there no balm in Gilead? Is there no physician there? Why then is not the health of the daughter of my people recovered?—JEREMIAH

CONTENTS

OF

THE CONCLUDING ADDRESS.

———

AN ADDRESS TO THE SERIOUS READER.

HAVING taken my leave of the thoughtless and gay, who regard an appeal to their reason, as little as they do the warnings of their conscience, I return to thee,* serious and well-disposed reader. I am too much concerned for thy soul's welfare, to lay down my pen, without showing thee more perfectly the way to the kingdom of heaven, by testifying to thee "repentance toward God, and faith in our Lord Jesus Christ."

Thou art happily weary of feeding upon the husks of earthly vanities. I have a right, therefore, as a steward of the mysteries of God, to bring out of the Divine treasury the pearls of evangelical truth; and I gladly cast them before *thee*, persuaded, that far from awakening thy anger, they will excite thy desires, and animate thy languid hopes.

Instead of ridiculing, or dreading a heart-felt conviction of thy lost estate, thou now seest it is a desirable privilege, an invaluable blessing. Ready to mourn because thou canst not mourn, thou complainest that thou hast only a confused view of thy total depravity. Thou wantest the feelings of the royal penitent when he said, "Behold, I was shapen in iniquity," &c; "I acknowledge my transgressions," and "my sin is ever before me;" but conscious thou canst not raise them in thy heart by natural powers, thou desirest some Scriptural directions suitable to thy case. Give me leave to introduce them by a few

PRELIMINARY REFLECTIONS
On the nature and depth of penitential sorrow.

I. Thou knowest that "except thou" truly "repentest, thou shalt" surely "perish," and that there is no true repentance, where there is no true sorrow for sin. "I rejoice," says St. Paul to the Corinthians, "that ye were made sorry after a godly manner: for godly sorrow worketh repentance to salvation, not to be repented of; but the sorrow of the world worketh death." Hence it appears that there are two sorts of sorrow springing from opposite sources, *God* and *the world;* the one a "godly sorrow," and the other "the sorrow of the world." Learn to distinguish them by their various causes and effects, so shalt thou avoid the danger of mistaking the one for the other.

The sorrow of the world, which many cover with the cloak of religion, arises from fear of contempt, dread of poverty, secret jealousy, revenge dissatisfied, love disappointed, baffled schemes, losses in business, unkindness of friends, provocation of enemies, or the death of some idolized relative. Nay, this sorrow may sometimes

---

* This address is only calculated for *serious persons,* who cordially assent to the doctrine established in the *rational demonstration of our fallen and lost estate.* As other readers have been dismissed with the portion of truth that belongs to them, they are desired not to meddle with *this,* lest their cavils confirm St. Paul's observation, "We preach Christ crucified, to the" self-righteous "Jews a stumbling block, and to the" self-conceited "Greeks foolishness."

spring from a mixture of self-righteous pride and slavish fear. Some cannot bear to be robbed of their fond hopes of meriting heaven by their imaginary good works. They lose all patience when they see their best righteousness brought to light, and exposed as "filthy rags;" they are cut to the heart, when they hear their apparent good deeds deserve punishment as well as their black enormities: or, like condemned malefactors, they dread the consequences of their crimes, while they feel little or no horror for the crimes themselves.

Exceedingly fatal are the effects of this sorrow in the persons whom it overcomes: their indignant hearts, unable to bear either disappointment, contradiction, or condemnation, rise against second causes, or against the decrees of Providence; fret at the strictness of the law, or holiness of the Lawgiver; and pine away with uninterrupted discontent. Hence, spurning at advice, direction, and consolation, they wring their hands, or "gnaw their tongues with anguish;" impatience works them up into stupid sullenness, or noisy murmuring; they complain that their "punishment is greater than they can bear;" and, imagining they are more severely dealt with than others, they hastily conclude, "Behold this evil is from the Lord, why should I wait for him any longer?" Thus black despair seizes upon their spirits: and if grace does not interpose, they either live on to fill up the measure of their iniquities, as Cain, Pharaoh, and Haman; or madly lay violent hands upon themselves, as Ahithophel and Judas.

This sorrow cannot be too much guarded against, as it not only destroys many persons, but does immense hurt to religion. For those who are glad of any pretence to pour contempt upon godliness, taking occasion from the instances of this sorrow, harden their own hearts, and prejudice all around them against the blessed "godly sorrow," which every minister of the Gospel endeavours to excite; maliciously representing it as one and the same with the mischievous "sorrow of the world."

Their mistake will be evident, if we trace godly sorrow back to its source. It does not spring merely from fear of punishment; but chiefly from humbling views of God's holiness, the impurity of the human nature, the exceeding sinfulness of sin, and the transcendent excellency of the law which condemns the sinner.

And this happy sorrow differs not less from the other in its effects, than it does in its cause. The persons who are blessed with it, far from murmuring or fretting at the Divine commandment, see it to be "holy, just, and good," both in its preceptive and penal part. They so absolutely acquiesce in it that they would not alter it if they could. They clear God, accuse themselves, subscribe their own sentence, and acknowledge, "it is of the Lord's mercies we are not consumed." Each of them can say, "Wherefore should a living man complain, a man for the punishment of his sins? It is good that he should both hope, and quietly wait, for God's salvation: I will therefore watch to see what he will say unto me, for he will speak peace unto his people." Thus in a constant use of all the ordinances of God, they meekly wait, wrestling with their unbelieving fears, till victorious "faith comes by hearing" of the matchless love of Jesus Christ; and then, "fearing the Lord and his goodness," they "sing the song of the Lamb," and run upon his delightful errands.

As thou seest, serious reader, the nature, necessity, and excellence of "godly sorrow," thou art probably desirous of being informed how deep thine must be, to constitute thee a *true* penitent. Know then, that it must be deep enough to embitter thy most pleasing, profitable, and habitual sins, and to prevent thy resting without a clear sense of thy peculiar interest in Christ. It must be profound enough to make him and his Gospel infinitely precious to thee, and to produce, under God, the blessed effects mentioned in the fifth part of the preceding treatise.

To be more particular: a true penitent may certainly, without despair or madness, go as far in godly sorrow, as David does in his penitential Psalms, or our Church in the first part of the Homily on Fasting. "When good men," says she, "feel in themselves the heavy burthen of sin, see damnation to be the reward of it, and behold with the eye of their mind the horror of hell, they tremble, they quake, they are inwardly touched with sorrowfulness of heart for their offences, and cannot but accuse themselves, and open their grief unto almighty God, and call on him for mercy. This being done seriously, their mind is so occupied, partly with sorrow and heaviness, partly with an earnest desire to be delivered from this danger of hell and damnation, that all desire of meat and drink is laid aside, and loathing of all worldly things and pleasures comes in place, so that they like nothing better than to weep, to lament, to mourn, and, both with words and behaviour of body, to show themselves weary of this life."

Nevertheless, it must be observed that godly sorrow needs not be equal, either in degree or duration, in all penitents. Those whose hearts, through Divine grace, open as readily and gently as that of Lydia, happily avoid many of David's pangs and Job's terrors. The powerful and instantaneous, or the gentle and gradual manner, in which souls are awakened; the difference of constitutions; the peculiar services that a few are called to, and for which they are prepared by peculiar exercises; the horrid aggravations that have attended the sins of some; and the severe correction which the Lord is obliged to give others, for their stout resistance against his grace; all this may help us to account for the various depths of distress, through which different penitents pass in their way to Christ and salvation.

The Lord does not needlessly afflict the children of men, any more than a tender father unnecessarily corrects his disobedient children; he only wants us to forsake our sins, renounce our own imaginary righteousness, and come to Christ to be partakers of his merits, holiness, and felicity. The sorrow which answers these ends is quite sufficient, though it should be ever so light, and of ever so short a duration. On the contrary, a distress as heavy as that of Judas is unavailable, if, instead of driving us from sin to Jesus Christ, it only drives us from profaneness to hypocrisy, or from presumption to despair.

If, still perplexed, thou askest what thou must do to get a sense of thy depravity productive of true repentance; I answer, that an affecting discovery of the guilt, nature, and danger of sin, is only attained by the assistance of God's Spirit, "who alone effectually convinces the world of sin." John xvi:8. But the Lord has graciously appointed means, in the right use of which he never denies a sinner the convincing and converting power of his blessed Spirit; and what they are, thou art informed in the following

DIRECTIONS

Proper for a half-awakened sinner, desirous of being duly convinced of his corrupt and lost estate.

II. Beware of "fools," that "make a mock at" sorrow for sin, and at "sin" itself. Beware of those "blind leaders of the blind," who, "having a form of godliness, deny the power thereof:" instead of pointing thee to the throne of grace, and bidding thee "behold the Lamb of God that taketh away the sin of the world," they will only direct thee to the church walls and communion table: and, perhaps, if they see thee under dejection of spirit for thy sins, they will recommend the play house, the card table, or what they call a "cheerful glass." "From such turn away," or they will persuade thee that repentance is melancholy; conviction of sin despair; and the love of God enthusiasm, 2 Timothy iii:5.

That they may not be able to laugh or frown thee out of the way of salvation, dwell in thy thoughts on God's awful perfections. "Justice and judgment are the habitation of his throne." The unspotted, resplendent holiness beaming forth from him, as from an immensely glorious Sun of righteousness, will show thee thy sins as innumerable as the flying motes discovered in a dusty room, where the natural sun can penetrate. Consider that they are committed by a worm of earth, against the Majesty of heaven; and they will all appear to thee infinitely great: especially if thou measurest them and thyself by the true rule, the oracles of God; casting away the three false standards which self-deceivers measure themselves by, namely, the good opinion of their worldly minded neighbours, the defective examples of their fellow sinners, and the flattering suggestions of their own blind self love.

Follow the example of "the noble Bereans: search the Scriptures daily, whether these things are so," Acts xvii:11. View, in that faithful mirror, the picture both of the natural and of the regenerate man, and ask thy conscience which thou resemblest most. If imitating the godly man described in the first Psalm, thou "meditatest in the law of the Lord day and night," the straitness of the heavenly rule will soon show thee how very far gone thy thoughts, words, actions, tempers, and nature are from original righteousness.

To this meditation add a frequent survey of the follies of thy childhood, the vanity of thy youth, the worldly mindedness of thy riper years, the capital transgressions which conscience accuses thee of, and the "hardness of heart," and "alienation from the life of God," that the Scriptures charge thee with. Confess all to the Lord as thou art able, remembering that "the wages of sin is death," who flies fast upon thee with the wings of time— *death*, who often gives no warning, and ushers in *judgment*, with all the horrors of *hell*, or the joys of *heaven*; and pray that these awful realities may affect thee now, as they will in thy last moments.

Frequently reflect how total must be our loss of spiritual life, which cannot be repaired but by a "resurrection," a "new birth," or a "new creation," Colossians iii:1; John iii:7; Galatians vi:5. And how desperate the disease of our fallen nature, which cannot be healed but with the blood of a Divine Physician. *Consider* attentively, consider *Him*, whose piercing look softened the obdurate heart of cursing Peter, whose amazing sufferings brought a hardened thief under the deepest concern for his salvation, and whose dying groans "rent the rocks, shook the earth, and opened the graves." The tender flower of evangelical sorrow grows best in the shade of his cross; a believing view of him, as suffering for thee, will melt thee into penitential tears, and seal upon thy relenting heart the gracious promise, "They shall look upon him whom they have pierced, and mourn," Zechariah xii:10.

In the meantime improve the daily opportunities which thou hast of studying human corruption in the life and tempers of all around thee, but chiefly in thy own careless and deceitful heart: take notice of its pride and self seeking, of its risings, and secret workings, especially when unexpected temptations trouble thy imaginary peace of mind: for at such a time thy corruption, like the sediment in the bottom of a vial that is shaken, will show its loathsomeness and strength.

Converse, frequently if thou canst, with persons deeply convinced of sin. Attend a plain, heart-searching ministry as often as possible; and when the sword of the Spirit, the word of God, pierces thy soul, beware of fretful impatience. Instead of rising with indignation against the preacher, and saying as proud Ahab did to the man of God, "Hast thou found me, O mine enemy?" account him thy best friend that wounds thee deepest, provided he brings thee to Christ for a cure: and when the arrows of the word fly abroad, drop the shield of unbelief, make bare thy breast, welcome the blessed shaft, and remember that the only way of conquering sin is to fall wounded and helpless at the Redeemer's feet.

Nevertheless, the impressions of the word will soon wear off if thou dost not importunately entreat the Searcher of hearts to light the candle of his grace in thy soul, that thou mayest clearly see whether "thy inward parts" are "holiness to the Lord," as thou fondly supposedst; or "very wickedness," as the Scripture testifies. It is only in God's light that we can clearly discover our blindness.

This "light," it is true, "shineth in darkness," but frequently "the darkness comprehendeth it not." That this be not thy dreadful case, do not *grieve* and *quench* the convincing Spirit, by persisting in the *wilful* omission of any duty, or *deliberate* commission of any sin: nothing but *obstinate unbelief* darkens the mind, and hardens the heart, more than this. Therefore, instead of burying thy "one talent" with the "slothful servant," earnestly pray the Lord to make thee faithful in thy convictions, and to deepen them daily till they end in a sound conversion.

In order to this, do not slightly heal the wound in thy conscience: it is better to keep it open than to skin it over by improper means: many, through a natural forwardness and impatience, have recourse to them, and ruin is the consequence of their mistake. That thou mayest avoid it, serious reader, I entreat thee to pay a due regard to the following

CAUTIONS,
Proper for a penitent who desires to make his calling and election SURE.

III. When thou hast affecting views of thy lost estate, beware of resting, like Felix, in some pangs of fear, fits of trembling, and resolutions of turning to God by and by, "when" thou "shalt have a convenient season." Neither give place to desponding thoughts, as if there was no appeal from the tribunal of justice to the throne of grace.

Run not for ease to vain company, bodily indulgence, entangling affections, immoderate sleep, excessive drinking, or hurry of business. "Cain built a city" to divert his trouble of mind; and multitudes like him, by "the cares of this world, the deceitfulness of riches, or the desire of other things," daily *choke* the good seed, the precious *word* of conviction, Mark iv:19.

Be not satisfied with faint desires of living the life of the righteous, or idle wishes of dying their death. Remember that "the desire of the slothful kills him:" and if thou hast experienced some drawings of grace, meltings of heart, or breathings after God, sit not down at last, as the Laodiceans, in a careless state, "neither hot nor cold." It is far better to go on thy way weeping, and seeking "the pearl of great price" till thou really find it, than to rest contented with a hasty conceit that thou art possessed of it, when thou art not.

Stop not in an outward reformation, and a form of godliness, like many who mistake the *means* or *doctrines of grace* for grace itself; and because they say their heartless prayers both in public and private, or go far and often to hear the Gospel preached in its purity, fondly hope that they are the favourites of God and in the high way to heaven.

Under pretence of increasing thy convictions, do not bury them in heaps of religious books. Some read till their heads are confused, or their hearts *past feeling.* Thus, though "ever learning, they are never able to come to the knowledge of the truth." *Hear,* then, as well as *read,* the word of life; but think not thyself converted when thou hast "received it with joy." The stony ground hearers went as far as this: "Herod himself heard John gladly, honoured him, did many things," but left the most important undone: for he never dismissed the incestuous woman he lived with; and at last sacrificed to her revenge the honest preacher he once admired.

Do not confound the *covenant of works* made with *innocent* Adam *before* the fall, and the *covenant of grace* made with *sinful* Adam *after* the fall, Genesis ii:17, and iii:15, and Romans v:11-21. They are excellent in their place, but when they are mixed together they destroy each other's efficacy. The dreadful thunders heard in Paradise Lost, and the melodious songs uttered in Paradise Regained, do not strike *at once* the same spiritual ear. The galling yoke of the law of works, and the heavy load of its condemnation, are dropped when we take upon us Christ's easy yoke, and submit to his light burden. In a word, the first Adam gives place to the second when we "find rest unto our souls." Let then the *curse* of the law of innocence be swallowed up by the *blessing* of the Gospel; or rather let it make way for the grace of Christ in thy soul, as an emetic makes way for a cordial in a disordered stomach. If thou takest them together their respective use is prevented. The first covenant loses its *humbling* efficacy, and the second its *restorative* power. Therefore, if thou hast really "received the sentence of death in thyself," leave the curse of the first covenant in the grave of Christ, "crucified for thy sins;" and welcome the pardoning, renovating grace of Christ, "risen again for thy justification."

On the other hand, rest not contented with speculative knowledge, and unaffecting, though clear, ideas of the Gospel way of salvation. Light in an unrenewed understanding, mistaken for "the mystery of faith in a pure heart," like an ignis fatuus, or false light, leads thousands through the bogs of sin into the pit of destruction, Acts viii:13.

Pacify not thy conscience by activity in outward services, and a warmth in God's cause: party spirit or natural steadiness in carrying on a favourite scheme, yea, or seeking thy own glory, may be the springs that set thee on the work. Jehu faithfully destroyed Baal and Jezebel, but his zeal for the Lord covered the secret desire of a crown. Take care also not to mistake gifts for graces; fluency of speech for converting power; the warmth of natural affection for Divine love; or an impulse of God's Spirit, on some particular occasion, for an evidence of spiritual regeneration. Balaam spoke and prophesied like a child of God, and "many will one day say" to Christ, "Lord, have we not prophesied, spoke all mysteries, cast out devils, and done many wonderful works in thy name?" To whom he will answer, "Depart from me, I know you not."

An Appeal to Matter of Fact and Common Sense

Avoid the self conceit of many who feed on the corrupted manna of their past experiences, and confidently appeal to the wasted streams of those consolations which once refreshed their hearts; when, alas! it is evident "they have" now "forsaken the fountain of living water," and "hewn to themselves broken cisterns that hold no water;" unless the mire of evil tempers, selfish views, and heartless professions of faith, may pass for "the streams which gladden the city of God."

Neither do thou heal thyself by touches of sorrow, by tears, good desires, or outward marks of humiliation for sin, as King Ahab. Nor by excessive fasting, retiring from business, or hard usage of the body, as many Roman Catholics; nor yet by misapplying the doctrine of predestination, and setting down notions of election for evidences of salvation, as many Protestants. No, nor by "doting about questions, strifes of words, and perverse disputings, which eat as a canker," as some in St. Paul's days, and too many in ours, 1 Timothy vi:4.

To conclude: Think not thou art absolutely made whole when the power of outward sin is weakened or suspended, when thou hast learned the language of Canaan, canst speak or write well on spiritual subjects, art intimately acquainted with the best ministers of Christ, and hast cast thy lot among the despised children of God, taken their part, shared in their reproach, and secured their esteem and prayers. Judas did so for years: "Saul was" once "also among the prophets." Ananias and Sapphira were supposed to be good believers for a time; the foolish virgins joined in society with the wise, and were perhaps unsuspected to the last; and Peter himself stood in need of *conversion,* long after he had outwardly "left all to follow Christ," Luke xxii:32. So important is that charge of our Lord, "Strive to enter in at the strait gate, for many will seek to enter in and shall not be able."

To these cautions against the various ways by which the generality of penitents skin over the wound of sin in their conscience, permit me to add an

EVANGELICAL EXHORTATION,
Pointing out the Divine method of a sound cure, which, though least regarded, and last tried, by most sinners, is not only effectual in some, but infallible in ALL cases.

IV. Wouldst thou, serious reader, be made whole in an evangelical manner? To thy convictions of original and actual sin must be added a conviction of unbelief. Feel, then, that thou hast neglected Christ's great salvation: own thou didst never ask, or never persevere in asking, the unfeigned, saving, powerful faith, by which "the atonement is received" and enjoyed, Romans v:11. Acknowledge that the faith thou hast hitherto rested in was not "the gift of God," that grace "of his own operation, wrought in thee according to the working of his mighty power," and mentioned Ephesians ii:8; Colossians ii:12; Ephesians i:9. And confess it was not the right Christian faith, because it chiefly grew from the seed of prejudice and education, as the faith of Jews and Turks, and not from the seed of Divine grace and power, as the faith of St. Paul, Galatians i:14, and because it never yielded the heavenly fruits which Gospel faith infallibly produces: such as, "a vital union with Christ," Galatians ii:20; "the pardon of sins," Colossians i:14; Acts xiii:39; "peace with God," Romans v:1; "dominion over sin," Romans vi:14; "victory over the world," 1 John v:4; "the crucifixion of the flesh," Galatians v; "power to quench the fiery darts of the wicked," Ephesians vi:16; "joy unspeakable," 1 Peter i:8; "and the salvation of the soul," 1 Peter i:9; Hebrews x:39.

Be not afraid of this conviction of unbelief; for it generally goes before Divine faith, as the fermentation of a grain of corn in the earth is previous to its shooting its stalk toward heaven. "God concludes," shuts us up "in unbelief," says St. Paul, "that he may have mercy upon us," Romans xi:32. "When the Comforter is come, says our Lord," "he will convince the world of sin, because they believe not in me." This is the transgression which peculiarly deserves the name of sin, as being the *damning* sin according to the Gospel, Mark xvi:16, the sin that binds upon us the guilt of all our other iniquities, and keeps up the power of all our corruptions. Its immediate effect is to "harden the heart," Mark xvi:14; and "make it depart from the living God," Hebrews iii:12; and this hardness and departure are the genuine parents of all our actual sins, the number and blackness of which increase or decrease, as the strength of unbelief grows or decays.

A conviction of this sin is of the utmost importance, as nothing but an affecting sense of its heinousness and power can make us entirely weary of ourselves: nothing but a sight of its destructive nature can prevent our resting without a complete cure.

But when thou art once convinced of unbelief, do not increase the difficulty of believing by imagining true faith at an immense distance. Consider it as very near thy heart. That which convinces thee of sin and unbelief can, in a moment, and with the greatest ease, convince thee of righteousness, and "reveal in thee Christ the hope of glory." How quickly can the Spirit take of the things that belong to him, and show them unto thee! "Say not" then "in thy heart, Who shall ascend into heaven, or descend into the deep" to get me the seed of faith? But let St. Paul show thee "the new and living way." "The word is nigh thee," says he, "even in thy mouth and in thy heart, that is, the word of faith which we preach; that if thou shalt confess with thy mouth the Lord Jesus, and shalt believe in thy heart that God hath raised him from the dead, thou shalt be saved:" for "we are saved by faith; faith cometh by hearing, and hearing by the word of God." "Hear" then "the word of the Lord."

Are thy sins really grievous to thee? Is the burden of them intolerable? Wouldst thou part with it at any rate? Dost thou fully renounce thy speculative and barren faith? Hast thou received the sentence of eternal death in thy conscience, acknowledging thy case (for any thing thou canst do without Christ) helpless, hopeless, desperate? And art thou truly brought to the grand inquiry, "What must I do to be saved?" See, feel, confess, that thou standest in absolute need of a Divine Physician, an almighty Redeemer; and that the God-man, Jesus Christ, joins both those extraordinary characters in his wonderful person. Submit to be "saved by grace," by free grace, through his infinite merits, and not thy wretched deserts; and instead of opposing, continually study God's wonderful method of saving sinners, the worst of sinners, *by faith* in his blood.

"There is no name but his under heaven whereby we must be saved;" neither is there cure, or "salvation, in any other," Acts iv:12. As "by him all things were created," so "by him they subsist," and by him they must be restored. The power of his word and breath made man a living soul; and now that we are dead to God, the same power, applying his blood and righteousness, must "create in us clean hearts," and "renew right spirits within us." This, and this only, heals wounded consciences, washes polluted souls, and raises the dead in trespasses and sins.

An Appeal to Matter of Fact and Common Sense

Wouldst thou then be made whole? "Determine," as St. Paul, "to know nothing but Christ, and him crucified." Aim at believing, realizing, applicatory views of what he is, and what he has done and suffered for thee. Through all the clouds of thy guilt and unbelief, which will vanish before our "Sun of righteousness," as mists before the material sun, "behold him as the Lamb of God that taketh away the sin of the world," and thine. See the immense dignity of his person; "he is God over all, blessed for ever;" and yet he condescends to be "Immanuel, God with us, flesh of our flesh, and bone of our bone." Consider the inexpressible value and inconceivable efficacy of his precious, all atoning blood. It is the blood of the sacred body assumed by the eternal Logos, when he "appeared in the likeness of sinful flesh," both as a victim and a priest, to suffer the penalty of his own righteous law for us, and "to put away sin by the sacrifice of himself;"—the blood "of the Lamb of God, slain to sprinkle many nations,"—the blood of that mysterious Being, who fills "the bosom of the Father," and the everlasting throne, at whose feet all the heavenly powers "cast their crowns;" and to whom, in the midst of the acclamations and adorations of "an innumerable company of angels," in the midst of "sounding trumpets, thunderings, lightnings, and voices, the spirits of just men made perfect ascribe salvation," free, full, immensely dear-bought salvation. And, to say all in one word, it is "the blood of God made manifest in the flesh," Acts xx:28; 1 Timothy iii:16. For "JEHOVAH our righteousness" is "the seed of the woman, and the son of man." The Godhead and the manhood are wonderfully joined in him; and in consequence of this mysterious union, he is not only a proper "Mediator between God and man," but the sole medium of reconciliation and union between the offended Majesty of heaven and the rebellious sons of Adam. As the brazen serpent lifted up in the wilderness, when viewed by the wounded Israelites, was the only means by which the poison of the fiery serpents could be expelled, and health restored to their tortured, dying bodies: so Jesus lifted up on the cross, when beheld by the eye of faith as bleeding and dying in our stead, is the only way by which sin, the sting of death, can be extracted out of our guilty, perishing souls; the only antidote that can restore us to saving health and eternal life, John iii:14. Apply whatever we will, beside this sovereign remedy, we may poison, but can never heal, the envenomed and mortal wound.

But remember, sinner, that faith alone can make the blessed application. Adam fell by rejecting in unbelief the word of threatening, and thou canst never rise, but by receiving in faith "the word of reconciliation," Genesis ii:17; 2 Corinthians v:19. Instead then of confusing thy thoughts and scattering thy desires by the pursuit of a variety of objects, remember that "one thing is needful" for thee,—Christ and his salvation, received by faith: "for, to as many as receive him, he gives power to become the sons of God, even to them that believe on his name. Beseech him, therefore, to manifest himself to thee by his word and Spirit. "He is the Author and Finisher of faith," the "Giver of every good and perfect gift;" ask of him a heart-felt confidence that "God so loved" thee, "as to give his only begotten Son, that thou shouldest not perish, but have everlasting life;" a firm confidence that, as the first Adam wilfully ruined thee, so he, "the second Adam," freely "loved thee," and "gave himself for thee;" and that thou "hast redemption through his blood, the forgiveness of sins," not "according to" thy merits, but "the riches of his grace."

The least degree of this Divinely wrought confidence will begin to attract and unite thy soul to Him, who "is our life" and "peace," our "strength and righteousness." The everlasting Gospel will then be music in thine ears, and power in thy heart. Its cheerful solemn sound will raise thy drooping spirits, and make thee fix the eye of thy mind on the "sign of the Son of man," the uplifted banner of the cross. And O, while the self righteous see nothing there but the "despised, rejected Man of sorrows," what wilt thou discover? "God in Christ, reconciling the world unto himself!" "God manifest in the flesh to destroy the works of the devil!" Jehovah "Jesus, the Captain of our salvation, treading the wine press of the fierceness of the wrath of the Almighty! Of the people there was none with him, therefore his own arm brought salvation unto him."

While the Gospel "trumpet is blown in Sion," and the self-hardened scoffing infidel, hears it with disdain and ridicule, what joy will the awful declarations convey to thy penitent and listening soul! With what rapturous delight wilt thou hang upon the lips of the messengers of peace, the sons of consolation, who preach free salvation by the blood of Jesus! While he himself, "confirming the word of his servants," says to the melting heart, with his "still, small," and yet powerful, renovating "voice," "Behold, I sit upon my throne making all things new:" "The words that I speak are spirit and life:" "I do not condemn thee, thy sins are forgiven:" "Be thou clean:" "Thy faith hath saved thee:" "Go in peace, and sin no more," Revelation xxi:5; John vi:63; Luke vii:48, 50; Matthew viii:3; John viii:11.

And O! what will thy believing, enlarged heart experience "in that day of God's power," and thy spiritual birth! Christ, "the true light of the world, the eternal life of men, coming suddenly to his temple," and filling it with the light of his countenance, and the power of his resurrection! Christ "shedding abroad in thy" ravished "soul, the love of thy heavenly Father," thy bitterest enemies, and all mankind! In a word, "the Holy Ghost given unto thee!" Or, "Christ dwelling in thy heart by faith," John i:4; 1 John v:12; Romans viii:15; v:5; Galatians i:16; Ephesians i:13; iii:17.

Being thus "made partaker of Christ," and "of the Holy Ghost," Hebrews iii:14, and 6:4, thy loving heart, thy praising lips, thy blameless life, will agree to testify, that "the Son of man hath power on earth to forgive sins," and that "if any man is in Christ he is a new creature; old things are passed away, behold, all things are become new," Matthew ix:6; 2 Corinthians v:17.

Till this is thy happy experience, pray, (as the drawings of the Father and convictions of the Spirit will enable thee,) earnestly pray for living faith, for a "faith" that may be to thee "the substance of" the pardon thou "hopest for," and "the evidence" of the great sacrifice thou "dost not see," but which our Divine Surety really offered upon the cross for *thee*. Consider how deplorable a thing it is that thou shouldest be prevented from claiming, receiving, enjoying the delightful knowledge of thy interest in the Redeemer's death, when his pardoning love, and "the word of his grace," offer it thee "without money and without price," and absolutely nothing but infatuating unbelief, or spiritual sloth, keeps thee from the invaluable blessing. Be not satisfied idly to wait in the Divine ordinances, till thou "seest the kingdom of God come with power;" but, as the "violent" do, "take it by force."

Prisoner of hope, be strong, be bold,
Cast off thy doubts, disdain to fear:
Dare to believe, on Christ lay hold;
Wrestle with Christ in mighty prayer:

An Appeal to Matter of Fact and Common Sense

> Tell him, "I will not let thee go,
> Till I thy name, thy nature know."

Be attentive to the calls of the Spirit, and follow the drawings of the Father, till they bring thee to the Son; and keep thine eye upon the dawning light of the Gospel, till "the morning star arise in thy heart." Venture, confidently venture upon the boundless mercy of God in Jesus Christ. If a spirit of infirmity bows thee down, yield not to it; "seventy times seven times" try to arise and look up, calling aloud for help against it. Say, if possible "with tears," as the distressed father in the Gospel, "Lord, I believe," or, Lord, I would believe, "help thou my unbelief" or with tempted Job, "Though thou slay me, yet will I trust in thee."

In this manner knock, with the earnestness of the importunate widow, till the door of faith open, and thou begin to "see the salvation of God." But stop not here at the threshold of Christianity. "Have boldness to enter into the holiest by the blood of Jesus." Go on "from faith to faith," till thy "day of pentecost is fully come," till thou art" endued with power from on high, baptized with the Holy Ghost and with fire," and "sealed with that holy Spirit of promise," which Christ "received of the Father," and "abundantly shed on his servants and handmaids," when he was "glorified:" compare Matthew iii:11; Ephesians i:13; John vii:39; Acts i:5, 8, and 2:33, 39, and 8:15, and 19:2; John vii:39; Titus iii:6.

In the meantime use all the means of grace with an eye to their end; "stir up the gift" of hope "that is in thee;" and, to raise thy drooping expectation, receive the encouraging testimony of God's redeemed, praising people, whose hearts and tongues are ready to testify to thy ears what the following lines declare to thine eyes.

V. "That which we have seen and heard declare we unto you, that you also may have fellowship with us; and truly our fellowship is with the Father, and with his Son Jesus Christ. For the life was manifested, and we have seen it, and bear witness, and show unto you that eternal life which was with the Father, and is manifested unto us." Yes, "we have found him, of whom Moses and the prophets did write." From blessed experience we declare that the Messiah is come, and his essence is *love incarnate*, his name *Free Salvation*, and his delight the eternal happiness of the children of men. "He is the chief among ten thousand" prophets, priests, kings, and saviours; "he is altogether lovely. We staked our souls upon his eternal truth, and it was done to us both according to his word and our faith. Therefore, with humble joy we declare, that he answers the prayers, and delivers the souls of perishing sinners, as graciously as he did in the days of his flesh.

Upon trials, a thousand times successfully relocated, we proclaim him the help of the helpless, the hope of the hopeless, the health of the sick, the strength of the weak, the riches of the poor, the peace of the disquieted, the comfort of the afflicted, the light of those that sit in darkness, the companion of the desolate, the friend of the friendless, the way of the bewildered, the wisdom of the foolish, the righteousness of the ungodly, the sanctification of the unholy, the redemption of captives, the joy of mourners, the glory of the infamous, and, in a word, the salvation of the lost.

Though he was the Creator of men and angels, he vouchsafed to be born of a woman, that we, the wretched offspring of degenerate Adam, might be born again, born of God. Though he had stretched forth the heavens like a curtain, and bespangled them with stars innumerable, he wrapped himself in the scanty, fading garment of our flesh, and put on the veil of our miserable humanity, that we might be invested with the glory and communicable perfections of the Divine nature. Though he was the King of kings and Lord of lords, he did not disdain to take upon him the form and office of a servant, that we might be delivered from the slavery of Satan, and that angels might be sent forth to minister for us, who are the heirs of salvation. Though he was the "fulness of him who fills all in all," he worked that we might not want; toiled, that we might rest; and endured hunger and thirst, that we might taste the hidden manna, eat the bread of life, and drink with him the mystic wine of his Father's kingdom. His omnipotent word covers a thousand hills with verdure, and clothes millions of creatures with rich furs, glittering scales, and shining plumage; but, O infinite condescension! he submitted to be stripped of his plain raiment, that our shame might not appear; he became naked, that we might be adorned with robes of righteousness and garments of salvation. Though his riches were immense and unsearchable like himself, though heaven was his throne and earth his footstool, he became poor, and was destitute of a place where to lay his head, that we might be rich in faith here, and heirs of the kingdom hereafter. Though he was, is now, and ever shall be the joy of the heavenly powers, and the object of their deepest adoration; he was voluntarily despised of men, that we might be honoured of God: he was acquainted too with griefs, that we might rejoice with joy unspeakable and full of glory. Though supreme Lawgiver and Judge of all, matchless love made him yield to be judged, and unjustly condemned at Pilate's bar, that we might be honourably acquitted, and gloriously rewarded before his awful tribunal. Though archangels laid their crowns at his feet, and seraphim veiled their faces before him, unable to stand the dazzling effulgence of his glory, he suffered himself to be derided, scoffed, spit upon, scourged, and crowned with thorns; that we might be acknowledged, applauded, embraced, and presented with never-fading crowns of righteousness and glory. "The Lord of Hosts" is his name; he is deservedly called, "Wonderful, Counsellor, the everlasting Father, the mighty God, the Prince of Peace;" cherubic legions fly at his nod; and yet, astonishing humiliation! "his shoulders, on which is laid the government" of the world, felt the infamous load of a malefactor's cross; and barbarous soldiers, followed by an enraged mob, led him as a lamb to the slaughter, that we might be delivered from the heavy curse of the law, and gently conveyed by the celestial powers into Abraham's bosom. "Let all the angels of God worship him," is the great decree to which the heavenly hierarchy submits with incessant transports of the most ardent devotion: and yet he was crucified as an execrable wretch, guilty of treason and blasphemy, that we, daring rebels and abominable sinners, might be "made kings and priests unto God," partaking of *his* highest glory, as he partook of *our* deepest shame: and, to crown his loving kindness, he expired in the midst of rending rocks and a supernatural darkness; that we might feel his tender mercies, and be indulged with the light of heaven, when we go through the dreary valley of the shadow of death, to reap the joys of eternal life.

> Survey this wondrous cure;
> And at each step let higher wonders rise
> Pardon for infinite offence; and pardon
> Through means that speak its value infinite!
> A pardon bought with blood! with blood Divine.

An Appeal to Matter of Fact and Common Sense

> With blood divine of Him we made our foe!
> Persisted, to provoke! though woo'd and awed,
> Bless'd and chastised! bold, flagrant rebels still,
> Bold rebels 'midst the thunders of his throne!
> Nor we alone! a rebel universe!
> Yet for the foulest of the foul he dies.

But this is not all: having "through the grace of God tasted death for every man," and perfumed the grave for believers,

> He rose! He rose! He broke the bars of death!
> O the burst gates, crush'd sting, demolish'd throne,
> Last gasp of vanquish'd death! Shout, earth and heaven,
> This *sum of good* to man; whose nature then
> Took wing, and mounted with him from the tomb!
> Then, then, we rose; then first humanity
> Triumphant, pass'd the crystal gates of light.   YOUNG.

O the depth of the mystery of faith! O the breadth, the length, the height of the love of Christ! All his stupendous humiliation from his Father's bosom, through the virgin's womb, to the accursed tree; all his astonishing exaltation, from the dust to the grave, and the sorrows of hell to the joys of heaven, and the highest throne of glory; all this immense progress of incarnate love,—all, all is ours! His mysterious incarnation re-unites and endears us to God; his natural birth procures our spiritual regeneration; his unspotted life restores us to a blissful immortality; his bitter agony gives us calm repose; his bloody sweat washes away our manifold pollutions; his deep wounds distil the balm that heals our envenomed sores; his perfect obedience is our first title to endless felicity; his full atonement purchases our free justification; his cruel death is the spring of immortal life; his grave the gate of heaven; his resurrection the pledge of glory; his ascension the triumphs of our souls; his sitting at the right hand of the Majesty on high the earnest of our future coronation and exalted felicity; and his prevailing intercession the inexhaustible fountain of all our blessings.

Come then, conscious sinner, come to the feast of pardoning love; taste with us that the Lord is gracious. Let not a false humility detain thee, under pretence that "thou art not yet humbled and broken enough for sin." Alas! who can humble thee but Jesus, that says, "Without me ye can do nothing?" And how canst thou be broken, but by falling upon this chief corner Stone? If humiliation and contrition are parts of the salvation which he merited for thee, is it not the quintessence of self righteousness to attempt to attain them without him? Away then, for ever away, with such a dangerous excuse!

Nor let the remembrance of thy sins keep thee from the speediest application to Jesus for grace and pardon. What! though thy crimes are of the deepest dye and most enormous magnitude; though they are innumerable as the sand on the sea shore, and aggravated by the most uncommon and horrid circumstances; yet thou needest not despair: he has "opened a fountain for sin" of every kind, "and uncleanness" of every degree: "his blood cleanses from *all* sin."

He is a Redeemer most eminently fitted, a Saviour most completely qualified to restore corrupt, guilty, apostate, undone mankind; the vilest of the vile, the foulest of the foul, not excepted. He is *Almighty,* and therefore perfectly able to restore lapsed powers, root up inveterate habits, and implant heavenly tempers. He is *love* itself; compassionate, merciful, pardoning *love,* become incarnate for thee. And shall he that spared not his own life but delivered himself up for us all,—shall he not with his own blood also freely give us all things!

Behold, O behold him with the eye of thy faith! cruelly torn with various instruments of torture, he hangs aloft on the accursed tree, between two of the most execrable malefactors; and there, insulted more than they, he bears our infamous load of guilt. "He knows no sin," and yet "he is made sin for us:" he "becomes a curse to redeem us from the curse of the law; his own self bears our sins in his own body on the tree; he is wounded for our transgressions, and bruised for our iniquities; the chastisement of our peace is upon him. God hath laid on him the iniquity of us all, and with his stripes we are healed."

See, PARDON FOR LOST SINNERS is written with pointed steel and streaming blood on his pierced hands and feet; the double flood issuing from his wounded side more than seals the dear-bought blessing: the hand writing against us is nailed to his cross and blotted out with his precious blood; his open arms invite, draw, and welcome returning prodigals; and there encircled, the worst of sinners may find a safe and delightful retreat, a real and present heaven.

O sinner, let thy heart fly thither on the wings of eager expectation and impetuous desire. By all that is near, dear, and sacred to thee,—fly from eternal death,—fly for eternal life. The *law,* violated by ten thousand transgressions, pursues thee with ten thousand curses: the sword of *Divine vengeance* flames over thy devoted head: *sin,* the sting of death, has been a thousand times shot into thy wretched breast; its subtle and dire poison continually works in thy hardened or distressed heart: *guilt,* the sting of sin, the never-dying worm, perpetually benumbs thy stupid soul or gnaws thy restless conscience: *raging lusts,* those sparks of the fire of hell, which nothing but the blood of the cross can quench; or *fierce passions,* those flashes of infernal lightning, that portend an impending storm, frequently break out in thy benighted soul; a heart-felt pledge of tormenting flames: *Satan,* whom thou hast perhaps invoked by horrid imprecations, goes about as a roaring lion, seeking to ensnare his careless votary, or devour his desperate worshipper: death levels his pointed spear at thy thoughtless or throbbing heart: *hell* itself is moved from beneath to meet thee at thy coming; and *the grave* gapes at thy feet, ready to close her hideous mouth upon her accursed prey.

Fly then, miserable sinner, if thy flesh is not brass, and thou canst not dwell with everlasting burnings, fly for shelter to the bloody cross of Jesus. There thou wilt meet "Him who was, and is, and is to come:" "Immanuel, God with us," who appeared as the Son of man, to "make his soul an offering for sin," for *thy* sin; and saved thy life from destruction by losing his own in pangs, which made the sun turn pale, shook the earth, and caused the shattered graves to give up their dead.

He is even now near to thy heart; he stands at the door and gently knocks by the word of his grace. If thou hearest his voice, and openest by believing, he will come in; the word of reconciliation shall be powerfully ingrafted in thy heart; thou shalt know, experimentally know the *truth,* and the *truth* shall make thee free. Assured that he hath by himself purged thy sins, abolished death, and brought life and immortality to light through the Gospel, thou shalt sup with him and he with thee; thou shalt eat the bread of God which came down from heaven to give life to a perishing world. Evangelical *truth,* received by faith, will heal, nourish, comfort, and sanctify thy soul.

But perhaps thy guilty heart receives no consolation from these lines. Thou still considerest Christ only as a severe lawgiver, or as an inflexible judge; and not as the "propitiation for thy sins," and thy gracious all-prevailing advocate with the Father. O, how dost thou wrong both him and thyself by such false conceptions! And how soon would thy gloomy fears give place to triumphant joy, if thy thoughts of him corresponded with his gracious designs concerning thee!

Wouldest thou know him better, behold him through the glass of his word, and not through the mist of thy fears; and thou wilt see that, far from watching over thee for evil, he fixes upon thee the piercing eye of his redeeming love; waits that he may be gracious to thy soul, and calls, continually calls for thee. O! if thou hast an ear, listen; and as thou listenest, wonder at the kind, reviving words which proceed out of his mouth.

VI.* "Comfort ye, comfort ye my people," says the Lord; "speak ye comfortably to Jerusalem, and cry unto her, that her warfare is accomplished, and her iniquity is pardoned; for in me she hath received of the Lord's hand double for all her sins: he is well pleased for my righteousness' sake; I have magnified the law, and made it honourable; I have been lifted up, and now I draw all men unto me. My delights are with the sons of men, and therefore am I exalted, that I may have mercy upon them. Behold, I come with a strong hand, my reward is with me, and my work before me. Every valley shall be exalted, every mountain and hill shall be made low; the crooked shall be made straight, and the rough places plain; my glory shall be revealed, and all flesh shall see it together.

"Hearken unto me, ye stout hearted, that are far from righteousness; I bring near my righteousness, it shall not be far off, and my salvation shall not tarry. Seek ye me while I may be found, call upon me while I am near: return unto me, and I will have mercy upon you; and though ye have only done evil before me from your youth, I will abundantly pardon: for my thoughts are not revengeful as your thoughts, nor my ways unloving as your ways: in me you shall be saved with an everlasting salvation.

"Come, therefore, unto me, all ye that travail and are heavy laden, and I will give you rest: my yoke is easy, my burden light, and my rest glorious. Ho! every one that thirsteth, come ye to the waters, and he that hath no money; come ye, buy and eat all that can revive, strengthen, and delight your souls; yea, come, buy wine and milk, without money and without price. Wherefore do ye spend your money for that which is not bread, and your labour for that which satisfieth not? Hearken diligently unto

---

* This part of the address is almost literally transcribed from the Scripture, and it is designed for none but mourners in Sion, dejected sinners, who are backward to come to Christ, that they may have life. These want "line upon line," and invitation upon invitation; and it is well if, after all, they are encouraged to come. As for full souls, I know they will loathe this honeycomb. But while they complain, "It has too many cells, and they are filled with the same thing," some poor hungry hearts will say, "'One thing is needful' for us. We cannot have too much virgin honey: its sweetness makes amends for the want of variety. If the manna falls abundantly round our tents, it will stir us up to praise, and not to murmur. Fulness of the bread of life will not make us wax fat and kick like Jeshurun, but bless God for his rich profusion; and with the disciples, we shall even 'gather the fragments, that nothing be lost.'"

me, eat that which is good, and let your soul delight itself in fatness. Incline your ear, and come unto me; hear, and your soul shall live: I will make an everlasting covenant with you, even the sure mercies of David, and you shall all know me from the least to the greatest; for I will forgive your iniquity, and remember your sin no more.

"O, if thou knewest the gift of God, wretched sinner, and who it is that saith unto thee, *If any man thirst, let him come to me and drink,* thou wouldest have asked of him, and he would have given thee living water; a well, a fountain of it would have sprung up in thee unto everlasting life; yea, out of thy belly, thy inmost soul, rivers of living water, the greatest abundance of the purest joy, would have flowed for ever. I, even I, am He that blotteth out thy transgressions for my own sake, and will not remember thy sins: I will guide thee continually, and satisfy thy soul in drought; and thou shalt be like a watered garden, or like a spring of water, whose waters do not fail.

"O how often would I have gathered thee, in years past, as a hen gathers her brood under her wings! How often would I have led thee as an eagle fluttereth over her young, spreadeth abroad her wings, taketh them, and beareth them! but thou wouldest not. Nevertheless, this is still the day of my power, mercy, and love: I pardon those whom I reserve, and I will yet be pacified toward thee, for all that thou hast done. I was angry with thee, but mine anger is turned away; my thoughts toward thee are thoughts of peace, and I am become thy salvation. Come, then, let us now reason together, and though thy sins be as scarlet, they shall be white as snow; though they be red like crimson, they shall be as wool."

Why does not thy drooping heart, O sinner, leap for joy, or melt with gratitude at these tender invitations of thy Saviour? Thinkest thou they do not belong to thee? Dost thou suppose that Jesus, who is all purity and holiness, must turn away with abhorrence from such a guilty, polluted, and abominable creature as thou art? One so void of all good, so full of all evil, so completely lost and undone as thou seest thyself? Art thou afraid that thy relapses into sin have been so frequent, and thy backslidings so multiplied, that hope, which comes to all, can no more come to thee? Or does the enemy of thy soul suggest, thou art careless, hardened, and sunk in stupid unbelief? Does he insinuate thou hast so long trifled with Divine grace, art gone such lengths in horrid wickedness, or hast contracted such unconquerable habits of indulging thy carnal mind, or following thy vain imaginations, that infinite mercy can no longer pardon thy sins, or infinite power change thy nature? Art thou even tempted to believe thou hast committed the sin against the Holy Ghost, and art almost, if not altogether, given up to a reprobate mind? O! check those gloomy, despairing thoughts; resist the devil, and give place to more true and honourable sentiments of Jesus.

Wherefore dost thou doubt, O thou of little faith? Is any thing too hard for the Lord? Are not all things possible with God? Can the Almighty, who became incarnate to die as man in thy place, want either ability or willingness to help thee, be thy case ever so deplorable and desperate? Is not darkness or light, sickness or death, all one to Him, who is "the Light of the world, and the Prince of life;" and who, with a word or a touch, raised the dead, whether they were yet warm on a bed, cold in a coffin, or already putrefied in a grave?

Confine not then, poor dejected sinner, thy Saviour's boundless mercy within the narrow limits of thy unbelieving thoughts. Get Scriptural views of his pardoning love, and true discoveries of his redeeming power. To guess aright at the prodigious extent of his mercy, lift up the dim eyes of thy struggling faith, and behold a great multitude, which no man can number, standing before the throne, with their robes washed and made white in the blood of the Lamb.

Among those countless monuments of Divine mercy, those illustrious trophies of free grace, see David, who, after having been admitted to close communion with God, plunged for ten months in the horrible guilt of adultery, treachery, hypocrisy, and murder. See Paul, once so fierce an enemy to the truth, so fiery a blasphemer of Jesus, so raging a persecutor of the saints, that his very breath was "threatenings and slaughter against them!" See Peter, who, after a great profession of faithfulness, and upon an apparently slight temptation, denied three times his Master, his Saviour, and his God, in his very presence. Peter, guilty of lying, cursing, and perjury, immediately after he had been apprized of the imminent temptation, and armed against it, both by receiving the holy sacrament at our Lord's own hand, and being admitted to see his wonderful agony, and glorious miracles. These, and thousands more, agree to tell thee "for this cause we obtained mercy, that in us first Jesus Christ might show forth all long suffering, for a pattern to them which should hereafter believe on him to life everlasting."

If all these witnesses do not silence thy doubts, and encourage thy hopes, Jesus himself, the faithful and true witness, will yet plead the cause of his dying love against thy unbelieving fears: thy gracious Advocate with God will yet be God's condescending Advocate with thee. O! let thy clamorous conscience keep silence while he preaches to thee the everlasting Gospel of his grace. And if to-day thou hearest his voice, harden not thy heart, come out of the cave of unbelief, wrap thyself in the mantle of Divine mercy, and worship the pardoning God, the God of never-failing truth and everlasting love.

Gracious Saviour! make thine own words spirit and life to the soul thou hast formed by thy breath, and purchased with thy blood. Blessed Comforter! while thy precious sayings strike the eyes of this hopeless reader, let the love which thou sheddest abroad, soften, melt, and revive his poor, oppressed heart, and let salvation come this day to the house of a son or daughter of Abraham! A touch, a breath from thee will break the bars of iron, burst the gates of brass, and make the everlasting doors lift up their heads, that the King of glory may come in.

"Who is this King of glory? Who is this that cometh from Edom, with dyed garments from Bozrah? This that is glorious in his apparel, travelling in the greatness of his strength?

"I that speak in righteousness, mighty to save. I have trodden the wine press alone; mine own arm hath brought salvation unto me, salvation for the lost: it is gone forth: my righteousness is near; the isles shall wait on me, and on my arm shall they trust. The Spirit of the Lord God is upon me: he hath anointed me to preach good tidings to the meek: he hath sent me to bind up the broken hearted, to proclaim liberty to the captives, and the opening of the prison to them that are bound; to comfort all that mourn, and, by the blood of the covenant, to send forth the prisoners out of the pit where there is no water.

"Fear not, therefore, thou worm Jacob; I am the first and the last, he that liveth and was dead, and, behold, I am alive for evermore. Yes, I ever live to make intercession for thee; and because I live, thou shalt live also. All power is given, all judgment is committed unto me in heaven and earth: I have the keys of death and hell: a Jonah, who cries to me out of the very belly of hell, is not out of the reach of my gracious and omnipotent arm.

"Who art thou that hast feared continually every day, because of the fury of the oppressor, as if he were ready to destroy? I, even I, am He that comforteth thee. I bring glad tidings of great joy, which shall be to all people. I have triumphed over all thine enemies on the cross. I have led captivity captive, and received gifts for men, even the promise of the Father, that the Lord God the Spirit may dwell in them. At my command the great, the evangelical trumpet is blown; and they that are ready to perish in the land of Assyria, and the outcasts in the land of Egypt, do come, and are welcome to Mount Sion. Hasten with them, thou captive exile, hasten to me that thou mayest be loosed, and that thou shouldest not die in the horrible pit of thy natural state.

"Thy helplessness is no hinderance to my loving kindness: I break not the bruised reed, I quench not the smoking flax: I uphold all that fall, I raise up all those that are bowed down: I say to the prisoners, Go forth; and to them that are in darkness, Show yourselves: I strengthen the weak hands and confirm the feeble knees: I say to them that are of a fearful heart, Be strong, fear not; behold, I will come with vengeance and a recompense; I will come and save you.

"My tender mercies are over all my works. When the poor and needy seek water, and there is none, and their tongue faileth for thirst, I the Lord will hear them; I the God of Israel will not forsake them. I will open rivers in high places; I will make the wilderness a pool, and the dry land springs of water.

"It is true thou hast sinned with a high hand, both against thy light and against my love; but how shall I give thee up, Ephraim? How shall I deliver thee, sinner? How shall I make thee as Admah, and set thee as Zeboim, those rebellious cities on which I poured my flaming vengeance? My heart is turned within me, my repentings are kindled together. I will not destroy thee; for I am God and not man. I have seen thy ways, and will heal and lead thee, and restore comfort to thee; for I create the fruit of the lips. Peace! peace to him that is afar off, and to him that is near; I will heal him.

"Thou hast not chosen me, but I have chosen thee; thou art my servant; fear not, for I am with thee; be not dismayed, for I am thy God. My strength is sufficient for thee; I will help thee; yea, I will uphold thee with the right hand of my righteousness. They that war against thee shall be as nothing; for I the Lord thy God will hold thy right hand, and make my strength perfect in thy weakness. I will bring thee by a way thou hast not known. I will make darkness light before thee, and crooked paths straight. When thou passest through the waters, I will be with thee; and when thou walkest through the fire, thou shalt not be burned, neither shall the flame kindle upon thee; for I am the Lord, thy Saviour, and thy God. I have carried thee from the womb, and even to hoary hairs will I bear and deliver thee.

"Therefore, hear now this, thou afflicted and drunken, but not with wine; I will not contend for ever, neither will I be always wroth; lest the spirit should fail before me, and the soul which I have made. I turn the water of affliction into the wine of consolation. Behold, I take out of thy hand the cup of trembling, even the dregs of the cup of my fury; thou shalt no more drink it again: I will put it into the hand of them that afflict thy soul: and in the room of it I give thee the cup of the New Testament in my blood, shed for the remission of sins: it is now ready, draw near, drink thou of it, and taste that I am gracious.

An Appeal to Matter of Fact and Common Sense

"Come near, that I may speak a word in season to thy weary spirit. Why standest thou afar off? Come near, I say, that my soul may bless thee. Let me show thee my glory, and proclaim my soul reviving name: The Lord! the Lord God! merciful and gracious, long suffering, and abundant in goodness and truth, keeping mercy for thousands, and forgiving iniquity, transgression, and sin! Let me wash thy heart from iniquity, guilty sinner; for unless I wash thee, thou hast no part with me. Unless thou art born again of water and of the Spirit, thou canst not see the kingdom of God: but this is the covenant of promise which I make with thee: I will sprinkle clean water upon thee, and thou shalt be clean; a new heart will I give thee, and a new spirit, even my own Spirit, will I put within thee, and thou shalt be completely born of God; and at that day thou shalt know that I am in the Father, and thou in me, and I in thee.

"Who is he that condemneth? It is I who died for thy sins, yea, rather, who rose again for thy justification, who am even at the right hand of God, who also make intercession for thee. The same compassionate love that made me weep over ungrateful Jerusalem, and groan over dead Lazarus, made me bleed and die for thee. O that, in this thy day, thou mayest know the things that belong unto thy peace, and the efficacy of that sacrifice by which I have for ever perfected them that are sanctified! O that unbelief, so injurious to me, and so pernicious to thee, may no longer hide my love from thine eyes!

"What! afraid of my purity, art thou ready to cry out as my apostle, Depart from me, O Lord, for I am a sinful man? And dost thou tremble at my words as a criminal at the sentence of his judge? O be of good cheer, it is I, be not afraid. Am not I thy light and strength, thy shield and buckler, thy tower and resting place, thy strong hold, whereunto thou mayest always resort, thy castle and fortress, the horn also of thy salvation, and thy refuge? As for thy sins, if thou desirest to part with them, they will no more hinder me from visiting thee, than the sickness of a patient prevents a physician from giving him his attendance.

"I know thou art a sinner—a great sinner: for this cause came I down from heaven to Bethlehem,—to Gethsemane,—to Calvary. I know thine iniquities are more in number than the hairs of thy head; like a sore burden, they are too heavy for thee to bear: and therefore have I borne them for thee in my own body on the tree. I came not to call the righteous, but sinners to repentance: I am the man that receiveth sinners, and eateth with them: I am the friend of returning publicans and harlots; all manner of sins and blasphemies shall be forgiven them through faith in my blood: God was in me, reconciling the world unto himself, not imputing their trespasses unto them; and now, I beseech thee, be *thou* (for one) reconciled to God; for in me God is reconciled to *thee,* thy sin is covered, and thine iniquity forgiven.

"Great as thy crimes are, poor mourner in Zion, I upbraid thee not with them; my infinitely meritorious sacrifice hath long ago atoned for their heinousness, and now I cast the mantle of my pardoning love over their multitude; thou art ashamed of them, and shall I be ashamed of thee? Far be the thought from thee; I glory in extending my boundless mercy to such miserable objects as thou art. This is a faithful saying, and worthy of all men to be received, that I came into the world to save sinners: and if, with my servant Paul, thou seest thyself the *chief* of them, let me do the *chief* part of the errand on which I came; look unto me,—partake with him of my *richest* salvation,—lose thy cares in the bosom of my mercy,—and receive the atonement I made for thee; but receive it *now:* for I have heard thee in a time accepted, and in the day of salvation have I succoured thee: behold, *now* is the accepted time; behold, *now* is the day of salvation, the day in which I bind up the breach of my people, and heal the stroke of their wound.

"Whence arise, O poor sinner, thy backwardness and misgivings? I have ransomed thee from the power of the grave, and thou art mine: I come to heal thee, and to reveal to thee the abundance of peace and truth: I bring thee a cure for thy wounded conscience, and saving health for thy sin-distempered soul!

"In a little wrath, and for a small moment, I have hid my face from thee; but with everlasting kindness will I have mercy on thee; for I am the Lord thy Redeemer. Believe it, and faith will work by love, and love will cast out fear: thus shalt thou take hold of my strength, that thou mayest make peace with me; and thou shalt make peace with me, for I am strength to the needy in his distress, a hiding place from the wind, a covert from the tempest, as rivers of water in a dry place, and as the shadow of a great rock in a weary land.

"Come, then, be not of them that draw back from me to perdition, but of them who believe to the saving of the soul. Far from casting away thy little confidence, which hath great recompense of reward, hold it fast; resist even unto blood, striving against the damning sin of unbelief; trust in me for ever, for in me, Jehovah thy righteousness, is everlasting strength; and let me no longer complain that thou (one of my oppressed people in spiritual Egypt) wilt have none of me, and wilt not even come to me, that thou mightest have life more abundantly.

"Not by works of righteousness which thou hast done, but according to my mercy I saved thee. I am the Lamb slain from the foundation of the world. What my gracious purpose planned before time, I have executed in time. My life and death have completed the wonderful bridge by which thou canst go over the great deep fixed between a holy God and thy sinful soul. Concerning a main arch of this mighty work, with one of my last breaths I said It is finished; and I now confirm the glad tidings with regard to the whole. With my right hand, and with my holy arm, I have gotten myself the victory, and parted for thee, not the waves of the Red Sea, but the dreadful billows of the fiery gulf. And now I return to see thee safe over. Leave only the world and sin behind; and, walking by faith, follow me through the regeneration to a throne of glory.

"Whence arises, sinner, this backwardness to trust in my promise, and venture after me? Dost thou suspect the sincerity of my tenders of grace? And by thinking that I secretly except thee from my mercy, when I offer it to thee openly, dost thou still make me a dissembler, a liar? O wrong me not so far; I am the Truth itself; I abhor dissimulation in my creatures: and I, that say a man should not use deceit, shall I use deceit? Shall I have concord with Belial? Shall there be an agreement between the faithful Witness, and the father of lies? Shall I sentence him that loveth a lie to the lake that burneth with fire and brimstone, and be guilty of making one myself? Horrible to suppose! Reject the blasphemous thought, sinner: it wounds me in the tenderest part.

"No, no, I do not put on a mask of pretended love, to hide a rancorous, unforgiving temper; the general invitation that formerly passed my lips, is still the very language of my heart. Whosoever will, let him come and take of the water of life freely; and the promise which I formerly made, is still firmer than the pillars of heaven, Him that cometh unto me I will in no wise cast out. Let these words, like incorruptible seed, beget thee again to a lively hope, and help thee to stir thyself up to lay hold on me and my great salvation.

"I grant, that no man cometh unto me except the Father draw him; but does he not say, I have loved thee with an everlasting love, therefore, with loving kindness, with the cords of a man, with the bands of love, have I drawn thee? Does he not draw thee even now? Who stirs thee up to repentance? Who raises in thee a desire of coming unto me by prayer? Who indulges thee at times with sweet hopes and alluring joys, to encourage thee to come? Is it not my Father and thine, thou poor starving prodigal? And that nothing may be wanting on his part to make thee come, to drawing does he not add driving? Does he not obstruct all thy prospects of creature happiness, and blast all thy worldly, yea, and all thy self-righteous schemes? And while he touches thy heart with the rod of distress, does he not lay the scourge of affliction on thy back, and put this gracious invitation in thy hand? Away, then, with thy hard thoughts of my Father; he and I are the flame of eternal love: I and the Father are one.

"Neither say thou in thy heart, This is a day of trouble, rebuke, and blasphemy; the children are come to the birth, and there is not strength to bring forth. Shall I bring to the birth, and not give strength according to the day? Dost thou fear that my zeal, my strength, and the sounding of my bowels toward thee are restrained? Am not I Jesus still? Is my love waxed cold, that it cannot pity? Is my hand shortened at all, that it cannot save? Is mine ear heavy, that it cannot hear? Or have I no power to deliver? Behold, at my rebuke I dry up the sea; I clothe the heavens with blackness; and if in the greatest storm I say to the raging billows. Be still! there is a great calm: fear not then: the zeal of the Lord of Hosts,—my zeal, will do this, and more, for thy soul; yea, I will do for thee exceeding abundantly above all that thou canst ask or think.

"I see what passes in thy heart, O thou unwise and slow of heart to believe all that I and my prophets have spoken: I read thy new excuses. Thou sayest thou dost not suspect me, my faithfulness, and my power; but thyself, thy helplessness, and the treachery of thy own desperately wicked heart. What, shall this sore evil hinder thee from coming to me, who alone can remedy it? Wilt thou pray to be excused from believing on such an account as this? O drop this last, this most absurd plea, and walk in the steps of the faith of thy father Abraham, Romans iv:16. Consider not the deadness and hardness of thy heart, but the reviving, softening love of mine; not thy want of power, but my omnipotence; not the suggestion of Satan, but the declarations of my Gospel. Wrestle not only against flesh and blood, but against the powers of internal darkness, and the spiritual wickedness of an unbelieving thought. Strive to enter in at the strait gate of faith. Against hope believe in hope, that I quicken the dead, and call the things which are not as though they were. Stagger no more at my promises through unbelief, but be strong in faith, and give glory to God, by being fully persuaded that what I promise, I am able and willing to perform.

"In me thou mayest find the richest and readiest supply of all thy wants: I am both the resurrection of the dead, and the life of the living: he that believeth in me, though he were dead, yet shall he live; and he that liveth and believeth in me shall never die. Believe then, and thou shalt not come into condemnation. Believe, and thou shalt receive power; thou shalt see the glory of God; thou shalt be established; yea, and sealed with the Holy Spirit of promise. Believe, and thou hast everlasting life, and shalt not come into condemnation. Believe, and a grain of faith will remove mountains of guilt and unbelief. Believe with all thy heart: all things are possible to him that believeth, and he shall inherit all promises; for to him that overcometh, (and *faith* is the victory,) will I give to eat of the hidden manna, and to sit with me on my throne; as I also overcame, and am set down with my Father on his throne. *Only believe,* then, and through faith thou shalt subdue the kingdom of darkness, work righteousness, obtain promises, stop the mouth of the roaring lion, quench the violence of temptation's fire, escape the flaming point of Satan's darts, out of weakness be made strong, wax valiant in fight, turn to flight the armies of thy spiritual adversaries, and receive thy dead soul raised to life again.

"Thou hast played with the fiery serpents; they have bitten thy heart, but I have already sucked the worst of the mortal poison. In the perilous attempt my soul was seized with sorrow even unto death; and an unheard-of agony, attended with a bloody sweat, came upon my body. A racking cross was the bed I was stretched upon: sharp thorns proved the pillow on which I rested my fainting head. The bitterest sarcasms were my consolations; vinegar and gall my cordials; a band of bloody soldiers the cruel wretches appointed to tear open my veins; whips, nails, hammers, and a spear, the instruments allowed them to do the dreadful operation. For hours I bled under their merciless hands; and thy fearful curse, O sinner, flowed together with my blood. In the meantime noonday light was turned into the gloom of night, a dire emblem of the darkness that overspread my agonizing soul; and at last, while earthquakes rocked me into the sleep of death, I gave up the ghost with cries that astonished my bitterest enemies, and made them smite their breasts in pangs of involuntary sympathy. Thus, to make thee partaker of my saving health, I took the shameful and painful consequences of thy mortal distemper upon me. And now, sinner, despise no more such amazing love, requite it with a believing look. Consider my wounds till thy conscience feels their wonderful effect. Behold my atoning blood till thou canst witness it heals all thy infirmities.

"Knowing the terrors of the Lord, I persuade men. Come, thou poor prisoner of hope, turn by faith to the strong hold of my protection. Up! for God will destroy this Sodom, the wicked world where thou lingerest. Up! for the great and terrible day of the Lord approaches. As I live, there is but one step between thee and death, and another between death and hell.

"Let my love even constrain thee to arise, and to follow me, that I may receive thee unto myself, and complain no longer that, with respect to thee, I have laboured in vain, and spent my strength for nought. Surely, sinner, I deserve thy grateful love, for I have fought thy fiercest enemies. Dreadful was the battle! My flesh was torn, my blood spilt, my life lost in the obstinate combat: but I have slain the lion and the bear. I have vanquished death and the grave, and rescued thy poor, helpless soul; and now let thy good Shepherd rejoice over his lost sheep; let gratitude compel thee to come into the fold of my Church, and join the little flock of my faithful followers. And if thou canst not come, do but look wishfully at me, and I will lay thee on my shoulders rejoicing, and carry thee in triumph into the richest pastures of my grace.

"Once more I turn suppliant; once more I stand at the door and knock. Saul! Saul! it is hard for thee to kick against the sharp goads of my love. Martha! Martha! one thing is needful, choose the good part, choose me. O Absalom, my son! my son!

give me thy heart; I have died for thee; do not crucify me afresh: lay down the spear of unbelief, and thine is my grace, my glory, my kingdom, the kingdom of heaven.

"Be not afraid to surrender; rebellious as thou art, I love thee still: can a woman forget her sucking child, that she should not have compassion on the son of her womb? Yea, she may forget, yet I will not forget thee. If thou wilt not take my word, believe my oath: because I can swear by no greater, I swear by myself: *As I live, I have no pleasure in the death of the wicked,* but that the wicked turn from his way and live. Turn, then, turn unto me, for I have redeemed thee: I have cast all thy sins into the depths of the sea, and will subdue all thy iniquities.

"And if thou canst not believe my oath, credit these scars. See, I have graven thee upon the palms of my hands. Long, too long have I waited for thy return, thou poor, wandering, weary prodigal. Let me see in thee the travail of my soul, and be satisfied. By the mystery of my holy incarnation and dreadful temptation, by my agony and bloody sweat, by my infamous death and glorious resurrection, I beseech thee, come to the pardoning God by me. If thou hast nothing to pay, I forgive thee all the debt: whether it be fifty or five hundred pence, or ten thousand talents, I frankly forgive thee all. Only let me heal thy backslidings, and love thee freely; let my left hand be under thy head, and let my right hand embrace thee. See the wounds which I have received for thee in the house of my friends! Reach hither thy finger, and behold my hands; and reach hither thy hand, and thrust it into my side, and be not faithless, but believing. Cleave to me with full purpose of heart, follow me through the regeneration, and thou shalt not only be one of my jewels, but a crown of glory, and a royal diadem in the hand of thy God: yea, as the bridegroom rejoiceth over the bride, so will I rejoice over thee, and give thee a name better than that of son and daughter:—I, the Holy One of Israel, will be thy life and glory:—I, thy Maker, will be thy husband and thy all."

And are these, O sinner, the gracious sayings of God to thee? The compassionate expostulations of God become incarnate for thee? Did God so love thee as to set forth his only begotten Son, as a propitiation through faith in his blood, thus to declare his righteousness, for the remission of sins that are past? May the Almighty now be just, and yet the justifier of him that believeth in Jesus? Is there no difference, no respect of persons with him? And is the same Lord over all, rich unto all that call upon him? Then shout, ye heavens! triumph, thou earth! and thou, happy sinner, know the day of thy visitation: be wise, ponder these things, and thou shalt understand the loving, kindness of the Lord.

Be no longer afraid that it will be presumption in thee to believe, and that God will be offended with thee if thou makest so free with Jesus, as to wash instantly in the fountain of his atoning blood. He not only gives thee LEAVE to believe, but he INVITES thee to "do it freely." Nay, he COMMANDS thee to believe, for "this is his COMMANDMENT, that we should believe on the name of his Son Jesus Christ." He even enforces the precept by a double PROMISE, that if thou believest, thou "shalt not perish, but have everlasting life." And that nothing may be wanting to stir thee up to this important business, he is gracious enough to threaten the neglect of it with the most dreadful punishment; for "he that believeth not shall not enter into his rest," and "shall be damned;" and he that to the end remains "fearful and unbelieving, shall be cast into the lake that burneth with fire and brimstone, which is the second death."

How canst thou doubt, then, whether thou art welcome to receive "the Son given," by believing on his name?

Come to him just as thou art, and he will make thee what thou shouldst be. When he counsels thee to buy of him the gold of faith, and the garment of salvation, take him at his Gospel word: come, without regarding thy stuff; the poorer thou art the better: the oil of his grace flows most abundantly into empty vessels: his charity is most glorified in the relief of the most miserable objects: his royal bounty scorns the vile compensation of thy wretched merits: he sells like a king, like the King of kings, without money and without price. "Ask and have," and "take freely," are the encouraging mottoes written upon all the unsearchable treasures of his grace.

Be of good comfort, then! Arise, he calleth thee! Stretch out thy withered hand, and he will restore it: open thy mouth wide, and he will fill it: bring an empty vessel, a poor hungry heart, and he will give into thy bosom good measure, pressed down, shaken together, and running over.

And now, what meanest thou, sleeper? Why tarriest thou? Arise, and wash away thy sins, calling on the name of the Lord. Lose not time in conferring with flesh and blood; much less in parleying with Satan, or consulting thy unbelieving heart: here delays lead to ruin: the Philistines are upon thee, instantly shake thyself. If thou art not altogether blinded by the god of this world, and led captive by him at his will, this moment, in the powerful name of JESUS, burst the bonds of spiritual sloth: break, like a desperate soul, out of the prison of unbelief: escape for thy life: look not behind thee: stay not in all the plain. This one thing do; leaving the things that are behind, Sodom and her ways, press forward toward Zoar, and escape to the mount of God, lest thou be consumed. By the new and living way consecrated for us, in full assurance of faith, fly to the Father of mercies, pass through the crowd of Laodicean professors, press through the opening door of hope, take the kingdom of heaven by violence.

With halting, yet wrestling Jacob, say to the Friend of sinners, "I will not let thee go, unless thou bless me." If he makes as if he would go farther; with the two mournful disciples, "constrain him to stay;" or rather, with the distressed woman of Canaan, follow "him whithersoever he goeth;" take no denial: through the veil, that is to say, his flesh, torn from the crown of his head to the sole of his feet; through this mysterious veil, rent from the top to the bottom, rush into the blood-besprinkled sanctuary; embrace the horns of the golden altar; lay all thy guilt on the head of the sin-atoning victim; read thy name on the breast of thy merciful High Priest; claim the safety, demand the blessings, receive the consolations, bestowed on all that flee to him for refuge; and begin a new, delightful life, under the healing and peaceful shadow of his wings.

But perhaps thou art now devoid of active power, and broken in spirit. The hurry of thy self-righteous nature subsides. Wounded and half dead, thou liest in the way of misery, waiting for the passing by of thy heavenly Deliverer. Thou hadst set thy heart upon being blessed in one particular manner, and God in his wisdom thinks it best to bless thee in another. Thou wouldest scale the New Jerusalem and storm heaven; but he chooses it should come down into thy soul as a fruitful shower descends into a fleece of wool. Be still, then, and know that he is God. Let him break thy self will, which hides itself under godly appearances; and let him practically teach thee that salvation is not of him that willeth, nor of him that runneth, but of God who showeth mercy.

Meekly dive into the amazing depths of these words, "In quietness and rest shall be your strength. Stand still, and see the salvation of God." The fire, the earthquake, and the rending of the rocks are over; silence takes place, the still small voice will soon follow. Thou art for a time taken from the foaming billows of self agitation, and led by the still waters: a calm succeeds the impetuous storm, and a passive waiting thy restless, fruitless endeavours. Thou art in the case of one fallen into the sea, who, having struggled long and hard to escape drowning, is obliged to yield at last. Yield then, weary sinner, yield to thy happy fate. Fully surrender to the God of thy life. Entirely abandon thyself to Jesus. Freely trust him with thy present and eternal salvation. Whether thou swim or sink, let thyself go into the ocean of mercy. Catch at no broken reed by the way, but calmly venture into the unfathomable depths of redeeming love. Lose thus thy life, and thou shalt find it. The power of God will soon be "made perfect in thy weakness," and when thy strength is renewed, earnestly wrestle again. Thus go on, alternately striving and waiting, according to the leadings of the Holy Spirit, till, having passed through all the inferior dispensations of Divine grace, thou enter by faith into the rest that remains for the people of God, and take possession of that kingdom of God, which consists in righteousness, peace, and joy in the Holy Ghost.

VII. In that kingdom, happy believer, the times of refreshing fully come from the presence of the Lord; mercy and love embrace thee on every side, and thy sprinkled conscience enjoys the peace of a sin-pardoning God. Then smiling justice, more than satisfied by the meritorious death of Christ, sheathes her flaming sword, and declares, "There is now no condemnation to them that are in Christ Jesus: they are justified from all things, and freely forgiven all trespasses." And now thou art more than conqueror through Him that loved thee. Standing by humble faith in his omnipotence, thou canst do all things, through his grace strengthening thee. Sin has no dominion over thee. The cruel and bloody tyrant that reigned unto death is dethroned; and grace, rich grace, sweetly reigns through righteousness unto eternal life. Triumphing in Christ over thy fiercest enemies, and putting thy victorious foot upon the neck of the *last,* thou challengest his utmost rage, and shoutest, "O death, where is thy sting? O grave, where is thy victory? Thanks be to God who giveth us the victory, through our Lord Jesus Christ!"

Now thou seest and feelest that God is LOVE. Thou dwellest in him, and he in thee. *Love,* the fulfilling of the law, diffusing itself through all thy heart, influences thy looks, words, and actions, and makes thee spring after Jesus into the chariot of cheerful obedience. Thy heart is as his heart; and while active grace draws thy willing soul along, God's free Spirit pours the oil of gladness upon the fervid wheels of thy affections. Supported and animated by thy Lord's presence, thou swiftly movest, thou delightfully fliest in all the ways of duty; mountains of difficulties sink into plains before thee; wisdom's roughest ways are ways of pleasantness, and all her paths are peace.

Now thou rejoicest to be thought worthy to suffer shame for Christ's name, and countest it all joy when thou fallest into divers trials. With him the cross loses its dreadful aspect, and enormous weight. When thou findest it in the high way of holiness, instead of consulting with flesh and blood how thou shalt go aside to avoid it, thou immediately takest it up, and it proves a comforting staff, a never-failing prop.

Christ crucified works this miracle of grace; for him thou receivest with every cross; and the moment thou dost so in the power of his Spirit, God, even thy own God, gives thee his choicest blessing; he crowns thee with loving kindness and tender mercies; and with the inexpressible complacence of a Father who receives a lost son, with the triumphant joy of a Saviour who embraces a raised Lazarus, he says to the myriads that surround his throne, "One more sinner repenteth unto life! Hallelujah! He hath escaped the avenger of blood;—he hath passed the gate of the city of refuge! Hallelujah! Shout, ye *sons* of the morning! My angels, strike your golden harps! Dance every heart for joy, through the realms of heaven! Let bursts of triumphant mirth, let peals of ravishing praise, roll along the transporting news;—let all your exulting breasts reverberate, let all your harmonious tongues echo back our glorious joy! For this my son was dead, and is alive again! This your brother was lost, and is found!"

And, irradiating thy soul with the light of his reconciled countenance, he says to *thee,* from a throne blazing with grace and glory, "Penitent believer, receive the adoption of a son. Because thou receivest my Son, my only begotten Son, into thy heart, I admit thee into the family of the first born. Be thou blameless and harmless, a son of God without rebuke, in the midst of a crooked and perverse generation, among whom I allow thee to shine as a burning light in a benighted world. Son, all that I have is thine; be ever with me, and thou shalt inherit all things. Yes, whether Paul, or Apollos, or Cephas; whether my first apostles, or my choice ministers; or the world, or life, or death, or things present, or things to come; all is thine, for thou art Christ's, and Christ is mine. As thou hast received him, so abide and walk in him, worthy, of me, unto all pleasing; being fruitful in every good work, and increasing in his knowledge, till thy faith is turned to sight, and I am all in all."

Start not, believing reader, at these sayings, as if they were too glorious to be credited. They are the true sayings of God. The Lord himself spoke them for thy comfort. They are the precious pearls which I promised thee out of the unsearchable treasures of Christ. If swine trample them under their feet, wear thou them on thy breast. Instead of being offended at their transcendent excellence, magnify the God of all consolation, who, having "delivered up his own Son for us all, with him also freely gives us all things:" consequently, the richest mines of Gospel grace. And, giving vent to the just transports of thy grateful heart, cry out with the beloved disciple, "Behold what manner of love the Father hath bestowed upon us, that *we* should be called the sons of God! Unto him who" thus "loved us, and washed us from our sins in his own blood, and hath made us kings and priests to God and his Father to him be glory and dominion for ever and ever." Amen.

APPENDIX TO APPEAL.

CONCERNING THE EVANGELICAL HARMONY THAT SUBSISTS BETWEEN LIVING FAITH
AND LOVING OBEDIENCE.

THE mystery of our salvation is thus opened by St. Paul: "By *grace* are ye saved, through faith which *worketh* by love." This apostolic declaration subdivides itself into the following propositions, which, on account of their clearness and importance, may with propriety be called GOSPEL AXIOMS. 1. "Ye are saved by *grace.*" 2. "Ye are saved through a faith which *works* by love." These propositions, like two adamantine pillars, support the whole doctrine of Christ concerning *faith* and *works, grace* and *rewardableness;* or *mercy* on God's part, and *obedience* on our own:—a doctrine which, though clear as the day, has nevertheless been so obscured by endless controversies, that thousands of Protestants and Papists know it in its purity no more.

According to the FIRST of these axioms, all that go to heaven give Divine *grace* the glory of their salvation; because they are all saved by mere favour, through the redemption that is in Jesus Christ. And according to the SECOND axiom, all that go to hell are obliged to clear Divine *justice,* because they are condemned merely for their avoidable unbelief, and obstinate disobedience. Upon this evangelical plan the righteous are *graciously* rewarded, and the unrighteous *justly* punished; the doctrine of God's *mercy,* in giving grace for Christ's sake, and of man's *faithfulness* in using it by Christ's help, sweetly coincide; and from their blessed union springs the just proportion of every part of the Gospel.

These axioms are so strongly maintained, and so frequently alluded to by the sacred writers, that whoever rejects either the one or the other might reject one half of the Bible. Attentively consider them asunder, and your unprejudiced reason will perceive their *equity.* Impartially compare them together, and instead of finding them incompatible, (as some prepossessed persons would persuade us they are,) you will see that they *harmonize,* in so exquisite a manner, as to answer the most excellent ends in the world.

To give you an idea of their working in the breast of believers, permit me to compare them to those two opposite and yet consentaneous motions of the heart, which anatomists call *diastole* and *systole.* The one forcibly dilates, the other powerfully contracts, that noble part of the human body; and both together, by means seemingly contrary, cause the circulation of the blood, and diffuse vital powers through all the animal frame. Just so passive *faith* andf70active *love.* The one perpetually *receives* favours from God, the other perpetually *bestows* them upon man; and thus, by continually performing their contrary (not contradictory) offices, they make spiritual life circulate throughout the believer's soul, and enable him to diffuse kindness and good works throughout the social body of which he is a member.

The Works of John Fletcher

From the animal we pass to the planetary world; and we shall see another striking emblem of the harmonious opposition which subsists between the two Gospel axioms. There we eminently discover the *centripetal* and the *centrifugal* force. Though opposed to each other, they are nevertheless so admirably joined together, that from their exquisite combination results the harmonious dance of the spheres: I mean, the circular motion of the planets around the sun, and around each other. Such is the wonderful effect of *evangelical promises* and *legal precepts,* when they meet in a due proportion, in an upright heart. The *promises,* which are all wrapped up in the *first* Gospel axiom, powerfully *draw* believers to Christ, who is the Sun of righteousness, and the centre of the Christian system; the *precepts,* which the *second* axiom necessarily supposes, drive them forward in the straight line of duty. Being thus delightfully attracted, and powerfully impelled, like planets of a different magnitude, in the firmament of the Church, believers rapidly move in the orb of evangelical obedience, where the *original* light of Christ warmly shines into their own souls, and their *borrowed* light mildly gleams upon their fellow mortals.

If ever you saw a person thus swiftly and evenly moving in the immense circle of religious and social duty, freely receiving all from his God, and freely imparting all to his neighbour, you have seen one of the "stars in the Lord's right hand;"—you have seen one who practically holds the two Gospel axioms;—one who *believes* as a sinner, and *works* as a believer;— one in whose heart the doctrines of *faith* and *works, free grace* and *free obedience, Divine faithfulness* and *human fidelity,* are justly balanced;— one who keeps at an equal distance from the dreadful rocks upon which *Antinomian believers* and *antichristian workers* are daily cast away. In a word, you have seen an adult Christian, a man who "adorns the doctrine of Christ our Saviour in *all* things."

If the two Gospel axioms are of such importance, that the health and vigour of every Christian flow from the proper union of their power in his heart, is it not deplorable to see so many people every where rising against them? *Self-conceited moralists* violently attack the *first* axiom, and *selfhumbled solifidians* will give the *second* no quarter. Those opposed assailants have all, I grant, a zeal for God, but not according to knowledge; for the *former* know not that they rob God of *his glory,* and the *latter* do not consider that they pour upon him *our shame.* The *one* refuse to acknowledge him the *grand Author* of our *bliss:* the *other,* to mend the matter, represent him as the *grand Contriver* of our *ruin.* Both, nevertheless, have truth on their side; but, alas! it is only *a part* of the truth as it is in Jesus; and truth divided, like an animal cut through the middle, is dreadfully mangled, if not entirely destroyed.

You are also desired to observe, judicious reader, that as a just proportion of sail and ballast, next to a favourable wind, makes a ship sail with speed and safety; so the just balance of the two Gospel axioms, next to the Spirit of God, makes a believer run swiftly and safely the race that is set before him. He does not properly *run,* he merely *hops* in the way of truth, who, discarding one of the Gospel axioms, moves only upon the other. *Antinomian Laodiceans,* therefore, and *antichristian Pharisees,* are equally blamable. For the piety of the *former* stands only upon the *first* axiom; and the devotion of the *latter* has no other basis than the *second.* The *one* will hear of nothing but *faith;* the *other* will be told of nothing out works. But the *sound* believer is for a *faith* that *works* righteousness.

"Faith unfeigned" and "obedient love," are of equal importance to the true Christian. Those precious graces, which answer to the Gospel axioms, like a well-proportioned pair of heavenly steeds, mutually draw the steady chariot of his profession across the valleys of discouragement, and over the hills of difficulty which he meets with in his way to heaven. If I might carry on the allegory, I would observe that all the advantage which the right hand steed has over the other, is, that it is *first* put in the traces; but this is no proof of his superiority, for he will be taken off at the gate of heaven; and "obedient love" alone shall have the honour of drawing the Christian's triumphal car through the realms of glory.

Reader, if in the theory and practice you maintain both Gospel axioms; if, instead of setting up the one in opposition to the other, you stand upon the Scriptural line in which they harmonize; you have surmounted the greatest difficulty there is in the Christian religion: you "hold the faith once delivered unto the saints." And now prepare to *contend for it:* arm yourself for the fight; for *Antinomian believers* will attack you on the *left* hand, and *Pharisaic unbelievers* on the *right*. But be not afraid of their number; patiently receive their double fire. They may gall one *another,* but they cannot hurt *you.*

Truth is great, and *love* powerful: if you fight under their glorious banners, though the arrows of contempt, and the brands of calumny will fly thick around you, you shall not be dangerously wounded. Only "take the shield of faith," with this motto, "By grace I am saved through faith;" and quench with it the fiery darts of self-conceited legalists. "Put on the breastplate of righteousness," with this inscription, "Faith works by righteous love, the mother of good works:" this piece of celestial armour will keep off the heaviest stroke of *self-humbled gospellers.* And animated by the Captain of your salvation, through the opposite forces of those adversaries, urge your evangelically-legal way, till you exchange *"the* sword of the Spirit" for a "golden harp," and your daily cross for a heavenly crown.

Such is the happy medium that the author of this book desires to recommend. Some time ago he thought himself obliged to oppose good mistaken men, who, in their zeal for the *first* Gospel axiom, wanted to represent the *second* as a "dreadful heresy." And now he lets these papers see the light, not only to prove to the free thinkers of his parish that the *first* axiom is highly rational, but to convince the enemies of the *second* axiom, that, though he has exposed their mistakes with regard to *works,* he receives the *genuine* doctrines of grace as cordially as they; and is ready Scripturally and rationally to defend salvation by *faith,* against the most plausible objections of self-righteous moralists.

He just begs leave to observe, that the preceding pages guard the *first* Gospel axiom; that the *Four Checks to Antinomianism* guard chiefly the *second:* that *the Equal Check to Pharisaism and Antinomianism* guards both at once; and that those tracts contain a little system of practical and polemical divinity, which, it is hoped, stands at an equal distance from the errors of moral disbelievers, and immoral believers.

This book is chiefly recommended to disbelieving moralists, who deride the doctrine of salvation by grace *through faith* in the day of conversion, merely because they are not properly acquainted with our fallen and lost estate. And the *Checks* are chiefly designed for disbelieving Antinomians, who rise against the doctrine of a believer's salvation by grace *through* the *works* of faith in the great day, merely because they do not consider the indispensable necessity of evangelical obedience, and the nature of the day of judgment.

In the *Appeal*, the careless, self-conceited sinner is awakened and humbled. In the *Address*, the serious, humbled sinner is raised up and comforted. And in the *Checks*, the foolish virgin is reawakened, the Laodicean believer reproved, the prodigal son lashed back to his father's house, and the upright believer animated to mend his pace in the way of "faith working by love," and "to perfect holiness in the fear of God."

END

An Appeal to Matter of Fact and Common Sense

www.ingramcontent.com/pod-product-compliance
Lightning Source LLC
Chambersburg PA
CBHW031232090426
42742CB00007B/168